D1276488

Personality
and the Good

Personality

and the Good

PSYCHOLOGICAL AND ETHICAL PERSPECTIVES

PETER A. BERTOCCI
Borden Parker Bowne, Professor of Philosophy
Boston University

RICHARD M. MILLARD
Professor of Philosophy
Boston University

DAVID McKAY COMPANY, INC. : NEW YORK

Preface

No one can teach college students very long without realizing how intense is their interest in what motivates human behavior and what ought to motivate it. The impact of their education comes home to them in terms of choices among values. They see quite readily that the questions "Who am I?" and "For what should I aim?" are connected with a larger question: "How do I know what can give significance to my living?" It is the assumption of this text that an introductory college course in ethics should help the student understand issues immediately related to answers to such questions.

Furthermore, the development of technical psychological interest in the nature of values has encouraged us to write a text in ethics that gives more than usual attention to psychological thinking about mental health and values. As a matter of fact, many college students who have had a course or two in psychology but none in ethics think that the psychologist defines the nature of the good life as well as anybody can. And college students of ethics are seldom sufficiently aware of the bearing of psychology on ethical conclusions.

Why not, then, approach this matter more systematically and attempt a text in which the student may study some psychological and ethical analyses especially relevant to the formulation of a philosophy of the good life? Why not place the thinking of influential psychologists alongside the reflection of ethicists, and why not suggest a systematic approach to basic ethical problems growing out of such analysis? Then the student can follow, within the covers of

v

one book, the exposition of basic perspectives on both human personality and the good life, the presentation of problems that both psychologists and ethicists must face.

It is immediately apparent that such a venture, especially when attempted in an introductory text, calls for selectivity that will provoke the criticism "not thorough enough." Philosophers will miss the exposition of significant historical and contemporary ethical views, and psychologists will feel that other areas of psychological exploration (especially objective and operational perspectives) need to be added. And both will be correct. We have guided our selection by the conviction that it is better to focus on certain fundamental problems, even at the expense of important historical and contemporary figures in psychology and ethics.

We begin our book, therefore, with an exposition of the theories of personality advanced by psychologists whose writings not only are influential but lend themselves readily to our purpose. They offer more explicit answers to the question: "What can exploration in the psychology of personality tell us about the nature of the good life?"

In each chapter of Part I, we, being primarily philosophers, have not ourselves sought to criticize psychological findings that purport to be scientifically adequate. As the exposition proceeds, however, the student will become aware of significant differences among the psychological approaches and their exponents, philosophical considerations aside. But as we move along, we take note of issues and interpretations that are especially important philosophically.

In Part II, we are, therefore, ready to consider problems about the nature of human wants, of human freedom, and of human obligation, problems that emerge from recent psychological discussion and tie in with persistent problems in ethical theory. Here we also suggest possible solutions that we favor at present.

Half of Part III is given to an exposition of basic philosophical perspectives on the nature of duty, values, and the good life, the stress being placed on the underlying issues that create differences in ethical conclusions. In the second half of Part III, we suggest a theory of value and of the good life in the light of our previous psychological and ethical analyses.

In Part IV, a system of ethical principles is proposed that may serve not only to correlate important streams of ethical reflection but also to bring out the relevance of such reflection to concrete problems of moral choice. Here our underlying concern in this text takes explicit form. It is that the beginning collegiate course in ethics should help the student to formulate both the values and the principles by which his choices may be guided. In such a course, the complexity of moral problems and moral choices must indeed be made clear, but the relevance of ethical reflection in the midst of the search for values should also be made evident. This does not mean that we have given the last word on any subject, but it does mean that we have tried to show how the study of ethics is pertinent to every-day choices.

In Part V, we conclude our study with the discussion of four areas of central importance for the development of personality. The choices a person makes with regard to the ideals of the social order in which he lives, with regard to love and sex, and with regard to the place of religious experience are crucial in the formation of character and personality. In each area, choices will reflect the maturity of value experience and of judgments made in other regions of life. What one thinks and believes about love, about the relation of moral and religious experience, will have a transforming effect on his own personality and on his thinking about the goals of social and political life. There are vital options here; and although we, here as elsewhere, have indicated our preferences, we have tried to make the issues stand out.

We might well call brief attention to an underlying theme that grew on us as this study proceeded. An adequate psychology of personality cannot be predicated on the thesis that the *ought* is reducible to the *is;* and an adequate ethical theory of the good cannot be predicated on the thesis that the *ought* has no roots in the *is.* Although either thesis may be correct, neither can be assumed at the outset. If *psychoethics* is taken to mean that, in the investigation of the nature of the good life or personality, the different dimensions of man's nature must be kept in mind, without allowing any one or any group of them to dictate arbitrarily to the others, then our book is an essay in psychoethics.

This book was written for a one-semester course. But if selectivity is necessary, we make the following suggestions: In Part I, preference might be given to Chapters 1, 2, 4, and 6, as minimal psychological background for the rest of the book. If teachers of ethics need to shorten the time devoted to psychological perspectives in Part I, they may find that Chapters 6 and 7 serve, between them, to raise and expound major psychological issues concerning the nature of man and of human motivation especially relevant to ethics. On the other hand, psychologists who wish to interest their students in valuational and ethical issues relevant to psychological study might concentrate on Parts I, II, III, and V.

Although we both have worked with common aims on every part of the book, the division of labor involved Bertocci in the writing of Parts I, II, III and Chapters 29 and 30 and Millard in writing Part IV and Chapter 28.

We have been singularly fortunate in the help we have received. To Gordon W. Allport, Professor of Psychology in Harvard University, we are indebted for the rarest kind of friendly encouragement, advice, and criticism in the venture as a whole and on early drafts of the manuscript. To Angelo P. Bertocci, Professor of Comparative Literature in Boston University, we are especially grateful for many acute suggestions and for the kind of help that frees a manuscript from much awkwardness and obscurity. To Yeager Hudson, Borden Parker Bowne Fellow in Philosophy, 1961–1962, we are indebted for painstaking attention to formal details, and to Thomas Buford, Donald Dunbar, George O. Hartmann, Allie Frazier, and Bertha M. Bardsley we are grateful for help on time-consuming tasks connected with preparing a manuscript. Mrs. Bertocci and Mrs. Millard accepted heavy obligations for preparation of the final manuscript and proofs in a spirit that makes this work especially meaningful to us.

The influence of Edgar S. Brightman on a large segment of fundamental theory in this book will be obvious to the reader. Our debt to our teacher is also a debt that students can feel only to a man whose thinking and living enlivens and animates the search for wisdom.

PETER A. BERTOCCI
RICHARD M. MILLARD

Boston University
October, 1962

Contents

"... If our eyes could see the beauty of virtue,
we should love it warmly ..."

—GOTTFRIED WILHELM LEIBNIZ

PART I:

The Good Life in Psychological Perspective

1

The Human Predicament

~~~~~~

I. *THE STRUGGLE AGAINST CHAOS*

A human being will not accept chaos. Nor can he long tolerate chaos. When he can no longer cope with it, he begins to get sick, both physically and mentally. When chaos has won out, he is dead. But as long as he is alive, he is seeking to reduce chaos in some way or other.

Obviously, the word "chaos" can refer to many different states. From the point of view of neat housekeeping, what is chaos to a mother in a child's playroom, may not be chaos to the child. For a freshman, the chaos of registration days has an order and purpose for the administration. In general, then, what is considered chaotic depends on the needs, desires, and purposes of the persons involved. "Chaos" always means danger and destruction to some plan of order.

One unique thing about a human being, however, is that he has to fight chaos on different levels in the same lifetime. This means that to be human is to undergo different *kinds* of order. For example, the process by which a person takes in, digests, and uses food involves a biochemical process quite different from that by which he organizes the ideas he "takes in." For an "undigested" idea is one whose logical relation to other ideas the mind does not see. Similarly, when a person enjoys beauty, the order he experiences is not of a biochemical or intellectual sort. Likewise, the yearning for moral integrity and for holiness involves overcoming "chaos" that can be defined only within each of these areas of experience.

3

But the struggle against chaos does not go on simply within each realm. Assuming that a person could achieve order separately in the search for beauty, he would soon find the threat of chaos in the conflict of beauty with economic, intellectual, and moral demands. We know all too well that the search for beauty may conflict with the requirements of morality, and the search for holiness has often encouraged health-destroying ascetic disciplines.

To restate: When a human being seeks health, beauty, truth, morality, holiness, he seems to be following different processes that, on the surface at least, are not like each other. Yet in each pursuit he seems to fight disorder and chaos. Hence the "predicament" each of us faces as a human being: We find ourselves reaching both for some sort of order in each of these different pursuits, and for harmony among them. Still, we do not know whether they are so related that they can be harmonized with each other. Nevertheless, we hesitate to cut any of them out of our lives lest we miss the best in life.

If we are to deal with this predicament intelligently, we need to know how the different aspects of our obviously complex natures work and how they are related to each other. In this chapter we must familiarize ourselves with some of the facts and issues that confront systematic thinking about the "predicament." We begin with the biological order of existence.

II. WHAT IT MEANS TO FIGHT CHAOS IN THE BIOLOGICAL REALM

Living beings, as distinguished from inorganic things, regulate and reproduce their life process. That is, changes in a living body seek to protect the effective functioning of its capacities. From the first stirring of life in a simple cell to the more complicated organization of cells we know in the human being, there goes on a striving for self-maintenance. As far as we can tell, the prize in the age-long evolutionary struggle called the "survival of the fittest" has gone to human bodies.

The "wisdom of the body" is forcefully set forth in Walter B. Cannon's book by this title.[1] The contrast between human and subhuman struggles against chaos may be illustrated in a homely way. What child has not come home from some pond joyfully clinging to

[1] *The Wisdom of the Body* (New York: W. W. Norton & Co., 1932).

a frog, determined to keep it alive a long time by feeding it well? He ties its leg to the back fence with a long string, he provides ample food, he is anxious to give it every care. Yet, to his surprise, the frog dies. The child just happens not to know that the frog, never having had the capacity (enjoyed by his more advanced kin, the birds and mammals) to prevent the free evaporation of water from his body, must dry up and die. The frog cannot regulate his body temperature and keep it constant, despite change in the external environment. In cold weather, therefore, he will be found at the bottom of his pond waiting for the return of warmer weather. The human infant provides an interesting contrast. He is safe in his mother's womb because of the mother's capacity to maintain her internal bodily temperature against climatic changes outside; but after birth he survives because he himself can maintain temperature in a changing environment.

In general, the higher its place in the evolutionary process, the more able is a body to maintain the constancy of its functioning by rectifying internal conditions and thereby adjusting to a wide range of disturbing factors. The shivering we do when we are "cold" is an emergency measure by which the body activates processes that create heat and readjust the balance. We could not hope to live at high altitudes where nature provides less oxygen than the body needs under average conditions unless the red corpuscles in our blood, which carry the oxygen from the lungs to the rest of the body, increased appreciably. With less oxygen available in the lungs at any one time, the needy body would not get enough oxygen unless the blood circulated more rapidly and unless more carriers were produced. But increase in blood corpuscles calls for greater activity of the blood-creating agents in the marrow of the long bones.

Such "natural defenses of the organism" are simple compared to the intricate complications that ensue when the organism as a whole is in danger. Obviously, in the course of evolution, those organisms survived which were able to prepare for emergencies as rapidly as possible. When we human beings, for example, experience fear and anger in dangerous situations, marked and rapid changes take place. Our breathing is faster, and, as a result, more oxygen can be supplied to the lung tissue and from there be transmitted to the laboring parts of the body. These organs accumulate waste more rapidly and therefore need more oxygen and food. This need cannot be met unless the heart beats faster and pumps more blood, with its white and red corpuscles, to meet the emergency. But this operation is more efficient if digestive processes are shut down and the blood energy shifted to the fighting apparatus. The sugar reserve in the liver must be tapped more freely. Cooperating with the sympathetic nervous system in this process are the adrenal glands, whose secretion into the blood stream helps in releasing sugar from the liver, in distributing the blood to the necessary organs, and in causing the blood to coagulate.

In manifold ways, then, the human organism is able to coordinate its physiological processes so that it can maintain itself in a condition that, although variable, is relatively constant or, to use the technical term, homeostatic. And, unless we could depend on these processes to maintain the internal equilibrium of our bodies, we would have to spend all our energy and time just keeping alive. What is gained by the self-balancing homeostasis is "freedom for the activity of the higher levels of the nervous system and the muscles which they govern." [2] Thus our brain, freed from the regulation of routine necessities, can attend to directing the more complicated interactions involved as we learn to meet the problems we face in developing our economic, intellectual, social, aesthetic, moral, and religious interests. Our bodies, of course, do more than fight the chaos they cannot accept. Fighting chaos is a prerequisite for positive achievement. At the bodily level we fight chaos in order to maintain normal stability as a basis for wider intelligent activity.[3]

III. *A SEMANTIC CAUTION ON BIOLOGICAL COOPERATION AND SURVIVAL*

We have been emphasizing that in man the greatest variety of organic self-fulfillment is possible only because of the mutual support operating among parts of the organism. This interdependence, which enhances the healthy survival of the organism, is often called "cooperation." But one should note that we are introducing the use of a term that has a meaning in social living different from the one it has here. When we speak of cooperation between persons, we refer to their pursuing a common goal when they did not have to. But when we say that the adrenal glands "cooperate" with the sympathetic

[2] Cannon, *ibid.*, p. 284.
[3] See *ibid.*, p. 305.

nervous system, there is really no question of the adrenal glands' doing otherwise and still maintaining themselves.

This distinction may seem mere stickling on a small point. But from the very beginning we must be alert to the need for using words carefully, especially when we use them in a context possibly different from the one in which they were first used. To cooperate socially suggests free coordination of persons who did not have to cooperate. But no such "freedom" is involved when bodily organs are said to "cooperate" with each other for mutual survival.

An equally important caution involves the use of the phrase "survival of the fittest." It is used to describe the biological fact that some animals survived and others did not in the process of evolutionary development. A variety of reasons can be given for the fact that some organisms were better able to cope with environmental demands and thus perpetuate their progeny; but the important point is that, because of their biological equipment in relation to the environment, they were able to outsurvive other organisms. The individual biologically weak in relation to a given environment did not survive.

The caution we wish to underscore is that the meaning of "the fittest" here *in this biological context* is ability to outsurvive competitors. But note the trouble we get into the moment we try to transfer this meaning to human affairs. Suppose that, in a business situation, the man who is not willing to use lies against his competitors, even though they use lies against him, loses out. Are the competitors better men? Indeed, are they ever better business men, if one keeps the community's needs, rather than "profits" for the individual, in mind? Clearly, we shall be inviting trouble unless we pause to ask the exact meaning of a term, especially when we move it from one area of experience to another. Thus, "creative" in biology means *self*-reproductive. But does "creative" in art and in social life mean the same?

IV. *MUTUALISM AND SURVIVAL*

With this semantic caution in mind we must now call attention to a recent shift in thinking about what is involved if the individual organism is to survive.

Earlier theorizing seemed to stress the importance of individual strength and prowess as a condition for survival. Recent scholarship finds such a "tough" interpretation of natural selection one-sided at best. Beginning with the one-celled amoeba and moving to the highest forms of animal life, another factor is present, which is perhaps better named "mutualism," rather than "cooperation." That is, animals survive best when their behavior involves them in preserving the group of which they are a part. Animals survive not merely by being independent individuals but, in most cases, to the extent that they can mutually support each other's struggle for survival. Thus, if the different kinds of cells that make up sponges are separated and then passed through a muslin filter without destroying them individually, the cells regroup to form a new organism. From the bottom of the scale of life to the top, the rule seems to be: United we survive; disunited we die. As Ashley Montagu summarizes the evidence:

> Certainly aggressiveness exists in nature; but there is also a healthy non-ruthless competition, and there also exist very strong drives toward social and co-operative behavior. These forces do not operate independently but together, as a whole; and the evidence strongly indicates that of all these drives the principle of co-operation is the most dominant, and biologically the most important. The coexistence of so many different species of animals throughout the world is a sufficient testimony to the importance of that principle. It is probable that man, in his own biological and social evolution owes more to the operation of this principle than to any other. Indeed, without this principle of cooperation, of sociability and mutual aid, the progress of organic life, the improvement of the organism, and the strengthening of the species, become utterly incomprehensible.[4]

We must once more stop to comment that we cannot safely conclude, from the fact that animals and men survive longer only insofar as they live in mutual interdependence, that men ought to be altruistic, or even that such mutual dependence is always good. *Selfishness and altruism at the human level need independent definition and*

[4] M. F. Ashley Montagu, "Social Life and Cooperation," in P. A. Sorokin, *Explorations in Altruistic Love and Behavior* (Boston: Beacon Press 1950), p. 83. Reprinted by permission of the Beacon Press, copyright © 1950, The Beacon Press. See also Montagu's *The Direction of Human Development, Biological and Social Bases* (New York: Harper & Brothers, 1955), pp. 24 and 27 and Chapters 2, 3, and 4. Also see Warden C. Allee, *Cooperation among Animals, with Human Implications* (revised; New York: Henry Schuman, 1951).

argument. In any case, more argument is needed before we conclude that, at the human level, ability to outsurvive others is the adequate or ultimate test of "good." Certainly the fact that a gang of hoodlums cooperates to rob a community and survives efforts to capture them does not mean that the hoodlums are better persons.

Nevertheless, no moralist can ignore the facts that "such a thing as a completely asocial variety of animal probably does not exist" [5] and that "the most important basis for selection is the ability of associated components to work together harmoniously in the organism and among organisms." [6] Nor can a moralist forget that when a human being consciously seeks to work harmoniously with others for a certain enterprise, he is following the dominant path taken by the cells in his body and by his animal ancestors.

Still, neither can a moralist forget that when a Socrates decides to drink the hemlock that will put an abrupt end to the mutuality of the cells in his body, when a Christ decides to allow crucifixion to end bodily processes, or when a soldier throws himself on a hand grenade to protect his comrades, he is deciding, for some ideal, to destroy all the armies of mutuality in his body. We cannot assume, either, that Socrates, Jesus, or the soldier is right, but *surely the problem of choice that every man confronts is not always one only of survival but of kind of survival, and sometimes it is one of survival or surcease.* Yet, as far as we can see, if the physiological processes of a person had the only vote, they would say: Survival at any cost! And if man's nature can be described solely in terms of bodily needs, there would be no other moral ideal than survival as such.

V. *HOW SHALL WE CONCEIVE OF HUMAN NEEDS?*

As a matter of fact, however, no psychologist or sociologist defines the course of man's existence simply as a matter of satisfying physiological needs. And yet, if there are nonphysiological needs, we must understand how they operate; whether they exhibit processes different from homeostasis, and how they are related to the total life of a person.

In the present stage of psychological and sociological knowledge,

---

[5] Montagu, in Sorokin, *op. cit.,* p. 85.
[6] P. R. Burkholder, quoted by Montagu in *ibid.,* p. 84.

there is much difference of opinion in regard to the interpretation of available data. Although we cannot deal with the underlying issues at length, we must, in the remainder of this section, present one problem which in various ways will dog us throughout this book. To keep our discussion concrete we shall review briefly the conception suggested by a sociologist who grounds the direction of human development in biological and social bases.

Ashley Montagu, like many other writers, holds that the basic needs of man are what he calls physiological tensions. The reduction of these tensions lead to acts that restore the equilibrium (homeostasis) of the organism. Let us consider hunger as a typical example. The physiological hunger-tension is the urge or need to ingest food and thereby to restore organic equilibrium.[7] The other basic physiological tensions besides (1) hunger for food are (2) oxygen hunger, (3) thirst, (4) sex, (5) fatigue, (6) restlessness, (7) somnolescence, (8) bladder pressures, (9) colon pressures, (10) fright, (11) pain. As Montagu interprets the data, each of these tensions is activated by a biochemical "warning mechanism" in the body. Dryness of mucous membranes activates thirst, tonic disturbance activates bladder pressure, and other warning mechanisms activate the other cravings that call forth neuromuscular action that re-establishes equilibrium and homeostasis.[8]

Now, Montagu considers all of these physiological cravings "vital" since they are "basic needs the satisfaction of which is necessary if the individual and the group are to survive."[9] Learning and culture play "no part in the original basic structure" of such tensions or in the "basic physiological acts calculated to bring about the appropriate adjustments."[10] The point at which the influence of learning and culture is felt is in the manner in which these tensions and physiological acts are expressed.

But a curious jump occurs from one level to another as Montagu goes on with his exposition of basic needs. For he adds that "there are also several nonvital basic needs which must be satisfied if the organism is to develop and maintain adequate mental health." The jump is from homeostasis-health, which has a definite physiological meaning, to "mental health," which has a far from definite physiological meaning. Shall we say that a "mental" or "psychic" factor has

[7] See Ashley Montagu, *The Direction of Human Development,* pp. 110 ff.
[8] See *ibid.,* p. 117.
[9] *Ibid.,* p. 118.
[10] *Ibid.,* p. 111.

been added, without adequate explanation, to the conception of a human being? Montagu would answer in the negative. "These non-vital basic needs," he says, "have their origin in the same kinds of physiological states as do the vital basic needs." [11] But he never states —and no one to our knowledge can state—what these "same kinds of physiological states" are.

Assertions are being made by Montagu which are unverified by any actual data. They are based on a possible theory that what we call mentality is no more than a functioning of the living organism.[12] This theory may be true, but it is not self-evident and, as a matter of fact, seems contrary to Montagu's actual description of his nonvital basic needs.

For example, Montagu describes the first of these basic nonvital needs as the urge "to be with others." Yet he calls the accompanying physiological tension the "feeling of nondependency or aloneness." But do we experience nondependency or aloneness as a physiological process? And do we actually experience the "feelings of security or interdependency" [13] as a physiological state?

Is the situation improved when Montagu describes the second non-vital need, supposedly originating in physiological tensions? He calls it the "general need or tension" for "expression." Expression, in turn, leads to actions of communication "and the resultant homeostasis," or "social" recognition. But do any of us experience the need for "expression" and "social recognition" as a physiological tension (like a gnawing hunger)? This clearly is a read-in description based on the prior convictions that "there is no such thing as a mind *and* a body, there is only a living body . . . and mind represents but one aspect of its functioning." [14]

Much as this description finds approval in some psychological and philosophical circles, closer examination reveals that this "one-aspect" theory gets its holders into trouble. To take Montagu's own description, as one typical example of that trouble: He has told us that a

---

[11] *Ibid.*, p. 118.

[12] On an earlier page Montagu, without any explanation, introduces the sentence: "There is no such thing as a mind *and* a body, there is only a living body, an organism, and mind represents but one aspect of its functioning" (*ibid.*, p. 59). He adds: "Mind as we know it phenomenally, as a process of behavior, is knit into the whole network of living as a natural event" (p. 77). Furthermore: "Unless the potencies of [the]. . . neuronal net undergo such social organization and patterning, mind cannot develop" (p. 77).

[13] *Ibid.*, p. 118.

[14] *Ibid.*, p. 59.

human being has physiological tensions that must be satisfied if he
is to survive. But in addition to these, man is said to have other basic
but nonvital needs—such as the need for security and for social recognition. Now an individual who wishes merely to survive physiolog-
ically does not need "social recognition" or the "feeling of security."
If he did, then recognition and security would be called *vital basic
tensions;* Montagu says they are basic but not vital. But why basic?
And basic to what? To mental health, is the answer. But is mental
health to be identified with bodily health, or even with bodily
longevity? Is mental health one aspect of bodily health? The answer
is not an easy affirmative. We know too many persons who go on
living in poor health but whose mental health we envy. And many
physically "healthy" persons are neither mentally healthy nor admirable by almost any standard of good living.

What is the underlying point of this discussion? Not to deny that
mental and physical health are related in many ways. But to insist
that, if we do know what physical health is, we certainly cannot use
it safely as a model for mental health. For mental health, while it
may be enhanced by physical health, is not simply the by-product of
physical health. Shall we assume, without adducing evidence, as does
Montagu, that nonvital basic needs "have their origins in the same
kinds of physiological states as do the vital basic needs"? [15] We still
cannot escape the fact that the feeling of psychological security and
the need for social recognition are not experienced simply as needs
to keep our bodies intact and strong. We cannot overlook the fact
that "mental health," even if it means survival, does not mean merely
physical survival, but actually *adds* new demands that cannot be
defined in terms of physical survival. Indeed, satisfying the demand
for social recognition frequently endangers physical health and survival.

On the other hand, if with Montagu we accept as "a satisfactory
short definition of 'mental health' " the "ability to love and the ability to work (Freud)," [16] do we not clearly have a new meaning for
"health"? It takes only a surface look to see that the needs to love
and be loved, the needs to work and to cooperate with others, call
for more than a physiological meaning of "chaos" and of "health."

As we said to begin with, the human struggle against chaos must
be fought, both on the same and on different levels, at the same time.

[15] *Ibid.,* p. 118.
[16] *Ibid.,* p. 150.

We shall be led astray if we assume that health on one level means health at any other level, or health for all together. We must now see, in further detail, whether we can apply the "order of survival" to the order of "mental health."

VI. ARE THE CONDITIONS OF PHYSICAL HEALTH AND THE CONDITIONS OF MORAL HEALTH THE SAME?

All things, insofar as they are alive biologically, strive to stay alive with a minimum of physical pain and, probably, a maximum of physical pleasure. We know what chaos means at this level—for example, decrease of physical comfort, more pain, and, sooner or later, death. What "the good life" means *at the biological level,* then, is simply a matter of comfortable individual continuity. Survival for each cell means self-maintenance in mutual interaction with other cells in a favorable environment. In biological terms, "health" might then be defined as that optimum state of the individual that promotes survival. Illness involves a battle that is going on in which all the factors making for biological strength are pitting themselves against the forces that would destroy health. The *strongest* fighters, if they have the environment on their side, win. Biologically, the words "mercy" and "kindness" and "courage" have no meaning. And we have already seen that "cooperation" in the sense of "chosen mutual aid" makes no sense at this level of biological survival.

If we keep these facts in mind, we shall not be seduced, as indeed some moralists have been, into using the conception of *physiological health* as the model for the good life. If, as human beings, we are only complicated physiological beings, then we might say that the test of any action is whether it helps a man to live longer (no matter what the pain or displeasure incurred). But Lewis Mumford's words put our problem neatly: "without food man can survive for barely thirty days; without water for little more than three days; without air hardly for more than three minutes: but without hope he might destroy himself in an even shorter time." [17]

In other words, how many times have men asked themselves: Is life worth living without hope or without feeling secure in social recogni-

[17] Lewis Mumford, *The Conduct of Life* (New York: Harcourt, Brace & Co., 1951), p. 30.

tion? There is no doubt that physically men want to live as long and as comfortably as they can. But neither is there any doubt that for human beings the word "survival" means more than just not dying, and the word "comfort" means more than a clean bill of health and a good house. A man can have health and comfort and still be miserable.[18]

In our day the acquisition of mental health has come to be considered as important as physical health, partly because we know that the two are somehow interconnected. How often we hear actions recommended "for the sake of mental health." But is mental health identical with moral health? Is mental health preferable to the good life? Or is it itself a product of the good life? Certainly there are many persons whom we consider physically and mentally healthy and yet not good. Obviously crying for definition are the terms "mental health" and "good life." Let us first consider what we mean when we distinguish the psychological level of life from the moral.

VII. *THE PSYCHOLOGICAL STRUGGLE AGAINST CHAOS*

What, then, do we mean by the struggle for order, and against chaos, at the psychological level? We do not mean an order of events, unrelated to the physiological system of nutrition and self-maintenance. But we do mean that a human being is more than a complicated physiological system concerned merely with perpetuation of that physiological organism.

Human life, we have seen, is not a continuous series of events concerned with survival as such. For we do not merely live through an event, as an animal does, without seeking meaning. An event has meaning for us insofar as we can connect it with other events, some of which may have happened, and some of which have not happened and may well never happen. Thus, a handshake for us is not a mere event in the physical and physiological order. It is one that has a

18 Dr. Harold G. Wolff, Professor of Neurology in Cornell University Medical College and editor in chief of *Archives of Neurology and Psychiatry,* stays close to the facts when he says: "In short, prolonged circumstances which are perceived as dangerous, as lonely, as hopeless, may drain a man of hope and of his health; but he is capable of enduring incredible burdens and taking cruel punishment when he has self-esteem, hope, purpose and belief in his fellows." ("What Hope Does for Man," *Saturday Review,* Vol. 40, p. 45, Jan. 5, 1957). See also Viktor Frankl, *From Death Camp to Existentialism* (Boston: Beacon Press, 1946).

meaning dependent on what the two persons are thinking and hoping. Again, a painful cut and profuse bleeding are physiological
events that portend disaster both to wounded animal and to human
being. However, while the animal experiences the pain, it does not
know that the event may mean being incapacitated for the future;
it does not know the many ways in which this event will affect friend
and foe. Compare, for a moment, the effect of serious illness on any
human mother as compared to an animal mother. The animal mother
experiences pain, but the meaning of that pain, what it can mean
for her children, is shut away from her and she will not experience
the anxiety of the human mother.

This capacity for rendering events meaningful by connecting
them with other events and with wants and desires, both in the
present and in the future, is a mere suggestion (all that we need for
the moment) of what we mean by the psychological level of existence.
This psychological level, inclusive of the physiological order and taking account of it, has many ends of its own. As psychological beings
we seem to desire to avoid another kind of chaos, the chaos of uncon-
nectedness of experiences, of irrelevance among them, and of continuous disorderly frustration of our wants. We can go on existing
as do animals, up to a certain point, but then we say "life has no
meaning" because we cannot find any pattern in events. Unless events
and experiences have *some seen relation* to our desires, physiological
and nonphysiological, there is no psychological order in our lives.
Our *psychological problem* is to find the relation between our interests and needs and the world in which they exist. These needs, such
as the need to be loved and to love, can for a long time at any rate
remain ungratified without disturbing physiological health, but they
create mental dis-stress and lead to mental dis-ease. Another kind of
well-being is disturbed when love is unrequited, curiosity unrelieved,
and sympathy unexpressed. And we feel such distress "mentally"
even though no bodily ill is noted.

If the reader's curiosity is so disturbed that he now wishes for a
solution to the problem of the relation of mind and body, part of
our purpose will have been accomplished. The reader will note, incidentally, that his "disturbance" is hardly physiological and that his
psychic state is more zestful if not more enjoyable! But, what is more
important, we wish to underscore the importance of a clearer understanding of this mind-body relation if the nature of man is to be
understood. The demands of this study force us to challenge certain

assumptions, such as the one made by Montagu, and perhaps come to a working understanding for this book.[19] Fortunately for our general ethical purpose, we may proceed, once we have agreed that human experience includes both "the wisdom of the body," and the "wisdom of the mind" and that these affect each other in ways to be examined at every turn.

No human being, it is generally recognized, conceives himself simply as a dynamo of electrons, or as a marvellously intricate digestive system, or as a smooth-working and complementary harmony of the central and peripheral nervous systems. To use Montagu's terms, we do experience nonvital basic needs, and these needs produce problems for us to solve, especially because we can be conscious of degrees of frustration in our lives. We are psychological beings and we have psychological problems because we have needs that cannot be satisfied by any bodily treatment alone.[20] We must now be more explicit about what it means to have a psychological problem.

Let us begin very simply with our everyday experience. Each of us finds that he needs and wants to eat. He cannot do so without having the ability to get hold of his food and also to masticate and swallow it. Let certain muscles in one's esophagus be paralyzed and the task of swallowing becomes difficult if not impossible. Now, while knowing that he needs to eat and that food is to be had and probably can be successfully assimilated, he will probably not look forward to eating. On the other hand, assume that he lived in an environment in which food was very hard to acquire, or even that the process of eating remained a trial, he would always look toward food with anxiety. For in this case, if hunger remains unfulfilled, he must starve.

---

[19] Psychologists themselves are far from agreement on this mind-body problem, but it seems to satisfy most psychologists to operate on the postulate that "an individual's psychic attributes are rooted in some way in the physiological functions of his body" (G. W. Allport, *Personality: A Psychological Interpretation* [New York: Henry Holt & Co., 1937], p. 80). The editorial staff of *Psychosomatic Medicine*, on the other hand, "take it for granted that psychic and somatic phenomena . . . are probably two aspects of the same process" (*Psychosomatic Medicine*, 1 [1939], 1, quoted in James H. Vander Veldt and Robert P. Odenwald, *Psychiatry and Catholicism* [New York: McGraw-Hill, 1952], p. 62). We shall not be delayed by a discussion of these presuppositions, neither of which seems to us to account for the actual facts of psychosomatic medicine. (See Peter A. Bertocci, *Introduction to the Philosophy of Religion* [New York: Prentice-Hall, 1951]; Brand Blanshard, *The Nature of Thought* [London: George Allen & Unwin, 1939]; C. J. Ducasse, *Nature, Mind, and Death* [La Salle, Ill.: Open Court, 1951]; and Charles S. Sherrington, *Man on His Nature* [2nd ed.; Edinburgh: Cambridge University Press, 1951].)

[20] See Chapter 7.

Here, in this simple illustration, we have the pattern of the human problem psychologically. Our living is constituted by the effort to discover how our needs (wants) and abilities can be fulfilled in a given environment. Let us call our wants and needs *motives,* because they move us to use our abilities, and because they provide the impetus to seek an environment that will gratify them. If we find that our abilities are inadequate to gratify our wants, even in a favorable environment, we experience conflict.

To take another example, the vocational counselor of a sixteen year old has told him that he probably has the capacities to become an excellent mechanic. But the young man finds himself wanting to be a lawyer, even though his tests, along with his past achievement, indicate that he does not have the ability to meet college requirements. Here the fundamental conflict appears between a motive or motives, abilities, and environment.

Nor is the problem always caused by a necessary conflict. The conflict may spring, for example, from his false conception of need, of abilities, or of the environment (or of all together). Thus, this sixteen year old may want to be a lawyer, not because he knows he has the ability to become one, but in order to be like his famous grandfather who went from law into statesmanship.

It is clear that if a person is going to avoid fruitless, unnecessary conflicts, he must have the clearest conception possible of his own motives, of his abilities, and of the real environment in which he lives. *The psychological situation, then, is one in which there can be conscious or mental awareness of conflict between motives, abilities, and environment, or any combination of these. The human problem* is to know as much as possible about each factor in the human situation and to keep motive (need or want), ability, and environment together, reducing *needless* conflict.

These words are easy to say, but they hide an enormous number of difficulties. One thing, for example, seems certain. At no one moment are we adequately aware of all our "real" needs and wants; nor are we certain what our capacities are and can be; and, of course, the complexity of other people, the many dimensions, known and unknown, of the environment, always stand as a challenge to any adjustment we may seek to make.

Yet most of the time we find that we must learn to con-form our motives to our abilities, and con-form both motives and abilities to the real demands of the environment. Sooner or later we all realize that we cannot have everything we want, and that, in any case, we have to make the most of our abilities if we are to get the most from our environment.

Yet there is an assumption here: to get "the most" is better than to get a "moderate" amount. The moment we ask what the nature of "the most" is, or why it is better than "moderate," we have passed beyond the psychological level of analysis to the *moral level*. At this level we are consciously facing our conflicts with a view to discovering what is the best way of dealing with them in view of what is possible in the physical, physiological, and psychological orders of existence. Let us review the ground we have covered in a way that will clarify what is involved when we say that human beings have moral problems.

VIII. *THE MORAL STRUGGLE AGAINST CHAOS*

Conflict comes into life, and chaos threatens, when an individual wants or needs what he cannot get. Biologically, we have seen, chaos threatens when any part of the organism functions or dis-functions in a way that endangers the surivival of the whole. And yet, while sheer survival seems to be a clear-cut norm for physical health, we have some difficulty in considering it the only one for physical health. An individual or even a group might outsurvive others and still have a miserable existence. For example, a person with a lingering disease that all but kills him, does survive, but, as a result of the continuing weakness, we do not consider him healthy. Why? Because the notion of physical health refers not only to survival but to a quality of *physical survival*.

But the moment we move from the physiological to the psychological order we find that survival means more than physical vitality. So we introduce notions like *mental health*. We now seek a quality of existence which, while not excluding survival-strength, involves quite a different conception of health. We now talk, for example, about "healthy" attitudes toward oneself, toward illness, misfortune, and death, toward others, and toward "life as a whole." But here we are talking about attitudes that we praise or condemn as "good" or "bad," or "right" or "wrong," and we seem to be in the middle of moral controversy.

As we think about this confusing situation we begin to wonder whether in the concept of mental health [21] we have a kind of mongrel whose parentage is far from clear, even though we go on living with it and have many varieties of mental healers. We cannot throw the term away, but we must realize how ambiguous the concept is.

What is suggested here [22] is that mental health, in the last analysis, has no standards or norms of its own that are independent of what we are now calling the moral order of life. The moral order, on the other hand, is more inclusive than the physiological demand for survival or the psychological demand to reduce needless conflict. And the transition from the physiological and psychological to the moral order takes place the moment a person operates from a *reflective policy*. A person has entered the moral realm when he chooses with some plan of action in mind by which he hopes to get the most out of life. Now he is not concerned with survival or even quality of physical survival; neither is he concerned with the moment-to-moment and day-to-day struggle to relieve needless tension and gratify his wants. Having reflected on the problem of *how to get the most from his physiological and psychological orders of existence in this kind of world, he acts from policy.*

We cannot be concerned in this chapter with what that policy should be, for that is the problem of our entire book. Within the moral order, progress begins when one asks as fundamental a question as that asked by Socrates, the father of Western moral reflection: Is the unexamined life worth living? What in life is most worth achieving? How do we know that some things are more worth getting than others? How much should one get for himself? How much should one depend on others? How much should he get for others, either when they cannot get it for themselves, or when they demand it of him? These and a hundred other questions are part of the human predicament at the *moral level,* that is, at the level of man's reflective search for the things that matter most.

We must stop for a preliminary definition of terms. It should be carefully noted that the word "moral" contrasts with "nonmoral," not with "immoral." An immoral act is one *chosen* in opposition to

---

[21] See the stimulating discussion in Marie Jahoda, *Current Concepts of Positive Mental Health* (New York: Basic Books, 1958), especially pp. 76 ff.

[22] G. W. Allport, in "Personality: Normal and Abnormal," *Personality and Social Encounter* (Boston: Beacon Press, 1960), p. 164, recognizes the same problem we face here with regard to health when he considers the psychological attempt to distinguish the normal personality from the abnormal. "No psychologist has succeeded in telling us why man ought to seek good health rather than ill, or why normality should be our goal for all men."

the reflectively approved ideal (and what the nature of that ideal should be is to be discovered). When any of us declares an act "immoral," he believes that the act in question is not in accordance with the ideal as he sees it. We also call such acts "unethical" (as opposed to "ethical" acts, which are held to actualize the ideal). "Immoral" and "unethical," then, are terms that we use synonymously, in opposition to "moral" and "ethical." Each of these terms is used only when one has a standard or ideal of conduct in mind.

What causes confusion is the fact that we also use the word "moral" for *any action that is chosen* as opposed to *action in which choice* (so far as we know) *could play no part.* This latter class of (involuntary) actions we call "nonmoral." Because they are not chosen or are beyond possible control of the person (say, his falling into an invisible hole in the dark, or his developing a cancer), they are not moral (ethical) or immoral (unethical). Thus, any act of choice is a candidate for moral or ethical judgment. *That is, an act of choice can be considered moral or immoral (to some extent), but an act in which, so far as we know, choice could not enter is neither moral nor immoral, neither ethical nor unethical, but nonmoral (or amoral).*

Obviously, there are many, many instances in which it is very difficult to know whether an act is moral or nonmoral. One of the very important questions we need to raise has to do with the nature and extent of human choice.[23] Not all ethicists will agree; but in this book we shall hold that all chosen acts are either moral or immoral (ethical or unethical); and all acts in which choice is not involved, no matter how admirable or detestable, are nonmoral. Thus, that we have vital needs and experience the urges and desires that we do is a nonmoral fact about our lives. These urges and desires enter the moral (ethical) arena of our lives when we approve of them and select them—in any degree. Much more needs to be said on these matters, but here our purpose is to clarify what we mean by the "moral" or "ethical" realm as opposed to the nonmoral realm.

Obviously, unless man were already a psychological being, there would be no *moral* problem. The *nonmoral psychological struggle against chaos* (the search for connectedness) readily passes into the *moral struggle against chaos* the moment a person tries to control the wants and capacities that would keep him from getting the most out of life, as he conceives the most to be. A "reflective policy" does not mean that human beings always do or should sit down, think out a policy, and then start living. All we wish to indicate is that any

23 See Chapter 8.

problem becomes a moral problem the moment one deliberately decides which of at least two conflicting experiences he is to prefer in a given instance.

The moral philosopher—or ethicist, as we shall call him for convenience—is the person who sets to work systematically to consider the choices man ought to make given his nature and the total world in which he lives. Most persons make their choices under the influence of their social environment, the world in which they live, and their *conception* of these. But they also choose in the light of what they believe their own natures are and can be. Obviously they make their choices, at any one time, with the amount of reflective sensitivity that their total experiences and education make possible.

In this book the authors are concerned with clarifying some of the basic issues that any person seeking to work out a systematic reflective policy for human thought and conduct must consider. Crucial are the problems that emerge from the consideration of man's own nature. Moral philosophers never have been able to move very far without a theory of human nature, and some of the profoundest psychological insights into the nature of man may be discovered in their writings. On the other hand, it may be, as Allport says, that "a fact and a moral imperative are more closely interlocked than traditional writers on ethics may think." [24]

We have already in this chapter tried to indicate the need for careful analysis and interpretation of psychological "discoveries." But the attempt in the next five chapters will be to expound the thought of psychologists whose thinking is especially germane to questions concerning the nature of the good life. These thinkers differ significantly among themselves; they are only a small part of the spectrum of contemporary psychological investigation. But they have been selected because each psychologist's analysis of the "human problem" not only is representative of significant thinking about the nature of the good life, but is, at critical points, germane to basic questions of historic ethical import.

IX. REFLECTIVE SUMMARY

Words like "choose," "cooperate," and "survival" shift their meaning as we move, for example, from the biological to the moral sphere. Thus, the meaning of "survival of the fittest" in the biological realm,

---

[24] Allport, "Personality, Normal and Abnormal," p. 165.

if extended uncritically to the ethical realm, would lead to the conclusion that the traitor who survives the innocent person whom he
betrayed is a better person. Is he?

The concept of "health" is an especially slippery one, for mental
health is not reducible to physiological health. Whatever the exact
relation between mind and body, such mental demands as "social
recognition" and "feelings of security" cannot be expressed wholly
in terms of physiological balance. Thus the conditions of physiological and mental health must not be assumed to be the same.

But is there any difference between mental health and the good
life? The good life, at this stage in our inquiry, seems to involve a
reflective choice of some standard, some best way, of satisfying physiological and mental needs. It involves much more than relieving this
physiological imbalance or reducing that psychic tension. It is action
chosen according to reflective policy. The nature of mental health,
it would seem, cannot be decided upon finally until we know what
the standard of the ethical life is. This we cannot discover without
considering the nature of man.

It seems clear that some of man's actions are chosen and some are
beyond the realm of choice.

The following diagram may help to avoid confusion in terminology.

	I	II
	Moral Action	Nonmoral action
	(from choice)	(not from choice, involuntary)
	↓	↓
	moral, ethical, right, good (for *chosen* action in accordance with an approved standard)	An action can be *good* or *evil* because it aids or impedes realization of the approved standard. Such action is good or evil but not *morally* good or evil.
	↓	
	immoral, unethical, wrong, bad (for *chosen* action not in accordance with an approved standard)	

Thus, a moral action (from choice) can never be amoral or nonmoral but only ethical ("moral") or unethical ("immoral"). The
question remains, to be discussed later, whether, and to what extent,
man is free to choose.

In the remainder of Part I we shall see what some psychologists whose work has been mainly with abnormal personality and other psychologists whose work has been largely confined to normal personality have to suggest about the dynamics and patterns of personality development that they consider healthy and unhealthy.

2

The Human Situation
As Freud Sees It

~~~~~~

We begin our study with Sigmund Freud (1856–1939), because his conception of the human predicament has been widely adopted and has influenced the whole manner of approaching the problems of developing human beings.

I. *THE CONSCIOUS AND THE UNCONSCIOUS*

We may appreciate Freud's pioneering all the more if we contrast his way of looking at human behavior with the way in which most of us usually view it. When something "goes wrong" with a person, we are likely to look for the trouble in some deficiency of physical or intellectual capacity, or in some unintelligent way of dealing with the physical and social environment. We assume that if a person can know his strengths and weaknesses, if he chooses a path dictated by insight into the demands of the environment, he will not have any serious trouble in life. There is nothing wrong with this way of thinking, as far as it goes—until we realize that we are assuming that all of a human being's energies and abilities are open to the person's own inspection.

Plato, Aristotle, Jewish and Christian students of the good life, and a long list of ethicists and psychologists have been quite aware of the obstacles that every person faces in controlling himself with the aid of his best knowledge. Still they work on the basic assumption that once a person makes adequate allowance for his deficiencies and limitations, he can pilot his ship through rough emotional waters without shipwreck. As they see it, when human beings try to be what they are not, when they misunderstand themselves, or when they labor under forced ignorance of their place in relation to other persons and to God (as religious thinkers would add), they come upon evil days.

But how different the human situation looks if we suppose that the whole of our conscious, reasoning existence, as well as the processes in our physical bodies, are not the determining forces in our lives! Assume that our flow of thought and our bodily processes are affected by unconscious wishes, assume that the ideals of truth and goodness, or the vision of God, are not so much controlling guides in our lives as contrived disguises of powerful and nonmoral forces within our natures—how changed our everyday conception of ourselves and our predicament becomes!

It was just this that Freud suggested when he held that the oldest, most powerful part of our lives never has seen the light of our conscious existence. In his terminology, our conscious *ego* probably developed out of the *unconscious* reservoir of emotional seething (the *id,* inclusive of the pleasure-seeking libido).[1] The *id* knows no reason and accepts no loyalties to anything but its own cravings; the *id* is asocial, and sure to use every avenue open to it that will guarantee self-gratification with a minimum of pain. Indeed, our ego, developed to help the id achieve as much gratification as possible, cannot expect to change the fundamental nature of the unconscious id, because, for one thing, the ego cannot know its own hidden sources in the id.

It must be clear that what Freud thus "added" to the human constitution was not just another power. He postulated a mysterious psychic dynamo from which our conscious egos develop and which keeps on having an unseen influence of what our egos do. Unless we discover enough about the id's nature, unless we find suitable ways of allowing it to gratify itself, many forms and degrees of mental dis-ease may afflict us. For example, we may find ourselves

[1] There is much more to Freud than we can touch upon in this chapter, where our concern for matters especially relevant to ethics, as well as space limitations, forces us to be schematic and to overlook refinements and variations in Freud that advanced readers would appreciate.

unable to remember certain events, we may find our bodies behaving in the most unexpected ways, we may be having the most disturbing dreams and fixed ideas, or we may find ourselves completely exhausted or mentally anxious—and yet see little "objective" reason for being so. Why? Because these "abnormal" manifestations or "symptoms" are the very means by which the id is getting as much gratification as it can, despite barriers that seek to inhibit expression.

Freud was convinced that the basic aims of the unconscious could not be changed by conscious activity. But he also believed that the instinctual needs of the id could be *displaced*. That is, the id can find other ways of seeking gratification besides the original or direct way. This discovery of a relatively servile function for reflective, conscious life and of an insatiable, undisciplined, unconscious "cauldron" of seething, psychic energy may well be said to be the permanent residue of Freudian thought about man, accepted by schools of therapy that would not accept other Freudian tenets. These we must now examine.

II. *THE PROBLEM FACED BY THE ID*

Perhaps the next Freudian shock was the characterization of the unconscious libidinous energies as sexual. Yet much unfortunate misunderstanding has been caused by attributing a common-sense conception of sex to Freud's view of the libido.

It is usually thought, for example, that the satisfaction of man's nutritive needs will keep him alive while the gratification of his sexual needs, with onset of puberty, will ensure posterity. For Freud, this separation of nutritive needs from the sexual and the conception of "normal" sexuality as a narrow, potent channel of human energy that finds gratification only in intercourse between the opposite sexes are oversimplified. As Freud sees it, the life-affirming unconscious is inclusive of preservative forces such as hunger, thirst, and sex.[2] Just as the nutritive needs are gratified in different ways, so the sexual energy may express itself in different forms.

Accordingly, the unconscious libido is essentially the persistent craving for self-preservation with as much pleasure as possible.[3] Be-

[2] See Calvin S. Hall, *A Primer of Freudian Psychology* (Cleveland: World Publishing Co., 1955), and Calvin S. Hall and Gardner Lindzey, *Theories of Personality* (New York: Wiley and Sons, 1957).

[3] For our purposes, no reference will be made to self-destructive instincts that Freud also assigned to the unconscious id.

cause the dominant pleasure of the libido is that derived from sexual gratification, the libido may be conceived as the pervasive craving for sexual gratification, a craving that can take different forms from birth onward. For example, the child nursing at the mother's breast is gratifying not only a nutritive need, but also the more fundamental libidinal (sexually toned) demand for pleasure. Similarly, the pleasure that comes with urinating and defecation is an early manifestation of the libidinal urge and not merely a cleansing of the body. If the libidinal urge develops "normally" or "healthily," this process will result in the capacity to give and take pleasure in sexual intercourse and rearing children.

For our purposes it is important to remember that this libidinal part of our nature is not only unconscious but insatiable; it knows no law, chafes at every restriction, and demands some compensation or substitute whenever restricted. Much to its distress, however, the libido is bound to have its pleasure-seeking frustrated by a body that can be hurt and by a physical world that frequently seems both indifferent to its desires and callous to its cries of pain. And when body and Nature are not buffeting it about, its desire for pleasure keeps on running into the stone walls of human customs and the "hard hearts" of those who turn deaf ears to its pleas. It cannot live without these insistent desires, and yet only misery and disaster confront it when it is heedless in its desiring. If it is to achieve any basis for survival with some sort of security, the id must wake up, as it were, to environmental demands and to its own insurgent demands.

This need for a guide was met somehow in the course of evolution. The ego, as Freud describes it, was differentiated from the id-energy for the purpose of performing this important function as traffic policeman. The traffic policeman is authorized and supported by the public to keep that same public moving in different environments with a minimum of frustration. It often may seem to the public that the policeman impedes traffic or takes on more power than has been assigned him, but this risk the public must take if it is to avoid disastrous bottlenecks at important intersections.

On the other hand, the ego (the conscious, reasoning self) does not have an easy time. To change the figure, its situation in relation to the id may be compared to the relation between a congressman (ego) and his constituents' desires (id) in a democracy. The constituents, let us say, desire freedom, but they often are not very clear about the best way to get it in a very complicated world. The congressman, therefore, is delegated with power to serve the interests of a constituency that "knows what it wants when it wants it," but can have no long range plan or understanding of all that gratifying its wants involves. The congressman, to be sure, may not know adequately what his constituents want, but he is better situated than they to view the complex national and international scene. It becomes his responsibility to work out suitable compromises between the demands of his constituency and the demands of the environment. He may discover too late that some "compromise" was not satisfactory, for the constituency has taken other action that in fact renders the situation worse. Similarly, in the life situation, the id will not take frustration "sitting down," as it were. By displacement it will try to eke out some gratification, which, though giving temporary relief, later turns out to be a nuisance.

III. *HOW THE LIBIDO FIGHTS FOR HAPPINESS*

With this general background, let us consider the main problems that the individual faces in his development. We must imagine a growing ego that cannot be fully aware of, or control, the outer world—and cannot be fully cognizant of, or shape, the aims of the id. It is clear that fear of pain and danger, that insecurity and conflict, will be the order of the day. Anxiety will result from fear (a) that id impulses will not be gratified, or (b) that id impulses, if gratified, will conflict with the demands of the world upon which its very existence depends, or (c) that id impulses are in conflict with the censoring superego (the largely unconscious conscience, to be described shortly).

The important point here is that unwanted anxiety results from these conflicts. It is anxiety that renders a person ineffective; the person needs to reduce it by every means in his power, rational or not. Indeed, the development of his personality may be seen as the individual's mode of reducing anxieties and of insuring the gratification of desires for pleasure with a minimum of pain.

Take, for example, the situation in which a pleasure-seeking child gradually becomes aware that his mother, the first enduring source of his gratification, cannot be exclusively his. The child, incapable of realizing that mother does not have to be exclusively his in order to satisfy his needs, wants to be sure she is his. He may misunderstand his father's claims on his mother. His father seems to enjoy mother's consent, and, alas, the child cannot hope to compete successfully with his father. What to do? Disown one's claim? "No, I can't," says the id. Get rid of the father then? "I can't do that," replies the ego—"and if I show too much hostility, I may rue the day. Besides, there is much in my father I like, and it's safer to have him on my side." There seems to be only one thing left to do. Compromise, for it will be safer than to allow the id full sway. "Instead of hating father, I'll identify with him and have mother's love indirectly." By following the motto "if you cannot lick them, join them," the child through *identification* with father (or authority) makes a prudent, if not wholehearted, adjustment to assure some pleasure in an otherwise hopeless situation.

But this is not the only way to escape anxiety. Why keep on bumping one's head against a stone wall? Why not bury a conflict that threatens one's peace of mind? Instead of fighting a losing battle with some desires, is it not better to *repress* them? That is, refuse (without being consciously aware of it) to admit that one has such a trouble-making sexual desire. "I never had such a wish. I'm not that kind of person!" Thus one may save oneself a "headache" today, only to be faced with more trouble tomorrow. For, on Freud's view, not to recognize the presence of the desire is not to snuff it out, and the repressed desire lives to fight day after day, gnawing away at the protective wall of identification. The result is vague anxiety lest "something awful" happen. For, having repressed the unwanted desire, one has never learned its nature or how to deal with it.

We see here why *repression* foments chaos in life. For the repressed impulse is not frankly faced and "understood." At the same time it is not destroyed, for it goes on working secretly. If the impulse is faced frankly, and *suppressed,* then there will be painful endurance, but the problem is in the open. When the repressed impulse goes on working secretly, the person gets no practice in controlling it and never develops confidence in dealing with it. At the same time he is using more energy than he realizes to keep it from breaking into the open. Thus, debilitating anxiety ensues— which the individual tries to avoid without ever getting at the real cause of the trouble.

However, as we have noted, the ego, through identification, does find partial satisfaction over against the day, possibly, when a more pleasurable solution may be found. This process of identification, especially with the father (for the boy) and the mother (for the girl) is important as a "solution" to anxiety, because father and mother are not only the primary authorities in the life of children, but their bridge to the rest of the world. The approval of mother and father represents the permissible pleasures of the broader environment. Their prohibitions, however, become the "No Trespassing" signs that one had better obey, "or else." Children, therefore, accept them and live by them, whether they understand them or not, because they are helpless to change them. Traffic is so much less fatiguing if one knows where the stop signs stand and where the one-way streets are. True, the powerful motor may be racing while a car is standing still, but the sooner the traffic rules become "second nature," the more likely it is that the car and its occupants will get home safely.

In Freudian terms, such introjected commands become part of the controls that libidinous desires have constantly to confront. What were once controls outside the child are now controls that are part of him (introjected). It is easy to see why Freud felt that the basic structure of personality was formed in the first five years. For at the time when the child is most dependent, least able to understand and criticize, and also primarily within the control of parents, certain signs—"Stop," "Go," "Caution," "Dangerous Curve"—become part of his "adjustment" to life.

We should understand that this process of incorporating into one's life what is deemed conflict-reducing and gratifying goes on throughout life, by and large unconsciously. Imagined and conceived objects, principles, or beings take their place with real beings in the process of reducing conflict. Freud believed that these early identifications perform an important social function simply because they exercise the unreflective, fairly rigid, inner policing function that keeps the libido within the bounds required for social order. Actually, this superego, as Freud called it, also affects the freedom of the ego, because the censorship goes on largely in the unconscious. We must take a closer look at this relation between the id, the ego, and the superego.[4]

IV. *THE FUNCTION OF THE SUPEREGO*

It would be well to consider the superego a kind of *automatic* conscience representing in the life of the person "what you can and

---

[4] On this and many other points related to this chapter, see Philip Rieff, *Freud: The Mind of the Moralist* (New York: Viking Press, 1959).

can't get by with." It keeps many impulses from reaching the ego. It acts not as a judicious critic carefully appraising each desire, but as an agent that helps to keep order by seeing that the conscious ego is not bothered at all by some impulses. Actually the ego might approve of some of these wishes, but it is not given the chance to sit in judgment because of the automatic, inhibiting work of the superego.

But the content of the superego is made up of the incorporated prohibitions demanded by parents and society at one stage of the person's life and in certain situations, despite the fact that these prohibitions might well be removed by parents and society in other situations. Yet, as things stand, the superego keeps on censoring in accordance with the past experience and thus keeps impulse from being more carefully reviewed by the ego. As we have said, however, these closed-out desires do not die simply because they are unwanted by the superego. The id, accordingly, may act up and threaten the superego's "defenses" and thus cause anxiety. Subterfuges (as in dreams or neurotic and psychotic symptoms) may be sought to give some gratification, but never the kind of gratification that suffices.

To summarize: From the point of view of the id, the ego and the superego, developed to further the blind pleasure-seeking demands of the id, often seem to have taken too much into their own hands and forgotten that their function is to make life easier. The ego, in turn, often finds itself hampered by the superego, which is not ruling realistically in the light of new situations. At the same time, the ego is faced with the possibility that the id will break through and listen to no counsel. In short, a strong but rigid conscience may keep a clean house, but too clean for living! Yet, without a control, the id would be all over the place, getting itself into more trouble than it could handle. The problem of life, as the ego sees it, is to weigh the demands of the id against the demands and opportunities of the environment. Through identification and introjected prohibitions, one kind of order and security is introduced, but the order may be too expensive—rigid, short-lived, and anxiety-creating.

Fortunately, therefore, there is another basic way in which the energies of the id can be gratified without creating so much anxiety. Normally, when the libidinous id cannot reach its preferred object in the environment, it finds some substitute source of gratification. If such displacements are socially acceptable, anxiety and repression are avoided. This displacement of libidinous energy may encourage, in varying degrees with different people, creative, intellectual, and artistic activity. When conflict in a life is thus resolved by channeling the energy into a socially acceptable and admired mode of behavior, the displacement is called *sublimation*. Thus, as Freud suggested, Leonardo da Vinci sublimated his yearning for his mother, from whom he had been separated early, by painting madonnas. Displacement, as this example shows, is influenced by the resemblance, in the mind of that person, of the substitute to the original object and by the restrictions of society as they filter through to the individual.

We need not elaborate other defense mechanisms—for example, fixation, rejection, and projection—by which conflict between the libido, superego, ego, and external influences are resolved. It is important to note that each involves the denial or distortion of the real situation in order to reduce tension and that each takes place unconsciously. They do save the libido from serious conflict, but only at the expense of a larger possible growth; they are penny-wise and pound-foolish. In actuality, they are compromises that cost too much in the attempt to provide self-gratification on a day-to-day basis.

Thus, the energy of every personality is channeled into different habits and attachments, into varied outlets that also may serve to dam up the primitive flow of energy. Every personality, at any stage, experiences gratification and discontent. Indeed, "civilization and its discontents" means that civilization is a stage of personal discontent, albeit discontent on the way to further gratification. The id must pay some price, as it were, for the securities of civilized life; but the price is illness and insecurity, if it schemes to eke out its pleasures in secret or if it seeks to manipulate "reality" instead of meeting its requirements.

Indeed, as Freud reflects on the development of the person from infancy to adulthood, he sees the problem as one of moving from the self-gratification of the child engrossed in discovering and enjoying his body (narcissism) to certain forms of displacement. Toward the end of adolescence, the individual should be attracted to others, and not for narcissistic reasons only. The adult, furthermore, should be concerned with others, with vocation, with marriage and family, and with civic responsibilities—and directed by other-regarding motives. Narcissism in adulthood means trouble, both for others and for the individual himself, for the person is still living in a world of childish dreams and distortion buttressed by defense mechanisms that would be unnecessary if he could forego immediate pleasures and live for more inclusive and long-range, but less assured, goals.

V. *THE CONDITIONS OF MENTAL HEALTH IN FREUDIAN TERMS*

With such basic Freudian concepts before us, we turn to answer the question that we set out to answer: What seems to constitute mental health and illness on Freud's view? It may be that when Freud said, "Where the id was, there shall the ego be," [5] he gave us the inner clue. That is, it is only as the changing person becomes aware of his libidinal cravings and is able to discipline them in accordance with reality that a healthy state of mind may be maintained. But to this general principle we need to add more specific content.

First, Freud's background as a physician seems to have led him to presuppose what actually seems to come out in his system—that there is an optimum state of fulfillment of function striven for in every stage of libidinal expression. A certain amount of evil and suffering will always be present in life simply because human beings at any stage are limited both in capacity to understand and to overcome the environment in which they live. But, for Freud, what a "philosophical" biologist might call the general "will to live" is transformed into a self-engrossed libido [6] simply claiming gratification—as much as possible, at whatever expense to anyone—provided that punishment can be escaped.

When Freud puts this unconscious energy beyond the knowledge and control of the reflective ego, he is indeed urging that we cannot expect to understand an individual's development if we think of him merely as a reasonable creature whose task it is, to use a Platonic image, to rein in the relatively wild steeds of desire so that the good of society may be guaranteed. Each person has implacable unconscious desires for pleasure welling up within him from springs deep

[5] Freud, *New Introductory Lectures in Psycho-analysis* (New York: Norton, 1933), p. 112.

[6] The exact relation between the psychic libido and the growing physiological organism is a matter of debate, but some thinkers believe Freud thought of the libido essentially as springing from bodily excitations and tensions. See Ruth L. Munroe, *Schools of Psychoanalytic Thought* (New York: Dryden Press, 1955), p. 75 and *passim*.

within his nature. And, Freud assumed, there will inevitably be trouble.

And well there might be, for on Freud's view, however he may insist that the wholesome individual must be reality-oriented and altruistic in motive, the child is unconsciously and consciously a self-engrossed pleasure-seeker, who cannot but regard the world around him as a means to pleasure. Despite Freud's emphasis on the process of sublimation, it never becomes clear how this narcissistic infant, whose ego and superego are in the last analysis different lines of defense against its own insecurity, is ever to find it possible to care about truth or other persons *for their own sake.*

Yet what does Freud say is necessary if this irrational, egotistic infant is not to be excessively anxiety-ridden? The answer seems to be made in terms of a balance of trends and countertrends in the quantitative energy-distribution of the individual. Mother and father and society must understand the nature and growth of the infant. Instead of being overrestrictive, especially in the early stages when the child's ego is developing and, as a result, he so readily misunderstands and misconstrues "reality," they will allow him to develop as much confidence as possible both in himself and in those around him.

Here, curiously, the appeal is to the rational nature of the individual, supposedly inundated by the irrational forces of the id. However irrational Freud may believe human nature to be, his whole system of therapy is based on the assumption that once society and parents understand the individual, and once he gets insight into himself—and this is made easier in a friendly atmosphere of tolerant concern, for which in turn there are no original roots in human nature—he will develop into a responsible adult. Any hope that there is for humanity rests on educating human beings in such a way that their uncertainties will not dam up and produce exaggerated, unrealistic anxiety.

To put the matter differently, on the Freudian view, the human situation seems to be one in which the childish catch-as-catch-can, self-absorbed demand for "sexual" gratification must come to draw a balance with the more far-sighted, more disciplined, and more enlightened calculation of a society. Society, in turn, must defend its "civilized" ways against the demands of children and the still undisciplined demands of adults. If the growing person cannot maintain an adequate balance, neurosis sets in. Here, any "compromise" pleasure experience is still permeated with suffering. If there is to be satisfaction more gratifying than this anxiety-nourished flight from one uncertain pain to another anxiety-nourished pleasure, it can only be gained when the individual learns to choose, in an understanding environment, those ends that do not separate him from those around him and especially from those upon whom he depends.

Secondly—developing this conception of mental health as striking a balance between irrational desire and dependable order—Freud seems to think that mental ill-health always stems from the fact that parents and society are seen by the individual as hostile to his legitimate self-expression. Because the individual, by nature, cannot really accept their control, he becomes a hostile maneuverer whose task is to overcome opposition by cunning disguises that enable him to get by. But he is, at the same time, a hostage who cannot afford to incur constant hostility.

Thus, instead of being able to express himself "authentically," [7] a person forever lives within the context of his own (frequently misunderstood) fears and the restrictions and taboos of the social environment. Because he always operates from concealment, as it were, he is forced to develop "in-authentic" values, which do indeed alleviate "situations," but which, because they are anxiety-induced, "never culminate in an experience joyous in itself." [8]

The psychotic individual, who needs institutional treatment, has paid the highest price for saving himself (as he believes) from the excessive demands of those who do not understand or care. As a psychotic he lives beyond the reach of people as they are. The symptoms of his illness are the ways in which he, facing his conflicts with his limitations and insight, "suffers" the most economical distribution of his energy. It would seem that to invite illness is to live as a child when one is chronologically an adult, that is, to demand protection for oneself without criticism of one's desires, to assume that one is correct in his strivings and that the world "owes" one a living. The person who is ill tends to gratify himself by fits and starts; he goes on being hungry for he is not really satisfied; he never confidently enjoys the pleasures that he does have, for he lives "on the sly" psychologically so far as others are concerned.

Yet an impartial observer who saw the individual's struggle from

[7] We borrow here from Lewis Samuel Feuer's interesting treatment, *Psychoanalysis and Ethics* (Springfield, Ill.: Charles C Thomas, 1955), p. 13.

[8] *Ibid.*, p. 13.

infancy onward might say that, if the impulses of the id had not been controlled arbitrarily by unwise or unsympathetic agents in the environment, the individual might well have endured his frustrations and moved step by step into the responsibility for the understanding and sympathetic care of others that adulthood demands. Thus, as Franz Alexander puts it, mature love appears as

a new feature in the emotional structure, when the young male and female feel secure. In adolescence the sexual object serves primarily to increase self-confidence, as a proving ground for the ego. In maturity love assumes for the first time a generous, giving quality, the evidence of strength and energy which the mature organism no longer requires for its maintenance. This type of love is what Freud called genital sexuality.[9]

We must note, however, that although the individual has gone outside himself, the suggestion is that we cannot expect him to do so until his need for self-maintenance is surfeited.

Third, Freud prefaces the famous statement "where the id was, there the ego shall be" with the interesting statement that the purpose of psychoanalysis is "to strengthen the ego, to make it more independent of the superego, to widen its field of vision, and so to extend its organization that it can take over new portions of the id." [10] This surely means that the individual must move between fearful self-protection, buttressed by an inflexible, self-protecting conscience, to more confident and flexible exploration of its own desires ("new portions of the id") in new ways. If the id can become more mobile, and if the "conscience" can become more tolerant, the ego can go on with its corrective work freer from crippling anxiety. [11]

A person, it is implied, suffers if he does not take into account as much as he can about himself, others, and the world. Yet he must not lose himself to any of these. As Freud's foremost English follower and expositor,[12] Ernest Jones, puts it, there is a great difference between a superego or conscience rooted in, and nourished by, fear and one rooted in, and nourished by, affection. For the kind of

[9] *Fundamentals of Psychoanalysis* (New York: Norton, 1948), p. 55. See also Alexander's *The Medical Value of Psychoanalysis* (New York: Norton, 1932).

[10] *New Introductory Lectures on Psychoanalysis*, pp. 108–12.

[11] See "The Resistance to Psychoanalysis," *Collected Papers* (London: Hogarth Press, 1950) Vol. V, written in 1925.

[12] See Ernest Jones, *The Life and Work of Sigmund Freud* (3 vols.; New York: Basic Books, 1953–57).

conscience one feels both reflects and determines the kind of relation one has to others, to one's own gratification and restraint, and to one's basic anxiety. If only the child can learn to endure libidinal tension in the presence of frustration without fear of loss and without building up defenses of guilt and hatred that lead only to frustrations of another kind; if, in a word, he can deal with his tensions and conflicts not by either denouncing or defending them, but by suspending them until a more propitious time for all, then he may come to find the freedom that Jones calls "control." He may then have the opportunity to develop a "normal" or healthy mind, that is, a mind that, being *Angstfrei,* can accept life joyfully "with all its visitations and chance." [13]

VI. *FREUDIAN THEORY VERSUS THE GREEK AND JUDEO-CHRISTIAN VIEW OF SALVATION*

We may conclude our exposition of Freud by comparing his view of "human salvation," so to speak, to other historic solutions. It seems clear that Freud, in his concept of sublimation and in his therapeutic scheme, assumes that if a child can be kept from undue, defensive anxiety, his natural development will include more of the interests and abilities of others, more of "reality" in the process of his own development. Again, if the child gets understanding, patient, good-humored care, he will, as he matures, not think of the world simply as his own preserve. Insight and forbearing care, a growing recognition of his problem, an awareness of the world, a society that disciplines because it cares—with these a fragile infant may grow into a healthy, free personality. There seems no doubt that Freud, to use common parlance, was "realistic" enough to see that the serpent of protective, aggressive selfishness would always be present.

Actually, then, Freud, as we have suggested, joins many thinkers in the Judeo-Christian tradition in claiming that there is something egotistic in man that cannot be exculpated by human effort alone. For these Judeo-Christian theists, only as God comes into the individual's life and is made the center of loyalty can he find strength

[13] Ernest Jones, "What Is a Normal Mind?" in *International Journal of Psychoanalysis,* XXIII (1942), 7.

to overcome narcissistic self-preference. It is otherwise futile and self-deceiving for man, individually and socially, to attempt to pull himself up by his own bootstraps. Freud, however, would not allow a religious factor to play any part in salvation from selfishness. Only understanding of oneself will sufficiently free the forces of personality from anxiety to allow altruistic living.

It is tempting to say, as some have, that such a command as "know thyself" is as Socratic and Platonic as can be expected. Clearly, for Freudian therapy to succeed, the individual must depend, with the aid of the psychoanalyst, upon the power of rational self-insight. Yet, to say that Freud's emphasis on self-understanding puts him in agreement with Greek reliance on reason is to be misled by a superficial similarity. Socrates and Plato regarded "knowledge" as something very different from the purely scientific understanding of causal sequences that the biologically oriented Freud accepted. They would insist (and here Aristotle and the Stoics would have agreed) that no one could be said to know himself and others apart from knowing the very structure of the universe in which human beings live. Socrates' God, Plato's *The Good,* Aristotle's contemplative *Prime Mover,* the Stoic *Reason,* were not simply beings "out there" alongside which man exists and to which he must adjust. They were Beings, to put it generally, related to everything existing, and without them there would be chaos in the universe. They were latent in every person's life; and they made themselves felt as positive aids to growth insofar as men curbed their desires and lived with each other and in their world as reasonably as possible.

Freud's libidinous energies, on the other hand, do not spring from any pervasive Order which makes for goodness. His thought is much closer in its presuppositions to that of Epicurus who had no belief in reality as an ultimate Unity to which man felt, or could feel, kinship. Epicurus thought of the good life as the maximizing of pleasure and minimizing of pain—and he conceived the highest pleasure to be of the mind. What could be better than to withdraw with kindred spirits away from the world and from any responsibility for others? For Freud, as for Epicurus, man is stranded in a universe that allows for a somewhat precarious existence, but certainly has no special concern for him. For Epicurus, as for Freud, knowing does not *unite* man to Reality. To know is to calculate one's chances for self-preservation and reproduction in an indifferent world. Neither Freud nor Epicurus believed that man's reason unites him to the

Universe in such a way that he can find new strength and insight if he meets the conditions.

Indeed, Freud felt that such beliefs, in a provident God, or in a Father to whom men could turn for understanding and care, were infantile props that only despairing, childish minds could dream up. Religion is a perpetual "illusion" in which the individual, amid the suffering inflicted by Nature and by selfish man, objectifies his deep-seated wish for security. This illusion keeps men from understanding the true source of their morality and from investigating the dependable ways in which the human lot can be improved.[14]

Thus we come back to our earlier statement that Freud leaves us the faith that man can manage to endure disappointment and chance, can join in positive concern for others, because he can see himself with detachment and insight. Whether his doctrine of the id and libido allows such confidence is a serious question. And when he denies to reason *any* insight into the inner nature of reality, or shuts human feeling away from *any* possible creative religious relation to the universe, he disposes too easily of matters that merit more careful consideration than he gives them.

VII. *A BASIC PROBLEM CONFRONTING PSYCHOTHERAPY AND ETHICS*

In this chapter we have thus far tried to understand what is involved in mental health as conceived by the leader of psychoanalytic thought, whose basic ideas now form a part of our heritage. And we have, at the same time, introduced fundamental problems that face all searchers for the life good to live. How shall we think (a) of man's nature, (b) of the part that biological and emotional needs play, (c) of the way in which man develops moral standards and a sense of obligation, (d) of the function and power of reason, (e) of the justification of egotism or altruism, and (f) of the role of belief in God? We must now become alert to a basic issue that will pursue us in succeeding chapters.

In his effort to give therapeutic counsel to persons obviously disturbed or in conflict, both within themselves and with others, Freud developed hypotheses about the reasons for their disturbances. To

[14] See Gregory Zilboorg, *Freud and Religion* (Westminster, Md.: The Newman Press, 1959), for a critical treatment of Freud's analysis of religion.

put it in our own language: What *ought* to have happened to these patients in order for them to have avoided these disturbances, and to have grown up "healthy"?

This procedure may seem quite different from an attempt to decide what the good life is by selecting a good man (or good men) and analyzing out the principles by which he lives. Aristotle, for example, said that the ethicist could not discover what made up the good life unless he studied the good man. Aristotle, accordingly, was forced to analyze the nature of the good man and the effect of cultural influence on him. And he discovered that the good life was manifest in the human being who harmoniously fulfilled the potentialities of his nature. As an ideal before him, no doubt, he kept the image of a good man (like Socrates or Pericles) as the standard by which to judge actions as good or bad. But his own analysis of the problems of becoming a good man was greatly dependent on his idea of the capacities of man's nature. Was it really otherwise with Freud?

As Freud attempted to discover why a person became "disturbed," he too, like Plato and Aristotle, was forced to provide an "anatomy" of the psyche and to develop principles to guide men in avoiding maladjustment and becoming "normal" or "healthy" persons. But where did he get his idea of the healthy and the normal? Was there some pattern of human attitudes and actions by which he was judging the degree of illness or health? Can the psychotherapist who is helping someone "find health again" avoid aiming at some ideal that he himself believes is approachable and worthy of effort, that is, which ought to be approached both by himself and the patient? While he may not conceive of himself as "a moralist," can he really avoid being one and developing some "basic" commandments?

Freud certainly would have insisted that it is best for all persons to "face reality" in their own nature, and in the world. Indeed, the psychotherapist might ask himself: "Why sit down and take one's own time and energy, another's time, energy, and money, unless you both believe that there is a pattern of living better than the one now followed by the patient?" "Whatever else a man ought to be," we can imagine Freud urging, "he ought to be as objective as possible about his life."

But, we may ask, where does even this part (objectivity) of an ideal of life come from? If we believe that it is valid, surely it is not because all people *are being objective* all the time. "They *ought* to be," a Freud would say. Well, why? Why is it better to be objective than subjective? This question needs to be faced, but Freud never tells why being objective is the ideal. It is clear, nevertheless, that like Aristotle, he is guiding himself by some ideal of the good man that never gets explicit justification.

As a first generalization, then, we may say that, in effect, all ethicists and psychotherapists cannot begin even to think about health and ill-health, good and bad living, without some frame of reference or ideal to guide them, as they go to work in judging and analyzing.

But does it make a difference whether one is explicit or not, as Aristotle was, about his predicament as a therapist or moralist? Let us ponder this question as we consider why, probably, Freud was not explicit. Persons, presumably, came to him as a doctor, complaining of ailments for which physiological medicine had no treatment. Freud did not push before the patient some explicit "ideal personality." The patient came because, in thinking, feeling, and acting, he was at some point seriously deviating from what was considered normal in his immediate social environment. The standard was as "practical" for the patient as that, and he was hoping that treatment would improve his relations to his family, his friends, and his work—and to himself. This may seem very uncritical procedure, for it may turn out that not the patient but the family is at fault.

But here it may help if we realize the difference in the situations that the ethicist and a psychotherapist confront. The psychologist does not proclaim what the good life is, but works with people who admit that they are "in trouble" and who want to decrease their conflicts in their situation as *they* see it. They come begging for help, especially if some bothersome physiological symptom or uncontrollable mental or emotional state is involved. The ethicist (or priest, rabbi, or pastor) faces a different situation even when people seek him out. He "stands for" or proclaims an ideal for men to follow.

About all the ethicist can do, if he wants to see his ideas in practice, is to try to get people to listen and to agree with him. His job, in the last analysis, is to get them to feel disturbed about their lives; from his perspective, they are morally sick and in trouble. But, if he is as persistent as a gadfly, he may, like Socrates, be forced to take the hemlock, because people will think the trouble is with him. When Socrates diagnosed the trouble of many Athenians as being the failure to see that "virtue does not come from wealth, but that wealth, and many other good things which men have, whether private or public, comes from virtue," [15] they invited him either to desist, to leave town, or to perish. The psychotherapist, then, is not the ethicist, although his role approaches that of the ethicist when the psychotherapist writes a book in order that people may "understand themselves and their problems."

But let us not lose sight of the more important theoretical issue involved here.[16] Should the psychotherapist try to help the patient get back to where the patient wants to be, or where he himself thinks it better for the patient to be upon the authority of his own observation and reflection upon life? Whatever the answer, the question finally to be faced is: Whence comes the standard?

The psychotherapist here might say: "I, a member of a certain society and culture, am confronted with a patient who is another member of that society and culture. He has come to me for help in relieving his disturbance, and this will indeed entail considerations of adjustment he may have to make in relation to his physical and social environment. We both, no doubt, make certain assumptions— more than we articulate—about what is desirable in our culture. But I, at least, find in the course of my analysis certain things about human nature which I could not have discovered unless there was this 'breakdown' and this analysis. And there gradually has emerged in my mind a picture of what might have been if something else had taken place rather than what did take place. The culture did not allow for this man's ability or needs, and he, in turn, did not take account of certain of its demands and opportunities, or even of his own nature. My ideal of health for him comes from a more complete analysis of him in relation to his social milieu and his probable future. Isn't this a better approach than being guided by some ideal of the good life?"

The answer here is not easy, and our concern is to give not a solution, but to point up a problem that will continue to interest us. Can either the psychotherapist or the patient get away from "the ideal of the good man *as such*"? Has not the patient, in coming, already made a judgment upon himself that is the result of many other experiences he has had and judgments he has made? Has he

[15] Plato, *The Apology of Socrates* (New York: Liberal Arts Press, 1948) p. 36.

[16] See Heinz Hartmann, *Psychoanalysis and Moral Values* (New York: International Universities Press, 1960), for further discussion of some of the issues treated in this section.

not judged himself and his experiences in the light of some conception, however inarticulate—even if it be no more than the ideal of
one who "gets along better with society"? Is it not failure in his
effort, be it only "to get along better with society," that has brought
him as one who is "in trouble" to the psychotherapist? Does the
psychotherapist not judge him both in the light of what he says and
in the light of his ideal of health?

In a word, must not psychoanalysis be guided by—and assume—
moral presuppositions, that is, (latent) conceptions of what the good
life is or might be? There is no doubt that psychoanalysis may put a
premium on some factors in the personality to the neglect of
others. If, for example, the therapist believes that mutual sexual
gratification is an important ingredient of a good life, his analysis
may ferret out factors related to sexuality and neglect those not
related to it. And if he thinks that no life is "good" in which there
is less pleasure than pain, he may focus on pleasure-making and
pain-relieving factors in the personality at the expense of other
factors.

From our argument, then, it follows that any analysis of personality
is more subtly influenced by the analyst's convictions about the good
life than might seem to appear on the surface. This does not mean
that psychoanalysis must stop until we can be sure what the good
life is. But it does mean that it is better for the psychotherapist to be
aware that such presuppositions are influencing analysis of what
"human nature" is, what it can be, and what it *ought* to be. Perhaps
a person never *ought* to be what he cannot be. Even so, the issue still
remains: What ought he to be in the light of what he can be?

To conclude: Any view of the nature of man that emerges from
psychotherapeutic analysis must be seen as reflecting some presuppositions about illness and health. It is not as if we could observe
human nature in the abstract, take its measure, and then say what it
could and could not do, or even what it could do best. Accordingly,
in studying man, we study not a concoction in a test tube, or the
life history of a plant that can make no assumptions or generalizations about its own life, however uncritical. We actually study a
being whose reflections on life make a difference to the quality of his
life and the judgment he passes upon himself as good or bad. Thus,
the ethicist and the psychotherapist must, like all of us, take life on
the wing, or "in the making." They must keep their eyes fixed on the

human beings before them. At the same time they must realize that, because they themselves are also involved in the process of living, it is important to be as clear and explicit as possible about the ideal they have in mind. This ideal they must check constantly by what goes on in the men to whom it is applied.

In a word, what we actually observe at any moment are men at some stage in the process of realizing some ideal; and therefore we cannot observe them apart from some ideal goal which observer and subject believe they ought to approach. We can only shuttle back and forth from conceptions of the ideal to the existent and realize that all observation and thinking goes on within that process. We cannot say: Let us first discover what man's nature is like and then let us decide what he ought to become. Nor can we say: We know what he ought to become. Not unless we can find some basis for believing that his nature at least allows him so to become. We are forced to start with convictions about man's nature, about what he can be, and about what he ought to be. As we go along, we improve our conceptions both of the actuality and of the ideal, and we continue to adjust one to the other.

We make these comments tentatively in the hope that they may sensitize us to a basic problem that confronts any ethicist and psychologist of personality, and the psychotherapist in particular. The relevance of these remarks can be tested by the reader as we turn now to other psychological interpretations of human nature and healthy personality.

The reader will note that we are not stopping to evaluate Freud's theory of the unconscious and other psychological doctrines crucial to Freud's theory of man and his development. We have hinted that it seemed to us doubtful that Freud could justify his belief that men who, by nature, are dominated by self-absorbed pleasure-seeking can be expected to become altruistic. Other important issues might have detained us, especially Freud's interpretation of conscience, of free will, and of religion. But rather than enter into the debate about the dynamics of personality growth here, we shall do better first to study the conceptions of personality set forth by other significant psychotherapists and psychologists of personality. Much of what they say will be relevant to basic tenets of Freud and to ethical issues. As we move along, we shall call attention, at appropriate places, to considerations important for the solution of historic problems about the nature of the good life.

VIII. *REFLECTIVE SUMMARY*

Usually men assume that they are aware of what they are about and keep adequate control of their actions by reasonable planning. Not only did Freud challenge this assumption, but he made the modern world aware that unconscious forces cannot be neglected in understanding human behavior.

Freud's own view is that man's consciousness and reason, late evolutionary acquisitions, originate in the need of an insatiable, undisciplined, nonmoral, unconscious id that cannot trust itself to come to terms with reality. This unconscious id is never open to man's conscious inspection. Explosions in the id may shatter the defenses of the ego, rather than be governed by the ego's realistic commands. Yet the essence of Freud's therapy is that the individual by way of detached, rational analysis can gain insight into his debilitating conflicts and avoid or overcome illness.

Freud does not make his case more acceptable when he adds that the unconscious is broadly sexual, governed by a ruthless pleasure-principle that is bound to conflict with the demands of family and environment generally. The human being's struggle is now centered in a conscious and unconscious connivance within himself to resolve conflicts. The superego is an inner automatic damper that forestalls major conflicts with a hostile environment and manages to maintain an uneasy compromise between the id and the world. The personality that a person thus acquires is the means he uses to escape anxiety in the attempt to realize as much pleasure as possible for himself.

Yet Freud says that a healthy personality must move from rigid, growth-inhibiting controls to flexible and understanding responses, from self-absorbed gratification to concern for mutuality and responsibility in human relations—including sexual, vocational, and family life. Is not Freud expecting a miracle to occur in order to get such reality-oriented and altruistic fruits from implacable self-seeking roots? The health requirement of positive love is hard to ground in a creature whose nature it is to escape anxiety about his own narcissistic pleasure. How move from a conscience (superego) rooted in fear to one nourished by affection?

This general view of human nature and personality involves Freud, on his own premises, in a questionable faith that man by self-

understanding—not by religious loyalty to any God or cosmic Reason
—can develop realistic maturity unhampered by infantile props, religious or otherwise. Freud seems to assume rather than argue the limitations he puts upon reason, and his view of the superego and of religion does less than justice to the whole of moral and religious experience, as we shall see.

In Freud we come face to face with the problem of the nature of the standard by which to judge personality defects and illness. We must ask the therapist: Whence, in your dealing with mentally ill persons, do you derive your standard of what they *ought* to be? Clearly both patients, therapist, and society operate on some conception of what human beings ought to become and can become. Because some view of what human nature is and ought to become is involved in observing and evaluating human behavior, the importance of keeping the underlying view of man and of the guiding ideal as explicit as possible is evident.

3

The Human Situation According to Jung, Adler, and Horney

~~~~~~

Freud, as we have seen, focused attention on the unconscious springs of human behavior. But was he correct about the fundamental urges operating below the surface and about their relation to the conscious purposes and behavior of the individual? The answers to these questions are beyond the special competence of the ethicist as such. Yet, to say the least, he cannot but be concerned about the powers attributed to human nature and the ways in which they are said to operate to support or impede the development of the good life. If the ethicist believes that the standards for the life good to live are rooted in or somehow related to human strivings, he will want to examine with special care any theory of human motivation and of the development of motives.

Our purpose in this chapter is to familiarize ourselves with three other significant theories of motivation and mental health. Whenever it seems especially relevant, we shall indicate ethical issues. But because in Chapters 4, 5, and 6, we shall study psychologists who, as they work at their own theories of personality development, are appreciatively critical of Freud, Jung, and Adler, our main concern in this chapter is to enlarge the background needed for later discussion.

I. *CARL JUNG*

Carl G. Jung (1875–1961), who Freud once hoped would be his successor, found it impossible to grant his teacher's emphasis on sex [1] as the controlling factor in personality formation. But like Freud, Jung is convinced that the total psychic energy of a person is somehow related to the energy used in bodily growth and decay and that most of it operates unconsciously.

Although Freud, however, held that all the creative and cultural pursuits are sublimations of an erotic libido, Jung maintains that creative expression is more fundamental than the sexual life to the healthy development of a person. Jung agrees with Freud that both the unconscious and the conscious factors in life must be balanced if malfunction is not to result. But Jung sees the whole problem of human life differently because different ingredients form the structure of man. Yet, as we shall note, Jung conceives of these ingredients differently because he does not think that mental illness can be adequately explained on Freudian principles. It seems clear also that his definition of mental illness, and degrees of illness, depends on what he believes health involves.

Jung's conceptions lend themselves even less to brief description than do Freud's, but even a truncated view of them may help us see what conditions are to be met if a person is to realize "integration" of his personality.

A. *The Human Heritage*

On Jung's view, man's motivational energy is far from exhausted by demands of personal survival and racial continuity. Everyday life, let alone the history of human culture, shows that man gives himself to many forms of activity that have little or no "survival" value. Man is never content with mere living, even mere comfortable or "pleasant" living. For, says Jung, man in essence is a maker, a creator.

But why is this? Why is the individual, why is "civilization" discontent with standing still or just living another pleasant day? Because

---

[1] There are critics of Jung who believe that his interpretation of Freud's sexuality is too narrow and that much of his criticism would apply, if at all, only to the earlier phases of Freud's thought. See Ruth L. Munroe, *Schools of Psychoanalytic Thought* (New York: Dryden Press, 1955), Chapter XIII.

every individual is pregnant with an unconscious psychic inheritance, with dormant tendencies that echo ages of ancestral struggle. Would it not be queer if each individual came into the world with physiological reactions (like reflexes) a part of him, or with the marks of evolutionary selection (like the appendix) in his body, and yet with a mind showing no traces of his ancestry? Why consider the newborn babe a psychic vacuum, with no traces of his ancestral psychic struggle in him?

Jung, accordingly, asks us to set aside a biological, shrunken image of man. Men at all times, everywhere, have not struggled merely to survive. Despite their differences, they have felt great challenges, scaled many heights, dreamed stirring dreams, and created visions of what life should be. Some experiences and visions they have found more satisfying than others, and some failures have driven them to despair. For Jung it is inconceivable that such successes and failures should leave no impression on the psyche. Thus he believes that, together, they are felt by each individual as part of his psychic inheritance.

Obviously, the problem of the relation of psyche to body lurks in the background. Yet, unless one is committed to making the psyche completely dependent upon the body, he can at least harbor the possibility that in the psyche, which a man inherits along with his body, there are traces that will influence not only how he "takes" the world now, but also what he will "go after." Such an inheritance Jung invites the skeptical reader to consider seriously when he hypothesizes the conception of the *collective unconscious*.

To expand: Each of us, Jung would say, has not only a unique *personal unconscious*, developed since his infancy, but he carries in his collective unconscious internal traces symbolic of the human race's basic ventures in living. These "archetypes," as Jung calls the traces, might be considered universal human themes by which our ancestors have lived. However, they are not finished, clear-cut goals, but "thought-feelings," that is, suggestive thrusts into our lives of immemorial ancestral wrestlings. They lie dormant within us, but far from dead. Their tendency is to re-enact themselves. Each of us needs to work out these "themes" in a new way in our new situations.[2]

[2] See C. G. Jung, *The Integration of Personality* (New York: Farrar and Rinehart, 1939), p. 50, and *Contributions to Analytic Psychology* (London: Kegan-Paul and Co., 1928), p. 162.

But is there any real evidence for such archetypal thought-feelings? It must suffice here to say that this far-ranging scholar found his hypothesis helpful in understanding much more than the psychopathology of everyday life. He scoured the mythological and artistic life of many peoples and was impressed by the underlying common "images" or symbols by which they live and depict their problems.

A simple example is that of the most significant symbol, the mother archetype. Present with variations among all people, it symbolizes the recurring *psychic conflict situation* so well illustrated during infancy. Every person, like the infant, feels a need for unity with the source of nourishment, warmth, and security. But "mother" may be not only the tender life-giver, and source of comfort; she may be the terrible punisher, the devourer of her children. Thus, the "image," the mother archetype, is not a fixed picture, complete once and for all; rather, it represents "one of the most vivid experiences man can have" [3] and comes alive when he has critical experiences of wanting security without losing his own identity. The father archetype is another important one; it symbolizes the need for authority and for creativity.

There are many such archetypes, often interrelated, that seek to find expression in the life of the individual. Again, archetypes are not to be thought of as creative in some simple-minded way. To illustrate, the Adam and Eve, the Cain and Abel stories in the Judeo-Christian tradition do not solve problems of the relation of men to each other and to the source of being once and for all. They suggest underlying "thought-feeling" reactions to human existence. So the Christian symbol of the Cross may "express" the kind of problem that human persons confront when they are overwhelmed by their sense of sin, by the amount of suffering sin creates in the lives of both the good and the bad. The Cross may then symbolize (in different ways theologically) the need for being saved from sin and its consequences. Symbols such as this have gripped men because they represent both some aim and some unfinished business in human life.

B. *The Nature of Human Conflict*

Keeping this conception of unconscious archetypes in mind, we can consider the persistent problem of living. For the individual, Jung realizes, is molded in a given society, in a given part of the

[3] Munroe, *op. cit.*, p. 553.

world. His parents and his society demand of him a certain conformity to their standards and ways of doing things. Yet he often finds that these requirements stir a hornet's nest within him. Consequently, his ego must somehow reconcile the demands of the "inner life" with the outer world. The result is a gradual conscious and unconscious development of the role in terms of which he resolves his inner and outer conflicts. This dramatic "mask," or *persona*, as Jung calls the role, actually operates to control individual expression in ways reminiscent of Freud's superego, for it assures an individual's "adjustment" to the group at the expense, if necessary, of his private yearnings.

Freud explained a large part of an individual's superego, as well as his present behavior, in the light of his past. Here again his disciple regards this analysis as only partially true. A person's orientation and behavior, Jung maintains, is to be understood not only through his past, but in the light of the significant problem he faces now and in the immediate future. Similarly, if a person is to stay healthy, he must balance gratification of the unconscious drives with the needs of the present. That is, the individual cannot allow the archetypal "wisdom" of the ages to blind him to opportunities for present creativity. Nor must he fall into the "safe" conventional ruts of the present and neglect the creative struggle that he shares in his inner nature with all men past and present.

With this perpetual conflict going on in him, it is not surprising to find the individual contriving different defenses in order to bring about "peace." For example, the exaggerated *introvert* escapes from "the demands of the world" into the secret enjoyment of the unconscious. But he never adequately finds new ways of gratifying his libido. On the other hand, the exaggerated *extrovert* is fleeing from conflict by being very attentive to the demands of the outside world. But he is never really adapting himself to it. It is, however, just as unhealthy to become shallow by adjusting to every new situation—but never changing anything—as it is to refuse to risk danger by withdrawing and becoming defensive. It is as unhealthy to *regress* to the "secure" infantile memories of "tender" childhood as it is to lose one's individuality by *identifying* with too narrow a *persona* or role.

The total situation is, of course, much more complicated than suggested here. For on Jung's view every person has to work within the particular set-up of capacities and tendencies that distinguishes him.

Thus he cannot be either simply introvert or simply extrovert, because if he is introvert in manner of expression, the extrovert in him will be driven to deeper unconscious development. Furthermore, any general slant of personality will be affected by the way in which a person manifests his cognitive functions of sensing, intuiting, feeling, and thinking. Thus a prophetic Gandhi, introverted and basically intuitive, becomes a different leader from, say, a military extrovert who is more "sensory" in orientation.

The important point for us, however, is that the individual must learn to organize all these basic factors in his life into an integrated team—what Jung calls a *self*. Both inner collective and personal unconscious tendencies, operating in the context of dominant temperamental and knowing capacities, must learn to live with the claims and necessities from outside—without destroying the creative potential of the person. "All or none" attitudes will not do. They invariably result from a peculiar fear to create a more harmonious individual. For there are far-reaching risks to be taken if one is not to become an acrobatic juggler with life.

Note the difference in emphasis and outlook here. Freud says that "where the id was, there shall the ego be"; insight into the past causes of the present is paramount. The emphasis is on replacing ignorance with knowledge. But insight in retrospect must for Jung be supplemented by insight in prospect. Thus Jung says: "Personality can never develop itself unless the individual chooses his own way consciously and with conscious, moral decision. Not only the causal motive, the need, but a conscious, moral decision must lend its 'strength' to the process of the development of personality." [4]

C. *The Crucial Faith in Development of Integration*

Jungian psychotherapy thus attempts to cure neurotic behavior by analyzing the symbolism that expresses the tension between the creative and uncreative—whether it be overdevelopment of the sexual at the expense of cooperation with others, whether it be overemphasis on the *status quo* at the expense of positive change. The task is always to effect a mode of living in which the past (including the unconscious) can contribute to the future, and the future, in turn,

[4] C. G. Jung, *Integration of Personality*, p. 289. There is much here to remind one of Rank's positive view of the ego and will. See Otto Rank, *Will Therapy* and *Truth and Reality* (trans. Jessie Taft; New York: Alfred B. Knopf, 1945).

can relate itself to the good in the past. Chaos results only when man rejects his dynamic potential for creative self-development and differentiation. In *Modern Man in Search of a Soul,* Jung observes that most persons over thirty-five who came for treatment were really suffering from thwarted or dwarfed creativity.

At this point it is interesting to state the difference between Freud and Jung in terms of their interpretation of religion. For Freud religion is an unfortunate illusion fulfilling an immature wish for a cosmic Father. But Jung believed that his older patients especially were in need of the creative thrust that religious (and artistic) living would have provided. For in religion the individual seeks an immediate experience of God—as we see in the varied symbolism of all peoples in their attempt to understand human existence and suffering. Jung holds that, whether religion be true or false, this archetype, this seeking, is denied only at the expense of mental health.

We close this section by suggesting several basic contrasts in the Freudian and Jungian view of the problem that man must solve if he is to avoid illness and be integrated. For Jung each man must use his potential for creativity, which links him to all men past and future, to work out his role as he interacts with his fellowmen and with the Universe in which he finds himself. While Freud introduced the modern mind to the forces of an unconscious realm, he conceived the problems of personal and social survival as a matter of so managing one's libidinous demands for pleasure that there might be a good balance of pleasure over pain in human existence. Freud's emphasis is on relieving erotic tension, on achieving gratification for desires that are essentially self-centered. In Jung's view the unconscious becomes the arena of creative demands—let pleasure and unpleasantness fall where they may. In mankind and in each person, the premium is on mind in the making; to decay means to be uncreative.

Again, on Freud's view, a person's future seems to be determined by certain rigid demands for pleasure, which, however devious in manner of gratification, are never themselves transformed. In other words, an individual's personality at any stage reflects the compromise made between unalterable urges within and the environmental forces impinging upon him. On Jung's view, there is demand from within and from without, but the demand for creativity calls for *transformation* of the situation in which the individual himself is a factor. Obviously, the creativity will operate within the limits of man's total constitution, but the theory of man and of the resulting good life includes creativity as part of every ferment in personality formation. In Jung, therefore, we have an excellent illustration of the way in which the conception of the kind of struggle going on in man affects the conception of the goal of human health. Or is a certain conception of health guiding the analysis of what the dynamics of growth are?

II. *ALFRED ADLER*

Alfred Adler (1870–1937) was another early disciple of Freud who came to conceive of basic urges in a different way and thus gave a different account of mental illness. Again, we must be satisfied with suggesting basic emphases in relation to mental illness.

A. *Conflict and Compensation*

When does a person begin to strike us as mentally ill? When his responses to situations are rigid and seem to bear no reasonable relation to the supposed provocation. For example, we can understand why a man might brag with small provocation; but when a man brags without any provocation, and does so consistently, we are surprised and soon wonder what is wrong with him. We can understand why a man might, once in a while, count the stairs he climbs, but when he seems compelled to count all the stairs he climbs every time he climbs them, we suspect that something more besides counting or stair-climbing is involved.

Adler, like Freud and Jung, started his career as a medical doctor. He became impressed with the part physical defects played in the total life of many of his patients. He also noted that many of his neurotic patients had some physical handicap or physically inferior organ. As a doctor he knew that often the body itself makes up for defects and also that the enforced use of some other organ makes it unusually strong—as when a person who has a handicapped hand or arm perforce develops the other hand or arm more fully than most people do. Persons with eyesight never take advantage of the sensitivity of fingertips; but those same nerve endings become "eyes" for the blind who have learned to read braille.

Much of our *compensating* for defect is indirect, as these examples show. In indirect compensation we use, or take fuller advantage of, other capacities to make up for some defect. But when a stuttering Greek boy, Demosthenes, trained himself to become a great orator by talking with pebbles in his mouth, he compensated directly by transforming the organ involved. Whether compensation is direct or indirect, crippling limitations in themselves need not cause neurosis.

It therefore became clear to Adler that defects are part of a larger problem the patient faces. Defects could be the occasion for, or even the manifestation of, a deeper problem in his life. Indeed, it often seemed that when a person was fighting a losing battle with the deeper problem, his infirmity spread to, or found expression through, a weaker organ. Often, also, the person seemed to have developed the physical infirmity as a way of trying to solve his problem.

Is there some one underlying urge which is frustrated by defects or takes advantage of them in order to avoid further conflict? Seemingly Adler gave a different answer to this question, or expanded his first answer, as time went on.[5] But there is no doubt that it was the search for power, the lure of superiority, the "wish to be a complete man," to use his own words, that pervaded all of Adler's thinking about the inner dynamics of man's nature. It is also clear that he, probably more than Jung, was concerned about understanding the individual in the light of his present problem and future needs. And for him, sex, far from being the primary dynamo in motivation, is only one of the many ways by which a person can try to feel adequate.

The all-important consideration, however, is the way in which a person conceives of his ability to deal effectively with his particular handicap. An organic defect, for example, may be an insurmountable barrier that forces the ambitious individual to seek a completely different means of achieving superiority. But the defect may itself be a largely unconscious way of coping with a situation that threatens him with failure. Thus, on test days the schoolboy becomes nauseated. The person who hates to give after-dinner speeches finds the best excuse for absence from banquets in the gastronomic disturbance he develops.

The situation, then, physical or social, is not the sole determining

[5] Calvin S. Hall and Gardner Lindzey, *Theories of Personality* (New York: John Wiley, 1957), pp. 116 ff. The student is referred to the excellent exposition of Adler through systematic presentation of his writings in Heinz L. Ansbacher and Rowena R. Ansbacher, *The Individual Psychology of Alfred Adler* (New York: Basic Books, 1956).

factor in the development of one's way of dealing with life. The emphasis must be put upon the response that a person himself makes to the situation. Indeed, a person's conviction about his status, however acquired, determines what the situation will be for him. For what a person does depends on what he *believes* he can do in that situation, as *he* sees it, as *he* strives for "perfection."

The importance of having a realistic appraisal of oneself in one's world becomes obvious. In a day when the term "inferiority complex" is on everybody's tongue and one somewhat glibly refers to his inferiority complex as itself explaining why he is not doing so well as expected, there is refreshing humor in the remark of a student who was doing poorly in a course: "Oh, I don't have an inferiority complex! I'm just inferior in this subject." Thus we emphasize again that not the limitation, but the attitude toward it, can become the determining factor in the development of a complex.

B. *The Problem of Growth*

To look at the individual's problem genetically, the one thing all children have in common is the feeling of inferiority dictated by their weakness and necessary dependence on others, especially their parents and brothers and sisters. As Adler put it: "to be a human being means the possession of a feeling of inferiority that is constantly pressing on toward its own conquest." [6] Yet the child comes into a strange world, whose modes of behavior are already established and not especially sympathetic to the infant's growing sense of frustration. Obviously if the child were an insensitive thing making no demand upon life, it would not matter whether he were first child or last, or whether his father and mother loved him. But the situation is vastly altered if, as Adler puts it, "a child, from its early infancy, is engaged in a constant struggle to develop, and this struggle is in accordance with an unconsciously formed but everpresent goal—a vision of greatness, perfection, superiority." [7] For now what love means to the child and what hate means to that child are related to the child's concern to overcome his particular inferiority status in that situation. From this point of view, one can see why it matters to a first-born to have a

[6] Patrick Mullahy, *Oedipus, Myth and Complex* (New York: Hermitage Press, 1948), p. 116, originating in Alfred Adler, *Social Interest: A Challenge to Mankind* (trans. John Linton and Richard Vaughan; London: Faber and Faber, 1938), p. 73.

[7] Alfred Adler, *The Education of Children* (London: Allen and Unwin, 1930), p. 5, quoted in Mullahy, *op. cit.*, p. 518.

second dethrone him, or for the second to feel in many ways subject to the first and himself dethroned by a third—and so on. For the child, the family becomes a constellation of forces that can make possible or threaten one's status—and so do school, play, and other social situations.

Adler also stresses as fundamental the attitude that the growing child develops toward himself, toward his vocation, and toward love. And because other persons are constantly involved in this whole struggle for status, security, and superiority, Adler came to emphasize the importance of social feeling—so much that it may be, as some commentators think,[8] that he thought of social feeling or social interest as an innate need along with the drive to superiority. To say that social interest is innate does not mean that the growing person does not need to learn how to express it intelligently as life moves on. Indeed, what Adler discovered is that early in life, even by the age of five, a child develops a *style of life,* a characteristic way of dealing with his need for social feeling and superiority, that affects all his responses to his physical and social environment.

C. *The Healthy Style of Life*

The great danger, accordingly, is that the person will develop a goal incompatible with his abilities, or that events or social pressures and changes will bring into his life problems for which his style of life is unprepared. A new child in the family, a more enterprising partner at work, the good fortune or deserved success of others, and myriad other situations will challenge the adequacy of one's own social feeling and sense of status. One can, for example, stand still and protect hurt vanity by developing a "sour grapes" attitude toward others and their achievements. Thus, instead of being creative, appreciative, and co-operative as the patterns and involvements of life change, instead of developing a style of life that can assimilate and grow in and through conflict, the person may construct fictions and fantasies about himself, the world, and others that will "protect" his preferred conception of himself. But in this latter direction lies weakness of personality and mental illness, for reality will not conform to narrow and false styles of life.

In retrospect, we may say that Adler, in contrast to Freud and Jung, sees the battle of life going on more completely at the con-

[8] See Hall and Lindzey, *op. cit.,* p. 117.

scious, though not necessarily critical or well-informed, level of life. Lured on by a vision of perfection, a person will be creative either realistically or unrealistically as he faces growth in his own life, alterations in the world, and changes in his relations to people. His attitude toward sex and sexual differences, toward physical and intellectual strength or infirmity, toward social success or adversity, will reflect his way of keeping his self-respect intact. If he is adequately appreciated and supported in his strivings, he will develop with more poise and self-confidence, and he will be encouraged to co-operate with others. But in any case he cannot remain uncreative. If his creativity is invested in techniques for protecting himself against feeling worthless—the one thing he cannot and will not stand —he will develop a *style of life* that will separate him from others and keep him from seeing his true status and the possibility for real growth within it. His life will be a constant battle *against* instead of a positive struggle *for* a life goal that can include real enjoyment. The Adlerian and the Jungian both see the need for the development of a "self" that takes full account of the needs of others in the attempt to find oneself.

D. *On What Is Concern for Other Persons Based?*

The time has come to raise again a question that we raised with Freud. We asked whether Freud, in endowing the individual with the obdurate demand for self-seeking pleasure, did not in fact make it impossible for a person to develop concern for others as anything more than a means to the gratification of his own self-love. Whence, then, the mature, heterosexual love that Freud holds to be the condition for healthy adulthood? A similar problem might well arise in connection with Adler's conception of the individual as driven by the lure of superiority. For if the individual is dominated by the struggle for power, can he ever come to appreciate other persons for their own sakes?

It is hard to know whether, especially in his later thought, Adler introduced *social feeling* as a balance in the individual against this self-absorbed striving for superiority. It may be that superiority-striving and social feeling are opposing forces within the individual that have a fairly even chance of being balanced in an adequate style of life. Or it may be that in Adler's thought the lure of superiority, like Freud's libidinous pleasure-principle, is the dominating motive that has to be tamed *for its own good* by recognizing the needs and demands of others.[9] It is one thing to say that in the unlearned structure of a human being one can find an urge to assist in meeting the felt needs of others, and another to say that meeting the needs of others is a way of achieving one's own good, in service to a self-absorption that knows no concern for others for their own sakes. Obviously, the role which "altruism" plays in human life, or can play in the human search for goodness, is at stake.

To put the issue sharply: Does man as man find it difficult on occasion to resist an urge to meet another's conceived need, just as he finds it difficult, say, to resist his urge to eat, drink, ask questions, and explore? Or does man as man develop an interest in others' needs simply as a means of gratifying his own nature, which has no impulse in it to assist others for their own sakes? It would not, of course, be necessary to find such an other-regarding tendency all fitted out with built-in mechanisms for helping others or for diagnosing their needs intelligently. But it would be important to know whether there are any inborn yearnings to help others within a growing child, tendencies that the child has to confront and learn how to gratify intelligently, just as he needs to learn to gratify hunger or thirst.

It seems clear that Adler, whether he is clear or not in his basic description of the motivational "givens" of personality, does insist that an adequate style of life must accept the responsibility for vocation, for love, and for marriage in a way that does not make pawns of other people. And Freud, too, held that there could be no adequate solution of a human being's problem if he did not sublimate the pleasure-principle enough to make allowance for the pleasure-principle in others.

We must, nevertheless, wonder whether Freud and Adler are justified in having confidence that such results can be expected from human beings. If the only dependable, unchanging orientation in man is one that directs him to protect his own pleasure and superiority at all costs, if in man there is no demand that finds gratification in living with others for their own sakes, then must we not conclude that love, friendship, social concern are contrived make-shifts to which we are forced to resort, but in which we can have no confidence unless they constantly serve our original demand for self-pleasure and power?

A critical question that we must take with us, as we move on, is:

[9] See Wayland F. Vaughan, *Lure of Superiority* (New York: Henry Holt, 1928).

If man is so predatory, or near-predatory, can any man ever, with justification, trust another—if we mean by "trust" something more than "be assured that he will fear me and work for my good in order to protect his own interests"? Let it be observed that we normally do not think of trust, love, friendship, and social concern as being based solely on such motivation as fear, power, or parasitic pleasure. Are these, then, "words"—simply ways in which we whitewash impulses actually fit for the jungle but somehow "trained" for "civilized" living?

In this connection a further comment may be made as we continue to bear in mind the dynamics of egoism-altruism in relation to health. Both Freud and Adler conceive of the cause of neurosis differently, yet both insist, the one by way of sublimation, the other by introducing social concern, that health cannot be achieved unless persons accept responsibility for the potential of others. Narcissism and the lure of power lead to neurosis unless they are somehow subdued, transformed, redirected, or supplanted, and the individual enters into responsible relationships with others. If such products can be achieved in human nature, must it not be because, in some sense, they are possible to human nature? May it be that it would have been better to judge origins by products, roots by fruits, in assigning powers to man? At any rate, we must bear this problem in mind as we study other psychologists' views of human nature, mental illness, and health.

III. KAREN HORNEY

Our study of Freud, Jung, and Adler [10] has introduced us to different ways of conceiving the human struggle against chaos and for health. We are now already impressed by the fact that these words "chaos" and "health" mean almost nothing apart from the "filling in" that each thinker provides through his specific theory of human needs and goals and the ways of working them out.

When one approaches the work of Karen Horney (1885–1952) with the question "What constitutes mental health?" he must be prepared for disappointment as far as direct answers are concerned. For this cofounder of the Association for the Advancement of Psychoanalysis

[10] Freud's original school of thought is called "Psychoanalysis," but Jung's and Adler's views are called "Analytic Psychology" and "Individual Psychology" respectively.

and the Dean of the American Institute of Psychoanalysis has written mainly about the causes of neurosis and leaves to the reader's inference how she believes a healthy person would respond to life.

A. *Basic Anxiety*

As Horney, with Freudian concepts in mind, analyzed patients, she, like Jung and Adler, came to believe that Freud's theorizing was too narrow when he hypothesized that sexual pleasure was central in human motivation. What, then, does she see as the dynamic of motivation? To put it in one sentence: Every person yearns for security, and when this is denied he experiences *basic anxiety,* which drives him to protect and increase any security *he* feels.

It should be clear at the outset that Horney does not think that a child must of necessity experience basic anxiety. The individual is not bound to be frustrated, as Freud's male or female child must be, in the demand made on the parent of the opposite sex. But when we consider the fallibility of human parents, that they themselves have unresolved problems and are prey to many weaknesses, what are the chances of a child's being loved as he needs to be loved? How many "nice" parents, for example, are so concerned that their child makes good that they never see that this very attitude encourages the child to feel disapproved of and even unwanted when he cannot successfully please his parents?

How easy, then, for a child who wants security to resent both his parents and the world in general! How easy for him to develop hostility that does not in fact make him more secure. For it may well occur to him that this very hostility he feels toward them may worsen the attitude of his parents and others toward him. The net result is more insecurity and more hostility!

What to do then? Repress this hostility, or successfully disguise it? Here Horney (with Jung) accepts the crucial concept of repression. We must remember that repression is not suppression. That is, it is not a matter of facing an impulse or desire, rejecting it as unsuitable, and, once having bottled up the unwanted emotion, going on to something else with the remark: "Well, that takes care of that." A repressed desire is one which, having been rejected "out of hand" without any understanding, goes on in the unconscious, smouldering, waiting, as it were, for the right draft to quicken it into flame. Thus, the feeling of being lonely and helpless in an indifferent or hostile world can go on generating a hostility so powerful that it constantly threatens to erupt.

It is in this situation that *basic anxiety* reigns. It is "a feeling of being small, insignificant, helpless, deserted, endangered, in a world that is out to abuse, cheat, attack, humiliate, betray, envy." [11]

B. *The Neurotic Symptom*

We have already noted that on Horney's view basic anxiety is not congenital but rather results from adverse factors in the environment: as domination, indifference of parents, disparagement, lack of "reliable warmth," overprotection, either too much or too little admiration. One cannot consider these and other adverse factors without realizing that much depends on how the child envisages or conceives what the parents do, that almost anything could disturb a child's sense of security and create basic anxiety.

What seems to interest Horney especially are the many ways in which this basic anxiety can be turned into neurotic symptoms. A neurotic symptom is a rigid way of feeling or acting with little, if any, justification for such rigidity. The reaction is always far out of proportion to the "provoking" situation, and it is rigid because the person, feeling unable, unconsciously, to deal adequately with the situation, puts up defenses that become automatic barriers against his desperate feeling of helplessness. The neurotic symptom is the end of a long causal chain, which we may diagram schematically thus: subjective feeling of helplessness and lack of love → feeling of resentment and hostility toward those whose affection we need → unendurable fear of reprisal if hostility is expressed → repression of hostility, which means that hostility may still spill out → basic anxiety, lest one stay unloved and insecure or increase insecurity by expressing his own hostility → neurosis, state of defense that represents "safety" in a tense "cold" war in which neither one, himself nor his enemy, makes any progress.

Actually, such neurotic symptoms involve the person in a vicious circle, for the more hostility he feels, the more reassurance is needed to relieve anxiety, and the more disappointed the victim is by the way others treat him. Consequently, anxiety takes its toll of his

[11] Karen Horney, *The Neurotic Personality of Our Time* (New York: W. W. Norton, 1937), p. 92; (see pp. 89–92). In *Our Inner Conflicts* (New York: W. W. Norton, 1945), p. 41, she defines basic anxiety as ". . . the feeling a child has of being isolated and helpless in a potentially hostile world."

energy. He feels fatigued, loses his enthusiasm for life, is not as effective as he can be, and loses faith both in himself and others. It is not hard to imagine an individual's state when (a) he knows he needs to depend upon himself and yet has never built any confidence in himself, (b) he knows he needs others and yet feels that they are the cause of his weakness. No wonder he loses flexibility in adjustment. Meanwhile anxiety leads to exaggerated, rigid response.

C. *Defenses Acceptable in Our Culture*

In our culture the person who finds his anxiety unbearable will try to defend himself in four principal ways. First, because he needs constant reassurance that he is loved, he will demand unconditional love, whether he himself loves or not. "After all, if I am loved, I'm safe." But because his desire for love is a means to his own security, and because he never considers others except in relation to his own need to be loved, he never seems to get enough loving. Thus he discourages or offends even those persons who seem (to others) to be giving him due consideration. So anxious is he to be loved that the very fear that he will be inadequate to any demands that they seem to make upon him will be enough to cause insecurity.

Second, because safety may come through power, he may make an uncompromising demand for power if he thinks he can attain it. Thus, he may seek prestige through raw power, or by wealth of knowledge, or by prowess in some endeavor or other. But, again, because his power through achievement is motivated, not by any desire to be helpful or cooperative, but only to ensure his own security, his very achievements boomerang. For who is more insecure than the person who must win or be "on top" all the time? Such a person tries to prove he is secure by humiliating others or disparaging their achievement. This type of response to anxiety is especially prevalent in a competitive society like ours.

A third way of defending oneself against anxiety is by being rigidly submissive—"wouldn't hurt a flea." The neurotic now "represses all demands of his own, represses criticism of others, is willing to let himself be abused without defending himself and is ready to be indiscriminately helpful to others." [12] But such "harmless" people succeed very well in losing the respect of even good people.

The fourth defense against neurotic anxiety is to try to withdraw

[12] Horney, *The Neurotic Personality of Our Time,* p. 97.

from any dependence upon other persons, for in this way "no one can hurt me any more." A person who tries this defense can become very assiduous in his chosen field. He can become a compulsive perfectionist, for by "being perfect" he will be above reproach. The main trouble is that his need to be defensive keeps him from having any sense of humor about the activity he is using as a basis for being irreproachable and unapproachable.

D. *Health as Unity of Self*

We have spoken thus far as if security and the basic anxiety resulting from a threat to security were the interconnected motivational springs of personality. Actually, however, Horney seems to take for granted all along that this demand for security and the resulting hostility come into play only if the unity of the individual "self" is threatened. As Munroe says: "the need to value oneself and to be valued" seems to Horney one of the obvious "givens" of human nature.[13] This longing for unity "is no mystical desire but is prompted by the practical necessity of having to function in life—an impossibility when one is driven in opposite directions—and by what in consequence amounts to a supreme terror of being split apart." [14]

In the light of this need to maintain a sense of unity, we should now say that the demand for security has a fairly definite goal: to defend this more basic need for unity when it is threatened. Actually, the growing and changing individual develops *an image of what he is as a "self"*, and it is this which he then seeks to preserve against hostile threats. The reader will note similarities between this notion or image of self-unity, the Adlerian "style of life," and Jung's creativity. The emphasis is now put on an end or goal that defines a human being. To be human is not simply to be molded or to "respond" to environmental forces, but to *select* from the environment what will meet the demands of the individual and to *resist* what threatens that "sense of self."

This concept of the self and self-image will get further treatment in the thought of Fromm, Maslow, and Allport. Our attention must focus here on what happens, on Horney's view, when the individual

[13] Ruth L. Munroe, *op. cit.,* p. 346. This underlying need becomes more explicit in Horney's *Neurosis and Human Growth* (New York: W. W. Norton, 1950). But even in *Our Inner Conflicts,* pp. 56 ff., she wrote that inner conflict is keenly felt because of the "longing for unity within ourselves."

[14] Horney, *Our Inner Conflicts,* pp. 56–57, quoted in Munroe, *op. cit.,* p. 454.

in his social milieu develops an image of himself that, although not true to his real abilities and needs, he nevertheless insists on preserving against all challenges. The individual becomes neurotic. For a neurotic, in the last analysis, is a person who insists on maintaining a rigid unrealistic image of himself against all "foes." The result is that all his struggle, tragically, is to keep intact a self-esteem that he considers ideal, but that bears little reliable connection with his own real potentialities. The "ideal self," being unrealistic and yet necessary to his position, itself calls for further defenses. The result—a psychological structure built upon sand when, in fact, stone is at hand for a better structure. No wonder the neurotic experiences an ever deeper and more desperate sense of the futility of existence.

If, in bringing this brief exposition to a close, we reach for a positive conception of what Horney seems to hold as basic to normal and healthy existence, we have a clue in this contrast of the real self to the self-image. The individual who is healthy has been able to keep his conception of himself in reasonable contact with his real potentialities and needs, without distorting the relationship between himself and others. If only a growing person can feel respected for himself and not merely for what he can do in competitive situations, if only he is not saddled or does not saddle himself with expectations outside the realm of his capacity and need, he will avoid the basic anxiety which underlies his neurotic defenses to procure "reunity." He will experience uncertainties and anxieties, but he will not be straining for what is beyond his level of achievement and he will allow his ideals to grow on what is possible to him in his cultural situation.

Significantly, Horney herself believes that the human predicament is far from hopeless. "My own belief," she says, "is that man has the capacity as well as the desire to develop his potentialities and become a decent human being, and that these deteriorate if his relationship to others and hence to himself is, and continues to be, disturbed." [15]

We cannot leave Horney without a further comment on her view of the incidence of neurosis. To be sure, what one believes to be his relationship to others is always important. But in Horney one finds the view that the times in which one lives will determine whether one is considered neurotic in the first place. Horney is so anxious to stress that felt conflicts are caused mainly by cultural patterns and

[15] Mullahy, *op. cit.*, p. 237. From K. Horney, *Our Inner Conflicts*, p. 19.

not by any pattern of motives native to all people that we may wonder whether she interprets her own data correctly.

For while it may be true that "our times" will *influence* even the definition of a neurosis, it is hardly the culture that determines the need to maintain unity or the need to be loved and respected. The way people become "neurotic" or "rigid" will indeed depend on the defenses a given culture accepts or encourages, but this is quite different from the suggestion that underlying anxiety is the result of culture. One would rather expect Horney to say that any human being anywhere wants to keep from splitting apart in conflict, that he will feel basic anxiety whenever this occurs under his cultural conditions, and that he will build defenses reflecting the repression that is going on in order to avoid overt clashes. Again, cultural conditions may accelerate the conditions leading to neurotic anxiety, but whether anxiety becomes neurotic depends on factors other than what the environment offers.

E. *What Motivates Altruism?*

Thus Horney leaves us with another phase of an earlier problem. Does the standard for development emerge—as Freud especially seemed to emphasize—from within a person? Are societal influences and processes to be evaluated by their capacity to help the individual gratify his innate needs? Or is the standard for the individual socially imposed upon him, with the result that he is declared neurotic or healthy by the standard set in the cultural situation? And if we fly from either alternative as too one-sided, by what criterion shall we judge any standard as the one that is "healthy" for both the individual and society? Will Fromm, Maslow, and Allport help us here?

But Horney has moved us a step further in our consideration of the question that we raised earlier in connection with the roots in human nature of a genuine social concern. When Horney faces the question "What is the controlling need of a human being?" what she says amounts to "I want to be secure," which may be translated "I want to be loved." The focus here is certainly still on the threat that the individual so readily feels to himself. Without further light on what is to be protected, Horney is not so clear as Freud with his id-instincts, or Jung with his demand for creativity, or Adler with the yearning for superiority or social feeling. The word "secure" is meaningless until we know the answer to the question "Secure for what?" The same applies to the meaning of "I want to be loved." Insofar as Horney's view can be interpreted as self-centered and parasitic, the same concern about the basis for altruism must haunt us. Here, again, however, the idea that seems to underlie all thinking about the weakness of personality is that it is only when the person demands love without responsibility for others that maladjustment ensues.

Yet, and especially consistent with the thought of Jung, in Horney's conception of the need for self-unity we see emerging another emphasis that will be interestingly developed by Fromm, Maslow, and Allport. When the stress is laid on the development of the potential of a person, without special preoccupation with oneself as threatened by others, a new kind of motivation is being involved. The focus is on growth or development of potential in whatever situation one finds himself. As we see this conception developed in other psychologists, new problems will descend upon us. But the reader already realizes how difficult it is to achieve a well-grounded view of human nature and the good life open to it.

IV. *REFLECTIVE SUMMARY*

Jung, Adler, and Horney agree in rejecting what they consider Freud's shrunken image of man. They question Freud's reliance on the individual's past and on the pleasure-seeking, unconscious, "sexual" struggle in order to explain personality formation. They stress rather the forward-looking, purposive outlook of the individual, although they hold differing views about the motives lying behind the goal to be realized. Jung does make use of unconscious striving, but in his contention that the basic demand of an individual's nature is to give creative expression to his own kind of being as he deals with perennial (archetypal) and contemporary problems, he joins Adler and Horney in shifting the emphasis to the present transactions between individual and environment.

Freud, Jung, Adler, and Horney agree that there can be no health for the individual apart from appreciative and cooperative interaction. But these words "appreciative" and "cooperative" (and others like them) are empty shells until we note what each psychologist fills them with, in terms of the motives to be gratified.

Thus, for Jung "integration of personality" must have creative expression as its mainspring and mainstay. Adler, in turn, sees the individual striving to overcome the inferiority that always haunts him, as a result of organic or other defects, real or imagined. It may not be too far-fetched an interpretation to say that this inferiority-superiority struggle takes place within the social situation in which the individual wishes to excel or find "completion." His style of life, therefore, is to be understood as his more or less systematic way of working out his conflicts as he sees them in the light of his conception of himself in his social situation.

In Horney, on the other hand, it is harder to reduce the individual struggle to any polarity as definite as dependence-creativity or inferiority-superiority. Even these polar tensions and others seem to be different ways in which the individual articulates his underlying plea: "Don't you see how helpless I feel? I want to be loved, to be valued, to feel secure. If I am not, I experience hostile and aggressive feelings. I cannot in fact be myself, develop confidence in myself, if I am always torn up by basic anxiety." Indeed, for Horney the motivational struggle may take so many forms, and each in response to social structure, that her emphasis seems to fall even more on the cultural influences that create the individual interaction than on innate or instinctual needs that demand gratification. Still, for her as for Jung and Adler, a healthy personality means that the individual has "found" himself in cooperation with others.

Now, as we have said, the goal of "health" or the condition of "healthy personality" seems identical when expressed in a general formula such as "finding oneself" or "fulfilling oneself in cooperation with others." But to what do these formulas refer in terms of concrete personality formation? Is a society in which individuals find themselves by being creative equivalent to a society in which they demand respect for their own excellence? And are either, or both, of these societies equivalent to another in which individuals demand that they be accepted for themselves with their capabilities and liabilities?

And, going one step further, the same question that bothered us in connection with Freud returns. If the individual, on these views, is so insistent in his claim to be himself creative, to be himself complete or superior, to be loved and valued for himself, will his so-called cooperation with others not be at most a refined, conniving, niggardly, and reluctant "deference" rather than positive outgoing concern for others? What will Fromm say at these points?

4

Erich Fromm:
Man's Search for Freedom

~~~~~~

In Erich Fromm (born 1900) we find a psychoanalyst who, profiting
from the work of Freud, Jung, Adler, Horney, and others, takes the
first positive, articulate, and systematic step into the realm of ethics
and social problems. His orientation to human existence is not so
much medical as it is sociological and philosophical. He moves constantly from an analysis of man in his basic relation to nature and
society to what he believes man and society *ought* to become. But—
and this is the all-important theoretical step which none of his predecessors took explicitly—on Fromm's view, man cannot be what he
ought to be unless he becomes what he really is.

In three successive books, *Escape from Freedom* (1941), *Man for
Himself* (1947), *The Sane Society* (1955), and then in a summary,
The Art of Loving (1956), one can almost see the movement of
Fromm's thought from (a) an analysis of man's status as a free being
to (b) the nature of the good that man can find only in himself to
(c) the kind of society that will at once develop from, and encourage, the most creative use of freedom. But we shall better understand the total outlook of Fromm and gain more perspective on the
ground we have covered thus far in this book, if we stop here to
contrast his perspective on man and morality with that of a great
tradition.

I. *MAN, THE ETHICAL IDEAL, AND RELIGION*

For the majority of mankind, East and West, the ethical life calls for *conformity* of human behavior to some Agency or agencies beyond man. In the Judeo-Christian tradition, as exemplified in the stories of Adam and Eve and Moses' reception on Mt. Sinai the Commandments of God, we see an underlying pattern illustrated. On this view, God creates man (unlike animals) in his own image and puts Eden at his disposal. The one condition exacted of man is obedience to God's command, whether or not man understands the reasons for it. When he disobeys God, he forfeits the joys of Eden and is made to work for his livelihood. When man does not offer his best to God and when he accepts no responsibility for being his brother's keeper, as the story of Cain and Abel teaches, he is disobeying the will of God.

In all this, the dominant pattern—and one repeated in other traditions—is that man finds his good not by consulting human nature, but by knowing and heeding the will of God as God chooses to reveal it to man. We shall not enter here into the different theological interpretations and refinements of the relation between God, Nature, and man. For there is no doubt that it is this simple, crude, yet clear-cut notion that has lent itself more than any other to easy understanding and acceptance by Jews and Christians. But it is this notion that Fromm is to reject. It is the notion, to repeat, that the good life is something superimposed on man, that man must live under the judgment of a Being, call him Father or not, who demands obedience from man's nature at any cost as the condition for man's security and happiness, both in this life and the next.

This conviction that the good life is to be lived under the guidance of God has been supported by other convictions as to how God made his ways known to man. The dominant tradition has been that man could be aware of God through religious faith or that God revealed himself to men of faith. In the Jewish tradition, this meant that God made his will known through leaders like Moses, Abraham, and Isaiah; and in the basic Christian tradition this line of revelation continued into the life of Jesus, the supreme and final revelation of God's will for man. The underlying assumption in such views is that man can both know God's will and be aided by

God to do it. The act of "faith" is not a "simple-minded" act of credulity. "Faith" is a kind of knowing and doing in which the believer affirms, attests, and enjoys a sense of comradeship with God the Father. The moral ideal is grounded in God and is revealed in the life of faith.

There have been influential thinkers, however, who explained the authority of moral ideals in man's life in a different way. Granting that the authority of the good life rested ultimately on God's nature, thinkers like Joseph Butler (1692–1752) and Immanuel Kant (1724–1804), believed that man knows the moral ideal not by way of a revealing act of faith but by way of a unique moral consciousness or conscience. A man's conscience, the final arbiter in his life, of right and wrong, is what it is because, in the last analysis, it is the presence of God's command in him. Man's "I ought . . ." is ultimately God's "Thou shalt . . ."

There are different versions of the exact nature of this moral consciousness, and we shall deal with them in further detail in Chapters 9, 10, and 11. For our purposes here it is important to bear in mind that, on these views, the conscience, or moral consciousness is a way of knowing what man ought to do *but without consulting man's needs or desires or abilities.* Just as the senses as such do not consult man's needs or desires in becoming aware of a physical world, so the moral *sense* or the *moral reason* becomes aware of commands to which the rest of life is subject. It is felt (and it is argued) that man is responsible for the moral ideal of which he becomes aware regardless of what he wishes, needs, or desires, and regardless of whether he can do what the moral ideal commands.

Now it will be evident to the reader of these pages so far that, with the possible exception of Jung, this particular approach to man and morality is either neglected or ignored, when it is not explicitly denied. There are various reasons, but we may speak of two here.

II. *MAN, THE MORAL IDEAL, AND SCIENTIFIC METHOD*

First, as we have seen, the psychoanalytic approach to mental health followed the lead-lines of medicine and biological research. By the time Freud began theorizing, the evolutionary conception of man was already assumed to be true in the scientific and scholarly world. Man was seen as a biological development having much in common with the animal world, not *with God*. If man is made in any image, it is the image of the higher animal rather than the image of God. The physiologist who wanted to discover what makes the human body work as it does has no need to make use of the idea of God. To believe in, or to deny, God is not important to a person who is tracing the route of a stimulus through the nervous system. In such a task, a physiologist gets more help from considering man's relation to animals than by thinking of him as a somewhat tarnished image of God. Seeing how his experimental animals respond to his probings will give him clues as to what goes on in man under similar conditions, but it seems obvious that his belief or unbelief in God is hardly relevant to such investigation.

Biology and medical science, accordingly, made the assumption that one does not heal a body by prayer to an external God, but by understanding the cause and effect relationships within the body and between the body and the external world. Thus, when Freud, the doctor, approached the problem of mental healing and health, it was understandable (whatever other reasons might be given) that he should make no appeal to the religious life of persons. Indeed, we have seen that he explained religion as an outworn and danger-ous defense mechanism. The "living faith" in God, he held, is an "illusion" better outgrown.

Similarly, conscience and the feeling of obligation got no recogni-tion at all in Freud's earliest theorizing. Later, as the superego, con-science became the internalized monitor not of the will of God but of the will of society as channeled through parental training. And in Freud's thinking we have already noted the faith that if only one could have insight into himself in relation to physical Nature and to other human beings, there would be adequate basis for mental health. For Freud the sources of the good life are within human nature, a nature untrammeled and unhampered either by Jungian ancestral archetypes or Greek, Jewish, or Christian convictions that the highest human living is in some sense an image of the Structure of Reality. This whole mode of approach, we suggest, came as an extension of the biological outlook on man's development and be-havior.

Closely allied to this outlook was a second intellectual attitude to which the growth of biological science is itself traceable, namely, a *scientistic* attitude toward truth. We are purposely using the word "scientistic" because we do not believe that "scientistic" and "scientific" mean the same thing, or that *scientism* is the same as *science*. The scientific way of answering any question or solving any problem is to develop theories or hypotheses that not only are consistent with the evidence at hand, but are confirmed by further evidence. In general, when a scientist wants to know what follows what, he develops an hypothesis suggested by the data he has and then goes on to set up an experiment over whose different factors he has sufficient control to discover whether the situation works out as it should if his hypothesis is true.

Why is the scientist never satisfied with hypotheses held to be true on any other grounds? Because in the *ideal* experiment two things happen. First, as we have just said, he can so control the factors involved that he can tell whether the outcome is the particular result he predicted. Second, what takes place in the experiment is open not only to his own gaze but also to the inspection of others. It is understandable that the scientist as a truth-seeker would prefer public evidence achieved through the repetitive control of experimentation. His assurance of "true" hypotheses will depend on how close he can come to such sensory, public, controlled evidence in confirmation of his hypotheses. Who would deny this ideal of truth?

But we must still distinguish the scientistic from the scientific attitude. Some scientists and philosophers have decided to restrict scientific research *only* to questions whose answers can be checked by sensory and, therefore, public observation. They would even restrict the words "true" and "false" to hypotheses thus checked or in principle checkable. Now such a sensory method of acquiring truth and such a sensory test of truth applies best wherever the processes that take place occur in space. This "sensory" scientific method has been applied especially effectively in physics and chemistry, but not so effectively in geology and astronomy because experimentation with celestial bodies and with millennial changes is impossible. In biology, although the processes go on in space and are observable in principle by the senses, experimental control is much more difficult to achieve.

Actually, in all these sciences—chemistry, physics, geology, astronomy, biology—hypotheses are sometimes developed and accepted that have not been confirmed by actual experimentation. Yet the evidence for the hypotheses is sensory; or the hypothesis is assumed to be checkable by sensory, public observation once adequate techniques are developed. Thus, hypotheses about the other side of the moon or about biological genes, accepted because they are most consistent with sensory data, have not yet been checked by sensory observation (although photographs have now been taken of the moon, and many believe that the electron microscope has "photographed" genes). Actually, insofar as biology rests on chemical and physical processes it has the weight of the strictest sort of scientific procedure behind it. But as biological processes become more complicated, especially in man, it is simply impossible either to develop or to check hypotheses provable on a purely sensory and public basis. Some types of blindness, paralysis, ulcers, and other ailments do not yield entirely to hypotheses supported wholly by sensory data.

In fact, there are theorists, called vitalists, who believe that being alive even as a plant or an amoeba involves activities that are not observable by sense. The biological evidence does not yield to one easily acceptable hypothesis about the nature of living processes.[1] And, as we suggested in the first chapter, the mind-body problem is always present to harass scientistic psychologists. Nevertheless, the whole approach to man and morality has been much affected by this *scientistic* approach to truth. If scientistic thinkers had their way, the only processes anyone, even the psychologist, should study, the only answers he should consider true, would be those open to public, sensory tests.

It must be emphasized, however, that while Freud, Jung, Adler, and Horney have not been systematically clear about the mind-body problem, they have all developed hypotheses by no means checkable by sense or public observation. Their appeal in support of these hypotheses has been to such phenomena as *resistance, anxiety, feelings of inferiority and insecurity,* which are certainly not known by eye, ear, nose, or any other sense. Today, however, the resistance of scientistic psychologists to such hypotheses resembles the resistance to Freud by medical men when he urged that the *libido* and non-sensory psychic proccesses like *repression* be taken seriously even if they could not be observed by the senses. Had Freud given in to scientistic scholars, there would probably be no psychosomatic medicine. That there is indicates that many scientific minds have not been willing to force themselves or reality into what they felt was

[1] See, for example, Charles Scott Sherrington, *Man on His Nature* (London: Cambridge University Press, 1951), and Edmund W. Sinnott, *Cell and Psyche* (Chapel Hill: University of North Carolina Press, 1950)

scientistic dogma. For such scientific minds the problem is always to gather as carefully as possible all the evidence relevant to the particular problem, and not to worry particularly about whether it can be sensed or not. At the same time, scientific minds grant to scientistic minds that the truth on which there can be most agreement is that unearthed by controlled experimentation and checkable by sense experience.

To be more specific, what we have witnessed in the psychotherapist is greater concern for the problem he is trying to solve than for a preferred type of evidence. Jung's theory of archetypes in a collective unconscious is surely the hardest to check by sensory processes; for Freud's id and superego, Adler's need of superiority, Horney's demand for "self-security," there will be no sensory check and there is little strictly experimental data (in the scientistic meaning). However, if these investigators, as they tried to understand mental illness were unwilling to be restricted by scientistic dogma and this scientistic climate, their training in medicine kept them closer to biological modes of thinking than to the religious and the philosophical. While they have made some hundred-yard dashes into speculative concepts like *the libido, the personal and collective unconscious,* they have resisted hypotheses that smacked of hoary philosophical "speculation" or other-worldly religious faith.

The importance of these developments—and we have barely sketched them—has been far-reaching for ethical theory and for the theory of man and the universe. Only the future will tell to what the different paths in the great debate over methodology will lead. We have purposely chosen in this book to begin not with philosophical and religious view of the good life, but with the scientific-scientistic perspectives of psychotherapists who give a wide berth to such philosophical and religious presuppositions as special rational, moral, aesthetic, or religious sensitivities.

There have been, of course, great philosophical movements that join in refusing to accept moral-religious "insights" into the universe. No lesser thinkers than Democritus, Epicurus, Hobbes, Condorcet, Comte, Marx, Santayana, and Dewey have denied any affinity between the highest in man and the Cosmos. They have affirmed instead that moral ideals are the outgrowth of human experience criticized by (some form of) reasoning. Because they deny any superhuman Agency, Realm, or Purpose to which something in man bears witness, and because they hope through the scientistic-philoʂophical study of man and Nature to discover the ideal program of moral and social action, these thinkers are called *Humanists* (as opposed to Superhumanists) and *Naturalists* (as opposed to Supernaturalists), or, better, *Naturalistic Humanists.*

In *Man for Himself* and *The Sane Society,* Erich Fromm, who calls the society he advocates a Humanistic Communitarian Socialism, stands within this tradition, and he comes to it mainly on the strength of psychoanalysis and sociology, although Spinoza, in particular, as well as Marx and Hegel have had considerable influence. In him, as we have said, we shall find the most systematic and self-conscious attempt to put psychological science to work in developing an adequate theory of human goodness. We shall not try to expound his (still sketchy) ethics as such here, but shall restrict ourselves largely to his theory of human nature and the conditions that man must fulfill if he is to realize his potential.

III. *MAN'S PROBLEM AS FROMM SEES IT*

We may state the human problem in Fromm's own words:

> What is essential in the existence of man is the fact that he has emerged from the animal kingdom, from instinctive adaptation, that he has transcended nature—although he never leaves it; he is part of it—and yet once torn away from nature, he cannot return to it; once thrown out of paradise—a state of original oneness with nature—cherubim with flaming swords block his way, if he should try to return.[2]

Here we note immediately that man is embedded in nature; he issues from an "original oneness with nature" and is not created by God; nor is he driven from nature as Adam and Eve were from the Garden of Eden in a fallen state of sin. And he may not return, ever, to paradise.

Man, then, has somehow "emerged" from Nature. But, in thus emerging, he emancipated himself "from the original animal harmony with nature" and thus has a different problem from that of animals. Interestingly enough, the author of *Genesis* I had also

[2] *The Art of Loving* (World Perspectives, Vol. 9, ed. Ruth A. Anshen; New York: Harper and Brothers, 1956), p. 7. Copyright © 1956 by Erich Fromm. Reprinted by permission of Harper & Row, Publishers.

noted that man is different from animals; he explained the difference by saying that this creature did not represent something new in the universe, but was made in the image of God. The contrast is complete: Man in the *Genesis* view could converse with God in the cool of the evening and be guided by him; man on Fromm's naturalistic view finds himself different from the animal, *freer* than the animal, but also more bewildered. Thus Fromm says: "Man can only go forward by developing his reason, by finding a new harmony, a human one, instead of the prehuman harmony which is irretrievably lost." [3] The whole hope of the Old and New Testament is that man, though driven from the Garden of Eden because of his free disobedience, may return to and live once more in fellowship with God, and do this with the help of God. But as Fromm puts it: "When man is born, the human race as well as the individual, he is thrown out of a situation which was definite, as definite as the instincts, into a situation which is indefinite, uncertain and open. There is certainty only about the past—and about the future only as far as that it is death." [4]

In this passage and many others we find Fromm turning away from the definiteness of Freud's libido and the fairly fixed modes of libidinous expression in oral, anal, and heterosexual development. In other words, although Fromm grants that man has inherited physiological responses, he denies any directive instinctive structure. About all man has left of his past is at best a psychic yearning to return to this primordial safety. Thus Fromm clearly severs the umbilical cord uniting psychoanalysis and biologically rooted instinct. He is almost as firm in this as he is in rejecting *Genesis*. In what situation, then, does this leave man?

In a graphic statement Fromm asserts:

Man is gifted with reason; he is *life being aware of itself;* he has awareness of himself, of his fellow man, of his past, and of the possibilities of his future. This awareness of himself as a separate entity, the awareness of his own short life span, of the fact that without his will he is born and against his will he dies, that he will die before those whom he loves, or they before him, the awareness of his aloneness and separateness, of his helplessness before the forces of nature and of society, all this makes his sep-

[3] *Ibid.*
[4] *Ibid.*, pp. 7–8.

arate, disunited existence an unbearable prison. He would become insane could he not liberate himself from this prison and
reach out, unite himself in some form or other with men, with
the world outside. . . .

The experience of separateness arouses anxiety; it is, indeed,
the source of all anxiety. Being separate means being cut off,
without any capacity to use my *human powers*. Hence to be
separate means to be helpless, unable to grasp the world—things
and people—actively; it means that the world can invade me
without my ability to react. Thus separateness is the source of
intense anxiety. . . .

The deepest need of man, then, is the need to overcome his
separateness, to leave the prison of his aloneness. The *absolute*
failure to achieve this aim means insanity.[5]

From such passages and others it soon becomes clear that Fromm
does not think of anxiety in Horney's way, as a response to hostility
arising out of one's feeling of helplessness especially in childhood.
Anxiety is an experience forever present in man's life because there
will never be a time when man can overcome the conditions that
make him feel alone in nature or strange or separate. The problem
in man's life is to overcome this separateness and to do it forth-
rightly and productively. One could succeed in overcoming "the
panic of complete isolation" [6] by withdrawing so far from the world
in one's mind that the world from which one is separated disappears.
But this is insanity. Thus, every man's life might, as it were, be
plotted by the degree to which he moves from such complete withdrawal to the stage of union with Nature and fellowmen that
Fromm calls *productive*.

For there is another side of this picture, which, as thus far depicted, seems so grim. Man is separated, yes, but this also means
that man is free from preordained instinctive patterns of behavior.
The very same powers that cause anxiety are those that make men
free to discover what *he* as an individual is, free to know how he
can relate himself to others, free from being pushed, free to plan
"the belonging" without which he feels so destitute. But in this

[5] *Ibid.*, pp. 8, 9.
[6] *Ibid.*, p. 9.

process of finding freedom man is a pilgrim whose progress is impeded by many obstacles, the greatest of which is the social milieu into which he is born but in which he must discover the nature of his real freedom. Let us see how the child's problem grows.

As a member of the human species the infant is already free from the bonds that give an animal security. Every step of growth is a step that makes more freedom possible, yet at the same time reduces security. For the steps in the direction of separation are not matched by a nicely balanced corresponding power that allows for harmony and assurance. Anxiety resulting from isolation is thus built into the human situation, for the child does not relinquish security-giving "primary ties" easily. It is in this condition that the family, the representative of the prevailing social structure, has the greatest influence in the life of the child. For the child, as he reaches for union on the one hand and is carried along the path of individuation on the other, develops his basic personality within this environment.

It is much too simple to say that the child is molded by the social pattern or that the child simply selects according to his need and ability. For the child is always growing and the problem is always changing, reflecting the kind of relationship that is established from day to day. Nevertheless, it seems quite safe to say that Fromm allows the environment much more power in the shaping of personality than do Freud, Jung, Adler, or even Horney. Thus he says: "Those drives which make for the *differences* in men's characters, like love and hatred, the lust for power and the yearning for submission, the enjoyment of sensuous pleasure and the fear of it, are all products of the social process." [7]

Fromm, in short, sees that the individual who has lost his primary ties may well be all the more tempted to find security by escaping from his freedom into a safe conformity with family, social groups, and the larger economic and political structure. But when the person becomes dependent on approval and tends to conform, he still feels insecure and anxious, and he uses his energy to compensate for or cover up his anxiety.[8] If one were looking for the "mortal sins"

[7] Patrick Mullahy, *Oedipus, Myth and Complex* (New York: Hermitage Press, 1952), p. 242. From Fromm, *Escape from Freedom* (New York: Farrar and Rinehart, 1941), p. 12.

[8] See *The Sane Society* (New York: Rinehart, 1955), p. 271. Copyright © 1955 by Erich Fromm. Subsequent quotations from this work are reprinted by permission of Holt, Rinehart and Winston, Inc.

in Fromm's analysis, he would turn to the catalogue of "escapes" from freedom which Fromm elaborately develops but which we can only mention here.

IV. *ESCAPES FROM FREEDOM*

Much of Fromm's writing is a description of how, in the individual's struggle to find the right solution to these conflicting needs for union and freedom, he is shaped by the prevailing economic, political, and philosophic trends of his times. These various "orientations," to use Fromm's word, a person can develop in dealing with his problem of freedom. For example, there is the person who is so anxious to be loved, so fearful of disapproval and lonesomeness, that he will "take anything" from those he depends upon. In direct contrast to such a "masochistic" orientation is that of the "sadist." This person dominates and exploits others for the same reason—that he may ensure not being separate or alone.

But Fromm's work is distinguished not so much by his analysis of such "unproductive orientations," which most of us recognize as being abnormal. He skillfully points out that much that is considered normal in the western world, and especially in an industrialized capitalistic democracy like America, does in fact turn its back on productivity. Thus, the person who wants to be stylish, who abhors being different, is actually an "automaton conformist." Or, if he is a "good mixer" and "sociable" and finds happiness in the things or people he has met, he may actually have developed a "receptive character." That is, he has disguised his insecurity by surrounding himself with things and people—as if he expected his happiness to come from circumstances outside himself, be it friends, gadgets, or God.

The "hoarding character," on the other hand, has little faith in anything or anybody outside of himself. He protects himself against insecurity by hoarding what he has; he demands a punctual and orderly world as a protection against his own fear of not being able to set things right.

And those persons who are always "selling" their personalities, making sure that they adapt to every new demand, actually illustrate the "marketing orientation" for they have given up their self-direction for safety. To the "marketing" personality, both other persons and they themselves are in fact commodities, things, to be used in exchanges that are useful and safe.

V. *THE AUTHORITARIAN VERSUS THE HUMANISTIC CONSCIENCE*

In all these "unproductive orientations" there is a common factor: the individual has sought to replace his primary ties not by cultivating his own nature but by finding and accepting some source of authority outside his own life. For Fromm, any person who regulates himself by standards that are external is escaping from freedom—with resulting self-distortion and loss of self-confidence. Indeed, Fromm dramatizes this battle by distinguishing two types of conscience at war with each other in the individual's life.

The *authoritarian conscience* is the internalization of external authority. When a person with an authoritarian conscience says that his conscience feels good, he really means that he feels secure in pleasing external authority and avoiding punishment or rejection. When he has a "guilty conscience," he is feeling insecure because he has offended authority and fears the threat of being rejected. His authoritarian conscience does not tolerate insubordination; it demands "all or none" intellectual and emotional submission. The person whom it rules feels sinful if he questions it or if he asks for its justification.

Fromm thinks that the notion of God in the Judeo-Christian tradition fits this authoritarian conscience, because God's authority is not to be doubted and his will is not subject to rational understanding. Any person whose authoritarian conscience allows him to bow and scrape subservient before any "transcending" authority, be it God or society, loses his productivity.[9] If he perchance asserts himself, he feels guilty, this guilt reawakening his primary desires for protective security.

But this side of the person's struggle, solidified in the anonymous authoritarian conscience, is not all there is to being human. Escape from freedom, yes, but that is not all. For a child is not "born to be broken" or to be an automaton. The child, even, puts up a fight to

[9] See *Man for Himself* (New York: Rinehart, 1947), pp. 141 ff.

be a "fullfledged human being." [10] So important is this struggle that Fromm says: "The scars left from the child's defeat in the fight against irrational authority are to be found at the bottom of every neurosis." [11] The story will be different if a child gradually learns to free himself from irrational authority and to link his life in responsible and understandable devotion to his own fulfillment and that of others.

At this point we may well ask: But is not Fromm pointing to another dimension in human nature? He is indeed. Working quite clearly from an ideal of what a "really" wholesome or good personality should be, he condemns as "unproductive" any personality ruled either by a Freudian conscience or socialized superego or by a conscience viewed as the voice of God. What Fromm now introduces, without blare of bugle or sound of trumpet, is a motivating force in each person that links him with every man's struggle for freedom everywhere. He calls it the productive or humanistic conscience. There is no understanding of Fromm's view of the dynamics of personality without the realization that he has this ideal of productivity in the back of his mind even when he does not refer to it or when he uses different names for it.

Yet, if we asked why the individual should not seek security and fatten on it (even as Horney, in the main, seems to suggest), what would Fromm say? He would insist that the individual must (ought to?) follow what his intrinsic human nature is. We shall understand Fromm better if we look at this humanistic conscience more carefully.

The "humanistic conscience is not the internalized voice of an authority whom we are eager to please and afraid of displeasing. It is our own voice, present in every human being and independent of external sanction and reward." [12] The word "voice" here is metaphorical, of course, even though it reappears on the next page when Fromm, still seeking to define the humanistic conscience says: "It is the voice of our true selves (not of God or society) which summons us back to ourselves, to live productively, to develop fully and harmoniously—that is, to *become what we potentially are*." [13]

What Fromm seems to have in mind is the struggle that any liv-

---

[10] Erich Fromm, "Conscience," in Ruth Anshen (ed.), *Moral Principles of Action* (New York: Harper and Brothers, 1952), p. 188.

[11] *Ibid.*

[12] *Ibid.*

[13] *Ibid.,* p. 189.

ing being puts up in order to be what it is its nature to be—except that Fromm seems to assume that it is our true nature to be harmonious. Again, he says: "It is the reaction of our total personality to its proper functioning or disfunctioning." [14] Thus, the humanistic conscience seems to be the self-assertion of the "true self" to become what it can be, rather than accept, for safety's sake, any externally imposed alternative.

Stated differently, Fromm is actually saying that *human nature is so constituted* that it sets up its own demand, namely, that its own potentialities be realized totally and harmoniously. The humanistic conscience is that which in each of our natures calls us to the best *we* can be; it demands that, whatever the terms Nature and other men set down, our own abilities and needs be heeded. And the price a man pays for not heeding it is unproductiveness, however much safety he may feel. If "we listen to every voice and to everybody but not to ourselves," [15] if we never take time to be alone and learn to listen to our *true* self-interest, we shall indeed be afraid to die—for *we* have never lived.

But why is there this impoverishment if one does not obey the humanistic conscience? Why is this better than the authoritarian conscience? Ultimately Fromm seems to have postulated a kind of power-making-for-freedom as intrinsic to human nature. In *Man for Himself,* he appeals to the principle that *"the power to act creates a need to use this power and that the failure to use it results in dysfunction and unhappiness."* [16] But it is not yet clear what "unhappiness" is, what "dysfunctioning" is. Some conception of what human nature ought to be seems to guide Fromm in his definition of human nature. At the same time, he seems to be developing his conception of happiness by what he thinks is constitutive of human nature. We need to look into this matter further.

It seems clear that for Fromm the "ought," the ideal, is present in some fashion within what he regards as the lasting, most dependable trends of each human being. And what are these? Those he shares with all humanity. The command is: "Be thyself, and as completely as possible!" To be one's *true* self is to allow what is not yet actual to become real. And, it is contended, a person cannot do so if he

[14] *Ibid.,* p. 188.
[15] *Ibid.,* p. 190.
[16] We owe this to Ruth Munroe, *Schools of Psychoanalytic Thought* (New York: Dryden Press, 1955), p. 465, who gets it from *Man for Himself* (New York: Rinehart, 1947), p. 219.

simply conforms. As Fromm puts it in *The Sane Society:* "Conscience by its very nature is nonconforming; . . . Conscience exists only when man experiences himself as man, not as a thing, as a commodity." [17]

What happens when this humanistic conscience makes itself felt? The answer: A person "senses his gifts or talents, his ability to love, to think, to laugh, to cry, to wonder and to create, he senses that his life is the one chance he is given, and that if he loses this chance he has lost everything." [18]

The critical reader may well ask: But why is the more lasting and the more universal in man better than what is not? Why ought a man to follow what he has in common with others? These questions never receive an answer. Fromm does not explain why a universal trend in basic human nature ought to be the standard.

This raises a crucial question that many moralists have raised, one that we must raise again later. Can what man *ought to be* ever be completely derived from *any* description of what he *is* and *has been?* Fromm seems simply to have assumed that because certain trends can be found in all people, the standard "ought" should be found in what is found in all people, the standard "ought" should be found in what is thus universal to man. Clearly there are other questions to be raised.

VI. *THE PRODUCTIVE PERSONALITY*

Such questions aside, in relation to the views thus far expressed, Fromm articulates a conception of happiness and mental health that runs somewhat as follows: "The aim of life," he says, "is to unfold man's love and reason and . . . every other human activity has to be subordinated to this aim." [19] Fromm distinguishes between reason and intelligence. Intelligence is the ability by which we work out our biological survival; it is the process of manipulating ideas and things so that we solve practical problems. Reason, on the other hand, "aims at understanding; it tries to find out what is behind the surface, to recognize the kernel, the essence of the reality which sur-

---

[17] *The Sane Society*, p. 173.
[18] *Ibid.*, p. 205.
[19] *Ibid.*, p. 173.

rounds us; . . . its function is not to further physical as much as mental and spiritual existence." [20]

But reason cannot function adequately without "relatedness and a sense of self." [21] Indeed, it is such reason that is missing in "alienated man." For he "takes his reality for granted" and therefore "wants to eat it, touch it, manipulate it," [22] rather than think creatively about the underlying meaning, "which cannot be eaten or manipulated."

Clearly an extraordinary conception of a "happy person" is emerging in this ideal of a creative person. One thing is sure. A "happy" person can never be "secure." As Fromm puts it:

> How can a sensitive and alive person ever feel secure? Because of the very conditions of our existence, we cannot feel secure about anything. Our thoughts and insights are at best partial truth; . . . our life and health are subject to accidents beyond our control. If we make a decision, we can never be certain of the outcome; any decision implies a risk of failure, and if it does imply it, it has not been a decision in the true sense of the word. We can never be certain of the outcome of our best efforts. The result always depends on many factors which transcend our capacity of control. Just as a sensitive and alive person cannot avoid being sad, he cannot avoid feeling insecure. The psychic task which a person can and must set for himself, *is not to feel secure, but to be able to tolerate insecurity, without panic and undue fear. . . .* [again]: *Free man is by necessity insecure; thinking man by necessity uncertain.*[23]

This insistence on the importance of tolerating insecurity, in fact, is the background for Fromm's rigorous condemnation of "many writers" in psychiatry and psychoanalysis who "postulate security as the main aim of psychic development and consider a sense of security more or less equivalent with mental health." [24] He even condemns H. S. Sullivan, "the most profound and searching [25] of these

---

[20] *Ibid.,* p. 170.
[21] *Ibid.*
[22] *Ibid.,* p. 171.
[23] *Ibid.,* p. 196.
[24] *Ibid.,* p. 195.
[25] *Ibid.* See H. S. Sullivan, *Conception of Modern Psychiatry* (Washington: William Alanson White Psychiatric Foundation, 1948); *The Interpersonal Theory of Psychiatry,* ed. Helen S. Perry and Mary L. Gawel (New York: Norton, 1953); and Patrick Mullahy, *Oedipus, Myth and Complex,* Chapter X.

writers." If "being happy" is identified with "having a good time" or being free from sorrow or sadness, then he insists that this "consumer attitude" is far from the experience of fullness, of self-discovery, of union with others. One other excerpt will bring out the essential thrust of his position:

> From the standpoint of normative humanism [note] we must arrive at a different concept of mental health; the very person who is considered healthy in the categories of an alienated world, from the humanistic standpoint appears as the sickest one—although not in terms of individual sickness, but of the socially patterned defect. Mental health, in the humanistic sense, is characterized by the emergence from the incestuous ties to family and nature, by a sense of identity based on one's experience of self as the subject and agent of one's powers, by the grasp of reality inside and outside of ourselves, that is, by the development of objectivity and reason. The aim of life is to live it intensely, to be fully born, to be fully awake. . . . To be able to be alone, and at the same time one with a loved person, with every brother on this earth, with all that is alive; to follow the voice of our conscience, the voice that calls us to ourselves, yet not to indulge in self hate when the voice of conscience was not loud enough to be heard and followed. The mentally healthy person is the person who lives by love, reason, and faith, who respects life, his own and that of his fellowman. . . . The alienated person . . . cannot be healthy.[26]

VII. *PRODUCTIVE LOVE*

The reader will already have guessed that "the art of loving" is the parallel to the life of reason. Here again the problem is for the individual to grow beyond the immature narcissistic state of wanting to be loved, to grow away from wanting to be loved simply for what he is. "Infantile love follows the principle: *'I love because I am loved.'* Mature love follows the principle: *'I am loved because I love.'* Immature love says: *'I love you because I need you.'* Mature love says: *'I need you because I love you.'* "[27]

[26] *The Sane Society,* pp. 203–4.
[27] *Art of Loving,* pp. 40–41.

For Fromm (we must stop to comment), love goes much further than mature heterosexual relations, as of course it did for Freud. But the need to love beyond sexual dimensions is for Fromm integral to human nature, whereas for Freud it was a sublimation of the libido. Love for Fromm is the search for union of a creative sort; its purpose is to protect both one's own potential and growth and that of the other person or persons. Again, productive love is giving and not receiving, a giving born of respect and understanding of the other.

It is in this context that Freud is criticized for not seeing that "the sexual desire is one manifestation of the need for love and union." [28] But Freud is even more wrong in thinking of the sexual desire as "the result of a chemically produced tension in the body," [29] which, being painful, must seek removal in sexual gratification. Indeed, Freud is not wrong so much because he overemphasized sex; he is wrong in "his failure to understand sex deeply enough." [30] Sexual love is rather the "craving for complete fusion, for union with one other person." [31]

VIII. *TO BECOME HUMAN, LOVE!*

We see now that Fromm has come full circle and suggested his answer to the problem of man. To begin with, man is free, frightened, and faint because of his reasoning capacity and his loss of fixed instinctive adaptation. But if he will use reason and not mere intelligence, if he will love and not just seek to be loved, he will solve the problem of his existence productively.

It may seem curious that words like "union" and "fusion" are used to characterize productive love in its different aspects. Such words are used by many mystics, Christian and non-Christian, who speak of becoming one with God, or with the One, or the Ultimate. In the typical, nonmystical Judeo-Christian tradition, it is love that "unified" God and man, but the relation is not conceived as fusion or union except metaphorically or poetically. God and his children are to be unified in purpose, but not in being. Fromm, as we saw earlier, rejected this theistic view of God because he thinks it must

[28] *Ibid.*, p. 35.
[29] *Ibid.*
[30] *Ibid.*, p. 37.
[31] *Ibid.*, pp. 52–53.

involve an externally imposed authority as the basis for human ethics. We must note, however, that while rejecting any view of man as the image of God, he clearly affirms an inner kinship between men because they are one with all there is.

Thus here he says: "Erotic love, if it is love, has one premise. That I love from the essence of my being—and experience the other person in the essence of his or her being." [32] And Fromm goes on: "In essence, all human beings are identical. We are all part of One; we are One. This being so, it should not make any difference whom we love. Love should be essentially an act of will, of decision to commit my life completely to that of one other person." [33] But fearful lest love conceived as an act of will might make it a matter of indifference whom we love erotically, Fromm stresses: "We are all One—yet every one of us is a unique, unduplicatable entity," [34] and therefore, although we are to love all persons in a brotherly way, "erotic love requires certain specific, highly individual elements which exist between some people but not between them all." [35]

Thus it is that Fromm would try to keep productive freedom in willed love and at the same time emphasize an element which knits all men together. Love in this sense carries a step further the relatedness that reason seeks. In loving alone can we "really know" the essence of man and the universe. [36]

Thus it is that the words "love" and "self-love" take on deep significance in Fromm. For in all his writing he contends that although we seem to start life as encapsulated, narcissistic beings, from the beginning we also feel lost ties. Our problem is to overcome human separateness and fulfill our longing for union not by alienating ourselves from our deepest selves, but by *loving ourselves* enough and thus moving into productive relationships with others and nature. Our reason will lead our freedom into relatedness; and if we love ourselves we shall be drawn into union with all others in whatever degree respects this situation and person. In short, persons are not selfish because they love themselves too much; they are selfish because they cannot love themselves as people who can and need to love. [37] The mature person loves other persons in the process of

[32] *Ibid.*, p. 55.
[33] *Ibid.*, pp. 55–56.
[34] *Ibid.*, p. 56.
[35] *Ibid.*, p. 57.
[36] *Ibid.*, p. 33.
[37] Cf. *Art of Loving,* pp. 57 ff., and *Man for Himself,* Chapter IV.

being his complete self, for this is what it means to be fully human.

Indeed, it is this conception of love that guides Fromm in his analysis of religious love. As we have seen, he moves along Freudian lines when he says that the God of Judeo-Christian monotheism is the product of immature thinking and feeling.

> The God of Abraham can be loved, or feared, as a father, some-times his forgiveness, sometimes his anger being the dominant aspect. Inasmuch as God is the father, I am the child. I have not emerged fully from the autistic wish for omniscience and omnip-otence. . . . [On the other hand], the truly religious person . . . does not pray for anything, does not expect anything from God; he does not love God as a child loves his father or mother. [Indeed], he has acquired the humility of sensing his limita-tions, to a degree of knowing that he knows nothing about God. . . . He has faith in the principles which "God" represents; he thinks truth, lives love and justice, and considers all of his life only valuable inasmuch as it gives him the chance to arrive at an ever fuller unfolding of his human powers.[38]

The word "God," it is evident, has now undergone a transforma-tion too. For the Fromm who earlier said that the premise of love is the individual's being a part of One now says that to love God is "to long for the attainment of the full capacity to love, for the realization of that which 'God' stands for *in oneself.*" [39]

The essence of Fromm's interpretation of religion seems to be condensed in a parallel that he draws between love of parents and love of God. The child, Fromm says, moves from attachment to mother as "all-enveloping love" to father as "guiding principle for thought and action" and finally to the mature stage of establishing "the motherly and fatherly principles in himself." He thus becomes "his own father and mother." [40]

> In the history of the human race we see—and can anticipate— the same development: from the beginning of the love for God as the helpless attachment to a Mother Goddess, through the obedient attachment to a fatherly God, to a mature stage where God ceases to be an outside power, where man has incorporated

[38] *Art of Loving,* pp. 70–71.
[39] *Ibid.,* p. 71 (italics added).
[40] *Ibid.,* p. 81.

the principles of love and justice into himself, where he has become one with God, and eventually to a point where he speaks
of God only in a poetic, symbolic sense.[41]

If the religious ideal is condemned because it keeps man from
deepest self-reliance, one can expect any social system to be condemned insofar as it keeps man from becoming his full self. We do
not need to spell out Fromm's barbed critique of dictatorial fascism
and communistic socialism and capitalistic democracy. For we can
readily see why he would criticize each system to the extent that it
puts a premium upon conformism and discourages that faith in one's
own creative core that is the source of faithfulness to others. On
Fromm's view, man can save himself only by creating a "sane society" in which "man relates to man lovingly, in which he is rooted
in bonds of brotherliness and solidarity, . . . in which everyone
gains a sense of self by experiencing himself as the subject of his
powers rather than by conformity. . . ."[42]

IX. *DOES FROMM TAKE FREEDOM SERIOUSLY?*

As we look back, we cannot but be impressed by Fromm's passion
for living from within—and by so doing linking ourselves to the
total growth of others. The search for freedom is man. He must
reach for no power beyond himself, be it God, parents, society, or
state, to give him security; but by living from within, he must creatively build his own individuality through responsible self-acceptance. "No power transcending man can make a moral claim upon
him."[43] We have already hinted that in considering conscience
"man's recall to himself,"[44] Fromm is merely assuming that man
has an enduring, inescapable "intuition" or awareness that he ought
to be the most complete kind of being *he* can be. And Fromm's
whole normative humanism is based on his psychological analysis of
orientations that keep man from becoming "truly human." Yet what
the "real" self is in a positive sense—as we saw in the case of Horney
—is very difficult to gather, even when all is said and done. There is
always difficulty in knowing what the real self is when by definition

[41] *Ibid.*
[42] *The Sane Society,* p. 362.
[43] *Man for Himself,* p. 170.
[44] See *ibid.,* pp. 141 ff.

it is the fulfillment of potential that is not defined positively. Despite all that is said about love and productivity and happiness, we are clearer about what they are not than what they are. In order to be illuminating, "making man more human" must be guided, we suggest, by a more articulate theory of what constitutes man, and his values.

But here we would focus on another problem that is especially important for Fromm, though it pervades all the psychologists whom we are considering. It is the nature of freedom. And we must begin by discriminating two types, which should not be confused. There is the freedom that comes from fulfillment, and this we shall call *ethical freedom*. Thus, in Fromm's terms, the productive personality is free because it has superseded the obstacles to living and is realizing its potential. Anyone is free, then, to the extent that he is what he can be.

But presumably, in order to achieve such *ethical freedom,* the individual who is uncertain about the future will be confronted by alternatives, decide to think or not to think about them, and, in any case, make *some choice,* say *yes* or *no.* This is *moral freedom,* and its exercise may or may not lead to ethical freedom.

One would suppose that Fromm, in view of his insistence that man accept the responsibility for productivity and refuse a short-sighted security for a larger creativity, would give theoretical emphasis to moral freedom. But in fact, he denies it. Here the scientistic fear of the unpredictable blends with what he believes are the discoveries of psychoanalysis. We are deluded if we take our feeling of free will seriously. "We are prone to believe that we act freely because, as Spinoza has already suggested, we are aware of our wishes but unaware of our motivation." [45] But in fact our motives are the result of our character orientation. "The will is not an abstract power of man which he possesses apart from his character," [46] and if we knew enough about a man's character we could predict his decision. For "the will is nothing but the expression of his character." [47]

To be concrete, on Fromm's view, the person who is *ethically free,* "the productive person who trusts his reason and who is capable of loving others and himself *has the will to act virtuously.*" [48] Here, clearly, freedom of choice, *moral freedom* is denied, but ethical free-

[45] *Man for Himself,* p. 232.
[46] *Ibid.,* p. 233.
[47] *Ibid.*
[48] *Ibid.* (italics added).

dom asserted. "Will" and "lack of will" do not refer to any human basic capacity, because a person with will is a certain kind of person (productive), and one who lacks will is unproductive.

We might ask Fromm, then, whether the fact that one "escapes from freedom" is anything he can do anything about through the act of choice. Is his character *his* in the sense that *he* is responsible at any point, in any degree, for the choice he has made? Is it not contradictory to say that our reason and our conscience are "our most precious capacities which it is our task to develop and to use," [49] if we go on to say that they are "forces within the structure of our total personality . . . determined by the structure as a whole?" [50] In what sense can we use our reason and develop our conscience if at every point in our lives our decisions are the product of our character orientation up to that time? Our purpose here is simply to call attention to a very knotty problem, to which we shall return. But we may ask whether reason is not itself a false guide if a person cannot choose to think twice and thus to govern himself in thinking at least by evidence and not by personality structure.

X. *REFLECTIVE SUMMARY*

In Erich Fromm several lines of thought become explicit and emphatic. Man is not a spark of the Divine, but the high point in natural evolution. Man can look for no special awareness (moral consciousness, for example) of moral commands or values in some Source beyond himself. Indeed, all appeals, rational or religious, for direction from sources outside man are outworn props no longer needed by men who will ground their conclusions about man and his values in observation of human experience.

In fact, Fromm vacillates between a scientific posture (in, for example, his refusal to hold, as scientistic psychologists do, that human motivation is basically physiological and biological) and a scientistic posture (in rejecting unique moral and religious intuitions as relevant sources of evidence about human values). But in his own ultimate appeal to "the voice of the true self," in his insistence that man is not a commodity, to what kind of evidence is he referring?

Fromm is anxious to reject backward-looking explanations of per-

[49] *Ibid.*, p. 234.
[50] *Ibid.*

sonality or any view that smacks of impositionism. His central theme is that such views discourage man from accepting the responsibility for freedom, wherein his true happines lies. For human self-development is fraught with uncertainty. In emerging from his oneness with Nature, man gives up once and for all a primordial security, a union with Nature that not even harmony with fellowmen can replace. Nevertheless his task is to be all that he can be as a separate individual, to replace his primary ties by a productive freedom that binds him responsibly to the harmonious growth of others.

The inner anxiety man feels as a result of this tension between individuation and union makes it easy for him to seek safety through social conformity and other ways of avoiding punishment and rejection. Yet, insists Fromm, there is no happiness for man unless he learns to tolerate insecurity and develops from within himself a personality responsive to change and sharing the universal need to love as well as to be loved.

Although we shall make use of many of Fromm's insights, there are some difficulties and ambiguities in his basic concepts. Thus, the freedom that Fromm is talking about is an unwilled freedom that expresses the total development of the unique individual in harmony with others. Yet while it is clear that such freedom-in-fulfillment must be different from mere plasticity, it is far from clear that it is rooted in any capacity to will freely between alternatives. Must "escape from freedom" mean refusal to become one's "real self"? On Fromm's view, we wonder whether one is *morally* free to accept or not to accept responsibility for Fromm's *kind* of freedom, namely, the freedom that comes through self-fulfillment. In the last analysis, it seems to us, Fromm denies moral freedom, despite the fact that his whole discussion presupposes that man can choose, to some extent at any rate, his orientation toward his fulfillment.

Finally, Fromm seems to presuppose, rather than give careful reason for, a view of man's "real nature" that in fact guides his analysis of what man ought to become. The assumption seems to be that man ought to be productively free simply because he cannot be what he "truly is" unless he does become free. But is this much more than reading the desired good back into the nature of man? Why say that what a man is to become or ought to become is what he really is?

5

A. H. Maslow: Human Nature and the Self-actualizing Person

~~~~~~

Erich Fromm, we have seen, opposes impositionism in every form. The standard for man must be found within himself and not imposed upon him by family, by community, by church, by state, or by God. Yet when man accepts his "freedom," when he becomes his real, creative self, he binds himself by ties of productive love to the good of others. In the thinking of Fromm we have seen the development of a trend of thought, discernible in Jung, Adler, and Horney, in which it becomes increasingly clear that the pleasure-hungry, libidinous individual whom Freud took to be normal and who "fulfilled" himself by cunning and conniving protective devices, is in fact a sick person. In the words of Kurt Goldstein, "The tendency to maintain the existent state [of self-preservation] is characteristic for sick people and is a sign of . . . decay of life" rather than "the tendency of the normal." [1] This thesis finds further support in the psychotherapy of Carl R. Rogers. Rogers holds that the human being has a self-creative potential, and not a narcissistic libido, which must be freed in and through the process of psychotherapy. [2]

[1] Kurt Goldstein, "The So-called Drives," in Clark E. Moustakas (ed.), *The Self* (New York: Harper & Bros., 1956), p. 17. But extended support for this thesis is to be found in Goldstein's influential book, *The Organism* (New York: American Book Co., 1939).

[2] See Carl R. Rogers, "What It Means to Become a Person," in Moustakas *op. cit.*, and especially *Client-centered Therapy* (Boston: Houghton Mifflin, 1951) and *On Becoming a Person* (Boston: Houghton Mifflin, 1961).

I. *THE PSYCHOLOGICAL REASONING AGAINST "REDUCTIONISM"*

If we ask ourselves why this change in thinking about human nature has taken place, we discover first that these thinkers simply found the Freudian-type hypothesis inadequate to the data that they faced in their therapeutic situations. But they also freed themselves from *scientistic* restrictions in their methodology. As we now approach the work of Abraham Maslow we shall see another explicit step away from such restrictions. To Fromm's explicit anti-impositionism, Maslow adds antireductionism. If we see why, we shall better understand Maslow.

Antireductionism has two themes in its platform. First, it urges that psychologists resist the temptation to use animal nature and animal behavior as a trustworthy model for understanding human beings. Secondly, whatever similarities a human being may have to other human beings, it is fatal to reduce him to "one sample" of human nature. The antireductionist, in short, maintains that *man,* however else he is surveyed, is to be studied in his own terms and that *each man* is to be understood on his own terms.

It is important to note that this concern for individuality—which is to develop into the ethical doctrine of respect for each individual —now stems not from the Judeo-Christian doctrine that God loves and cares for each person, sinner or saint. It springs from concern for truth, and nothing but the truth, about human nature, no matter how difficult and baffling the search for it may be. Whatever their religious or philosophical convictions, a large roster of influential psychologists—the list would include, besides those already mentioned, G. W. Allport, Hadley Cantril, Paul E. Johnson, K. Koffka, W. Köhler, K. Lewin, H. Mowrer, Gardner Murphy, H. A. Murray, H. S. Sullivan—finds that the data of human nature simply cannot be adequately explained if one tries to understand human experience and behavior by reference to processes that take place, presumably, in animals. Their conviction marks a great gain in the struggle against what we have called scientism in American psychology.

These thinkers, to be sure, welcome discoveries about human nature that have resulted from comparing the behavior of animals and human beings. The psychologist cannot ask animals for their introspective reports, so he is restricted to noting the sequences in their behavior. What he thus discovers is open to check by other investigators, for much in animal behavior can be studied under conditions that are experimentally controlled. But public inspection and experimental control, we have seen, so dominate the scientistic mind that it soon approaches the understanding of human action by limiting itself to what is observable in a similar public and controlled way. The scientistic psychologist rejects human introspection as a source of knowledge about persons because every individual can gaze only into his own consciousness and his reports cannot be verified by others.

Now, every thoughtful believer in introspection realizes that introspective descriptions of experience need to be scrutinized with the utmost care. But it is also true that human beings have lived for centuries without seriously mistaking what is in the minds of others when they talk about their perceptions, emotions, intentions, and thoughts. And, more important for the psychotherapist, whatever entrée he has into the "depths" of the patient's mind he can have only because, through his own introspection, he can surmise what the patient is experiencing. Generalizing a point that Allport has made in a similar connection,[3] we think that our introspective reports should be believed until we have good reason to suppose the contrary.

It is not hard to see that if a psychologist includes among his data his own introspective reports and the reports of others he will be forced to give up the *scientistic* conception of accuracy. But this scientistic ideal, we recall, arose from the attempt to pattern the science of psychology after the methodology of the physical sciences. In these sciences, the behavior of entities can be studied without reference to motivation; we do not ask what motive the billiard ball has in moving to the corner pocket. But we cannot tell from the overt behavior of a human being what his needs and purposes are; indeed, to misunderstand a person's inner motivation is to misunderstand his behavior. No reader of this book will have had reason to underrate the importance of motivation. If the psychologist allows his desire for prediction, accuracy, and public validation to keep him from the most circumspect study of human experience in every

[3] See G. W. Allport, "The Trend in Motivational Theory," in Moustakas, *op. cit.,* pp. 25–43.

phase and at every level, he may save his scientistic accuracy, but he may lose much of the human being and of the scientific spirit.

It is the willingness to follow human experience in all its ranges that unites the psychologies of the men we have mentioned above, despite their own occasional pronouncements. Realizing that they are moving against the currents of psychological scientistic orthodoxy, they insist on making psychology not so much science-centered as person-centered. This is especially true of Maslow and Allport, whose thought we study in this chapter and the next. They would be criticized as being too intuitive or too unscientific by those scientistic, "operational" psychologists who want every conception and every problem defined in terms of the differences observable to our senses. Allport and Maslow in fact would not reject operational approaches when human nature allows them, but they refuse to condemn either psychological science or human nature to such a restricted approach.

II. *MASLOW'S PLEA FOR "THE WHOLE MAN"*

In the thought of A. H. Maslow, then, we have an especially good example of the move from scientistic accuracy to scientific adequacy in the study of man. Early in his psychological career Maslow concentrated on comparative and experimental psychology, biology, and neurophysiology. But as he turned with greater emphasis to the human organism and human experience as a whole, he became increasingly dissatisfied with a presupposition that pervaded psychological thinking in these fields. The tendency was to view man as though everything he did was done simply for the sake of survival. Suitable for creatures struggling merely to reduce threats to their safety, it crowded out too much of actual human nature.

With this approach was coupled another tendency in psychological studies that Maslow had to challenge. When psychologists did get away from studying man in the light of his evolutionary ancestry, they focused on giving a good description of the average man. For if one studied "many persons" one could gather "reliable" statistics. But Maslow saw that we might get a distorted conception of human beings by assuming that what most often happens is the clue to what infrequently happens. If it is dangerous to consider the animal as a norm for interpreting human behavior, it is also hazardous to allow the average man to become the *norm*-al man or even the healthy man.

We have already seen how Fromm inveighed against this last conception; he believed that the "average" man allowed his desire for security within his culture to keep him from productive self-fulfillment. But Maslow goes a step further and raises the question: Are the healthiest, maturest, most productive, or, in his own word, "self-actualizing" persons simply off-average persons who are understandable as variations of the formula for the average and subaverage and sick? Or are they to be understood on their own terms, as unique wholes?

And now Maslow takes the giant step and asks us to consider whether self-actualizing persons may not be the ones (like Aristotle's good men) who represent the flowering of the human species, since they bring into being potentialities not realized by others? Indeed, are they not the ones who can tell us most about what human nature is and can be and thus throw light on the nature of development? Let the psychologist, then, not overlook these few, if they are few, even though they are hard to select with the kind of precision either scientist or philosopher would like.

It may be difficult for the beginner to realize how daring, in the orthodox climate of recent scientistic psychology, is this suggestion —which indeed has as its philosophical ancestors in Plato and Aristotle. For it says: Let us look to the end, to the ripest fruit of a developing process, and not to the beginning *only,* if we want to understand the process as a whole. Although this idea is implicit in much of what we have discussed before and especially in Adler's conception of a life style, the main trend (as illustrated in the actual psychoanalyses reported by Freud) is to conceive the nature of man in the light of what goes on in infancy and childhood and, indeed, to go back of that (as in Jung's studies) to the prehistoric archetypes of the collective unconscious.

Maslow, in fact, criticizes Freudians for yielding to the easy temptation of allowing their analyses of sick minds to influence their view of the total growth process and, bluntly, to regard "normality as a special case of the abnormal." [4] For it may turn out to be the opposite: it may be that "psychological illness is primarily a struggle toward health." [5] Indeed, Maslow goes as far as to say:

[4] From mimeographed lecture, "A Philosophy of Psychology," 1956, p. 11.
[5] *Ibid.,* p. 12.

The trouble with many psychologists is that they are content to work with but a portion of the human being, indeed even to make a virtue and a desirable thing out of it. They forget that ultimately their task is to give us a unified, empirically based conception of the whole human being, of human nature, in general, *i.e.*, a philosophy of human nature.[6]

It is high time, he contends, that psychologists do justice to the person who is concerned not alone with meeting emergencies and gratifying survival needs, but also in experiencing life for its own sake. It is this self-fulfilling, self-actualizing person that Maslow keeps before him as he tries to gain insight into the different levels of human need.

III. *THE HIERARCHY OF HUMAN NEEDS*

The goal of each and every human life, then, is self-fulfillment, "living up to his potentialities." [7] But human beings have many other problems that they need to solve on the way to this goal. What is especially interesting about the "often largely unconscious" [8] basic needs of man is that each represents a special and basic universal personality problem that must be adequately satisfied before significant higher development can take place.[9]

What this means is that human beings everywhere, regardless of differences in ability, regardless of differences in culture, have certain basic needs that create similar problems for them. Maslow is not yet ready to say that these basic needs are universal for all cultures, but contents himself with asserting that they are "*more* ultimate, *more* universal, *more* basic than the superficial conscious desires" [10] of human beings.

As Maslow proceeds to describe these "instinctoid" needs, he keeps his eye fixed on how they appear in human nature rather than in animal nature. Thus he says that we must not be drawn into thinking of human instincts as strong and overpowering, as we may well find them

[6] *Ibid.*, p. 6.
[7] From mimeographed lecture, 'Personality Problems and Personality Growth," 1954, p. 9.
[8] Maslow, *Motivation and Personality* (New York: Harper and Brothers, 1954), p. 101.
[9] See *ibid.*, especially Chapters V–IX.
[10] *Ibid.*, p. 102.

to be in animals. After all, a need may be innate and common to all men without having the right of way in human life.

Indeed Maslow calls his list of needs "instinctoid" to emphasize two facts: first, they do not express themselves as rigidly as animal instincts do; second, they are not learned in a culture, however influential environment and culture may be in directing the way and extent to which they are gratified. In short, in Maslow's conception, there is an underlying structure of human needs which orients each man to his environment at the same time that he is subjected to the influence of what he learns in his environment. As we proceed to describe these needs we shall discern an order among them. They may not be equally strong but their proper expression is vital to the fulfillment of human life.

We are already familiar with the first two types of instinctoid needs. Basic are the *physiological needs* that serve the homeostatic balance of the body and keep it alive—the needs for food, water, sleep, warmth, exercise, and procreation. At the next level come the needs for *safety and security*—which call for protection when one is in danger or helpless. These two sets of instinctoid needs provide for the sheer existence and survival of the body.

But even at this level we must introduce a unique pattern of thought that almost always runs through Maslow's conception of how needs are organized or related to each other. His thesis is that unless some needs are gratified, others will not even appear. Thus, a person can get hungry enough to throw safety considerations to the winds. Or, if first-level needs do not find adequate gratification, they will keep on interfering with the gratification of "higher" needs. Thus, as Maslow says, "undoubtedly these physiological needs are the most prepotent of all needs." [11]

Maslow defines such prepotency as meaning "specifically . . . that in the human being who is missing everything in life in an extreme fashion, it is most likely that the major motivation would be the physiological needs rather than any others." [12] Assume, for example, that a person is lacking food, safety, respect, love, and beauty. On Maslow's view the person would "most probably [note!] hunger for food more strongly than anything else." [13] But, Maslow goes on to say that as long as the organism is dominated by physiological needs "all other needs may become simply non-existent." [14]

[11] *Ibid.,* p. 82.
[12] *Ibid.*
[13] *Ibid.*
[14] *Ibid.*

An important issue is at stake here, and we must pause briefly to consider it. It may well be true that physiological needs are prepotent, for there comes a point at which a hungry and thirsty person dies. But the prepotency is not so consistent when we consider the relation of frustrated safety needs to the next higher ones, the needs for love, for freedom, and for community. In other words, it may be true that for the "chronically and extremely hungry man . . . freedom, love, community feeling, respect, philosophy, may all be waved aside as fripperies that are useless, since they fail to fill the stomach." [15] But is this a safe generalization for the man who does not feel safe and secure physically? Will he need to feel safe in order to want freedom and to respond with love and respect for others?

Before answering, we should remind ourselves of those men who, for example, have been willing to starve to death for some principle. Millions have faced death and endured starvation and torture for their country. There is no doubt that the pattern of prepotency that Maslow suggests often applies to most of us, and it usually applies to growing children, especially when higher needs or purposes are not developed. But that this relative prepotency of needs reigns in our adult lives even most of the time may be seriously questioned.

Maslow himself allows that the self-actualizing person is not so subject to this law of prepotency. But may it not still be questioned whether we can accept the general formula [16] that the chronic gratification of a lower need releases higher needs, on the ground that those that are gratified "cease to exist as active determinants or organizers of behavior"? [17] Would it not be safer to say that if hunger is gratified it may no longer be *an* "issue" in the motivational life of the individual? Or, similarly, that a child who has been brought up in a safe, orderly, predictable, organized world that he can count on is less likely to make safety *the* issue in his life?

To continue with Maslow's hierarchy of instinctoid needs, the next, and third, level consists of the "belongingness and love needs." Maslow stresses the importance of these by asserting: "In our society the thwarting of these needs is the most commonly found core in cases of maladjustment and more severe psychopathology." [18]

If this third level of instinctoid needs reminds us of Horney, the fourth level, the *esteem needs,* recalls Adler. The need for self-esteem

[15] *Ibid.,* pp. 82–83.
[16] See *ibid.,* p. 83.
[17] *Ibid.,* p. 84.
[18] *Ibid.,* p. 89.

is universally present in the desire "for mastery and competence, for confidence in the face of the world, and for independence and freedom" [19] as well as in the desire for prestige, recognition, and appreciation. We already have seen, in Adler's thought, that the thwarting of these needs gives rise to such feelings of inferiority and helplessness that neuroses are encouraged. Healthy self-esteem, says Maslow, is based on "*deserved* respect from others rather than external fame or celebrity and unwarranted adulation." [20]

Let us assume that one has reasonably gratified these four kinds of needs. Will he find himself still restless and discontent? Maslow's answer is unequivocal: Yes. For, in the last analysis a person must do "what he is fitted for." [21] Here Maslow states explicitly the formula that, we suggest, is implicit in all the psychological approaches to the good life, from Freud to Fromm through Allport (as we shall see). For he says: "What a man *can* be, he *must* be. This need we may call self-actualization." [22]

The difference between psychologies, of course, lies in the conception of what it *is* that man can be and become and how that becoming is conceived. As we have already seen, Maslow stresses the principle of prepotency in the emergence of drives.

Thus, as Maslow turns to the highest (the fifth) level of needs, namely, *the need for knowledge for its own sake,* he says that "clear emergence" *usually* rests "upon the prior satisfaction of the physiological, safety, love, and esteem needs." [23] As he himself generalizes, "the most single principle underlying all healthy human development" is "the tendency for a new and higher need to emerge as the lower need fulfills itself by being sufficiently gratified." [24]

Two misconceptions must be avoided, however. First, these needs must not be pictured as layers that rest on each other in tight little compartments, for they are all different aspects of a continuous, dynamic experient. Second, and this is crucial, although some psychologists may give the impression that the first four types are the really crucial ones for "health and happiness," Maslow insists that these self-actualizing needs and peak experiences (to be mentioned soon) are just as important, and indeed more so, to *satisfied* living.

[19] *Ibid.,* p. 90.
[20] *Ibid.,* p. 91.
[21] *Ibid.*
[22] *Ibid.*
[23] *Ibid.,* p. 92.
[24] "Defense and Growth," in *Merrill-Palmer Quarterly,* 3 (1956), 44–45.

The higher needs, in other words, are not simply "frosting on the cake" but are capable of lifting the whole experience of life to a higher level.

We may pause to note the importance of this point, because a whole conception of education and social planning could be at stake. For if the higher needs are as important to human fulfillment as "the lower," the differences will be felt, sooner or later, in the lives of students who make the search for knowledge and for aesthetic appreciation a serious goal in their education. Nor can a society intent on developing wholesome persons make technical training primary and "pure investigation" and aesthetic sensitivity secondary. As Maslow points out, in order to guarantee the satisfaction of basic needs, including self-actualizing needs, the individual must enjoy a modicum at least of freedom of speech and investigation, along with freedom of action consistent with similar demands of others, and freedom of self-defense against injustice. Maslow's main point here, however, is that persons may become mentally ill because they are not fulfilling their intellectual capacities, because they are not gratifying their basic desire "to understand, to systematize, to organize, to analyze, to look for relations and meanings, to construct a system of values." [25]

Similarly, as much as persons need protein for bodily health, they need to perceive and create beauty for self-fulfillment.

IV. *DEFICIENCY MOTIVATION VERSUS GROWTH MOTIVATION*

Actually Maslow is preparing us to see two underlying trends in human motivation that have not been carefully distinguished. There is a difference between *living* and *preparing* to live. It is one thing to live merely to make up for deficiences, to live for safety now and "for the future." This kind of living is quite different from that of a healthy child who overflows spontaneously moment after moment. Deficiency motivation controls the first kind of living; significant growth is present in such "coping" with life. But growth also issues from trying out one's powers for their own sake—*"exploring, manipulating, experiencing,* being interested, choosing, delighting, *enjoying,"* [26]—without any hunger to feed.

[25] *Motivation and Personality*, pp. 96–97.
[26] See "Defense and Growth," *op. cit.,* p. 37.

Thus, in his own way, Maslow puts the struggle for both security and for growth (which we noted especially in Jung and in Fromm) within the individual.

> One set [of forces] clings to safety and defensiveness out of fear, tending to regress, hanging onto the past, *afraid* to grow away from the primitive communion with the mother's uterus and breast, afraid to take chances, afraid to jeopardize what he already has, afraid of independence, freedom and separateness. The other set of forces impels him forward toward wholeness of Self and uniqueness of Self, toward full functioning of all his capacities, toward confidence in the face of the external world at the same time that he can accept his deepest, real, unconscious Self.[27]

In this constant conflict that goes on between these "defense forces" and "growth trends," the child will be freer to choose *unknown* "growth-through-delight" if parents and environment generally can gratify his basic needs for safety, belongingness, love, and respect. For thus the child is released from the threats and insecurities that discourage venturesomeness.

However, Maslow is also introducing here, beyond his principle of prepotency, *a principle of intuitive preference,* as we may call it. Maslow is saying that the anxieties and delights of growth motivation are in constant competition with the anxieties and delights of deficiency motivation.

Suppose we ask Maslow: On what grounds do you say that individuals "grow forward when the delights of growth and the anxieties of safety are greater than the anxieties of growth and the delights of safety"? [28] Maslow replies by enunciating what he thinks is a simple, stubborn fact of introspection:

> . . . growth takes place when the next step forward is subjectively more delightful, more joyous, more intrinsically satisfying than the last; . . . the only way we can ever know what is right for us is that it feels better subjectively than any alternative. The new experience validates *itself* rather than by any outside criterion. It is self-justifying, self-validating.[29]

Growth experience is not chosen because someone else tells us "it's

[27] *Ibid.,* pp. 37–38.
[28] *Ibid.,* p. 38.
[29] *Ibid.,* p. 36.

good for us," or will make us live longer, or will bring external rewards. "In a word, this is the way in which we discover the Self and answer the ultimate question Who am I? What am I?" [30]

We must stop here to emphasize an underlying conviction, because of its obvious consequences for ethical reflection, as we shall see in detail later. For if one is to make choices by giving preference, fundamentally, to self-validating *delight,* to what is he trusting his own future and the destiny of others? To the belief that human nature is intrinsically good? To the belief that if untampered with, human nature develops wholesome fruit? As Maslow himself puts it: "We rest here on the faith, that if free choice is *really* free and if the chooser is not too sick or frightened to choose, he will choose wisely, in a healthy and growthward direction." [31] Yes, but how can a parent or teacher or society know when the child feels safe enough to dare to choose the new step ahead? Maslow replies: "Ultimately, the only way in which we can know is by *his* choices, which is to say that only *he* can ever really know the right moment when the beckoning forces ahead overbalance the beckoning forces behind, and courage outweighs fear." [32]

In passing, we may observe that while it may be true that all our valuations are based on actual experiences of "delight" (and its gradations and opposites), human beings have learned through sad experience to look beyond the face value of experiences before giving them a final assessment. The question that must be raised is that of the criterion by which we are to evaluate experiences, be they on their faces delightful or not. To say that the child himself can resort in the last analysis only to his own experience as it comes along may leave us, in evaluating, in a more desperate situation than is really our case. But we shall return to this whole matter later.

V. *PEAK EXPERIENCES AND SELF-ACTUALIZERS*

We now turn to a characterization of the kind of persons that emerge when spontaneous growth tendencies, deep in their natures, are not choked off at the level of deficiency-defense motivation.[33]

[30] *Ibid.,* p. 37.
[31] *Ibid.,* p. 39.
[32] *Ibid.,* p. 40.
[33] See *Motivation and Personality,* p. 224.

As might be expected, on Maslow's view, the division is not between sick people and well (average) people, but between people in different stages of self-fulfillment. The psychologically sick person is the one who has never known enough safety, love, respect, in short, the one who "has never had enough good relationships with other people." [34] Different neurotic symptoms are the different ways in which the patient tries to hold on to as much health as possible in his defensive stage of coping with life.[35]

The self-actualizing person, by contrast, is "growth motivated rather than deficiency motivated." [36] It is important, however, not to assume that self-actualizing people are simply higher levels on the continuum (a) crippled, (b) average, (c) self-fulfilled. For Maslow's studies suggest that self-actualizing people "have so much to teach us that sometimes they seem almost like a different breed of human beings." [37] The very fact that they are growth motivated means that they have different perspectives on themselves, other persons, and the world. Self-actualizers do not live merely to meet deficits. Having weathered the cries *for* safety, *for* respect, *for* love, they are free to develop from within and even to tolerate deficiencies in the lower basic needs. They live expressively, from within; they are environment influenced but not environment centered.

To be more concrete, we review briefly some of the characteristics that Maslow finds in self-actualizers—persons like Lincoln, Jane Addams, Einstein, Spinoza, Beethoven, Goethe. Maslow grants that, statistically speaking, the group is small, but his thesis, we remember, is that it is to persons like these that we must look for insight into what man can best become.

1. Self-actualizers are more efficient in seeing themselves and others as they are. They do not confuse wish with reality and are not frightened by the unknown; they reason out their problems on the basis of fact; and when faced with disorder and uncertainty, they do not wish them away but make tentative decisions by which they live until they have new evidence.

2. Self-actualizers are able to accept their own human nature, its weaknesses and good points, and live with it. They live without pos-

---

[34] *Ibid.*, p. 318.
[35] Cf. *ibid.*, p. 190.
[36] *Ibid.*, p. 183.
[37] Maslow, "Cognition of Being in Peak Experiences," mimeographed form of Presidential Address before the Division of Personality and Social Psychology, American Psychological Association, September 1, 1956, p. 1.

ing, without feeling unnecessary guilt, and without exaggerating their own good points and the weaknesses of others.

3. They are spontaneous; that is, they are not hampered by the artificialities of convention when an important issue is at stake. Yet, they do not buttress themselves by being unconventional.

4. Because they are problem centered and not ego centered, they develop a concern for the basic issues of life and "work within a framework of values that are broad and not petty, universal and not local, and in terms of a century rather than the moment." [38]

5. Along with this sense of perspective, these self-actualizers are detached about their own problems and those of others without being diffident or indifferent. They are able to be alone and stand alone and do not need the constant reassurance and compliments of others.

6. Persons with the above traits become more autonomous or independent of their culture and environment. These characteristics in turn are possible *because* they are dependent on themselves for their development and growth and not on circumstances. Furthermore, because they are beyond deficiency motivation in regard to love and safety, they do not think of other persons as the only source of their needs for safety, love, respect, prestige. They are growth motivated. The essentials of the good life for them do not depend on what other people can give. "Self-contained," these persons can maintain a relative serenity and stability in the midst of circumstances that would drive other people to distraction.

7. It must not be thought that these detached, autonomous, self-contained persons do not have a real concern for the welfare of others. Indeed, Maslow comments that the basic reason for their "getting to this point of independence from love and respect, is to have been given plenty of this very same love and respect in the past." [39] Despite the fact that they are "very different from other people in thought, impulse, behavior, emotions," [40] they have a family feeling toward their weaker, foolish, and sometimes nasty and unsympathetic fellowmen. They are not condescending even though aware of the limited perspectives and appreciations of others.

8. Furthermore, as one might expect, self-actualizing persons are not only more selective in close friendships, but their ties are more obliterating of ego boundaries. Thus, widespread elder-brotherly

---

[38] Maslow, *Motivation and Personality*, p. 212.
[39] *Ibid.*, p. 214.
[40] *Ibid.*, p. 217.

feeling lives side by side with discriminating friendships. When these persons are hostile, the hostility is deserved and directed to the good of others rather than to mere self-defense.

9. It is not surprising that such persons have a "democratic character structure." They are not authoritarian and "are friendly with anyone of suitable character regardless of class, education, political belief, race, or color." [41] Their basic reaction to other persons is to them as persons deserving of "a certain quantum of respect" no matter how bad they may be.[42]

10. Finally we bring together several of Maslow's other attributes, for they center around the capacity of the self-actualizing person to experience himself, others, events, and the whole of things differently. Whether self-actualizers are experiencing the ordinary event, beauty, sex, or knowledge, there is a creative quality of wholeness and freshness in their experience. Indeed it is to this quality that they owe their strength. Most people just see things as means to an end; they tend to label things and experiences as "another one of those." But self-actualizers "have the wonderful capacity to appreciate again and again, freshly and naively, the basic goods of life, with awe, pleasure, wonder, and even ecstasy, however stale these experiences have become to others." [43]

Interestingly enough, the high point of these recreative experiences, be they mediated by beauty or sexual orgasm, suggests the kind of experience that religious mystics have reported. As Maslow puts it:

> There were the same feelings of limitless horizons opening up to the vision, the feeling of being simultaneously more powerful and also more helpless than one ever was before, the feeling of great ecstasy and wonder and awe, the loss of placing in time and space with, finally, the conviction that something extremely important and valuable had happened, so that the subject is to some extent transformed and strengthened even in his daily life by such experiences.[44]

At this point Maslow comments that "it is quite important to

---

[41] *Ibid.*, p. 220.

[42] *Ibid.*

[43] *Ibid.*, pp. 214–15. Maslow's underlying philosophic stance here seems to be a combination of Bergson and Whitehead. The former insists that the intellect, expressing the needs of *homo faber*, staticizes the creative flow of things; the latter that we stop confining our cognitive attention to what is "clear and distinct" and realize that reality may be met in the fuzzy and conceptually unclear.

[44] *Ibid.*, p. 216.

dissociate this experience from any theological or supernatural reference, even though for thousands of years they have been linked." [45] He prefers to use the Freudian term "oceanic feeling" for such experiences, "because this experience is a natural experience, well within the jurisdiction of science." [46] He thinks that if we divorce the experience from supernatural reference we can reject the traditional theological interpretation of the mystical experience as qualitatively different from all others and place it on a "quantitative continuum from intense to mild." [47] Thus, the "tremendous intensification of *any* of the experiences in which there is loss of self or transcendence of it." [48]

Actually such oceanic or mystical experiences are only one kind of "peak experience." "Peak experiences," furthermore, are not confined to self-actualizing persons. Peak experiences are "moments of highest happiness and fulfillment," which may occur to many people and which help to make self-actualizing persons. Peak experiences may be moments of love, of parental experience, of aesthetic perception, of intellectual insight, of nature experiences. The important thing about them is that they are not experiences that come when the main interest is to "make ends meet."

For they come when what is experienced is experienced with complete absorption, "detached from relations, from possible usefulness, from expediency, and from purpose." [49] These peak experiences of pure delight fill one with "awe, wonder, amazement, humility and even reverence, exaltation and piety." [50]

And, as Maslow sees it, a very important difference arises when one looks at life from the perspective thus reached. Now the whole of existence is seen as beyond good and evil as we normally experience these. Evil especially is regarded as a "partial phenomenon, a product

[45] *Ibid.*
[46] *Ibid.*
[47] *Ibid.*
[48] *Ibid.*, p. 217. It is interesting to note that Maslow, usually arguing against reducing the qualitative differences between experiences, is willing, for the sake of a "scientific" description, to run together into one kind what may well be different types of experiences. To consider the aesthetic and the religious experience of one kind with other peak experiences, and to place them on a "quantitative continuum from intense to mild"—the mild being open to most individuals—is to invite much resistance from those who know these experiences "from the inside." In any case, much more argument would be required than is given here. It will be informative to compare this view of religion with Freud's and with Allport's later. Our own interpretation must wait until Chapter 30.
[49] "Cognition of Being in the Peak Experiences," *op. cit.,* p. 3.
[50] *Ibid.,* p. 11.

of not seeing the world whole and unified, and of seeing it from a self-centered point of view." [51] In any peak experience there is such a poignant and piercing quality that tears or laughter may be evoked, which "may be paradoxically akin to pain, although this is a desirable pain which is often described as 'sweet.' " [52] At its height, some writers have described the peak experiences as a kind of "eager dying." [53] There is in these experiences a *"loving and uncondemning acceptance of the world and of the person,"* [54] and the person feels more of a unity, more completely himself, than he ordinarily does.

In the end, these peak experiences, which might be called self-actualizing moments, help persons to become self-actualizing persons. For, as Maslow summarizes, in these peak moments, the individual experiences

> an episode, or a spurt in which the powers of the person come together in a particularly efficient and intensely enjoyable way, and in which he is more integrated and less split, more open for experience, more idiosyncratic, more perfectly expressive or spontaneous, or fully functioning, more creative, more humorous, more ego-transcending, more independent of his lower needs. . . . He becomes in these episodes more truly himself, more perfectly actualizing his potentialities, closer to the core of his Being.[55]

With this quotation we bring to a close an attenuated description of what human life can become and must become if it is to fulfill its potential, on Maslow's view. We can now see why he says that human nature "seems not to be intrinsically evil, but rather either neutral or positively 'good' " [56] and that the evil in man's nature "appears most often to be a secondary reaction to frustration of this intrinsic nature." [57] Man's inner instinctoid nature, unlike the instinctive nature of animals, is indeed not "strong and overpowering and unmistakable" but "weak and delicate and subtle." It is therefore "easily overcome by habit, cultural pressure and wrong attitudes toward it," [58] and human beings can so easily neglect or discount it.

[51] *Ibid.*, p. 11.
[52] *Ibid.*, p. 16.
[53] *Ibid.*
[54] *Ibid.*, p. 21.
[55] *Ibid.*, p. 26.
[56] "Personality Problems and Personality Growth," *op. cit.*, p. 2.
[57] *Ibid.*
[58] *Ibid.*

Nevertheless, this tendency to fulfillment does not disappear when neglected or denied, and it may be seen at work even in the mentally ill, who are ill because they do not—and perhaps just because they will not—give up their demand for self-fulfillment.

Indeed, although Maslow does not pay much explicit attention to the problem of the superego and the conscience, it is clear that this inner self, driving to fulfill itself, functions (like Fromm's "self") as the "intrinsic conscience" insisting "that we be true to our inner nature" [59] and not sell out to conventional safety. But Maslow's concern, in some respects more explicit than Fromm's at this point, is as much for the average person who "gets by" as for the neurotic and the psychotic. The latter are crippled and often realize it; many seek help and are grateful for it. But the "average man" can have "subtle value illnesses," [60] which represent a stunting of inborn potentiality; in some respects these persons are worse off than the neurotic. When he says "I'm as good as the next man," he may be expressing the symptoms of an inner cancer that eats away for a long time; he may never die of the cancer, but he has never really lived.

VI. THE PERSISTENT QUESTION: FROM WHAT IN MAN DOES THE STANDARD OF GOODNESS COME?

A. The Search for Universal Needs and the Theory of Natural Law

In Maslow's psychology, we see a strong emphasis both on the universal in man (instinctoid needs and prepotency) and on the unique in man (especially exemplified in self-actualizers). His thought provides a good point from which to review the ground we have covered from an angle that makes contact, once more, with the history of ethical reflection.

The main question that we have been asking of Freud, Jung, Adler, Horney, Fromm, and Maslow is this: On your view, what must a human being do not only to withstand "breakdown" but also to achieve positive health and strength? There is a common theme in

---

[59] *Ibid.,* p. 4.

[60] *Ibid.,* p. 13. The above exposition has not had the benefit of Maslow's latest book, *Toward a Psychology of Being* (Princeton: Van Nostrand Co., 1962), which appeared too late for use here, and in which some of the papers referred to above may be found.

all their answers, despite important differences in detail. Discover, they say to us, those tendencies that define the central needs of human nature and give them adequate expression in the life of the family, the building of a social order, and in more private avocational pursuits.

All this may sound obvious until we emphasize that for these psychologists it is the unfolding and development of what is in man that counts for his happiness and his misery. The environment, physical and social, may act to impede or obstruct the gratification demanded by certain needs intrinsic to human nature. But, and this is crucial, neither the environment nor the individual can snuff those needs out or supplement them. The individual is subject to these "forces," and he must either obey their mandate or suffer the different degrees of malformation or maldevelopment of which his nature is capable. Whatever plasticity each author may allow the individual, so that the individual can adjust his needs to environmental restriction and opportunities, the fact nevertheless remains that his "health" depends on the degree to which the goals or ends implicit in human nature are realized. The good life, happiness, health—call it what we will—is a function of the fruition or fulfillment of these needs that constitute the individual human being, be they very specific like the physiological, or nonspecific like creativity, freedom, security, superiority, or self-actualization.

But how do we know what is most human? What needs constitute an individual human being? Our authors answer: Those needs common to all men, the common denominators of human want, the universal motives that characterize all human striving regardless of the environment. True, no one of our authors would deny differences among human beings or the degrees of strength of these universal motives. Nor would any suggest that there is one identical "happiness" for all persons despite differences in individual ability. But in a chorus they insist: The fundamental needs are the universal ones, those which all human beings share consciously or unconsciously. And it is these needs that are prepotent and form the groundwork of a given life. When individuals and society try persistently to ignore, neglect, deform, or supplant these, either mental illness or a supine mediocrity results.

As the student of the history of moral philosophy reads this account of the basic needs underlying "health," he is reminded of the historic ethical doctrine of *natural law*. To be sure, this doctrine has suffered from unclear definition and much variation—and largely because different moralists, like these psychologists, construed the nature of man differently. But, granted this checkered history, it is safe to say that what natural-law theorists sought to do was root the essential good of man in the structure (laws) of each man's nature and not in societal training as such. Such ethicists, theologians, and political philosophers were seeking a good possible to all men, because it involved the proper development of their inner being. Consequently, whatever other source there might still be for arriving at the moral standard, the nature of the moral standard was to be found in the core of human nature.

In Plato, Aristotle, the Stoics, in important strands of Christian moral philosophy, as well as in the Naturalistic tradition that we shall study later, we find different theories of how man's inner nature is related to Reality or to the Divine. But, again, there is convergence on the idea that the good for man is what conforms to the laws of a human being's nature. The good for man is ultimately one that does not vary with time and place, with societal or cultural differences, for it is a law of his nature. The good is not something that a society can impose upon the individual, for society must itself recognize and be molded by the tendencies in his nature.

In a day when men have been faced by the doctrine that the authority for the good lies in the state, as in fascist and communist thought, one can understand why there has been a new interest in natural law among moral philosophers, political theorists, and theologians. Thus Jacques Maritain, speaking within the Thomistic and Roman Catholic tradition, defines these "unwritten" laws: "There is, by virtue of human nature, an order or a disposition which human reason can discover and according to which the human will must act in order to attune itself to the necessary ends of the human being." [61] Over and over again in the history of common sense and philosophical morality, an action is declared wrong because it goes contrary to "human nature." Moral controversy about property rights, mercy killings, marriage and family organization, or about church and state have been "settled" by reference to the permanent structure of human nature.

Indeed, it is because, on this view, the human being has ends or

[61] *The Rights of Man and Natural Law* (New York: Scribner's Sons, 1943), p. 61. For this quotation we are indebted to the compact historical treatment and critique in Walter Muelder's article, "Personalism, Theology, and Natural Law," *The Philosophical Forum*, XIV (1956), 3–20.

goals to be fulfilled in his nature as a person that there developed the doctrine of "natural rights"—of "inalienable rights" to "life, liberty, and the pursuit of happiness," as the American Declaration of Independence put it. Whether these rights, these "constants of creation" as Emil Brunner calls them,[62] are given by God to all men at birth or are part of the demand that man's nature makes upon a Nature indifferent to him, marks a basic difference between Theism and Humanism, as we saw in discussing Fromm's work. Here the important point is that all these attempts to discover the good and man's rights appeal to something permanent in the nature of man, that which constitutes him the kind of being he is.

It might, therefore, be said that modern psychology and psychotherapy, especially in the movement of thought from Freud through Maslow, represents another chapter in the attempt to frame an ethical standard by reference to the intrinsic nature of man. The attempt to understand the nature of mental illness gradually led to strivings to discover what enduring motivational needs underlay the struggle for health. There have emerged—and we have not discussed Carl Rogers, H. S. Sullivan and others—different conceptions of the structure of intrinsic motives or needs as we have seen. But is it not now clear that these psychologists are in fact carrying on the intention of the natural-law moralist as they ferret out permanent, universal needs? Whether these psychologists have produced a truer picture of the underlying structure and whether they have unwittingly oversimplified the problems of moral living because of the restrictive scientific or theoretical presuppositions on which they work are things for us to decide as we go along.

B. *The Biomorphic Model of the Good Life*

Let us repeat, then, that our authors thus far have sought the standard of health in the dynamics of universal needs in interaction with environment. But we must note further that they seem to be influenced in their search by an assumption about human nature and health. The assumption may be correct, but we should make it explicit.

This assumption is embedded in a "model" that seems to control psychological thinking about human growth and health. The model is that of a growing cell or seed. That is, the stance that our psy-

[62] *Justice and the Social Order* (New York: Harper & Brothers, 1945), p. 89.

chologists take toward the human beings whom they study reminds one of a botanist who watches seeds develop after he has planted them in different soils and subjected them to different conditions and who then notes which plants produce the sturdiest, disease-resisting fruit. The standard for "the best plant of this variety" (Aristotle's "good man") is said to grow from within the nature of the seed as it unfolds its potential under different environmental conditions. Of course the environment is vital to growth, but it is on the "potential" of the plant and what *it* can become that attention is focused—a tomato plant never produces cucumbers, though the quality and size of the tomatoes are indeed affected by the soil content and climate.

Now, to be sure, all our authors are aware of the differences between the most delicate and intricate plant and the complex of billions of cells that compose the human being. But does not the analogy of a plant-seed *real*-izing (or *act*-ualizing, or *ful*-filling) its potential with greatest resistance to disease still remain uppermost in their thinking about the health of man? It is this biomorphic (or even horticultural) model of growth that underlies the thinking of the psychologists studied here.

Are we not told more explicitly by some, like Fromm and Maslow, but implicitly by all, that a person *ought to become what he can become?* Have we not been told that the real, the true conscience of a person is somehow the voice of his own real potential as opposed to the "dictates" of the social or physical or divine environment? In other words, on these views "the ought" that any individual "ought" to obey is the inner law of growing nature at the point at which he is most like other individuals. A person ought to be what he, as a *human* being, *can* be, just as a cell must fulfill *its* function in relation to other cells or a seed must become what *its* nature prescribes.

In passing, then, we raise two questions to which we shall return in separate chapters: Is this an adequate description of the experience of "ought" as we have it? In any case can we adequately derive the nature of what man "ought" to be from what he "is"? Here, however, we must press two other questions that the biomorphic model of health suggests to us.

Can it be that under the influence of this model we emphasize the "natural growth" aspect of life at the expense of those more dramatic moments when life seems most of all a "choice"? The process by which a plant realizes its potential does indeed reduce to the interaction of its nature with the environment, with the plant "adjusting"

simply because there is nothing else for it to do but what is forced
on it in each situation. But can we fairly think of human experience
as a forced growth at every point in its development? Granted that
there are limits to our given and potential nature, are we not free
within these limits to guide our growth by reflective goals? If this
is so, "natural" growth means something significantly different for
human beings. The meaning of freedom must be included in the
description of what is "natural" to man.

What is at stake here is the nature, extent, and meaning of human
freedom—if there be any—in relation to the definition of the life
good for man. Fromm and Maslow make great use of the idea of
freedom, but, as we hinted in our comment on Fromm, the idea fails
to be carefully defined. What does it mean to say that man "escapes
from freedom," that man himself must choose his values, that satisfaction of lower needs leaves man "free" to realize higher needs, that
peak experiences "free" one from deficiency motivation? What is
clear is that there are obstacles for growth to fulfillment. What is *not*
clear is what the full meaning of choice is.

We have just commented that psychological attempts to rest the
goal of human development within the intrinsic needs of human
nature force on us a further discussion of the meaning of "ought"
and of "freedom" in human experience. Perhaps an even more disturbing question is whether such attempts to define the common or
universal nature of man actually provide us with any criterion for
judging the nature of human health.

Before attempting an answer to this question, let us study what
happens if the search for unlearned, universal human needs is declared misleading and futile. We turn, therefore, to the thought of
a psychologist, Gordon W. Allport, who challenges the presuppositions of such natural-law ethics and, in fact, works out a much more
systematic and inclusive theory of human personality than any of the
writers thus far mentioned.

VII. *REFLECTIVE SUMMARY*

Maslow would agree with Fromm's anti-impositionism. His own
antireductionism is another step in focusing attention on man himself. We must move, he urges, from the scientistic demand for accuracy to the more liberal scientific concern for adequacy as we

study man. We must do more than reduce man to a complicated animal, or a creature mainly intent on survival.

Furthermore, we must stop making the assumption that our best light on man comes from studying "normal" or "average" man. We may learn much by looking back to animal origin, by analyzing illness, by discovering how the masses of men live, but we stand to lose our most illuminating data if we neglect the study of accomplished persons and of human experiences that, however unusual, reveal dimensions of development that persons can and ought to realize.

We can understand why so many individuals do not become self-actualizing personalities if we realize that each person can live at several levels of need. These range from the level of sheer physical survival and security to those for love, esteem, and self-actualization. The higher levels tend to emerge only as the lower prepotent levels are gratified. If a person is desperately hungry or feels very insecure, he is not likely to care much about his need to belong and to love.

The healthy personality is only realized as one is able to move beyond "coping" with lower needs to the spontaneous and positive activity in which self-actualization consists. A person who is not sick may still not be well. For example, in gratifying needs for safety, esteem, and love, he may still be stultifying his need for fuller intellectual and aesthetic satisfaction. Indeed, the self-actualizing personality seems to operate on a different level from the coping personality. He is spontaneous not because he is unafraid, has self-insight not because he has stopped posing, has concern for others not because he is either anxious "to please" or "to help," but because he sees himself with a detachment that comes when one emphasizes growth rather than competitive achievement.

Four inadequately resolved problems are especially suggested by Maslow's views. (1) Does he make enough of the fact that many persons fulfill higher-level needs even at the expense of physiological, safety, and other "lower" needs? (2) Can we assume, in the last analysis, that a human being, if allowed relative freedom, will move dependably, guided by "self-validating delight," to his own reach of perfection, as a flower in a good environment might? (3) This biomorphic model of growth suggests the underlying thesis that a person ought to become what he can become. But is this an adequate description of what our experience of obligation is, and does this conception of our growth as an inner evolution do justice to our experience of free choice (despite what Maslow says of creativity)?

(4) Is knowledge of man's universal nature an adequate criterion of the nature of goodness?

The underlying question perhaps is this: On what grounds do we decide what is higher and lower in personality? Why is the universal a better test than the unique or vice versa?

6

Gordon W. Allport:
The Maturing of Personality

~~~~~~

I. PERSONALITY AS UNIQUE

A. Shall We Study Man or Men?

We have been asking of Freud, Jung, Adler, Horney, Fromm, and Maslow one main question: What must a human being do, not simply to avoid mental illness but to achieve positive health and strength? There is a common theme in all their answers, despite important differences in detail. Discover, they have said, those tendencies that define the central needs of human nature and give them adequate expression. For the environment, physical or social, may act to impede or obstruct the expression demanded by basic human needs, but it cannot snuff them out. The individual is subject to these inner "forces," and he must either obey their mandate or suffer the different degrees of malformation or maldevelopment of which his nature is capable. Accordingly, the good life, happiness, health—call it what you will—depends on the fulfillment or fruition of those needs that constitute human nature.

What is the clue to the basic or central needs of a human being? The answer is: Those needs which any man shares with all men, the universal motives that characterize all human striving regardless of the environment. True, no one of our authors would deny differences among human beings. Nor would any of them urge that there is one identical "happiness" for all men, despite differences in ability. But in a chorus they say: The universal needs are the fundamental ones. And the pattern of individual and social health and happiness must consist in the kind of expression these basic needs demand. The social and physical environment must be taken into account, but psychic underground earthquakes and serious surface disturbances will result if these universal needs are cribbed and confined "too much."

A revolution is in the making, obviously, when a psychologist comes along who refuses to think of a concrete human personality either as a particular variation or as a combination of universal needs. To put the contrast between Gordon W. Allport and our other authors sharply: they, with increasing emphasis on the plasticity of the human being, have noted the differences between men and animals, between mature men and average men, but the differences are set within a common humanity of needs. In Gordon Allport the emphasis is in the other direction, namely, on the uniqueness of man, with a minimizing of common or of universal needs. "John" (if we may use a proper name for "the individual") must not be seen as an example of the "need for achievement"; nor is he an intersection point on which all the common needs of man-in-general converge.[1] His needs are his own. Even hunger and sex, even reflexes and the need for rest are inextricably woven into a unique pattern of motives. It is always misleading to use common labels for the motives of an individual man.

The question the ethicist will have in mind is: How on this view can we ever discover any standard of goodness for all men? Or for any man? In studying Allport's view of personality, accordingly, we shall not only be seeking for the differences between his views and others, but for the novel and constructive way in which he asks us to conceive the dynamics of personal living and the direction of the good life. Because some of the concepts he uses will be needed later in our discussion, we shall seek to acquaint the reader with them as we move along.

B. Why Emphasize Man's Uniqueness?

Allport urges that the uniqueness of each personality should never be sacrificed to the desire for simplicity, for public knowledge, or

[1] See *Becoming* (New Haven: Yale University Press, 1955), p. 23.

for universal laws. But this emphasis illustrates an underlying philosophy of psychology that all but turns its back on what most psychologists in the first half of the twentieth century took for granted. Their concern for "public" facts, or for laws applicable to all individuals, neglected the unrepeated and unrepeatable factors in the individual. Many felt, and still feel, that the destiny of "psychology as a science" is threatened if the psychology of personality aims to understand the single individual as such.

Every criticism of such *scientistic* psychological approaches to personality that we have already noted in our introduction to Maslow finds echoes in Allport's work. For him there must be a policy of the "open door" to every facet of personality, high or low, whether easy to get at or difficult to conceive and measure. For him every personality is unique and not simply "a sea of statistical averages." [2] Indeed, if any American psychologist or philosopher catches and develops William James's sense of the throbbing concreteness and variety of human experience, it is Gordon W. Allport.[3] Like James, Allport abhors neat formulas and methodologies that falsely pretend to exhaust reality.

II. *GROWTH IN PERSONALITY*

A. *The Structure of the Individual*

The outstanding fact that all study of human nature should keep central is that "man alone has the capacity to vary his biological needs extensively and to add to them countless psychogenic needs reflecting in part his culture (no other creature has a culture), and

---

[2] *Ibid.*, p. 20.

[3] Allport's work reveals the influence of teachers like William McDougall, Münsterberg, and W. Stern (all of whom had a strong penchant for philosophy), and of far-ranging scholars and value theorists like Richard Cabot and Ralph Barton Perry. Always, however, he has harnessed his theoretical interests to dogged empirical discipline, never turning his back on experimental research and techniques. The Allport-Vernon-Lindzey *Study of Values,* for example, has long been a statistical aid in revealing the value profile of individuals. But its emphasis is on the person's unique pattern of values and not on averages or types.

This chapter was written with the argument of *Personality, A Psychological Interpretation* and other writings in mind and was read with generous approval by Professor Allport. The new book, *Pattern and Growth in Personality* (New York: Holt, Rinehart and Winston, 1961) is an excellent restatement and development of the essential position in the light of data and discussion since 1937 when the first book appeared.

in part his own style of life (no other creature worries about his life-style)." [4]

In fact, man's very genes start him toward uniqueness. Each man has gene-linked characteristics associated with family, stock, and race; but even here there are individual differences in neural plasticity, responsivity, and in that mysterious emotional climate, temperament, that also differentiates persons. And, of course, each man is endowed with reflexes, physiological drives, and homeostatic processes that usually make for sheer survival with push-button efficiency. But Allport leans heavily upon what he calls the gene-given "capacities to learn," that is, potentialities in neuropsychic nature that, being inherently plastic, make changes in response possible.[5]

Indeed, one is tempted to unify these learning potentialities into an *original disposition to develop individuality,* because Allport himself, confessing vagueness about their nature, speaks of an "underlying disposition to adapt and to modify behavior." [6] As Allport sees it, then, given basic physiological drives and these neuropsychic "capacities to learn," the normal individual "will in time develop a conscience, a sense of self, and a hierarchical organization of traits." [7]

A striking "model of man" begins to emerge as we reflect on Allport's view to this point. Man is no passive reactor to stimuli from without; he is not jerked this way and that by the strongest forces brought to "condition" him, as behavioristic and operational psychologists seem to think. Nor does his present striving emerge from underground springs of universal needs that are finding this and that outlet. Allport's central conviction is that man's uniqueness lies in his capacity for transforming his "human" nature into individual nature. Man is an act-or, not a re-actor.

What is notably missing in this analysis, we remind ourselves, is any list of universal needs. Why? Because they can never do justice to the myriad ways [8] in which persons achieve an endless variety of goals. Allport, to be sure, often appeals to such "needs" as security, superiority, and love, but his insistence is that these, when they

---

[4] *Becoming,* p. 22.
[5] See *ibid.,* p. 26.
[6] *Ibid.,* p. 27.
[7] *Ibid.,* p. 26.
[8] "All stencils [of needs] fit concrete cases only with the loosest approximation." (G. W. Allport, "Motivation in Personality: Reply to Mr. Bertocci," *The Nature of Personality* [Cambridge, Mass.: Addison-Wesley, 1950], p. 100). See P. A. Bertocci, "Critique of Gordon W. Allport's Theory of Motivation," *Psychological Review,* 47 (1940), 501–32.

occur, can be explained economically by the fact that individuals endowed with similar physiological demands and learning capacities will usually, if exposed to similar environments, develop similar forms of life—including the so-called "universal" or "instinctoid" needs that other psychologists claim to be unlearned. To say that men are "similar" gives us a basis for comparing people, but runs the danger of distracting attention from each unique individual pattern.

B. *Growth in Individual Motivation*

Allport, then, resists explaining a person's motives by saying that they represent the channeling of more basic universal needs. But he is equally adamant against such formulas for development as "the basic personality of a person is fixed by the time he is two—or five!" His attitude is that we should trace motivation in each individual life as we find it.

These convictions Allport supports by his theory of "the functional autonomy of motives." This phrase covers such life situations as the following—to start with one of his own illustrations. A former sailor still has a craving for the sea. He may have first acquired his love for the sea as an aid in his struggle to earn a living. In other words, his "motivational craving" was conditioned to seagoing. But now, years later, he is a wealthy banker and the original nutritive motive for going to sea is destroyed. Yet the craving for the sea persists unabated.[9]

What has happened here? A man has continued to pursue an activity from a motive different from the one that started him off. This does not look like the mere new channeling of an old drive, for the banker no longer needs to go back to the sea to earn a living. What seems to have happened is that the craving for the sea has another function and operates "on its own," as it were. Allport says that it is accordingly "functionally autonomous" of the motive with which it was once connected.

Surely, this is a common occurrence. Which of us cannot name many experiences like it? We all went to school to please mother, but we certainly do not now continue our studies for this reason. The girl we married we first met for the sake of completing a four-

[9] *Personality, A Psychological Interpretation* (New York: Henry Holt & Co., 1937), p. 196, and cf. *Pattern and Growth in Personality*, Chapter 10.

some. Many of us buy cars to get places and then get interested in cars for their own sake. Instances of functional autonomy may be multiplied without end.

We must not miss the enormous effect that this functional autonomy of motives has on the theory of personality. For according to this principle, each new motive, far from depending upon the continued activity of the original motive, becomes itself a basis for other motives, which in turn become functionally autonomous of it. This means, concretely, that the personality developed is now no longer fettered either to the past or to the present or even to what the person "starts with"—a fact of importance for the ethicist especially. For now even though man is born "intrinsically selfish" or "intrinsically altruistic," these motives can be transformed and supplanted by new ones as his life undergoes change. An individual's motivation is always to be understood in terms of his own present concerns.

Keeping this transforming rather than channelizing process of development in mind, let us, for the sake of concreteness, follow John in terms of certain basic problems that he will "normally" face as he grows. He begins life as an infant motivated by certain nutritive and physiological demands (Maslow's nutritive and safety needs) and with the dispositions to realize and individuate his potentialities. During infancy, while John is dependent on others, he is little more than a parasite. Even at two he is self-absorbed, disregarding the desires and property of others. The younger he is, the more impulsive he is. For, after all, he is quite unable to think out long-range goals, and he is absorbed in becoming aware of what he can do in relation to others. Yet as he moves toward adolescence he weaves together patterns of interest, some more important to him than others. In particular, he develops much more sense of responsibility to others than could have been realized from his "unsocial beginnings."

Curiously enough, Allport would say of John that as he grows, "self-love" will always remain "positive and active" in his nature, though "it need not remain dominant." [10] To counteract the "totally unsocialized" beginning of the individual, Allport seems to appeal to "capacity" for eventual socialization—an appeal that should not be necessary for a proponent of functional autonomy. Allport's general point, nevertheless, is clear. John, an infant "totally unsocialized," may be expected, because of "a 'disposition' for eventual

[10] *Becoming*, p. 30.

socialization," to transform his motivation and become altruistic with the help of "conscience, imagination, and extension of the ego." [11]

This transformation does not, of course, take place "out of the blue." It will not take place at all unless John experiences "a generous amount of security" up to his fifth year. Without this "normal affiliative groundwork" John may become aggressive and hateful in reactive protest and fall short of a "productive life style."

Here Allport reminds us especially of Adler, Horney, Fromm, and Maslow. Yet, lest these remarks be taken to give too much power to environmental influence, we must hasten to say that this early security does not produce, but leaves John free for, "creative becoming." This, in other words, is Allport's way of saying that John must not be seen merely as a mirror of his culture. John selected from, and reshapes to a marked degree, what he encounters in home, school, and society. Indeed, John's development may be seen even as the attempt to reconcile two modes of becoming: "the one that makes him into a mirror, the other that lights the lamp of individuality within." [12]

Thus Allport ascribes to normal human beings a basic pattern of becoming. This means that although he rejects any pat set of instincts and emphasizes the transforming and supplanting of motives, Allport does not leave the flow of individual life without aim or direction. The uniqueness of the individual is lawful, and certain "effects" may often be predicted from certain "causes." As we have noted, the individual who does not receive love and security as well as physical nurture in early childhood may not be free to develop his persistent demand for autonomy. Parents, educators, moral philosophers, and social theorists are urged, in the name of what a human being (implicitly) *is*, to remember that the individual is seeking to, or needs to, develop a balance between self-love and altruism.

C. *What Gives Unity to the Unique Individual?*

Our concern so far has been to sketch beginnings and orientations in John's development, as Allport presents it. As John matures and learns, what is remarkable is that he is not merely developing many

[11] *Ibid.*
[12] *Ibid.*, p. 35. (We shall need to recall this emphasis when we come to discuss free will.)

modes of conduct. Before long he finds himself with a rough "system" of responses, with an emerging personality. He is not just an omnibus of responses or a collection of habits. His responses are connected with each other in many ways; and, however varied their nature, he begins to have enduring organization in his responses to what goes on in him and outside of him. This organization, indeed, is John's personality—unique, complex, oriented, changing, and yet enduring. Unless this were so his friends would not recognize "John," and John would be a fire-works of surprises for everybody and himself.

No, John has his own style of life, as Adler put it. But a process is going on which is of special interest to psychologist and ethicist. For, if we look closer, John's style of life reveals that some "modes of adjusting" just happen to be there somehow—something John "picked up somewhere"—and others are very important and persistent.

To be concrete: John, let us say, wakes up at seven every morning, takes two slices of toast, never more than one cup of coffee, reads the editorials or the financial page in the paper first, is "grouchy" until ten, and so on—this is "John." But these actions are not "really" John. For any one of them he will push aside if he is awakened by a telegram telling him that he must be in New York by late afternoon to sign a contract allowing him to continue the work he loves. We are now getting closer to the center of John's personality. If, on going to New York, John finds that the proposed job means being away from wife and children frequently, that the people he is to work with are mainly "go-getters" who do not care what happens to the underdog, he will feel conflict, for his "work" and "professional advancement" are at stake. Yet he declares: "Life is too short to give up family life and live in a social jungle; no boost in pay is worth these sacrifices."

We have now moved from what we might call the periphery of John's personality to a set of goals, values, concerns that define "where he lives," the center of his life. This interrelated web of attachments, which in fact represent what life so far means to him, this is the *proprium*. Interwoven in this proprium, consciously and unconsciously, are "the things that matter most" to him—and John may not realize it until they are threatened. "Oh yes, anything for a chance to go on to an advanced stage of my work! But not at the expense of keeping life generous, friendships warm and loyal, business contracts honorable, and above all, maintaining family life for Jack and Andy and Gertrude."

If we pressed John deeper we might find that even these "values" do not mean more to him than "freedom of conscience," for example.

This sketch of John bears out Allport's main contention that personality includes

> habits and skills, . . . matters of fact and cultural values, that seldom or never seem warm and important. But personality includes what is warm and important also—all the regions of our life that we regard as peculiarly ours, and which for the time being I suggest we call the *proprium*, . . . all aspects of personality that make for inward unity.[13]

We need not for our purposes go into the different aspects of this developing unity: the recognition of our bodily process as intimately "ours"; the sense of day-by-day, week-by-week, and year-by-year continuity that we call our self-identity; the strengthening of self-seeking "ego enhancement" by greater concentration of what is "mine, not thine"; the balancing of ego enhancement by identification of self with objects, people, or causes that enlarge what we mean by "me" to include others; and, more pervasive than all, the knowing self.

The important fact about the proprium for us is this: Because of it John forges ahead in life not simply trying to "reduce" tensions but actually "looking for trouble," if need be. What is crucial for him is that the *values closest to "him,"* his *propriate motives,* be realized, preserved, and increased. However else John's body, his memories, his reasoning and imagining contribute to his total life, he will never be understood unless we can differentiate these "things that matter most" in his life from those that, in relation to it, are peripheral attachments. For it is this proprium, this "ego," this cluster "of long-range goals, regarded as central to one's personal existence" that "distinguishes the human being from the animal, the adult from the child, and in many cases the healthy personality from the sick." [14]

Later (Chapters 15 and 17), when we come to consider the organization of values and the constitution of character, this notion of the

---

[13] *Ibid.,* p. 40.
[14] *Ibid.,* p. 51. Cf. Peter A. Bertocci's, "The Psychological Self, the Ego, and Personality," *Psychological Review,* 52 (1945), 91–99.

proprium as "central" will be helpful. All the more, then, we must stress that the concept of the *proprium* enables Allport to account not only for the unity and continuity of personality as such, but also for central, "warm," value motivation in terms of which a personality is organized. Thus if we are to understand John in terms of the values he holds dear we must know what values are "in" his proprium, as opposed to those "in" the periphery of his personality. We would expect John's "conscience" to be well represented in his proprium, but we cannot be sure of this until we see how Allport understands "conscience" and its development.

D. *Conscience and the Personality*

We have met conscience already in Freud as the superego, the interiorized monitor of the socialized child. This inner warden punishes or inhibits the child at points where parents, usually standing guard for "society," had insisted on restriction. Fromm, we remember, distinguished the authoritarian, security-seeking conscience from the humanistic, the monitor of the "true" self's demand for responsible freedom. For Allport the authoritarian conscience, or what he calls the "must" conscience, might suffice to explain the moral life of a child (and of the immature person generally), but it will not account for important aspects of human moral behavior. For, if John's conscience is simply an introjected social code, we cannot explain the existence of his private code of values in loyalty to which he breaks with codes established by parents and culture.

Two points are to be noted, then, in Allport's analysis of "conscience." First, he realizes that John may incorporate parental approval into his own self-image. In other words, parental standards may become propriate. John has now to move beyond the authoritarian superego.

Second, Allport stresses a new factor in the development of conscience. In moving beyond the stage of the "must" conscience, John comes to feel a kind of obligation that is quite different in "feel" and quality from the fear and anxiety of the negative "I must not, or else." This development is the "ought" conscience. In Allport's words, "Whenever I make a self-referred value-judgment—as if to say, 'This is in keeping with my self-image, that is not'—then I feel a sense of obligation that has no trace of fear in it." [15] Again,

---

[15] *Becoming*, p. 72.

"fear becomes ought as propriate development begins to outweigh opportunistic." [16] That is, John, in sifting his values, finds some to be more worthwhile and necessary to him than others, and these become the values toward which he feels "ought," not "must." John's external sanctions give way to internal ones, "experiences of prohibition, fear, and 'must' give way to experiences of preference, self-respect, and 'ought.' " [17]

In sum, John moves from "must" to "ought" only as his self-image and value system develop to the point where specific habits of "obedience" are supplanted by self-imposed ideals. When John reflectively confronts a conflict of values and decides that a certain action is in accordance with his self-image, he feels that he "ought" to perform that act. If he does not try to perform that approved action, he will experience guilt—which is not fear or anxiety but a different state of mind altogether.

We must underscore this new ingredient in the person—an "ought" that is not fear. It seems to have escaped other psychological thinkers, though it has a long history in theological and moral philosophy; and we shall need to return to it again.[18] In Allport's view, furthermore, this "ought" conscience, for the most part, is "generic" in content. It represents not so much details of living from moment to moment, but rather broad directions or commitments. John may believe in the ideal of democracy or of brotherly love, but the concrete meanings of these commitments have to be worked out from situation to situation. Nevertheless, it is these long-range goals, involving his image of himself, his interrelated schemata of values, that keep John living "forward," even though he may never realize them completely. Meanwhile, in terms of such long-range goals, John develops a *style of life* that helps him to achieve definiteness in evaluating himself and his relationships to other people.

The proprium, including the dynamics of the generic "ought" conscience, we must recognize as accounting for the actual stability, the continuity and unity, as well as the onward pull, that characterize the uniqueness of John's striving. But even now we are still dealing with rather comprehensive concepts for describing what takes place in John. We need to take a closer look at the structure of John's personality.

[16] *Ibid.,* p. 74.
[17] *Ibid.,* p. 73. See Chapter 9 below for the authors' analysis of this experience.
[18] See Chapter 9.

III. *PATTERN IN PERSONALITY*

A. *Habits, Attitudes, Traits, and Personality*

Habits tie a person's action to definite stimuli. William James wisely called them the "fly wheel of human society," for they free us to put our minds on other things.

But what takes place in John when he holds an attitude *pro* or *con?* The sight or thought of a particular dog seems to awaken a predisposition in John's neuropsychic system that he has learned through his experience with that dog. As long as he has a *pro* attitude toward the dog, the dog may expect a certain favorable response to him to persist. Let the reader think of his own attitude toward mother, father, a particular friend, or enemy, the fountain pen mother gave him at Christmas, or his Alma Mater. All arouse in him, as a result of his past experience with them, an ingrained response that is not easily erased. Obviously, within a moral context, it becomes important to develop favorable (or *pro*) attitudes toward worthwhile objects and objectives and unfavorable (or *anti*) attitudes toward evil actions and principles.

But even attitudes do not fully account for the stability in human personality. For, as we have seen, they remain directed toward some object (or class of objects), and they require such stimuli to activate them. But another stage of preparedness and directedness is reached when John develops traits, for example, neatness, studiousness, sincerity, talkativeness, punctuality, kindness, honesty, and good humor. Traits also are imbedded in John's personality as a result of learning, but they represent a marked advance in the organization of his responses. For a trait does not, like a habit or attitude, need an object for its expression. Let us see what this means, and why it is important.

We say that most habits and attitudes become "second nature," because we respond so "naturally" in terms of these ingrained dispositions. By habit, we "unconsciously" brake our car at a stop light; the sight of the American flag immediately arouses a certain attitude in us. But we need the stop light to bring the habitual action out and the flag to elicit our favorable attitude. Traits, however, need no specific object to stimulate them, because they are not geared to a particular stimulus.[19]

Thus, if John is polite, sincere, or talkative, we can predict with considerable assurance how he will behave *regardless of particular stimuli and situation*. When he enters almost any social gathering, he will seek occasions to exercise his politeness or create opportunities for talk. His traits render many different situations "functionally equivalent" occasions for courtesy or conversation. It is truer to say that his traits represent demands that his acquired nature now makes on the different environments he enters. Thus for the neat person a disorderly situation is "a mess." In short, when we say, "John is neat," we are saying that in situation after situation, differing among themselves (at home, in school, at the fraternity, in restaurants, or with his car), he will probably respond as if they were the same to him. For John, neatness has become functionally autonomous and also propriate. In his childhood it was neither.

Let us note the practical difference in terms of moral development that a habit, attitude, or trait makes. Imagine, for example, the stage of development that John would be in when neatness was for him only a habit or an attitude. He may have a habit of washing his hands and being clean about his room and desk. His attitude toward being neat about his room, on the other hand, we may call not favorable; therefore we hardly expect him to muster up energy to change the habit. But if he has a trait of neatness, there will be much more likelihood of his being neat in both these cases and in a larger range of situations, because these different situations are rendered similar by his trait of neatness.

Before moving to a larger perspective on John as a whole, let us review what we know about him in basic terms.

Given certain physiological drives and a complex of capacities, John faces the problem of becoming as creative as possible in his environment. He will always be engaged in a constant struggle to keep tendencies of self-love from overinhibiting his need to affiliate and participate with others, but his underlying task will be to work out a style of life—embracing habits, attitudes, traits, and other interests—that will give unity, variety, and growth to all his activity.

[19] The concept of intention is added explicitly to Allport's motivational scheme in *Pattern and Growth in Personality*, pp. 220–25, with a view to stressing the forward-looking, longer-range thrusts in motivation, involving the fusion of emotion and cognitive processes.

We shall not understand him if we do not know what habits, attitudes, and traits are especially enduring and central in his striving for meaning and values. And he cannot undergo the minor and major conflicts in his life without developing, often without realizing it, some pattern of values and principles that become propriate and to which he feels "obligated" both as "musts" and as "oughts."

B. *The Pattern of Mature Personality*

What, then, as Allport sees it, can the psychological study of personality lay down as guiding fact and principle for the development of individual potential?

It is in his definitive analysis of the theory of prejudice that one sees Allport grappling with the problem: What is it that encourages a person to become intolerant, change-resisting, hostile, and aggressive? Allport analyzes in considerable detail what we have already seen to be the underlying struggle between self-absorption and proper regard for other persons. It becomes clear that a person's whole development may be seriously handicapped if in early childhood he feels unwelcome and unloved, the victim of capricious and harsh parental discipline. If he feels secure, he is more likely to develop sympathy for the "underdog" and not take out his bitterness on other people. If he himself is treated with love and respect, he can be inclusive and democratic in his attitude toward those unlike himself, for he does not have to save his "ego" by the expensive device of exclusion. "Affiliation is the source of all happiness. When hatred and animosity grow in life, they are the crippling distortions of this *naturally affiliative trend*."[20] Indeed, "the original orientation of all men is toward a trusting and affiliative philosophy of life."[21]

Again, summarizing some research findings on human motivation in factories, business offices, schools, and in the armed services, Allport comments:

Men are basically eager for friendly and affiliative relations with their fellows of a sort that respect their own sense of integrity and self-esteem. There is thus a double finding that must be taken into account in our theorizing: people want close, warm,

[20] *Nature of Prejudice* (Reading, Mass.: Addison-Wesley, 1954), p. 441 (italics added).
[21] *Ibid*, Cf. pp. 441 ff.

love relationships with their fellows—but at the same time they are exceedingly sensitive to slights to their *amour-propre*. Indignity to one's self-esteem quickly generates hatred.[22]

"The truest statement that can be made of a normal person is that he never feels that he can love or be loved enough." [23]

If John is to avoid a defensive and narrow orientation toward life, he must be a participant. Let John's parents, teachers, church, community, and employers take heed of a fundamental principle for encouraging maturity. *"Maximize situations where the individual [child or adult] can participate fully and on terms of equal status in projects of joint concern to him and to his associates."* For "in so doing we shall realize affiliation, safeguard self-esteem, and reduce hostility." [24]

This broad principle gives a general formula for developing a rounded and mature personality. From day to day the challenge takes on specific and concrete forms. It comes out graphically in the following quotation:

Take, for example, Citizen John who moves and has his being in the great activity wheel of New York City. Let us say that he spends his hours of unconsciousness somewhere in the badlands of the Bronx. He wakens to grab the morning's milk left at the door by an agent of a vast Dairy and Distributing system whose corporate manoeuvers, so vital to his health, never consciously concern him. After paying hasty respects to his landlady, he dashes into the transportation system whose mechanical and civic mysteries he does not comprehend. At the factory he becomes a cog for the day in a set of systems far beyond his ken. To him (as to everybody else) the company he works for is an abstraction; he plays an unwitting part in the "creation of surpluses" (whatever they are), and though he doesn't know it his furious activity at his machine is regulated by the "law of supply and demand," and by "the availability of raw materials" and by "prevailing interest rates." Unknown to himself he is headed next week for the "surplus labor market." A union official collects his dues; just why he doesn't know. At noontime

---

[22] "A Psychological Approach to the Study of Love and Hate," in P. A. Sorokin (ed.), *Explorations in Altruistic Love and Behavior* (Boston: Beacon Press, 1950), pp. 148–49. Reprinted by permission of the Beacon Press, copyright © 1950 The Beacon Press.
[23] *Ibid.,* p. 152.
[24] *Ibid.,* p. 164.

that corporate monstrosity Horn and Hardart, swallows him up,
much as he swallows one of its automatic pies. After more activity in the afternoon, he seeks out a standardized day-dream
produced in Hollywood, to rest his tense, but *not* efficient mind.
At the end of the day he sinks into a tavern, and unknowingly
victimized by the advertising cycle, orders in rapid succession
Four Roses, Three Feathers, Golden Wedding and Seagram's
which "men who plan beyond tomorrow" like to drink.

John has been active all day, immensely active, playing a part
in dozens of impersonal cycles of behavior. He has brushed
scores of "corporate personalities," but has entered into intimate
relations with no single human being. The people he has met
are idler-gears like himself meshed into systems of transmission,
far too distracted to examine any one of the cycles in which they
are engaged. Throughout the day John is on the go, implicated
in this task and that—but does he, in a psychological sense, *participate* in what he is doing? Although constantly *task-involved*,
is he ever really ego-involved [that is, is his proprium in-
volved]? [25]

What then shall we do about Citizen John? Well, industrial psychologists are taking this problem to heart.

What the industrial psychologist has discovered is that when
the work-situation in which the individual finds himself realistically engages the status-seeking motive, when the individual
is busily engaged in using his talents, understanding his work,
and having pleasant social relations with foreman and fellow-
worker, then he is, as the saying goes, "identified" with his
job. He likes his work; he is absorbed in it; he is productive.
In short, in McGregor's terms he is industrially *active;* that is to
say, he is participant.

When, on the other hand, the situation is such that the status-
motive has no chance of gearing itself into the external cycles
of events, when the individual goes through motions that he
does not find meaningful, when he does not really participate,
then come rebellion against authority, complaints, griping, gos-
sip, rumor, scape-goating, disaffection of all sorts. The job-satis-
faction is low. In McGregor's terms under such circumstances
the individual is not active; he is industrially *reactive.*

[25] *Nature of Personality*, pp. 146–47. We have substituted "John" for the "Sam" of
the original.

In the armed forces, in federal employment, in school systems, the same principle holds.[26]

But what shall be done for Citizen John in his larger relationships as a democratic citizen? It is clear that he cannot be equally ego involved in every one of the wheels within wheels of his private and social life, let alone all of the ramifications of civic life. Some selection is necessary.

Here Allport suggests that most people can engage in some aspect of the following major fields of activity: occupational, educational, recreational, political, religious, and domestic. "We might assert," says Allport, "that a healthy ego should find true participation in all of them. Or allowing one blind spot to the bachelor, to the constitutional hater of sports or of politics, to the agnostic, there is still a balanced diet of participation in, say, five fields." If John is not engaged as a participant in some of these "his life is crippled and his existence a blemish on democracy." [27]

What do these passages tell us? That it means little to say that John must be a participant unless we see his participation taking form in a pattern of value that defines important segments of his life and, in their balance, keeps him from charging wildly in all directions. But even this, as Allport sees it, is not enough.

Selective participation needs to be supported by inner stamina as John faces responsibly the fact that important values sometimes need to be sacrificed, especially as the inevitable crises in his life are confronted—sickness, old age, serious disappointments, and death itself. More than action as such is needed to cope with such problems. John may have a key value that for him sums up his attachment to life. Often, but not always, this value is a "mature religion."

C. *The Mature Religious Sentiment*

Both the roots and the fruits of religion are complex. Many emotions (especially fear, love, joy, awe) may enter into the religious sentiment. The whole range of human desires can play a role in religious belief. One person's religious sentiment may arrest his development, another's may be a neurotic escape or a security-giving defense that will encourage prejudice and intolerance. As we might expect, the religious sentiment is unique as personality is unique, and it will both reflect and influence the person's total orientation.

[26] *Ibid.*, p. 147.
[27] *Ibid.*, p. 152.

Once again, Allport is not satisfied with views of religion that conceive it as the channelizing of some drive or instinctive need. He would see the religious sentiment in the variety of ways in which it appears in a life, and not be satisfied with some simple formula. Thus it is not merely a form of fear or a longing for justice and truth; religion is neither "just emotional" nor "just cold reason." If we see the religious sentiment in the context of a person's search for meaning, we shall find that ". . . we are dealing with a mode of response wherein a combination of feelings is tied to a conception of the nature of things that is thought-provoking, reasonable, and acceptable," [28] at least as far as the individual's search for the "why of things" has gone. In a word, the why of creation, joy and sorrow, zestful living, sickness, courage, death is as crucial in John's search for meaning as his "scientific" seeking for the causes of health, sickness, and death. The religious sentiment is John's response to living and, at the same time, his guide to further experience.

What would be involved, then, in the development of a *mature* religious sentiment? Here, Allport, hewing strictly to the psychologist's task, does not define maturity by the content of belief (which must concern philosopher and theologian). He is guided by his conception of a mature personality. He is saying that although the psychologist cannot prescribe the positive content of religious belief in detail, he can suggest the conditions under which religious convictions will make for an impoverishment of life on the one hand and for richness and unity on the other. It is with this aim in mind that we should first review the observations that Allport makes about the mature personality.

John, as we have already seen, does not achieve a mature personality unless he moves beyond the self-absorption of early childhood. It is not enough, however, for John to supplant childlike gratification of biological impulses with sheer gadding about with "a lot of interests." There must be more reflective organization of interests. But it is important that his "center of gravity" be outside himself in a job to be done. "Paradoxically, 'self-expression' requires the capacity to lose oneself in the pursuit of objectives, *not* primarily referred to the self." [29] When John is able to become absorbed in goals that involve the good of others, he is found to organize his values outward. Such *self-extension* is the first mark of a mature person.

[28] *The Individual and His Religion* (New York: Macmillan & Co., 1950), p. 17.
[29] *Personality, A Psychological Interpretation,* p. 213.

But Allport notes how easy it is for an individual "with a cause" to take himself overseriously unless he buttresses self-extension by *self-objectification*. This calls for insight into oneself—"that peculiar detachment of the mature person when he surveys his own pretensions in relation to his abilities, . . . his own equipment in comparison with the equipment of others, and his opinion of himself in relation to the opinions others hold of him." [30] Such an individual is sure to have a *sense of humor*, which someone has defined as the ability to sit on a star and look at yourself and your ventures—with a good-natured grin.

But Allport is convinced that self-extension and self-objectification must feed into and issue from a "unifying philosophy of life." This conviction does not mean that John can deliver a lecture on his philosophy of life. Like most people, he is not trained to do so. But he is nevertheless living by some conception of his place in the scheme of things. Some feeling for priority among values moves him from day to day. Otherwise he would be at the mercy either of impulse, the latest fad, or of conventionality.

But may John not organize his life around nonreligious values, for example, the aesthetic or the social? Allport's reply is: Yes, although the religious sentiment is by its very nature the most embracing. The mature religious sentiment is most appropriate to a mature personality just because it "lays itself open to all facts, to all values, and disvalues, and claims to have the clue to their theoretical and practical inclusion in a frame of life." [31] If John believes, as the mature religious person does, that his life is oriented and committed to *"what he regards as permanent or central in the nature of things,"* [32] the main stream of his experience will not be dammed up by partial or unstructured ecstasies; he will not lose power by being drawn with abandon into many outlets and rivulets that at so many moments of human life might seem to be the mainstream.

Equally important, John, insofar as he is religiously mature, will realize that he cannot know all. Therefore, no matter how firmly he may hold to what he believes to be the true faith, "he knows perfectly well that doubt concerning it is still theoretically possible," *and* he learns to act wholeheartedly even without absolute certainty.[33]

To summarize: the mature religious person, the mature person-

[30] *Ibid.*, p. 214.
[31] *The Individual and His Religion*, p. 54.
[32] *Ibid.*, p. 56.
[33] *Ibid.*, p. 72.

ality lives with conviction and yet with eyes wide open. He knows
"that he is *finally* uncertain of his ground. But he feels that . . . in
a world where optimistic bias and faith are largely responsible for
human accomplishment, it would be silly for him to lapse into unproductive skepticism, so long as he has a chance of being correct." [34]

The reader of William James is here reminded of the latter's
famous essay "The Will to Believe" (first entitled "The Right to
Believe"). James held that whenever a vital belief—such as belief in
God—cannot be decisively confirmed or disproved by evidence and
reason, it is the path of wisdom and valor to believe. If, in other
words, belief in God brings power to help the individual create
values, then it is his "right" to believe in God unless evidence to the
contrary is overwhelming.

A note of caution is imperative here. James is not justifying the
attitude: "You have everything to gain and nothing to lose by being
religious, so believe at all costs." James would not have justified religious belief in the face of decisive evidence, at the cost of intellectual integrity. He is urging that when the evidence does not force a
decision, a person has the right to take the side that he believes will
encourage total human development, including intellectual growth.

Applying this "will to believe" specifically to the development of
mature personality, what conclusion may we draw? If a critically developed religious sentiment encourages a person's discrimination of
values, sharpens his insight into himself, and deepens his sense of
humor, if, further, it inspires extension of himself, by creating in
him an allegiance to a cause which he believes is the Source of all
good, he certainly cannot be considered immature or infantile if he
commits himself to such a religious faith.[35]

Before we pass on to the next characteristic of the mature personality, it is hardly necessary to underline the difference between this
view of the place of religion and Freud's. Freud believed that to outgrow infantile wishes was to outgrow religion. Allport grants that
there is much self-protective, infantile "religion" that must be outgrown. But he holds that a person may become mature with the
assistance of that selective, critical, comprehensive, and adventurous
organization of value that religious living can encourage.

So also would Allport grant to Fromm that immature "religion,"
simple acceptance of a conventional shield, might well serve as an

---

[34] *Ibid.*, p. 73 (italics added).
[35] Cf. *The Individual and His Religion*, p. 79.

escape from freedom. And, as Fromm seems to believe, it might separate men from each other. But Allport would argue that growth toward maturity in religion enlarges tolerance and human-heartedness.[36]

Let it be clearly understood that the final philosophical problem of the truth of belief in God is solved neither by Allport nor Freud nor Fromm nor by any other psychologists, although their own considered views are visible in their conclusions. Allport does not deny that a personality can be mature without a religious sentiment as such. Obviously, all will depend on the nature of his unbelief. The mature unbeliever will be a disbeliever for well-considered reasons, just as the mature believer will believe for equally sober reasons. Allport's central contention is that religious belief as such cannot be branded infantile, immature, or mature from a psychological point of view. Psychologically speaking, in the last analysis, the important question is: Can the religious sentiment play the all-important maturing function of giving focus and inspiration to "becoming"? The mature believer and mature unbeliever may well be close to each other because they have been trying to weave together in theory and practice as many of the streams of existence as possible.[37]

IV. CRITICAL OBSERVATIONS

In the last two sections we have seen Allport grappling with the problem of defining the mature personality. Actually, as we see it, he is caught in the psychologist's dilemma when it comes to talking about a mature personality. As a psychologist, his task is to describe what does or probably will take place, not what ought to take place. This raises a very difficult set of problems, which we must continue to discuss in this book. For surely what a man ought to become cannot be unrelated to what he is. Yet because man may "become" in so many ways, how shall we know which form of becoming is mature and which immature?

To be concrete, it is clear that Allport favors self-extension to self-absorption, that he favors a unifying philosophy of life that is preferably but not necessarily religious. He values participation, tolerance, and affiliation above self-protection, prejudice, and indiffer-

[36] See *Personality and Social Encounter* (Boston: Beacon Press, 1960), Chapter 16.
[37] *Becoming,* pp. 94–95.

ence to the needs and abilities of others. But if one seeks in Allport's writings for the reasonable justification of these preferences, he gets no clear guidance. As a psychologist with his eye trained on the sequences involved in human patterns of feeling, thought, and action, he throws much light, for example, on the causes and effects of prejudice, of relative disorganization in personality, of insufficient self-insight, of unwillingness to participate or allow others to participate. Evidence is adduced, theories of development are carefully argued. But where does Allport find the norms for saying that some kinds of relationship are better than others?

Our point is not that he as a person does not have either grounds for or rights to his convictions on these matters; it is that, like all our other psychologists, he slips into a theory of *the good life, the mature life* without making clear what his presuppositions are.

Clearly, the moment the psychologist begins to move beyond a description of what men *do* value, of what men *can* and *do* become, to what men *might* better become or *ought* to become, he is involved in philosophical issues for which his specific analyses as a psychologist or psychotherapist are not adequate—however firm he may be in his own ultimate conviction.

Allport himself is aware of this. In later essays, he makes it clear that no psychologist, as psychologist, can tell us what standards a normal or sound or mature person ought to achieve. In short, the psychologist as psychologist cannot define the life good to live.[38] The psychologist or psychotherapist can only borrow his standards from philosophy, from religion, or from prevailing folkways.

At the same time, Allport holds that psychology can be of fundamental assistance to ethics by showing that certain theoretical goals are unrealistic because they depart too far from the potentialities of human nature, that other goals lead to consequences that would "generally" be acclaimed as good or bad. He sums up by saying: "Modern social science, for all its imperfections, can now aid us in selecting from among the moral imperatives prescribed by various philosophers as guides to social policy." [39] His plea, in short, is for a cooperative relation between ethical theory and psychology.

The psychologists' predicament in relation to norms might be all the worse for those who, like Allport, wish to allow for the maxi-

[38] See "Personality, Normal and Abnormal," in *Personality and Social Encounter*, Chapter 10.
[39] "Normative Compatibility in the Light of Social Science," in *New Knowledge in Human Values*, ed. A. H. Maslow (New York: Harper, 1959), p. 137.

mum variety in the course of becoming. For Freud, Maslow, and Fromm might say that a man, given certain unlearned needs, ought to become what these innate needs are always demanding that he become. Preference should always be given to actions that allow such needs to "be expressed" with a minimum of conflict. The advantage that these theories have is the suggestion of a fairly definite criterion—for example, a definite hierarchy of self-actualization as advanced by Maslow, or a specific need for freedom, fundamental to the structure of the "real" self, as used by Fromm as a criterion for different orientations.

Allport, we have seen, will not accept any such "guiding" needs inherent in human nature (apart from physiological drives). He no doubt would say: "I may be in a bad plight with regard to norms, but my house of values is not built on the sands of innate needs that everybody disagrees about and that create more problems than they solve. Anyway, can you go from what men universally are to what men universally ought to be?" Our own final reply to this must await later consideration.

What we wish to suggest here is that although Allport does resort to "capacities" rather than instinctoid needs, although he does say that he is willing to talk about common needs for the purpose of comparing man with man (without thinking of them as ingrained in human structure), we wonder whether in fact he does not, more than he realizes, *depend upon* some of these trends as being more basic guides to value preferences.

Once more, to be specific: Are not the needs to grow-in-individuality, the needs to be loved and to love, the need for participation, and the need for integrity, in fact universal? If they are not found in persons, must not Allport say that this is owing to the fact that their natures have been arrested in development and perhaps crippled? However strong and well supported is Allport's desire to rid us of universal stencils in personality motivation, it is noteworthy that he has not been able to forego a list of trends toward self-fulfillment without which the persistent struggle in an individual's life is hard to understand.

We are suggesting, in other words, that Allport's theory of personality and his view of maturity become more intelligible—whatever their final worth for ethics—if we conceive these needs that he would consider acquired as limits within which each individual must operate if he is to be "human."

Indeed, this kind of persistent generic "capacity" alone makes it possible to understand the development of personality as Allport conceives it. Take as fundamental his "capacity for meaning." It is present in the infant, child, preadolescent, and adult in a way that must be accommodated to his abilities and environmental learning. But can the facts of continuity in a given personality be explained if we say that John cannot have a "need for meaning" because this need is expressed differently in the familism of preadolescence, in the gang participation and bull sessions of adolescence, as well as in his mature religious sentiment or philosophical outlook as an adult? The person grows because inner potential is being actualized in accordance with *its* own nature in interaction with the nurturant environment.

To summarize our suggestion: John will always be unique in the way in which he grows. But if we say, as Allport does, that his striving for greater meaning, for participation, and for love are some of the conditions that must be met if John is to fulfill himself, are we not in fact urging that there is a structure for growth in *human nature as such* that may, indeed, be expected to develop in stages? Having gone this far, we can go on to say that it is only as the individual *learns* to relate these needs or "capacities" with self-insight, with a sense of humor, with an increasing loss of self-centeredness and positive outreach in value inclusiveness that *his* "nature" can blossom effectively.

We repeat, any set of universal needs will not solve the problem of why certain forms of meaning and growth, why certain organization and expression of unlearned needs is better than another. But if man's nature can be described *in part* in terms of certain universal needs, would we not have some considerations for judging whether a given theory of the good life is running counter to certain needs or whether it can expect support from ingrained yearnings? Insofar as the search for instinctoid needs reveals persistent sources of striving, be they considered ultimately good or bad, the theory of the good life will be assured of relevance to important trends in human nature if it takes adequate account of instinctoid urges.

Allport might justly warn us about allowing any list or definition of needs to be too restrictive. But, if we are at all correct, unless we do have some notion of long-range goals persistent through changes (such as the need for affiliation, participation, creativity or growth, and meaning) we are exactly in the plight Allport would be in if he did not slip in the "needs," as he seems to, by the back door.

What emerges from these comments on Allport, which we think, apply basically to all of our psychologists, is the importance of developing a fairly explicit theory of human needs and abilities even if it should turn out that these needs and abilities cannot be final or positive guides to the nature of the good life. No adequate theory of what man ought to be can be relevant to the human situation unless it takes full account of what it is that human beings are likely to need and want. Indeed, what "ought" stands for in human experience, whether it is derived from needs or speaks for human society, and exactly how it is related to wants and abilities remain the central questions.

In Part II, therefore, we hope to propose a theory of man, of human needs, of human obligation, and of human freedom that may recommend itself especially in the light of the kinds of psychological problems we have been studying. In Part III we shall be forced to reconsider Parts I and II in the light of specifically ethical theories about how we know what the good life is.

V. *REFLECTIVE SUMMARY*

Our psychologists thus far have urged that positive mental health involves adequate expression for unlearned universal needs and tendencies. But Allport revolts against this view because the uniqueness of personality as he sees it cannot be explained by the modification of universal needs. He substitutes a striking concept of human growth. Man now is a victim neither of conscious nor of unconscious urges; he is no passive reactor to or mirror of culture. He is an actor who, in his environment, consistently transforms his own motivational tendencies of yesterday, not by extending them to some new object today, but by supplanting them in the light of new needs today.

This functional autonomy of motives is particularly significant for ethics because it can mean, for example, that even if a person starts life as a selfish pleasure-seeker, his future is not necessarily a cunning channeling of drives in order to escape reprisals. A man can become functionally autonomous of unsocial beginnings and, with normal affiliative treatment, develop a productive life style.

Allport's view seems to give personality a certain freedom even from the individual's own givens, a freedom that is not "taken back," as it is in Fromm's view when freedom is said finally to consist in being one's "true" self. Yet for all this emphasis on creativity, on freedom from slavery to instincts and infantile drives, the question persists whether Allport's own description of dynamic factors in the growth of personality does not in fact actually resort to more universal and more constitutional needs than his theory allows. For in referring to participation, affiliation, and even autonomy as needs that cannot be stifled without deformation of individual potential, is Allport not in fact asserting that, however pervasive functional autonomy in motivation, the individual's demand for these lines of expression will be found operative in some mode or other?

Even if this criticism has merit, it is still the fact that Allport gives an unusually explicit account of the way in which individual pattern and growth is to be conceived. The proprium (ego) is an acquired inner unity of preferred skills, motives, and values; it in turn serves to form, organize, stabilize, and direct further strivings of the individual. The specific content of the proprium will feel the effect of the development of personality beyond the rather infantile "must" conscience to the more reflective, generic principles of the "ought" conscience. The varied dimensions of stability, the present "go" and the longer-range continuity of striving are provided by attitudes, traits, intentions, and style of life.

The mature personality, the product of discriminating balance between many interests and values, involves self-extension, self-objectification, compassionate involvement, self-acceptance, and a unifying philosophy of life. Allport is explicitly aware of the positive, expansive function that a mature religious sentiment—as opposed to a rigid, restrictive, self-protective, infantile sentiment—can have in the search for meaning or in fusing emotion, reason, and action in practical commitment to what is felt to be ultimate.

Allport is also fully aware of the psychologist's dilemma when it comes to defining the ideal of mature personality. Because his task as scientific psychologist is to define what is, he cannot prescribe what ought to be. At least, as Allport himself suggests, the psychologist can keep the ethicist from making egregious errors about what human nature is and what it can become. At best his observations of human patterns and goals and of their effect upon personality can be suggestive for the ethicist.

From our study of psychological views of human development, three problems much disputed in ethics emerge: the nature and range of human freedom, of obligation, and of motivation. To these problems we turn, in more philosophical vein, as we prepare for the normative study of personality and the good life in the remainder of this book.

PART II:

Basic Problems in Psychological and Ethical Theory

7

The Psychological Framework
for Ethical Reflection

~~~~~~

Psychologists, as we have seen, cannot decide what they mean by a sick mind or a healthy mind without asking: What is the standard for the good life? How do we know it? How do we conform our lives to it?

But these are the questions that have been and are the concern of moralists and theologians. Shall we ask the competent psychologist to stop working in this area and let them take over? No. For, as the history of ethical and theological reflection confirms, there is no way of keeping psychology, ethics, and religion from converging on this problem of defining and realizing the good life. Whether we concentrate, as does the ethicist, on the question of the nature of the good or, as does the psychologist, on the nature of personality and its development, we cannot escape the overarching question: What is the nature of the good life in the light of the given nature of man and of his relation to the total environment?

In this book we have chosen to see first how far the study of an especially relevant portion of recent and current psychological probing could take us. Any ethical system is clearer if the conception of human givens with which it works is explicit. In this chapter we shall begin to outline a tentative ground plan of human nature, which profits, we hope, from the psychological analyses we have studied. We start by setting forth what we mean by saying that man is a knowing-wanting being. We shall try to be definite even though we cannot do full justice to the topic.

I. *THE PERSON AS A UNIFIED, SELF-CONSCIOUS KNOWER*

A. *A Human Being Is Capable of Self-Consciousness*

A person's awareness is not limited to sensing, feeling, wanting, remembering, imagining, perceiving, and thinking; he can become aware that he is undergoing these states. "Man is a self-conscious being," implies more than immediate experiencing. For if man simply sensed, remembered, imagined, and wanted, without being able to relate his experiences to each other and be aware that he is doing so, he would never realize that he can make mistakes; he would simply rehearse his past experiences. *To think is not merely to have ideas in mind; it is to relate them to each other and to new experiences in order to solve some problem.*

B. *Man in Thinking Is Guided by Logical Norms*

As we seek similarities and differences, as we classify experiences and events, we find ourselves fulfilling or frustrating an inner demand for consistency. Whatever the psychic processes that tumble our images and ideas into consciousness, the moment that we start organizing our ideas, we experience a curious constraint if we find inconsistency among them. We are, of course, often unaware that we are inconsistent. But no one can show us that we are inconsistent without appealing to this norm, which he expects to guide us. And something in us is disturbed if we "know what we mean" when we say, for example, that "Since all men are two-legged, this man is three-legged."

We are not asserting that man is always logical or consistent, and we are not asserting that if he is to describe or explain events truly, all he needs is to be consistent with his premises. All we assert here is that, whatever the other conditions that a man must meet if he is to discover the truth, man never makes headway in his search unless he avoids inconsistency. He simply cannot be resigned *intellectually* in the presence of contradictory statements. Now, because any self-conscious planning involves the organizing of ideas, we can see how crucial to his view of the world is this inner demand that ideas be consistent with each other.

May we not conclude: Just as man's body exemplifies and survives in accordance with laws of physiology, so his theoretical gropings take form in accordance with this minimal logical demand by which he unwittingly is guided to some extent as he examines and connects his experiences with each other, and by which he guides himself as he seeks to correct a logical error. In a word, if a man breaks the law of physiology he may ache physically; if he breaks the laws of logic he may "ache" intellectually. If he is to escape serious physiological or intellectual disorder, he will have to conform sooner or later to these laws.

We are stressing this demand for logical consistency here because it seems to have been lost sight of by those who have sought the "dynamic" causes of human behavior in man's nonthinking nature. This latter emphasis would have tragic consequences for psychological science itself if those who sought these dynamic causes did not obey logical laws, or if they did not expect those they treated to become logical in thinking about their desires. Indeed, the whole impact of Freud's thought, when he asserts that ego shall be where id was, is that logical connections shall inform and transform the life that had simply been pushed about by instinctive impulses of the amoral and alogical id. We reassert: There is more to finding the truth than logic; but, as someone has said, no one breaks the laws of logic without the laws of logic sooner or later breaking him. Further comments about the relation of reason and desire [1] are better postponed until we have suggested our theory of needs later in this chapter.

C. *Man Is a Complex, Self-identifying, Continuant Agent or Personal Self*

The reader of these pages so far has found the word "self" used in different ways—and should he invade the field of epistemology and

---

[1] See the treatment of this theme in Brand Blanshard, *Reason and Goodness* (New York: The Macmillan Co., 1961), Chapter XIII, "Thought and Desire."

metaphysics, he would encounter even greater variety. For our purposes in this book we shall briefly suggest an interpretation of what the word "self" can mean if we stay close to what we actually experience.

There is continuing structure and change in each of us. Without memory and imagination one's experience could never build up to anything, and without the ability to think logically, "the building" could never be more than the haphazard piling of experiences upon each other. But the inescapable fact for every one of us is that from moment to moment and from day to day we are "my changing-same self." If we were not the same we would not even know that we change. How can we express this amazing yet inescapable fact?

Actually, we suggest, our remembering, recognizing, recalling are phase activities of the pervasive, permeating unity we find ourselves being. Tomorrow I shall remember today as "my" yesterday; today and tomorrow are phases of a unified me. I am not today and tomorrow merely spliced together; today and tomorrow are my experiences related temporally. Certainly, there could be no thinking function unless a memory-binding unity ("I") existed each moment and "carried" its past with it.

Person-al experience, then, is not simply one moment after another; it is not simply a "flow of experiences," of sensations, perceptions, images, thoughts, desires, emotions, feelings. Human experience is *experienced as a flow* only because, we suggest, there is this complex, active, time-binding continuant, which from birth onward changes and matures with every new encounter. This self-identifying unity of activities—of sensing, remembering, imagining, thinking, wanting, emoting, feeling (and, we shall see, oughting and willing) —we shall call *the person or personal self.*

This personal self is not an homunculus behind its activities, carrying them "somehow" in its own unchanging nature, as some soul psychologies would have it. This personal self is the kind of event we experience it as being, a complex unity of the activities designated, which has this remarkable capacity to maintain its identity-in-change.[2] Our view has its difficulties, of course, but none, we

[2] Nor is this person identical with the "self," the ego, personality, or proprium of much recent psychology. For the latter are all developments of the personal self as described here. They are modifications, more or less continuous in their acquired nature, of the activities of the person in his interaction with the environment. See Bertocci, "The Psychological Self, The Ego, and The Personality," in *Psychological Review,* 52 (1945), 91–99.

think, comparable to the problems of the objector who denies that he is a unity-in-process. For he will have difficulty explaining why he is the same person at the end of the sentence that states his objection as he was at the beginning!

D. *Man Is a Psychophysiological Being*

We have been urging that the person is a self-identifying, active continuant, and we have pointed out some of its activities—staying fairly close to capacities that all thinkers would grant as basic to the human species, however they might disagree in exact description. Had we identified these activities with either mind or body or completely with either consciousness or the unconscious, the thunder and lightning of psychological and philosophical controversy would have been released about our heads. As we suggested in the first chapter, however, the mind-body (or psychosomatic) relationship is a problem that cannot be side-stepped or solved dogmatically.

Fortunately, the ethicist, in large stretches of his work, does not need to resolve this problem in detail. Whatever many psychologists say when they are theorizing about the matter, when they actually describe human behavior, they talk about needs that are not organic and localizable in the body. They talk about needs that are psychogenic, whether or not they specify that these are derived from the bodily needs. Surely phenomena such as the libido, anxiety, repression, sublimation, mental health, maturity, "self," ego, proprium, freedom, responsibility, psychic dependence and independence, creativity, "peak experiences," the need to love and be loved, to "belong"—just to mention a few—do not yield to description solely in physiological terms. The analysis of some neuroses and psychoses that involve no bodily disablement presents barriers to him who would explain them in physiological terms alone. Such neuroses and psychoses respond not to physiological therapy, but only to therapy that brings changes in perspective or meaning.

No, if we take what we find and do not try to force the data into a simple monolithic theory, we must say that each of us as a person is a psychophysiological being. The personal self that we have been talking about is dynamically related in a give-and-take with a body, but it is not identifiable with the body. By this we mean what is open to the observation of each of us. We all have bodies that operate homeostatically, that is, in accordance with physiological law. But we could not think and live and interact with each other, with the natural world, unless we conformed also to some extent to the laws of thought, laws that we do not make up any more than we make up the laws of homeostasis.

At the present stage of knowledge, at any rate, nothing but madness seems to lie ahead for the dogmatist who would explain the nature of his being by studying processes that go on solely in the brain and body. He would in actuality seek to understand the meaning of logical contradiction and incoherence, of anxiety, guilt, and love by the delineation of what goes on in the nerves and glands only!

If we set metaphysical theories aside for the purposes of this book, what seems clear is that psychic and organic processes and activities are dependent on each other, in varying degrees, for their functioning and that derangement or deficit in either physiological or psychic processes can have effects upon the other member. Thus, we may define *the person, for ethical purposes, as a complex, self-identifying, continuant unity whose activities involve psychic and physiological events.* The exact relation of the psychic and physiological in a given situation is better determined not by formula but by analysis of that situation. A man eating ravenously after days of hunger is gratifying a bodily need; but is his psychobiological nature not heartened at the same time by the thought that at least he will survive?

We should not have taken space for this brief analysis of the human person did it not influence the specific analysis of many psychological and ethical issues. For just as there are localizable physiological needs, there may well be, as we shall suggest, psychic or mental needs. Perhaps the most pervasive difference forced on us by this view of the person as a psychosomatic being is in the definition of "survival." For now, when we speak of survival, we cannot think simply in terms of continuous bodily living. The loss of hope, or love, or freedom to think, even though organic life goes on, may mean psychic death. Obviously "the good" for a *psychosomatic* being will be much more difficult to define than it would be if we could confine ourselves to physiological strength and longevity.

With this general view of the person in mind, we now propose a tentative analysis of basic human needs. We must first remind ourselves why the difference between unlearned, universal needs and learned, variable needs is important for ethical theory.

II. *THE PERSON AND HIS UNIVERSAL NEEDS*

A. *The Ethical Importance of Universal Needs*

As a person proceeds to think about the directions in which his life is to go, he is very soon forced to come to terms with at least two outside factors, his social environment and the forces of Nature. While his actual interchange with Nature is his own, his views of natural events are influenced by the views of his culture as he understands them. A Trobriand Islander is born into a culture where he is told that in dealing with "natural events" he is at the same time dealing with the forces of black magic—for example, "all serious illness and all deaths, except perhaps those due to suicide and murder, and death in battle, are due to magic; and only magic can cure illness." [3]

Cultural influences on his orientation to his environment aside, the person who is trying to discover how to gratify his wants is soon forced to realize that some events in nature take place regularly, do not depend upon his wanting them, and force him (as well as his culture) to make some adjustment to them if he is to get *what he wants*. How many events there are, of which a human being has to become aware, if he would maintain health. What will happen *if. . .*! What may happen *if. . .*! Such expected sequences of natural events are the basis of fundamental "do's" and "don'ts" in the societal code.

Thus, the laws of physical nature provide a stubborn context within which all human wants and abilities are measured; they provide a constant framework which, once known, can be taken for granted; and they lay down the natural limits within which physical action can take place. Human beings get physically hurt if they do not adjust their lives to these sequences.

We have been stressing this simple point because we wish to draw a parallel in connection with human needs. Are there any dependable sequences within the wanting-life of man that provide similar limits and that man neglects at serious expense? Let us assume for purposes of our discussion here that anything we want we claim, while we want it, to be valuable (value claim); anything we do not want we claim at that time to be disvaluable (disvalue claim). Much

[3] A. Macbeath, *Experiments in Living* (London: Macmillan & Co., Ltd., 1952), p. 120.

more will be said about this in Chapter 14, but let us use this distinction between "value claim" and "disvalue claim" to stress the tentative character of the search for values as well as to underscore the relation to want, desire, or need.

If a person has dependable recurrent wants (usually called *needs*), which he cannot alter, they will lead to recurrent value claims and recurrent disvalue claims. The moralist then must know whether such stable sources of value and disvalue claims exist and what they are. To state this in ethical terms: If a person has dependable wants, as well as variable wants, and if those wants insistently and persistently make themselves felt in his own life and in the lives of others, regardless of social or physical environment, then the ethicist knows that there are certain dependable value claims or disvalue claims that will recurrently surround, and perhaps constitute the framework for comparison with, his variable value claims. If man is to understand what it involves to live "with himself," whatever nature or whatever society demands from him, he needs to know what these wants are that are "universal" in different periods in his own life and in the lives of others.

To give oversimplified illustrations: If a person knows that his unlearned wanting nature will make recurrent demands for nourishing food, he will need to include such food in his diet, whatever else he eats. Again: If he is not loved by his father, it is unfortunate; but it is worse if nobody loves him—assuming that to be loved is a universal need. Briefly, a person needs to know "the sort of objects" that his wanting constitution demands, just as he needs to know what the recurrent pattern of the world around him is, or its "constitution."

It may be clearer now why as ethicists we are interested in the nature of unlearned universal needs. If there are some universal needs, there are some universal value claims, untouched by environmental influences. If there are universal value claims, they may guide us to principles by which we may guide our criticism of relatively temporary and culturally conditioned value claims. Of course, we cannot assume that a universal value claim has necessary priority over the more variable value claims. But it is evident that recurrent, relatively unalterable value claims deserve special consideration in the ordering of life. To satisfy them may be prerequisite to mental health and the good life even though their satisfaction alone will not constitute all that the good life involves.

Again, it has been all too easy for some psychologists and other people to assume that universal needs are more valuable than more variable wants. Actually, the question of "good or bad," of "how good and how bad," cannot come up until we know what our constitutive and universal needs are, how they are connected with each other, and how they will interact with the total environment. Also, we need to know whether some universal needs exercise a measure of control both on other universal needs and on more variable desires. Furthermore, if some of the needs (like those for food and shelter) can be satisfied only by specific objects, whereas others (like the need to be loved, let us say) are more general and plastic and do not prescribe their gratifiers so rigidly, we need to know this. And if it should be that, as Maslow suggests,[4] some needs are not only universal but more insistent, with the result that, unless they are gratified, disturbances will be set up in the person that will destroy the possibility of realizing other values, then we begin to see a principle emerging for ordering value claims. None of these problems has an easy answer, but no ethicist who would speak for man can neglect them.

B. *A Tentative Analysis of Universal Needs*

The reader of Chapters 1 through 6 does not need to be told that psychologists are hardly of one mind on the question of the number and nature of universal needs. Our previous discussions of motivation theory, and especially of Allport and Maslow, provide special background for the suggestions we wish to advance here. We begin by stating what we would regard as untenable[5] in any theory of universal needs.

First, untenable is the view that all desires are derivatives of one underlying need such as "the will to live," the libido, the need for superiority, the need to be loved, or the need for freedom. And our main reason for saying this is that these so-called underlying needs simply have no meaning apart from the derivatives. What is the will to live if not the need to eat, to be safe, to explore, and so on? How do we know what it means to be "one's self" unless we know what needs are involved in being a particular self?

[4] See Chapter 5 above.
[5] The reader might fruitfully compare the statement here with Allport's "Requirements for an Adequate Theory of Motivation," in *Pattern and Growth in Personality* (New York: Holt, Rinehart and Winston, 1961), pp. 220–26.

Second, any view of unlearned needs in man is untenable if these needs are defined as inflexible and rigid in mode of expression or gratification. Nor is the goal of a need to be conceived too narrowly in man. The need to explore, the need to master, for example, are not confined either to specific stimuli or to specific modes of expression. We shall adopt Maslow's adjective "instinctoid" for the constitutional needs in order to emphasize that while they are unlearned, they have *much greater generality* of goal and *much more flexibility* in expression than instincts as we find them in animals. In man, needs are not little spring-door mechanisms that operate in the same way under different conditions of maturation and learning.

Third, we are eager to emphasize the extent to which nurture can take "nature" and drive it into different forms of expression—which in turn can become "second nature." So ingrained can the means of expressing a need in a given environment become that the individual often finds that he cannot express that need in any other way, except perhaps under conditions of direst emergency. For example, although Americans normally find it unthinkable to eat human flesh, American soldiers as starving concentration-camp prisoners have considered eating the flesh of other men. Thus let it be clearly understood in what follows that although we shall insist on *given, unlearned, general objectives,* we deem it very important to know to what extent basic needs can be influenced by learning and culture.

Finally, any theory of human motivation must pay adequate attention to (a) the unique variety in unity of each person, (b) the persistent tendencies whose satisfaction is the condition for the expression of other needs, (c) the fact of maturation that may alter the strength of needs, and (d) the limited adaptability of the total unlearned endowment of the individual. In every person, then, our thesis will run, there is a structure of unlearned motive-need and ability (talent, intellectual, and otherwise) that persists, though not rigidly, through the changes that go on in him and confront him from without.

1. *Tissue Needs*

Under the heading of tissue needs we would group all the needs whose gratification is necessary to physiological self-maintenance; for example: hunger, thirst, temperature, exercise, sleep. The demands of these needs in relation to each other, the way in which their gratification is dependent on the specific environment and on the physiological strength and cognitive abilities of the individual is fairly clear.

If a human being had no other dimension of need than tissue needs—if a steak were a very tasty piece of meat and not at all a prestige symbol, if clothing were simply a means of protection against the elements—then man could indeed be said to "march on his stomach" and "live" by his abilities to get shelter from the environment. He would be an impoverished higher animal, though more flexible and able than any other animal. "The good" in his life could be defined in terms of inclusive gratification of tissue value claims.

Yet, even at this organic level, the problem of deciding the ethical ideal for "organic" living would be more complicated than it seems. Bodily processes create minimal demands which, if they go ungratified, cause distress and weakness. Thus, some persons can get along with less sleep than others, but all must sleep at some time or other. The problem is: How much more than the minimum should one have? Here the person goes to the medical expert for help. But again, the medical expert can tell him what he needs to do *if* he decides that his own physical health is more important than the demanding work he is doing. Even at a simple, individual, physiological level, we see, there are a host of value claims to be selectively criticized by him who would lead "the good" physical life.

Even larger issues lie in wait. Why and how shall he share food, shelter, and pain? Why should the "inconvenient" unborn child, the weak, crippled, idiotic, or senile person be protected against pain and death if this endangers the physical comfort of the physically able? Most of us have "accepted" solutions to these problems. But we raise such questions to bring out the fact that fundamental moral issues would still exist even if man's needs were basically physical. With every need or type of demand that we add to human endowment, the ethical problem becomes more complex.[6]

2. Defensive Needs

In the ground plan of all human beings, we suggest, there are two emotions, fear and anger, that stir the person to wide ranges of

[6] This would be the place to include the need for sex experience. Because we shall deal with it in Chapter 29, we wish here simply to say that it is one of the hardest to define in the context of human experience, as any reader of Freud alone will know. We do not intend to slight it.

behavior. Fear and anger [7] never function "on their own" independently of other needs. One may eat to eat, but one is not angry merely to be angry; nor does he become afraid just to be afraid. Anger and fear occur when something in the world, *as the individual cognizes it,* threatens his other value claims. What is a threat to one person finds another smiling; what frustrates one is a challenge to another.

Again, if man had only physiological needs and if fear and anger subserved only these needs, the whole human situation would be different. It might well be that the ties that bind family, clan, and other societal institutions together could be explained only on the basis of contracts made to allay fear of harm and death. The ultimate value might now be survival of the fittest, and "fittest" would be described in terms of safety for these physiological needs.

One does not have to look far to find persons who would say that the root of all human motivation is each man's need to maintain himself against nature and his fellow man. A man, on this view, makes only those concessions to others that he deems absolutely necessary to his own safety and then only in such a way that the balance of power may be forever in his own favor.

Thomas Hobbes gave philosophical expression to this view when he hypothesized that man "in a state of nature" was concerned only with his own private wants and safety. Yet even Hobbes's self-centered man in a state of nature stopped to reflect. He realized that death has a way of equalizing all men. No Goliath can escape a stone well aimed by a stripling! Hobbes's man is thus driven from a "state of his nature" into a social contract with other men aimed to protect him against others. The state, Leviathan, is held by Hobbes to be inviolate, for only thus can one hope to find security.

The reader of Hobbes's social and political ethics [8] may well

---

[7] Were there sufficient space we should defend our use of these *emotions as needs,* a very unconventional procedure among psychologists. William McDougall, to be sure, held that every "instinct" and "propensity" had its internal accompaniment as emotion. Thus, "anger-pugnacity" and "fear-escape" would be his terms.

The reader is urged to consult McDougall's *Energies of Men* (New York: Scribner's, 1932), as well as *Introduction to Social Psychology* (Boston: Luce, 1921) to discover later and earlier aspects of McDougall's theory of motivation.

We are much influenced by McDougall, for it seems clear that many human needs are *felt* (phenomenologically) by the experient as stirred-up states of mind that seek release or gratification. But to hold, as McDougall does, that all needs have emotional counterparts, seems to go beyond our evidence. Hence we shall name the emotional state whenever we can identify it in experience.

[8] See Sterling Lamprecht's suggestive introductory essay on Hobbes in the Appleton-Century-Crofts edition of *De Cive* or *The Citizen* (1949).

wonder how Hobbes, beginning with a human nature thus narrowly restricted, could come to demand that men in society "ought" to be forgiving, grateful, and gracious. But we have seen this same problem occur in Freud. And we have seen Allport grapple with it both by resorting to functional autonomy and later by adding the affiliative capacity to the nature of man (see above pp. 123–125, 132–135).

We are here touching upon another hotly debated psychological issue of importance to the ethicist. If the newborn babe has throughout life no other innate tendencies than tissue and defensive needs, how have his "higher needs" evolved? They certainly are not necessary if all that man wants is physical sustenance and security. Can it be, as is often maintained, that these "higher" needs are the effect of intelligently "expressing" tissue and defensive needs?

But, how do the "hungers" for love, for freedom, for knowledge, for beauty, for holiness develop from tissue and defensive needs? How does the hunger for freedom come out of a hunger for food? We can see how overt *behavior* called love, for example, could develop, but *the inner emotional urge* for love—that seems to be another matter! To say that the need to be loved or to love is the kind of need that we feel when we are hungry (and so on) is to disregard evidence each of us cannot mistake. The feeling state "I *want* to be loved" and the feeling state "I *want* to respect" certainly do not feel like any variation of hunger, of other tissue needs, or of fear and anger. Because we believe that man is a psychophysiological being whose psychic nature is stirred to want in its own way, we go on to propose the next three needs.

3. Achievement Needs

Curiosity and *mastery* appear, in different terminology, in older lists of instincts and even in contemporary discussions [9] of motivation. We cannot stop to argue the "instinctoid" nature of these needs, although we should argue once more that their inner emotional thrust could not be learned, but we can try to clarify their essential import.

[9] See H. A. Murray *et al., Explorations in Personality* (New York: Oxford, 1938), O. Klineberg, *Social Psychology* (rev. ed.; New York: Holt, 1954), C. Kluckhohn and H. A. Murray, *Personality in Nature, Society, and Culture* (New York: Knopf, 1949), Robert W. White, "Competence and the Psychosexual Stages of Development," in *Nebraska Symposium on Motivation* (Lincoln: University of Nebraska Press, 1960), and Carl R. Rogers, *On Becoming a Person* (Boston: Houghton Mifflin Co., 1961).

a. *Curiosity-Wonder*

Curiosity-wonder is characteristic, in some form and some degree, of human beings regardless of their environment. We must remind ourselves here of Maslow's warning that in man we should not expect "instinctoid needs" to be always overpowering. Among human beings, exploratory behavior of neither child nor adult can be classified entirely as means to practical ends. Even animals seem to explore with no ulterior purpose. The child and adult probe and inquire when they are otherwise satiated, and often they get so interested in their probing that other needs take second place.[10]

The emotional stirring involved in such probing is *wonder*. The occasions for wonder are myriad and cannot be specified ahead of time, though what stimulates wonder is an "unknown" deemed to be knowable. To wonder and to have that wonder gratified by better understanding brings to the person a quality of psychic gratification that must be felt to be appreciated. It is its own reward, as well as being instrumental to other rewards.

b. *Mastery-Elation*

Other things being equal, human beings, regardless of environment, feel the *need to master* and the emotional quality of *elation* as the obstacle is being overcome. This, we suggest, is the inner emotional spring in what so much psychological literature refers to as the need for superiority, or participation, or recognition. How destitute a human being feels if he can overcome none of the obstacles he finds in his way. And how natural to try. It is this trying, this inner *wanting to overcome,* that we would declare cannot be taught —although it can be encouraged or discouraged.

Anger does, of course, mobilize energy to attack obstacles, and the need to master may seem to be simply one form of anger. But such a reduction of mastery-elation to a form of anger-aggression overlooks the fact that human beings feel elated when anger is not present. Furthermore, when anger against restriction succeeds in achieving the objective desired, the felt quality of elation is not the felt quality of anger reduction.

[10] For recent emphasis on "cognitive" motive, see J. Nuttin, *Psychoanalysis and Personality: A Dynamic Theory of Normal Personality,* trans. G. Lamb (New York: Sheed & Ward, 1953); D. C. McClelland, *Personality* (New York: Sloane, 1951); H. Cantril, *The Why of Man's Experience* (New York: Macmillan, 1950).

Here, again, we seem to have a motive that can, as Adler thought, become the central motive in a person's life. But do most of us want superiority or power as such, or do we want to overcome obstacles on the way to gratifying our various desires in the physical and social world? The satisfaction that we find in play activities—from bicycling to bridge, from baseball to chess, and even in many games of chance —is unexplainable apart from the obstacles we set ourselves to overcome. For a human being to feel that he can meet the problems growing out of other needs and those forced on him by environmental pressures is to feel a kind of *fulfillment* that gives zest to living.

Once more, in the need to master we experience not some psychic, overpowering ground swell of the do-or-die variety, although this can develop. Yet to feel "in control" rather than "panicky" gives quiet confidence and poise to a person for which there is no "external" measure. Even when mastery does not pervade the whole of one's being, as with Maslow's self-actualizing personalities, mastery in segments of life provides the "elation" that comes when a person feels: "I am a cause and not just an effect."

Reflecting for a moment on curiosity-wonder, and mastery-elation, we remind ourselves that these instinctoid needs do not, like hunger, thirst, sex, fear, and anger, create a "threatening" turmoil in the person. They nevertheless make themselves felt not only as "servants" to all other needs, but as partners in the total task of "finding oneself." It becomes increasingly clear that all instinctoid needs are not separated channels of human energy or coiled springs—though they seem to behave as such when denied. If we could keep in mind that a human being is not an emotional person first and a thinker afterward, but a reflective feeler or emotionally involved thinker, we would be fairer to the actual facts.

In other terms, we should see that although we may list needs abstracted from their context, one after the other, they are really foci of what we are calling the *wanting-knowing structure of a given person who is trying to express these interconnected needs in accordance with his abilities in a given environment.* The individual interprets each situation both in the light of his past experience and also in response to the want-tensions felt at a given time. Thus, the child not fed when he is hungry, not cared for when ill may feel all the worse because he wants to understand this state of affairs. To be physically in need and unable to understand or to master the situation evidently makes for what we might call a confluence of needs.

But actually the needs do not "flow together," because they are particular foci of the total person at that moment.[11]

4. *Affiliative Needs: Tenderness, Sympathy, Respect*

a. *The Need to Be Tender*

In the presence of an object conceived to be helpless (but not necessarily suffering), a human being, other things being equal, feels the emotion *tenderness*. The quality of tenderness, like the quality of anger, fear, wonder, or elation, must be felt to be known.

If any human being told us that he never felt tenderness, we should have to say that he was emotionally insensitive at one point, just as some persons are deaf to some sounds. Other things being equal, any being *conceived of* as helpless—the new-born babe, kitten, puppy, a needy person conceived as helpless—evokes a tenderness that moves the person *to want to protect* that being. The phrase "conceived of" must be given special emphasis, for the person may not see helplessness as helplessness. The phrase "to want to" must be noted, for when the "object" is conceived as helpless other factors may still enter the situation and keep a person from doing what he feels, momentarily, the urge to do.

Important to our conception of man is this thesis—to be further borne out by our analysis of sympathy—that a human being is not emotionally insulated against the need of others for help. Another may feel tender where I, given my view of the same situation, may feel angry. But the fact remains that in his life and mine, at some point or other, tenderness is evoked, even though it may be short-lived, suppressed, and even repressed.

It is unfortunate that psychologists have tended, when they recognized this need, to tie it to biological maternity or paternity. Without denying for a moment that it is usually so linked, we should regard maternal and paternal tenderness as one very potent expression of the generalized tenderness-protection need. Even their own infant,

---

[11] This is the basic objection that we have to Maslow's provocative suggestion that the tissue and safety needs, for example, are prepotent. The most we can say at the psychological level of description is that when there is conflict it is very difficult, in any given situation, to keep some needs from prevailing over others. It is hazardous to predict what an individual will do. For in a conflict situation, a person, child or adult is at every moment a total unified being in some state of wanting-knowing, trying to resolve a particular problem. Some want may win out, but the individual is left feeling the total complex, which involves the unsuccessful wants and his interpretation of this situation. The unsuccessful needs may still be having considerable effect on the total person in transit, and on the emerging emotional ferment.

who is actually helpless, may be *conceived of* as a threat to their security by his mother and father, and this conception may lead to their abandoning him, for example. The child who tries to jab out the eyes of a kitten, the adult who destroys ants, are not "set" to see these animals simply as helpless. When they are so set, we would contend, they may still hurt and destroy, but not without *feeling an inner retraint imposed by the emotion of tenderness.*

In the *want* to protect that accompanies the felt tenderness, we have the basis for some of the most characteristic sources of human joy and suffering. If we ask ourselves whether we would want to live without ever feeling tenderness for anything, we gain some insight into the place it has in our lives.

b. *The Need to Sympathize*

The emotion of *sympathy* not only feels different from tenderness, but, other things being equal, is evoked when a person appreciates the suffering of a sentient being. The felt urge is to relieve the suffering, so we call this need sympathy-succor.

Obviously, the same situation may evoke both sympathy and tenderness, *but sympathy does not feel like tenderness, and tenderness does not feel like sympathy.* In sympathy, the stimulus situation (as conceived) involves suffering rather than helplessness. Here again, the felt urge to stop suffering need not be obeyed. Yet it is a fact that felt sympathy "hurts" in its own way when unrelieved.

We suspect that psychologists who have refused to regard tenderness and sympathy as instinctoid have been misled by the stereotype of instinct as an overpowering urge invariably evoked by the same object. But our phenomenological approach forbids such external analysis. We are insisting, rather, upon felt inner tensions within the psychological field of the experient, who is always responding to his environment with his whole past and his conceived future. A person may recognize suffering, realize that its alleviation now will cause other unwanted results, and therefore not act now, much as he wants to. It is this *want to relieve* that we regard as unlearned and unteachable.

It is important to note that we are not stating that sympathy and tenderness—like all but the tissue needs—are present in the newborn infant. They obviously must await maturation of cognitive ability. But we test universality of needs by their presence neither in animals nor in infants. It is each peculiar felt "want to," often intrinsically emotional in nature, that we regard as crucial to our theory of universality, our theory of independence of specific culture and environment. For, we suggest, none of these particular "want to" experiences could be taught or learned unless it was latent in the person.

To be concrete: Can we teach a person to "want to" relieve, to feel sympathetic, if this is no part of his nature? We can teach the action pattern, but not the inner "want to" relieve when he feels sympathy. Among the most poignant and valued states in human experience are the states of wanting to relieve—even when one cannot actually alleviate the suffering.

Indeed, were there space we would do more than call attention to the probable repression of sympathy that occurs in the lives of most of us. It simply hurts too much to want to relieve suffering when one cannot or dares not for other reasons. "Hardening of the heart" can only occur because the heart is "soft," other things being equal; and we all experience the unique gratification that comes when we can relieve the suffering of others.

Still, to add one more comment, we must not be seduced into regarding tenderness and sympathy as the roots of altruistic behavior. Such a temptation must be resolutely resisted, even though great thinkers like David Hume [12] have rooted altruism in sympathy. In Chapters 14 and 27 we shall insist that altruism and selfishness are not emotional states as such. We cannot neglect the fact that felt tenderness and felt sympathy, uncritically expressed, may hurt rather than help the person suffering. Unintelligent "help" may spring from the desire to reduce one's own "feeling bad." As parents soon learn, when care of children is based on immediate response to their own need to protect and to succor, the children are spoiled. In a word, every human emotion can be expressed selfishly or altruistically.

c. The Need to Respect

What happens to any person, other things being equal, when he is in the presence of an object that he conceives to be worthwhile (according to whatever standard he acknowledges)? Our reply is: he feels the emotion of *awe* or of *respect*. How he will behave when he feels this emotional stirring depends on what he can do and what he believes that situation requires, but to say that his attitude and behavior will tend to be "submissive" is as close as we can get. Hence we call this need respect-submission. How emotionally poverty-

[12] David Hume, *An Inquiry Concerning the Principles of Morals*, ed. Charles W. Hendel (New York: Liberal Arts Press, 1947), Sections I, II, III.

stricken we would consider a human being who stood in awe of nothing, who respected nobody!

We must not yield to the temptation to "reduce" respect (and the "submissive" behavior it provokes) to a form of fear. Anybody who thinks for a moment of the beings he respects will realize that his inner state is not a fearful one. He may fear the being also, but respect certainly does not feel like fear. It requires psychological abracadabra to reduce respect to fear. One respects mother, father, wife, country; one may or may not fear each of these.

The area of experience that comes to mind when we use the word "respect" is the religious.[13] But we would suggest that while respect, developed to the degree we would then call "reverence," is no doubt involved in the religious experience, the latter has other components as well. Here we would note that respect is evoked by a whole range of values, from those involving the manifestation of skill and power, to moral, aesthetic, and religious values. Put very simply, to admire is to feel respect for what we admire. We simply are not made to be unresponsive to differences in value. And while respect is related to many other emotions and dispositions, ranging from gratitude to sorrow, it imposes its own psychic tone in all those situations that the person contemplates and admires.

5. The Need to Be Creative

The urge to create, though related to all other needs in the unity of the person, is not merely a form of these other needs. One might well call this need the yearning for novelty, the protest against monotony, drabness, and routine, the demand that life be not merely "one darn thing after another."

This demand for novelty, again, is usually found in connection with the expression of other needs (for example, to eat something different, to master something new), but it involves a peculiar kind of restlessness, and it often involves the person as a whole.

It is this need, perhaps, that comes closest to expressing what Fromm has in mind in his conception of the need to have *freedom for*, as well as *freedom from*. As he suggests, the security-loving, "conventionalized" personality is, in fact, ill because he has rejected the lure of freedom (or creativity). But, before Fromm, was it not Jung who insisted that the fundamental problem in each life is to keep the yearning for creative, individualized integration from being

---

[13] In our next chapter we shall be using the term "respect" in the context of moral experience. The degree and quality of respect, or of any other emotion, depend on the life context in which it is experienced, on the situation as conceived.

suffocated? And is Maslow's self-actualization not the name for the thrust in every life for the fullest expression at every stage of development?

Yet there is a difference between creativity [14] as we view it and creative self-actualization in Maslow, Fromm, and Allport. Self-actualization, for them, is the underlying demand for human beings to become all that their natures allow. Furthermore, we have noted, for them such creativity is largely synonymous with the good life. But in our view this demand for novelty, so crucial indeed to growth motivation, does not necessarily result in growth, or in "goodness" or "maturity." Lives can be mangled because this restless demand for novelty does not guarantee fulfillment; creativity may result in a violent knocking about from pillar to post. We must resist the "honorific" connotation of "creativity." The demand for creativity needs further evaluation, as does any other need.

This fact, however, does not keep creativity from becoming a pervasive motive; rather it accentuates what may well be the fundamental problem of life: how to keep true value in every area open to novelty; how to keep "becoming," in Allport's terms, without jeopardizing the achievement of the past. From day to day in myriad ways, the changing person may avoid some lures to adventure and follow others.

Creativity is, as we conceive it, not the whole of the self, not the basic urge, but one tendency in the person that cannot be neglected without having life lose its zest. Our language does not have a word for the emotive psychic tone felt when a person is enjoying "novelty," but the word "zest" may suggest the state. Perhaps creativity-zest could refer to this wholistic demand, which can seduce, as it can crown, personal striving.

C. General Comments on This Theory of Motivation

1. Is Pleasure the Necessary Goal of Living?

Pleasure, Freud and psychological hedonists to the contrary notwithstanding, is not, on this view of motivation, a necessary or independent need or goal of action. Human beings are not so constituted that the search for pleasure is the underlying spring of all their be-

[14] There is much in Robert W. White's theory of "competence" as "one general motivational principle" that is common to our analysis of creativity, of mastery, and of curiosity. See his "Competence and the Psychosexual Stages of Development," in *Nebraska Symposium on Motivation 1960* (Lincoln: University of Nebraska Press), pp. 97–140. and "The Concept of Competence," *Psychological Review*, 66 (1959), 297–333.

havior. It may be that pleasure *ought* to be the ruling ethical principle—but it is simply contrary to experience to say that man is
necessarily moved only by concern for the maximum of pleasure and
the minimum of unpleasantness. It would be equally untrue to fact
to say that man is indifferent to the lures of pleasant experiences.
One of the ethical problems facing each person is to decide how to
evaluate the value claims of different pleasures.

We would suggest that the reader check in his own experience an
observation we would make about "pleasure." We simply do not find
ourselves seeking something called "pleasure." What gives "body"
to pleasure is not something called pleasantness. Pleasantness is always a *kind* of pleasantness it is because it comes from the *kind* of
experience which yields it. In other words, experiences *of* pleasantness are not of something by itself, as one might say of the colors of
objects. The blue of a necktie and the blue of a wall could be the
same, but the "pleasure" of coffee-drinking and the pleasure of
cocoa-drinking are, as experienced, different. When we want coffee
instead of cocoa, we want the coffee not for "pleasure" but coffee-
including-pleasure. The "pleasure" that coffee brings cannot be
switched to cocoa. And this surely means that there is no such thing
as pleasure-in-itself. What we seek, at least to begin with, is not
pleasure, but certain "objects" that attract us because of what they
are.

To live for "pleasure," then, means to live for nothing ever experienced concretely by anyone. To be sure, pleasure comes as we
relieve the tension that wants set up. But then the pleasure is the
particular pleasure involved in gratifying *that* want. And even as we
express any given need, the gratifying will have an experienced quality that is not "pleasure," but the unique, unrepeated pleasantness of
that particular experience. Thus the "pleasure" of eating wanted-
strawberry-ice-cream is not a "pleasure" identical with that of eating
wanted-vanilla-ice-cream.

We return, then, to the conclusion that we cannot seek "pleasure"
but only this quality of pleasure or that quality of pleasure involved
in this or that specific experience. There is nothing in the structure
of human nature that enthrones pleasure and necessarily enslaves
men, though many are the persons who have made "pleasure" their
goal and been enslaved by it. We would contend that they actually
made certain clusters of experience, involving certain qualities of
pleasure in certain quantities, their goal. That pleasantness and
unpleasantness are important value and disvalue claims is undeniable,

but that "the pleasure principle" could ever be the guidepost for selection among values is cause for amazement—even when it comes from Epicurus, Bentham, and other noted thinkers.

2. *What It Means to Say that Man Is Nonrational*

Does not our description of instinctoid human needs justify the conclusion that man is a nonlogical or nonrational human being? It does if we specify carefully what we mean by such a statement. It does if we mean that man is motivated to think and behave by needs and emotions that do not first consult the laws of logic or the requirements of reason. Even curiosity involves, we urged, the propulsive power of wonder.

But it does not if we mean that man cannot be guided by the norms of logic and evidence, in other words, that he is hopelessly irrational. For our view is that man, in the wanting or conative side of his nature, is activated by nonlogical, nonrational needs that predispose him to favor certain areas of his environment and experience. But this is not to say that these needs are irrational, that they necessarily resist organization into any coherent pattern. Needs are not "forces of unreason" that supposedly undermine all human attempts to be rational; they are forces that clamor for expression without circumspection, and they make their own claims, but they are not intent on destroying each other or the person.

Of course men are irrational; it is no easy matter to be reasonable. But we are not unreasonable simply because we have nonrational urges. Indeed we would be less likely to say this if we remembered that each need is not a separate part of a person. Each need, like every focus of human activity, goes on within the complex unity of the person. The person, we have urged, is also and at the same time a reflective being; his reflection goes on within a total nature that is activated by such nonrational factors as instinctoid needs, acquired desires, sensory-perceptual experiences and, as we shall suggest, by nonrational capacities like will and obligation. All nonrational factors in the person call for further organization and direction as he seeks to reason—to relate them to the total environment and to the future as he can envision it.

What part reasoning ought to play in human experience is an ethical question,[15] and the psychologist helps the ethicist by making clear what happens to human beings when they use reason to find excuses rather than to "face reality."

[15] See Chapter 19.

What we are here asserting, in short, is that man is at least a think-ing-wanting being, whose capacity for self-conscious reflection poses problems of selection among value claims whatever their source. In our next two chapters we shall argue that man is also a "willing" and "oughting" being, and we shall try to designate the part each activity plays in the dynamics of human nature.

3. *Instinctoid Needs and the Good Life*

Whatever other sources of information may be available to the ethicist, he cannot (we would now assert with greater confidence) disregard the fact that human beings do have a complex structure of instinctoid needs in which a skeletal dynamic framework of universal value claims take root. But from such a framework we cannot deduce the actual good for human personality. The motivational givens do not constitute the good. Yet they do provide substantive raw material for the good life, because they persist in their basic expectancies be-yond any particular mode of gratification. This common human nature, these common value claims, cannot be disregarded as individ-uals try to work out their schemes of true values. Macbeath keeps a nice balance as he formulates the problem any society must face in relation to these basic needs.

The fact is that no society can afford to allow its members un-limited scope for the exercise of their most powerful impulses, while no society can completely repress them. All societies there-fore have rules governing the conditions in which they may find expression, and these rules differ from people to people. Yet within wide limits which are not easily ascertainable, human nature seems to be so plastic, so easily molded by cultural condi-tions, that it settles down not unhappily under many different kinds of regulations. . . . We have, however, to remember that what has to be satisfied is not particular impulses or urges or desires, but persons, and persons who are members of societies, and that what they require is a way of life in which their differ-ent impulses find expression and satisfactions in ways which are compatible with one another and with similar satisfactions by other people.[16]

[16] A. Macbeath, *Experiments in Living* (London: Macmillan & Co., 1952), p. 138. This study of the nature and foundations of ethics in the light of recent work in social anthropology is a remarkably clear, interesting, and scholarly work, whose stimulus, especially in this chapter, we gratefully acknowledge. See also for helpful evaluation of this problem of basic needs, *Anthropology and Ethics* by May and Abraham Edel (Springfield, Ill.: C. C Thomas, 1959).

Each person, then, experiences needs that, never completely exhausted at any one time in his development, are expressed in the great variety of value claims as he tries to "tend" to them in accordance with his ability in the different social and physical environments that he confronts. At the core of his unique personality the person will probably develop a citadel of values with which he identifies what his "life" means (Allport's proprium). Psychologically speaking, the way in which he expresses his basic needs, as he goes along, will depend, within limits, on what values constitute his proprium. The ethicist asks: What values ought to be propriate, as opposed to peripheral, in personality if the person is to achieve the good?

The very mention of personality as having a learned structure that will influence consciously and subconsciously the future development of striving leads to the critical question: To what extent is a person free to develop his future personality or choose other modes of striving? This is the next borderline problem in psychology and ethics.

III. *REFLECTIVE SUMMARY*

How shall we think of man? What are the activities that are present in the growth of any particular pattern of personality? Why can personality change without losing continuity and pattern that reflect present, dynamic interplay with the environment? In rudimentary form our answer can be expressed in ten theses.

1. Unless man is a unified, self-conscious knower, aware of himself as the same person even as he changes, there would be no option and continuity in human life. In communication with other persons and in his private thinking he is guided by, and constrained by, norms of logical consistency; he is also able to guide his actions by thinking consistently about his ideas and their relation to events and by developing reasonable hypotheses about himself and the world. To be sure, man "rationalizes," but unless he can reason coherently, all his theories, including this one about his being an unreasonable rationalizer, are futile. Whatever else is true of him, then, a person is a self-conscious knower who can guide himself by norms of consistency and reasoned investigation.

2. However, a person experiences himself not only as a self-conscious knower but also as a complex unity of remembering, feeling, desiring, perceiving, and, we shall argue, of willing and oughting.

3. While this personal unity of activities is constantly affecting and being affected by his body, the laws of his physiological body are not the laws of thinking and of these other activities. For psycho-ethical purposes we may consider a person a self-identifying active unity continuing in and constituted by basic unlearned psychic and physiological capacities.

4. It is this complex psychosomatic agent who gratifies his needs as he interacts with the environment and thus gradually develops that more or less systematic and unique mode of adjustment that we call "personality." The personality changes in response to the person's conception of what he needs and what is possible in the environment, but if the person in his basic activities were as changeable as personality, there would be nothing to restrain and guide the development of the different modes of adjustment that constitute his personality. Thus, the stage of ethical development of a personality reflects the selectivity of the person whose cognitive capacities, temperament, physique, and basic needs are being engaged in total response to the world.

5. On this larger psychosomatic view of the person, we realize that "survival" involves both psychic and physiological dimensions of the person, that the human struggle is for psychic expression as well as biological continuance. Psychic welfare is not grafted onto biological drives, for psychic capacities and needs are involved in all post-infantile striving.

6. Our view of innate, universal, human motivation reverts to "a list" of instinctoid needs in order to emphasize the fact that there is more than one basic thrust or dimension in human motivation. But all instinctoid motives are contemporaneous; they are phases of the dynamic unity of the person involved in every stage of personality formation. It is important to note that on our view the instinctoid motives, although defined as involving inflexible generic objectives, are flexible in manner of expression, in accordance with the capacity of each person to learn from his experience and to modify his means of achieving these generic goals.

7. If there are such dependable, unlearned motives regardless of specific environmental demands, the ethicist must realize that all men will make similar claims to gratification, even though these claims will be modified and expressed as specific value claims as the person works out the problem of their fulfillment in specific environments. It is these generic needs, seeking gratification in different situations that pose the basic problems of selectivity and choice for persons.

8. Thus, tissue, defensive, achievement, and affiliative needs, and creativity, are motivational facets, distinguishable but not compartmentalized, of the total activity of the unified person. Each need represents the person as propelled in a different direction, each adds its own psychic tone to any phase of development, for each is constantly involved within the ongoing motivational pattern of personal life.

9. Because these instinctoid needs are tendencies in man "as such" and pull him in different directions—toward self, toward others, toward aggression and hostility, and toward sympathy and respect— we cannot say that man is selfish or unselfish "to begin with." Man is neither sinner nor saint "by nature," but he can become either—by second nature, or learned habit.

10. In defining the good life, therefore, attention will need to be given to the contribution of rational and nonrational factors in the life of a person. The cognitive and noncognitive capacities and needs are at work in the organization of personality as the unique person develops his own unique responses to the claims of his own nature and of the environment. In this process of development the question always comes up: How free is he to modify his past, to select his future?

8

The Nature of Human Freedom

∽∽∽∽∽∽∽∽∽∽∽∽∽∽∽∽∽∽∽∽∽∽∽∽∽∽∽∽∽

Human beings grow and develop. They vary their responses to the environment, and their further growth and development is influenced by the particular effects of their interchange with the environment. This transactional way of conceiving human change applies, however, to plants and animals as well as to men. The variation possible in a plant is not as great as that in animals; the course of evolution has seen the development of a fabulously intricate nervous system in man that enables him to vary his responses in ways unimaginable at the plant and animal level. The question before us is: How shall we conceive the nature of the variations that take place in man? Does man's greater versatility in fact conform to the model useful for describing plant and animal change? Or must we introduce a new activity, willing, to explain changes that seem different from the developments in plant and nervous systems?

I. FREEDOM AS FULFILLMENT OF POTENTIALITY

Tomato seeds under favorable environmental conditions develop into sturdy tomato plants, which in turn develop ripe tomatoes. The pattern involved: specific seeds developing their potential in interaction with the potential of the physical world that affects them. It is assumed that in a favorable environment the potential of the seed

175

will develop into a plant that flowers and goes on to produce a mature fruit. To turn to the animal world for illustration, we may think of a chick growing from a fertilized egg to the point at which it can break the eggshell. When the chick interacts with the more complex world, it develops potentialities and built-in responses that enable it to discriminate those portions of the environment necessary for its growth into a chicken.

Whether we think of tomato seed or chick, we cannot escape the notion of a definite kind of organism with limited but plastic potential, which, given the proper environment, will *perforce* become all its own potential allows. The tomato plant and the chicken are the end products of interacting conditions suitable to their intrinsic abilities and their potential. In this biological (or biomorphic) model of development, the future is the product of what the individual, given its limited potential, can become in a specific environment.

If the environment is favorable, the sturdy tomato seed cannot become a diseased plant, and the chick cannot become a sickly hen. But the healthy tomato plant and the healthy chicken have power to do what the diseased cannot—survive and reproduce—and thus have "freedom" the diseased cannot exercise. Clearly, *freedom on the biological model is the fulfillment of potential with a view to optimum fulfillment of potential,* as opposed to restriction or distortion of growth. Are the human situation and human freedom essentially different from this?

The answer is "no" from most of our psychologists. Under the influence of this biomorphic model, they say that the personality at any point is the joint product of what is allowed by the total environment in interaction with the abilities and potentialities of the human organism. To be "free" is to fulfill one's own given potential for growth. To become free is to guide growth by understanding one's potential, by knowing the conditions that keep that potential from growing, and by getting rid of the obstacles to growth, so that the individual's needs and abilities may blossom.

In this perspective, the problem of human freedom becomes, in essence, horticultural or zoological. To be sure, it is stressed that human growth is governed by more complicated factors than we now know how to control. However, the growth-to-maturity process, the "freeing" of one's potential for fulfillment, is in essence no different from that of a plant or animal. The one important difference seems to be that, in addition to having greater capacity and plasticity, man is able to think and therefore work out possible solutions to problems that he confronts before action itself takes place. But this ability to think also increases the opportunities for mistakes that he can make about himself and his world. Society can aid the individual best by helping him to understand himself and his "good" and "bad" responses so that he can become *himself* more.

Thus, despite differences among themselves, our psychologists conceive of the problem of human growth as a kind of engineering problem in which the only concern is to know and take proper account of the stresses and strains as one actualizes his potential in varied situations. The terms "freedom" and "creativity" and even "choice" occur frequently, but in the last analysis, the growth, change, or development that they have in mind involves the becoming that a given individual, with his potential, *must* [1] become in the environment that presses in upon him. The change is "free" if some notion of an implicit goal is injected as the "end" of the development. "Freedom" is denied to the extent that the goal is not reached or is reached in distorted fashion. The boy who has sound limbs is "free" to walk, and in walking he exercises that "freedom." The lame boy is not so "free" to walk, and he exercises his "freedom" under "restraints."

As we shall see, especially in Chapters 14, 15, and 17, freedom as optimum fulfillment of a person's potential is a good description of what we shall call *ethical freedom*. But, as it seems to us, the biomorphic model of growth-to-maturity does not do justice to what actually goes on in the human being. The need for another notion of freedom may become clear as we criticize Fromm's conception of freedom.

II. *FREEDOM AS AGENCY IN CHOICE SITUATIONS*

Erich Fromm [2] saw that the human situation is drastically different from that of the animal. Man is free from the instinctive controls that give animals built-in safety equipment. Insecure, faced by a wide

---

[1] The word "must" may seem too strong here, but it is intended to convey the idea that what happens as a result of interaction between individual and environment would be entirely predictable if we knew fully what the past and present forces in a given situation are.

[2] See Chapter 4, pp. 76–81; 90–93.

range of possibilities available to him through the quality of more plastic physiological, emotional, and intellectual equipment, he is tempted to forfeit the freedom that would come in fulfilling his nature by looking for security in passive "cooperation" with others. Yet, the freedom his nature demands is a kind of creative participation that will often endanger present security.

Now, while the word "freedom" keeps on occurring in Fromm's thought, it is clear that it refers to different stages of development. As already hinted, it seems to be a word used to describe the two-fold fact (1) that man, because of the greater plasticity of his greater endowment, can perform more functions than an animal, and (2) that man will in fact be fulfilling his nature if he can escape the deformation and distortion that occur if he passively conforms to environmental pressures for the sake of security. "Freedom" thus means more plasticity and opportunity at one pole of development and actualization of potential at the other.

But if we leave the matter here, the essential biomorphic model of freedom is still in control. A dog has more plasticity and endowment than a tomato plant. If his dog nature is not cramped by too much domestication, let us say, he will be freer than a plant both in potential and in range of achievement. Although the word "chooses" often occurs in Fromm's and other psychologists' writings, it seems only to mean that the course of development did in fact take this rather than another form. But is this all that a human being means when he says that he chose to act rather than not to act in a certain way?

This may be the case, but it certainly does not allow for another way, and, we suggest, the usual way, that normal human beings experience choice. Built on the analogy with the changes that go on in plants and animals, it is at odds with another description of what freedom involves. In Western thought this other view was suggested in the "Myth of Er" in Plato's *Republic* and in the third book of Aristotle's *Nicomachean Ethics;* it was boldly set forth by St. Augustine and gained further influence through its exposition in the thought of Kant. This view, which we are about to present in our own way, is opposed to the biomorphic view of freedom and focuses on a kind of experience possible only to reflective and discriminating beings.

Do we experience ourselves always as a center of converging forces of which the most powerful has its own way? Often when a certain sequence of events is going on in us and when it would seem that a given convergence of forces is about to produce a result we do not approve, do we not find ourselves *willing* to alter that course, in accordance with the approved goal? Consider several examples, purposely put in the first person, because they involve introspective reports.

I am seated at a polite dinner party in a friend's home, I have enjoyed the food, and, while listening to a social lion speak of his many accomplishments, I suddenly find myself about to yawn. This chain reflex will indeed take priority over everything else, and it may so take me by surprise that "I couldn't do anything about it." But this very manner of expressing myself indicates that there are other times when "I," unable to control the initial phases of a physiological response, do find it possible to start other neuromuscular processes, which stifle the yawn.

This simple experience is a sample of the many other physiological events-in-process we find ourselves called upon to control and change: sneezing, hiccoughing, nodding, giggling, stumbling. We need simply to remind ourselves of the many "natural" physiological events that we ask the growing infant and child to control to realize how much we fully expect human beings to be able to initiate new processes of control, new directions of action, when other processes are already operative. In all such situations there would be no initiating were no plasticity possible.

But when I do have any plasticity I find that I can make some difference to the process-in-course by willing an end other than the one that was about to take place. Many times the end that I will does not ensue, but usually there is at least a delaying action. I may still be defeated five minutes later, but my willing served to release factors into that situation (*how* I do not know) that altered the situation.

Before turning to another illustration, let us formalize what is meant by "free will" in this other emerging model. On the occasion of a person's becoming aware of a situation going on in him of whose outcome, left to itself, he does not approve, he finds that he can initiate some alteration in accordance with another end of which he does approve. He may not succeed in achieving his approved goal, but as he observes himself from within, he knows that his act of willing has made some difference to the total state that he is experiencing.

Note, we are not saying that in willing he is free to do anything he may wish. A human being can will only within the limits prescribed by his total plastic and unplastic endowment. Furthermore, for him to be free in willing does not mean that he always succeeds in achieving the goal he approves. But it does mean that his willing in behalf of a certain goal not favored by the activity-in-process makes some difference to what ensues.

Accordingly, at such choice points, we cannot describe what happens to him without including his activity of willing. Let us see if this description of "free will" can apply to another more complicated level, such as that exemplified in the dynamics of prejudice as Allport describes it.

Because I want very much to be loved, I find myself feeling bitter and hostile generally ("toward everything") because I am not loved or approved by the people whom I want to love me. Let us say, following Allport,[3] that the total situation in my personality is plastic enough so that my tension can be resolved either by blaming myself or by blaming others. (I am assuming, although it probably is not true in the child, that to some extent I am consciously aware of these possibilities.) Let us say, further, that the cultural situation in which I live and my earlier home training make it convenient for me to resolve this tension extropunitively by developing a prejudice against Negroes. But now, having read psychological accounts of prejudice (like Allport's) and perhaps having had psychological counseling, I am aware that my attitude toward Negroes is prejudiced. The problem is: Knowing that I am prejudiced and, in part at least, why, can I do anything to change this prejudice in accordance with my ideal of fairness?

The situation becomes acute when I find that my fraternity brothers are considering inviting a Negro to join the fraternity. Much to my later chagrin, I find my first reaction negative, and I say "no" even before I have thought about it. But when asked why I object, I then find myself reconsidering the situation as I listen to discussion of the merits of the candidate. As I introspect, I find myself rebelling against the good things they are saying about this Negro; I don't like to hear them; I invariably minimize the good points; and I keep recalling all the bad things I have heard about Negroes—or I urge that this choice will not make friends for the fraternity. At the same time, I find myself annoyed at myself for harboring such ideas and acutely aware of my earlier resolve to be fair to every individual Negro I meet.

[3] *The Nature of Prejudice* (Reading, Mass.: Addison-Wesley, 1954), Chapter 9.

In a situation like this, which admittedly is oversimplified, does not the essential structure of many of our experiences come out? "I" seem to be a field of conflicting emotions and ideas, some for and some against a possible outcome. Yet if "I" let the situation "take care of itself," there is little doubt that my long past of prejudice, added to the present association with a Negro who does not catch my fancy, would mean that I would vote against him. At moments like this, William James's description is apropos: The reasoned ideal seems so helpless against the flow of passion and dislike.

Yet, it is exactly at times like this that I find I can at least will the ideal. I exert myself (in a way that can be experienced but not described) in favor of that ideal. William James would have said that at times like this my problem is to bring and keep the ideal I approve of in the focus of my consciousness. But whether or not this is an adequate description of the process by which "I" make an effect, there is no denying that when I will, I alter *to some extent* the stream of action that had "taken over" before I willed. Again, it is true that I do not always succeed in altering the situation enough to achieve the approved end, but no one who lives through this sort of conflict can deny that there is some inner *experienced* effect, if no overt behavioral victory. And, often, victory both in felt experience and in behavior does ensue, much to the surprise of the person himself—as when he finds that his will to endure unwanted pain and suffering for the sake of a larger end does win the day.

Let us see how this analysis of free will might apply to the problem of prejudice formation and reconstruction. There is no intention here of denying the psychological description of prejudice formation in terms of extropunitive response rather than intropunitive response. But to put the question bluntly: Did the person who blamed someone else do so simply because hostility has its way against the other possible emotional responses present? In Allport's description,[4] for example, no reference is made to the person's effort or will, and the assumption is made that the prejudice is the outcome of psychological processes regnant at that time. This may indeed be the true description in many instances, when the individual does not even get to the point of willing. But this is not the description of the only situation that can occur.

We submit that while from within the intropunitive and the extropunitive pathways are often seen as tempting possibilities, the in-

[4] See Peter A. Bertocci, "Gordon W. Allport's *The Nature of Prejudice* and the Problem of Choice," *Pastoral Psychology*, Vol. 5, No. 48, (Nov. 1954), 31–37.

dividual does not feel forced to take one. Furthermore, often, even at the moment when the individual feels himself to be a battlefield of conflicting impulses, his act of willing one goal brings relative order into the conflict that is going on. This act of willing is one of the factors producing the ensuing psychological situation. Thus the very fact that the experient makes the effort to be intropunitive, tries to take the blame on himself, rather than "scapegoat" the other fellow in the conflict situation, makes a difference to the total state of mind, for a period of time at least, even if the willed goal is finally defeated.

In asserting that often the conflict between wants, between emotional forces, is altered by the very *effort* of the experient in favor of an approved ideal, we are offering a different conception of "freedom" from the biomorphic one that begins with relative plasticity and ends with relative fulfillment. This freedom-in-fulfillment points to an important ideal, as we shall ourselves urge. But it leaves out of account the *moral freedom* that persons feel. Such free will, to use the traditional terminology, has been called "free" to emphasize at least three contentions: (a) such willing is part of the intrinsic capacity of a human being who has matured to the point where he can think alternatives, (b) such willing is an initiating influence in (many) human situations where alternatives seem possible, and (c) such initiating "will" is not *the product* of the rest of the personality's configuration of needs, wants, habits, abilities.

Few libertarians, as they have been called, have denied that the effectiveness of willing would not be influenced by the remaining regnant processes and possibilities within the personality. In other words, to believe in "free" will is not to believe that willing can effectuate any of its goals regardless of other factors in the personality and in the environment. Opponents of "free" will have talked as if belief in such freedom involved taking the act of willing out of the nexus of factors influencing each other in a person's life. But actually no such view is intended here. The insistence on freedom grows out of a common experience that persons have. Granted that factors from within and from outside may converge in their experience, they often feel the act of choosing as an additional aspect in the total situation, an act that has in fact often changed the future from what seemed to be the prospect before willing began.

At this point, the reader must be the final judge as to whether he does find himself having experiences in which this willed effort—which is different in its "feel" from "wanting to" or desiring—is a pervasive factor on those occasions in which he asserts himself, as it were, against the dominant tendency at a given juncture in his experience, and in favor of an approved, nondominant goal. One thing seems certain: if willing feels different from wanting, even as hearing a sound is different from seeing a color, that distinction must in fairness be made by any psychologist interested in clarifying what goes on. Even if we are wrong in saying that it is "free," that such willing introduces a new tone into the conscious state seems undeniable.

As for the "freedom" of the will, it also seems necessary to say that at the moment one is at work controlling the situation in the direction he sees fit, he certainly is not *conscious* of being forced to take this initiative, though he is conscious of a strain in which other factors in his situation are pitted against his willed end and often slow down or keep his initiative from succeeding.

It is, of course, always possible to *say* that the outcome is in fact predetermined by factors in his nature of which the person is not aware, that if we knew enough about every action we would know, for example, that the individual who thought he had a choice between being intropunitive and extropunitive actually had no choice, because the hostility due to being unloved had so piled up as to make no other issue possible. But to say this is to go behind the *experienced* situation and to postulate an unexperienced state of affairs in order to save the theory, gained from the nonhuman realm, that no event could in fact be different from what it is if we knew enough about it.

But why should this deterministic theory be credited when it seems to be in clear conflict with a simple experience like the following? I am tired, discouraged, and somewhat bitter because my motives have been misunderstood. At the same time, knowing that this is the state of affairs, and bringing to this state other feelings, thoughts, and ideals, I find it difficult but possible, say, to be polite but not forgiving. In such a situation I experience a freedom to alter and control a state which, without my willing, would end in my "flying off the handle."

True, as the example suggests, I am never quite sure in such situations how far I shall in fact be able to accomplish my approved goal— I do not know, to coin special phrases, how much *will-power* my *will-agency* can enjoy. But that I feel the will-agency making some difference as my effort makes itself felt, I cannot doubt.

These two terms, "will-agency" and "will-power," are introduced not because we have two discontinuous experiences, but to focus attention on two phases of the total psychological matrix in which willing is present. My initiating effort, will-agency, continues until the conflict is resolved in one way or another. For example, I keep putting one foot in front of another in that last quarter mile of the mountain climb despite aching back and fatigue; but this approved act is constantly opposed by every ache and the almost dizzying fatigue that soon may actually overpower my will-agency, with the result that I "give up" and sit down. Will-agency has will-power as "measured" roughly in terms of the efficacy that will-agency seems to have in the total situation.

This distinction is not unimportant. For, on the view here suggested, *freedom to initiate* action toward a goal (will-agency) is not the result of other factors in my past and present. The *freedom to effectuate* that goal in different degrees (will-power) is indeed influenced by the remaining factors in the situation. In other words, no scientistic or scientific psychologist, no ethicist, need fear that the will-agency can be a completely chaotic force in personality formation. Will-agency cannot break habits and attachments "at will," for will-agency is always hedged about, or works within, the total complex of "forces" that are at play within the personality at any given time.

Before turning to evaluate other important psychological considerations that have been advanced against free will in this sense, it will be well to review other relevant phases of the view being suggested.

III. *WILL-AGENCY, WILL-POWER, AND THE DEVELOPMENT OF PERSONALITY*

First, willing does not enter into experience until the person is mature enough to become aware of alternatives.[5] Unless an individual can think of possibilities, he cannot but wait dumbly for conflicting tendencies in his nature to come to a head and pass into the future— in the way that the future growth of a plant or animal emerges from the ingredients biologically needed for self-maintenance. Will-agency is usually not involved when wanting or desiring by themselves will bring about an approved objective. I do not will to be friendly and

[5] See Peter A. Bertocci, "The Moral Structure of the Person," *Review of Metaphysics*, Vol. XIV, No. 3 (March 1961), 369–88.

fair when my desire can carry me to that end. But let my desire to be friendly meet an obstacle—other desires, other habits, and possible harm—and I find myself pulled up short. I may, on consideration, still approve of being friendly, but these desires, habits, and circumstances still stand opposed to that end. Judging from the experienced situation, friendliness will not result if "I" do not intervene. It then seems that I have to shift gears "psychologically" in order to initiate effort in favor of the friendliness I still approve of, even though opposing desires threaten it.

But in willing the friendliness that my desire would ordinarily have carried through, I have introduced a new tone into my experience. Yet insofar as I get anywhere with my "initiative," I do not feel as if I am adding anything that is not "myself" to the struggle. My effort does not take *nothing* and make *something* out of it, as some opponents of free will seem to fear. I do "pull myself together" ("oomph," to use C. I. Lewis's expression [6]): I find other ideas, feelings, or desires released in me, which I might not have experienced otherwise unless I had "turned" to support the approved goal. It is as if I were a general deploying forces I had but was not using purposefully.

The "will," then, as will-agency is not a "faculty," a "part" of me. It is my self initiating a course of action that would not have occurred unless the will-agency (rather than want-agency) had taken hold. Will-agency is one kind of activity that a person can perform under conditions in which, presented with alternatives, a person initiates action in favor of the approved end at that moment.

Second, will-agency does not guarantee the outcome by itself. Although no simile is adequate, will-agency in a given situation may be compared to a coiled spring pressing against restraining factors. Will-agency has, at that particular point, all the other components of the personality to deal with. Some components may be on the side of the approved alternative; and others on the other side may be stronger than anticipated. Some patterns of need, feeling, and ability are stronger than others. A person with well-established prejudices, with strong attachments of a propriate sort, is not going to find it easy to break their hold when they are involved in a choice situation. Actually the agent himself cannot know how much will-power will-agency can have in the crucible of his personality at any particular point.

[6] See C. I. Lewis, *The Ground and Nature of Right* (New York: Columbia University Press, 1955).

We can now ask: For what then can we hold the person morally responsible? Only, it seems to us, for changes in his life that, as far as anyone can tell, are or have been within his power (will-power) to make, *granted that* he has exerted will-agency. Again, moral responsibility (as opposed to legal or any other kind) rests on him to do (will-agency) the very best he can do (will-power) in any situation wherein alternatives are possible. It is by no means clear, in many situations at least, whether a person had alternatives and what he could actually succeed in doing. It is well to be cautious in assigning moral responsibility, but that moral responsibility exists seems clear.

This view of will-agency and will-power does not deny that there are factors in a person's unconscious that are involved in determining the outcome of the struggle in the choice situation. But what is denied is that the influence of unconscious forces or motives is such that what eventually happens at the conscious level is the sheer working out of the struggle below the surface. Although this may sometimes indeed be the situation with regard to some specific act, the acceptance of this *complete determinism* for all acts outruns the known facts.

But it is important to give this general position its due, so we shall here examine the thesis that the so-called conscious will cannot in fact change the course of psychic events. As John Hospers puts it:

> We talk about free-will, and we say, for example, the person is free to do so-and-so if he can do so *if* he wants to—and we forget that his wanting to is itself caught up in the stream of determinism, that unconscious forces drive him into wanting or not wanting to do the thing in question.[7]

On our view, the verb "will" would be substituted for "want" in

[7] John Hospers, "Meaning and Free-Will," *Philosophy and Phenomenological Research*, X (1950), 321; and reprinted in part as "Free-Will and Psychoanalysis," in *Readings in Ethical Theory*, ed. Wilfred Sellars and John Hospers (New York: Appleton-Century-Crofts, Inc., 1952), pp. 560–75. The discussion in the text will not be limited to Hospers' article, but is indebted to this excellent presentation of what may only roughly and loosely be called a psychoanalytic theory of unconscious motivation, since this particular denial of freedom is neither necessitated by psychoanalytic doctrine nor held exclusively by psychoanalysis. The reader is also referred to *Freedom and Determinism*, ed. Sidney Hook (New York: New York University Press, 1958), for presentations of different perspectives. One of the best recent extensive treatments of the problem is Austin Farrer's *The Freedom of the Will* (New York: Charles Scribner's Sons, 1958). For a brief but excellent presentation of a libertarian position, see C. A. Campbell, *Selfhood and Godhood* (New York: The Macmillan Company, 1957), Chapter IX.

this quotation, for willing is not a kind of wanting any more than wanting is a kind of thinking. But let us examine the psychoanalytic view at closer range.

IV. *DOES UNCONSCIOUS CAUSATION JUSTIFY PSYCHOLOGICAL DETERMINISM?*

We are already familiar with the doctrine that the conscious ego developed out of the stormy libidinous unconscious for the sake of effecting compromise between the insistent pleasure-seeking of the libido and the demands of the physical and social environment. But as this ego developed during uncritical childhood days, it was forced to depend upon mother-father-social forces, whose demands came to form a fairly rigid set of inhibitions that acted as a block to many of the impulses and desires of the unconscious. We need not be confined to the Freudian view of the unconscious-conscious connection to grant that the relatively uncritical solutions of conflict in early years form a strong bulwark, for good or ill, with which the conscious ego faces future need fulfillment. But is it true, as some proponents of psychic determinism would hold, that both our acts of will and the deliberations leading to them "are but facades for the expression of unconscious wishes, or rather, unconscious compromises and defenses"? [8]

There are many case histories in the records that read as if this were the only way in which the action of an individual could be explained. Is a man a gambler? Does he lose his own money, his wife's, and become impoverished? Let us assume that it might seem that *he* had decided to stop gambling but later returned to it. It might seem to him that *he* decided to go back to gambling. As Hospers suggests, what this man does not know is that he is still trying to punish his mother for her denial of his infantile wishes. He is rejecting all the things identified with her who had "trained" him so well presumably. Further analysis shows that equilibrium could not be maintained in the underground struggle between the superego and the libido. For while he is successful in rebelling by gambling, the fact that he cannot quit while winning is the punishment the superego is demanding of the "naughty" gambler.

It would be easy to multiply instances of this sort in which sup-

[8] Sellars and Hospers, *Readings in Ethical Theory*, p. 564.

posedly "free" conduct can be traced back to patterns of response or "mechanisms of adjustment" that were developed as compromises early in life and now have right of way. What we must ask is whether such tracing back does not beg the question at issue. What is assumed is that a libertarian position such as ours cannot do justice to such facts. Let us see whether our interpretation is controverted by known fact.

To begin with, the person who feels free (to any extent) does *feel* free, and he is convinced that as long as he wills, his willing is a factor in the present matrix of consciousness, whatever the extent of its efficacy may be. For us as observers to tell him that he is not feeling free is like telling someone who is experiencing pleasure that he is not. Whatever, then, the past may be, whatever in the unconscious is pressing on consciousness, the moment a conflict does reach the present, the moment the agent believes an alternative is possibly open to him in the situation that he is now experiencing, at that moment he can act willfully (will-agency). This is the minimum that must be granted, whatever the final consequences of his willing (will-power) may be.

What can be called in question is the amount of power free will has. A person may be wrong about the probable outcome of his freedom and yet feel free. As we have said, whatever the extent to which he tries in the direction he approves, he may be fighting a delaying but finally ineffective action. In the terminology suggested above, his will-agency, contending with psychic patterns too strong for it, may find that it does not have the will-power to win that particular battle. But to believe in free will is not to believe that one wins at all choice points, but only that one is not the complete victim of nonwilled forces in one's personality and in the environment. When asked "Why don't you control your temper?" an irascible man replied, "You'll never know how much of my temper I *do* control."

Let us, then, apply this reasoning to the example of the gambler, who did stop for a while before beginning to gamble all over again. On our view, this example might well indicate that will-agency did have the power, for a while at least, to stop the disapproved action and then was forced to capitulate to stronger oppositions. Such intervals of discontinuance, to be followed by continuance, are common in the life of many inveterate smokers and drinkers. Their stopping too could presumably be explained away by saying that during such periods the superego was in fact in control, only to be upset once more by the cunning libido. And there is no infallible proof that this could not be the case.

To make the same basic point in another way. Suppose we assume that the personality structure is fixed, if not by the age of two, then assuredly by the age of five. Indeed, let us say that a masochistic neurosis has already set in by the age of five, so that, as Hospers puts it, "the masochistic snowball was on its course downhill long before we or anybody else knew what was happening, and long before anyone could do anything about it." [9] Does it indeed follow that the individual can be said to be a mere puppet, moved henceforth by this masochistic style of life? Will every conscious decision be in fact controlled by this subterranean neurotic streak? Or can he sometimes resist the more obvious manifestations of his own obsession? We are struck by the degree to which neurotics who cannot control the compulsion as a whole can and do control specific expressions of it.

Again, we cannot tell about the individual case; we cannot tell beforehand what changes can be effectuated by will-agency. But let us remember that to the extent that psychoanalytic treatment ever helps an individual to change his psychological orientation, it does so presumably because other latent "bottled up" factors in the total person are freed to have more effect on the undesired trend. Well and good, but once the individual is thus "freed" by removing emotional blocks, once the ego is where the id was, is not the individual once more confronted by the problem of making those choices in his life that will not send him back to his masochistic orientation?

In other words, in psychoanalytic thought, we take it, the ground for wanting the ego (reason) to be where the id was is so that *alternatives* will be open to the individual, which, presumably, he can deal with more effectively—in our terms, his conscious will-agency can have more power than it had. Were this not so, were there no more relative freedom in choosing, the process of psychoanalysis would simply be the transaction whereby the prisoner, released from one set of chains, finds himself bound by another set. Again, psychoanalytic process of "freeing" simply means, if psychic determinism is granted, that the prisoner is freed from a gloomy cell of the dungeon

[9] *Ibid.*, p. 568.

in which he is, to a brighter cell perhaps, but he himself does not choose any alternative that reason may light up. In which case, the whole point of having reason enter the dungeon vanishes. The subject is still the victim of changing factors in his nature and to no extent an agent who can deploy these factors in accordance with an approved future. If this is all that can ever take place in personality —an alteration of forces with no willed changes possible—another conclusion follows that destroys psychoanalysis as a science, but we shall turn to this later.

For the moment we re-enforce an earlier hint by a direct question. Does it follow that because a person has developed a masochistic unconscious trend, no more freedom remains within his person-ality? Surely a masochist still has choices even within the trend of his masochistic orientation, let alone the areas of his life that may be relatively untouched by this psychic structure. Masochistic he is, but is there only one way in which the expression of that masochism is predetermined?

Again, granted that a homosexually oriented personality may have no freedom for heterosexual response, is there no freedom left in his personality? The choices of a confirmed homosexual do not include the range of heterosexual possibilities, to be sure. But is he excluded from the range of preferences and alternatives within his homosexual orientation?

Let us assume that his homosexuality is a symptom of serious emotional maladjustment of constitutional nature and could not be changed even by psychoanalysis and that will-agency is impotent to alter it. May he *as* a homosexual not have (a) choice to give in, or not, to all instances of homosexual temptation, (b) choice of his partners, and (c) choice in the other areas of action both related to and remote from this trend? In a word, while his total life problem will indeed be significantly affected by his homosexuality, he still has areas of choice.

To generalize: Although persons with fixed neurotic trends no doubt experience a shrinking of the horizon of choices, and although their problem is no doubt more difficult because forces presumably beyond their control are at work, their situation is not basically different from that of the person who has been incapacitated by an accident or by such an illness as a stroke or a heart ailment. That is, their choices in the future will be within a different framework. But to say that they have no freedom is simply to allow a deterministic doctrine to dictate what experience is rather than allowing experience to guide doctrine.

With the distinction between will-agency and will-power in mind, it may be possible to provide a meaningful interpretation of the kind of situation in which psychological literature abounds. We are told of persons who, having been subjected to rather traumatic experiences in early life—such as premature weaning or the loss of needed parent—spend the rest of their lives trying to regain a lost state or trying to ferret out some new way of preserving their egos in altered social situations. In each instance we cannot tell how much will-power there will be, but to deny will-agency is to simplify the inner situation, contrary to experience. The person may indeed not feel responsible for his neurosis, but he may feel responsible for what he does with the possibilities still left open, given that neurosis.

Psychic determinism, then, is hardly a foregone conclusion or the most probable inference from the fact that what we are at any time is the product of (unknown) inherited psychophysiological limits and the course of maturation and learning. From this fact, determinism follows only if will-agency is eliminated from our natures to begin with. But what empirical data are left unexplained if we hold that as an infant's capacities mature and as he becomes able to think alternatives, he also finds himself having will-agency to direct his inherited dispositions and his present learning within the limits of his total nature and the environmental situations? He may at many moments of choice believe that he can do more than he may actually be allowed to do by latent learned and constitutional "structures," and he cannot himself know when he will meet obstacles that will impede the realization of his approved goals.

But only mere theory *not based on anything we as persons actually experience* can hold that the experience of freedom is itself everywhere determined by underground forces or that it is also an experience determined by these forces to be utterly ineffectual. For what we experience is considerable freedom to guide and control our activities in many areas and little if any freedom to alter our course of development in others. Neither the determinist nor the libertarian can move from *some* to *all* without going against experience to the contrary. On the other hand, if we are to take the conscious life at all seriously, indeed, if the reasoning ego is to become even a Freudian aid to the unconscious, it cannot be completely determined in its action by the unconscious.

V. *DOES DETERMINISM UNDERMINE THE SEARCH FOR TRUTH?*

We have come to the threshold of the most devastating of the consequences of psychic determinism. For if "the unconscious is the master of every fate and the captain of every soul," [10] there is no longer any foundation for trust in the truth of any conclusion. That is, if conscious deliberations and conclusions are the products only of the strongest factors in the unconscious complex at a given moment, is there any ground left for trusting the deliberations of one man more than those of another? Indeed, why should we trust a psychoanalyst's conclusions about his patient's troubles more than the patient's? For the psychoanalyst's conclusions are not the result of an unbiased search for truth, but the consequences of the chain of events in his unconscious over which he has no rational control. If there is no will-agency, if a person, further, has no will-power to control his inquiry by the demands of logic or of the evidence, why should he trust his own conclusions? Because of the supposed control of every factor in a person's life by his unconscious, or by present stimuli and past habits for that matter, the consequences of the denial of will-agency are much more serious than they seem on the surface, and we must be sure to understand why.

We are not, of course, suggesting that there is among human beings any completely unbiased judgment, based on what "the evidence itself" demands. Every given instance of an "objective" judgment may well be surveyed with the possibility in mind that, despite the competence of the judge, the judgment is more in tune with logic and evidence. But surely the ideal we have in mind for any "true" judgment is that, "as far as humanly possible," the competent observer controls his own predilections enough to come to a conclusion based on the available evidence. To the extent that we think a person has "a special ax to grind" to that extent do we become all the more critical of his conclusions in an area where that ax can be ground. And we know that, no matter how well trained we may be in given areas, we need to watch ourselves when we come to conclusions that involve our loves and our hates. In short, the more complicated problems become and the more value-involved the

[10] *Ibid.,* p. 572.

issues are, the more do we demand both judgment of competently trained persons and independent judgment from a panel of judges representing different basic perspectives on the values involved.

But, again, why all this fuss about "allowing the evidence to speak for itself" if every human conclusion is in fact compelled only by the strongest or psychologically most compelling run of events in the past and in the present? All our precautions to protect "truth" are of no avail if the unconscious, be it benevolent or malevolent,[11] is forcing conclusions based on its nature rather than on the relatively impartial scrutiny of events? If the truth-seeker cannot think —and we mean by "think" the consistent relating of evidence to the hypothesis involved—or if, at the very point at which he no longer wants to think lest the evidence lead to a disliked conclusion, he is unable to go on thinking, his conclusion may be no more than the cunning sputtering of hidden and unconscious motivation. If a person cannot "think twice" and review his conclusion in the light of evidence and logic, there is that much less ground for trusting his conclusion. Nor is there any point to urging that public observation and checking is better than private for there is no longer any ground for supposing that the judges involved can hold themselves to the requirements of truth as opposed to capitulating to the strong psychological stream of events within them.

VI. *FREE WILL, PRAISE, ADMIRATION, AND OBLIGATION*

We close this chapter by gathering the main lines of our discussion and making several distinctions that need to be observed.

First, the possibility of free will in human beings presupposes plasticity in the physiological and psychic capabilities of each person in his varying environments, but it is not a synonym for the fact of variability. In thinking of human freedom, it is not enough to say, as Dobzhansky does well to remind us, that "there is no such thing as a purely inherited or a purely environmental trait, since all traits arise during the process of development." [12] The issue with regard to human free will concerns the possibility of the person's directing his growth, within the limits of his internal and external "givens,"

[11] *Ibid.*, p. 575.
[12] Theodosius Dobzhansky, *The Biological Basis of Human Freedom* (New York: Columbia University Press, 1956), p. 23.

in accordance with an envisaged goal. A person cannot *become* what the limits of his nature and of his environment do not allow; free will does not mean that he can never successfully *will* what his nature, given and acquired, does not allow.

But the crucial difference between plant, animal, and human being is not merely in potentiality but in man's capacity to learn from the past as he thinks out possible solutions to problems he confronts. As thinker, the person is a moral agent at one point at least, namely, at the point at which he must try to decide what to think in the light of the data available. If what he thinks is determined entirely by his strongest desires, or by his prepotent associations, there is no ground for trusting his conclusions concerning the data. In his decision to think rather than be victimized by psychological associations, or in his decision not to think and to allow psychological associations to take over, every person takes a step of great importance for the rest of his moral judgments and actions.[13]

Second, while we never know accurately how circumscribed the power of will-agency may be, will-agency does influence the course of a life in the sense suggested—that is, if the end contemplated and willed had not been willed, some other course of action would have ensued. As one's will-agency tries to realize a goal, it may be pushed from pillar to post, by the structures that pile up in personality. But even the neurotic and the crippled have some choices in the areas left open in their lives.

Third, on this view, then, *will-agency is that capacity of a person* (who has reached the point at which he can be in conflict and envisage "a way out") *to effect a change that is consistent with the approved end of the moment of choice. Will-power is the amount of change that can be effectuated as seen from the point of view of the end contemplated.* To say that a person has no will-power is to say that he cannot effectuate approved objectives in any discernible degree. To say that he has no will-agency is to say that whatever occurs in his life, be it thinking, desiring, or acting, is simply the denouement of converging forces without any reference to a critically approved end (for criticism itself here is meaningless).

Fourth, while we may admire or disapprove actions, we blame or praise them also only if, and to the extent that, we believe that they are fully chosen and in accord with the ethical ideal we ourselves

---

[13] For further discussion, see the first chapter in Peter A. Bertocci, *Free Will, Responsibility, and Grace* (New York: Abingdon Press, 1957).

approve. Do we not often admire and praise a person for the same action? For example, we may admire the rich man for putting a fistful of bills into the collection plate and we may praise him also; we may admire the accomplishments of a brilliant student and we may praise him also. But frequently we find ourselves admiring a certain action without feeling that we can praise (morally approve of) the action. Thus we admire the giving of much money to charity and yet find ourselves unable to praise the man for so doing *unless* (a) we believe that he did not have to do it, but chose to, (b) we agree with the motive behind his giving, and (c) we believe, according to our ethical standard, that the amount of the gift was appropriate. Again we admire the brilliant student who "so easily" masters difficult material, but we do not praise him morally unless we think that (a) he does not have to apply the unusual ability he has, and (b) he can apply it otherwise than for the accomplishment of which we approve.

It seems clear then that we confine (moral) praise and (moral) blame to actions that we approve or disapprove in accordance with our ethical standard and that we believe were fully chosen by the moral agent. We never feel justified in blaming a person for not doing what, as far as we know, it simply is not in him to do. We may be wrong—and how frequently and fatefully we are wrong!—about what another is "free" to do, but there is little doubt that we blame him in accordance with the degree to which we believe he was free to do other than he did and in accordance with our conception of what ought to have been done by him in that situation.

Thus, the notion of free choice takes us to the consideration of what the ethical standard is by which men ought to judge themselves and others as they seek to discover what the good life is, given their wants and abilities and their will-agency. We cannot assume that one ought to fulfill his nature and thus achieve *ethical freedom*. The careful consideration of this problem lies ahead. But we now need to ask: What is involved in the experience of obligation?

VII. *REFLECTIVE SUMMARY*

Many thinkers, including our psychologists, conceive of human freedom on a biomorphic model, as optimum fulfillment of potential for growth. But this biomorphic model does not do justice to the human experience in which a person, feeling a conflict of forces in himself, alters the unapproved course by initiating action toward an end he does approve.

Such moral freedom, we suggest, is not itself a product of other formations in personality. It is a native capacity or function of a person capable of reflection. This initiating effort persists along with other formations in personality and its effectiveness is therefore influenced by them. But its own action is a formative factor in the matrix of personality development at a reflective level—even though the person does not succeed in achieving his approved goal.

More analytically, will-agency is not a separate part of a person's life; it is an activity of the person that "feels" as different from impulse, want, or desire, and it often operates against the impact of their power. Still, the power that will-agency actually develops in a given situation is a by-product of the complex factors operating in personality at a given stage.

This fact, that the person's will may operate with and within a total complex of personality should discourage some determinists' fears that if "free will" exists there might be chaos in personality. Indeed, a person can be held morally responsible only for changes in his life that have been and are in his power to effect. A person may be wrong about the probable outcome of his choice and yet feel free to effect the actual outcome, even if he does not finally succeed in doing so to any appreciable extent. Indeed, a person may be incapable of warding off a neurosis but still be capable of influencing its concrete expression at some point.

There are more far-reaching consequences of the denial of free choice than are usually realized. If there is neither will-agency nor will-power, the psychoanalytic process is in fact a farce, because whatever liberation of reason from past emotional blocks might be effected by psychotherapy would still leave the patient the victim of the strongest psychic formations in his life. Indeed, if everyone's actions are completely determined by such formations in personality, why should one trust a psychiatrist's conclusions more than the patient's? For if determinism is true, we cannot assume that the psychiatrist is free to be impartial in his analysis of the patient. If the analyst's conclusions are guided not by the evidence but by regnant predilections, why trust him?

If a man is completely determined by the strongest forces in his life and if he cannot depend upon himself ever to give reasonable interpretations, he can never be a "truth-finder" in any area of experience. Blame and praise, as opposed to admiration and condemnation, are not justified; for moral responsibility presupposes not abilities alone but the capacity to use them, within limits, for ends that the person reflectively approves. It must still be remembered, however, that if a man is free to choose between alternatives (moral freedom), the problem he faces is to choose those ends that do allow him *ethical freedom,* that is, the optimum fulfillment of his potential.

9

The Human Experience of Obligation

Let us visualize a domestic situation. A husband is shaving as his wife prepares breakfast. He smells the toast burning and knows that his wife is not in the kitchen. Suppose that he unhurriedly continues to shave, with the result that the toast is burnt to a crisp and the kitchen fills with smoke, thus adding to his wife's work.

Even this simple situation moves us to a very interesting form of judgment. We do not stop with the observation: "The toast was burning while he was shaving." That sentence describes what occurred. What we find ourselves adding is: "He ought to have stopped shaving and taken out the toast." This judgment refers to what *has happened* but also asserts that this state of affairs *ought not* to be! When we say "ought" we have in mind not a situation that *is taking place,* not one we *want* to take place, but one that we believe ought to occur, whether we want it or not.

What does this situation tell us about our nature? A husband fails to rescue burning toast, thus allowing waste to take place and adding to his wife's distress. Why do we add an "ought" response? Why do we not simply add: "We do not want this to happen"? What we do say is: It *ought* not to happen. And when we feel "ought" in a situation, we are "bothered" in a way that is different from the disturbance we feel when we do not *want* a certain state of affairs.

Human beings, we generalize, are not satisfied simply to let things happen. Something in them sometimes rebels. In some situations they do not simply *think* that it *could* be otherwise or simply *want*

198

it to be otherwise. They say it *ought* to be otherwise, and by "otherwise," they mean "better." In such situations they feel "obligatoriness"—a peculiar command or imperative to seek something better.

This ought-imperative, as we may call this experience, is so direct that it seems impossible that there should be so much disagreement about its function in human experience. We shall in this chapter outline four interpretations of this experience.

I. *OUGHT AS THE IMPERATIVE*
   TO ALTRUISM

It was Bishop Joseph Butler, about two hundred years ago, who insisted that conscience, as he called the ought-function, is different from any other passion. Why? For when the passions are in conflict, the strongest passion wins. Conscience never overcomes passion by sheer power. Present in the struggle between competing passions, the ought-imperative simply "sits in judgment," as it were, and expects to be obeyed without forcing obedience. Conscience does not overcome passion as, for example, fear overcomes anger or anger overcomes sympathy. Yet it never fails to have authority! In Butler's own words, conscience "magisterially exerts itself," [1] for what it condemns is wrong even if conscience is disobeyed. A condemned desire, in other words, may get its way but not be approved.

As Butler sees it, then, more than a power struggle between passions goes on in man. The end of a particular battle, with the strongest passion winning out, does not tell the whole story. It makes all the difference in the world whether the winning factor was *right* in winning. This, says Butler, is what we mean by the "moral nature of man" or "his real proper nature." To win without conscience on the side of the victor is not to win, but, in a peculiar way, to lose.

We are not here concerned to expound or to grant everything Bishop Butler said about conscience, but can there be any doubt about the human situation as thus far depicted? Human nature is not simply a battleground of opposing desires and needs. It is a battlefield between desires that are deemed right and wrong, good and bad. We do not simply feel the conflict of desires; nor do we simply judge them right or wrong. We experience the "demand" that right

[1] *Five Sermons*, Sermons II, Section 8 (New York: Liberal Arts Press, 1950), p. 38.

ought to win, even when it does not. The ought-imperative still stands even if it does not win the day. Butler expresses this aspect of his view in a passage whose last lines are eloquent:

> Thus that principle by which we survey and either approve or disapprove our own heart, temper, and actions, is not only to be considered as what is in its turn to have some influence, which may be said of every passion, of the lowest appetites, but likewise as being superior; as from its very nature manifestly claiming superiority over all others, insomuch that you cannot form a notion of this faculty, conscience, without taking in judgment, direction, superintendency. This is a constituent part of the idea, that is, of the faculty itself; and to preside and govern, from the very economy and constitution of man, belongs to it. *Had it strength, as it has right; had it power, as it has manifest authority, it would absolutely govern the world.*[2]

Butler, in fact, went beyond this conviction that conscience is authoritative if not compelling. He held that conscience claims authority for a particular moral verdict, namely, altruism. We are not concerned to agree or disagree with this verdict now. For we wish in this chapter to focus attention not on the subject of the ought-imperative, but on its peculiar magisterial authority. Note that if two persons disagree about a given verdict, or *what ought* to be done, each still insists that his verdict *ought* to be followed. In other words, there may be argument about *what* one ought to do, but there is no argument about the fact that what a person believes to be right is felt by him to be obligatory.

II. *OBLIGATION AS AN AUTHORITATIVE GUIDE TO THE UNIVERSAL GOOD*

Actually when we come to Kant's view of obligation it is almost impossible to separate *what* one ought to do from the feeling of *ought,* but we shall still do so. Kant would agree with Butler that conscience claims authority "without so much as knowing in what degrees of *strength* the several principles prevail or which of them have

---

[2] *Ibid.,* p. 41 (italics added). From *Five Sermons* by Joseph Butler, copyright ©️ 1950, by The Liberal Arts Press, Inc., and reprinted by permission of the The Liberal Arts Press Division of The Bobbs-Merrill Company, Inc.

actually the greatest influence." [3] Butler, to be sure, believed that altruism found support both in our want-nature and our ought-nature. Kant would not assert such harmony. But both Kant and Butler agreed that the authority of obligation does not spring from the want-function.

Thus, Kant points out that when we feel obligated to act, we do not act *from* want or inclination. We might also *want* to do what we are doing from obligation, but the experience of obligation is not rooted in our inclination. What is more, the feeling that we have is different. For example, I may like the taste of the medicine I take for an illness, and the fact that I like it does not, in itself, make the act wrong or bad. But the total psychic tone is of one sort when I both like the medicine *and* feel that it is my duty to take it; it is different when I take the medicine even though I do not like it. In both experiences, however, there is something peculiarly the same. Kant refers to this peculiar psychic tone in duty or "ought" in these words: "Respect is a feeling . . . specifically distinct from all feelings—which may be referred either to inclination or fear," though "it has something analogous to both." [4]

Kant has other things to say about what the basis of this feeling of respect is (we have omitted them purposely here). But we must emphasize that this respect, in Kant's mind, does *not* spring from an inclination, positive or negative. Why? Kant replies: ". . . I cannot have respect for inclination, whether my own or another's; I can at most, if my own, approve it; if another's, sometimes even love it, that is, look on it as favorable to my own interests." [5]

Kant does not stop his description here. But is he not correct in asserting that we do not respect ourselves if we do only what we want *because* we want it, without further consideration? And is it not also true that we never *respect* ourselves for doing that which we *must* do, either out of the strongest positive wish or the strongest fear.

Yet if respect does not attend positive inclination or fear as such, what does it accompany? Kant answers: rational law.

[3] *Ibid.*, p. 12.
[4] Immanuel Kant, *Fundamental Principles of the Metaphysics of Morals* (New York: Liberal Arts Press, 1949), p. 19. Because this respect in Kant's view is not connected with any feeling or emotion, this use of the word "respect" must be distinguished from our use in Chapter 9 when we described respect-submission as an emotional orientation to any object of admiration, not of fear. The psychic tone Kant has in mind might be called *moral respect.*
[5] *Ibid.*, p. 18.

But although respect is a feeling, it is not a feeling *received* through influence, but is *self-wrought* by a rational concept, and, therefore, is specifically distinct from all feelings of the former kind, which may be referred either to inclination or fear. What I recognize immediately as a law for me, I recognize with respect.[6]

Kant here seems to have his finger on certain important facts about ourselves. He is saying that we can respect a rational law because it is not forced upon us but is thought out by us. If I find myself liking certain persons, I am under the control of a habit, and I may continue to like them and favor them. But suppose I think about these persons and can say to myself that whether I like them or not, they are worthy of favor. I may then go on favoring them on both grounds, my liking and my rational approval. But it is the second, the idea of their worth, that I can impose upon myself, saying: "I ought to favor these persons, whether I like them or not." It is the second that produces *respect,* not the first.

Yet, a further step is required in Kant's view, if the action is to be worthy of respect. The action must be in accordance with a principle that I would be willing to have enforced upon me if I were in the other person's place; that is, a principle applicable to all persons at that choice point. We must be able to think that action according to this principle is worth any person's approval when he thinks about it clearly. Thus Kant says:

What I recognize immediately as a law for me, I recognize with respect. . . . The immediate determination of the will by the law, and the consciousness of this, is called *respect,* so that this [respect] is regarded as an *effect* of the law on the subject, and not as the *cause* of it.[7]

Clearly, Kant is saying that the occasion for respect is not a law forced upon us (like the law of gravitation) but a law we have thought out (not made up arbitrarily) and approved. This law we are not *forced* to obey but feel we *ought* to obey even if we do not. Note also that the respect we feel does not create the law; the law is the occasion for our feeling respect. Again, as Kant puts it: "The

    [6] *Ibid.,* p. 19. From *Fundamental Principles of the Metaphysics of Morals* by Immanuel Kant, copyright © 1949, by The Liberal Arts Press, Inc., and reprinted by permission of The Liberal Arts Press Division of The Bobbs-Merrill Company, Inc.
    [7] *Ibid.,* p. 19.

object of respect is the *law* only, that is, the law which we impose on *ourselves,* and yet recognize as necessary in itself." [8]

When Kant speaks of a moral law "necessary in itself" as the sources of our respectful response, what does he have in mind? Well, would we have *respect* for sincere friends just because someone told us that we know from past experience that sincere friends are helpful? Such a generalization from past experience might be true, but would it be authoritative? Would not authoritativeness depend upon our being able to say that all persons ought to respect sincere friends whether we or they like it or not? We are not approving or disapproving of this particular statement, but simply using it to illustrate what we believe Kant means when he says that we can only respect and impose upon ourselves actions in accordance with rational law.

It is this same line of reasoning that leads Kant to say that we cannot hold up a specific "exemplary" person as a moral proof of an ethical ideal. To enjoin a person: "See how Lincoln acted? Do likewise!" is to forget, Kant would say, that a person cannot respect an example without respecting the principle thereby exemplified. But the universal principle in turn cannot be based on what human beings have done or are doing, but only on what would apply universally to every kind of rational person, finite or infinite.

We shall not here try to define further what such moral imperatives require in Kant.[9] Our concern now is to focus on the fact that, as Kant sees human nature, the ought-function has the same magisterial authority noted by Butler, even if it has not the power to effectuate itself. The ought-imperative, they both agree, is not constituted by or derived from any of the want-urges of our lives. Butler, however, believed that our moral consciousness is a "reflective" awareness of our duty to be altruistic. Kant held that the respect involved in moral obligation was rooted in universal and necessary principles. It may be that Kant is wrong in linking moral obligation only to principles (in his sense) of action. But it is unfortunate, we believe, to neglect Kant's differentiation of moral respect simply because we cannot agree with the total analysis of the conditions under which it occurs. It may well be that Kant, convinced that respect could not issue from want-urges, is wrong in holding that only a reason that does not depend upon the guidance of past experience can be authoritative. We repeat: it is one thing to disagree about

[8] *Ibid.*
[9] See Chapter 21.

what it is to which we feel obligation; it is another to deny the peculiar kind of magisterial authority, whatever the particular oughts to which it is tied. That there is an authoritative, yet not compelling imperative, in experience seems clear, whatever the changes in the specific end or ideal to which we feel obligated.

By and large, moral philosophers have been so intent on discovering *what* it was to which one feels obligated that they have, with Kant, assumed that there was some particular attribute of the object that made it obligatory. They analogized thus: Just as one sees red, presumably because the object seen is red, so one feels obligation when and only when the object is seen as obligatory. Now this may be the truth. But it may also be true that one feels the ought-imperative toward an unspecified goal or object.

We shall say more about this later. What is worthy of repetition here is that persons who disagree about the specific objects of conscience still feel equally conscientious about the ends that they believe are obligatory. This suggests, at least, that obligatoriness is not the effect of the object as such, but a state produced in the subject when any object or end is viewed in a certain way. And, as we shall suggest, the experience of obligatoriness, this feeling of respect or magisterial authority, must be affirmed as a function of human nature regardless how much persons disagree about what it is that is imperative.

As an historical fact, however, many moralists and psychologists have seemed to argue: "If persons can disagree about what the object of obligation is, it must be because there is nothing in human nature itself that is uniquely moral. Therefore, both this magisterial authoritativeness, and any object to which it is directed, had better be considered to be the result of learning and training." This is the view that we have met among some of our psychologists, and we must reconsider it in this context.

III. OUGHT AS INTERNALIZED MONITOR OF SOCIETAL NORMS

Freud, we remember, held that the function of the superego is to relieve the conscious ego of sole concern for resolving unpleasant conflicts by squelching trouble-promising libidinous impulses before they could cause disturbance. The superego, however, does not start out with some special mandates of its own. What it objects to, or allows, depends entirely on the prohibitions and permissions of the social situation in which the person has been reared.

Running through Freud's thought is the unargued but basic conviction that right and wrong are to be determined by the "pleasure-principle which draws up the programme of life's purpose." [10] This search for "happiness," as he calls it, has a positive phase and a negative one: ". . . it aims on the one hand at eliminating pain and discomfort, on the other at the experience of intense pleasures." [11] As Freud sees it, this pleasure principle or program "dominates the operation of the mental apparatus from the very beginning." It is bound to cause anxiety because it is "in conflict with the whole world. . . . It simply cannot be put into execution, the whole constitution of things runs counter to it." [12]

This "programme" will be threatened by the weaknesses of our own bodies, by the physical world, and especially by other human beings who are also trying to work out their "programmes." In this situation, the growing individual cannot avoid trouble. Life for him becomes a matter of working out as well as possible the maximum of pleasure available with a minimum of risk to further enjoyment of pleasure. Once the individual realizes that he needs other individuals as fellow workers in keeping him safe against danger and that he needs members of the opposite sex to insure gratification of his sexual needs, he works out all the other "rights and wrongs" in the way of personal habits, customs, and institutions.

What is called for in Freud's view is no special kind of "moral" consciousness, but the use of imagination, memory, and intelligence in the service of the aggressive demand that not too many sacrifices be made to insure a balance of pleasure over unpleasure.[13] "Civilized man has exchanged some part of his chances of happiness for a measure of security." [14]

In order to understand how such "security" is achieved, recall how Freud conceives the initial newborn babe—although the reader must be warned that the student of Freud is presented, not with a neatly worked out theory of conscience, but with tentative analyses and theoretical stumbling and fumbling, which Freud would be the

[10] *Civilization and Its Discontents* (New York: Robert O. Ballou, 1930), p. 27.
[11] *Ibid.*
[12] *Ibid.*
[13] *Ibid.*, p. 91.
[14] *Ibid.*, p. 92. Cf. also pp. 140–44.

first to admit. Perhaps the clearest picture resembles something like this.[15]

The growing infant sees in the parent the source of his security, but also the block to his pleasures. If he follows his aggressive pleasure tendencies, he is in constant danger of being found and discovered. If he inhibits his pleasure-seeking, he feels frustration and anxiety; if he does not inhibit it, he feels anxiety at being found out. Yet he cannot bear to destroy the parent and consequently face the greater anxiety of even less security. At the same time, he "loves" the parent who, in giving him security, "loves" him. This see-saw ends up in his "identifying" himself with the parent, or taking the side of greatest balance of pleasure possible.[16]

Thus the superego represents the internalized authority of the parent who is at the same time loved and feared. This "conscience" becomes the relatively automatic compromise that the individual has made as he faces "reality" with a view to getting as much pleasure as possible and with as little anxiety or risk as possible.

If the child, then, overcome by the pleasure principle in a concrete situation, succeeds in getting by the censorship of the conscience, he cannot help still feeling the anxiety that springs originally from "biting the hand that feeds me." Indeed, soon the child feels anxiety not only about the deed but also about the mere thought of the deed that is disobedient. Thus the child comes to feel guilty or anxious [17] both when he disobeys and when he intends to disobey the internalized keeper of the peace.

We thus see what has happened progressively by the time the child has become an adult. The renunciation of instinctive pleasure demands resulting from his fear of punishment by an external authority may exist side by side with, or give way to, renunciation resulting from dread of the internal authority of conscience. "To go against" conscience creates the same anxiety or guilt that earlier was elicited by fear of external authority. Conscience stands over against pleasure-desires as aggressively as did the realities of the en-

[15] See *ibid.*, Chapter VII.

[16] "Originally, it is true, renunciation is the consequence of a dread of external authority; one gives up pleasures so as not to lose its love" (*ibid.*, p. 112). See also Freud, *The Ego and the Id* (London: Hogarth Press, 1950), p. 39. The superego arises, as we know, from an identification with the father regarded as a model.

[17] Freud uses the terms synonymously or at least never distinguishes them. He uses the term *remorse* "for the reaction after an actual performance of an aggressive deed." (*Civilization and Its Discontents*, p. 129).

vironment in childhood. Early anxiety led him to develop a conscience and now conscience, being the standard accepted as a necessary compromise with the nurturant environment, is the cause of
anxiety.[18]

To comment: as one reads Freud with Butler and Kant in mind,
one misses completely the contrast they insisted upon between the
ought-function and inclination or wants. When Butler and Kant
observe their experiences of obligation, they describe them as feelings of respect, which might seem like, but are not, any kind of desiring or disliking (such as fear). The power of ought is not the
power of fear. Conscience has authority in a life even when it has
been overpowered by fear and disobeyed. The authority of the
Freudian superego, however, is based on its *direct power* to deny
gratification of pleasure or on its symbolic or *potential power* to
control gratification without endangering security. A subtle but important distinction and issue are at stake.

The "authority" of Freud's superego, we are suggesting, is the
mixed power of fear and passion for pleasure. This is the power of
anxiety. Butler and Kant would never agree that the *moral* authority
involved in "respect" is the power of anxiety. They deny, we suggest,
that when we disobey conscience we are experiencing the kind of
uncertain fear and dread we call "anxiety." They deny that guilt
should ever be equated with anxiety or that *moral* approval is equivalent to parental and social approval.[19]

But how do we settle a question of this sort when two minds can
be so much at odds? We can only urge that the reader himself first
search for the differences suggested between anxiety and guilt, between fear of any sort and respect or *ought.* He must allow these
experiences to speak for themselves and be careful not to allow other
convictions about human beings to influence his interpretation of
the experience of obligation.

Freud, for example, like many other psychologists cannot see "obligation" in early childhood, so he conceives of the ought as a residue
of the struggle for security and love as the infant grows. But granted
that no "magisterial authority" is felt in early childhood, may it not

[18] "Renunciation (externally imposed) gives rise to conscience, which then demands
further renunciations" (*ibid.,* p. 114).
[19] Freud remarks: ". . . the sense of guilt is nothing but a topographical variety of
anxiety" that "in its later phases . . . coincides completely with the dread of the
super-ego" (*ibid.,* p. 125).

come into being at a later stage? (Allport, we noted, held that a "must" conscience precedes an "ought" conscience.) It may well be that the ought-function appears only after the child has matured enough to think about alternatives of action before him. In other words, the fact that the ought-function appears later does not mean that it is a product of social approval and fear.

It is all the more interesting to recall, in this context, Fromm's demand for a distinction between the authoritarian conscience and the humanitarian. The humanitarian conscience is not preceded by, or reducible to, the authoritarian conscience. For it speaks for the basic need of the individual for responsible freedom, while the authoritarian conscience (in Freudian fashion) develops from the demand for security. Here again, however, the ought-function seems to be interpreted in the light of a preconception of what man's nature is rather than analyzed for its own sake. The ought-function, for Fromm, seems to be linked with the inner demand for a specific goal, freedom, in contrast to universal principles (Kant) and altruism (Butler).

In actual fact, then, at the hands of the psychologist as well as the traditional moralist, the ought-function remains a kind of moral eye that, be it in the name of self, society, or God, monitors the individual in the midst of the conflicts of life. In the next two chapters we shall study more extensively views of the ought-function as a way of knowing what is right. In the remainder of this chapter we shall describe our own *non-cognitive view of moral obligation* in the light of our discussion so far.

IV. *OUGHT AS AUTHORITATIVE IMPERATIVE TO AN UNSPECIFIED BEST*

The debate between thinkers like Butler and Kant and psychologists like Freud resolves itself, in the last analysis, into the question: Is what we feel when we experience "I ought" a kind of want or desire, or a fear of consequences (that is, "must")? In our terms, is the ought-function reducible to the want-function?

Now, one can take the position that any human function *could* become some other. We might say that the sensation *blue* could become the emotion *anger*, but, for that matter, we might also say that the emotion *anger* could become *fear*. But is there anything in our experience that would justify such claims? If any experience can become any other experience, if anger could *turn itself into* fear and if tenderness could turn into contempt, we should be in a sorry psychological mess. Fortunately there seem to be limits as to what can become what. Hence, with Butler we had better say, "Any experience is what it is and not another thing," and proceed to justify our claim that the fear emotion can become the ought-function.

We propose therefore to analyze our adult experience of obligation, because, after all, we shall surely make errors in tracing the genesis of an experience if we do not describe it accurately in its adult form. Nor can we know whether our analysis of the past of an experience in childhood is correct unless it can lead us to the present as we know it.

A. *Obligation Experienced in Reflective Choice Situations*

We begin, then, by an assertion that is consistent with our analysis of will. We feel obligation only to objectives we believe to be, to some extent, within our capacity to achieve. When we say, for example, "Justice ought to prevail," would we ever feel obligated to bring justice about unless we believed (correctly or incorrectly) that we could improve on the present situation? Any act that ought to be done, clearly, must be believed to be at least partly within the agent's capacity. There can be no ought-experience where there is no present will-agency.[20]

We must next mark the fact that neither will-agency nor ought-experience takes place unless the individual can hold before himself "now" goals or ideals for the future. He could not do so unless he could think in terms of concepts. The "justice" that I feel obligated to will must be kept "before my mind" in thought. Hence, the capacities to think, to will, and to feel obligated are inseparable, though distinguishable, aspects of human experience.

If they are inseparable, we can infer that because the infant cannot think logically or inductively, we should not expect the ought-function to be present in infancy or until the child has matured enough to be able to think alternatives and, accordingly, to begin to choose. A human being becomes a *moral* agent only when he is

[20] See Chapter 8.

capable of self-consciously reflecting on his experiences and posing alternative goals conceived to be within his power to some extent.

B. *Experience of Ought as Imperative, Not Impulsive or Compulsive*

Thus far we have said that a human being feels obligated only when he can confront himself with alternative plans of action at least partly open to him. Now we come to the main question: How shall we describe this experience of feeling obligated? Here there is no appeal beyond introspection, and the reader must check what we now suggest by his own experience.

We call attention to three salient phases of the experience of obligation. First: Let us assume that a person, at a choice point in his life, says: "I think alternative A is better than alternative B." What takes place in him the moment he has reached this verdict, that A is better than B? He experiences: "I ought to do A and not B." Second, if instead of doing A he does B, or anything else inconsistent with A, he feels moral guilt (which is not anxiety). Third, when he seeks to do A and not B and believes he has done all he can, he feels *moral approval* (not social approval). Let us consider each of these factors in order.

In the experience of obligation we stand before a fact that, however finally interpreted, means that human beings are stirred and motivated not only by wants or by the "will-to-survive." For in the experience of obligation, the emphasis is on the quality of survival. One presumably can go on living if he does B rather than the reflectively approved A. But he feels *ought* about A and not about B. "A" has magisterial authority (Butler); toward it we feel the kind of respect Kant found in *ought*. We shall not catch the unique psychic quality of *ought* if we think simply of the admirable or even "worshipful" quality, presumably, of the object approved. As Kant and Butler both emphasized, there is a quality in the experience of ought by itself that makes it stand in sharp contrast to experiences of want, must, and their cognates. True, when we want an object we are spurred toward acquiring it. Yet moral experience is not in itself a felt "pull" toward an object.

Let us take a closer look. The "pulls" of desire may indeed overcome the ought-function. Yet what we ought to do, whether we desire to or not, has a different "pull," a pull that does not feel like want and has that impressive power that we call authoritativeness. Mandelbaum has used the word "requiredness" for this "experienced demand" when a person apprehends a situation in which a certain action is deemed fitting.[21] Whatever the word we finally use, the salient character of this experience of "I ought" is that it does not feel like "I want" or "I must." We experience obligation as an imperative: it is a command we are not forced to obey, for then ought would feel like must.

Furthermore, we cannot escape the imperative once we have "judged" an alternative to be *better than* another. At the risk of being overbold, we defy a person to confront a situation in which he is convinced that he has choice to conclude sincerely (for whatever reason) that alternative A is better than the others and then *not* feel that he ought to do it.[22]

Suppose a person in this situation said to us: "When I decide that A is better than other alternatives, I feel 'I must do it,' or 'I want to do it.'" Here we find ourselves in the kind of situation that we would be in if a person said to us that he is experiencing blue at the same point that we are experiencing red. Once we are sure we are using words carefully, that we know what he means by "red," and that he simply does seem to have the experience we are calling "blue," there is nothing further to do than to hope that all or even a majority of other "impartial observers" would not, in the presence of this object, say that they too see blue. Similarly, at choice point we suggest that the experience of obligation as *lived* through is itself neither a "feeling compelled" to obey nor a simple "wanting" to obey, and we hope that other "impartial observers" will agree.

In any case, it is usually in a situation where "wants" or "musts" conflict that one finds himself making the choices to which obligation attaches. A Socrates confronted with the "musts" of ceasing from his philosophizing or leaving Athens or taking the hemlock may want most to stay in Athens and philosophize and he may least want to die. Once he has decided which of these courses is the most valuable, he feels obligation to that course—along with fear or other emotions for himself and others.

[21] See Maurice Mandelbaum, *The Phenomenology of Moral Experience* (Glencoe, Ill: The Free Press, 1955), Chapter II.
[22] Compare the treatment of ought by Brand Blanshard in *Reason and Goodness* (New York: The Macmillan Co., 1961), pp. 329 ff.

C. *Ought Experienced as Imperative to the Conceived Best, But Not Itself a Cognitive Experience*

We now wish to make a further suggestion that should not be accepted or rejected finally until the reader has evaluated the discussion in the next two chapters. Simply put, our suggestion is this: The experience of obligation is always felt *only* to that objective which is deemed the best of alternatives in the situation of choice. We shall not here ask how he knows what the best is, for that is in fact irrelevant to the experience of oughting. Why do we say this? Because persons who disagree about what the best is nevertheless feel obligation to what they deem (rightly or wrongly) to be the best at that time.

In a sense this is the most poignant fact about the human situation: persons differing about what the best means nevertheless feel obligated to the best as they now define it. Conscientious Athenians stand resolutely against a conscientious Socrates; conscientious objectors to a given war stand resolutely opposed to conscientious believers in that war; conscientious members within a home, a school, a society, oppose each other—"much as we would like to agree with you." Indeed, we go so far as to say that "no self-respecting person," no person of integrity, would do less. We may dislike our enemies and disapprove of much that they do and fight them even to the death if we deem that necessary. But we honor them for their willingness to live and die for what they believed right. We do not admire, honor, or respect their conclusions and objectives, but we honor them because they did what they felt they ought.

It may now be clear why, as we *conceptualize* this experiencing of obligation, we do not tie it to any particular object or objective to which the person feels obligation at the time. The imperative is to the particular object or principle only if it is conceived to be better than the other alternatives open to him. Thus we say that the essential thrust of obligation is never to freedom, or justice, or love, but to "the best I know." "I ought to do the best I know"—this is the absolute imperative as felt in every conscious choice situation from which some decision emerges. If justice in some form is felt to be the best, then we say: I ought to do justice.

We are not saying that at choice points we or anyone else are articulately aware of "I ought to do the best I know." But we are saying that after reflection, profound or superficial, spontaneous or extended, the feeling of obligation will attach to what in that situation, correctly or incorrectly, was in fact deemed to be the best (or better).

In sum, our view is that the particular right or wrong, the good or evil, to which a person feels obligated will be found on analysis to be that which he, correctly or incorrectly, believes to be the best alternative in the situation that has opened before him—given his past, his nature, and the responses open to him at that point. And the only direct evidence we can offer the reader is what he finds by analyzing his own experience.

Some other factors from our total moral experience may help to confirm this conclusion or to allay doubts. Thus, we must agree with the possible objection that no one experiences an "ought to do the best" as such. For actually we confront only concrete situations in which the choice, for example, is "to eat or not to eat," "to lie or not to lie," not "the best or the next best." But our formulation is based on the fact that as we look back and survey our concrete choice situations in their great variety, we find one common factor: each decision to whch we felt obligation was deemed the best in that situation. Therefore we conceptualize the experience of oughting as always being "I ought to do the best I know," fully realizing that the best is not some specific quality like honesty or justice.[23]

On such grounds, we urge that in human experience, whatever our *duties* (or particular *oughts*) turn out to be, a man's obligation is always to the best as he knows it. Do we not feel obligated to the "better → best," even though our decisions about our specific duties change? For example, as long as a parent believes that a certain objective is best for his child, he will feel morally obligated to work for its accomplishment. But should he change his mind and decide on another objective as best, his ought transfers to that. On such a view, at any rate, we can account for the persistent loyalty within the same man, and among men, that keeps them loyal to the best as they see it, even though *what* they believe the best is will vary as they grow.

[23] We are glad to find support for this interpretation of moral experience in the interpretation of Kant by A. R. C. Duncan in *Practical Reason and Morality* (London: Thomas Nelson and Sons, 1957), throughout, and especially Chapter IV, pp. 68–69. Also, those who know the work of A. C. Garnett, *The Moral Nature of Man* (New York: Ronald Press, 1952), will recognize that the view here propounded is in essential agreement with his "subjective" sense of obligation, but differs from his view of objective obligation.

D. *Ought Supported by the Fact of Rationalization*

Furthermore, support for this "ought to be the best I know" comes from the common experience of finding "good" reasons, not real reasons, for a given choice. When we so rationalize, are we not concerned to throw that light upon a situation that will allow it to appear "right?" But why bother with making things look right, if we felt no imperative to measure up to the best?

This evidence is not conclusive, of course, for one might always say, in this situation, that the person wants to make things "look right" because of his upbringing. Does not saying this, however, simply push the question back to: Why do we bother to want ourselves to look right *in this way?* Why do persons who do what might seem to be wrong either to themselves, or to others, or both, hurry to justify their action by making it "right"? Is it residual fear? But here we are back again to the fact that ought is not felt as fear. The "discomfort" that leads a person to rationalize is a peculiar "moral" discomfort. It is this *uniquely moral ache* that we must further characterize in developing our second main thesis now regarding the experience of ought.

E. *Ought as Irreducible to Introjected Social Approval*

What do we experience when, having decided that A is best, we do not will A? Many, influenced by Freud, will tell us that we experience anxiety.

Now, there is no denying that we feel fear-anxiety [24] when we do something for which we have been punished in the past and for which we expect punishment in the future if we are discovered. If a man knows that for disobeying the will of the state he will be imprisoned and dispossessed, if a man knows that a certain course of action, which he believes to be the best, may well lead to disastrous results for himself and for those he loves, he will indeed experience fear-anxiety. We grant, then, that fear-anxiety, in some degree, usually attends any expected punishment or danger.

Our question, however, is: Does he feel only fear-anxiety when he

[24] We shall use the hyphenated word "fear-anxiety" to indicate the range of emotional stirring from what may be fairly definite fear to that uncertain sense of a possibly impending doom that characterizes anxiety.

deliberately goes against what he has agreed is the best? Our own introspection leads to a clear-cut negative. *Along with fear-anxiety,* in a situation where we believe that we could have done otherwise, we feel a state of unique emotional unrest for which we would reserve the word *guilt.* So different is the psychic tone of guilt that we find it difficult to see how ordinarily acute observers have used anxiety and guilt as if they were synonymous.

F. *Moral Guilt as Irreducible to Fear-Anxiety*

If we are correct, in guilt there is no fear-anxiety, although fear-anxiety may accompany guilt because of dangers involved. The feeling of *guilt* itself is not a feeling of impending uncertain punishment, but a different kind of gnawing discontent. In a given situation, there may be fear-anxiety of other punishments, exacted by the agent or other persons, but the guilt feeling is a kind of unrest and tension having its own peculiar quality. After one has been punished or if one for some reason is not punished, the guilt is still present.

Here we may be told, guilt is the residue of past situations in which fear-anxiety were ingredients: guilt is past censorship associated unconsciously with the present misdeed. Obviously there is no way of disproving this. But we return to our basic methodological stand: if an experience now does not feel like fear-anxiety, there is no good reason to invent the possibility that it began as something other than what it feels like.

Further confirmation of the suggestion that guilt is not reducible to fear-anxiety may be found in the fact that although someone else may accept punishment due me for a misdeed, no one else can take away my guilt. If another takes my punishment upon his shoulders, he removes my fear-anxiety, but not my sense of guilt. I must live alone with my guilt; and only the healing and the renewal that life and time grant me will enable me to live with it and through it without being permanently damaged.

Many other problems might be taken up here, for example, the meaning of repentance and forgiveness (see Chapter 17), but space forbids further discussion beyond the central point that we need to emphasize here. Guilt attends default in fulfilling what I believe I ought to do, and guilt has a life of its own, not dependent on whether one has been or will be punished. Guilt often lives side by side with anxiety, it may even give rise to anxiety, but it is not anxiety.

G. *Moral Approval as Unique and Irreducible*

The third main tenet in this noncognitive view of obligation emerges from introspection of what takes place when the moral agent *does* pursue the course he believes to be the best, knowing that this will have a disturbing effect on the pattern of his own life and incur the wrath and hostility of others. Let a man brought up in the midst of plenty, accustomed to social privilege and the favor of his peers, let this man decide that his whole way of life and that of his family and friends is a kind of social and economic parasitism; let him further decide to give up his economic power and privilege and use all his ability to improve the lot of the economically and socially underprivileged; and let him have the realization of the hardship that will ensue both for himself, his family, and his social group. What will a person in such a situation undergo?

Surely he will experience upheavals of feeling and emotion; ingrained habits of living will indeed "revolt" as his will-agency seeks to break their power. He will experience much insecurity and anxiety within; and these will be matched by the fears and anxieties caused by the hostility of those he now opposes, the disappointment of dear ones, and his own sobering realization that if his decision is wrong he will have hurt many persons. But do these emotional states exhaust all that he will undergo as he proceeds to will the best he knows?

If we are correct, in the midst of his personal emotional agony, in the midst of social disapproval, he feels a quiet, persistent emotion for which we shall reserve the words "moral approval" (to contrast with social approval). Can any of us deny the fact that often we are able to go on, despite the personal insecurity and the social disapproval that hurts so much, simply because there is in us that which stands fast and is felt as a peculiar sort of approval? It is *as if* something were saying: "Whatever else happens, this is what you are to do!"

At moments like this we can understand why Kant said that nothing filled him with such awe as "the starry heavens above and the moral law within." And is not this unflinching ought-to-do-the-best, wth the accompanying sense of moral approval, what is really behind Fromm's statement that the "real self" makes itself felt as that which should be realized despite insecurity? The power of obligation is not that of an electric current or of thunder and flashing lightning or of some overpowering passion. It is no gust of wind that carries everything before it. But as one does what he believes to be the best, he cannot escape the inner moral approval that is probably the core of what we mean by self-respect.

Again: Can this moral approval be a residue of past social approval? All we can say is that in any given situation we are able to feel the difference between social approval and moral approval. If I gain social approval by doing what I think is best—all the better! I can feel both social approval and moral guilt at the same time, for the action that gains the approval of others is not the one I believe to be the best.

V. *THE MORAL STRUCTURE OF THE PERSON: PERSPECTIVE*

We conclude this chapter by considering what total conception of human nature and the moral situation emerges if we are correct in our analysis of obligation in this chapter and of free will in the previous one.

The basic unlearned endowment of human nature has two components that are not granted in most recent "scientific" psychology and indeed by influential moral theorists. These components are the notion of (limited) free-will-agency, and of moral obligation. We must not bog down in the important genetic question as to when these appear in the human being, for our contention is that genetic psychology cannot know what it is tracing unless the analysis of what we know most directly in adult experience is adequate.

For ethical purposes, it is enough to say that the child begins to have *moral* experience when he can reflect upon experiences he has undergone, compare them to each other, and arrive at some conclusion about better and worse. *By moral experience we mean a complex psychological state in which the person believes himself to be able to move toward alternative goals and finds himself feeling that he ought to will that alternative which he believes to be the best.* When examination of the course of life cannot take place, there is nothing but the flow of the strongest need, desire, or impulse. Here agency is meaningless, and the experience of ought is never reached.

We shall leave it to the genetic and developmental psychologist [25] to tell when and under what conditions these facets of human na-

[25] Jean Piaget, *The Moral Judgment of the Child* (New York: Harcourt, Brace, 1932).

ture occur, but we shall refuse to have them explained away as "the results" or "by-products" of other factors, which, *as we experience them,* simply do not have the same psychic quality and "body." A person is a complex unity of sensing, remembering, imagining, thinking, feeling, needing, willing, and oughting. He is capable of intellectual error and wrong ethical choice, but he is *morally evil* only when he does not will the best he knows. If he wills other than the best he knows, he may achieve his goal, but experience guilt. If he wills the best he knows and, because of circumstances beyond his present control or will power, fails to achieve his approved goal, he will be sad, he may experience fear-anxiety, but he will have a peculiar sustaining *moral approval.*

At the risk of overstating the situation, we suggest, then, that the unique thing about a human being is not simply that he has deep-seated urges more flexible than those of animals, not simply that he has a memorial and imaginative and reasoning range that makes choice possible, but that he is a creature who, in the midst of desire and conflict, finds himself obligated to the best as he sees it. His society and his past experience may well influence what he comes to believe is the best, but every society is forever nourishing human beings who may upset that society by demanding a best not yet envisioned. For in the crucible of persons not driven by, but lifted by, this curious "ought to the best," a ferment constantly goes on that demands that change be growth toward the best conceivable at that time.

To what shall we change, what is worth keeping, and by what standard shall we judge ourselves and others? This is the central question of moral philosophy, and this will absorb us in the remainder of this book.

VI. *REFLECTIVE SUMMARY*

What distinguishes the view of moral obligation set forth in this chapter? It parts company with any theory that regards "obligation" as the product of learning; it parts company with any theory that identifies "obligation" with particular "duties" or introjected prohibitions or commands. To feel "ought" is not (as we shall later argue) to be morally conscious of, or know, what general principle or particular action is called for in a situation.

Ought, we contend, is analyzed out of a complex experiential situation in which the person believes that there is some alternative
that he deems the best in that situation, and that he believes he can
enact. In every reflective choice situation, "ought" is the imperative
to will the best one knows. What that best is, and how we know it,
whether it be the commands of our parents that are so habitual as
to be "second nature," or whether it be the "voice of God" or of
"society," remains to be seen. But whatever the specific meaning of
"best," however controversial its content, there is no denial of the
magisterial authority (not power) of felt obligation.

What this means, further, for a theory of the nature of man, of
the ground plan of his nature, is that man is not simply a complicated organization of flesh, muscle, gland, nerves, and gray matter,
or a complex mixture of cognitive activities, or a creature moved by a
network of motives, innate and acquired, or even as agent-self free
to will within limits goals that he has thought out. To say that man
is a psychophysiological creature—of which the physiological, the
rational as well as nonrational motives and will are interpenetrating
activities—this is important. But to leave it there by saying that
ought is the by-product of the interplay of man and his social environment is to neglect the unique feeling of imperative, not compulsion, that alters the complexion of man's experience when he
feels his dynamic "ought to the best I know." On this view man is
not only, as James so well said, "a fighter for ends" but a fighter for
quality among ends.

One phase of the psychic tone introduced into human experience
by action in accordance with obligation is moral approval, which
may or may not be accompanied by social approval. A person who
does what he believes to be the best in his power may be disappointed in what he accomplishes; he may regret social disapproval
and feel anxious because of it; but he still feels the unique "satisfaction" of moral approval. What a person imposes upon himself as
"his" good brings approval of this unique sort, once he does all he
can to achieve it. This, we suggest, is the essential truth some psychologists (like Fromm and Maslow, for example) are not quite adequately expressing in their views that man gets "growth" satisfaction through creative self-expression.

The other phase of the psychic tone that ought gives to the moral
struggle is the guilt one feels when—however much he may succeed
in achieving a goal, and however much he gains social approval—he

himself knows that he has chosen what he believed was contrary to the best. Despite the fact that he now may feel no anxiety, he still feels guilt.

Finally, we re-emphasize the fact that the experience of ought and the experiences of willing, reasoning, and desiring are not independent "forces" or "faculties." They are distinct and irreducible phases of a complex but unified person. This desiring, reasoning, oughting, willing person seeks, from moment to moment and day to day, to find that mode of living that will enable him to preserve and increase what he believes to be best—in the world by which he is nourished and challenged. The question now before us is: What kind of guidance, if any, does man get in his search for that best?

PART III:

The Good Life in Ethical Perspective

10

Man's Relation to the Ideal: Classical Realistic Perspectives

~~~~~~

I. *THE INNER CORE OF "CONSCIENCE"*

Many believers in God cannot believe that He would create them without providing an inner guide to goodness. "After all," they seem to reason, "if animals have such built-in mechanisms as instinct and reflex by which they know what to avoid and what to approach, surely man must have an inner compass that points relentlessly to his true good!" Many are the forms of this belief in an inner monitor, but perhaps the most popular and crudest form is belief in "conscience" as the voice of God within man, which tells him what is right and what is wrong.

We call this view crude because it leads its exponent so readily into the very trouble he is trying to avoid. He wants a steady authority for his moral choices. But how trust an Authority whose dictates to one person contradict those to others in the same situation?

Nevertheless, can it be that there is a kernel of truth in this crude belief, which we should heed? Quite often persons have heard a "voice" telling them to do what, at the time, they did not want to do or were unprepared to do. When persons feel that what they ought to do is contrary to their wishes and present capacities, they readily infer that such binding commands must come from a Source beyond themselves. (Even those who cannot believe that they are receiving a mandate from God often decide that it must be the voice of Society.)

In western philosophical thought, Socrates gave expression to an interesting variant of the view of conscience as the direct revealer of God's will. Socrates believed that the uncriticized life is not worth living. So effective was he in stimulating Athenian young people in particular to examine the grounds for their beliefs that defenders of "the Athenian way of life" were able to have him condemned to death.[1] When asked how he could be so sure that it would be better for him to die than to give up his examining and teaching, Socrates replied, among other things, that he had not felt on this occasion the warning that his "inner voice" gave him on other occasions.

The noteworthy thing about this "voice" was that, rather than constantly telling Socrates what to do, it acted as a veto once he had elected a certain course. Socrates was convinced that it was God warning him not to continue in the path taken.

We know so little about the reasons for Socrates' thinking as he did that it would serve no useful purpose to discuss his view further. But here, clearly, is one moral gladiator who, firm in moral conviction and action, did not regard his "conscience" as a direct source of positive information from God about the good, but as a negative monitor warning him not to continue on a course of action. Perhaps the main effect of Socrates' stand was that it opened up the whole question whether man's basic moral loyalty is to be simply loyalty to a continuation of existence at any cost. According to Socrates, man is morally bound to do the bidding of his own inclination, or of his society, or state, only if this is God's will for him. The silence of the negative monitor is God's signal to "go ahead."

In this chapter and the next, we shall present the reasoning of thinkers who, going beyond any crude belief in conscience as *vox Dei*, or as a negative sign of God's will, believe that man in his experience of obligation is guided by values he does not himself create. Fundamental to the thought of such philosophers is a simple analogy. We assume, they say, that the pleasure we feel when we are experiencing a pleasant object is caused by something in the object. Likewise the obligation we feel when we experience a certain "yes" or "no" within us is caused by something in a commanding source. If there are no obligation-inspiring "objects" in the world, man would not feel obligation. For the thinkers we shall be considering, a person's awe-

[1] See Plato, *The Apology of Socrates* (New York: Liberal Arts Press, 1948).

some response to an objective value, ideal, or Source, is the valid inner core of conscience.

II. *THE PLATONIC VIEW OF MAN'S AWARENESS OF THE IDEAL*

Socrates' basic claim to inner guidance was developed and refined in the thought of Plato, one of the Athenian young men who was converted to philosophy by Socrates. The significant and unique thing about man, Plato urged, is his search for truth, beauty, and justice. But how does man come by these ideals, which he acknowledges even when he is not faithful to them in his living?

Plato's answer took the following form: When I look about me in the world of things and people, all I see are imperfect objects, beings, and actions. There is no exception to this fact. In the realm of sense and desire there is nothing perfect. But if all my ideas and ideals come *from* this imperfect world of things and actions, as many of my contemporaries tell me, I am faced by an enormous contradiction. The perfect and the imperfect cannot be the same. Sheer inanity, if not insanity, lies this way!

Here I am, then, in an imperfect world with ideals of perfection. How are they related? Surely the imperfect cannot be the source of the perfect? To be specific, how can an imperfect world, or an imperfect man like myself, or an imperfect society like the one in which I live—how can these be the source of my ideas of perfect Truth, Beauty, and Justice? Plato saw no way out of this impasse. We cannot avoid it by denying that we have such ideas of perfection. For if we have no idea of perfect truth, justice, and beauty, how can we make the comparisons that result in our saying that a statement is untrue, that a state of affairs is unjust, and that a painting, say, is ugly? Yet if we cannot arrive at these ideals by learning from an imperfect world, how do we come by them?

Here Plato took a courageous theoretical step that no later thinker has been able to disregard. Unlikely as it may seem to persons used to thinking that the world they live in has only the dimension open to the senses, there is a way out. It is to hypothesize that there is another dimension to the world and to realize that the total universe has in it both the perfect and the imperfect. Yet the imperfect cannot explain the perfect. And the imperfect is knowable as such only insofar as it approximates the perfect. Consequently, with the path from the imperfect to the perfect closed, and the imperfect making no sense without the perfect, we must conclude that the True, the Just, and the Beautiful are the ultimate, enduring, and unchanging realities that are imperfectly expressed in everything else. We are not clear about the exact relation of The Comprehensive Good to the changing imperfect things, but it makes more sense to say that the imperfect in some way imitates, or less completely expresses, The Good than to say that The Good is derived from the less-than-good.

If this is the nature of the world, we can draw the inference that in man there is the same tension between perfection and imperfection that exists in the universe everywhere. And certainly our own experience seems to give excellent witness to this world plan. For, as we have seen, we judge ourselves to be imperfect because we seem to be aware of the perfect, and we strive for the more nearly perfect, being imperfect! This means, concludes Plato, that we must see our lives not only as in contact with and nourished by the things our senses and desires need, but as having another dimension, a special *rational insight* or kind of intellectual functioning, which makes contact with and is inspired by the realm of Truth, Beauty, and Justice (or The Good in its many perfections).

In fact, Plato is convinced, we could not have gone through the process of reasoning we have just been experiencing unless we were already to some extent following or exemplifying the Patterns of Order (or Ideas, as Plato called them) that are the really real beings in the universe. If we were simply flesh and blood, if our reasoning were patterned after what the senses and desires yield, there could be no explaining why we criticize ourselves by these Ideas. Had we better not say, then, that our natures are "akin" to the Ideas and would be hollow if they had no tie with them? Indeed, are we not doomed to fruitless frustration in the degree to which we allow the immediate promises of our desires and the seeming certainties of the sense world to dominate our lives?

To recast Plato's argument briefly for our specific problem: Plato could not explain the imperative lure of the ideal (our ought-function) without conceiving the nature of the universe and of man in much broader terms than it is revealed to us in sense and desire. Why should the ideals to which we feel obligated be less real than the colors we see through vision? If there is red in sensory consciousness, we explain it by referring to red beyond our experience: as we say, *we* sense it; we do not make it up. Why should it be otherwise with Justice? If we in our moral consciousness find that Justice is the Ideal toward which we strive, however fumblingly, why should we not say that it too is "there," beyond our minds, waiting, as it were, to be recognized both in thought and action? [2]

On the basis of our discussion of Plato we are ready to define *ethical realism*. *Ethical realism* is the theory that in oughting we are aware of standards of excellence that are at least independent of the act of knowing and, for that matter, perhaps ultimately independent of our existence. In Plato, we have seen, the moral experience is itself a source of his conviction that the universe in which we live is a whole of Goodness. Our ought-function expresses the underlying structure, the ontological nature, of things.

It is interesting to note that Jung's notion of a collective unconscious and the archetypes that link the individual to the whole human past has some resemblance to Plato's insistence that each of us brings *to* his senses and desires patterns that make themselves felt as we try to solve the problems of living. Jung does not clearly hold, it would seem, that these archetypes have existence independent of man. Plato, especially in his early thought, held that each soul brought into this life with it an inarticulate remembrance of former togetherness with the Patterns.[3]

The contrast between a Platonic and Jungian perspective and that of a scientistic psychology especially is remarkable. For the scientistic psychological approach to human problems, emphasizing as it does the sensory, the public, and the quantifiable as the foundation of truth, and placing all mental equipment within the framework of man's physiological nature, has cut itself off from possibly conceiving of man as being sensitive both to a "natural" and to a nonnatural realm of being. But Plato defined human sensitivities, in the light of the search for values, in terms that linked the human being not solely to biological and social needs, but to a framework that embraced both man, society, and the cosmic "natural" world. Insofar as Freudians and even neo-Freudians, or insofar as scientistic psychol-

[2] This line of reasoning, which, as here given, emphasizes inferences from experience is not unfair, we believe, to Plato's essential argument as found in dialogues like the *Meno, Phaedo, Phaedrus, Symposium,* and *Republic* in particular. But it would create the wrong impression if we suggested that this indirect inferential approach was the only one Plato took. He would probably say that this indirect approach is an attempt to defend what is actually given to us in direct experience.

[3] Cf. *Meno* and *Phaedo* especially.

ogists insist on seeking for the patterns of life within the want-need structures of human nature, the Platonic challenge will continue to be: "But how can you move from what you want, from what you sense, to that which by your own confession you aim at—The True, The Just, The Beautiful? How do you get from what is, from what you want, to what ought to be, to what you ought to want? How, we repeat, do you get to the ideal if the only source of your knowledge is the imperfect world of sense and desire as human beings know these?"

We shall never understand the ethical realist until we realize his perplexity over views that would derive any conception of perfection from imperfections. If, he insists, men are completely ignorant, that is, completely insensitive to the demand for truth, how shall we account for the actual fact that men of every caliber seek to know truth? For the realist, it is this stubborn conviction that the higher cannot come from the lower that stalks the seeker every time he is tempted to give up his conviction that the ideal is at least dimly present to him in his moral striving.

It is not that ethical realists "look down upon" their senses or their desires and vital needs. If anything, they find that trust in their senses "lets them down." It might seem, they say, that we know a circle through our senses. But is not any circle, as our reason defines it theoretically, a perfect circle? Yet how can we think a perfect circle if our senses are the only source of our knowledge? For any circle we sense is not a perfect circle. If we sense only imperfect circles, and if our senses are the only source of our ideas of circles, how can we think perfect circles?

Can we escape this theoretical impasse by saying that our perfect circle is an imperfect circle with the imperfections *imagined* away? No. For we must then ask: What, other than memories based on sensory experience of imperfect circles, guides our imaginations to know what parts to leave out, in approaching the idea of a perfect circle? Anyhow, would we know that the data of sense perception are imperfect if within or before the mind there was not a standard constantly and quietly operative? And what is true of circles, which might seem to be founded on perceived lines, is all the more applicable to ideals like justice that can never, in any way, be observed by sense.

Whether the ethical realist is right or wrong, he should certainly shake us from any easy assumption that we simply can derive our ideals of truth, beauty, goodness from the experiences of sense and desire. As we might expect, however, any basic and startling solution such as the ethical realist gives will be subjected to searching critiques, which in turn give rise to attempts to expound the essential insight in other terms. We are not here even attempting an historical account that is accurate in detail or representative of every variation. But nonrealistic views of value and value-knowing will direct, as we shall see, a large part of their attack upon the realistic view of the moral consciousness. We must, therefore, consider ways of value-knowing that develop this essential theme, which we have found in "crude" conscience, negative monitor, and rational insight. For such theories of value-knowing involve both theories of human knowing and obligation and theories of value.

We have in fact already touched on two variations in the thought of Bishop Butler and Kant. We stressed in the last chapter their emphasis on the peculiar psychic tone of the experience of obligation. What we did not stress was the fact that both Kant and Butler also believed that this experience of obligation is *cognitive,* that is, that the ought is a *knowing* of a standard by which the expression of desires and abilities of persons should be guided (hence the term *moral consciousness*). We return briefly to Butler's account here, for his view offers an illuminating contrast to some psychological and sociological accounts of the relation of obligation to the nature of man.

III. BISHOP BUTLER: REFLECTIVE CONSCIENCE AND THE IDEAL OF ALTRUISM

Butler believed that self-love is a strong component of human nature. He also believed, however, that it is balanced by an equally potent concern for others. Says Butler:

> It is not a true representation of mankind to affirm that they are wholly governed by self-love, the love of power and sensual appetites; since, as on the one hand, they are often actuated by these, without any regard to right or wrong, so, on the other, it is manifest fact that the same persons, the generality, are frequently influenced by friendship, compassion, gratitude; and

even a general abhorrence of what is base, and *liking of* what is fair and just, takes its turn amongst the motives of action.[4]

Butler does not think that this balance between the dispositions favoring self-love and those favoring benevolence is a matter of training, as other moralists like Thomas Hobbes would have us believe. Both self-regarding and other-regarding tendencies, Butler holds, are present in human nature; we are not to think of benevolence as a "play-it-safe device" for increasing one's own security.[5] Yet, although this analysis of human "propensions" finds an underlying balance that our intelligence must respect if self-fulfillment is ever to take place, Butler insists that such an account of human motivation is incomplete. For it neglects "a principle manifestly superior to a mere propension," [6] a principle that claims absolute direction of all in human nature, namely, conscience. Recalling now the qualitative psychic tone of this "principle of reflection," we must complete our picture of Butler's view of obligation by noting that for him "conscience" is a method of knowing that benevolence is the specific ideal that is authoritative in man's life.

We can see why Butler believes that this "magisterial" presence of benevolence makes a great deal of difference in actual behavior. For if one can feel reasonably propelled to realize the ideal of benevolence to which his emotional nature also propels him, he will feel that he ought to be benevolent even when he is emotionally discouraged. To use one of Butler's illustrations: The parent whose affection for his children leads him to make due provision for their education will find that "the reflection that it is his proper business, what belongs to him" will carry him "through more labor and more difficulties for the sake of his children than he would undergo from that affection alone, if he thought it, and the course of action it led to, either indifferent or criminal." [7]

Thus it is that Butler contends that the *whole* nature of man is adapted to a course of action in which self-fulfillment is in harmony with, indeed impossible without, honest and fair treatment for others.[8] In general terms, Butler stands to Hobbes as Montagu,

[4] Butler, *Five Sermons* (New York: Liberal Arts Press, 1950), pp. 10–11 (italics added). Copyright © 1950, by The Liberal Arts Press, Inc., and reprinted by permission of The Liberal Arts Press Division of The Bobbs-Merrill Company, Inc.

[5] Cf. *ibid.*, p. 23.

[6] *Ibid.*, p. 11.

[7] *Ibid.*, p. 26.

[8] Cf. *ibid.*, p. 45.

Fromm, Maslow, and Allport stand to Freudians in rejecting the view that man is nothing but a selfish individualist. This battle over the roots of altruism in man is one that has gone on for ages, and it goes on today.

What we would stress here is the fact that many ethicists, like Butler, have taken special pains to root altruism in the "magisterial" authority of obligation. Indeed, in much of the literature, when "obligation" is being discussed it usually turns out that the specific obligation of being altruistic is alone in mind. In the thought of Kant, as we shall see, obligation involves *the* universal principle that all persons ought to respect personality in themselves and others as an end and never as a means only. Kant did not have Butler's confidence that man's emotional-conative nature would reliably undergird altruism. His view of moral obligation and of man's moral nature is so influential a version of ethical realism that, leaving until a more appropriate place his specific reasons for the belief that the moral consciousness reveals the duty to be altruistic, we cite and analyze a fertile passage from the German philosopher.

IV. *IMMANUEL KANT: OBLIGATION TO DUTY FOR THE SAKE OF DUTY*

In the first three paragraphs of his famous work, *Fundamental Principles of the Metaphysics of Morals,* Kant startled ethical theorists by taking the emphasis off the specific action or principle of action that ought to be done and focusing it upon the inner intent of the person. But he went further and said that the only activity that can always be said to be good is this inner intent.

> Nothing can possibly be conceived in the world, or even out of it, which can be called good without qualification, except a *good will*. Intelligence, wit, judgment, and the *talents* of the mind, however they may be named, or courage, resolution, perseverance, as qualities of temperament, are undoubtedly good and desirable in many respects; but these gifts of nature may also become extremely bad and mischievous if the will which is to make use of them, and which, therefore, constitutes what is called character, is not good. . . .
> Moderation in the affections and passions, self-control, and

calm deliberation are not only good in many respects, but even
seem to constitute part of the intrinsic worth of the person; but
they are far from deserving to be called good without qualification. . . . For without the principles of a good will, they may
become extremely bad; and the coolness of a villain not only
makes him far more dangerous, but also directly makes him
more abominable in our eyes than he would have been without it.

A good will is good *not because of what it performs or affects,
not by its aptness for the attainment of some proposed end, but
simply by virtue of the volition—that is, it is good in itself.* . . .
Even if it should happen that, owing to a special disfavor of fortune, . . . this *will should wholly lack power to accomplish its
purpose, if with its greatest efforts it should yet achieve nothing,
and there should remain only the good will, . . . then, like a
jewel, it would still shine by its own light, as a thing which has
its whole value in itself.*[9] [Italics in this paragraph added.]

As if to ward off the temptation of any reader to think of the good
will as sentimental "good intentions," Kant adds to this passage a
parenthetical clause stating specifically that the good will is "not a
mere wish but the summoning of all means in our power." Let us
analyze this passage.

We mark first the distinction between *the right* and *the good*.
Kant is saying that, however we finally define the total good, or
happiness, there is one kind of action that "shines by its own light,"
and is good (right to do) even if it never succeeds. This action is the
summoning of all the means in our power to do the good. Furthermore, Kant adds that the good will "appears to constitute the indis-
pensable condition even of being worthy of happiness." [10]

Let us now set the words "the good, happiness, and right" in
historical context. For Kant and for most other moralists going back
to Plato and Aristotle, some state of total fulfillment is held to be
the good, or the goal of moral endeavor. Although "happiness" has
no one historical meaning, in whatever context, it is identical with
the good. Although happiness connotes pleasure to many, it must

---

[9] From *Fundamental Principles of The Metaphysics of Morals* by Immanuel Kant,
copyright © 1949, by The Liberal Arts Press, Inc., and reprinted by permission of
The Liberal Arts Press Division of The Bobbs-Merrill Company, Inc.
[10] *Ibid.,* p. 11.

not be identified with pleasure. Hedonists and utilitarians like Epicurus, Jeremy Bentham, and John Stuart Mill have believed that pleasure and pleasure alone constituted the ideal of happiness or *the good*. But for Plato, Aristotle, and other moralists including Kant, happiness involved more than (selected) pleasures. In any case, happiness is often the name for *the total state of being* called *the good,* by reference to which any action is to be evaluated as being *good* or *evil, right* or *wrong.* "Good" or "right" thus came to be applied to any action or intention that leads to the realization of *the good,* and "wrong" to actions or intentions that oppose such realization.

To get at the distinction that Kant wants us especially to see, a further word is necessary about the use of "good." In its most general sense, the word "good" is used for acts or events or things that are deemed to fulfill some other end. A good hat is one that is well made and fit for wearing; a good car fulfills the purpose of transportation; and a good deed is one which leads to the pattern of action deemed *the good.* It may be noted that in English we do not normally speak of a "right" hat, or car, though we can and do say that a hat may be just right in some aesthetic pattern.

It is when we come to "a good deed" that we must be especially watchful about our meaning and usage. A deed may be called "good" in this general sense if it is "just the action needed to fulfill a certain end" and therefore "right" as a means to this end. But there are many actions or intentions that we would call good and right in this sense (such as the giving of the right poison to induce immediate death) that we would not call right in another sense because they lead to an end which we do not believe is *the good.* We are thus forced to distinguish between the *morally good* or *morally right* and the good in this general nonethical sense. When a chosen act is good because it contributes to *the good,* it may be called *morally* good (*morally bad* or *evil* for the opposite). The synonyms for morally good and morally bad are *morally right* and *morally wrong,* meaning, once more, action or intention favorable and unfavorable to *the good* (or happiness) respectively.

It is just here that Kant makes a point that constitutes a significant difference for ethical theory. The good will, he says, is *good* or *right* not *for something beyond itself* but in its own light, regardless what the consequences for *the good* are. This raises the whole question:

Is the *morally good* or *evil* (or *morally right* and *morally wrong*) *knowable apart from its relation to the good contemplated?* We ask the reader to consider concretely the following situation, with the alternative meanings of the above terms in mind.

Let us say that, as A and B are walking together over a bridge, they hear a cry for help from the river below. Running to the rail they see a person struggling helplessly in the water. They both immediately dive in after the drowning person. But when A hits the water he is temporarily incapacitated by a stunning blow from a floating log he has not seen, and he almost drowns. The drowning person is left for B to rescue.

Let us ask this question: Was the act of A *morally wrong* or *evil* because he did not in fact rescue the person? We immediately begin to see the different perspectives that lead to the different uses of the words "right," and "good," and "the good." Many persons, with the Stoics and Kant leading them, would immediately insist that even if A's action did not save the person, even if in fact the consequences did not contribute to *the good,* it was still (morally) right, or *morally* good for him to do all in his power to effect the good. This means that the word "good" must not be assigned only if an act eventuates in *the good.* An act could eventuate in *the good* even when it was not intended to. Kant therefore holds that the only act that is unconditionally good—as opposed to all other goods that depend on good fortune or a favorable confluence of circumstances— for any person to perform is this act of doing the best he can to execute *the good* as he sees it. This act, and this act alone, is *morally right* or *morally good:* it *ought to be done,* whatever else is done. Kant is distinguishing a *morally good act* from a good act by focusing on the person's specifically moral intention as opposed to the final results of the act, which may not depend on the moral agent.

No sooner have we said this than we find ourselves wondering, and someone will be sure to urge: "When we compare the total relation of A to B to the saving of the person, does not the fact that B not only did his best, but actually accomplished it, force us to conclude that B's act is more valuable, is better than A's? To put A and B in the same class surely seems to be unfair, for one did bring about consequences that are good. Furthermore, to stress the motives of persons and not their consequences is to encourage a kind of sentimentalism in moral behavior. It is the accomplishing of the good, the deed and not the motive, that is basic. In fact, the only reason for considering A's action *morally good* or *right at all* is that it intended *the consequences* that were approved." What our questioner is urging, then, is that the morally good or right act does not shine by its own light, that no moral act is good for its own sake, but only, when we think it all out, because of its intended consequences in relation to *the good.* Indeed, this is the line of argument taken by ethicists who call themselves *teleologists,* because they judge the goodness of any act (or moral wrong and right) only in relation to *the good.*

This is the place, then, to articulate an important parting of the ways in ethical theory. In general, we may say that *teleologists* in ethical theory make the concept of *the good (happiness, eudaimonia, summum bonum)* the key concept in ethics. They judge every action as right or wrong, *morally good* or bad (evil) by its relation to *the good.* Such an ethics is called *teleological,* because the goal or end is the controlling basis of judgment. But others, like Kant, would hold that regardless of what the end is or the consequences are, there are also some actions that *are* right, come what may. Such actions are directly known to be right by morally sensitive persons. This view is called *intuitionism* and is clearly a form of *moral realism.* For it claims direct knowledge of the *morally good* (right), or direct knowledge of *the good,* in terms of which any action is to be judged good or bad, or morally right or wrong.

We should warn that many versions of what constitutes *the good* and the *morally right* may be found among ethicists and that a given ethicist may be an intuitionist in connection with part of his ethics and a teleologist with regard to others. Kant, for example, held that whatever other duties a person had, whatever his total good turned out to be, this good will is always a duty (morally right). But Kant finally defined the happy life, the *summum bonum,* as the life in which the man who did perform all his duties conscientiously actually fulfilled the whole of his nature. But on Kant's view a man, insofar as he is a moral agent, finds himself asking one question in all situations requiring choice: "Is the principle behind the action I am about to perform one which I would so approve that I would be willing to have it forced upon me and all other reasonable beings in all future time as a law of nature is enforced upon me now?" We shall more appropriately develop the meaning of this famous *categorical imperative* in Chapter 19. Yet Kant's view of obligation has furnished a most interesting development of theories of the moral consciousness.

We started this chapter with that crude form of the moral conscience in which it is held that at points of choice God specifically tells the moral agent what path to take. If this is an argument for the existence of God, it will lead to the damaging objection that because God has been held responsible for so many conflicting "moral insights," he is either confusing man or, if we take many of the "commands" seriously, he is no more an object of serious worship than the warring gods of Greek mythology. Such a God would certainly seem in need of moral conversion. Socrates' negative monitor cannot fare better. But it has been important to see what these views were getting at, namely, that man appears to have an experience which, though often in opposition to what seem clearly his own desires and nature, nevertheless makes demands upon him. These demands he is forced to respect even if they cannot best be accounted for by a theory of man's contact with a realm of being not open to his senses and desires but ultimately directive of what he ought to do in the world of sense and desire. In Plato we saw this view take full expression, for Plato tells us that man is a denizen of two worlds, one of sense and desire and the other open to human reason, that he is a being constantly guided by an inner controlling vision of *the Good,* in conformity to which man will find his nature capable of being fully realized.

For Butler, however, "conscience" does not reveal *the Good.* There is a "principle of reflection," which sits with "magisterial" authority (not power) in the midst of man's desires, re-enforcing the altruistic tendencies in man's nature but not reducible to them. In Butler's view obligation is directly aware, not so much of another Realm of Values, as of the principle of altruistic action (which, to be sure, he believes God has created in man). Kant, like Butler, conceived the experience of obligation to be a part of man's nature, God or no God. It is irreducible to the life of inclination and makes its demand in its own right, independent of consequences as such or *the Good* as such. The good will is the will to do all in one's power to preserve courses of action, which, as it turns out, all rational beings would agree might well be forced upon them, and which would make man worthy of happiness (the good) even if he never became good. In the next chapter we shall follow further this great stream of thought.

V. REFLECTIVE SUMMARY

Man is not adrift in a complex world without an inner monitor. In the midst of the conflicting demands and impulses of his nature, surrounded by a world of imperfect sensible objects, he feels the lure of perfections that cannot have their source in the imperfections of human existence. No amount of imagining and reasoning can derive the perfect from the imperfect. Only the dim awareness of perfection guides his analysis of and movement from imperfection.

It was this idea, basically, that led Socrates and Plato to insist that our real world is not simply an order of imperfect things but a larger structure, a larger Good, which our natures can know through our "moral consciousness" or "moral reason." In the universe there is this tension between perfection and imperfection, and man is a child of it. He is not valuationally blind to what ought to be; his task is to discipline his life of desire by the lure of the ideal. Thus, it is some final ideal, known by a unique moral consciousness, that the ethical realist first emphasizes in his view of man and of the search for the good life.

For example, Bishop Butler finds that even though human beings are emotionally inclined by self-love and benevolence, there is in man a "principle of reflection," which informs him that benevolence is the authoritative ideal for man, even in situations where emotional factors do not favor it. But Kant, equally convinced that man is aware of a universal principle of value, made it a point to insist that the obligation to this principle does not depend on a man's inclination or the consequences of his actions. For Kant the one undeniable good—free from all circumstance, desire, or possible consequences—is that a man do all in his power to obey this principle. Thus the morally good act shines by its own light. The good will depends no more on consequence for its goodness than does the universal principle that guides moral action depend on analysis of desires.

Briefly, ethical realism, in classical mode, emphasizes an authoritative inner moral light and an absolute duty to choose action consistent with the values or principles known by this moral consciousness, regardless of the clamor of desires.

11

Man's Relation to the Ideal:
Recent Realistic Perspectives

~~~~~~

I. SIR W. D. ROSS:
THE RIGHT AND THE GOOD

In beginning our discussion of several historic views of the moral consciousness, we described and illustrated the conviction that in fact permeates the "realistic perspective." On this view, the demands of the moral consciousness may be in direct and lasting conflict with the rest of one's nature. Many religious persons, all over the world, believe that God's commands are directly known and that they are to be followed whether they can be approved by human reason or not. Let the reader remind himself of the biblical account of Abraham's willingness to sacrifice his beloved son, Isaac. Plato insisted that while man's reason linked him to the cosmic Good and ultimately led him beyond itself to an ecstatic experience of the Good,[1] reason had to do constant battle with the appetites. Butler, we would have seen had we studied him further, believed that there is a basic harmony between self-love and benevolence that results from the wisdom of God, who created man, but we noticed that he gave "magisterial" authority to the reflective moral principle.

  With one voice such ethical realists urge: Obey your highest moral insights come what may of your desires, for in your desires

[1] See Plato's *Republic*, Books VI and VIII.

you will find no solid basis for guidance. In Kant we found the insistence that if an act is done *from* inclination and not *from* duty, that act may be in accord with *the good,* but it cannot be considered a morally good act. The right is to be done whether *the good* is ever accomplished in this life or not. Kant, like many others, was driven to believe that the disharmony between duty and happiness, the frequent conflict between doing right and endangering self-fulfillment would, if the universe is reasonable, be eliminated in the next life. But whatever conflict and disharmony between duty and happiness is present in this life and whatever happens in the next life, Kant had no doubt that man ought to do right in this life. It is this problem, how to conceive the relation between the right and the good, that we must follow in this chapter; and we could begin with no better contemporary representative than the learned Oxford scholar, W. D. Ross.

Permeating Ross's ethics is the conviction that the moral life is too complex "to fit into a simple creed" in which the right act is always that which has good consequences, either for oneself or for the greatest number of persons.[2] His main contention is that we simply do not judge all acts right and wrong by their relation to *the good*. And Ross buttresses this thesis by confronting us with the theoretical troubles that we face in trying to use a teleological standard exclusively. But, in the last analysis, he asks us to inspect our immediately given *(prima facie)* moral insights to confirm his view. What we shall do here, then, in our own way, is to ask the reader to inspect his experience in the light of some of the questions Ross would put to him.

A. *Special Obligations*

Is it not true, Ross might inquire, to begin with, that your duty to your mother and father or to other members of your family does not depend on the consequences of your loyalty to them? Do you not in action favor members of your own family, even if you think it would be better for yourself or society if you did not? Don't you think that a father and mother, in turn, ought to show preferential concern for their own children, even if the children of others are more promising?

[2] Cf. *Foundations of Ethics* (Oxford: Clarendon Press, 1939), p. 79. See also *The Right and the Good* (Oxford: Clarendon Press, 1930) and E. F. Carritt, *The Theory of Morals* (London: Geoffrey Cumberledge, 1928).

Ross's own answer to these questions is unhesitating: Yes! Each of these suggestions expresses a *special prima facie* obligation in certain situations. That is, we are so constituted as to approve morally of preferential action for members of our own families. This *special duty* to family members is one of several duties that, as we shall see, Ross believes we feel toward persons with whom we are involved in some special way. Here we must note that Ross is clearly saying that our moral consciousness (ought-function) *knows* certain actions to have special claims upon us. The claim we have been considering is an example of "the claim which those have from whom we have accepted benefits in the past." [3]

Consider another question: Does not the person whom I have wronged have a special claim for compensation from me? In other words, is not the person I have wronged more than "just another person" to whom my relations may be governed solely by asking whether compensation has good consequences for all concerned? Here, in a second special area, Ross states, the person I have wronged "has become someone with a special claim on my effort, over and above the claim which all men have to my beneficence." [4]

But in addition to these two *special* obligations involving rendering good for good and making compensation for evil, there is a third special obligation that is "so axiomatic that no moral universe can be imagined in which it would not exist." [5] This is the obligation arising from the fact that one has made a promise.

Why especially does the keeping of a promise seem so axiomatic to Ross? It is because when we promise something to another person, we voluntarily say to him that we bind ourselves to him in a certain way. We have said that we grant him a claim upon us which arises from this very promise. Thus, Ross says:

> A promise being this, an intentional intimation to someone else that he can rely upon me to behave in a certain way, it appears to me perfectly clear, that, quite apart from any question of the greatness of the benefits to be produced for him or for society by the fulfillment of the promise, a promise gives rise to a moral claim on his part that the promise be fulfilled. This claim will

[3] *Ibid.,* p. 76. This view, which sees right as not derived from good, is called "deontological" and the exponents "deontologists." See also the treatment of deontology in Brand Blanshard, *Reason and Goodness* (New York: The Macmillan Co., 1961), Chapter VI. This excellent book, felicitous in its setting of the march of reason in the search for goodness, was not available before this work was in almost final form.

[4] Ross, *Foundations of Ethics,* p. 76.

[5] *Ibid.,* p. 77.

be enhanced if there are great benefits that will arise from the fulfillment of the promise in contrast to its violation; or it may be overridden [note!] if the fulfillment of the promise is likely to do much more harm than good. But through all such variations it remains as a solid fact in the moral situation; and it arises solely from the fact that a promise has been made, and not from the consequences of its fulfillment.[6]

B. *When Obligations Conflict, How Do We Choose?*

We must pause to note that, as hinted in the bracket, Ross's view is not a thorough-going intuitionism, despite his insistence that promise-keeping has "a tendency to be right which does not arise from a tendency to promote the general good, but from the fact that a promise has been made." [7] For he insists that the special duty to keep a promise may be overridden if into the situation come other factors that do more harm than good. That is, promises are not to be kept irrespective of the consequences—as an out-and-out intuitionist would hold.

Nevertheless, Ross still insists that the promise-keeping is a rational, moral intuition in its own right and that it must not give way to utilitarian respect for overriding consequences. The reason for possible overriding would be that another obligation conflicts with the intuited obligation to keep promises. This obligation, not as specific as the special obligation, is to produce the maximum good possible.

Ross, let it be perfectly clear, is saying that different *right* acts, including special duties, do not have as a common factor the promotion of the maximum good. He holds us rather to an inescapable fact of our moral experience as he sees it: namely, there simply are different "rights." Among such *right* acts are the special obligations, which may be in conflict with each other, and the obligation to maximize the good. The *prima facie* special right of promise-keeping may be in conflict with the *prima facie* right of producing the maximum good possible. This is awkward, but we cannot simplify our problem of choice by urging that the duty to maximize goodness takes axiomatic priority over other *prima facie* duties, as a teleologist would hold if he were deciding the conflict. To a given act may be attached different *prima facie* duties that are in conflict. If this

[6] *Ibid.*
[7] *Ibid.*, p. 79.

sounds complicated, we are not to blame the moralist but the data of our moral experience, which do not seem to obey our desire for a simple overruling principle.

In this view, when we approach the problem of what to do in certain circumstances, we find ourselves "seeing" a certain imagined act as "fitting" or "unfitting" in those circumstances. Any act, however, is complicated and many-sided, bringing, let us say, harm to some benefactors and good to others who have not helped us. The same act that breaks a promise here builds confidence there. The fact that we cannot pronounce "straight off on rightness or wrongness in the totality of these aspects" [8] does not keep us from feeling nevertheless that we have certain *prima facie* obligations to the situations as seen in different perspectives. But, as we become clearer about complicated choice situations, even *prima facie* obligations may give way to the choice that maximizes goodness. Thus an act *prima facie* wrong may turn out to be the right act when it is seen to be the most right of the obligations open to us. We are not obligated once and for all to do that which is obligatory on immediate inspection.

To comment: Ross has been forced to make a distinction between *prima facie* or immediately felt obligatoriness and *actual* obligatoriness. Thus the tendency of an act to fulfill a promise and "the tendency of an act insofar as it seems to produce the greatest good" may both be right *prima facie,* but if it turns out that the fulfilling of the promise is not likely to produce the greatest good in the total situation, the promise might well not be kept.[9] Accordingly, when *prima facie* obligations, special or not, conflict, a moral agent balances aspects of the total situation and comes to a decision as to which is actually obligatory in that situation. It is in this way that Ross hopes to meet the usual criticism that moral intuitions give no guidance when choices are complex. For if in a given situation, *prima facie* obligations do conflict, any one of them may be overridden if the total moral situation calls for it.

C. *Good Character as Right and Highest Good*

It might seem that, for Ross, some *prima facie* obligations are not standing obligations, but only obligations "if and but." This would

[8] *Ibid.,* p. 84.
[9] See *ibid.,* p. 89.

be the wrong interpretation. For "an act of promise-breaking is morally unsuitable insofar as it is an act of promise-breaking, even when we decide that in spite of this it is the act that we ought to do." [10] And usually, as our "natural moral consciousness" informs us, when keeping a promise to A involves us in slight preponderance of harm to B, we should still keep the promise and not be asking about every promise: Will it lead to a preponderance of good? For the fact is that we do recognize grounds of rightness other than productivity of good results.[11] Again, there simply is no easy formula for deciding which *prima facie* duty is to be preferred when *prima facie* duties conflict. For right acts, then, are *right* because they are right; they are not to be chosen because they are *good* teleologically.

Yet it is right, we have also seen, to produce as much *good* as possible—or a balance of good over evil. It would help us to choose among goods and also guide choice when "right acts" conflict if we could know whether any priority exists among *goods*. As it turns out, Ross, reminiscent of Kant, claims that among goods, the highest is the duty to build good character in ourselves. To build a good character means to cultivate our sense of duty, so that we shall not only perform rights acts but also perform them as much as possible from a sense of duty.[12]

An interesting and important distinction is involved here, and an illustration will bring it out. If I pay my debts because it is my duty to pay my debts, I am doing the right thing, whatever in addition my motive may be. But if I pay my debts, not only as my specific duty but also from a sense of duty, the act has *moral* worth, which it would not otherwise have. Note: I do not do my duty *from* a sense of duty. That is, I do not pay my debt only on the ground that I ought to develop my character. I pay my debt because a debt simply ought to be paid. But I ought to cultivate *the motive of doing my duties* (or character) as the highest good. My duty to pay my debts does not become right because I have the right motive (to develop my character); but I ought to have the right motive and I ought to do that duty! In other words, any duty is to be done, ideally, both because it is a duty and because I am the kind of person who feels morally bound as a person to do his duties, whatever they turn out to be.

[10] *Ibid.,* p. 85.
[11] See *ibid.,* p. 91.
[12] *Ibid.,* p. 122.

Why is it important to perform an act of duty from a sense of duty? As we have seen, an act is right because a person sees that it is right in a given situation. But because these intuitions of rightness are so specific and so different, why does our doing of right not simply involve us in performing a series of discontinuous duties? Because we also have a duty to produce as much good as possible, and because the highest of goods is the good of character. But character develops only as a man does his different duties from a sense of duty. Thus, the duty to do the right not only because it is right but because we are morally obligated as persons to do what we find to be right infuses our moral efforts with a unity they would not have otherwise.

We make our transition from the nature of right to the nature of goodness by stressing the approach to ethical knowledge that is exemplified in our analysis so far. It is Ross's underlying conviction

> that both in mathematics and in ethics we have certain crystal-clear intuitions from which we build up all that we can know about the nature of numbers and the nature of duty . . . ; we do not read off our knowledge of particular branches of duty from a single ideal of the good life, but build up our ideal of the good life from intuitions into particular branches of duty. [And Ross adds the significant sentence] In the course of our thinking we come to know more, but we should never come to know more if we did not *know* what we start with.[13]

This last statement will give special pause to those who say that what is right and wrong is learned in every respect from social experience. One can hear the echo of a Plato who held that man could never know anything if he had to begin in complete ignorance!

But Ross has made an important addition to his thesis that we have *particular* intuitions of right and wrong. For what unifies the doing of specific duties is the fact that the person himself is morally obligated in a choice situation to a *nonspecific* good that supports all other "rights" and "goods." This nonspecific good is the duty of exerting himself to do what seems "morally most suitable" in a given set of circumstances. We are not simply to do right acts, but we are to do them from good motives of producing the greatest good possible (including the highest good, character). What this amounts to is that *the good,* whatever else it is, must contain due consideration

[13] *Ibid.,* pp. 144–45.

of *prima facie rights,* including special obligations and the obligation to produce the greatest good possible.

D. *The Good in Contrast to the Right*

We must now ask how Ross would define good when it does not
mean acts of obligation (general and special). After all, not even the
general duty to maximize goodness can be followed unless we know
what constitutes this goodness. We may begin with the question:
Are there "things that are good through and through," and not good
as a means to something else? Ross's answer is affirmative, and he
once more asks us to introspect and see if we can agree with him on
the following main points.

(a) Do we actually, for example, think that all things are good
only if, or *because,* we approve them or are interested in them (or
because they bear some other *relation* to a state of ourselves)? Or do
we call some things good because they are worthy of approval in
themselves? Let us begin with the conscientious life to which we
have already referred. Do we believe character to be good because
we approve it, or do we approve it because *it* is worthy? Ross has no
doubt that the conscientious life is good in itself, that it is worthy
of our approval, and not worthy *because of* our approval. And he
would say the same of benevolence and of other moral dispositions.
Whether conscientiousness and benevolence *also* are liked, or have
good results, or no, has nothing to do with their goodness. This is
what the moral consciousness knows, says Ross, and this is the end
of the matter.

Nevertheless, suppose we denied these intuitions, and any others
like them. Suppose we asserted that all goods or values are values
because someone is interested in,[14] or likes, what is considered valuable. We would find ourselves, claims Ross, in a serious situation.
"If things were only approved, without anything being worthy of
approval, the act of approval would simply be nonsensical." [15] Indeed, the very fact that we often tell ourselves that some of the
things we approve are not worthy of being approved illustrates that
we do believe that some things at least are worthy of being approved. If all our value judgments consist simply of approvals and
disapprovals, how could we get to "*worthy* of approval" and "*worthy*

[14] See next chapter.
[15] *Foundations of Ethics,* p. 262.

of disapproval"? If we start only with "is approved," how do we get
to "worthy of approval"? [16]

This argument, however, is simply Ross's way of forcing us to do
justice to what he believes is, in the last analysis, the intuition that
nothing makes the conscientious life good but itself. And the same
type of consideration applies to knowledge and to aesthetic experience, as we shall now see.

(b) Is intelligence good because we approve it, or is it good and
thus seen to be worthy of approval? Is not knowledge intrinsically
preferable to ignorance and error? Consider, for example, the use
of intelligence "which notices differences where *they* exist and iden-
tities where *they* exist, which draws from premises only the conclusions which they warrant." [17] Is it not certain that "whether or not
all or most men always have liked and always will like these things—
which we cannot possibly know—they are intrinsically better than
their opposites, better worth having, more *worthy* of admiration,
whether they receive it or not?" [18] There is no doubt in Ross's mind
that the mental activity that leads to knowledge is good not because
it is liked but because it is itself "an admirable activity of the human
spirit." And the same goes for artistic creation.

(c) By this time the reader himself may have asked: Is not pleasure in this same situation? Surely we think pleasure as such is good?
Ross would agree, but he considers several facts notable.

First, while we admire or commend moral dispositions and actions,
intellectual and artistic creation, we never commend or admire the
feeling of pleasure as such. Nor do we admire a man or think him
good merely because he feels pleasure.

Second, granted that pleasure is intrinsically good but not admired, it would seem, in view of man's widest obligation to maximize goodness, that we ought to produce it. But Ross believes that
no man ever feels obligated to produce pleasures that are the manifestation of a bad moral nature (for example, cruelty). Furthermore,
"we feel ourselves under no obligation to produce even innocent
pleasures for ourselves." [19] On the other hand, we do feel that we
ought to produce pleasure for others when it is not a morally bad
pleasure; and we certainly feel that we ought to minimize pain
when it is not a morally good pain.

[16] See *ibid.*, p. 266.
[17] *Ibid.*, p. 267.
[18] *Ibid.*
[19] *Ibid.*, p. 272.

Rather than pursue Ross's interesting comments about pleasure further, we must focus attention on his observation that while non-vicious pleasures are not worthy of admiration, they are worthy of satisfaction, because we find ourselves justifiedly satisfied when we see people innocently happy.[20] And Ross is emphatic that the good of other persons' innocent pleasures, and our producing of them, is not constituted good by the fact that we are satisfied, but by the intrinsic nature of the pleasures themselves. Yet because we feel no *prima facie* obligation to produce pleasure irrespective of whether it is our own or others', because we do not, in any case, think pleasure to be an admirable activity (but a satisfying one), Ross concludes that pleasure is not intrinsically good, only good under certain limited conditions.

This conclusion about pleasure has consequences for practice. For "the *prima facie* duty of producing what is intrinsically good always takes precedence over the *prima facie* duty of producing pleasure for others." [21] Specifically, virtuous activity, intelligence, and aesthetic creativity confer goodness on their possessor and take precedence over pleasures as such. While pleasures, my own or those of others, are never worthy of admiration, the innocent pleasures of others are morally worthy objects of interest to me, but never objects felt to be obligatory by the experient himself.

There are many other facets of Ross's moral philosophy that merit attention, but we must turn to another type of moral realism, which will be all the clearer if we stop to underscore the general characteristics of Ross's ethical theory.

E. *Summary: The Person, the Right, and the Good*

(1) Fundamental is the conviction that when human beings say that an act or a state of affairs is right or good, they do not mean that it is right or good *because* they are interested in it or need it. In certain situations certain acts are seen to be suitable, and certain activities are seen to be good, apart from their needs and desires. The right and the good are characteristics of acts and activities open to human beings in their relation to themselves, each other, and the world about them.

(2) This presupposes that man has a moral consciousness that

[20] See *ibid.*, p. 276.
[21] *Ibid.*, p. 284.

discriminates (a) certain actions as right, or morally suitable, in certain situations, and (b) certain activities (for example, knowing versus ignorance, benevolence and conscientiousness versus selfishness and neglect of the claims of duty, aesthetic creativity versus aesthetic dullness) as unrestrictedly good.

(3) This does not mean that the moral consciousness solves all our particular problems of choice. Nothing can take the place of acute balancing of rights when they conflict or circumscribe assessment of goods in their relations to each other and to rights in concrete situations. The authors of this book, for example, hold that the core of moral obligation is the obligation to do the best one knows, without specifying how we know the best. Ross, agreeing that the widest obligation is to maximize the good, goes on to specify several obligations that arise in special circumstances and to discriminate certain goods as the best—such as the development of character, knowledge, aesthetic sensitivity, and concern for the innocent pleasures of others.

(4) Ross, therefore, does not set forth definite rules or a definite prescription for the ideal life. He contends that any morally sensitive person cannot but keep certain obligations and goods in mind as he tries to maximize the right and the good in every situation. Nothing can take the place of this sensitivity to good and to right, for these cannot be defined in terms of ingredients other than their own nature—any more than the quality of yellow can be defined by wave-lengths or any other color.

II. *THE GOOD AND THE PERSON IN THE ETHICAL REALISM OF VIVAS*

Eliseo Vivas of Northwestern University, in his vigorous book *The Moral Life and the Ethical Life* [22] agrees with Ross that values are objective, but he interprets the nature of the right and the good differently.

A. *Right as Meaningless Apart from Good*

The point of greatest disagreement between Vivas and Ross involves the notion of right. "The rightness of an action," says Vivas,

---

[22] Chicago: University of Chicago Press, 1950.

"does not unqualifiedly consist in its suitability, conceived as a character shining like the flush of youth on its cheek." [23] Vivas is concerned lest "what Ross takes to be the crystal-clear intuitions of men
who are good and enlightened . . . could be but the bland prejudices of a well-trained man in the unperturbed enjoyment of his
upper-class, hermetically sealed, pre-Buchenwald, pre-Hiroshima,
imperial British insularity." [24]

Furthermore, Ross fails to see that "right" has meaning only in a
choice situation where the individual is trying to decide which of
alternative values is fitting (right) in view of the context of acknowledged goods or values. Acts cannot be right in themselves; *right,* as
a moral concept, *has no independence.* Nor are there independent
obligations to make claims on a person apart from their capacity to
"fit" as "the best completion" to a value system which the individual
acknowledges.

Vivas' view calls for a shift from a polar tension between the right
and the good to the centrality of the good, that is, the ultimate authority of values. The *ethical realism* of Vivas, therefore, concerns
the primary objectivity of the good and not the co-equal objectivity
of the right.

Two other facts stand out in the total moral situation as Vivas
conceives it. First: what makes man a person is not that he, as *man,*
has certain familiar psychophysiological capacities, but that these
capacities have been informed and unified (more or less) by a hierarchy of values that he acknowledges. Man-in-culture is not what he
is because of his culture, but his culture is what it is because of the
values he finds required of him. These values, once selected and
organized, become his "conscience," that is, the basis for his selection
of other values and even of the value that he puts upon himself as
a person. Man's problem, therefore, is so to use his powers and capacities that he can discover, appropriate, realize, and thus become
a carrier of these values, without which he can never become what
he "truly" is.[25]

This statement of the problem might sound as though man must
first examine his own capacities and powers and then select and
organize "values" in accordance with that nature. But actually,

[23] *The Moral Life and the Ethical Life,* p. 253. This is not entirely fair to Ross, who
granted that *prima facie* obligations were not crystal-clear in the sense that they could
be enacted without further thought.
[24] *Ibid.,* p. 253.
[25] See *ibid.,* p. 241.

Vivas believes just the opposite. He intends to define *man* by the values he acknowledges, and not the values by man's nature. As he sees it, the order and hierarchy of values is not created by man. In some sense, values are in the very constitution of things, and it is man's choosing of them that allows him to become a *person* or personality.

To put this important concept differently, whether man likes it or not, he is the kind of being who responds to values; in the vernacular, he is "a sucker for" values.[26] "The good chooses us through the effect of its requiredness upon us, which we merely acknowledge. *We do not create it; we discover it.*"[27] Once more: "The values which, through his own free decisions he [man] sought to incorporate and through whose incorporation he grew into a person were not themselves created by him. They found him and exercised on him their requiredness."[28]

But the meaning is not that man has no freedom or creativity in the moral situation. For it is always a given man with his conscience or the present organization of values in his life who must further choose among the objective values. The values he chooses and incorporates further help to determine which way his powers and capacities shall go. In short, a man will become the person that the values he chooses allow him to become. But he always chooses from within a more or less organized, unified, hierarchized system of values, which constitute him or make him what he is. The decision is his, the acting his, but, just as the road a motorist takes will take him to a predetermined exit, the way of value a man chooses will develop him into the kind of person his values dictate. But his choosing them does not make them good.

Second: it is this theory of the good that provides the content of Vivas' conception of the right.

> What actually makes a choice right, or the best under the circumstances, is that it possesses a value-character or quality apprehended as objectively independent of the agent. The choice fits because it possesses this value character . . . which fits into the moral system of an agent seeking the solution of a perplexity.[29]

[26] See *ibid.,* p. 259.
[27] *Ibid.,* p. 240.
[28] *Ibid.,* p. 241.
[29] *Ibid.,* p. 238.

And the voice of conscience [30] is not that of a distinct moral consciousness aware of specific or special obligations, but "the voice of one's self" or "an aroused moral personality in the act of defending itself against disruption." [31]

B. *The Foundation of Radical Altruism*

The nature and justification of altruism is especially noteworthy in Vivas' version of ethical realism. A man, we have been told, becomes a person insofar as he incorporates values that give quality to his life. But the values he incorporates do not exhaust the range of values that he espouses as worthwhile, not only for himself but for others. A man could not consistently respect values unless he respected men who respond to and seek to incorporate values.

> This is to say that we recognize another person's moral claim in the same manner in which we recognize any other set of values which presents itself before our consciousness and elicits our espousal, because we respond to its collective requiredness. But this is not all, since we respond chiefly to the requiredness of one value above all, the value of the other person, which we acknowledge as a value by agreeing to consider his demands. Let me illustrate what is here involved. Peter says to Paul, "You ought to grant me this request, x." Paul, in acknowledging his obligation to consider its legitimacy (not to grant it), recognizes that Peter is a person and, as such, embodies a value and that to disregard Peter's request is to treat him as a thing. The satisfaction of the demand is thus an addition to the universe of values espoused by Peter and recognized by Paul, an addition which Paul cannot refuse to consider without turning his back on the requiredness of the values in question. [32]

It never becomes quite clear whether another man is valuable as a man rather than as a person. Does a man make moral demands

---

[30] In contrast to the view of the authors of this text, there seems to be no generic ought-function; and no specific obligations, in contrast to Ross's view of right. And yet in answering the question: Why should I be moral? Vivas says: "Man ought to be moral because he has two duties from which all his other duties derive, the duty to know God and the duty . . . to realize himself as a person" or "to live up to the highest value that one is capable of" (*ibid.*, pp. 248, 259). This last clause is close to our "I ought to do the best I know" and to Ross's widest of duties. But Vivas seems to assert here rather than justify these answers.

[31] *Ibid.*, p. 236.

[32] *Ibid.*, p. 260.

upon us simply because he is a "featherless biped" with certain powers? In a sense, this is an academic question, for the distinction be
tween man and person must remain a matter of the degree to which
values are incorporated.[33] But strictly speaking, the logic of Vivas'
position would force him to say that only values "require," and a
human being has value only to the extent that he does embody
value. Vivas does say that "a person is a human being who possesses
intrinsic value and who embodies a system of values." [34]

In the last analysis, however, Vivas himself seems to insist that the
"source of moral authority cannot be the will or any other aspect of
our [not-yet-personal] psyche," or of anyone's else psyche.[35] The
moral ground for altruism stems from the value-requiredness without which we cannot become or remain persons.[36] What gives a man
dignity is not his being a psyche or self with certain powers, psychic
needs, or interests, but the fact that his psyche acknowledges values,
feels itself morally responsible for this (selective) incorporation, and
thus *derivatively* becomes a source of value.[37]

Before continuing, we must note the contrast that exists in the
thinking of Ross and Vivas in this matter of altruism, for it will give
rise to another critical difference among ethical realists. Ross simply
holds it to be an intuitive demand that benevolence is a moral duty.
As we saw, the primary, admired goods of character, of knowing,
and of aesthetic experience and the limited goods of pleasure are to
be respected and promoted in others. But for Ross, all these goods
are qualities of experience *in persons* and are admired or approved
as such by a morally sensitive person. For Ross there are no "values
independent of persons," although the values as goods do not become values simply because persons approve or are interested in
them. Again, such values as Ross designates are experiences of conscious persons; they have intrinsic value as the fine activities of
spirit.

But Vivas conceives of values as a kind of ultimate component of
the total environment in which a self lives; "these values stand
toward their discoverer as something which is distinct and independent of, I would even say *prior* to, himself." [38] Thus values have

---

[33] Cf. *ibid.*, p. 326.
[34] *Ibid.*, p. 259 (italics added).
[35] *Ibid.*, p. 264.
[36] Cf. *ibid.*, pp. 264, 266, 326.
[37] See *ibid.*, p. 326.
[38] *Ibid.*, p. 267.

a status in the nature of things for Vivas; they may be said to be ontologically independent of man. Each man carves his own unique system out of them and thereby becomes a person worthy of respect. On Ross's view, values are found not "in the universe," or in God, but where persons recognize them, as qualities of human achievement and enjoyment that are obligatory for all persons. For Ross, values or goods do not "first" exist independent of *man* and then make him a *person* as he selects those which will make him truly what he is. For Ross, other persons are the sources of our moral concern simply because their values are admired by us and their innocent pleasures are satisfying to us.[39]

Thus, in the thought of Vivas and Ross we see two fascinating developments of the essential thesis of ethical realism, with Vivas much closer to the Platonic conception of values and man's relation to them, and with Ross dethroning them from their ontological status as such beyond man. At the same time Ross insists, as Plato and Vivas do, that the goods and the duties of life are not good or dutiful because men like them or approve of them, but because they are worthy of men's approval and obligation whether men like them or approve of them or not.

C. *The Dignity of Man*

The more specific problem we are here discussing, whether man has dignity and value intrinsically, or whether he *acquires* dignity and moral worth by embodying values, is not one to which Vivas is insensitive. Indeed, he regards his whole treatment of the moral life as incomplete, for he believes that no adequate account has been given of that rare dimension of life which he holds to be the moral demand that a true Christian in particular makes on himself. This is the obligation to love another person for his own sake regardless of the values he embodies. Vivas acutely and eloquently depicts that crucial problem in the moral life that arises when a person with his system of values confronts another whose values are not consonant with his own.

Are men, then, to be respected for the values they embody or which *inhere* in them, in the ways in which Ross, for example, seems

---

[39] It is not easy to decide whether the term "person" is used in the same sense by Ross and Vivas. It might well be that the distinction between "man" and "person" is one Ross would regard as unnecessary except to bring out the fact that what gives man's life quality is value-activity.

to suggest? Or are men to be treated not only as intrinsic values but as "superior to all the other values we espouse"? [40] In a word, is another to be respected by me because, as a human being, he has value incommensurable with any other values he may or may not embody? [41]

We stay close to Vivas' own statement of the issue:

> For what the Christian does is to say to himself, so to speak, the following: "Nothing I want, no value that attracts me, no secular good, whether it be power or wealth or knowledge or happiness, not even the value of life itself, which I espouse so desperately and for the sake of which, if necessary, I would be ready to sacrifice so much—no other value can compare with one special value I ought to espouse. And this is the value that resides intrinsically in each man because he is a person. So that, if I have to choose between injury to all my other values and injury to the person of another, the choice is clear because, no matter what a person may be, I must acknowledge this value above all others." [42]

Unless this is so, says Vivas, "it is not possible to respect a coward as much as a hero, nor is it possible to respect a brothel-keeper as much as a sister of charity." [43] For unless a person has intrinsic worth himself, distinct from the total worth of values he espouses, on what grounds can we do what the Christian demands—treat another person

> in such a way as to avoid violating his dignity no matter how unworthy morally he may be known to be. For him, beyond moral distinctions, lies the intrinsic worth of a man which neither vice nor weakness nor accident can annihilate. The keeper of the brothel has intrinsic worth, no less than the self-sacrificing nurse serving in the leper colony, and the rat-catcher or the garbage man no less than the king.[44]

That a great deal will theoretically and practically depend upon being able to justify intrinsic respect for man as opposed to respect for him as a carrier of value should now be clear. Vivas is not willing

[40] *Ibid.*, p. 288.
[41] Cf. *ibid.*, p. 289.
[42] *Ibid.*, p. 289.
[43] *Ibid.*, p. 329.
[44] *Ibid.*, p. 329, and see p. 345.

himself to establish the primacy of the person simply by the Christian contention that all men are created equal in God's sight. He is aware also that more needs to be said than he has said in this book.

But, avoiding technicalities, Vivas' argument runs as follows. The person deserves unqualified respect because any living being has intrinsic value and the human being exhibits the highest form of being (which Vivas calls "spirit"). His is the highest form of being because he alone is able not only to live and be in the world but to know that he is (self-consciousness), to know his environmental surroundings as objects to be known and appreciated for what they are in themselves and in relation to him (objectivity), and to be creative as he molds himself and converts his given nature by ideal values (freedom).[45]

Self-consciousness, objectivity, and freedom—these capacities mark man off from all lower beings. For they make man's existence, which is "never utterly devoid of value," [46] one in which he is able to reach beyond the realm of organic needs and know both the anguish and the joy that life, freedom, and creativity bring. "Between the poles of birth and death there is an area over which we have some mastery, since between them we can exercise in spontaneity the creativity of our spirit, can play with beauty, create truth, and mold even our own character." [47]

Here we see once more that the goods, which Ross made the source of moral admiration, reappear as the fine products of the spirit. Whether Vivas has actually made his case for the intrinsic value of persons, independent of any specific set of values, is questionable. He seems, in the last analysis, to be depending on an ethical intuition that human existence is valuable, whereas earlier he claimed only that objective values give men value. His reply would probably be that it is man's capacity for self-consciousness, objectivity, and freedom that renders him supremely valuable. After all, the difference between man, the existent, and the person, the existent who has incorporated objective values, is one of degree, for man is never "utterly devoid of value." True, Vivas has two contentions: man, regardless what moral status he achieves, is intrinsically valuable; and man cannot be given value apart from the values he incorporates. Does Vivas reconcile the two adequately?

[45] Cf. *ibid.*, pp. 332–33.
[46] *Ibid.*, p. 340.
[47] *Ibid.*, p. 343.

III. *THE UNDERLYING CHALLENGE OF ETHICAL REALISM*

Our concern in this and the previous two chapters has not been to attempt a critique of Plato, Butler, Kant, Ross, or Vivas, but to lay bare some essential contentions of ethical realism and the nature of its challenge to other theories of obligation and value knowledge. For ethical realism, as we have noted from the beginning of the last chapter, involves an underlying view of man and his place in the universe that is larger than any particular tenet. The underlying challenge involves not so much the problem whether man has a non-sensory, moral awareness of special obligations and values, though this is an important issue to settle. It is not even whether man's nature feels obligated to realize values once he intuits them or knows them in some manner or other. It is whether man's own needs and actions are *the* source of the values that man does admire and respect or that bring satisfaction to him.

The ethical realist is as interested as any psychologist in the nature of man. But he believes that any psychology (and his criticism has relevance to the psychologies we have studied) is inadequate to man's actual experience of obligation and values if it sees these as *functions of* man's feeling, thinking, willing, or wanting. Obligation and valuing tell a story also about man's environment and man's relation to it. No man is valuable simply because some other man knows him, likes him or dislikes him, or needs him to fulfill his needs. A man is valuable either because value is to be predicated of him as he is, independently of others' wishes or knowledge, or because he incarnates, exhibits, enjoys values that, as it were, stand over against him and all men and *give value* to individual lives.

In bare terms, the ethical realist holds that if there is no value already in the universe, be it in God, in a Platonic realm of Ideas, or man as the kind of being he is, then no values can "rub off" on man because of anything he may like or want. Just as the psychologist says that man must "adjust" his needs and wants and abilities to his environment or suffer (be it anxiety, distortion, malformation, or death), so the ethical realist says: Unless a man become aware of values as standards by which he is to guide and transform his nature, not only will he have no moral signposts to guide him, but he will never know when or to what extent his being has been fulfilled. For "fulfilled" is a value term. Psychological health has no meaning if we look only into man and neglect the values by which man's health is to be evaluated.

Finally, although Plato, Vivas, and Ross differ in their conceptions of the manner in which values, the good, and the right are finally to be conceived, they agree that the good is not made good by the person's experiencing or knowing it. Such ethical realism is the most outstanding, perennial contrast to the kind of theory of value that we have seen emerging from the thinking of psychologists like those we have studied (and from the thinking in the rest of this book). Indeed, it is because ethical realists have made human cognition of value a testimony to a realm not open to microscope or telescope that the theory of man becomes so different.

If we see man as a complicated animal, existent, changing step by step in accordance with essentially biological laws, striving among his competitors to stay alive and strong, we tend to see the whole world focused around the "fulfillment" of such needs and their derivatives. But if we take a normal adult, an ethical realist would say, we find him feeling obligations and responding to a realm of value. These values are as important to his "life" (when we are thinking about more than mere existence and staying alive) as is his sensory world for the movement of his body and the gratification of his organic needs. Thus man's capacities, especially his moral-rational nature, need to be seen in a different light. However they may be affected by society, they are never its product, and they exist rather as beacons of a realm of being by cooperative response to which man may find his highest fruition.

To be sure, writers like Fromm, Maslow, and Allport show increasing awareness of the problem of human fulfillment on its own terms; and to some extent they set aside the developmental for the sake of the peak experiences (or value-experiences) by which, they urge, development is to be judged. But when they come to the analysis of moral existence itself, they tend to revert to the developmental. They see the moral life as a function of human capacity and need rather than a sensitivity in man that indicates that he needs to adjust to a larger realm. Finally, all the psychologists stress the need that human beings have for each other, but Vivas' question "Does one value himself or others intrinsically, or because he 'needs' them?" does not enter into the scope of their analyses.

We are thus brought back to the crucial issue that has emerged so far: Do we assume that human life itself has independent value and how do we determine that value? Do we assign value to human life in terms of its kinship with a realm of value by which human life is to be informed? Do we assign value to human existence because it is the kind of existence that exemplifies the values we find ourselves obligated to and admiring (Ross)? Before we can return to this question and the poles so starkly defined, we must study those ethical thinkers who would turn their backs on all of these contentions and hold that the very conception of values as common to all men results from a false analysis of the human situation.

IV. *REFLECTIVE SUMMARY*

The basic contention of the ethical realist is that human beings have a moral consciousness of basic values which, independent of human cognition, and desire, yet demands human allegiance. Of the variations on this basic theme, the views of W. D. Ross and E. Vivas accent suggestive differences.

Ross holds that certain actions in certain special situations are right, that is, make a moral claim upon us—for example, loyalty to parents and keeping one's promise—whatever the consequences.

A conflict between such special duties is subject to the duty to maximize the good, although the duties themselves do not consist in their relation to the good.

Among the goods to be preferred, on Ross's view, the highest good is the doings of actions from a sense of duty; and this good, character, along with the duty to maximize the good, serves to give unity to moral choice. But other goods besides conscientiousness—for example, benevolence, aesthetic and intellectual creation—are good not because of their consequences but because they carry their own intrinsic worthiness with them.

Vivas cannot agree with Ross's contention that actions can claim to be morally *right* independent of their relation to goods (or values). For Vivas an action is right not because it is intrinsically "fitting" but because it fits into the realization of objective values. In Vivas' terminology, unless man did feel the claim of the hierarchy of values, he would never be a person, for it is only as these values are selectively incorporated into a man's life that he becomes a person.

Another notable difference between Ross and Vivas consists in the way each conceives of objectivity. Both agree that objectivity means independence of like and want. But for Ross the goods are inherent in persons and are to be respected as bearers of value, whereas for Vivas they are independent of persons.

Yet are persons to be respected only as bearers of values? Or are they themselves the highest values to be respected, irrespective of the values they incorporate? On Vivas' view, it would seem that persons in fact cannot be respected "for themselves," because their value must come from their ability to incorporate the objective order of value selectively. In Ross's theory, to respect goods is to respect persons in whom they exist.

Whatever the differences and problems, the essential view of man that emerges is impressive. Man is the kind of being who can fulfill himself not solely by consulting his interests, wants, and capacities, as he interacts with his environment, but by heeding the claims of rights and values whose worth does not depend upon man's knowing them or wanting them. Nor can man ever realize himself in his world without heeding the imperatives of his moral consciousness.

12

The Denial of Ethical Realism: Emotivism and Privatistic Relativism

~~~~~~

Three baseball umpires had been discussing the difficulties involved in judging strikes and balls. Finally the first umpire said: "Some's balls and some's strikes and I calls 'em as they is." The second declared: "Some's balls and some's strikes and I calls 'em as I sees 'em." The third asserted: "Some's balls and some's strikes but they ain't nothin' till I calls 'em."

While there are close parallels to these convictions in ethical theory, the situation is more complicated, as the reader has already noted. The first two umpires are closer to the position of the realist in value theory for they agree that there are strikes and balls (good and bad, right and wrong) regardless of whether they are accurately perceived. The third umpire represents the position of "subjectivists," who contend that whatever is going on outside their minds, there is no such thing as value until some mind "calls 'em." But there is more than one type of subjectivism in value theory, so we must, in this chapter and the next, study basic types. Because each type rejects ethical realism or "objectivism," let us call to mind once more the major contention of the objectivist.

I. OBJECTIVISM AND ITS DISCONTENTS

The objectivist in value theory maintains, we have seen, that when we experience rightness or goodness, we are undergoing an interaction roughly parallel to what takes place, for example, when we experience a red apple or any sensory object (on the uncritical, "common sense" view). We believe that the red apple we are experiencing does not depend for its existence on our being aware of it. Presumably the red apple was already "there" to be experienced. When we met the conditions for seeing it, the red apple became an object of perception. The "perception" of justice and love is not essentially different, although our moral consciousness, not our senses, is involved in "intuiting" them as good or right for us. Justice, for example, does not depend upon our being aware of it for its existence, but it makes a specific difference to us if we meet the conditions for becoming aware of it.

We may draw another parallel between our experience of a red apple and of justice. Let us say (again perhaps uncritically with "common sense") that the pleasant response we normally have to the red apple is a pleasantness *in us* that is caused by the red apple. Similarly, the objectivist maintains, the "ought" response in us is the effect of having beheld "justice." To experience and to know justice is to feel obligated to it. Neither our feeling of obligation nor the obligatory object is created by the experient, for the specific obligation in the experient takes place only because justice (or any other value) is what it is. Thus, the one thing all objectivists insist upon is that, despite the errors we make in intuiting and in acting, in our value experiences we are not the *makers* of the value any more than we are the makers of the red apple.

But what objectivist has not had his moments of serious doubt? No matter how vivid and convincing some of his own experiences have been, he has been bothered by the fact that other respected and sensitive human beings—and not undisciplined reprobates—have evidentaly been blind to his visions. At moments like these he might say: "May it not be that what I 'see' says more about me than about what is out there? And have I not discovered in my own experience that the moral certainties of one time in my own life were different from, and sometimes contradictory to, those I later experienced? In view of the changing 'certainties' in my own life, in view of the sincere disagreements that I discover with objectivists like myself even in my own culture, I wonder whether the values I assert as independent of my knowing and of my attitude to them are really independent?"

The objectivist might even continue his reflections in similar vein: "Nor must I underestimate the possibly disastrous psychological impact objectivism can have upon me. For if I believe that the values I espouse are not values because I say so, but because they are trends or even controlling factors in the very structure of the universe, I feel that regardless of what other people say or do, it is important for me to be loyal to these values 'though the heavens fall' and though other persons are (at least immediately) hurt. If I hold that the equality of all people is 'the way of things' or the will of God, without adherence to which men will become decadent, what prevents me from deciding that my duty is to see that others give allegiance to that good whether they, in their benighted state, see it or not. Such mistaken persons can so live and legislate that they can be impediments to real progress in value; I must, therefore, do all I can to keep them from social and political power. People like me have done a lot of good, as history shows, but some of us have not stopped at unmitigated cruelty. We have been so concerned to lift people out of their mere social customs and conventional morality and lethargy that we have been willing to sacrifice some of them, if necessary, to the cause righteous for all people! I'm afraid I must admit that this objectivist position of mine clearly does not necessarily lead to good practical results."

No thinking objectivist is unfamiliar with such reflections. He may say that the cruel results are accidents, not necessities of his position. A man may believe in ethical "absolutism" without being cruel in practice. This may be so, but perhaps we had better consider first the views of writers who have been driven by the objectivist's compunctions, among other things, toward subjectivistic theories which they believe better accord with the complex facts.

II. EMOTIVISM AND ITS CAUTIONS

Emotivism is a theory of value and ethics that has been considerably discussed in the last twenty-five years, especially in England and

America. The most influential representatives have been A. J. Ayer [1] in England and Charles L. Stevenson [2] in America. Emotivists have been self-critical and much criticized, and it would be unfair for us to suppose that the brief statement given here would adequately take care of the attenuations and extensions attempted by various emotivists. Emotivism has made its basic impact through a far-reaching challenge to every other type of ethical theory, subjectivist and objectivist. Its major onslaught seeks to destroy traditional views through a totally different analysis of human moral experience.

The objectivist points out an important distinction. It is elementary in logic and philosophy to say that any judgment or proposition that is not self-contradictory may be true or false. Thus, because there is nothing logically contradictory about the statement "All men are four-eyed creatures," it may be true. But this claim runs counter to the sensory evidence; so, even if there is no logical reason why it cannot be true, we say that in fact it is not true.

Similarly, turning to the realm of moral experience, there is nothing logically contradictory, says the objectivist, about the ethical claim that to hurt innocent persons needlessly is morally wrong. But any person who *perceives* the act of one person hurting another person, who knows that this hurt is being done to an innocent person, also intuits by way of the *moral* consciousness that this act is, in fact, morally wrong and feels the obligation not to do it and to condemn such action. He believes that "right and wrong," "good and evil" are equivalent to morally true and morally false. In other words, right and wrong are predicates that refer truly to what is there; the ball pitched over the plate waist-high is really a "strike" before the umpire calls it so. Right and good are ethical judgments, and they can be discovered to be true or false, says the objectivist. (His view is accordingly often called a *cognitivist* view of ethical judgment.)

On the emotivist view, however, the whole debate about truth and falsity of ethical judgments is a battle that should never have been fought. Why? Because we made the costly mistake of assuming that in morality we are talking about what characterized something going on independently of our own feelings or emotional responses (in the example given, the hurting of an innocent person needlessly). We

---

[1] A. J. Ayer, *Language, Truth and Logic* (2nd ed.; New York: Dover, 1952).
[2] Charles L. Stevenson, *Ethics and Language* (New Haven: Yale University Press, 1944).

failed to realize that our predicate adjectives, "right" and "wrong," are not *in fact* aimed at telling what is so about the act but only at telling what our emotional response is to the action. To understand this view, we must take a closer look at the way in which we treat our emotional responses.

A. *Emotions and Attitudes Describe Only Our Responses to Actions*

We do not want to claim that our emotional response to an object is true or false. We feel fear, anger, joy, or sorrow, and we do not think of their being true or false attributes of their objects. We fear mice, become angry at molestation, are sorry when we are hurt—but the fear, anger, or sorrow does not "say" anything about mice, molestation, or hurt as such. Another person may wonder at mice, be patient with molestation, and be angry when hurt. Surely our feeling-emotional responses as such do not tell us anything dependable about the objects (and, because we too change, even about ourselves often). Therefore, we do not use terms like "true" and "false" about emotions, as we would do if we believed that they told us anything about the object. We just do not dare to say with any confidence: mice are fearful, molestation is anger-provoking, and hurt is sorrow-causing. But we do say with confidence that mice are small rodents, molestation involves interference, and hurt can lead to illness.

If we carry this line of reasoning over to the ethical arena, we see why the emotivist asserts that the ethical debates were needless and without solution. The fundamental premise, that ethical judgments are assertions (about states of affairs) that can be true or false, is as mistaken as would be the statement that emotional characterizations of states of affairs are true or false. Accordingly, emotivists hold that ethical judgments do not in fact *say* anything—meaning, say anything about a state of affairs in any sense that could be verified by observing the state of affairs. All that an ethical judgment does is to *express* a person's emotional response to a situation. Some situations please him and he says: "Fine! Grand! Hurrah!" Others displease him and he expresses himself by words expressive of his negative emotional response. Thus his emotive response may be negative to a person's being needlessly hurt, but it makes no sense to call the response a judgment that is true or false.

What, then, happens to such ethical terms as "right," "wrong," "bad," "good"? They are expressions of attitudes in favor of (pro attitudes) or against (anti attitudes) some object or action. Attitudes are psychological formations in the personality that prepare a person to respond negatively or positively toward certain objects. ("I favor learning and teachers. I'm against 'grinds' and pedants.") Because attitudes are states of readiness to respond favorably or unfavorably to certain objects, they tell us about ourselves and our responsiveness and not about "balls and strikes as they is" or even "as I sees 'em." There are truths and facts about situations in the light of which every normal agent acts, but none of these is the "value" of these situations, which can reside only in the response.

B. *The Emotivist Substitute for Obligation*

We have noted that the emotivist uses a whole theory of what makes a statement true as a backlog for the fire with which he burns away the contention that ethical judgments are true or false. We must now see what the moral situation is as reconstructed in terms of emotivism.

In the first place, a "pro" or "anti" attitudinal state must be substituted for Butler's magisterial, authoritative state, for Kant's feeling of moral respect, or for our own claim that the feeling of ought is not one of inclination. The emotivist finds himself not "obligated" but feeling "warm" or "cold" in different degrees about different situations.

In the second place, moving beyond the state of mind, to the value object, the emotivist denies that there is a strike or ball for him to call. Thus, if I am told that six million Jews were systematically exterminated by Hitler, I may find myself bitterly indignant against Hitler and ready to demand that steps be taken that will prevent any recurrence of such actions. But I must realize that this means only that I feel this way about the situation as I conceive it. My attitude is not true; it is only against. There's no point in my telling my neighbor that he *ought* to condemn this situation as wrong. My only hope is that his *attitude* will *agree* with mine.

For attitudes, after all, are not true or false or right or wrong; they are only stronger or weaker. I may find that others have attitudes in *common* with mine but without any natural reference to the "truth" of what we hold in common. If I say to you, "Slavery is wrong," all I can mean is that I have a negative attitude to it and hope that you will have the same. I can try to persuade you to see the situation as I see it and hope that you will feel as I feel about it. Again, I can try to be sure that my neighbor sees the facts that I see about slavery, and I can hope that his attitude may conform to mine and that we can work together to get others to conform their attitude to ours and act to put down the source of our annoyance. But, let us be clear about it, in all moral situations we cannot hope for valid and verifiable judgments; we can only hope for common attitudes based on truths about man and the world. This moral outlook will keep us from ranting and raving about moral absolutes and help us to focus our attention all the more on the actual objective facts about any moral situation and, if we so wish, on how to get attitudes changed.

It is not hard to see why some have felt that if this view is taken seriously, the whole moral life is undermined. If there are no objective standards, "anything goes"! But it must be stressed here that this is not the conclusion that the emotivist draws and certainly not the aim he has in mind. He believes that he is being more scrupulous in giving an adequate account of such ethical agreements and disagreements as we have, that once we understand and apply his position we can more intelligently move toward mutual understanding and agreement in moral attitudes. The emotivist (and the relativist) position cannot be rejected simply because it presumably will produce moral reprobates.

Therefore, as a third main argument in the emotivist's favor, let us consider his account of the basis for ethical disagreement. Moral agreements and disagreements occur, he believes, not only because psychological constitutions and personalities are different but also because persons actually differ about the facts relevant to the attitudes they have and do form. And surely we must admit that often, when the facts about a total situation are cleared up, persons with differing attitudes move toward common attitudes. Persons who disagree about the desirability, for example, of smoking or racial segregation may often be found to disagree because they disagree about the relevant facts. Surely, when the facts are unclear, it is hazardous to take a firm position and condemn the opposition. But two people, originally with opposing attitudes, may well move toward a common attitude as they move toward a common conception of the actual facts.

This argument still leaves unmentioned the very knotty problem of differences in attitude when there is agreement about facts, and the emotivist is not unaware of this. But is any problem that the emotivist encounters in trying to decide how best to persuade a person to change his attitude any different from that encountered by any other ethicist? We think not. If the emotivist theory of value is correct, and if his theory of obligation is adequate, his view cannot be rejected because there is no clear light on how to change attitudes, given agreement about facts. The emotivist is aware that language calls up attitudes and that change in one attitude can affect other attitudes, in ourselves and in others. The actual effect we have upon each other, apart from action, is through whatever emotional appeal our words have.

We cannot deny that there is much truth in emotivism as a psychology of persuasion, as far as it goes. If our main concern were solely to give an account of agreement and disagreement in ethical theory, to provide some feasible way out of the problems that harass objectivisms, and to indicate where we need to focus attention if we are to move toward moral agreement, we should be very much tempted to go along with the emotivists. But as an adequate account of our total moral experience, the emotivist view seems partial and unconvincing.

III. CRITIQUE OF EMOTIVIST'S VIEW OF OBLIGATION

Much has been said in this book about the *prima facie* experience of obligation, about how different it feels from inclination of any sort. Our own view has been that, however wrong the objectivist may be in his contention that the experience of obligation *is* a cognition of a specific duty or a general principle, his distinction between inclination and obligation reveals incontrovertible psychological insight. Thus, it seems clear to us that the concrete flow of the moral life does involve attitudes; it does involve beliefs; but it also involves an experience of obligation that is related to beliefs and attitudes but can be reduced to neither; and it gives a psychic tone and a thrust to life that must not be lost from sight. Let us be specific by considering this view in the light of the analysis by an outstanding exponent of emotivism in ethics, Charles L. Stevenson.

Stevenson finds an equivalence between what we may call the imperative of command (Defend your country!) and the moral im perative (You ought to defend your country!). There is no doubt that both imperatives seek the same end, defense of country, but what is left out, it seems to us, is the very essence of the difference between ought and all the other experiences we have of feeling, emotion, and want-need. It simply is not the case, as Stevenson holds, that "you ought not to cry!" as said to children, "is roughly interchangeable with "Stop crying!" [3] The all-important difference, psychologically speaking, has been ignored.

Here each person's introspection, in the last analysis, must be the final court of appeal. Speaking for ourselves, any kind of command or exhortation that proceeds simply from another's "I want you to," hedged about by any kind of pleas and suggestions (Please do! Please don't! I wish you wouldn't! I wish you would!), simply does not carry the kind of authority that is felt when I say "I ought to." If I say, "You ought," I mean not simply that I want or urge you to because I favor this; I do not simply mean that in the situation you confront there is a choice that you will want to make when you have the proper beliefs about it. I mean that, given insight on your part into the situation, the choice I am referring to is demanded not by me or by my desires but by your own capacity to feel obligated to the best that you know. If there is any command or any authority, it is the command of something within you that moves beyond the "attraction" of likes and the repulsion of dislikes. To be sure, we feel magnetic or countermagnetic emotive and attitudinal "suggestions" in the total social situation that includes us, but the "magisterial authority" of the ought is not based upon any positive want or negative fear.[4]

To press our contention: Does the reader find that the essentials of his moral experience are adequately expressed in this formulation of Stevenson?

(1) "This is wrong" means *"I disapprove of this: do so as well."*

(2) "He ought to do this" means *"I disapprove of his leaving this undone: do so as well."*

(3) "This is good" means *"I approve of this: do so as well."*

Let us leave aside, for the moment, the definition of the value experience or disvalue experience as expressive of the felt pro-attitude or anti-attitude. Is the hortatory imperative "Do as well!" substitutable for the kind of self-expectant authoritativeness felt in the

---

[3] Stevenson, *op. cit.*, p. 21.

[4] The reader may wish to refer back to the discussion of obligation for further reminder of the considerations which lead us to a derivation of "guilt" and "moral approval" different from that usually given (Chapter 9).

imperative of "ought"? In a moral situation, do I actually deal with no more than your attitudes and your beliefs in relation to my attitudes and my beliefs, with a view to bringing about as much agreement as possible? Or do I not rather take it as a fact that you, in your experience, confronted by alternatives, will feel *obligated* to do the best you know? This sense of obligation arises and persists even if the organization of your emotional-want life at that time should not favor an excitement that results in action.

We must leave this aspect of the problem. We do so, aware that our whole analysis of obligation may be rejected by one who believes that the *prima facie* quality of ought-authority can be genetically derived from early conditioning and identification. So we turn to a more decisive test. Does the emotivist's theory of what a value is do justice to elements in his own analysis?

If we understand him correctly, the emotivist cuts away the attitudinal response (expressed in "I approve or disapprove") from the object to which it is a response. While he stresses the importance of beliefs about the objects of the attitude involved, it is distinctive of his view that valuing is not an appraisal of an act but simply an expression of one's attitude toward it.

Consider, for example, an act in which an innocent person is being needlessly hurt. Let us say that I have a favorable attitude toward it, and you have a negative attitude toward it. I say to the perpetrator of the act "Continue!" and you say "Stop!" but neither of us can say that anything about the act is right or wrong, of value or disvalue. All we can express is our attitude; no judgment about one's being better than the other makes sense. So, also, if the innocent person being hurt says "Stop!" all he is doing is adopting a negative attitude toward being hurt, even though he is innocent of any misdemeanor.

We can now see what makes the emotivist vulnerable to the claim that on his view, taken seriously and consistently, morality would be based on the shifting sands of desire.[5] For valuing does not tell us anything about the rightness or wrongness, the value or disvalue, of an innocent person's being unnecessarily hurt, but presumably only about our attitude toward it. If this is so, any attitude toward the act that is psychologically possible may be taken, for the act does not in any way control the attitude taken toward it.

But if this were actually the case, there would be no good reason for the emotivist's plea that all parties be adequately informed about

[5] *Ibid.*, p. 30.

the act as the basis for greater conformity in attitudes. Presumably there is something about adequate information that will guide attitudes formed toward the situation and lead to its being wanted or unwanted. But for proper information about "innocent person being unnecessarily hurt" to have an effect upon attitude means that in this situation, *something is involved which is independent of the attitude* by which the attitude is, or ought to be, guided! What is involved is that the person is being *unnecessarily hurt!* In other words, *something about the situation grounds the favor or disfavor* of the spectator. Favor and disfavor, or human responses, do not "create" any value there is, but they may presumably be guided by what is true about the situation.

Unless something about "innocent person being hurt unnecessarily" did justify disfavor or favor, why urge adequate factual information about the situation as the basis for increasing commonness in attitude? The very fact of seeking the facts of the case means that there is a connection between the objective situation and the subjective desire. Both the desire and the nature of the objective situation desired are involved in the emotivist's own theory of value. It is because human desire *in relation to* innocent-hurt (or, conversely, because innocent-hurt, in relation to human desire) makes the kind of difference that it does to both perpetrator and victim, to persons immediately involved and to others, that we have a basis for declaring one attitude more justifiable than another. Agreement in attitudes must be founded not in the psychological state of agreement but in the fact that such agreement stems from what is believed to be true about innocent-person-being-hurt-unnecessarily.

We maintain, in other words, that on the emotivist's own theory it turns out that some attitudes not only are preferred to others but ought to be preferred, because of the relation of the objective situation to human desire. To say: "This is wrong" means I disapprove of this: do so as well!" And to justify it or to hope for further agreement is to be forced to go beyond the psychological state of attitude to what might justify the attitude. It means not "I disapprove of this and that's the end of it," but "I disapprove of this and believe that you will (or ought to) also when you see what I see about the object of my present disapproval." In brief, the emotivist is himself forced to make a shift from attitude to a justified or worthwhile attitude as the basis for valuation by virtue of his appeal to objective considerations or to a basis for greater conformity in attitudes.

The emotivist—to make the final criticism—would be hard-pressed indeed to justify his preference for truth over falsehood. Does "I ought to accept the truth" mean simply "I approve of this," or is there something about truth and something about falsehood that justifies his favorable attitude? The very ground for preferring truth over falsity is that attitudes and actions guided by an actual state of affairs are better than attitudes that "express" only our state of mind or being.

The emotivist, we may summarize, tries to support his discontent with objectivism by the claim that there are in fact no judgments that can truly or falsely predicate values of actions or situations. All one does do is to approve or disapprove and hope for greater attitudinal agreement through factual agreement. But this means that there is something about the situation beyond him to which his attitude ought to conform if it does not. Approval or disapproval by itself is no ground for guidance. To say to another "Do as well" on the basis of one's own preference as such is preposterous unless I believe that my attitude is grounded in true belief about the object. But why is truth better than falsity? Why ought I to follow the truth and not falsity? Not simply because I happen to approve it, surely.

If such argument is all we can propose as an alternative to the discontents that we may justly feel about objectivism, we had better hold to objectivism. But emotivism has ancient and contemporary allies in two forms of relativism, and they remain to be expounded and examined.

IV. RELATIVISM AND ITS DENIALS

A. What Privatistic Relativism Means

A person is arguing for privatistic (often called "subjective" or "individual") relativism when he says: "One man's food is another's poison. People are so different in ability and in need, their life situations are so different, that it is foolhardy even to try to assert that what one man finds good is good for another. There is just no arguing about tastes. What a man values depends exclusively on his own likes, dispositions, and wants. Therefore, he alone must be the judge of what is good for him: and he must not make the mistake of telling others what is good for them." In other words, the individualistic relativist is called a relativist because he claims that *there is no standard for measuring value beyond his private evaluation.*

This theory seems very simple to understand, and it often is taken to be obviously true, especially by students who have just begun to reflect upon their own moral standards. For this kind of relativist does not proceed, as emotivism does, from a concern for truth and falsity in judgments, but from a concern to protect the individual from the imposition of standards foreign to him. Neither God, nor parents, nor society, says the privatist, can define for a person what is good for him, because he is different from them. It is unfair to judge a man by factors that do not make his differences from other persons, in other situations, count.

Thus the privatist, seeing the Ten Commandments as requirements that were drawn up *for* him and not proceeding from his own nature, rejects their validity for him. The very fact that the Ten Commandments are the same for all, that they are universal requirements for all people in all situations, is the source of their weakness. Why? Because, presumably, God did not consult human beings when he made them.[6]

But the privatistic relativist objects even when he is asked to judge his private preferences by the laws of any human tribunal, be it custom or the laws of any community, state or country. For him the standard (if such it may be called) exists only in the individual and is therefore relative to him. Once more, why? Because every individual is in some respect different from others, and any "law for all" is bound to infringe on his individuality.

Here many relativists are guilty of confusion. It is one thing to say that a standard is *relative* to an individual (dependent upon him alone), and another to say that it is *related* to him. It would be difficult to discover in the history of thought any ethical realist, objectivist, or absolutist who held that standards of value, however conceived, were not *related* to the nature of persons in some manner or other. What absolutistic father, for example, who believed in absolute equality, would demand that the same amount and kind of food be given to the two-year-old and the sixteen-year-old alike? Ethicists

---

[6] We are here not claiming that this characterization of the Ten Commandments is correct, although it is true that many relativists and nonrelativists would hold that it is. As a matter of fact, however, is it not a silent premise in Christian thought that the omniscient Mind who instituted these commandments knows what human beings can and cannot do, and that these commandments, therefore, were not imposed *without any reference* to the nature of human beings, as the relativist seems to argue?

who have believed in the same ethical standards for all have been concerned about how to make their standard relevant to individual differences. For example, Plato's whole system of education as developed in *Republic,* let alone *Laws,* was concerned with the discovery and training of individual differences in ability—within the pattern of universal standards.

Clearly, then, it would make no sense to say that, independent of man, standards exist that are held to be standards for him, unless he is in some way related to them and unless the individual's specific relatedness to them is discovered. The issue between the objectivist and the relativist is not, in theory, an issue of forcing standards indiscriminately upon all persons. However, it is this stereotype of the issue that we fear has been influential in discussion. It may indeed be the case that persons who hold that there are objective standards for all people everywhere are more likely to disregard individual differences at important points. But such disregard results from the frailties of human beings rather than of theory. In theory, the universalistic objectivist would want to take individual predicaments into account, at least as a basis for winning the individual's adherence to the universal goals.

No, the issue between the privatistic relativist and all others lies in his theory of the relation of values to persons. The privatist insists that the relation of the standard to the individual is one of complete dependence on the individual's desires as they are related to others and to the world. He denies that there is or can be *any* fixed standard, either in the nature of men or in the nature of the world, by which he can safely judge his own, or another's, actions to be better or worse.

Let us translate the privatistic view into a concrete situation. Sam says: "I enjoy having persons work for me at my convenience at as little cost to me as possible." Arthur says: "I enjoy having persons work for me only when I feel that it is not hurting them and when they believe that I am not just using them." Again, Sam says: "I enjoy money, and all the more when I do not have to work for it, and I don't care how I get it, as long as it doesn't seriously hurt me." Arthur says: "I enjoy money, but only when I feel that I have earned it." According to the privatist there is no rational way of deciding which of these statements expresses a standard to be followed by all persons, for one set of statements is true for Arthur alone and the other for Sam alone, and neither is true for both. Actually, there is no point in arguing which line of action Sam or Arthur ought to take because Sam and Arthur are just different! Sam must not fall into the temptation of assuming that his attitude toward slavery and money is one that would apply to Arthur. A similar logic applies to Arthur.

It is only when we see him in the stark nakedness of his position that we begin to see why, in practice, the privatistic relativist moves to *societal relativism* (or social relativism). For what happens between Sam and Arthur when Sam applies his theory to Arthur and his money? Arthur, as a theoretical privatist, cannot blame Sam for trying to do what he likes when he likes it. But let us assume that Arthur will not like Sam's attitude toward him and his money. If he does not like what Sam is trying to do, he must see to it, practically, that Sam fails. He cannot do so by persuasion, given his theory, for (unlike the emotivist) he has taken a firm stand on the ultimate differences between himself and Sam. If Sam persists, he can only stop him by action. This means that *in practice,* which is the only arena where disputes for the privatist can be "debated," the only appeal is to might. In theory the privatistic relativist cannot hold to the general principle that might makes right; but in practice the only appeal he has is to the big stick, for or against him. In practice, then, he is led to live by a principle that is the denial of all reason: the test of the rightness of any judgment is power to enact it. This principle means, for example, that among individuals and among nations, the winner is not only the stronger; he is right!

There are practical difficulties, then, into which privatistic relativism leads. Of course, if on theoretical grounds privatism could be successfully defended, we should have to make the best of it. But certain theoretical implications and factual considerations make the privatist's position doubtful if not hopeless.

B. *Difficulties the Privatistic Relativist Must Face*

First, one wonders whether the privatist is aware that he himself now seems to be embarked on a moral crusade under the banners: "Respect individual differences!" "A fairer deal to those who live in differing circumstances!" "Tolerance for all, no matter who we are or what we do!" He seemed to oppose any standards for all people, but actually he favors what might be called fairer standards! And here he joins ranks with those moralists who believe in fairness to the individuality of all concerned.

We may summarize the first difficulty by saying that insofar as the relativist bases his case on the unfairness of universal standards to individuals, he himself has a certain standard. And this standard is not based on his desires but on factors he believes to be objective in the human situation.

But second, our intellects protest when we are told that two contradictory statements may both be true about anything, either fact or value. On the privatist's view, it follows that if, as I like it, actions are to favor individuality, and, as you like it, actions ought not to favor individuality, *both* statements, favored as they are by different persons, are equally correct. Again, if I hold that honesty is good and you hold that honesty is bad, *both* statements are correct. Or, because there is no way of knowing which is correct, neither is correct! We simply should not take stock in value judgments, for they do not tell us a thing about anything but our own feeling states.

It is at this point that the emotivist (as we saw) enters and denies that we should ever say that there are moral judgments, and he draws the conclusion that so-called moral judgments are ejaculations of approval and disapproval. Be that as it may, our protest here must stand against any relativism that forces us in its statements to assert positively that contradictory statements about the same act can both be true. For then the word "true" has lost any vestige of the meaning (self-consistency and universality) that it must have to be distinguishable from "false."

The consistent relativist would force us to fight all theoretical battles out on the basis of might makes right. The emotivist softens this conclusion by emphasizing the importance of knowing the facts relative to any conflict of attitudes, and he at least anchors some of the factors involved in an ethical dispute in the situation common to both disputants. But on the analysis of the privatist, centering in the inevitable differences between persons, even this small hope of objectivity is lost.

In the last analysis, however, it is the pivotal claim of the privatist —that because of the incontrovertible differences that always exist between persons, there is no basis for asserting that universal value judgments can be discovered—that contributes his weakest point.

The fact of differences is conceded. Even the contention that there are more differences than similarities between persons is conceded. Whatever has been urged against universal needs and in favor of the uniqueness of personality organization from the first days of infancy must, in practice, be upheld. Furthermore, physical and social situations differ and create different problems for persons, even for similar persons. The Eskimo, the Neapolitan, and the Equatorial African, however much alike, would be forced by climate and by geographical condition to make different adjustments in order to preserve their health. But a physically weak and physically strong person located anywhere would be forced to make different adjustments to the same environment. No, the facts of difference, of uniqueness, are gladly conceded. And we would also insist that insofar as persons *do* differ (or live under different unavoidable prospective situations), these differences should always be taken into account at least in applying any general principles that might be found. The privatist must be heeded in any protest he makes against running roughshod over individual differences.

But the privatist's conclusions outrun his evidence. Even his brother-relativist, the social relativist, will tell him that a society (to take that social unit as an example) does and can "force" conformities on individuals that will yield enough uniformity upon which to base common ethical customs. The privatist, in a word, is much too casual in his thinking about the similarities that do exist or can be made to exist between human beings. All societies condemn cruelty to children, however the practices of one may seem cruel to another. All favor health and justice, although definitions and expectancies differ. All want to explain their world, although their standards of explanation differ.

In any case, the psychological considerations brought forth in Part I of this book, and in Chapter 7 in particular, at least support the search for more similarities in human constitution than appear on the surface.

V. *REFLECTIVE SUMMARY*

The emotivist tells us that we should refrain from making the mistake of attributing adjectives like "right" and "wrong" to actions or wants. All value predicates, he says, are expressive only of our emotional responses or attitudes toward actions, not descriptions of what ought to be. He substitutes for obligation pro and anti attitudes, in view of which he would persuade others to change their attitudes to conform to facts. For ethical agreements and disagreements are basically caused, not by supposed disagreement about "values" but by disagreement about facts relevant to attitudes.

Is it true, however, that the experience of obligation is interchangeable with an exhortation to do something because we feel favorable to it? In a moral situation, are we dealing with each other only on the basis of attitudes or beliefs? Or is there another authoritative imperative that each of us brings to beliefs about and attitudes toward what is good or bad, right or wrong?

The emotivist believes that true belief about the relevant facts in a situation are important to agreement. But it is far from clear why such facts are important if the moral judgment about them reflects, not something about the right and wrong, value and disvalue, *of the act,* but only *about the attitude* of the person feeling a certain way about it. Clearly, something in the situation judged must ground the pro or anti attitude. Unless something in the situation beyond the psychological state of approval or disapproval, something true or false presumably, does guide the attitudinal state, as that to which attitudes *ought* to conform, there would be no point in trying to persuade others, and we land in privatistic relativism.

The privatistic relativist is concerned to keep the individual from being imposed upon by ethical standards that do not spring from his own preferences. For him, therefore, individual desire is the only ground of valuation; neither customary nor universal standards for the individual are in fact justified, for all persons are different from each other.

On these grounds the privatist should never be able to persuade other persons to "agree" with him on actions he desires and approves; the final standard for settling serious disputes would have to be: "Might makes right!"

But practical difficulties aside, it actually seems that the privatist's theoretical stance is the contradictory universal moral appeal: "All individuality ought to be respected, whether we desire to or not."

The root difficulty in privatism, however, is in the basic claim that persons are so different that universal values cannot be defined. We shall examine this matter further in the next two chapters. But one wonders how there could be any living together at all if it were the final truth that the same situation, good simply because one person likes it, is bad simply because another dislikes it.

13

The Denial of Ethical Realism: Social Relativism and Naturalism

~~~~~~

I. *SOCIAL RELATIVISM*

A. *What Social Relativism Means*

The *social relativist* is a relativist because he believes that there is no standard of values apart from the customs, laws, and ideals of the society in which the individual lives. For the social relativist the larger social group of which the individual is a part is substituted for the individual's desires as the standard of judgment. The individual can guide his judgment of right and wrong or of what constitutes the good life only by the standard implicit in the customs, explicit in the constitution or laws, and exemplified in the institutions of his society.

For example, it is customary in America to be deferential, in certain ways, to women and children. If a person is not deferential, he cannot be imprisoned, but his behavior will be considered crude and insensitive. Some things, however are not left to custom. Laws, enforceable by the police, make explicit what kinds of employment women and children may be allowed, for instance. Such laws (in our democracy) formulate and express the desires or standard of the majority. Because they subject violators to some form of punishment, laws encourage the establishment of new habits or customs of procedure. This occurred in America, for example, after laws were passed protecting the establishment of labor unions and regulating certain relations between management and labor. Today, although there is criticism of the abuse of certain practices, the American has adapted himself to the practices themselves as a way of organizing industries.

It is always a question how far a given law that cuts across the grain of given customs will succeed. America, at the time of writing, is witnessing an important instance of this truth in connection with patterns of racial segregation. Since the decision of the United States Supreme Court favoring gradual desegregation of Negro and white, those Southern states that have the largest number of Negroes and in which the politically dominant whites feel that their way of living is threatened by the decision have reacted against the decision so strongly that they have opposed even those forms of desegregation and those tendencies that had been already at work. In other Southern states, the decision of the Supreme Court has accelerated the process of desegregation. There is no denying the dynamic interrelation of law and custom in regulating the behavior of individuals.

Whatever the pattern of action a given social group develops for assuring basic uniformities, the explanation given by the social relativist is simple. Despite the differences in capacities with which an individual is born, his "patterns of culture" shape his sufficiently plastic nature to their mold; and he judges himself and comes to be judged first by whether he is a good American, a good Englishman, a good German, a good Russian, a good Zuni.

These are the basic considerations from which the social relativist starts. If different nations do have any customs, laws, institutions, and ideals in common, it is all to the good; but when one nation differs from the other, the individual is guided by the customs, laws, and ideals of his own country.[1]

The social relativist, clearly, denies that the individual is the standard of right and wrong. He would settle theoretical and practical disagreements by appeal to custom and law within the group in

---

[1] An economic interpretation of national relativism would be found in words such as these of the Marxist theorist Engels: "We maintain that all moral theories are the products in the last analysis of the economic stage which society has reached at a particular epoch" (quoted by C. Kluckhohn in his essay "Universal Values and Anthropological Relativism," in *Modern Education and Human Values* [Pitcairn-Crabbe Foundation Lecture Series, Vol. IV; University of Pittsburgh Press, 1952], p. 96).

question. In a sense, he says to the privatist: The private individual of whom you speak is an abstraction of theory unrelated to facts.

But the social relativist begins to argue like the privatist the moment the question of universal values is brought up. Who is to judge which nation is right when Russia and America disagree? When a fascist state and a communist state disagree, and when both disagree with democratic states? The answer is: There can be no judge, for there is no standard common to all nations, peoples, and cultures. Each culture has developed its own solution to the problems of living, and no other culture can sit in judgment upon it or assert that if a specific culture gave up certain ways of thinking and acting it would be better off.

This is the stand that the social relativist takes. And there seems literally no end to the actual samples he can display from the storehouse filled by anthropologists [2] and other students of culture, all of which clearly bring out the fact that behavior praised, blamed, or accepted in one society or culture is judged differently in another. If the case for cultural relativism can be made by pointing to the contrast in the attitudes of different societies to the same behavior, what an impressive list can be drawn up, and how few are the important areas of human concern that are left out! Consider instances of "cruelty" to animals, the plucking of chickens alive to improve their taste and bullfights, in which the bull cannot, after all, win; compare the "abuse" of infants, for example, infanticide, or of the aged, for example, parricide; or move from the kinds of labor that children are allowed to perform to kinds of treatment accorded persons as slaves or as prisoners—and we see that societies differ in their evaluation of the same treatment given to relatively innocent and harmless animals and to persons who for some cause have been overpowered by another group.

Shall we further contrast the attitude toward sexual expression both in and out of marriage, the attitudes toward the relation of husband and wife to each other, to the families from which each comes, and to their children? We shall find no end of differences, it would seem, in what is right to do with regard to controlling the individual's sexual drive in relation to the concern of that little

[2] See Edward Westermarck, *The Origin and Development of the Moral Ideas* (New York: Macmillan and Co., 1906–8); Ruth Benedict, *Patterns of Culture* (Boston: Houghton Mifflin, 1934); May Edel and Abraham Edel, *Anthropology and Ethics* (Springfield, Ill.: Charles C Thomas, 1959); Alexander Macbeath, *Experiments in Living* (London: Macmillan, 1952).

group among humans, the family, which is so important at once to the welfare of the dependent individual and of any society.

If we now moved to property and land rights, to the distribution, control, and inheritance of whatever is considered "wealth" in a given society, the data would pile up into mountains of differences.

And if we entered that vast realm of judicial and political rights, we would be overwhelmed by the differences in the treatment that an individual or group in one culture can receive as opposed to those in another when the same behavior is involved.

How swollen, also, the list of differences would become once we examined the many varieties of rite, practice, and belief that are granted religious sanction.

In listing differences in treatment of the same behavior, we have stayed at the level of those interests and problems that no individual can possibly escape in any society: his birth, his "right" to live, to work, to propagate, to be buried; his relation to animals; his relation to his family; his accumulation and dispensation of property; his political power, involving freedom from harm, freedom to act, freedom to be tried before condemnation, punishment and reward related to his actions; his desire to pray or not to pray and worship his God or gods. We have not touched the whole problem of what is considered normal or abnormal psychologically in the behavior of persons or the myriad variations in personal traits allowed in one society and not in another. There simply is no denial of the differences in both means and ends, in detail and principle that the social relativist can bring to support his general thesis. Yet we must ask whether the evidence and the reasoning based on that evidence do indeed make cultural relativism a more probable hypothesis than any other. First let us see what consistent belief in social relativism actually means for action.

B. *The Practical Case against Social Relativism*

What the social relativist has to say about the way in which a person's society influences his standard of right and wrong tells heavily against privatism and some forms of ethical realism. Furthermore, what the social relativist says about the differences among social groups describes so well the concrete situation we live in as groups, as nations, as cultures, that any kind of universalist in value theory seems like a wide-eyed, unrealistic sentimentalist who insists on ignoring the facts of life. And yet, if nothing else, the practical situation that social relativism leaves us in stirs us to further analysis. It is our impression that many persons look upon cultural relativism as a position that would put an end to "what nations dispute about" and to national intolerance. If basic practical problems are in fact eased by social relativism, we are predisposed in its favor. But are they?

Here, for example, are two great nations (the United States and Russia, if you will) embracing millions of people and influencing many others. In their different physical environments, they have developed modes of living that have enabled them to survive. Now, however, they stand facing each other with suspicion, convinced that the "way of life" each has developed is the right way of life for itself, and, as a matter of fact, for other people also, if only they would change their systems. To such nations the social relativist might say: If only you both would realize that your system is good only for you, you would not be now seeking to impose your standards on each other. What you each are doing is judging the other by your own past history and experience instead of realizing that each of you has developed the system that has enabled him to survive.

Even to state this application of social relativism in the second half of the twentieth century gives one a sense of unreality. This application might have seemed more adequate in a day when peoples were more or less prevented by geography alone from meeting each other on the pathways of the world. How many nations today can avoid the others' needs, demands, or sphere of influence as each seeks to assure and improve its "standard of living"? Assume, then, that nation competes with nation not only for the raw materials and other physical necessities, but also for power over the others as a basis for its own security. If, at any one time, there is not enough for any two nations, how would we avoid conflict on social relativist presuppositions? Each nation would be considered the judge, the only judge, of the rightness of its cause. Each maintains that its way of life is good for it. But should one nation relinquish its hold on the raw materials it controls, if the other nation finds that this control of raw materials endangers its standard of living? Has the Weaker Nation a right to say that the Controlling Nation does not need these raw materials to preserve its standard of living, when that Controlling Nation thinks otherwise? Not on the terms of the social relativist, because one nation cannot claim to know what is best for another. Yet each nation is actually assuming that its people have at least as much right to live as the others.

It may now be clearer why the very "realistic" position suggested by the social relativist does not in fact help us to resolve the actual conflicts that come up between nations, conflicts due to the fact that they live in one physical environment to which both must look for physical sustenance and physical security. Whenever conflicts of this sort arise, there is no putting off the question: Which of us has more right to live? or, even, Which of us has more right to live at such a level as to force other people to live at a lower level of existence?

Furthermore, social relativism consistently applied does not encourage international tolerance. It may well provide a conception of morality that encourages each nation to defend the *status quo*. To assert that each culture has a right to its own values has one ring when you are a member of the more favored culture which enjoys security, a security often denied other cultures in part by the fact that your own controls their fundamental resources. But the same assertion has a far different ring to the member of the unfavored culture who feels that this argument in effect would deny him what your culture controls. You may not be asserting that your culture is better than his, but he wonders whether you believe so when you do not allow him to share more power over resources.

The fact seems to be that the American way, the British way, the German way, the way of the West, the way of the East are all different ways of approaching the problem of living. But each "way" is regarded by the other as condemnation of its own once its physical resources are endangered (not to speak of its ideals) by the demands and controls of the other. The social relativist may be describing a fact, but the moment this fact of diversity is raised into a statement of principle that might guide us in action, does it not encourage harm rather than good by favoring any *status quo* in practice? Has the principle of *apartheid* being practiced in South Africa not already proved to be self-defeating?

Let us spell out another consideration that is involved in such arguments between groups or nations. The have-not groups always appeal to a fact that the cultural relativist denies. Sooner or later they say to the "haves": "We are human, too! We may be Russians, we may be yellow or brown or black, we may be members of another culture, but we are human too, just as human and as good as you are. We do not challenge your power over resources, but we challenge your right to them if it means that we are to be forever denied. Indeed, now we challenge your moral right. And, if you do not now recognize our rights in the matter, the day may come when you will be forced to recognize our willingness to die in the attempt to obtain what we believe are our rights as human beings."

To repeat, this appeal to a common humanity transcending customs and culture is the kind of appeal that has always been made by groups against each other. And what we find ourselves faced with in the twentieth century is a world united by physical inventions and threatened by nuclear destruction, which can take place between "distant" countries within an hour. We can live with each other in uneasy trust, but some trust is required even for mere survival. Unless we can achieve a community of moral trust and moral purpose, we may destroy ourselves. Yet in this situation we must say, as cultural relativists, that there is no basis for supposing that there can be a common trust or a common moral purpose. For, on this view, there exist neither universal standards independent of man, which could be a source of unity, nor a universal human nature to ground any universal values or principles.

In what follows, therefore, we must re-examine (a) the claim, as we shall now put it more conservatively, that there is not enough in common between men to justify any appeal to common values, (b) the claim that men actually do not have any common values, and (c) that no adequate basis can be found, in view of existent and historical diversities, for discovering any common or universal values.

C. *The Theoretical Case against Social Relativism*

1. *Are Human Beings Similar Only within a Culture?*

There is no doubting, of course, that nation differs from nation, and culture from culture, in ideas of what is right or good and what is wrong or bad. Even between groups and parties within nations, let alone between religious denominations, there are important disagreements concerning values. Within a nation like the United States, for example, the moral sentiments concerning the treatment of the Negro still create different factions, which, in turn, disagree among themselves as to the customs and laws that should govern our interracial behavior. The Republican and Democratic parties each represent important disagreements as to the relation of government to the life of the nation, though at the moment of writing it seems that the differences in party lines are not so clear as the differences within each party on certain specific issues (such as taxation in relation to defense). Members of religious groups, whether Protestant, Roman Catholic, or Jewish, are to be found in both political parties, and they disagree with each other as to the proper attitude toward church and state, as to the degree of federal aid, if any, that should be given to schools.

An important, unheeded fact comes out in such illustrations of the differences in ethical loyalty within a nation. These differences, partly in moral principle and partly in moral practice, force one to realize that it is not clear where one "group" stops and another begins. Does it not, then, grossly oversimplify the concrete situation to say that an individual introjects the values of his culture, as represented in his mother and father? This conception makes it seem that individuals within "*a* culture" or "*a* society" would be stamped in infancy with a common brand, as it were. Actually, however, there are so many differences within groups, even among individuals within families, that one is forced to ask why scholars speak so freely about *a* culture. It would seem that they must have in mind the fact that there are common aims despite differences in practice.

Yet the social relativist bases much of his case against universalism on the thesis that persons are what they are because their particular culture makes them so. But if he believes that *a* culture can be defined, despite the many significant differences within it, then he must be focusing on points of broad agreement in aim and practice that do exist. If broad agreements do exist or come to be as a result of the interaction between persons in the common struggle for improvement, why argue that such agreements are not possible between nations also? If people, no matter how different to begin with, do come to have *a* culture, if they can come to sufficient agreement on some broad principle and some general practices, why continue to hold that greater agreement cannot be reached between cultures?

We approach our conclusion: If the social relativists emphasize differences, they must take them all the way back to individuals and become privatistic relativists. If they emphasize the fact that individuals and groups within *a* culture or *a* nation do come to sufficient agreement in their customs, institutions, and legal constitutions, then these facts should force them to reconsider their view that there is nothing universal about human nature. In a word, if 180,000,000 people can come to agreement on principles to which they give allegiance, it must be because human nature in its fundamental constitution and in its capacity for growth and learning does have and can have more in common than is allowed for in the relativistic emphasis on differences.

It is true, as even our own restricted study has indicated, that contemporary psychologists cannot agree on any specific list of drives, instincts, or needs common to all people. But that the search for common capacities and needs must go on is reinforced by the very fact that persons, despite differences in environment, can have problems sufficiently common to make possible the formation of a group, community, state, nation, society of nations, and universal culture.

In sum, then, either *a* group or *a* society is possible or it is not. The sociologist, the psychologist, and the historian, let alone all of us in everyday life, believe that such forms of social unity exist, and thus we think and act on that assumption. It is plain nonsense to talk about introjection of social norms unless there are social norms. But if these broad unities do exist despite the differences in human nature, on what grounds can the conclusion be drawn that still wider norms cannot be defined as guides to more universal standards of behavior?

Add to these considerations the fact that persons from widely different cultures can migrate from one to the other and gradually, in the melting pot of human interaction, come to understand each other and live with each other, and the conviction grows that there is nothing intrinsic to human nature that makes the search for and definition of more universal goals a vain one. It is this kind of concern that led to the search for and tentative formulation of universal motives attempted in Chapter 7. We must remind ourselves once more, however, that from the fact of universal motives we cannot move straight away to universal norms.

2. Does Difference in Custom Necessarily Mean Difference in Ideal?

In this section and the next we must be fully aware of a problem that always faces any careful investigation. The data, the actual events and behavior, may be roughly the same and yet give rise to different interpretations. We have already noted in Chapter 1 that for a long time biologists claimed that "the data supported" individualism as the force governing animals in their struggle for survival. This trend of interpretation has been all but supplanted by the theory that the group is the unit of survival.

In anthropology and social psychology, another interesting reversal of interpretation has taken place. Twenty-five years ago the trend was to mark the differences between societies and cultures and ideals; it seemed that there were no data to justify belief in cross-cultural similarities and values. An influential, not to say dominant, trend in social psychology saw the individual conditioned by the stimuli in the environment which molded him to fit its nature. This interpretation fitted in well with the anthropological trend. The data have not changed. Yet investigators today who search for similarities find support for cross-cultural values. And there is a supporting psychology for this new trend of interpretation.[3] In what follows, we shall keep these "reform movements in mind.

It is, then, a real question whether, *as a matter of actual fact,* cultures differ as much as they are said to differ. Communities, nations, cultures do differ in practice, but do these differences in practice always indicate differences in purpose, motivation, or ideals?

Let us illustrate our meaning. Each of us knows that his way of expressing the spirit of Christmas, for example, may be different from the customs of others at Yuletide. And each of us might debate whether his own way of practicing the Christmas spirit is more intelligent and appropriate than another's. Yet, while one man disagrees with another's practice, he gladly agrees that "his heart is in the right place." That is, there is more agreement in purpose and in ideal than is actualized through specific, but different, behavior.

Again, two men may agree that they should be kind and generous to the needy. But one man may give money to the needy beggar in the street, whereas the other turns him down. The man who turns him down may feel that this kind of giving is not the best way to be kind, that he does better to contribute to social agencies whose work would make such street-begging unnecessary and provide for both immediate and longrange assistance. These two men agree in motive and idea; they disagree, and importantly, on how to implement the ideal. We must, accordingly, not be deceived into thinking that these men do not agree in principle because they disagree on the way of working it out.

Let us illustrate this same point by reference to group action. In

[3] See Solomon E. Asch, *Social Psychology,* Chapter 13, "The Fact of Culture and the Problem of Relativism" (New York: Prentice-Hall, 1952).

one home, discipline may be harsh; the rod is not spared lest the child be spoiled. In another home, it may be the rule that physical punishment should not be used. In both homes, however, the ideal may be the same—the child should not be spoiled, but should learn self-discipline. The practices differ, but they are "functionally equivalent" in the service of identical ideals. One might condemn the parents who use physical punishment on the ground that physical punishment, while easy to administer, may create more problems than it solves, but one would not condemn the ideal of self-discipline and proper punishment.

To generalize: Persons having the same ideals—regarding the rearing of children, the goal of a school system or of an economic system —believe that this goal would be better achieved by different patterns of action. And each person might appeal to certain facts, scientific and otherwise, to support his views. But all too frequently, even when persons take pains to know all the relevant facts, the truth is that we simply do not have enough technical knowledge to lead to conclusive results. Thus socialists who believe that there should be a more equal ownership and public control of a nation's wealth do not necessarily differ in principle from capitalists who agree that persons should not suffer unnecessarily and should have opportunity to improve their condition, economically and socially. The capitalist and socialist differ in the means to be used to improve the common wealth, the capitalist insisting that a system of private enterprise with a minimum of government control will produce the greatest good for all. Neither side has evidence that is strong enough to limit the degree of difference in interpretation.

In closing this section, we use two more examples to illustrate our contention that, in fact, there is frequently much more agreement in purpose and ideal than the cultural relativist takes into account and that many cultural relativists miss such agreements of principle because they study patterns of culture only in terms of practices rather than in terms of goals and principles. Thus, Americans might gasp at the practice of a certain tribe that puts its aged to death before they become feeble. This is no way to reward or respect parents who have nurtured us through our childhood and adolescence! But let us not judge before we ask a question. What is the tribe's motive and goal? We discover that the supposed "savages" believe that a person who dies in a feeble state will, in the next life, remain eternally enfeebled. If we believed the same, could we devise a better way to honor our fathers and our mothers? This illustration serves also to indicate how people's ultimate convictions about human nature and destiny will help determine their practice.

Again, many Americans are shocked at the "barbarism" of a custom described as existing among certain Eskimo tribes. It seems that it was considered correct etiquette for an Eskimo husband to offer his wife for sexual intercourse to any other Eskimo whose hunting expedition has kept him from contact with any woman for a certain period of time. A little more knowledge will show that the custom was not meant, at any rate, to be cruel. If one conceives of sexual intercourse only as a basic physiological hunger, and if one conceives of a woman as a sexual convenience and servant, as do those Eskimos, such "hospitality" appears more logical. To think of women as "part of the furniture" results, in this instance, in strange courtesies. But they can be well meant.

Two facts emerge from our example. First, behind extreme differences in action and behavior there may actually be a common ideal, in this case, hospitality. Second, the differences in manner or custom of expressing the same ideal may spring from different interpretations of the same facts to suit different purposes, from inadequate factual information, from ignorance, and even from varying conceptions of the nature of the universe itself. As Asch says, the trouble with the social relativist is that he deals with social data "in a piecemeal way." Data must not be divorced from context; their situational meaning must be understood. When different actions are seen through the same situational meaning, then it may well be discovered that the same values are being sought.[4] It remains now for us to ask whether investigation has actually unearthed any common cross-cultural values.

3. Different Cultures Do Have Some Similar Ideals and Values

Most of our earlier discussion does more to point up the problem of interpretation of differences than to prove the fact of similarity. Without being unmindful of winds of doctrine, let us then record some of the conclusions that do eventuate when the piecemeal approach to cultural values gives way to situational meanings and is alert to functional equivalence.

Clyde Kluckhohn, the Harvard anthropologist, has been one of the leaders in combing the data with an eye to common cross-cultural

[4] Karl Duncker, "Ethical Relativity?" *Mind*, 98 (1939), 40–41.

values. His theoretical base is the realization that human beings everywhere are biologically more similar than different in need and potentiality and that they are forced by the realities of living together as human beings to hit upon common modes of mutual expectancy as the very foundation of their social survival. "Human life is—and has to be—a moral life (up to a point) because it is a social life." [5]

We here take the liberty of presenting in list form, but virtually in Kluckhohn's own words, some of the conclusions he came to:

1. No culture fails to put a negative valuation upon killing within the tribe. Noteworthy also, in connection with the importance given to life, is the fact that no culture fails to ceremonialize the fact of death.

2. No society has ever approved suffering as a good thing in itself. As a means to an end (purification of self-discipline), yes; as punishment—as means to the ends of society, yes. But for itself—no.

3. No culture fails to put a negative valuation upon indiscriminate lying. (Consider how long a human relationship, let alone a society, can exist when persons cannot trust each others' statements or, more formally, their promises and contracts.)

4. No culture fails to put a negative valuation upon stealing within the in-group. There are important variations, to be sure, in the conception of the extent of the in-group and in the limits of toleration of lying and stealing under certain conditions. (Note that here the underlying notion is really that of fairness and justice.)

5. No culture approves of rape or any achievement of sexuality by violent means.

6. Reciprocity is a value prized in all societies.

7. Truth and beauty (however differently defined and expressed in details) are universal values. This brings out the fact that in all societies there are values that go beyond mere survival or immediate

---

[5] Alfred Louis Kroeber and Clyde Kluckhohn with the assistance of Wayne Unterhein and appendices by Alfred G. Mayer, *Culture: A Critical Review of Concepts and Definitions* ("Papers of the Peabody Museum, Harvard University," Vol. 47, No. 1 [Cambridge: The Museum, 1952]), pp. 174–79.

significance. (One wonders why religious values, once variety of definition and expression are kept in mind, are not included in the list, if beauty—or better, aesthetic experience—is included.) [6]

8. Turning now to qualities of character, Kluckhohn (in clear-cut refutation of the theses of Ruth Benedict and, we suspect, of Karen Horney) says that the concept of the mentally normal has cross-cultural aspects. The "normal" individual must have a certain measure of control over his impulsive life. No one, unless he has socially approved justification, can threaten the life of his neighbor without being treated as insane or criminal. A broad "subcategory" under this is: No one is considered fit for social life unless his behavior is predictable within certain limits by his fellows.[7]

9. The writers are certainly not experts in this area, but they venture to extend Kluckhohn's list by asking whether it would not be hard to find a culture that did not put a premium upon courage (once more allowing the society to determine what the special situation for the courageous spirit should be)? And is there any society that regards health, physical or mental, a bad thing? We dare suspect that other common cross-cultural values might well be found if we worked with some such set of virtues as that to be suggested in Chapter 16 and if we worked with a larger set of needs to begin with than those which make for biological survival.

4. There is No Escaping Some Judgment About What All Persons Ought to Do

We must not allow ourselves to be seduced by any list of cross-cultural values into premature positive conclusions about the good life. We have had to deal with the privatist and cultural relativist

---

[6] Note also that the moment one includes beauty, especially, one can hardly say, as Kluckhohn does, that the existence of universals reflects a series of categorical "oughts" only in the sense that there are necessary conditions—given by nature, invested by man only in their specific formulations—of adjustments and survival always and everywhere. For aesthetic experience can hardly be said to be a necessity for survival, or for social life, but only for *quality* of survival and *quality* of social life. Indeed, this is also true of other values in this list. Kluckhohn, in seeming to be "hard-boiled" biologically, makes less of his data than he should.

[7] This list thus far is worked out on the basis of pages 417–19 in Kluckhohn's essay "Values and Value-Orientation," in *Toward a General Theory of Action*, edited by Talcott Parsons and Edward A. Shils (Cambridge: Harvard University Press, 1954). For theoretical background, consult Kluckhohn's "Universal Categories of Culture," in *Anthropology Today*, prepared under the chairmanship of A. L. Kroeber (Chicago: University of Chicago Press, 1953), pp. 507–23.

because their denial of universal values was a crucial attack, at the very outset, on our quest for truth about what human beings *ought* to do. What values, then, *ought* human beings to pursue as the basis for the life good to live? What ought all people to recognize as the standard for good living? This question will occupy us for the rest of this book. But we would here note that there are at least two *ought-judgments* unwittingly presupposed by the cultural relativist.

First, the conclusions of the cultural relativist are worth noting only because they involve honest, impartial, courageous (three character values!) analysis of the evidence in accordance with the norms of scientific method, critical inquiry, and logic. Could any cultural relativist—or would he—confronting a member of another culture who disclaimed any value at all for critical methods, concede that the latter ought not to follow critical methods of inquiry in discovering the truth? To put it crisply: Unless the cultural relativist can assert that all persons who make statements ought to support them by the most critical analysis of evidence and that this value ought to be universal, the cultural relativist has cut the limb on which he has been sitting.

A second underlying "ought" seems to have gone unnoticed. Society A, let us say, differs from Society B. The conclusion drawn from this has been that what Society A believes to be good for it is good for it, despite the fact that it is diametrically opposed to what Society B values for itself. What common meaning underlies this claim that there is *a* good for A and *a* good for B? Survival! The assumption is that because Society A has survived thus far with its pattern of values, and Society B has survived thus far with its different pattern of values, then they are both equally good! In the statement "What Society A thinks is good for it is as valid as what Society B thinks is good for it," this "good," common to both societies, is assumed to be survival. In short, what the relativist actually maintains is the proposition: "Survival is the only standard by which to judge any goodness."

Once we have drilled our way down to the rock-bottom assumption in the relativistic argument, we come up against the same old fundamental issue. Is the fact of survival in itself really a test of goodness? A cunning blow by a brute kills a trusting man; a surprise atomic attack devastates the nation who had agreed not to use its atomic weapons. In either case, could or would we say that the worse party died? The fundamental weakness, then, in all relativism, which supposedly denies all universal oughts, is that it really judges all societies by its hidden assumption that as long as people survive there is no other basis for judging *better* and *worse*. *The moral life, however, begins at the point at which we begin to decide what makes survival worthwhile or what kinds of survival are preferable.* Is there any experience within life for which survival itself should be risked? To answer *yes* is to suggest that some *kind* of survival is better than *mere* survival. To answer "No value is worth endangering survival itself" is to uphold survival as the universal standard of value and thus to give up relativism! The only way to defend any theory of value is to enter into a discussion assuming that truth can be discovered about values.

To summarize: There is no gainsaying the fact that human beings at some time or other have done and approved all kinds of contradictory actions. In this chapter and the last, we have considered movements of thought that have tried to deal with this conflict of moral judgments. The emotivists are driven to deny that value judgments are true or false in any strict sense of the word, and they see the problem as one of so influencing persons that they can find agreement in attitudes of favor and disfavor. The emotivists consider the facts of moral disagreement and decide that the search for universal truth in ethics is a misguided one. The relativists consider the facts of moral disagreement and decide that the search for universal truth is destined to end in failure because men and situations are so different.

Both of these positions, we have urged, ultimately rest on an appeal to the value judgment that all persons ought to seek and follow the truth, a value that is possible only when and to the extent that men control their feelings and attitudes by fact. Both emotivists and relativists, when pressed, are seen to presuppose more similarity between persons and their value judgments than their theories allow. Although the arguments against emotivism, privatism, and social relativism in value theory cannot be lumped together, the fact that keeps coming to the fore is that human needs and capacities, in interaction with the nurturing environment, do produce values both similar and different.

Does this line of argument suggest that values tell us something important about the nature of man and of the world in which he lives, something that is not so arbitrary and accidental as the emotivist and relativist seem to think? Values, perhaps, relate men to each other, in this world: they may not exist independently of man as the extreme ethical realist contends, for they seem to grow out of what man can make of man in the realm of nature. This is the guiding conviction of the naturalist in value theory, and this is the next theory we must study.

II. *NATURALISM IN THEORY OF VALUE*

A. *The Convergence of Naturalism and Psychology*

The naturalist agrees with relativists and emotivists that it is incorrect to ascribe reality to value qualities or norms and to suppose that there is any irreducible moral consciousness that reveals such values. He asserts that any possible knowledge of value that we can have must come by turning to human functions other than a special moral sense or moral intuition. We must depend for our knowledge of value on the same thinking powers that we use when we think about stones and trees, emotions and feelings. This means that we must turn away from supernaturalism and nonnaturalism and study what is involved when human nature develops in interaction with the physical world.

It is evident that the naturalist gladly accepts whatever support is forthcoming from the psychologist or psychotherapist who, as we have seen, has been led into questions of value by his concern to understand the bases of mental health. Today the movement "down" from theological and Platonic heavens and the movement "up" from the psychological and sociological studies of personality meet in the naturalistic concern to understand how man, with his constitution, may more effectively grapple with the problem of living with his fellowman in their common environment. Much of the exposition in our first six chapters was given to the analysis of this development from within psychology itself. Let us describe the convergence we have in mind.

The human being, as our psychologist saw him, is a psychophysiological creature with enough plasticity in his nature and enough reflective ability to be confronted with problems and to select those objectives that would meet the demands of his given constitution and the environment. These psychologists found themselves asking about the nature of value, the meaning of guilt, and the nature of the good life; they found themselves disagreeing with each other about the nature of man's innate equipment and the nature of the goals that would constitute the good life.

But these are the very problems concerning which ethicists, moving away from supernaturalism and nonnaturalism, are seeking enlightenment from the pychologist. Ethicists find themselves forced to decide on the most valid method for the study of man and to evaluate differing interpretations of psychological observation. Fortunately, for the most part, their academic training in philosophy involved them in a study of scientific developments, and their liberal-educational training exposed them to the physical, biological, and social sciences. They, therefore, are usually equipped to understand what the scientifically or scientistically oriented psychologist is getting at and to see the relevance of many of their findings to problems in ethics.

Indeed, the history of American psychology has been deeply affected by philosophically trained minds like those of William James and John Dewey. The work of both in psychology and philosophy forced them to return to problems of methodology and to critical thinking about the mind-body relation, reflexes and instincts, emotions and feelings, obligation, values, will, and religious experience. Most introductions to ethics give much attention to John Dewey's theory of value for he was the most influential recent exponent [8] of naturalism, although George Santayana's *Life of Reason* and other works have been important, along with the careful analyses of Clarence I. Lewis.[9] We shall here, however, restrict ourselves to the thinking of yet another naturalist in value theory, Ralph Barton Perry, who not only wrote a masterpiece in the field of value,[10] but has brought his life work in this area to significant summation in *Realms of Value*. Perry always moves in appreciative, if keenly critical, contact with psychological investigation. It would be difficult to find a philosophical scholar whose systematic work in theory of knowledge, metaphysics, ethics, and political theory is invested with more extensive historical learning.

[8] See especially *Human Nature and Conduct* (New York: Henry Holt, 1922) and *The Theory of Valuation* (Chicago: University of Chicago Press, 1939); for a development of this approach to value, see Ray Lepley, *Verifiability of Value* (New York: Columbia University Press, 1944).

[9] Clarence I. Lewis, *An Analysis of Knowledge and Valuation* (La Salle, Illinois: Open Court Publishing Co., 1946); *The Ground and Nature of the Right* (New York: Columbia University Press, 1955); *Our Social Inheritance* (Bloomington: Indiana University Press, 1957).

[10] See his *General Theory of Value, Its Meanings and Basic Principles Construed in Terms of Interest* (New York: Longmans, Green and Co., 1926), which incidentally might be compared and contrasted with W. M. Urban's *Valuation: Its Nature and Laws (Being an Introduction to the General Theory of Value)* (New York: The Macmillan Co., 1909).

B. *Perry's General Theory of Value*

How simple Perry's definition of value seems: *". . . a thing—any-thing—has value, or is valuable, in the original and generic sense when it is the object of an interest—any interest."* [11] Yet the very simplicity of this definition leads to its being misconstrued. The crucial words are "interest," "thing," "object," and we must know what Perry means by them if we are to lay the proper foundation for his ethical theory.

First, then, "anything" means exactly what it says. But the definition does not say that anything is a value. It says that anything is a value "when it is the object of an interest." An apple, a blue sky, a person, an ugly word, a worm—*any*thing, any experience—is a value only when and insofar as it is an object of interest. Once we have digested the fact that nothing in the world is excluded from being a value (or a disvalue), provided it is an object of interest, we can shift our attention to the meaning of "interest" in Perry's mind.

Second, then, what is an interest? A complete answer here would involve a whole psychology of the motor-affective life. But crucial in any interest is the kind of "expectancy" aroused by something in which the person feels "for" or "against" what is expected. Again, when a person is interested he is attending with expectancy; he is in a state of "being for" or "being against" what he expects to happen. Once we keep the focus on this core of meaning, we can use whatever words suggest this meaning to us: "desiring-avoiding," "liking-disliking," "hoping-fearing," or even "pro attitude" and "con attitude." For ethical purposes it does not matter how the psychologist-biologist ultimately describes the events that transpire in the person when he is interested. It is important, however, to keep from reading our own ordinary meanings into Perry's words. The "state of expectancy" needs closer scrutiny.

Perry has said that anything will be a value, a good or an evil, when some person is in a state of expectancy about what it will bring him. He also adds: "a thing is an object of interest [a value] when its being expected induces actions looking to its realization or non-realization." [12] For example: a child sees the uplifted hand of his parent,

---

[11] Ralph Barton Perry, *Realms of Value: A Critique of Human Civilization* (Cambridge: Harvard University Press, 1954), pp. 2–3.
[12] *Ibid.,* p. 3.

or sees his father scowl. The value it has for him will depend on the expectancy aroused in him, as a result of his past experience, by the uplifted hand and scowl. If the child wants what he expects, then he experiences value; if not, disvalue. His expectancy will lead him to take actions on his side that he has learned are most appropriate to such an occasion! What we must emphasize, therefore, as important to "expectancy" is the *conceived relation* between the person and the object. A value, accordingly, consists in the fact that something (anything) is *related to* (not relative to) an interest favorably or unfavorably.

It must be noted that Perry does not say that the interest *makes* the thing valuable (as the emotivist does) any more than he is saying that the thing makes the interest valuable. He does say that the conceived relation of anything, favorable or unfavorable, to anybody's interest, is what makes *the thing valuable to that person*. If another person claims a positive relation of something to him, I am bound, on Perry's definition of value, to acknowledge the fact that the thing is a value for him. The fact that I do not claim the thing to be either a value or a disvalue does not itself keep the thing from being a value to another.

To go no further would make Perry's view sound *relativistic*. It is in fact *relational*, because the emphasis is put on the relation of man to what he believes he can expect *from* the object. Were the object not related to an interest, it would not become a value; but the value does not on that account depend solely on the interest.

Indeed, as we think more concretely of Perry's *interested man*, the picture that comes to mind is not that of a man who, on a non-naturalistic view, contemplates "obligations," or feels irreducible *prima facie* duties, but man, on the "naturalistic" model, an active pursuer of interests, and as agent in behalf of what concerns him about himself in relation to the world that constantly affects him and his interests. In view of our discussion of the emotivist (Chapter 12), we stress that what is believed about the object and man's conative relation to it enters into the definition of value. And whether relativism is true or not depends not on the definition of value in terms of interest-object but on whether common values are in fact discoverable. We must look into this matter further.

Third, then, for a thing to become an *object* of *interest*, it is necessary that it become an object of cognition, that is, that the thing be "taken" as something from which or by which the interest may be favorably or unfavorably gratified. The "taker" may be wrong in his expectation because he has misconstrued the relation of the object to himself or vice versa. What the thing means to him may be different from what the thing actually is. To put this carefully: The object is *not the stimulus;* it is what the stimulus is taken to be by the subject. The object is *what he expects.* For example, it is not, as we usually say, "the apple I see" that interests me and becomes a value. It is what I expect from the apple in relation to the interest that is dominating me. The red "object" is the stimulus, but the possibility of the hunger gratification that I expect to result from my eating of it constitutes it a value. Again, the red "object" is the stimulus, but the possibility in another situation of gratifying my angry impulse to throw something is what makes it valuable for me. The "red object" by itself apart from its possible relation to an interest is not a value.

What is expected of any object will always be problematic. Thus, the person, presented with anything, takes it to be the basis for certain expectations, and it is to this "object" that he responds favorably or unfavorably, as the value anticipated. Thus, as Perry says, interest, "while it embraces expectation, is something more than expectation: it is for or against the expected." [13]

To summarize in our own terms: when we say that a person is in a value situation, we mean that he has become aware or believes that something will yield certain results related in some way to his interest. To be "interested in" is to be related to some expected object in a *pro* or *con* way that remains to be dealt with by further action and thought. For example, a work of art or food will interest the person in accordance with what he sees in it as related positively or negatively to some interest. Then, and only then, does each become a value or disvalue.

Fourth, a final word of caution against an all too prevalent psychological misconception. Perry believes that it is psychologically false to think that the only objects of interest can be pleasure (negatively, unpleasantness or pain), and "my" pleasure at that. There is no doubt that pleasure and pain attend interest and that interests are "my" interests. But only false theory and not actual observation of experience can lead us to assert (a) that because all interests are my interests, the only object of interest is myself and (b) that because pleasantness and unpleasantness attend positive and negative

13 *Ibid.,* p. 40.

interests, desires to avoid or decrease unpleasantness or to find and increase pleasure are the only motives behind interest. "*My* interest, attended with pleasures and pains, may be an interest *in* some other person, *in* food, wealth, sex, power, beauty, truth or anything whatever, including pleasure and pain." [14] Clearly, with one stroke Perry denies that man is so constructed that he seeks nothing but pleasure (psychological hedonism) or his own gain (psychological egotism), thus reasserting his own relational view of value.

C. *Perry's Theory of Ethical Value*

We have now before us Perry's theory of the nature of value in general. So far his sole aim has been to define what it is that makes up *any* value, be it economic, aesthetic, or moral. There would be no need for a theory of ethical value in particular if interests did not conflict with each other and if knowledge at every stage of life was complete. The specific problem of ethics, therefore, is the problem of dealing with conflicting interests and problematic objects of interests. Moral values as distinct from intellectual, aesthetic, economic, and religious values are values chosen as a result of conflict among any other types of value. As Perry puts it in a capsule: "Morality takes conflict of interests as its point of departure and harmony of interests as its ideal goal." [15] Once more, Perry's definition of ethics and morality sounds so simple and so optimistic that its impact needs articulation.

The "purpose of morality is the abundant life." [16] But the abundant life is gained neither by affirming every interest nor by denying interests, but by organizing them "that they may flourish." [17] We cannot tell, to begin with, what the ideal organization will be, but, to repeat, morality is not concerned with denials for the sake of denials. The elementary, inescapable fact is that a man has conflicts of interest that by their very nature force a denial of some sort. He cannot have his chocolate cake and eat it too! The problem he faces is to decide what interest he had better choose in order to protect other interests.

A sound morality, therefore, cannot enjoin more conflicts or denials than living itself would probably force upon us; its concern,

[14] *Ibid.*, p. 46.
[15] *Ibid.*, p. 87.
[16] *Ibid.*, p. 88.
[17] *Ibid.*

rather, is to find the ideal of life which will allow as many interests as possible to be included harmoniously.[18]

To this point, what stands out is Perry's conviction that the ethicist's business is not to pronounce for man as a brute or as an angel. Human interests are the raw material of the moral life; the moralist must see them for what they are before passing any judgment of "good" or "bad" upon them. He does not know what interests, be they negative or positive, will be included or excluded in the final round up. Interests conflict and converge, and they must be sorted and harmonized; and this attempt to achieve the most productive harmony (to be defined) is the aim of the good life.

Again, no particular interests as such, no "values" as such, have priority over other interests or values. The only way to respect a value, Perry is saying, is to take it on its own face value and affirm it until other interests and their "values" force a choice. Thus, the procedure is not to choose one *or* the other, but to ask how any choice will affect the affirmation of other values and interests. It cannot be emphasized enough that Perry has no preconceptions that "some interests are always bad" and "some good." Why? Because one cannot know what is a "good interest" and a "bad interest" until he relates them to each other. For Perry the only ideal that will be likely to honor "face values" or "face disvalues," is that of cooperative inclusiveness or "positive harmony."

We now can answer the question: What makes any value moral? Any value becomes a *moral* (good) value if its realization leads to a more inclusive cooperation with other interests and values. It is *immoral* (bad) if and to the extent that it does not. In Perry's own words: "Morality is man's endeavor to harmonize conflicting interests: to prevent conflict when it threatens, to remove conflict when it occurs, and to advance from the negative harmony of non-conflict to the positive harmony of cooperation." [19] It is clear, then, that the central notion in morality is adventurous organization rather than negation or affirmation of interests as such.

So important is the notion of harmony that it will be profitable to scrutinize it at closer range. Perry emphasizes cooperation, limitation, contribution, avoidance of inner discord,[20] but all these processes can be misunderstood unless we remember that the *kind of*

18 *Ibid.*
19 *Ibid.*, p. 90.
20 *Ibid.*, pp. 90–91.

harmony he advocates is one in which "the whole serves the part," in which the whole exists "only for the sake of the parts." "The parts are interests, and they are organized in order that they, the constituent interests themselves, may be saved and fulfilled." [21]

We may in this last sentence see Perry's model for the ideal of personal, social, and political life. For this very interest in the parts and their organization does not mean that the whole is not more important than some one or several parts. Although the whole must serve the parts, it will, by virtue of its inclusiveness, be greater than any of its parts. Yet this *kind of inclusiveness* can speak for the parts as a whole because it is the conjoint voice of the majority of component interests.

The ideal by which we can judge "good" and "bad" thus emerges. "What suits all of a person's interests is exalted above what merely suits a fraction; what suits everybody is exalted above what merely suits somebody." [22] Perry calls this process of integrating interests "reflective agreement." [23] The "will" of a person or of a social group is thus formed after all competing interests have presented their credentials before the bar of a reason that relates, sifts, and reconciles with a view to preserving as many interests as possible. In any given situation there may well not be "a nice, neat answer," but the effort to agree as far as possible is the path to be followed. The experienced seeker after goodness knows that "morality is a *pursuit*, not an infallible recipe." [24]

D. *The Moral Life and the Happy Life; The "Right" and "The Good"*

We shall retread some of the ground we have covered as we seek to understand how Perry would distinguish, if at all, between the moral life and the good life. For, as we have seen, some ethicists, like Ross, find it necessary to distinguish "the good life" from "the moral life." They argue that the moral life is part of the good life, but that neither is equivalent to the other. Thus a father might do his "duty" ("right") by his idiot child, although sadly aware that in this case his duty, fully executed, can actually do little to improve the child's intelligence or enlarge the scope of his values (the good). Such ethi-

[21] *Ibid.*, p. 91.
[22] *Ibid.*
[23] *Ibid.*, p. 92.
[24] *Ibid.*, p. 100.

cists hold that the duty (the "right," the "moral" act) does not derive its rightness from the consequences. For in the case of the idiot child, greater expense, increase of time and energy given to his welfare may result in no improvement or prospect of improvement. Nevertheless, they argue, one still has a "duty" to the child.

The fact that many "right" actions of this sort, done "from duty," seem to cost so much in other values has raised the question whether any action can be judged right or wrong apart from the consequences it promises for the remaining values. Every systematic moralist therefore finds himself asking whether such synonyms as "right," "morally good" or "morally valuable," "duty," "virtue" can be used of any act apart from its relation to other values, for example, pleasure, aesthetic pursuits, or the religious life.

Perry's solution to this question is already implicit in the theory of value and morality just expounded. *Any* object of positive interest is good, and any object of negative interest is bad to begin with. Yet any good act (or value) would become "morally bad" or "wrong" if it still is chosen when it is not in concert with other interests. Correspondingly, any evil act (or disvalue) would become "morally good" or "right" when its pursuit advances the total harmony of values. "Right" and "wrong," morally speaking, cannot be decided, accordingly, apart from the total consequences making for harmonious happiness in the lives of those concerned.

The ideal of happiness is a life in which every interest and value is applauded by all the rest, reflectively related both in the long run and in the short run. When this ideal is advanced by any act, it is a *morally* good act. The act becomes one's duty, despite difficulties to be overcome; but it is not to be done "for its own sake." If any act does not forward the ideal, it is morally wrong, and it becomes one's duty to oppose it, despite its lures. Thus a person who constantly sets himself to relate his actions to the ideal of harmonious happiness and does his best to realize it is leading a *morally good life* even if he does not achieve the good. And, as Perry urges, the *morally good life* is "a condition of *harmonious happiness*—a condition in which, through the increase and cooperation of its members, all interests tend to be positive." [25]

Against Ross, then, Perry decides that a moral act cannot be defined apart from its relation to the good life. It is the relation of an act to the happy life that renders it right or wrong. But we must

[25] *Ibid.*

emphasize again that the happy life (or happiness) is not to be identified with pleasure, although pleasantness, Perry believes, would be more pervasive in a life in which there was less conflict of interests than one in which there was more conflict. Nor is Perry willing that a person should buy a "shallow" happiness by being unwilling "to extend the range of his awareness to embrace all the interests at stake together with the actual circumstances which confront them." [26] Perry is all too aware that in a full life there will always be "some sense of negation" [27] because there are so many interests that cannot be realized. Yet man is responsible for the most harmony or happiness he can find through being as inclusive as possible.

To summarize: Perry's theory of right and wrong, in sharp contrast to Ross's, has no place for duties or rights that can be declared so apart from the good of the whole, individual and social. Right and wrong acts are means to the larger organization of values that embraces them.

E. *Rights and the Nature of Obligation*

The theory of the good life just developed has important ramifications for the theory of rights and the conception of obligation. Let us ask ourselves first: Do human beings have any rights which other persons are morally bound to respect regardless of the consequences to their own lives? Immediately there come to mind such "rights" as the "right to live," "pursuit of happiness," "freedom from fear," "freedom from want." In Perry's view, however axiomatic these rights may seem to us, they cannot be morally binding in themselves and can always be brought before the court of the largest organization of interests possible. No right is ever unrestricted; it is always a right deemed to be justified by the total concerns to be protected.

Still another important consequence, already mentioned, is re-enforced, for it is crucial to the democratic way of life as Perry conceives it. Within an individual life no interest has "right of way" without consultation with other interests.[28] The total individual is a law unto himself, or autonomous, when it comes to any partial interest. But just as the partial interest of an individual cannot be

---

[26] *Ibid.*
[27] *Ibid.*
[28] See Perry's *Puritanism and Democracy* (New York: Vanguard Press, 1944) for one of the best treatments of the religious and philosophical roots of the democratic ideal.

snuffed out without consultation, so also in the social whole each individual has *both* the right to be considered by others *and* the obligation to consult others as he seeks to realize his interests. Thus, be it in the individual or in the social life, there are no "final" or "absolute" rights.

Second: What happens to the experience of obligation, or the conception of conscience, on this naturalistic view?

Perry is fully aware of "the command" involved in the experience of "ought," "duty," or the "moral imperative." But he thinks that this "imperative voice" cannot be accepted at face value. The "imperative voice" is "an accident, due to the fact that the right action is associated with political, parental, or other authority." [29] Here Perry is joining those who hold that oughtness is a derivative of a mustness that the person faces if he wants under given conditions to arrive at the good.

There is no need here to elaborate on this view, which we have already met among our psychologists. A human being constantly finds himself in situations that are compelling. As a result of past learning, he feels his "sense of duty" as a constant reminder that in every situation it is imperative that something be done. Accordingly, to call attention to a man's obligations is to make him aware of his situation and its demands. Because on Perry's view, the total demand in all human striving is harmonious happiness, it is this goal that is behind oughts and duties. Obligation or ought, then, is not an ultimate, irreducible factor in a person, but one that arises inevitably in his experience as he seeks harmonious happiness.

F. *Comment on the Relation of Obligation and Value*

It will be apparent to the reader of Chapter 9 that it would seem to us that this derivation of the *experience of obligatoriness* simply does not do justice to the quality of the psychological tone and imperative that distinguishes obligation (moral approval and guilt) from "must" or social approval and disapproval. We take this occasion, therefore, to emphasize what seems to us to be an unwarranted jump in ethical theorizing on the part of some naturalistic ethicists and psychologists and of Perry in particular.

What seems to have happened is that obligatoriness and value have been tied into one neat package. The naturalist seems to argue:

[29] *Ibid.,* p. 109.

If one rejects a realistic view of value, one denies any uniqueness to moral obligation. If values are independent of man or of desire, then there may be a special cognitive function to become aware of this fact; but if values are not independent of man or of his desires, then obligatoriness also loses its cognitive function.

But in such packaging moral obligation is lost. One side, the Butlers and Kants and Rosses, have been so impressed with the quality of obligatoriness that they have added nonnatural values or duties to the world. The other side, the relativists, emotivists, and naturalists, have brought value down to the earth of human desire and then felt constrained to explain obligatoriness as a kind of desire, too. In so doing, the actually experienced, given character of obligatoriness has been, as it seems to us, reduced out of existence.

Our own basic thesis, in this area, is that obligatoriness, as a noncognitive functioning, is a capacity of a human being that is not the product of training. But its presence in human life forces us to include among intrinsic human *tendencies* not only needs and interests but also this imperative to do the best one knows in every choice situation. We have said, in a word, that the magisterial experience of "I ought to do the best I know" is as "natural" as hunger for food or as the demand to be consistent in reasoning. Oughtness does not come *from desire,* however trained. It is in human experience not because of social conditioning or identification. It is not the voice of God as such. It is noncognitive. Because of its presence in human experience, we have not only sentences like "I desire this more than this," but like "I ought to desire this more than this" and "I ought to pursue this desire and not that."

This, then, is our position. We stand opposed at different points to cognitivist and noncognitivist, to naturalist and realist. We are closer to the realist and cognitivist in our unwillingness to reduce away imperative quality in human life. But we have been impressed by the objections both to the realistic and to the emotivist and relativist theories of value. The naturalistic analysis of value seems most promising to us, although the naturalist's final interpretation of the place of man and value in the universe does not do justice, we think, to all the data (see Chapters 14 and 30).

In the view that we are about to expound, the influence of naturalism will be evident, especially as derived from John Dewey, Perry, and C. I. Lewis. Our specific relation to Perry's theory of value will come out as we proceed, so we need not stop here for further critique. But because of differences in the interpretation of the person and his place in the cosmos, we shall call our view *normative universalism* in ethics.[30] The remaining chapters in this book will develop the ramifications and involvements of this view, which, for the authors at least, harmonizes many important emphases in ethical and psychological theory without being a conglomerate eclecticism. But of this the reader must be the judge.

III. *REFLECTIVE SUMMARY*

Is the social relativist correct in claiming that because societies and peoples differ so much in the values that they prize, there are not and cannot be universal values and ethical principles? If individuals are similar enough to allow common values to develop in a society or culture, it is arbitrary to suppose that cross-cultural values cannot be achieved. Furthermore, what seem to be cultural differences in value are often differences not in ideals but in means of realizing them.

In any case, cross-cultural values—for example, disapproval of suffering as such, of rape, of lying and stealing within the in-group; and the approval of reciprocity, truth, and beauty—have been discovered. And when we analyze the presuppositions of social relativism, we note the underlying uncriticized conviction that survival is the basic standard for judging goodness and that all persons ought to use critical inquiry in their search for truth. Social relativism cannot withstand either its own presuppositions or known fact.

Ralph Barton Perry develops a theory of values in which value is related to man—without ending in relativism. For value, while linked to interest, is also related to what the experient expects from the object. Perry's theory of value is relational, involving both the nature of the experient and the nature of the object.

On Perry's theory, the ethical problem is to make wise choices among values in view of the conflict of interests and the problematic knowledge we have of the world. Wisdom in choice, that is, happiness, calls for the most inclusive harmony of values open to persons,

---

[30] Were it not for the fact that we wish here to focus on ethical theory, we would call this a *personalistic theory of value*. The acceptance of *normative universalism* does not necessarily entail an idealistic personalistic metaphysics, though we believe that such a metaphysics is in the last analysis the most reasonable philosophical account of values, persons, and events.

individually and in social relationships. The moral life consists in harmonizing the conflicts in value so that optimum inclusiveness is realized.

Thus, any act is morally right to the extent that it increases, as far as possible, the harmony among values, but no act is right or wrong in itself. Similarly, there are no axiomatic rights that are not to be assessed in terms of their relation to the optimum harmony among values. Indeed, on Perry's view, even the experience of oblig-atoriness stems from the search for harmony of value interests.

Perry's refusal to grant to obligatoriness any unique moral quality is probably influenced by his conclusion that there is no unique moral cognition. But the refusal to allow for moral cognition need not be accompanied by the refusal to note the irreducible moral tone in obligatoriness. We now ask whether a theory of value can be developed in which the noncognitive uniqueness of moral obliga-tion can be related to the moral pursuit of universal values in human experience.

14

Normative Universalism as a Theory of Values

~~~~~~

I. VALUES AND DISVALUES AS KINDS OF EXPERIENCING

When a person wants or desires, he becomes sensitive to something that he believes will gratify his desires. Initially, before reflection is possible, a person is in no doubt about gratifying a felt want. Perplexity arises when his desires conflict and the person is aware of the conflict. In short, the only "problem" a person has when he feels a desire is how to gratify it, not whether to gratify it.

Thus, if an individual had only one desire, and if it could always be gratified without further conflict, he certainly would never ask any questions about whether or not it would be better to gratify it. *No question of good and bad, right or wrong, comes up simply because a person has a desire for something—yes, any desire!* The only "bad" or "wrong" at this stage is to experience a desire or want (or, to use Perry's term, "interest") and not be able to fulfill it. And all that "bad" or "wrong" would mean at this stage is: "I don't want to remain ungratified." Why? Because a person is that kind of being who inclines to gratifying desires when he experiences them.

In other words, there is no question of *moral* right and wrong or *moral* good or evil until a person is psychologically mature enough to know conflict of desires, compare them and their possible or probable outcome, and make a choice. At this point we agree with Perry: there is no value apart from interest in and desire of some object. No interest or desire is morally good or bad, or right or wrong, in itself, apart from its relation to the gratification of other desires. The moral life begins at the point of choice, to some extent reflectively made, among values. A man cannot be ethical or unethical, that is, moral in contrast to immoral (not nonmoral), until he begins to choose among values. In most of this chapter, we shall develop further a theory of value in relation to the problem of choice among values. In the three succeeding chapters especially we shall consider the nature of the ideal person.

We have said that reflective choice presupposes experiences that gratify wants or frustrate wants. We wish to stress especially the dynamic and polar relation involved in all value experience. This is the important fact for value theory, whether we find ourselves "wanting something" and then experiencing the fulfillment or the frustration of that want, or whether we start with certain experiences and then find them want-fulfilling or want-frustrating. Value experience is constituted by experience-wanted (want-fulfilling); that is, the person is undergoing a total experience in which fulfilling of desire in and through some "object" is taking place. The word "object" does not necessarily refer to "a thing out there."

Thus, when I am finding the idea that solves my problem, I am experiencing (this kind of) value. Were there nothing about the object ever to make it wanted or unwanted, want-fulfilling or want-frustrating, "it" would never become valuable; on the other hand, wants unrelated to any object in and through which they could be fulfilled or through which they could be frustrated might be experiences (assuming such could be conceived), but no part of any value or disvalue experience. Again, if a person had no interest in any of his experiences, or if he had experiences in which he could take no interest or which would evoke no interest, there would be no value experience in the primary sense of the word. To put it laconically: where there are no needs, wants, desires, or interests, there are no values. Where no experiences are wanted or where experiences neither fulfill nor frustrate wants, no values come into being.

We add: *Any experience as wanted, or want-fulfilling, is a value experience; any experience as unwanted, or want-frustrating, is a disvalue experience.* Up to this point, again, our view is naturalistic in Perry's (and Dewey's) sense. It shares their psychological emphasis on the importance of desires (emotions, urges, wants) as integral to human existence and value experience. At the same time, it singles out the quality of the total experience, undergone or anticipated, as the actual value in enjoyment. For example, it is the felt kindness-quality in the experience I am having that I am glad to have and wish to continue until something occurs to make me change my want and its mode of gratification. My wanting does not constitute the experience of kindness as a whole, but kindness-as-want-fulfilling (and, by extension, as wanted) is the value experience.[1]

Thus, there are no values or disvalues that are not experiences of persons capable of wanting and of being frustrated; there are no values independent of wanting beings. The nature of the life good to live (or the ethical life) and the nature of the moral life (or choice in accordance with some conception of the best) involves organization and selection among human value experiences. This transition from value experiences as such to moral-ethical experiences requires fuller explanation.

II. THE MOVEMENT FROM THE PREANALYTIC TO THE REFLECTIVE STAGE OF VALUE EXPERIENCE

Each person in this first stage of enjoying or disliking some quality-in-experience (which probably never exists purely as such) is in what we may call the *preanalytic phase* of life. But the person is soon forced by the conflict between value experiences to compare, contrast, and select among them. The problem of choice, *the moral problem,* arises only as the person accumulates enough experience to know that, while gratifying certain desires involves further wanted experience, the gratifying of certain others brings some unwanted experiences. He must decide which desires to pursue and how to connect them with their consequences in "the world." If the child can learn to fondle the cat in such a way as to avoid (unwanted) being scratched, all the better! His moral problem begins the moment he compares, with a view to selection, the *quality of experiences themselves with the quality of their consequent experiences,* in this case the feel of the fur with the sting of the scratch.

[1] See the similar emphasis, developed quite independently, in Brand Blanshard's theory of goodness as presented in *Reason and Goodness* (New York: The Macmillan Co., 1961), especially Chapters XI and XII.

Obviously, this particular moral problem is not as important as many other problems he will face, yet it can illustrate the broad principle; the moral life begins when any person confronted by conflict in value experiences, or value claims, knows it and reflectively makes his choice. The alternatives, as in this instance, are often not momentous; but moral problems are moral problems even if of the trivial variety. "Shall I wear my brown shoes or my black ones today?" How important a choice is one can only know after he has experienced value and disvalue, but to have made any choice at all reflectively is to have embarked upon the moral life.

We may now distinguish the stage of sheer value experience as *preanalytic* and the moral stage of choice as analytic (or reflective) and proceed to match the differences between the verb "value" (I value) and the noun "value" (value experience).

For the important thing at this preanalytic level is that the verbs "to value" and "to disvalue," meaning the *grading* of wanted or unwanted experience (value experiences), have no relevance. Only when an experience wanted or unwanted is looked at again, as it were, is compared with other experiences, does valuing or "evaluating" begin. Before this, to be sure, there is "psychic quality" in the desiring-experience to be evaluated; there is "psychic quality" in the process of gratifying and "psychic quality" in the fulfillment and consequences of desiring what was desired. But these root experiences, these qualities of experience, are what we evaluate with a view to "the next thing to do" or future choices.

These distinctions are suggested in order to bring out the fact that *in evaluating* our value experiences we are not creating the value for the first time or in the primary sense; rather we are trying to understand their relations to each other and to other desires and aims in our lives. Our question at the analytic level is: "How will I know which value experience is more worthwhile? By what goal shall I judge value experience?" The thinking experient asks these questions because he no longer has that *unquestioning*, prereflective *psychological* assurance that comes from naively taking for granted that any desired object as desired is "right" or "good." Experience at "face value" gives way, because of conflict, to finding a basis for relating and valuing. Here the experient passes from the preanalytic (unevaluated value) stage of experience to the analytic or reflective (moral) stage of evaluating. He is now ready to exercise will-agency in relation to the best to which he feels obligated.

Let us review our whole thesis thus far, for the point will be important in later discussion. Insofar as we entertain the impulsive stream of life that simply courses through us, none of us quarrels with the reactions to things that we find occurring within us. Whipped along by impulse or merely enjoying some state, we ask no questions until something pulls us up short. Then we decide, on some ground or other, what to do. As remembering, thinking beings, capable of self-consciousness, we bring to bear on this decision factors that we believe relevant. Combining trial and error and insight, we stumble along into the future with its enjoyments and conflicts, hoping to improve our appraisals. Sooner or later we come to some decision, which we do not always explicitly hold before our consciousness, as to how we are going to settle conflicts. Life in this presumable preanalytic stage is lived and never questioned; when the questions do arise, only the analysis, comparison, and relating of the value experiences in stage one can form the basis for evaluating.

We might also say that in the preanalytic stage our value experiences lead us to make relatively confident *value claims* about these experiences, which we do not challenge until life forces us to. Let us repeat, however, that what we are saying about value experiences or value claims and evaluation is not in conflict with Perry's analysis of value or with his definition of the moral life (in contrast to the ideal of life). At our next step we diverge.

III. *THE TRANSITION FROM "THE DESIRED" TO "THE DESIRABLE"*

On the view of obligation that we are proposing, it is at this second, reflective stage that the imperative "I ought" makes itself felt. "I ought to do the best I know" and "I will" are functions of the person at the stage at which active choice among value experiences, in the light of some criterion of value, is believed to be possible. But "I ought" does not supply the criterion of value. Obligation (oughting) is not a nonnatural cognition (or any other type of cognition) of values in any sense independent of interest; nor is obligation (oughting) a residue of past learning. It is an irreducible imperative, present at the point of reflective choice, though it may go unheeded.

What we wish to emphasize here, as theoretically important, is that this *ought* enters into the judgment "I ought to be kind" not because of some ought-quality in kindness (as the ethical realist says). Ought enters into judgment because the person involved in choice is an oughting as well as a desiring-valuing person and has (in a way to be described) developed the conviction, in a given situation, that kindness is the best alternative for him to will. The actual shift from "the desired" to the "ought-to-be-desired" is not constituted by some ought-quality in the value experience itself, but by the fact that some value experience has been judged to be the best by a person whose nature it is to feel ought about the best in the choice situation.

To put it flatly: the movement from the desired to the desirable is *not* due to *introducing among the desires an imperative set of obligations or values that are not derivative from desire* (as the ethical realist would have it). No value experience as such *initially* involves or is characterized by ought. And thinking about, or evaluating value experiences, does not in itself produce ought. But ought is felt about any value experience deemed (by whatever standard or criterion) to be the best by the wanting, thinking, oughting person. In a word, we do not make an arbitrary shift from the fact that an object is desired (a value claim) to the conclusion that it ought to be desired. But the moment a person who experiences a value (or anticipates it) decides that it is the best in that situation, it becomes the object not only of criticized desire, but also of obligation. And the standard by which choice is to be made, we suggest for the moment, following Perry and E. S. Brightman,[2] is one of inclusive harmony within the total experience of the person in his total relation to other persons and the world (see Chapters 15 and 21).

With this general view of the relation of value and obligation before us, we must pause for consideration of the particularly relevant criticism of views such as ours made by the ethical realist Wilbur Urban.[3]

The view of value just presented presupposes, Urban would say, the value judgment "Life is good." For we have urged that individual value experiences as such cannot be judged good or bad apart from

---

[2] E. S. Brightman, *Moral Laws* (New York: Abingdon Press, 1933), especially Chapter IV; and see F. R. Tennant, *Philosophical Theology* (New York: Macmillan, 1928), Vol. I, Chapter VII.

[3] Urban, interestingly enough, gave scholarly expression to a theory of values much like ours in *Valuation: Its Nature and Laws, Being an Introduction to the General Theory of Value* (New York: Macmillan, 1909). But in *The Intelligible World* (New York: Macmillan, 1929), we find a sustained critique of his own formerly more naturalistic point of view, and in his text *Fundamentals of Ethics* (New York: Henry Holt, 1930), argument for an ethical realism.

their relation to a larger frame of value experience. But on what grounds, *within life experience itself,* asks Urban, can we justify the claim, for example, that life (desires, interests, needs) *ought* to be preserved? Have we ourselves not urged, he might remind us, that the mere continuance of life, because wanted, is not necessarily good? The normative value judgment "Life is good" cannot be *derived from* value experiences as we have described them, but is the result of a moral intuition that is not reducible to wanting some experience or other. What, then, can we say in reply to Urban?

Our rejoinder would take the following line: It is one thing to assume that mere living, mere survival, is *always* good. It is another to argue that the standard for deciding whether life is "good" must come from outside the living that constitutes our preanalytic stream of life. The reason we give for denying guidance from any source beyond the stream of living itself is that there is no way of knowing that "guidance" from any such source would be relevant for lives like ours. Any standard by which we criticize our living must be one that will guide further experience of our kind. How can we assume that any standard would be relevant to our lives unless its development has taken past, present, and possible human experience into account? We can criticize one human situation in living only on the basis of other human value situations.

Our countersuggestion to Urban, then, is that any standard for living can be a standard for us only because it is rooted in our total capacities as living beings. Would we, for example, accept "the will of God for us" unless we assumed that "He knoweth our frame" better than we ourselves do? The same follows, with due modifications, for our parents and other counselors. When a person, having struck snags in satisfying desires, comes to question whether the naive assumptions of the preanalytic stage can continue to be made, he is on his way to discovering what may be called the reflective, experiential standard. This always involves a judgment about some value experiences *on the basis of comparison with the remaining stock of relevant value experiences.*[4] The judgment "Life is good," in the last

---

[4] We are not calling this a naturalistic standard (though the naturalist would agree with what has been said essentially), simply because the word "naturalistic" tends to be most clearly defined by its denial of any supernatural world, rather than any positive circumscription of what is meant by "natural." At the present stage of the discussion, there is no ground for either asserting or denying the existence of any supernatural realm. All we are asserting is that the criticism or evaluation of any value experience, religious, aesthetic, or otherwise, can come only from appreciating it for its own sake and then understanding its interconnections with other experiences.

analysis, amounts to: Which life is good? Which of the lives (of want-fulfillment and so on) that, as far as I can see, are open to me ought I to want and to choose as a result of reflection upon the network of human desire and its relationships (see Chapter 7)? Assuming that such an answer to Urban is adequate, we need all the more to be explicit about the development of a standard of value in the personal life.

IV. *THE CRITERION OF VALUE*

To review: if our observations are correct, persons assume (pre-analytically) that any experience that is want-fulfilling is a value experience and any that is want-frustrating is a disvalue experience until they are brought up short by conflict and are faced with the necessity for making a more selective response. In order to emphasize the tentative and unexamined character of this phase, we call any wanted experience as such a *value claim* (or disvalue claim for want-frustrating experience). The question of "claim," we repeat, does not become *articulate* until "uncriticized" moments of value experience are forced to confront each other conceptually in a conflict situation. I have experienced (wanted) kindness; I have experienced (wanted) honesty; now shall I be kind, or shall I be honest and tell my friend what he hates to know?

It is at this point that a comparative *judgment* of the value claims, kindness versus honesty (and other values), needs to be made, and I decide what ought to be kept or to be avoided (to speak in minimal terms). Again, the boy who, having experienced ice cream and eggs (preanalytic), is asked to choose between them, may now judge: "Ice cream is better than eggs." (Meaning: the experiences I get from eating ice cream are more gratifying than those which come from eggs.) He is making a value judgment about value claims of the preanalytic level. (They could both have been disvalue claims or mixed.) He is grading his experience of ice cream through comparison with his experience of eggs. He may, if questioned, at first, say that he simply prefers the taste of ice cream to that of eggs, but further questioning might lead to his defense of his selection by reference to dietary needs.

As the analysis continues, many other need-want factors may be brought in, and he may in the end conclude that his original preference for ice-cream-value over egg-value cannot be accepted if he wants to fulfill more wants in his life, even at the level of taste and eating. Whatever decision may be reached in a given life, the point of our simple illustration is to show that the simplest value claims and the earlier judgments of comparative value may not be dependable.

In a word, the problem that a person always faces with regard to any (uncritical) value claims and any more critical value judgments is to ascertain whether the relation between value experiences will actually be sustained by relevant factors within his own life without excluding the relevant experience of others. To formalize the question, the experient must ask: Is the experiential relation I am grading on the basis of immediately apparent (*prima facie*) value experiences one upon which I can depend as I go on living—given what I am, what other persons are, and given the total nature of the environment which impinges upon me?

This second reflective step, in fact, takes us beyond the uncriticized *experience,* the intermediary judgments of relations between value experience, to the judgment of *dependable value.*[5]

A dependable value is a value claim judged to be best after systematic criticism of its relation to other relevant values and facts. Let us be explicit here. "Dependable" or "undependable" with regard to value claim refers to the status claimed by a person for the actually "enjoyed" or expected value experiences *in relation to other value experiences* in his own life and (sooner or later) in that of others. It follows that, in the last analysis, a person cannot appraise a value claim without connecting his value experiences and judgments of related (not relativistic) values to each other systematically. Here Perry's concern for inclusive, positive harmony among values, as the criterion for judging between values, emerges. To put this same idea in another way, we would say that the *criterion of value* (of the dependability of any value) is *experiential, growing coherence* within the total life of value experience in self and others and all the factors relevant to the creation of value experience. This means that the dependability test of any value claim is its capacity to "live with" other value claims in a supportive relation.

Our concern in the next three chapters will be to develop specific demands made on the experient by this criterion, for we shall attempt

---

[5] E. S. Brightman, to whom we are essentially indebted for this line of reasoning (*Moral Laws* [New York: Abingdon Press, 1933], *A Philosophy of Religion* [New York: Prentice-Hall, 1940]), distinguished *value claim* from *true value.*

a systematic ordering of different levels of value experience. But here we would stress that the search for a growing, mutually hospitable variety of value experience, in which no value experience is arbitrarily trusted or neglected, in which no human need or want or ability is slighted, involves the person in a constant critique of his own habits and customs. It will be no easy task for him to be the kind of "ideal observer" whose experiential and, at the same time, systematic concern for scope of human value experience will often conflict with concern for quality. As we shall see, there will be a constant struggle between range and variety of value experience and the depth or height of value experience. But the "ideal observer" [6] and systematizer of value experience will make full allowance for the facts of growth and change, for inclusiveness and quality, as he tries in his "cool moments" to work out the hypothesis about the organization of his value experience that will, with *greatest probability,* protect and promote the maximum range of value consistent with quality.

It may also be noted here that growing coherence is the basic procedure in deciding which of several scientific hypotheses is acceptable. That hypothesis which does justice to more of the data than any other hypothesis and that seems more fertile for further investigation is the one accepted as true until further evidence renders it obsolete. It is the mark of an educated man, as Aristotle long ago reminded us, to know the kind of accuracy available in different areas of life. In the realm of ethics, we suggest, growing, experiential, systematic coherence of value experience and action consistent with the best hypothesis is the best criterion we have. The dependable, either in the search for scientific truth or in the life good to live, may not be the everlasting: at every stage we are asking for that hypothesis which best solves the problem in the light of the relevant and available evidence and which keeps the door open for further evidence. If the ethical life can keep up with the many demands made upon human beings from within and without and lose nothing needlessly, it will be because it rests on a system of value that gives play to range, variety, and unity—in a phrase, to creative unity or harmony.

Finally, what we have been saying about the search for a standard by which to criticize value claims is based on the realization (a) that each of us makes mistakes in appraising values just as we do in interpreting our sense experience and (b) that no primary experience of

---

[6] See discussion in Richard B. Brandt, *Ethical Theory* (Englewood Cliffs, N.J.: Prentice-Hall, 1959).

value or disvalue can arbitrarily be considered ethical or unethical (moral or immoral). Our problem everywhere is to compare and connect dependably.

To close this section with an illustration of the kind of problem faced by every reflective experient of value, let us suppose for a moment that a young man is, in a cool moment, trying to decide what value to place upon the drinking of liquor. He will need to balance such factors as the taste, the physical effect upon him, the psychological effect, the financial cost, its place in fostering or injuring social relationships. But this is not enough. He will have to ask whether all the conditions involved in manufacturing and selling liquor are such as he can critically approve, and how his own consumption is related to this whole liquor system as it affects other persons. What may have seemed a matter of private practice thus comes to involve broad issues of social and political policy in which many *facts and values* need to be related. The problem of responsible choice is the problem of first adopting as far as possible the attitude of an impartial observer and then enacting the decision that seems to protect that scheme of values which promises, as far as he can tell, to protect the widest range, variety, and unity of values in his life. That this will involve him in a network of responsibility to others and to a social and political system will be argued later (especially in Chapter 28).

V. *VALUES AND THEIR RELATION TO VALUE POTENTIALITIES*

We must now articulate a neglected fact that is crucial not only to value experience but to the verification of a value judgment (for example, "A balanced diet ought to be chosen" or "Kindness ought to be done and cruelty discouraged"). Both in our exposition of Perry and in our own discussion we have emphasized the importance of conceiving value as a dynamic relation between an "object" and an "interest." But to stop here is to leave out of account the fact that what value experiences are, what they lead to, and which of them become available depends on two ever-present factors. These are the nature of the person experiencing and the nature of the object deemed to be the source of value. Summarily: the fact that I like an apple tells something about my psychophysiological constitution at a given moment *and* about the nature of an apple *in relation to* my constitution. Value experiences are *joint products* of human nature in relation to the world. A value experience is a fact not only about me but about the world in interaction with me. So also, the fact that I like being kind is a fact about me that takes root in and affects other potentialities in me and in others.

It is so important to remember that value experiences, especially when dependable, are not the mere products of wanting, but joint products, that we invent a new term, *value potentialities,* to stand in contrast to primary value experience. "Value potentialities" designates the fact that human beings are so made and the world is so constructed that there are *potentialities for value experience that do not depend upon wanting or interest for their being.*

Our theory of value up to this point has favored the nonrealistic and naturalistic contention that values cannot exist without persons who have wants demanding fulfillment. Here, however, we would stress the independence of value potentialities, which, as such, are not immediately felt by or dependent on wanting-knowing persons. In other words, on our view the ethical realist would have been correct had he said that value potentialities in and beyond man are independent of human desiring and objectively affect the life of desire by their natures. It is this emphasis of ethical realism on factors independent of felt want that we would gladly embrace in our theory of value. What is objective in value experience is not some value datum irreducible to desired experience, but capacities, in ourselves and in the world that sustains us, that are always operative and determining the range and quality of our value experiences. If ping-pong is better for some persons than poetry, it is because the value potentialities in playing ping-pong can create more and better experiences of value in these human beings, given the value potentialities of their natures, than can poetry, given its value potentialities. Let us clarify this statement by considering another simple illustration.

Every child finds himself liking many experiences, and many experiences at first seem valuable just because he wants them. Take him to Playland. Being an "unexperienced" child and not knowing his capacities, he wants one of everything, from eating to riding on the merry-go-round and the roller coaster. And, up to a certain point, he enjoys each. His mother and father have already, no doubt, selected those experiences for him which are least fraught with danger (given his potentialities for value as they see them). But he himself may find that much eating and much riding do not go together, as is evident from the sick headache and nausea that ensue. A whole gamut of experiences of disvalue follow because he (given his capacities) cannot "take" everything (given their properties).

Let us take a closer look. Given the child's psychological and physical constitution, a certain point was reached at which value experiences of eating not only decreased but stopped and were supplanted by the disvalues that his particular constitution permitted. His interest did not create the value-disvalue potentialities in the food and in his mind-body, yet these value potentialities would never become values or disvalues unless he came to see them and wanted (or did not want) them. He did not create the experience of food in the way it was enjoyed simply by wanting it; nor is he responsible for the fact that he is so made that this sequence of value experience and disvalue experience is what it is. He learns this; the human race before him has learned this; and his mother and father had already done some of the selecting for him.

What happens when he goes back to Playland? If he is not to repeat his earlier sequences, he will have to decide which value claims to forego and which to experience again. How many experiences go together in the light of their value potentiality, as far as he knows himself and them? The experienced values of Playland that harmonize with and protect most of the others of which he is capable might well be called the *dependable values* of Playland for him.

But in what does their being dependable consist, then? In their *coherence* with other experiences open to his capacity for value as well as on their own intrinsic value. But that *these* values cohere more than others does not depend *alone* on his wanting each of them: he does not create what could take place in him or the varying coherence or mutual support the amusements and their properties may have for each other, given the potentialities of different children. In other words, the fact of their coherence is a fact about his own human nature in interaction with the demands and opportunities afforded by Playland. A dependable value, then, is a value experience that, when analyzed, turns out to be dependable in terms of its relations to value potentialities in himself and his environment, in terms of its relation also to other values afforded by interaction between the person's given nature at a given stage of life and the given nature of the world around him.

Let us bring out what our illustration teaches us. The dependable value of an experience does not consist in what we think we want or do about what we want. At this point the relativist made his mistake. As we see it, the dependable value especially takes root in our actual natures and their potential for value experience and in the world we interact with and *its potential* for *us*. At any one point we may have hardly begun to *real*-ize or actualize what our natures make possible or the interacting world makes possible.

Once more, our search for dependable value is a search for supportive relations among experiences of value and disvalue and for the relation of these to the value potential in ourselves and in the world. What is in itself a value experience may lead to destruction or insecurity of other value experiences: that is, a given value experience loses in value by being the kind of value experience that, granted our nature and our world, hurts rather than facilitates other value experiences. In short, the more a value experience or pattern of value experiences is found on reflection to be coherent with other patterns of value experience, the more dependable it is. Human values at any one time will be as stable as their foundation in value potentialities in human beings and in the world allows them to be. Yet because we never know all that human nature can be or all that the world in which we live can allow in interaction with us, we do well to base our ventures in the life good to live on experiential, growing coherence.

If we are correct thus far, we may conclude that the *norm* for value experiences is neither in our wants alone nor in the structure of things alone, but in the interaction between our knowing-wanting selves and the world we inhabit. We do not know the norm by cognitive acts of a moral consciousness. The norm does not appear once and for all before any individual and thereby gradually before the race of men. It forever consists in an imaginative hypothesis about the interpenetrating value experiences of men that will enable them to realize the best in themselves and in the world beyond them. As we shall see, the norm is no fixed, unchanging stencil or pattern of value experiences; but neither is it anything any person desires. It will always be some form of actualizing the value potentials of persons as they interact with the value potential in each other and in the world. The norm for value experience is not *relative* to man, or *independent* of him; for it can only stand for that dynamic *relation* between man and the world which keeps man on tiptoe in his varied actualizations of the potential for value in himself and the world.

VI. *THE GENERAL NATURE OF NORMATIVE UNIVERSALISM AS A THEORY OF VALUE*

We have been arguing, in effect, that the experiences that each person selects as dependable values are the effect of factors in his own nature and of factors in the world around him with which his nature interacts. No person creates the basic structure of his own nature and its manifold possibilities and value potentialities; nor does he create the basic structure of the world around him and its value potentialities. The fact that a person can experience value is a fact about him; the fact that he can critically evaluate *what he does value* is a statement about the universe in which he lives. It is the kind of universe in which he and these dependable values and dependable disvalues are possible. Persons and their values are as much a part of the totality of things, whatever it ultimately is in metaphysical terms, as are stars, oceans, bumblebees, "the laws of nature," and sunsets. An adequate philosophy or metaphysics will need to find a coherent hypothesis that will fit both the facts and values found in human experience and the fact that human beings can know and value what they do.

Such is our theory of value. Our exposition of this theory will be complete only after different phases have been developed as this book moves on. But here we must relate what our theory means for the problem of universal values. Evidently in our theory of value, there cannot be, strictly speaking, universal values, *as experiences*. For no two persons are the same and therefore the value *experiences* of no two persons can be identical. Furthermore, our concern is not simply with values that all persons do (or might) realize, but with values that all persons ought to realize. On our theory of value, we can speak only of *norms of value*, that is, of idealized, conceptual patterns of value that all persons ought to will as far as it is open to them to will. Clearly, the emphasis when we speak of norms, in contrast to value claims and dependable values, cannot be on the particular value experiences that this or that person in this or that society may have, but on the pattern of values that a person ought to realize in this kind of world, given his nature as a person. For example, we might be able to say that all persons ought to be healthy and friendly and lovers of truth, without saying that they ought to eat meat, express friendliness in a certain way, and love physical science. A norm can be universal because it frames the ideal good which the value experience of persons must particularize in situation after situation.

We shall acquire our conception of such a universal norm, we said, by systematizing human value experiences in relation to value potentialities as coherently as possible, thus working toward the most dependable pattern known thus far. Insofar as human beings, despite their differences in ability and culture, do have common motivational needs and abilities and do have a basically similar world, we may expect to find both the same kinds of value experiences and the same normative patterns, along with infinite differentiation in detail (resulting from their differences in nature, development, and environment).

In our last chapter we found good ground for supposing that the relativistic view of values cannot be maintained in theory or in fact. But the task still remains to set forth a pattern of values that might act as an ethical norm by which persons can guide their search for value. Our concern in this chapter has been to show that although there are no values without persons, the values of persons are not dependent on human wanting alone but on value potentialities within them and beyond them, which help them to organize their experiences of value. The task in the next three chapters is to discover, if we can, whether a pattern of values—a norm—can be established by which all persons can generally guide themselves at any stage of value experience. Indeed, the remainder of this book will deal with various phases of the definition of the norm of values for persons.

VII. *REFLECTIVE SUMMARY*

No persons, no values! In this conclusion we are in agreement with the ethical relativist, yet we find his specific theory of values inadequate. We propose a theory intended to acknowledge his essential contention against the moral realist, but we agree with the moral realist in his contention that values involve factors independent of man. What experiences are good for man in this world depends, we decided, on factors in himself and in the world, value potentialities that man finds but does not create and that influence the kinds of value open to him.

We begin with the fact that value experiences (or disvalue experiences) involve some quality of personal experience as wanted (or unwanted). As the person notes the varied conflicts between value experiences, he moves from the preanalytic level of experiencing to the reflective level of choice, that is, from value experiencing to evaluating these experiences. Evaluating does not create the qualities felt in value experience, but it "grades" them and thus prepares the stage for oughting-willing some critically preferred value experience.

The shift from "desired" to "ought to be desired" or "desirable" is possible because, on our view, the person feels obligation to any value deemed best among alternatives he believes on reflection to be attainable. His criterion for deciding what value claims are dependable values involves systematic reflection on the interplay between his values given in his own experiences and recommended by others. Those values, within the total variety of value experiences, that he believes support each other and encourage growth in value are held to be dependable.

Further reflection shows that dependable values are joint products of the value potential in ourselves and in the world beyond us. It is incorrect, therefore, to suppose that value experiences, because they are experiences in persons, have no basis beyond man's own desires. Value potentialities, independent of man's will, both in himself and in the environment, are factors involved in all of man's choices. Indeed, the values man prefers are influenced by the ways in which value potentialities do or do not support his choices. For example, friendship is preferable to hostility because of the way it affects all the other value claims and values of both the friend and the befriended. Similarly, value potentialities do much to determine what value experiences are or are not possible, what value experiences are dependable and what are not, what value experiences are instrumental and what are intrinsic, what value experiences harmonize and what do not.

Accordingly, we conclude that the norms for value experience are not in man alone, nor in the structure of things beyond man alone. They are hypotheses about the best way (or ways) in which human nature, in the interplay with the total environment will preserve and increase the values open to him. These norms of value are not value experiences; they are hypotheses about what the world and man's basic nature will support and encourage; they are generalizations *about the objective ground of value,* in the light of which men ought to guide their concrete, individual, and social struggle for values.

If this is so, we cannot speak of values as if they were descriptions of man's experience alone. Dependable values are descriptions of the world in which man lives and thus are evidence of the kind of world in which he lives and is ultimately controlled—a theme to which we shall return in Chapter 30.

15

The Life Good to Live:
A Symphony of Values

〜〜〜〜〜〜〜〜〜〜〜〜〜〜〜〜〜〜〜〜〜〜〜〜

I. *PROBLEMS IN DEFINING THE NORM*

A. *How Shall We Conceive the Norm?*

Charles Morris,[1] in studying "paths of life," discovered that Americans want a life in which there is "dynamic integration of diversity." David Riesman [2] says that the contemporary American wants to live securely in a suburban community with his family and neighbors, his life relieved of monotony by hobbies and travel. G. W. Allport and James Gillespie [3] find that American students in liberal arts colleges, in contrast to their counterparts in seventeen other countries, want "a rich, full life." This concern of American students to avoid dull routine in favor of "color" and variety stands in special contrast to the concern of students in France, Italy, and Germany to "form a character" and "become a distinctive personality."

A more recent study by Philip E. Jacob [4] does not contradict such

[1] Charles Morris, *Paths of Life: Preface to a World Religion* (New York: G. Braziller, 1956).

[2] David Riesman, *The Lonely Crowd* (New Haven: Yale University Press, 1950).

[3] James M. Gillespie and G. W. Allport, *Youth's Outlook on the Future*, ("Doubleday Papers in Psychology"; Garden City, New York: Doubleday & Co., 1955), pp. 13–14.

[4] Philip E. Jacob, *Changing Values in College: An Explanatory Study of the Impact of College Teaching* (New York: Harper & Brothers, 1957). A critique of this study may be found in John E. Smith's *Value Convictions and Higher Education* (New Haven: Edward W. Hazen Foundation, 1958), and under the same auspices, by Allen H. Barton in *Studying the Effects of College Education, 1959*.

326

findings. The value profile of seventy-five to eighty per cent of American college students (not restricted to liberal arts) includes seven values in common:

First, American students are *"gloriously contented"* in regard to both their present activity and their future outlook, to career, family, and to enveloping sociopolitical life. They are "supremely confident that their destinies lie within their own control rather than in the grip of external circumstances." [5]

Second, they are "unabashedly self-centered," yet not as a pioneer might be, but as dutiful participants in the contemporary economic order.

Third, "social harmony with an *easy tolerance of diversity* pervades the student environment." [6] These students are not, however, crusaders for greater social justice.

Fourth, they respect sincerity, honesty, loyalty as "proper" *moral virtues* for decent people. As the Allport-Gillespie study also showed, these students "do not feel personally bound to unbending consistency in observing the code, especially when a lapse is socially sanctioned." [7]

Fifth, they favor religion "on most week-ends," but are not convinced that belief in God should be a deeply transforming factor in daily personal or social behavior.

Sixth, they are "dutifully responsive towards government," but "politically irresponsible" so far as accepting personal involvement in the political process is concerned.[8]

Seventh, while setting *"great stock by college* in general and their own college in particular," they seem to value their college education largely in terms of vocational preparation and social adjustment.[9]

Fortunately, it is not our concern here to evaluate the validity and accuracy of these studies. Even if we had more accurate and more inclusive studies of what Americans, or Germans, or Japanese *are* valuing or even if we discovered many international and cross-cultural patterns of value, such findings could be no more than raw material for our concern in this chapter. We are here embarked on the even riskier search for a possible pattern of values that all persons *ought* to realize. For this project we must indeed bear in mind the types of

[5] Jacob, *op. cit.,* p. 1.
[6] *Ibid.,* p. 2.
[7] *Ibid.,* p. 2.
[8] *Ibid.,* pp. 2–3.
[9] *Ibid.,* p. 3.

value, the ways of life, the ideals of personality that men have prized and do prize. But our task is to see whether it is possible to conceive an inclusive and harmonious pattern of values to which all persons ought to be loyal.

Such a pattern of values would define the meaning of happiness. However, we have not used the word "happiness" for the life good to live because this word is so often associated only with the utilitarian ideal of the greatest pleasure (happiness) of the greatest number. But the word "happiness" has a long history, and, when used in the Platonic-Aristotelian sense for a fully active life in which some pleasures are components, it stands for the most inclusive ideal of personality.[10]

This inclusive organization must do justice not only to what human needs and abilities are and have been, but also to what human beings, as far as we know, can become in relation to the environment in which they live (physical, biological, social, and—possibly—divine). The life good to live is the life that has breadth and depth, richness and unity, harmony and fertility, universality and individuality. But these are all mere words unless we can spell out in terms of concrete human value experiences what we intend them to mean.

Such an enterprise requires special preliminary cautions if we are to avoid misunderstanding of our intention in this chapter and the next two. We are not trying to *prescribe a particular set of value experiences that every human being ought to set about to realize mechanically, regardless of his present stage of development or his need development and capacities.* It will remain true that any given pattern of values or value proprium will be unique. Two philosophers —or a thousand—who *mirabile dictu* were in agreement could not prescribe the particular pattern of value experiences that Sam Jones, living at the corner of X and Y Streets, in 1965, should incorporate into his living.

Once more, we are not saying that every person, in the next ten years, ought to develop an appreciation of Beethoven's Fifth Symphony, join the carpenter's union and the Methodist Church, have three children, and take up swimming as a hobby. The concrete complex of value-and-disvalue-experiences that a person actually undergoes in any one day defies anyone's ability to calculate, let alone anticipate.

[10] See Aristotle, *Nicomachean Ethics,* 1097 a.

Furthermore, at any one stage in his development—say, in his fourteenth year, or as a junior in college, or as a parent of three children —a person's life has, more or less, an organized value structure (value proprium), which he himself, in a cool moment of self-evaluation, would prefer to change if he could. It would be the task of understanding members of his family, of friends, of technically trained counselors, to help him make specific decisions about the specific value experiences that he might well preserve, discourage, or seek. We are preparing, then, *no stencil to be imposed upon particular persons;* nor should we do so even if we could. There is nothing that can replace the "art of living," that is, the day-to-day insight into what value experiences should be sought by a particular person at a particular stage of development.

However, although choice must always be *related* to a given person and situation, such procedure in choice does not involve us in *relativism* in value theory. For, the question we face, along with Sam Jones and the members of his family and community and his technical advisors is, in terms that we suggested at the end of the last chapter: What *norms* ought a person to use as he seeks to guide his choice of values? Ought any person, for example, to avoid education, or should education be included in any ideal pattern of value experience? Without defining what an ideal education would be, it is clear that the ideal would be approached in different ways. Sam Jones may pursue the ideal of education through the experiences of algebra and other pursuits in logic, the study of history, and the understanding of civil engineering. Esther, his daughter, may pursue the ideal through linguistic and literary studies, with special interest in the modern French novel. But our concern is this: *Ought* education to be, if at all possible, a part of every human life? And, what part, speaking generally?

To summarize: we are seeking the norm by which a human being in the critical pursuit of value experiences ought to guide himself if he is to realize the best that is open to him, at the stage of development in which he is, in the light of the kinds of value-experiences he can probably enjoy given his potential as a human being. As he seeks to move from where he is to where he ought to be in value experience as a whole, nobody can shoulder for him the responsibility of choosing in a situation that inevitably involves compromise (not opportunism).

B. *How Do We Know Which Values Are Most Important?*

In Part IV of this book there will be a detailed analysis and justification of principles that ought to guide choice. Here we shall only
suggest principles involved if we are to be experientially coherent in
the search for value.

First: Assuming that values are wanted experiences, those values
are most important which *as experienced* have a quality that is preferable as such to the quality other values have. This principle we
might call *the principle of intrinsic quality in value experience.* To
illustrate: The eating of bread, the enjoyment of music, and the
experience of compassion are value experiences. We should say that,
if we had to choose between these three, the experience of compassion
as experienced is superior to the experience of music, which, in turn,
as experienced, is superior to the experience of bread. The reader
may disagree, but not without illustrating the point being made. He
too has been appreciating critically a certain quality in each experience; and, for the quality of this experience, after he compares it
with others, he claims a priority.

Second: Those values are most important which, rather than endangering other values, actually support and sustain and, if possible,
increase value experience. This principle we might call *the principle
of growth in value experience.* Suppose, for example, an able high-
school senior wants to have a professional career, get a college education, marry, establish a home, and be an active member of a community. Because he does not have enough money to pay for a college
education, should he accept a reasonable loan that is offered him? He
has grown very fond of a girl who promises to be a good companion
in marriage. Should he marry her first? As he confronts the problem
of choice in this situation, if he is willing to reflect on the probable
realtionship between these different sources of value, he will see that
proper college education will support all the rest of these ventures
and that it would be better for him to accept the necessary loan, post-
pone marriage, and go to college. What he is doing here is discovering
the probable *causal relationships* between these different courses of
action. Because education is the long-run support of all the other
ventures, it becomes the most important value.

Again, the reader may disagree; and if he does he will be bound to
point out the different relationships on which he bases his choice.

He too will be asking: Which value or pattern of values will make for the conservation and possible increase of the values involved? In our search for a norm, therefore, we shall use both the principles of *intrinsic quality* and *of growth*.

Before turning to a third principle, we must make a distinction between *intrinsic values* and *instrumental values*. The possession of money is a value not for its own sake but for the sake of other values. Even a miser hoards money, and probably not for the mere possession of coin but for the kind of security it gives him. Again, traveling or moving about from one place to another is not an end in itself but a means to aesthetic experience, fellowship, knowledge, or other values. We may thus define an *instrumental value as any value that is experienced or sought not for itself but as a means for securing other values that are sought for themselves, namely, intrinsic values.* It seems clear, as the above illustrations suggest, that some experiences are not enjoyed or chosen for themselves, but are considered "values" because they are "tools" to use in order to obtain other experiences that are deemed valuable in themselves. To be sure, intrinsic values may be instrumental also; a profession, education, marriage, social activity are intrinsic values that are also means or instruments for realizing each other.

The importance of the distinction between instrumental and intrinsic values resides not only in the fact that it brings out the causal connection between terminal value experiences and experiences that are not intrinsically valuable. It warns us, to be sure, of a constant temptation in moral choice: the treating of instrumental values as if they were the end goals of life. But—even more important—it also makes us fully aware that values, instrumental and intrinsic, are so interpenetrating that any normative pattern of values will, in the concrete striving of the individual, involve him in the search for the proper causal relations between instrumental and intrinsic values.

With these considerations in mind, we can see that in applying the principle of intrinsic quality and the principle of growth in value experience, a third over-arching principle emerges: *the principle of most inclusive harmony in value experience*. This means that persons ought to choose that pattern of values which enables them, without lastingly jeopardizing intrinsic and higher values, to include as many values as possible. In other words, *the life best to live, at any stage of a person's existence, is the life that keeps a creative and mutually sustaining balance between the largest range of values open to him.*

It should be evident that "the happy life" can never be a static, unchanging state, but has to be one of creative growth.

We are now ready to suggest the reasoning which leads to a pattern of values as the basic norm by which value experiences ought to be chosen.

II. *THE PATTERN OF VALUE EXPERIENCES*

A long-standing ethical tradition supports, in the main, the classification of values listed in Diagram I.

DIAGRAM I

(Enumeration of Types of Value Basic to Happiness)

Existence Values
Health Values
Character Values
Economic Values
Vocational Values
Recreational Values
Affiliative Values
Sexual Values
Aesthetic Values
Intellectual Values
Religious Values

Our concern is to gain insight into their actual and possible relationships to each other.

A. *Existence as a Value to Be Respected*

Usually existence is not included separately in the classification of values. For, as Socrates said, the purpose of life is not to live but to live well. We would not deny this. Yet we distinguish what we call *existential values* from other values in order to emphasize the fact that simply to be conscious, to be aware of ourselves and of the world around us, to be the kind of self-conscious persons we are, is not only desired but desirable. Once in a while we may speculate that it might be better to be, say, a cat, than to exist as a human consciousness. But how many persons, offered the choice, would actually choose cat existence to human existence? Even the so-called "peace" of deep slumber is considered good in part because of the faith that this slumber will be followed by conscious awareness. In short, the experience and practice of men everywhere forces upon us the conclusion that it is better to be alive than not to be at all. There seems no great proof of the contrary.

But why make a special point about the value of existence for its own sake? So that we may remind ourselves of the obligation to stay alive, other things being equal, and to protect the possibility of sheer existence. For those of us who live in relative security against murderers or against the power of any man to determine, be it by supposedly divine right or not, whether we should live or die, this question may seem abstract. But six-million Jews were systematically killed during World War II by men who took it upon themselves to determine on the basis of "race" whether a person should live or die. In our own day, when nations stand poised with nuclear weapons to destroy large portions of a vast population, we need to remind ourselves again of the obligation to preserve existence. This is "natural piety," and we do well to observe it.

Antivivisectionists crusade under the conviction that it is wrong to undertake scientific investigation when it endangers the life of animals for the sake of understanding living processes and helping in the prevention and cure of disease. Whatever else may be said against antivivisectionists, they remind us, as do vegetarians, that mere existence, be it of animals or of human beings, is not to be taken lightly. We have a responsibility not to destroy any sentient existent unless we can give good reasons for doing so. Albert Schweitzer in his insistence on "reverence for life" does well to remind us of the fact that the moment we lose our reverence for life, in any form, something in us dies and the quality of our own existence suffers.

We do not wish to prejudice the question as to whether any man ought ever to give up his life for others or take his own life in preference to some other alternatives. All we wish to emphasize here is that the existential value of "just living," even when the quality of that living may not seem very high (as in the late stages of cancer), is important enough to demand respect. From this point on, however, the choice is between qualities of personal existence. When we know what these qualities are, we are better able to discuss such questions as suicide, mercy killing, or the taking or sacrificing of life for any purpose.

This differentiation of sheer existence from all the values that give life qualitative value and disvalue may well be criticized. Is not "existence" an abstraction from the concrete undergoings that give living value and disvalue? Why, then, differentiate it as if it were something to be sought for itself, when in fact it is the only universal instrumental value?

Once more, the point is well taken and would be fully accepted were it not for our concern to articulate the fact that, as far as we know, existence is preferable to nonexistence; and, until anyone has good grounds for supposing that in any situation it is better not to exist, our obligation is to respect existence in any form. In the name of quality we have no right to destroy particular forms of existence without further argument. We are not concluding that no case can be made for euthanasia or suicide or mercy killings, but we would seriously question any argument based on the theory that existence is valued or valuable simply as instrumental to possible higher values. We might grant that there are specific situations in which a person would be better dead than in excruciating and hopeless pain that does no person or cause any good (see Chapter 26). But in any instance where nonexistence is a moral option, the case for it would have to be based on the consequence of this choice for other moments of possible existence in one's own life and that of others.

B. *Health Values*

It is one thing to be alive; it is another to be healthy. Bodily health refers to that *quality* of *bodily* existence that not only is free from disease but also assures that sense of vitality and physical fitness which protects both continuity, variety, and quality of existence.

Most of us do not distinguish as we should between being well (that is, without annoying pain) and being healthy. As a matter of fact, we tend to be satisfied to "just live from day to day." We know that an ounce of prevention is worth a pound of cure, but in the absence of gnawing pain or disability, we tend not to take such precautions as medical check-ups. In so doing, we endanger existence itself by not pursuing health.

There are, of course, the illnesses and diseases that come regardless of human planning and choice. But although we do not usually speak of it as such, having health is in good measure a moral problem. For health requires disciplined choice in obtaining that amount of food, rest, exercise, and recreation which is adequate and not excessive. Health often involves the sacrifice of experiences that, while pleasant in themselves, decrease the health-quality of our lives by weakness and fatigue and thus affect not only the length of life, but the tone of life from day to day. How many people are exhausted before they need to be, are ill more than they need to be, because they have not willed (other things being equal) to include in their lives only those experiences that increase strength and vitality and create that sense of physical well-being which characterizes the healthy person?

If the reader has thought of the good life merely in terms of negatives and inhibition, these remarks about achieving the healthy life, bringing to his mind visions of ascetic abstinence from many immediate pleasures, must seem to have fulfilled his worst suspicions. But the ethicist must face the facts and all the facts. There simply is no denying that, other things being equal, the person who has planned to be healthy has not lost either in quantity or quality of bodily pleasure; he actually enjoys a more complete range of bodily pleasures than does the person who "takes life as it comes" or "lives it up." Furthermore, other things being equal, it is the person who takes health too much for granted who loses days of work or does a mediocre job out of sheer lack of physical fitness. By being in no shape for maximum alertness, he may endanger the lives of others. He is forced to make demands upon others when he is ill; he may carry contagious disease; his state of health may impair his effectiveness as a member of a family or of society generally. Preventably bad health is, more often than we realize, immoral, as well as inimical to both the individual and the group.

What should emerge from this discussion of health values is a lesson in choosing among conflicting values. Because health values, given existence, (a) actually increase both the amount and quality of existence values, (b) mutually sustain and support each other, (c) are deemed more valuable, as felt, than the values of merely "being alive," and (d) do not jeopardize other values of life, they ought to be preferred to other bodily values, which, however appealing momentarily, endanger those values which promote health.

But the problem of selecting health values also sensitizes us to the fact that many experiences of bodily disvalue are present in human life, the results of nothing for which the human person can be held responsible—for example, environmental factors beyond human control, diseases, and the disvalues that come with physiological change and age. At the same time, reflection on the conditions for health makes us realize that we cannot have either duration of existence or a high quality of health unless we develop another whole area of life, which we may call the area of character.

C. *Character Values*

We have been insisting on the factor of moral choice in health. Health is more than a matter of physical endowment and adequate resources. The unhealthy are not found only among underprivileged and poverty-stricken people. Even if the community did provide free medical and pharmaceutical aid and free hospitals, we could not assume that this in itself would decrease failing health, sickness, and disease. For persons are often not *willing* to "take the trouble" to avail themselves of the doctor's and the clinic's service—as recent experience with publically available injections to prevent poliomyelitis has shown. To generalize, once the health potential is given in the person or in the environment, *health no longer depends upon physiological and environmental circumstances but upon the capacity of the person to control himself in the choice of conditions which promise enduring health-values.*

Thus, there is no escaping the fact that health can depend on character. *Character is the willingness to discipline oneself in accordance with approved conceptions of values or ideals.* Most of us are not as healthy as we can be simply because we are not willing to "give up" or "sacrifice" some value claims for others that seem more immediately attractive—thus the professor who, when asked what he did for exercise, replied: "I lie down and think about it!"

We have introduced this concept of character in connection with the concept of health for two reasons. First, because we wish to challenge the notion prevalent in so much advertising and in much of our thinking that a healthy body is the foundation of a good character and other values. This is a half truth. It is true that a person who is crippled or a person who is unhealthy loses a great many other values in life as well as the quality of health-value itself. But he does not lose character on this account. On the other hand, it is also true that the person deprived of health-value cannot achieve as much good even if he has good character. And this is the ethical ground for asking parents and society to guarantee as far as possible, to every infant and child especially, the adequate environmental conditions that make for health. Nevertheless, one cannot foster and maintain health without choice. The child who says "I'll do what I like when I like it, and only if I like it" will be lucky indeed if he keeps his physical health—or his mental well-being! On the other hand, let the child be willing to face any necessary hardship in keeping and developing his health—the hardship that that particular child can, so far as we know, face—and he has done his full share to deserve the physical health that is under his control. This is not to advocate a simple-minded doctrine of discipline for discipline's sake. It is to remind ourselves that physical health cannot be bought at the drug store or at the infirmary. Like every other value, it must be built up by the individual who is willing to forego other value claims, like immediate comfort and convenience, for the sake of the ideal of health.

But there is a second reason for introducing the notion of character in connection with this elementary transition from existence to health values. The very nature of human existence forces us to emphasize the importance of character control for the whole of life. For a human being to live is for him to change and be affected by the requirements of the environment. But change means alteration and disruption of established patterns. It means insecurity and can produce anxiety, anxiety so profound that it can lead to many physical symptoms of ill health. But change also means new opportunity, greater scope for one's capacity, and, for the growing person, new values.

The fact of change, in other words, is in itself charged with value and disvalue possibilities. The person of character exerts control (within limits, usually) in the face of change. He recognizes change for what it is; he does everything he can, with himself and with his environment, to will his approved ideal. Change finds the man of character examining the new situation in the light of his approved ideal with a view to transforming it in the light of that ideal. Change finds him trying to exert *creative control* in choice situations.

Let us now put flesh on this skeleton. What do we admire when we say about a person: "Now, there's a man of character!" We may be speaking of a student who has discovered, on coming to college, that even increased effort will not bring the same grades he acquired in high school, but who, nevertheless, is relentless in exerting himself to improvement. We may be speaking of a person who, in spite of illness and other handicaps, "stays with it." We may be speaking of a Job, who, unflinching in his conviction that he has not deserved the evil which has come to him, yet will curse neither God nor man.

Nor do we necessarily approve of the ideal that guides the man of character. We may even approve a certain gangster's character, though we do not approve his predatory goal. What we approve is his willingness to sacrifice for what he thinks is right. A Napoleon and a Lenin we may vigorously oppose, and yet still prize their indomitable wills. A Gandhi and a Schweitzer, a Socrates and a Francis of Assisi—again whether we agree with their ends or not—strike a responsive chord in us when we contemplate their ability to stay at the helm of their ships. We call those who die for principles that we admire "martyrs"; we call those who die for principles we abhor "fanatics"; but we all wish we had their power to stick to their guns "through thick and thin."

So many problems come up in connection with the exact nature of character and its place in the full life that the next two chapters will be devoted to a more complete analysis of the constituents of character. Here we shall raise only two questions and suggest tentative answers. First, is character, or creative control in accordance with approved ideals, an instrumental value, a means to some other end, like health? Character is indeed an instrumental value, but do we not experience "character" as an intrinsic value? When we feel that we are not supinely giving in, when we feel "steadfast," do we not experience a quality of life that, whatever the other consequences may be, is something good?

Here again, each reader must judge for himself as he analyzes this phase of his complex experience. Whatever else life brings us, if we come to feel that we are always the victims of the strongest desire when our reason says *no* to that desire, do we not realize that we have lost, or are missing, one of the supreme values of life? There is nothing that can substituted for character. Creative control seems to be the one thing *we* can contribute, nay, must contribute ourselves to the flux of life.

Second, is the person who has developed character less vulnerable to mental disorder and maladjustment? Character, as we shall see, is a complex of many trials or virtues, for example, honesty, courage, and kindness. We are not suggesting that character is the "cure" for mental balance or health, or the "preventive." Yet when we review the factors that, in different psychotherapeutic approaches, seem to be considered fundamental in causing neuroses, we note a persistent emphasis on the person's need for security, on his anxiety in the face of insecurity. If we ask ourselves: "What is worse than the insecurity itself?" we answer: "The abject fear of insecurity, the unwillingness to face it, which actually increases the insecurity." If the child or adult begins to look for ways of protecting himself from insecurity, he makes excessive and rigid demands on those upon whom he feels dependent for his security. At the same time he hates himself for being weak, and he may hate those he connects with his feelings of weakness.

This is the kind of person who comes to dread change, be it due to his own life process or to forces outside of him. It is his opinions that readily take on the protective coloration of the crowd. He easily surrenders freedom, prefers anonymity at any time to responsibility in a group—and yet he never enjoys the cordial feeling of cooperation. The person who accepts the responsibility for freedom, in Fromm's terms, must face uncertainty. If he "escapes from freedom," he does not escape the real insecurity that springs from his inability to exert control on circumstances. There is no person, child or adult, who is more insecure than the person who forever seeks security. To be healthy mentally (whatever else is demanded) means, as far as we can see, at least to be able to face insecurity as creatively as possible.

Character, then, seems to be both an intrinsic value and an instrumental value to bodily and mental health. As we consider its relation to other values, we become more fully aware of the interdependence and interpenetration of value experiences. Diagram II may be suggestive of the ground covered and of what is to follow.

DIAGRAM II

AFFILIATIVE	EXISTENCE	HEALTH
SEXUAL	CHARACTER	ECONOMIC
AESTHETIC	COGNITIVE	VOCATIONAL
RELIGIOUS	(Truth)	RECREATIONAL

This diagram clearly suggests the dependence of all growth in value experience on *Existence, Character,* and *Cognitive* (or *Truth*) Values.

D. *Economic Values*

Economic values have sometimes been listed, as by W. G. Everett and W. M. Urban,[11] along with bodily values. Strictly speaking, the economic value of any article is its comparative value in exchange. Actually, the place of economic values in the life good to live is not easy to determine, once we get beyond those economic values absolutely necessary to good physical health. Yet good men from the beginning of time have warned against the amassing of goods, gadgets, and riches. Why? Because they knew that the pursuit of economic goods may become so absorbing that men have little time and energy left for other values, which are more significant than an excess of economic goods. And some persons who have become wealthy at the expense of friendship, recreation, home, family, the pursuit of learning, the enjoyment of beauty, and the worship of God have known how empty the achievement of economic security can be. They show how easy it is for men to be deceived into thinking that once they have a good bank account or a good house or a budget safely in the black, they have by the same tokens assured a good home, a cultivated life, and friendships.

Such reflections take us back to our caution: no one can properly assess the place that "things" have in his life, above their importance for health, unless he has given adequate attention to the value of other nonmaterial phases of life. Sober reflection has always found economic goods to be instrumental to the other values in life.

Yet it is difficult to emphasize that economic values are always means to ends without leaving the impression that economic goods are unfortunate necessities that can only tempt men to a lower form of existence! After all, does not a man's love for his family become more satisfying because he can provide them, especially in the years when their needs are more numerous, with proper food, a good house, adequate medical attention, good schooling, safe roads and playgrounds, painstaking policemen, and a stimulating social, aesthetic, and religious environment? *No man grows better in an economic vacuum.* Much of his development as a personality involves his training of himself (creative control) to earn and take care of

[11] See the tables of value in Chapter XII of Everett's *Moral Values* (New York: Henry Holt, 1918) and Chapter VIII of Urban's *Fundamentals of Ethics* (New York: Henry Holt, 1930), as well as the treatment of values and their interrelation in W. H. Roberts' *Problem of Choice* (Boston: Ginn & Co., 1941).

economic goods. The person who is careless in his treatment of his own property may well be lacking not only in imagination for what property can mean to him, but also in scrupulous care of what property can mean to others. There is very little that one possesses that does not influence others for good or ill, and the person who simply wastes what he says "belongs to me" is usually blind both to his own good and the good of others.

Every person in a community, no matter what else he does, is inevitably measured and tends to measure himself by his capacity to become at least a self-reliant economic agent. A person's job usually represents his station in the community; a person confident in his job is usually a person free from unnecessary worry and more able to take a cooperative part in family, community, and civic life. A man's stake in life, his own sense of achievement, will be strongly influenced by the confidence he feels in his capacity to earn and to maintain his economic goods.

Indeed, a person's attitude toward his own economic goods often offers a clear view into his adjustment to life. As we have seen, capacity to acquire economic goods involves one's creative control; but it also creates social prestige and power. The man with possessions and wealth that other people would like to have soon finds that other persons envy him, that they want his favor, that they prefer him "on their side." Actually, he finds them quite suggestible to the power that he can exert over them, and it is the unusual man who does not succumb to the temptation to exert and extend the power his money and people's attitude toward money give him over them. Indeed, if he is careful and calculating in the use of his financial power, he may come to "have a say" in every aspect of the community's life, be it business, the school, the church, the charitable or political affairs of the community. Thus power accumulates through power.

Prestige power and political power, along with economic power, allow expression for the instinctoid needs to master obstacles, gain admiration, and be creative. To feel needed, to participate, to master are intrinsic values because they form a recurring source of gratification in human life. But enjoyable as gratification of those needs is, the specific expression they take may actually foster weakness and rigidity in a person who does not see that they must be expressed in accordance with the other needs and values of experience. Again, to master, to be creative, to participate in economic and political pursuits (as opposed to being a victim or slave or unappreciated member of any assembly line or political system) are universal values—and the economic, social, and political systems are at once the product and the battleground for the gratification of these needs. But unless the agent is discriminating in his choice of expression, he may lay up conflicts with other values that spring from these same needs.

A person's work or vocation, be it that of a construction worker, carpenter, lawyer, teacher, pastor, or housewife, readily becomes the center from which and by which many choices in value are made. And, we have been urging, the concern for economic gain, for social prestige, for health, and other values may easily lead him to choose a vocation on grounds that will not in fact lead to growth and challenge in value realization. One thing seems clear; namely, if the choice of a person's vocation is not guided by the person's abilities as well as by his interests and needs, he will soon come to lose basic confidence in himself and to depend upon other persons' abilities and performance. If a person's vocation, on the other hand, is supported by actual ability, so that he himself and others can depend on his performance, the foundation of his social life is neither shallow nor false, even if he cannot gain through his particular work as much economic security and social prestige as he might like. But a person who can feel that through his own powers, however modest, he can stand in a cooperative relation to the rest of the community undergoes a kind of gratification that makes him consider his work both an intrinsic and an instrumental value.

E. Recreational Values

The life good to live—or any comprehensive organization of values —must have a place in it for the values of recreation; and if we pass quickly over such values, which are probably sufficiently obvious to the reader, it is not to minimize their importance.

That we need to think freshly about the range and content of recreation will be apparent the moment we realize that the increase of leisure because of economic and industrial developments leaves persons with time on their hands that can be used for anything but re-*creative* activities. We might add, in view of what we have just said about vocation and work, that for many whose vocations perforce become a source of monotony and frustration, life can become richer through the hobbies and recreational activities that call more of their economically unproductive abilities, and perhaps more of their personalities, into play.

F. *Affiliative Values*

1. *Affiliative Values as Enhancing All Other Values*

The term *affiliative value* is intended to refer to a wide range of experiences beginning with momentary feelings of companionship and extending to experiences of lasting friendship and love.

Most of us live in the middle ranges between sheer loneliness and the sharing of human love at its best. But is it not true that every other good in life—and we speak cautiously—is rendered more valuable if it becomes part of a cooperative and appreciative human relationship? At the same time, let some good thing, such as vocation, become the source of estrangement and suspicion between human beings and the value of that thing begins to wither. Who cares for health at the expense of all friendly recognition and concern? Who wants a good house, a fine car, and a solid bank account if the house cannot be a home, if the car is a menace to companionship, and if the bank account is not appreciated by others as a fair reward for honest effort?

It might seem that the man of character has to follow the dictates of his own conscience despite the disagreement and opposition of others. We have insisted on the value of such creative discipline. But one must hope that his concern for character values will in fact ultimately be a creative basis for human relationships. It might seem also that the experience of beauty must be confined to privacy.

But is its value decreased when one can talk about it or feel kinship with another in appreciation of a common object?

It is so easy for those of us who live in the middle ranges, who always have a certain number of friends, someone at home, at school, or at work who cares about what we do, to take affiliative values for granted and thus underestimate their importance in the growth and spread of other human values. Yet he who would reach the higher ranges of companionship-in-care must leave the middle ranges of cozy friendships, intermingled as they often are with petty animosities and small loves. We may best articulate the kind of thing we mean by this last sentence if we consider several ranges of emotional development in the light of psychological investigation. (Later, in Chapters

27 and 29, we shall consider important problems in altruism and romantic love.)

2. *The Need for Understanding Care*

It is almost axiomatic in contemporary psychology that the infant and child need to feel loved. What the world means to a baby depends on the kind of attention mother, father, brothers, and sisters give it. If the emotional atmospheric pressure of a home cannot make a child feel that life is worth living, very few things can. Religious educators know that "God" can mean little to a child whose every desire for affection and for responsive help is spurned in the home. Studies of prejudice in adult life reveal that often the most rigid and uncritical prejudices are to be found among persons whose own childhood was fraught with insecurity and emotional rejection.[12]

For the child to want love, for the child to long for significance, for the child to need physical protection and sympathy in his times of need, for the child to know that mother and father (or anyone in the familial relationship) cares about what happens to him—all involve thousands of situations in which there can be gratifying value experiences despite frustrations and conflict. Yet no child can begin to discover order and pattern in his value experiences unless his parents or substitutes are mature enough emotionally and understanding enough to give him the kind of acceptance and guidance he needs as he develops.

In short, the fundamental affiliative unit is the parent-child relationship. Without parents who have learned to love, the child will suffocate psychically. There is much evidence to indicate that the child will never move out of his egocentric concern for self unless parents understand his problems and are themselves sufficiently other-centered to give the painstaking guidance and companionship the growing child needs.[13] Yet, no matter how understanding and concerned parents, family circle, and others may be, there is no way of sparing the growing person the disappointments that have their root in human ignorance and frailty. Given the careful nurture of a good home and a provident society, the individual in the last analysis has to make his own response to others in the midst of his and their

[12] See, for example, G. W. Allport, *The Nature of Prejudice* (Reading, Mass.: Addison-Wesley Publishing Co., 1954), Chapter 18, and T. W. Adams *et al.*, *The Authoritarian Personality* (New York: Harper and Brothers, 1950).

[13] See Bruno Bettelheim, *Love Is Not Enough: The Treatment of Emotionally Disturbed Children* (Glencoe, Illinois: Free Press, 1950).

disappointments, his and their needs. And here he must come to terms with his own forms of egocentrism and adopt attitudes that will discourage self-pity.

We go so far as to hazard the generalization (supported we believe by much of our analysis in Chapters 1–6) that at the core of much mental breakdown, when we trace it far enough, is the fact that at some point in life a crucial negative attitude was formed toward hardship. Why are some persons willing to face disappointment and suffering without becoming bitter, while others are not? If a person is unwilling to confront difficulty, disappointment, or pain, especially when he understands the good that can come as a result of his proper confrontation of these trials and risks, what has happened to him?

This is hardly the place for an exhaustive exploration. We do suggest that such a person at some time lost his confidence in his own *capacity for suffering* or in the worthwhileness of suffering even for an objective of which he rationally approves. And further, we suggest that, whenever this happens, part of the reason is that at some point of trial in his life, he did not have anybody to show him the kind of concern for his struggle and his welfare that made him feel that somebody really cared about what happened to him. Mother and father and friends cannot, to be sure, take failure, pain, and disappointment out of life. But they can make the growing person know that in his failure, in his pain, and in his disappointment, he is never forgotten. In the midst of difficulty he can feel their concern and their willingness to work with him in making the most of the poorest situation.

To put the point directly: human beings are encouraged to face the risks of life when they know that in their moment of need there will be compassionate hands to help when help is possible. It is all too easy for a child to grow out of his egocentrism into unabashed and aggressive selfishness or into such modes of selfishness such as withdrawal into self and uncooperativeness. If he is to grow from egocentrism into give-and-take affiliation, he needs to have parents who not only understand his situation but are firm, though friendly, in seeing to it that he realizes (a) that he simply cannot have all he wants, (b) that he simply cannot have it at the expense of others, (c) that neither his noisy demands nor his uncooperative expression of discontent will improve the situation.

Still, the child who can feel that *he* is not rejected has a quality of affiliation with his parents that is the basis for every other attempt at adjustment, either with people or with things. For, although pain is pain, failure is failure, and disappointment is disappointment, they are not *only* so when the individual knows that everybody is not indifferent to their presence in his life. And until a growing person does realize that he can "take" suffering and that disappointment can be faced and kept from spreading, nothing can help him face his problems more than the knowledge that others care for him for his own sake. In the psychiatric experience of rediscovery and healing, the catalytic agent is the patient's confidence that he is in an understanding, and not merely condemnatory, relation to the analyst, whose main concern is to help him to find himself.[14]

Much more could be said, and should be said, about the intrinsic and instrumental value of the kind of human companionship that assures to each of us, in time of trouble, a warm place in the sympathetic concern of others. But if human life were only a yearning for care, we should miss all the value experiences that come when *we move from the want to be loved to the want to love.* Even practically speaking, as we have noted, the need for care cannot be filled unless there are others who are concerned to care. Yet we can be so aware of our need for affection that we overlook even the intrinsic value of the need *to care for.* Before passing on, we must dwell briefly on this new level of need.

3. The Need to Care

Let it be noted that we are not here arguing the case for unselfishness or altruism as opposed to selfishness (though we believe we are providing some grounds for unselfishness). We are simply calling attention to experiences that human beings actually do have. And we are suggesting that, apart from the need that others have for the consideration flowing from active love, there are few values richer in quality than the experience of loving. Once more, there are different stages of this love, and we have limited ourselves to its basic thrust.

The person who can only call for care and never give it is a weakling. There may have been times when he felt the inner tug to

[14] See especially the therapeutic methods of Carl R. Rogers and Harry S. Sullivan, *e.g.*, Carl R. Rogers, *Client Centered Therapy, Its Current Practice, Implications and Theory* (Boston: Houghton Mifflin, 1951); *Counseling and Psychotherapy: Newer Concepts in Practice* (Boston: Houghton Mifflin, 1942); *Psychotherapy and Personality Change* (Chicago: University of Chicago Press, 1954); *A Therapist's View of Personal Goals* (Wallingford, Pa.: Pendle Hill, 1960); and Harry Stack Sullivan,, *Conceptions of a Modern Psychiatry* (Washington: William Alanson White Psychiatric Foundation, 1947); *The Psychiatric Interview*, ed. Helen Swish Perry and Mary Ladd Gawel (New York: W. W. Norton, 1954); *The Interpersonal Theory of Psychiatry*, ed. Helen Swish Perry and Mary Ladd Gawel (New York: W. W. Norton, 1953).

help and protect another, but simply could not bring himself to do it because of his fear that his help would not be appreciated. Whatever the reasons for his unwillingness to come to the aid of others, whatever the causes for the "block" he feels when he would "like" to help others, the fact is that he is one whose insecurity and weakness are a stumbling block to his own development as a person and to the best expression of his own needs to sympathize, feel tender, respect, and be creative. For there are few situations that challenge one's ability more than the differing needs of other persons. To develop one's knowledge and one's imagination enough to understand another and to be able to leap to his side not only emotionally, but with some helpful act and suggestion, is no easy task.

To take a positive interest in the needs of others without demanding appreciation and recognition involves a high grade of self-mastery and a deep insight into the art of helping. For it is of great importance to keep one's concern for another from becoming an imposition on that other, that is, from becoming simply another way in which one asserts oneself. At the same time, is it not a "peak experience" to know that others trust you, to see the gleam of "welcome" in their greeting, and to know that in your own life you have been able to share the good that you in turn have received?

The person who cannot really care for anything or for anyone but himself is all the narrower in the range and quality of his emotional development. For where there could be generosity there is miserliness and greed; where there could be kindness, there is indifference; where there could be trust, suspicion easily grows; where there could be gratitude, there is fear; where there could be companionship, there is loneliness.[15] Apart from the fact that such a person becomes a broken link in any group or society, has he not allowed to shrivel those emotions which give to life many of its most stirring and satisfying experiences?

G. *Sexual Values*

The nature and function of sex in human experience is not easy to appraise, as every reader of Part I will realize. We are, therefore, reserving Chapter 29 for the discussion of its place in the pattern of values.

---

[15] It will be noted that here we are treating kindness and other attitudes as emotional responses—in contrast to the analysis they will be given as virtue-traits in Chapter 17.

H. *Cognitive or Truth Values*

Normal human beings take for granted the value experiences involved in the many varieties of awareness and knowing. The intrinsic as well as the instrumental values that come into human life through most sounds, colors, tastes, smells, and tactual sensations are immeasurable. Each sense can bring pain and unpleasantness, but which of us would give up the value experiences connected with any one sense —take sight, for example—because pain can also come therefrom?

Nor would we give up the capacities of memory and imagination because they can bring forth both hope and despair, joy and sorrow, anxiety and anticipation into human life. But it is in man's capacity to weave experiences of sense, memory, and anticipation into a connected pattern with a view to solving some problem—that is, in his capacity to think—that we find the source of the greatest cognitive values and disvalues. For once a man has the capacity to think about experiences he has had, he is freer not only to understand what has happened, but also to plan courses of action with or without benefit of such understanding.

Indeed, while we are usually aware that thinking can be turned to unethical purposes, we tend to neglect the fact that moral discipline is required if we are to think straight and to think thoroughly about anything. For thinking, as opposed to free association, does not take place as a matter of course. How easy it is to "free associate" or to allow our thoughts to follow "luxuriously" in the stream of the strongest feelings of the moment. But often when we try to straighten thought out in accordance with the demands of logic and of the problem to be faced in a given situation . . . well, things do not go smoothly! Obstacles are met that need to be overcome; we easily get tired of trying to see relationships that are not obvious. And here we become aware of the neglected fact. It takes character (or creative control) to think and to think persistently, not only in the face of discouragement but at any time, if one is to meet the exacting conditions of discovering the truth. We come back once more to the centrality of character values for the life good to live.

What we must also see more clearly is that a person encourages personal maladjustment when he is not willing to do his utmost to discover the truth. Psychotherapists warn us without ceasing that a human being must "face reality" and not lean on defense mechanisms that keep him from knowing the truth about himself and the world about him. Briefly, let us see why this is so.

A young man is turned down by his girl friend. He may protect his ego by saying to himself: "She wasn't much; I'm glad that's over" or "There aren't any good girls, anyway." This sour-grapes mechanism may relieve his feelings and even give him a chance to swagger, but he might have used his thinking ability to discover, as far as possible, the real cause for his being turned down and to develop insight into himself that could help him in the future.

Indeed, if we analyze other defense mechanisms, we discover that they also involve different ways and degrees of fleeing from reality. It would seem that the person, in order to defend his emotionalized conception of himself, or in order to protect some value that seems paramount at the time, is not willing to face all the facts, think hard about them, and then work out some way of dealing with them that will improve the situation as much as possible.

To take a few examples: How easy it is for us to *rationalize,* that is, give some excuse other than the real cause that justifies our actions in our own eyes or in the eyes of others! How tempting to *project* our own weaknesses into the lives of others so that we can glory in punishing those weakneses there rather than blaming them in our own lives! With what ease we *identify* ourselves with some person or prestige group, instead of accepting the responsibility for all that we ourselves can do! Through *repression* a person may keep out of his conscious life facts that at the time seem intolerable to him, only to discover that he has to tolerate gnawing anxiety and thus cut himself away from other possible values.

Persistently modern psychotherapy points to the same conclusion: a person courts mental illness unless, as he grows, he comes to appraise his own abilities, desires, and accomplishments honestly and, facing his assets and liabilities as a person, is willing to do his utmost (creative control) to build a mode of life that is soundly based on those potentialities. To develop the human capacity for seeking the truth is not a luxury for him who would fulfill his potential life by the relevant facts about himself and his world—as opposed to manipulating the facts to conform to likes and dislikes.

Finally, what becomes increasingly clear is the dynamic interrelation between character and truth-finding in the search for values. To discipline oneself without the guidance of available truth is to invite fanaticism. But the truth available to man about either fact or value will not be discovered by one who will rationalize instead of accepting the discipline of reason. We cannot escape the facts: If there had been no human beings willing to discipline their thinking by the norms of logic and scientific method, if no human beings had been willing to put aside convenient prejudices that kept them from seeing the facts, there would be no significant understanding of the causal connections in the physical, biological, and social world upon which human beings depend for the preservation of existence, health, and social welfare. Without the willingness of men to bring order and increase quality in the life of desire and feeling, there would be no arts and no ethical and religious norms.

Nor can we minimize the importance of philosophical thinking that seeks to understand the interrelations of all our experience and knowledge. Truths may come in small bits and in large chunks, but if, as so much of our thinking seems to indicate, the truth should lie in an interpretative network of ideas, each of which throws light on the other, we shall be better off to know this fact. Every other value in life is endangered to the extent that the search for truth falters. At the same time, much of the sheer joy of living consists of thinking for its own sake. The creativity and the sense of mastery involved in unraveling the skein of fact and value bring a quality into life that is its own reward—and men who have an essentially contemplative life do not apologize for it but quietly wish that their fellow-men could enter into their joy.

I. *Aesthetic Values*

Man, we have said. is a wanting-knowing being spurred on by the obligation to do his best. No one with any inkling of what gives human beings intrinsic satisfaction could omit the unique quality of fulfillment in aesthetic experience from a definition of the best. In fact, aesthetic satisfaction has frequently been taken as the proto-type or key to intrinsic values in general, and with good reason. In order to appreciate or respond aesthetically to any object—a willow tree, a garbage can, a Braque painting, another human being, the RCA building, or the Faure *Requiem*—I must attend to it for its own sake.

The objects referred to in the last sentence may be considered in-strumentally in different ways. The RCA building I frequent for business transactions. The willow tree is a nuisance because its roots block the water line. The Braque painting covers that crack in the plaster. The weathered garbage can is sturdy and convenient to carry. I familiarize myself with the Faure *Requiem* in order to pass the course in music appreciation. In the "practical" attitude that I take to each of these objects, I am treating it as a means to some further end. Indeed, I do not respond to it as a whole but dissect the object and then treat it as if it were that dissected part. Such dismemberment has its purposes, obviously, but it yields no aesthetic experience.

Suppose now, that I stop, on a bright spring morning, to look at that willow tree. Strictly speaking, I am presented with a sensory pattern, but the pattern as I look at it, takes on life; it becomes a living whole of color, ranging from bright yellows to dark greens and browns. The willow tree has left behind its winter drabness and in its spurt of new life is soft and hard at once. It caresses the light, plays in the breeze, yet clutches the earth firmly. To catch the sun its branches burst into a myriad of twigs and new leaves. To catch the water and life-giving chemicals from the earth its roots spread into a tangled skein of rootlets that crowd out other plants and clog water pipes. For me in this moment the willow tree is a thing of beauty, of intrinsic perceptual meaningfulness. It has become an aesthetic object.

Let us examine this new perspective on the tree. The perspective includes all my past experiences of willow trees, springs, growth, awakening, reaching, clutching, softness, strength, and struggle. The willow tree has now taken on significant individuality. The tree has for me not just recognitional significance (Ah, that is a willow tree!) but emotional significance. It has become a fully embodied symbol—not of something else, but a self-embodied symbol containing the range of its meanings in itself. The richer the background of my own experience, the fuller the embodied symbol becomes. Again, this experience could not occur so long as my own primary concern was with clogged water pipes. To realize the significant individuality of the willow tree I had to forget myself, attain a certain kind of objectivity, become "absorbed in the tree." But the result of such self-forgetting is a peculiarly rewarding experience, an experience of insight and intrinsic value now.

No wonder the aesthetic values have been taken as the prototype for intrinsic values in general! In each realm of value experience the end for which we ultimately strive is such intrinsic value. Character values, cognitive values, affiliative values, recreational values, or reli-

gious values—when we begin to stress their uniqueness and importance as experiences to undergo for their own sake, we immediately
use aesthetic terminology: "awe," "sublimity," "grace," "zest," among
scores of other terms. Again, in aesthetic perception we begin to
grasp the richness, the emptiness, the beauty, the ugliness, the tragedy,
the fulfillment, the intrinsic significance of our environment.

Once more, as I shift from my normal "practical" perspective to an
aesthetic perspective, I actually rediscover the street on which I live—
or see it "as it really is" for the first time. It is no longer just a quarter
of a mile of sidewalk and asphalt down which I rush in order to get
home for supper. It becomes an amazingly revealing patterned landscape, with some houses ostentatiously yet vapidly pretending to be
what they are not—gothic castles, Georgian country houses, south-
western ranches on cramped city lots—and other houses honestly
admitting the conditions of suburban life and, making the most of
the contour of the land, unifying trees, gardens, and well-kept lawns
with quiet dignity.

This ability to perceive aesthetically, to look at situations and objects in terms of intrinsic perceptual meaningfulness, calls forth new
dimensions of our own being even as it transforms the world we live
in. The ability to perceive aesthetically is perhaps the best antidote
for what might be described as our squirrel-cage existence—overcon-
cern with endless chains of means without ends—or a morbid self-
absorption and self-pity. One is able, in aesthetic perspective, to see
the incongruities of so much of his actual behavior in the context
of his pretensions and laugh at himself. Or he suddenly becomes
aware of human foibles and of human accomplishments in context.
He can see, for example, the weathered face, gnarled hands, and
penetrating eyes of the lobster fisherman in a Maine village as characteristics of a life that has not been easy but that refuses to compromise with the elements or other men. Appearance takes on the
substance of the meaning of a life.

Suppose I try to capture or embody or interpret the uniqueness of
this fisherman in paint. I paint him not primarily to communicate
this uniqueness but to clarify it—to express, to capture it for myself
in a special way. I create with the paints a new embodied symbol.

If I am successful, I may be creating a symbol that makes it possible
for others to grasp not only what the fisherman looks like (in fact
there may be very little image-likeness) but what he means in his
uniqueness—emotionally, cognitively, perspectively, as seen through

my eyes and my experience, whether my intention was communication or not. Thus, whole new dimensions of nonverbal communication open up. A person who has never been to Maine, who has never known an ocean fisherman, but who is able to grasp what might be called the language of the painting, can experience the ruggedness, the saltiness, the significant individuality that I experienced as he recreates the fisherman from the perceptual clues I have left in the painting. The artistic medium might have been, of course, a poem, music, or a piece of sculpture.

Through artistic creation, therefore, the artist embodies and interprets his world. Others of the artist's own or subsequent generations can through the work of art re-enter that world, not simply as they might read it in histories, but rather in its more fully flavored life. Accordingly, if I want to experience medieval man's sense of mystery, of awe, of aspiration, of devotion, and of humility, I do so most effectively not by reading medieval history alone, but by visiting the cathedral of Chartres or Notre Dame.

Of course, if I have read history, both Chartres and Notre Dame are easier to grasp, but from the history I cannot grasp what my aesthetic experience of Chartres and Notre Dame makes possible. I may not be able to grasp the art forms of another culture or period without minimal knowledge of that culture or period, but I can probably never know the affective overtones, the sense of being at home, the aspirations, or the types of frustration and fruition of that culture or period apart from its art forms.

The artist can thus perform the social function of conserving a people's values, of binding a people together in their cultural history and of making available to all many of the significant emotional, as well as the cognitive insights of the race. "History may tell us what men did, but only the poet or other artists can make us relive the value of their experiences." [16]

Because the arts do make possible a level of sympathetic understanding and insight not otherwise available, they are usually among the first modes of communication to fall under censorship in a totalitarian state. The last thing a dictator or a totalitarian leader wants is sympathetic insight by his people into the perspective of others.

It is true, of course, that one may have a fair number of other types of value without enjoying aesthetic values. One can exist in relatively

[16] DeWitt H. Parker, *The Principles of Aesthetics* (2nd ed.; New York: F. S. Crofts & Co., [1920], 1946), p. 37.

good physical health, make money, bear children, and have friends without ever seeing the willow tree as more than a nuisance to clog water pipes or without enjoying Brahms's *First Symphony* or without ever seeing anything more in a Jackson Pollock than squiggles of paint. One can eat meat and potatoes almost as if eating were a necessary evil to be got over with as quickly as possible without ever enjoying a well-appointed table. The aesthetic values are not essential to biological survival. But so also can one survive without religious values, with a minimum of intellectual values, and with many acquaintances but no friends. What does need to be pointed out, however, is that without the aesthetic values the whole of life is immeasurably impoverished. If emotional and mental health are essential to health in the broadest sense, then the aesthetic side of life is essential to fully effective, not to say creative, living.

We would go one step further by suggesting that it is only as the aesthetic values interpenetrate with the other values that any of the other values reach their fruition in full intrinsic import. Character values without aesthetic values invite fanaticism and emptiness. Religious values without aesthetic values can in fact impoverish the life of spirit in drab buildings and buttonless clothes. Intellectual values without aesthetic values lead to the anemic life of the disembodied intellect.

That the life of value realization, that the good life itself, must favor, in the last analysis, living on the most significant and creative level of which each person is capable—and for its own sake—this is the very meaning of our phrase "symphony of values." Indeed, we can gladly agree with R. B. Perry: "Art, both in the creation and enjoyment of it, is thus true to the deepest motive of morality." [17] And we can hope with I. Edman: "In time the disciplined freedom of art may come to be considered the highest morality: the creation and enjoyment of art the most rational practice." [18]

J. *Religious Values*

No inventory of human values, especially if it is to include those forms of experience deemed intrinsically worthwhole and exerting far-reaching influence on other values, can omit religious values. But again, because religious experience and belief can bring both

[17] *The Moral Economy* (New York: Charles Scribner's Sons, 1909), p. 212.
[18] *The World, the Arts, and the Artist* (New York: W. W. Norton, 1928), p. 43.

good and evil to human life, they involve special problems of interpretation, which we shall consider, together with religious value, in Chapter 30.

III. *THE SYMPHONY OF VALUES AND THEIR ORCHESTRATION*

The "score" of the types of value experiences is now before us. A whole ideal of personality and the good life is involved in what has been said. Some further comments may clarify the total conception.

A. *Uniqueness of Each Value Experience*

First and foremost, every value experience (and type of value) has its own uniqueness. Each value is what it is, a fulfillment, a lived-through (*erlebt*) qualitative experience related to some want, innate or acquired. This may give the impression that we have in our experience a sheer plurality of value experiences. But no more is meant than that health, for example, is not in itself, say, a recreational or aesthetic value; or that while some values are roughly substitutable by others (the eating of a pear in place of an apple, for example), the rule, strictly speaking, is that no two value experiences are identical. The heightening of sensitivity and the training of taste, be it in food or in music, accentuate this fact. The rendering of the same musical composition by two musicians can create differing degrees of approval and disapproval because one cannot be substituted for the other.

We must, indeed, not forget that the *final* evaluation of any value experience will depend on the part it plays in sustaining and heightening a larger network of value interests. Nevertheless, no value is a "slave" to some other, even though it cannot claim priority without justification. A value experience is what it is and must be seen for what it is *in* the process of gratifying some need or need complex, and being related to other values. Whatever harmony may be discovered between values cannot be either automatic or arbitrary.

B. *Interrelatedness of Value Experience*

Our exposition of value themes may have brought into relief important contrasts between values. But we have been driven by the interlocking nature of human needs and abilities to recognize the interrelationship between values. Whatever priorities may exist among values must be seen in terms of their capacities to sustain and enhance value ventures as a whole. Thus, we have urged that character values and truth values are bipolar central goals simply because truth cannot be achieved without self-discipline (see Diagram II, p. 339). Yet self-discipline, unenlightened by truth about oneself and the world, may be unmitigated cruelty. At the same time, both character values (the virtues) and truth values are crucial to every other search for discriminating quality in value experience. Health, economic, vocational, recreational, aesthetic, affiliative, sexual, religious, and aesthetic values have lasting value only as they are built on truth and the willingness to discipline oneself in the search for truth.

We have purposely avoided talking about *a scale of values*—that is, higher and lower values—or spiritual as distinct from other values, because in the network of a particular individual's life especially, it is in fact not helpful to assume priority for any particular type of value. It is individual, systematic, dynamic growth in value coherence that must provide guidance about specific priorities. Every personality, analyzed psychologically, will have a different profile of value. Analysis might reveal that Sam Jones is "too high" in the cognitive and "too low" in the affiliative or aesthetic range of values to become more coherent in his experience of value. The value proprium in each personality may need changing in different ways as the person gains insight into the value structure he ought to live by. Our contention is that the norm for value realization is systematic, inclusive, dynamic coherence among value experiences as these express the nature of man and of his total interchange with the world.

C. *Values as Joint Products of Man and the Total Environment*

The reader has probably noted already that these basic forms of value experience do in fact stem from and give expression to the needs and motives outlined in Chapter 7. In physiological needs, in the demand for mastery and for affiliation, in the urge to sympathize and to express oneself sexually and creatively, in the need to know, to respect, to feel free from insecurity and fear, and yet to assert oneself with confidence and control—here values are born. And in the interpenetration of these needs and abilities as they meet the demands of the physical and social environment and then in turn seek to conform it to themselves, we can trace the alliances between instrumental and intrinsic values and discern the shape of the larger pattern of values open to human beings.

Values do not exist independent of human conation, ability, and knowledge. Yet their quality, structure, and pattern is dependent not merely on desire but on the potential for values in human nature as a whole and in the nurturant environment. The ideal of personality is not a will-of-the-wisp, but the attempt to understand the conditions under which human beings may fulfill their needs and abilities in relation to each other and the total environment. The ideal of personality, the normative pattern of value, is a joint product of man and his universe. It is the creation of man—challenged and nurtured in this kind of universe.

D. *The Organization of Value as Symphonic*

We seem to begin with pluralistic value experience and fragmentation and move to interconnection and organization. But this shift, after all, may well be expected. For, we remember, it is a unified personal agent, feeling obligated to the best, who is ever at work realizing or actualizing his potential in a world that at once challenges, invites, concurs, supports and frustrates. In traditional terms, this theory of the ideal personality is eudaemonistic; the ethical goal is self-realization.

But every theory of self-realization must bear inspection in terms of the self to be realized. On what might be called a "personalistic" view, which we have here in mind, no encapsulated "monad" or entity is involved; no self-centered, parasitic agent is envisioned; no unchanging and rigid "soul" ultimately impervious to the environment, enjoys a hidden existence. If anything, on this view, to become encapsulated, parasitic, or impervious is ethically to be a sick personality.

Nevertheless, the person is not the product of society alone, and he has a self-identifying unity in change as he guides himself by overarching ideals and norms. If "healthy," he is never simply a thoroughfare or crossroad of the world. He is engaged in his own search for meaning, for breadth, for fulfillment, and he finds that he must accept responsibility for as much as he can in the world around him. He is not content to seek a final peak experience or "perfection," for he continuously seeks to weave together patterns of value experience. If anything, as we shall see increasingly, he is a growing, responsible agent seeking fuller community among values open to him and between his own values and those of others. He moves from conflict in his own life and with others, not to an inane peace, but to creative harmony—seeking, like A. N. Whitehead's God, to see that nothing worthwhile is lost.

The problem in every life, in the last analysis, is to orchestrate value experiences, to find the proper place for each quality in the ongoing fulfillment of the theme of life. It is not simply to avoid tension and conflict, but to avoid needless tension and conflict. To orchestrate values is to invite creative conflict, that is, conflict in which staleness and monotonous security is always challenged in the very attempt to achieve a new harmony.

In our attempt to find a figure that would suggest the kind of *concert of contrasting movements* in the life of value realization, we find the basic pattern suggested in a symphony most helpful—hence our term *symphony of values* as the norm for personality growth. The theme of a symphony is rich and abounding as it moves from stage to stage and finds itself "fulfilled" in the new peaks of harmony through different instrumentalities. No movement is left idle and unchallenged, and there is a tension-in-harmony always on the move to another peak; at the same time, there is also the free play and the breath-taking adventure on the ridges of a musical slope. But throughout, a particular theme is fulfilling itself, as it were, almost to its own surprise. No single figure, of course, will do for the life of a person seeking symphonic orchestration of values. What must not be lost in any figure, however, is the fact that the ideal person is one who is willing to face the conflicts of value in life and to harmonize them as creatively as possible.

IV. *REFLECTIVE SUMMARY*

In what does happiness or human well-being consist? Our answer is that all persons, as far as is within their power at each step in their self-development, ought to develop personalities in which a core pattern of values is central.

How do we discover this ideal pattern of values? By noting the intrinsic quality of value experiences and the seeming order of interdependency among value experiences and the needs and capacities that undergird them.

The network of interpenetration between values defies summary or extended description, but certain broad lines of interreliance are observable. *Existence* values are obviously basic to all others and are not to be cast aside lightly in order to protect quality of existence for the individual or for other persons. Yet, existence respected, all concrete moral choices are between envisioned qualities of experience.

Thus, *health values* protect and enhance the quality of bodily existence, but they cannot be achieved without two other basic ranges of value, *character* and *truth values*. The willingness to control oneself by one's ideals and the willingness to discover as much truth as possible are crucial to the realization, preservation, and increase of all other values—although the matrix in which cognitive and character values grow will in turn be affected by all the other values.

Accordingly, *economic* values, including vocational values, affect the realization of other values. But accumulation of economic values is impossible without truth and sacrifice, and their distribution will be affected by concern for vocational, affiliative, and other values. Again, there is no value in life that is not enhanced by friendship and love, but such *affiliative* values, both loving and being loved, are dependent for much of their realization on *character, aesthetic,* and *religious* values. *Sexual* values, in turn, may deepen or destroy affiliative values, as we shall see; they are kept from becoming tawdry and enslaving by their marriage to the whole range of values. Our *cognitive* values also provide unusually good examples of the marriage between intrinsic and instrumental values, since the various forms of knowing are intrinsic goods even as they make possible other forms of value—and disvalue. Finally, both aesthetic and religious experience, whatever final theory we develop about their place in life, not only permeate all other values when they are taken seriously but can be peak experiences of intrinsic satisfaction.

In this family of values, the instinctoid needs and emotions and the capacities dwelt upon in Chapter 7 find fruitful coexistence in myriad concrete ways. Although no "class" of value is reducible to any other, the quality of value experience, we have noted, is sustained and enhanced by the concentration of needs and capacities involved in them. If there are any priorities among values, they are based on the fact that higher values—character and cognitive values, for example—are conditions for realizing and preserving the others.

But the notion of priority in some scale of values must give way to the fundamental fact that there can be no increase in value, let alone initial realization, unless there is a continuous, dynamic, selective interweaving of value themes, an interweaving that involves mutual support between the needs and capacities of a person and his interaction with the total environment.

There is a very important inference to be drawn from this fact. The ideal pattern of values in personality is what it is, not because persons desire them, but because they express the norm for making the most of given human potential and of the given value possibilities in the total environment. Thus the normative, universal ideal of personality is a reasonable hypothesis about "the way things are and can be" in the world as we know it. This ideal of personality is not only a fact about man but a fact about the universe.

What we also discover in the attempt to realize the person's potential is that such self-realization would be impoverished without creative insight into the value needs and natures of other persons. The symphonic organization of values in the individual ties him to the community of persons in the search for values. Thus the underlying motif in the symphony of values is not peace, but harmony-in-creative-tension.

16

Traits, Virtues, and Personality

~~~~~~

Any theory of the life good to live must clarify the nature and place of the virtues in an ideal personality. Nevertheless, in the last quarter century especially, ethicists have neglected the analysis of the virtues, that part of ethical philosophy the Greeks called *areteia*. On the other hand, as we have seen, psychologists of personality are studying not only the factors that constitute the inner core and structure of a personality, but the kinds of dispositions that strengthen or weaken mental health and maturity. If Aristotle was interested in the definition and function of moral and intellectual virtues, G. W. Allport and a host of other psychologists have been analyzing the causes of prejudice, intolerance, and conformity, as well as the authoritarian and other "styles of life." In dealing with the virtues, we can draw on both the psychologist and the ethicist; they will help us in our ultimate aim: to decide what are the components of an ideal personality. Despite ambiguities that will appear as we move along, we shall suggest an approach to the virtues that will take account of factors in development that neither the psychologist nor the ethicist can afford to overlook.

I. TRAITS AND VIRTUES

We must study the traits of a personality if we would understand not only how that personality is knitted together, but also what that personality is likely to do in varying environments. When someone tells us, "John is kind, honest, courageous, loyal, and industrious, Richard is thrifty, honest, courageous, cruel, and industrious," we begin to form a conception of how John and Richard would probably act in varying circumstances. We can form a conception of what the Hopi expect of themselves when Richard Brandt reports:

> The Hopi will tell us that people should be cheerful, keep their tempers, be prudent, reliable, industrious, manly, brave, cordial, friendly, cooperative, persistent, kindly, gentle, sympathetic, generous, thrifty, truthful, and hospitable. He disapproves of a person being envious, vengeful, excitable, boastful, lazy, argumentative, snobbish or conceited, or a gossip.[1]

A trait, we recall, represents an organization of the energies of a person that determines not so much how the environment will affect him, but how he will take his environment. Thus a person with the trait of politeness can be depended on to act politely in most environmental situations.

G. W. Allport tells us that there are about 18,000 [2] trait names in the dictionary, more than four per cent of the words in the total English vocabulary.

In view of the many traits that human beings can have, we naturally ask of any proposed lists of traits designed to describe a personality: Which of these are more important? Would the presence of some traits discourage the development of others? And, in any case, how does one judge which traits *ought* to be included in a good personality and in what pattern, if any?

But we need also to ask what the similarities and differences are between traits and virtues. Are all traits virtues (or vices)? Are all virtues (or vices) traits? Are some traits in part virtues and in part not? Can one have a virtue that is not a trait? These are questions that involve psychological issues still in debate. We give a tentative answer now, pending further discussion later.

All virtues (or vices) are traits in Allport's sense: a trait is "a generalized and focalized neuropsychic system (peculiar to the individual), with the capacity to render many stimuli functionally equiv-

---

[1] Richard B. Brandt, *Ethical Theory: The Problem of Normative and Critical Ethics* (Englewood Cliffs, New Jersey: Prentice-Hall, 1959), p. 97. See also Brandt's *Hopi Ethics: A Theoretical Analysis* (Chicago: University of Chicago Press, 1954).

[2] G. W. Allport, *Personality: A Psychological Interpretation* (New York: Henry Holt, 1937), p. 305.

alent and to initiate and guide consistent (equivalent) forms of adaptive and expressive behavior." [3] That is, a person with a trait like neatness, finding himself in a given situation, sees in it possibilities of neatness that would not occur to a person who is not neat; and he ordinarily proceeds to tidy things up in accordance with this particular trait. Insofar as a person has traits like honesty, courage, kindness, talkativeness, cruelty, he is likely to transform situations in accordance with these particular traits. All virtues, then, are traits because they are dispositions of this sort.

But are all traits virtues (or vices)? We reply: Only those traits are virtues (or vices) that are deemed to be the product of choice. Why? An action is moral or immoral, in our view, *to the extent that* it is the product of choice or will-agency.

But someone will demur: Are traits chosen? Have not a person's traits—his gait, his politeness, his irascibility, for example—been gradually built up? Are they not expressive of hereditary and temperamental givens in the person as he spontaneously responds to environmental stimulus and challenge? Furthermore, are not all traits gradually built, long-range, total postures? Choice actions, by contrast, are specific and focused in a given situation. How, then, can any traits be virtues?

Traits are virtues, we suggest, only to the extent that a person "coming alive" to the presence of a certain disposition, approves of it, affirms it and reaffirms it or actions consistent with it, in a given choice situation. Thus a young man becomes aware that he is polite or honest largely because of his home training. But to the extent that their development did not involve any reflective choice, these traits are not virtues. "There's no virtue in his honesty," we say. If, however, he now approves of them and sustains them in time of conflict, they become moral traits or virtues (or immoral traits or vices).

We grant that this results in a far from tidy situation. For how do we know to what extent a specific trait is or is not a virtue? Or that what we call a particular virtue is not a nonmoral trait? Because we cannot be sure offhand, we should all the more carefully take into account, in judging either ourselves or others, this ambiguity or complexity. Perhaps in his own life one can be clearer about the traits that he has developed or nurtured by dint of conscious effort, but he might well be careful about deciding whether another person's trait is or is not a virtue. We suspect that most of our traits are mix-

[3] *Ibid.,* p. 295.

tures of what "just grew" under different types of provocations involving more or less choice. Perhaps this preliminary, tentative
answer may be kept in mind and tested as we consider important
phases in the treatment of virtue traits, especially by Plato and
Aristotle.

II. *BRIEF HISTORICAL ORIENTATION*

A. *Plato*

For Plato any man who cares about making the most of his nature
will develop four virtues: justice, wisdom, courage, and temperance.
It is important to see why Plato considers these four virtues crucial.

Plato follows his teacher Socrates in his concern that men "tend"
their souls. His underlying conviction is that the soul becomes diseased and vicious if it does not nurture itself by certain values and
if it does not discipline itself in certain ways. Whatever abilities a
man has and whatever circumstances surround him, he can never
realize values consistently if he does not organize his life in accordance
with four virtues.

Thus, one is not being *just* either to himself or to others if he
allows his wants or appetites to run wild instead of coordinating them
with his abilities. The just person, for Plato, is he who controls the
gratification of his wants or needs by a true estimate, first, of his
abilities, and, second, of the function that they allow him to perform
best in the community. How will he gain this true estimate? Not by
asking only, "What do I like? In what am I interested?" but by rationally discovering what he can do as he develops both in interest and
ability. In order to achieve justice in himself and in the community,
he will need to develop the virtue of *wisdom*. Thus, for Plato, no
person can afford to encourage ignorance in himself; every person
must be as wise as he can, that is, know facts in relation to value and
act accordingly.

Plato, however, realizes that a person can seem to know his wants
and abilities and environment and yet not follow the path of action
indicated. For appetites and needs have a way of craving immediate
relief, and they frequently create sheer disorder in a life by demanding unbridled gratification regardless of ability and environment.
(How anticipatory of the amoral Freudian id!) Yet appetites cannot
be disregarded. Wisdom dictates that their gratification be tempered

(*temperance*) in accordance with the total situation in which a man finds himself.

But although the reason points the way to wisdom, it cannot enforce its own counsels. It is the task of the "will" (Plato calls it "the spirited element of the soul") to enforce the counsels of reason, despite risk and danger. The virtue trait that performs the task is *courage*. The "spirited element" must not allow itself to be so seduced by the appetites that it fails to enforce the counsels of reason.

Thus, for Plato, in the well-tended soul every human ability and need would make its own unique contribution and not usurp the function of another. Justice is the harmonizing (orchestration) of all the main capacities in a life: reason, appetites, and spirited element. To be just is to integrate personality, to affirm the specific purpose of each function in relation to the rest. Plato is convinced that only he who can develop these virtues will be free from enslavement to any one part of his life and able to participate in community life as a member, not as a parasite. Plato did not believe that "likes" should rule life; nor did he hold that they should be neglected and denied their proper place in the economy of the whole.[4] But each form of self-control is a virtue.

We cannot leave even so brief a discussion of Plato without adding that his view of the nature of man (and of the problems that face man in large part because of this nature) influences his definition of the virtues. For the virtue of wisdom in particular cannot be understood unless one keeps in mind Plato's theory of value (see Chapter 10). We have to bear in mind that for Plato reason is not simply a matter of drawing inductive generalizations about human nature in a societal and natural environment, but a process of becoming fully aware of the value structure, or backbone, of reality, the realm of Ideas. For Plato the man with wisdom is the man who has become aware of his essential kinship with the ultimate Good, which, as Plato says in the *Republic,* is the cause of everything's being and being known. This awareness of the Good, firmly held before him, would lead man to justice for himself and others.

We shall see the full bearing of this view of man and reality, if, out of chronological order and before turning to Aristotle, we merely

---

[4] There are those who think that Plato demeaned the life of desire—and there are certainly passages in which Plato in no uncertain terms condemns the desires out of resentment against their capacity to seduce. But on the whole his concern is for a balanced unity of every individual, in a society that takes full account of its citizens' abilities and needs.

mention the way in which Christian ethical thinking added to these classical virtues.[5]

Note, for example, a passage from St. Paul's letter to the Corinthians—"And now abideth faith, hope, and love, but the greatest of these is love." We shall consider the nature of love later, but no one can understand what Paul meant by faith, hope, and love, unless he asks: What conception of man's nature and man's relation to God is governing Paul's definition of these virtues? Man's sin, as Paul saw it, estranged him from God in such a way that only the redemptive death of Jesus, expressing the forgiving love of God, could give him power to keep from sin or further alienation from God and man. Paul and those who follow his views would hold that the classical virtues, with their emphasis on wisdom and justice, would never "save" man, given his intrinsic waywardness and sinfulness and his incapacity to control his own will. Thus, faith, hope, and love, defined in terms of a specific Christian theology, must for Paul constitute the inner core of man's proprium, because only they can properly inspire and direct wisdom, justice, courage, and temperance.

B. *Aristotle*

As we reflect upon Aristotle's treatment of the virtues, we realize that he places the emphasis not so much upon the nature of the person as upon the situations that any person inevitably faces. Aristotle did borrow Plato's idea that the good life had to involve the balanced fulfilling of the unique capacities of the individual—physical, emotional, moral, aesthetic, and intellectual. The Platonic concern for developing each individual in accordance with what he can do best reappears in Aristotle's conception of a virtue. For each virtue is a "bringing to excellence" of the individual as he learns to respond to certain inescapable problems that he must face as a person.

As Aristotle sees it, all of us experience fear, tenderness, respect, sympathy, elation, anger, pain, and pleasure—and, generally too much or too little! "But to have these feelings at the right times on the right occasions towards the right people, for the right motive and in the right way is to have them in the right measure, that is somewhere between the extremes; and this is what characterizes [moral] good-

[5] See the brief discussion of the central Stoic and Epicurean virtues in the next chapter.

ness." [6] The word "moral" must be emphasized because Aristotle would say that we cannot hold persons responsible for feeling such emotions as anger or fear, but we do hold them responsible for the choice of modes of expression, and this choice is what constitutes action virtuous or vicious. Thus, the virtues are not unlearned passion, but "states of character" or dispositions persons choose to learn and keep.[7] Briefly, then, for Aristotle, a virtue is *a chosen way* of bringing the emotional and intellectual capacities to the point of excellence (which he calls the mean between extremes) in response to well-nigh inescapable human problems.

In order to see what Aristotle's theory comes to in detail, let us so present nine of the virtues in his list that the accent on virtue as deliberate response to human situations becomes clear.

1. *Courage*

(a) The Situation: The problem facing each person in the presence of anticipated danger.

(b) The Choice: Although one cannot help being fearful in such situations, the task is to avoid the two extremes: rash and foolhardy behavior on the one hand, and cowardice on the other. The deliberate undergoing of the risk involved, in the right way, at the right time, in service to principle and not simply to feeling, constitutes the virtue *courage*.

2. *Temperance*

(a) The Situation: The problem facing each person now is not that of avoiding pain but of dealing especially with the enticing pleasures given through bodily senses. A person is tempted to devote too much time, energy, and money to these.

(b) The Choice: To select such pleasures to the extent to which they promote bodily health and physique; to prefer harmless pleasures insofar as they do not become too expensive or enslave one. The virtue here is *temperance*. It is the mean, the "just-right," between intemperance and asceticism.

3. *Liberality*

(a) The Situation: The problem of acquiring and distributing whatever money can provide (wealth).

[6] J. A. K. Thomson, *The Ethics of Aristotle: A Translation of the Nicomachean Ethics* (London: Allen and Unwin, 1953), p. 51.

[7] Aristotle, *Nicomachean Ethics*, Book II, Chapter VI.

(b) The Choice: The problem is to take from the right person and give to the right person for the right motive—that is, neither giving to nor taking from tainted agencies—and being willing to take a loss rather than make money at any price. The extremes to be avoided are prodigality both in giving and getting on the one hand, and meanness or niggardliness on the other. The virtue, or mean, is *liberality*.[8]

The next virtue, which we shall call *magnanimity*, or "greatness of soul," is a very interesting one, for it puts a stress on a quality which many believe is, or should be, quite foreign to any Christian list of virtues.

4. *Magnanimity*

(a) The Situation: What kind of claim for recognition or respect should an unusually deserving, able, and virtuous person make for himself as his honest desert? For what kind of honor does a man who is worthy of honor settle?

(b) The Choice: Accept only those honors which come from highly esteemed persons. Take external goods only as vehicles for the expression of respect. At the same time, do not look down upon the weak, but be more ready to help them than to be helped by them. In a basic sense, to be great-souled is to be above receiving benefits, or competing for prizes, which most persons seek. The great-souled man is above all honor and all good that come to him, for in the last analysis he is self-sufficient. He will not be depressed by misfortune or overjoyed by good. Only a man who is the "beautiful completion of the virtues"[9] will be able to do this. But it is this man alone who avoids the extremes of demanding more than he is worth (vanity) or expecting too little (smallness of soul). "The poor-spirited man is one who, though not undeserving, deprives himself of such advantages as he deserves, the effect of his failures to claim his deserts being to convince people that there must be something bad about him."[10]

5. *Pride*

(a) The Situation: Granted that the temptations faced by the superior person are different, the problem of justifiable pride confronts

---

[8] We omit any discussion of the Aristotelian virtue of *magnificence*, or the proper expenditure of large amounts of wealth, for no new principle is involved different from that of liberality.

[9] Thomson, *op. cit.*, p. 104.

[10] *Ibid.*, p. 108.

the garden variety of men as they ask themselves how much honor they have a right to expect and from whom.

(b) The Choice: There is no word for the mean between extremes here. One is tempted to use Adler's thought to expound what Aristotle had in mind in this instance. For only the person who has to go on proving to himself, or having it proved to him, that he is worth honoring will neurotically accept all and every honor regardless of his desert. A man of "proper ambition," however, will accept honor in return for his dedication to any good cause.[11]

6. Sincerity

(a) The Situation: The problem facing each person in representing his merits and demerits in such a way that the truth about himself is conveyed to others.

(b) The Choice: Adopt speech and action that will leave the correct impression about your real qualities—without underestimating them (and thus becoming self-deprecating) or exaggerating their value (and thus becoming boastful). The best word for this mean is sincerity.

7. Distributive Justice

(a) The Situation: The problem of distributing honor or money and other possessions among members of the group.

(b) The Choice: Keeping as clear as possible the basis for assigning merits (namely, quality of physical work or intellectual work, as for example in grading papers). Choose to distribute the shares proportionate to merit, so that no one gets too much or too little. This virtue, which aims to achieve equality, "personalities" aside, is called distributive justice and is to be distinguished carefully from the following, namely, corrective justice.

8. Corrective Justice

(a) The Situation: The problem of restoring equality when there is no simple standard of comparison in distributing good and evil,

---

[11] Before continuing, we must make one comment. The reader may be impressed here by the great concern that Aristotle seems to have that a man should have an ego or proprium that he protects because it is worth protecting and that a man respect himself as well as others. The description so far may seem to jar sharply with the Christian conception of man as a selfless servant of his fellowmen. There may indeed be a strong difference in the Christian strategy of giving one's life that one may save it. This whole question needs much more careful analysis than is possible here, but before final judgment is given, it is important that the remaining Aristotelian virtues be kept in mind, and, not the least, his discussion of friendship in Nicomachean Ethics, Books VIII and IX. See Chapters 26 and 27 below.

or when injustice has already been done and the need is to decrease loss or gain in the light of unique factors in the situation. There are times when unnecessary harm is done if each person is judged simply as one person. For example, granted that a father may have struck his son unjustly, would it be just for the son to strike the father an equal number of times or at all? (We are reminded here of one of Ross's special obligations, Chapter 11.)

(b) The Choice: Seek to find a basis of equality by which a judgment can be made that will hit upon the fairest proportion between conflicting claims and demands. For example, let us assume that a five-year-old boy lost his eye in an automobile accident in which the father of a family was the offender. A judge would certainly not be just if he rendered a verdict that the father of a family should have an eye removed. The problem is to find a basis of comparison that will take full account of the demands of each, and correct injustice as much as possible, without creating unnecessary new injustice.

9. Equity

(a) The Situation: The problem that a person confronts when the very universality or generality of the law forces him to do injustice to some individual situation. Why? Because "the *data* of human behavior simply will not be reduced to uniformity." [12]

(b) The Choice: Seek to make up for the defect inherent in legality by aiming, in the *spirit* of the law, at the just proportion. The resulting virtue is *equity*. The equitable man is not a stickler for his rights under law, especially when this is to the disadvantage of others whose unique situation the law could not embrace.[13]

As we reflect on these moral virtues, two points become clear. First, a virtue is not a negation of life; it does not put a quietus on life. Each virtue is the product of the *deliberate effort* to realize the best both in the person himself as he confronts problems created by his own nature and in his relations to the world in which he lives. Again, every virtue is a search for excellence, for development to optimum capacity in varied life situations. This conclusion could be further corroborated if we took time to analyze Aristotle's intellectual virtues (for example, prudence, intelligence, science, and art), for these virtues solve the problems of knowing the complex world in which a man finds himself.

[12] *Thomson, op. cit., p.* 146. Aristotle, *Nicomachean Ethics,* 1137b. See Chapter 27 below.

[13] See Chapter 25, Sec. II, *Principle of Specification.*

Second, we must avoid superficial understanding of Aristotle's doctrine of virtue as the mean between extremes. For example, it falsifies Aristotle's intent to say that he believed in "moderation in all things," especially if we take this to mean, as is often done, "nothing too much." For Aristotle's emphasis is on fulfillment, on acting in the best way possible in each situation, that is, on finding exactly the right amount for excellence. We might say that a virtuous man is a fanatic about excellence.

"Moderation in everything" neglects the fact that Aristotle explicity says that there is no moderation when it comes to something that is evil to start with. Thus, to refer to a very practical situation, if it should be shown that cigarette-smoking or drinking of alcohol involves debilitating effects to start with, the doctrine of the mean calls for abstinence and not "moderation." On the other hand, assuming that bread does no harm to the body or is a value to start with, one can eat "too much" or "too little" bread. This does not mean that the case for or against smoking and drinking can be built on the above analysis alone, but it does mean that Aristotle's doctrine of "moderation" cannot be used to support any action that is normally hurtful. For when it comes to a bad thing, moderation means abstinence. The doctrine of virtue in Aristotle demands that persons seek that amount of anything which will bring them to full activity or sustain excellence.

With this sketchy treatment of the major virtues suggested by Plato, St. Paul, and Aristotle in mind, we can now pursue further the question of the relation of trait-virtues to the development of personality and to values as a whole.

III. *THE RELATION OF VIRTUES TO THE SYMPHONY OF VALUES*

The virtues (and vices) are not the whole of the ideal personality. The life good to live consists, we have urged, in the symphonic orchestration of value experiences. Among these values are those traits which are deliberately chosen (in the sense described above) and which, as willed experiences, we have called virtues. These virtues are specifically *moral* values. Thus, all values and virtues are experiences that, coherently criticized, are deemed worthy of being chosen even if at a given juncture we did not in fact desire them.

From the coherent organization of value experiences there emerges a conception of "the best we know," to which we feel obligated. On our view, then, a person ought to realize values—inclusive of virtues —because, so far as he knows, this is the best way to fulfill his needs and abilities in relation to the environment in which he lives. Granting this general view, let us ask more specifically: What relation do the virtues, or *moral* as opposed to *nonmoral* values, have to other values in the formation of personality?

Let us consider Sam Jones, first in cross section at a given moment and then longitudinally, as an ethical formation that has had a past and is moving into the future. In cross section we would see a complex of value experiencing, a more or less well-defined organization expressive of the way in which he, up to that moment, has met the demands of the environment in accordance with his own needs and abilities. Many of these values are "incorporated" in habits, attitudes, sentiments, traits, ideals, and a style of life that compose Sam's personality structure at that moment. And Sam, at such an arrested moment, would probably say that there was much that he approved and much that he disapproved.

If, now, we change perspectives and look at Sam's personality longitudinally, as "becoming" or in a state of transition toward other ends than those realized at the moment, we see a somewhat different picture. There are discontents to be dealt with, ideals to be actualized, and inevitable changes to be taken into account as Sam anticipates the future. Present value experiences are threatened, and they will be sustained only if there are factors in his personality that at once resist particular change and yet give continuity from one moment to another, throughout the whole course of his life.

It is at this point that virtues, as traits, become very important. For, without traits, as we have seen, a person would be more likely to be "triggered off" by his environment. Habits, sentiments, attitudes have their being *in* some environmental situations and *toward* some object. Thus in the presence of the American flag, toward which he has a strong favorable sentiment, an American Boy Scout has formed the habit of coming to attention and saluting in a prescribed way. One cannot assume that, in view of this habit, he will sacrifice much for that flag. But if he has developed the trait of patriotism, he may be expected to behave in every way that seems to him to express loyalty to his country and thus to develop other supporting attitudes and habits expressive of patriotism. Thus, he may later volunteer for the armed services, pay his income tax honestly, consider new ways of improving his country. In other words, *given* a trait, at a given time, the individual is motivated to cope with different situations that take on the same meaning to him only because he has that trait. Different situations become opportunities for him to express his patriotism.

We can see, accordingly, why children need to develop not only *habits* of neatness or honesty, favorable *attitudes* toward neatness and honesty, but also *traits* of neatness and honesty. For given the trait of honesty, an adolescent, say, is more likely to develop the new habits and attitudes needed in a very wide range of environments —paying the correct amount in telephone booths, and stores, not cheating on examinations, and so on. Thus, a trait organizes both the past, present, and the probable future and in so doing gives stability to the life of striving.

With this explanation in mind we can, perhaps, see more clearly why virtues, as traits, are important in the formation of the personality. A virtue fosters and a vice hinders the realization of values. If one believes, for instance, in the values of friendship and of truth, he will be more likely to develop and conserve these values in his life if he develops the virtue-trait of honesty and kindness. One may go so far as to say that the realization of all other values will be relatively spasmodic and chaotic without the support of traits.

But traits do not develop all at once in the life of a person. We shall have to leave to the psychologist the task of deciding how traits come about, but it seems obvious that there will be much interplay between underlying needs, abilities, habits, attitudes, and sentiments. What requires stress here is that virtue-traits, as specifically *moral* values, do not exist apart from other (*nonmoral*) values as discussed in the symphony of values. I do not become courageous for the sake of courage, but in order to protect other values, such as health and friendship, that will be endangered unless I am willing to face risks. I do not develop either the habit of honesty or the attitude toward honesty or the trait of honesty unless I choose the value experiences of knowing the truth as far as possible, and the other value experiences that such knowledge promotes. All virtue-traits have value realizations beyond themselves which give them point.

We are entitled, then, to generalize about the relation of virtues to values. That life will be most successful in value realization in which the particular symphony of values is supported by habits, attitudes, and especially virtue-traits consonant with those values. Aristotle remarked, "As a result of virtue men tend to noble deeds."[14]

A.   The Virtues as Intrinsic Moral Values

1.   Are Virtues Instrumental Only?

What we have said thus far might seem to imply that the virtues (or vices) get their total value (or disvalue) because they are means to realizing nonmoral values. They have no value in themselves. Is this an adequate description of our experience? Our thesis will be that while virtues cannot exist in isolation and while they do enhance value realization in a total personality, their value is not instrumental only. This means that *if a person could have all the other value experiences and not have virtues in his life, he would be lacking in one of the most profound areas of value experiencing.* Why is this so?

The virtues, we have said, are specifically *moral* values, in contrast to aesthetic, economic, health, and other values. This means that their very existence depends (in varying degree, as allowed by the given life history) on the deliberate effort of the virtuous person. A virtue must be developed by the person himself; it expresses in a peculiarly intimate way his creative effort in the struggle for values. One may offer another friendship and money, but one cannot offer him courage and honesty. One can offer another a job, but he cannot give him industriousness and good humor. This supplies a very good reason for our differentiating the virtues as character values from other values (health, economic, vocational, aesthetic, and so on). For, again, virtues do express in a unique way what a person has done with himself in choice situations in which the value to be realized depended more on his own willingness to discipline himself than on the environmental offering. A man's virtues *character*-ize him; in his character a complex pattern of virtues is "marked in" and these entail a different form of self-discipline.

2.   Character is the Core of Self-Realization

We may now develop a thesis of our last chapter: the values of character and truth are crucial to the development of other values. What we are now pointing to is the fact that "character" is one word

[14] Aristotle, *Nicomachean Ethics*, 1101b.

for a whole complex of moral values that are, as forms of self-discipline, intimately related to the realization of other values. And it may not be clear that *as forms of self-development* the virtues by themselves become a kind of inner core (a specifically *moral* proprium) or backbone of the ethical personality. Character is always willed orientation involving certain forms of self-discipline (trait-virtues) toward some other value. But because the nature, extent, and pattern of the virtues constitute the on-going moral power of the person, character is an intrinsic good.

We may come to the same conclusion by clarifying the ambiguity that has attended the use of the word "character" in psychological discussion. The psychologist of personality may use the term "character" almost synonymously with personality, as G. W. Allport suggests,[15] for character, like personality refers to the stable organization of a life. In order to keep evaluation and description distinct, we might say that character is personality evaluated! Thus when we say, "How characteristic of him!" we are using that word in its strictly psychological sense.

But we mean something else when we say "Ah, that man has character." We not only mean that he has a persistent mode of adjustment "engraved" in him (according to the meaning of the word in Greek), as an organization of traits, but we also mean that we approve of the fact that he is self-disciplined. Indeed, we may not approve of the particular organization of another person's character, but we still approve the fact that he (in general) does not give up principle when sacrifice is involved. Whatever else may be "wrong" about him, we cannot but approve of his resolute rejection of the path of least resistance.

"Character," then, is a term that has a dual function. It is used descriptively by the psychologist, but the ethicist uses the term in approval of a person's self-engraved dispositions. Still, why do we praise a man for being courageous and blame him for being cowardly, praise him for generosity and blame him for being stingy? We blame or praise him for any trait to the extent that we believe him capable of doing otherwise than he did. (Obviously, the whole discussion of free will, in Chapter 8, will be relevant here.) Nothing in a person's nature or in the environment *necessitated* his being courageous or cowardly, generous or stingy. There might well be as

[15] Cf. G. W. Allport, *Pattern and Growth in Personality* (New York: Holt, Rinehart and Winston, 1961), pp. 30–32.

we have said earlier, traits that a person acquires with no choice involved at any point in the development. But these traits would be properly *admired* or *abhorred* without being *praised* or *blamed*. These traits would not be virtues; they might well be valuable components of his personality, but they are not his (moral or immoral) character.

As we warned in the first section of this chapter, we are not left in a very neat situation psychologically or ethically. It would be so much neater if we could divide all dispositions into (nonmoral) traits or (moral) virtues. But the dynamics of the development of personality simply do not allow this. Similarly, it would be reassuring if we could always be clear about blaming or praising another for his specifically moral achievements. No doubt, in judging another, we often praise or blame him for traits that in fact deserve either admiration or abhorrence. But the fact that we may make mistakes in judging a particular person must not blind us to the very important distinction between admiration and praise, scorn, and blame. We do not blame men for experiencing anger and fear, for example. To experience anger and fear is to be human; anger or fear or any other emotion is said to be amoral or nonmoral, because we cannot blame persons for having these emotions. But we do blame them if we believe that they did not have to experience them when they did, that they should have been able to control them or, failing that, control their means of expression. In the same way, we consider traits virtues (or vices) depending on whether we believe that they had to be developed.[16]

B. *The Dynamics of Character in the Development of Ethical Personality*

We are now ready to continue with our main concern: the place of virtues in the total pattern of value in personality. The virtues are deemed to be (at some points at least) the work of the agent-self as he chooses among responses open to him. We may say that they compose the main part of his character. (Attitudes and sentiments, insofar as they are voluntary, may also be said to be phases of character.) This means that a person's character is the moral laboratory of his life; it embraces a roughly definable area in which the agent is forging those traits (and attitudes and sentiments) that he ap-

16 Cf. Aristotle, *Nicomachean Ethics*, 1113b.

proves. And it also means that each virtue in itself is a certain kind of quality of personal being. This new quality of living (courage versus cowardice, for example) represents a way of solving some problems in the life of the individual. The act of being courageous remains as a quality of preferred experience, even after the other particular values gained through courage have ceased to be.

Thus, it takes courage to become indebted for the sake of one's education, but the educated man goes on having to face uncertainty and risk. Whether his character includes courage or cowardice will be important to his future development both as a student and in other areas of life. But the *moral posture* or *stance* of being willing to face danger for the sake of value does not depend on any other value. A virtue has value in itself as a *kind of living in choice situations*. It is settled disposition, a point of self-actualization, in a total personality. Although a virtue supports other values, its own value resides in characterizing a personality in a lasting way despite what other values come and go. Value experiences of beauty or play or health can come and go as the vicissitudes of life allow, but the virtues stay as relatively permanent foundations for all value realization in a personality. The fact that they are interrelated as moral virtues with other values should not deceive us into supposing that their value consists in that interpenetration alone. The virtues are "written into" our natures as actualized experiences that give each man his living form.

It may now be clear why *aretaics* is an important part of ethical theory. It makes a difference, and a serious one, which traits are included and excluded from the character, the moral crucible of a person's life. For to repeat, not only do the virtues survive other value experiences whose growth, development, and change they serve, but they are also value experiences in themselves. If anything, then, the virtues, or the specific *moral values,* are the most important values and disvalues in a personality, for they are the foundational substructures upon which many other values sooner or later come to depend.

Character, finally, is not identical with happiness or self-fulfillment, but there can be no lasting self-fulfillment without character. The artist, for example, may be able and inspired, but his patience and industry (and other forms of self-discipline) will largely determine what he does with his inspiration. The student may have a high I.Q., but his willingness to dedicate time to detail, sacrifice conflicting pleasures, and work for long-run, uncertain goals will be crucial to his becoming a scholar.

Perhaps all that we have done in this chapter is to return by a circuitous route to the Kantian insight that the good will, the will to do everything in one's power to execute the good, is the jewel that shines by its own light. Yet we have been providing the background for the hazardous undertaking upon which we shall embark in the next chapter, namely, suggesting that there is an irreducible minimum structure of virtues in the character that all persons ought to seek.[17]

IV. DIFFICULTIES INVOLVED IN DEVELOPING A SCHEME OF VIRTUES

Plato, we have seen, defined his cardinal virtues—justice, wisdom, courage, and temperance—in relation to desire, reason, and the spirited element. Aristotle developed a larger list based on pervasive problems-to-be-faced, in both the passional and the intellectual life (the latter we have not analyzed). Many Christians, with an eye on man's relation to God especially, emphasized the centrality of faith, hope, and love. But when St. Paul (I Corinthians, 13) tried to analyze the marks of Christian love in personality, his prism yielded such virtues as kindness, patience, humility, and generosity. Jesus, in the Sermon on the Mount, said that the blessed would be poor in spirit, meek, merciful, forgiving, that they would be peacemakers and willing to be reviled for their belief in him. No one can understand Jesus' teaching apart from his concern that man's supreme duty is to conform one's life to the vision of a loving Father of all men.

The path to the discovery of some basic scheme of virtues is beset by many snares. Indeed, a great recent ethicist, Nicolai Hartmann, who devotes a large part of the second volume of his monumental work on *Ethics* [18] to a very perceptive treatment of virtues, warns against trying to organize the virtues systematically. He maintains

---

[17] The advanced student will profit from the acute discussion of moral traits found in Maurice H. Mandelbaum, *The Phenomenology of Moral Experience* (Glencoe, Ill.: Free Press, 1955), Chapter IV. We doubt that the distinction drawn by him between an actional trait (like courage) and a dispositional trait (like gratitude) can be maintained.

[18] Nicolai Hartmann, *Ethics* (New York: The Macmillan Co., 1926, 1932).

that the variety and the richness of the life of virtue cannot possibly be caught in any scheme of virtues.

Before proceeding on our own venture, we must agree with Hartmann that "a complete diagram of the virtues" cannot be articulated and that in the last analysis, "we can only pick out what the consciousness of the age has elaborated and has to a certain extent made palpable." [19] We must also, with Hartmann, recognize that the variety of virtues is so great that we can easily blunder in achieving a proper gradation. Perhaps, with Hartmann himself, we should focus on two crucial moral values, justice and brotherly love, and allow all others simply to cluster around them. What we seek, nevertheless, is a rationale in terms of which the basic structure of ethical personality is not an omnibus either of values or of virtues.

V. REFLECTIVE SUMMARY

To know a person's traits is to know what he is likely to require of himself in a variety of situations. We might call virtues evaluated traits. But it seems to us that traits are *moral* values to the extent that they involve choice.

Throughout the ages many ethicists have tried to discover the virtues crucial to human happiness. For example, the Platonic virtues are descriptions of how each man ought to act if each basic part of his nature is to perform its function in accordance with what he can do best.

In the last analysis, the final selection of virtue-traits presupposes some view of the nature of man and of his place in the universe. Thus Plato's ultimate conviction is that men are akin to The Good and to each other in different degrees. Accordingly, each man's *wisdom* consists in realizing this truth and disciplining himself to become *courageous, temperate,* and *just.* St. Paul, in the dominant Christian tradition, maintains that man's sin has left him so estranged from God that only through *faith* in the redemptive death of Jesus is there adequate basis for the *hope* and the *love* that will properly direct *wisdom, justice, courage,* and *temperance.*

Aristotle, whose view of man's place is closer to Plato's, defines each virtue-trait in relation to inescapable situations that every human being, given his nature, will confront. On his analysis, we

[19] *Ibid.,* p. 226.

noted, each virtue seeks to bring his nature to its perfection in the situation confronted. Aristotle's emphasis on "nothing too much" must be interpreted in the light of his ideal of excellence for each person.

We conclude that a person's search for the good calls for developing moral values, that is, virtue-traits, among the other values of personality. Indeed, without virtue-traits the realization of other values is likely to be spasmodic. Virtue-traits, in turn, cannot be isolated from other values because they are always connected with the realization of some value or other.

Character, the organization of virtue-traits, is the moral crucible of ethical personality, but its value is both intrinsic and instrumental. The virtues of character are instrinsic forms of moral creativity, and, at the same time, they serve to produce and sustain other goods in the symphony of values.

17

A Scheme of Virtues

Our task in this chapter is to work out a scheme of what may be called cardinal virtue-traits, that is, traits that ought to be willed if personality is to be creative and self-actualizing. Obviously, there are other nonvolitional traits in a personality, important for the organization and enrichment of a particular personality.

Some traits, as we suggested in the last chapter, are rooted in constitutional factors and very early training. They grow without being noticed. Yet when a maturing person takes critical stock of them, he may approve some and condemn others. To what extent some traits may be strengthened and others uprooted remains a problem in each personality. Our distinction between will-agency and will-power is especially relevant when we confront the problem of working out, when choice is at all possible, which way our traits shall go.

However, the traits we shall be concerned with are cardinal virtue-traits, that is, traits whose development, sustenance, and preservation we believe to be crucial if we are to create and maintain the symphony of values and other virtues. Let us proceed by suggesting a scheme of virtues and the reasoning involved in its development. Then we shall raise some questions that such an hypothesis should legitimately face.

I. *PERSONAL VIRTUES*

A. *Honesty*

First then, we suggest, there is one virtue that nourishes all the other virtues and values of life. It is the will to become honest.

Before defining the meaning of this virtue, let us remind ourselves that the one "good" underlying all psychotherapy is, in the psychologist's sense, "Face Reality!" "Where the id now is, there shall the ego be," said Freud. No other psychologist denies his essential intent, that the source of healthy growth is the fullest realization possible of what one's own nature is and allows in relation to the environment. But much depends on what is meant by "knowledge."

"Know thyself," said the Greek. Gandhi writes at the end of his autobiography, "My uniform experience has convinced me that there is no other God than truth." [1] We paraphrase this Greek motto into basic Christian teaching, "You cannot know yourself unless you know your God and your proper relation to your brother." Despite their different conceptions of reality and God, Plato, Aristotle, and Marcus Aurelius would agree with Hindus,[2] Confucians, Buddhists, and Moslems in a common conviction that knowledge of, and action in accordance with, truth is basic to human welfare.

But the kind of knowledge sought, the kind of honesty involved, in all these great traditions is not a "knowledge of fact" alone. It is not a knowledge from which appreciation and moral concern are absent. We suggest, accordingly, that, be it in the psychotherapeutic situation, in introspective analysis, or in reaching for understanding of nature and God, the emphasis must be placed on a knowing that is also a savoring, a tasting. The Latin for "wisdom" is *sapientia,* and the root verb is *sapere,* to taste. The honesty we are seeking to define is closer to the meaning of wisdom, that appreciative savoring of the object, problem, or solution—which is never less than intellectual, yet also involves both feeling and action.

To achieve wisdom is the goal of the virtue-trait of honesty. Accordingly, we may define honesty as the *willingness to seek as accu-*

[1] M. K. Gandhi, *An Autobiography, or My Experiments with Truth,* trans. M. Desai (2nd ed.; Boston: Beacon Press, 1957), p. 503.

[2] For an instructive view of "schemes" of virtue the reader should examine Susil K. Maitra, *The Ethics of the Hindus* (2nd ed.; Calcutta: University of Calcutta Press, 1956).

rate and complete an account as possible of any situation (social, political, and cosmic) in which one is living. In dealing with others the honest person is concerned not merely with "telling the truth" but with conveying it as faithfully as possible to those with whom he is speaking. The contrasting vices are the *intellectual irresponsibility* that is satisfied to guess and offer a complacent opinion when something better is available, *rationalization,* in which one seeks to know not what is true but only to justify an action or intent, and *dishonesty,* in which one conveys to another information and suggestions calculated to deceive and mislead.

Two specific comments may clarify our use of the phrase "willingness to," for it will recur as we define other virtues.

First, we are emphasizing that a virtue is not dependent on inclination and desire, but is the willingness to "take hold" and establish the approved order among conflicting inclinations. This may involve suppressing some traits already existing, or opening the way for more complete expression of others or the development of new ones. If there were no needs, no wants, no desires, there would be no value experience; if there were no conflicts among needs and desires or among values, there would be no problem of reflective choice, no virtue. A virtue consists in the person's willful, deliberate orientation of his action toward the ideals or values that that particular virtue is serving. What the psychological mechanisms are by which this curbing and controlling of the manifold of inclinations is done is far from clear to us. Yet is there any denying, for example, that the brave man, feeling fear at the prospect of danger, somehow succeeds in controlling that fear so that other parts of his nature may be freed and guided to achieve the end he purposes?

Second, it may seem strange and inconsistent for us to call a virtue a trait, or *settled* disposition, and then talk of each virtue as "a willingness to"—as if there were not yet any settled disposition. While confessing to some perplexity here, we suggest that much of it may be relieved if we remember that in a growing personality different stages of development are always present. A personality is always "becoming." A person's neatness and kindness and courage always have to stand new tests, not only because life necessarily changes and he confronts new situations, but because his development of a certain virtue opens new areas of sensitivity and new "moral mountains" to climb. Furthermore, as we have already urged, once a trait has been established, either volitionally or nonvolitionally, the developing person, in cool reflection, may decide to keep reaffirming it as conforming more to his style of being than another. Hence, willful choice, resulting in whatever change the person can make at that time, is involved. No virtue-trait can be assumed to be settled (or uprooted) in part or as a whole, once and for all.

Thus we must bear in mind that to speak of a virtue-trait is not to designate a snug little component or compartment of a personality. The definition of a virtue-trait is in fact the definition of a critically approved trend in a personality (and vice would be a critically disapproved development). The specific exemplification of the ideal intended or willed in a given person will vary in degree. We can never afford to forget that a personality, except for those neurotic, psychotic, or pervasively "set" persons, is the more or less systematic, dynamic way in which the person is still finding fulfillment of his nature. Any one stage of development may be surprisingly plastic or fixed. Thus, the virtue-trait as defined may, at a given stage for a given person be more an ideal that he would will into a trait than the settled disposition already expressive of willed achievement.

For example, Sam Jones may be honest and courageous enough to overcome pain, but still a rationalizing coward when he faces certain disapproved pleasures. Again, Sam Jones's courage may be a "settled" disposition as far as overcoming obstacles to loyalty to friends, facing dentist's pain, telling "inconvenient" truths. But it may be relatively "unsettled" with respect to treating his enemies fairly, paying his debts, or giving to worthy charities.

True, many, including Aristotle, have said that one is not "really" virtuous if he has still to think about it. But the truth here—a person who is "really" good is one whose goodness is now "second-nature" —must not allow us to minimize an even more important fact. Because personality involves change, a virtue must always remain a stage "on the way" to the total fulfillment of the person as he grapples with the new complexities that ever face him.

We may now return to the virtue which we would call *the taproot* of the tree of virtues and values: honesty. As the willingness to be sensitive to and appreciative of the total circumstances in which one lives, honesty is the virtue responsible for truth-seeking—the value we discovered to be so important in the symphony of values (Chapter 15). Because a person must often make selective responses to complex needs and interests in confused situations, honesty involves the willingness to hold fast to what seems true at any stage in his development. Indeed, what situation in life can be either fully appreciated or adequately confronted without such willingness? No other virtue and value can produce goodness without honesty, and this is why we call it our *theme-virtue* or *taproot virtue-trait.*

And, clearly, honesty can never stop growing, because if it ever "settled" once and for all, the life of the person would become rigid at that stage of development. Accordingly, to say that a person is honest is to assert the belief that he *has* overcome a whole range of obstacles in the way to fuller appreciation of himself, of others, and of his world. And it is also to assert the belief that he will continue both to will and to succeed in overcoming temptations to dishonesty as he moves toward the ideal of becoming as wise as he can be.

B. *Courage*

It is difficult to discuss honesty without at the same time talking about courage. But no action, however "daring" in retrospect, can be called courageous unless there is some knowledge of the risks involved. Also, in many situations, one cannot be honest, or become honest, without courage. *Courage is the willingness to face insecurity and to make the sacrifices needed to achieve the goal deemed worthwhile but dangerous.*

We must pause again to comment on a problem that has haunted both moral theory and every moral agent: How does one get the courage, or how does one increase courage, to undergo risks or to give up present "goods" for greater value? St. Paul was convinced that his willing was by itself unable to realize the good he approved. As already noted, he believed that only as he was aided by God, through his faith in the redemptive death of Jesus, could he find the strength to live according to the ideal of love. "I can do all things in him [Christ] who strengthens me" (Philippians 4:13). Readers of St. Augustine, in turn, will know how St. Paul's view gave him hope for his spiritual struggle.

Indeed, much Christian thought is dominated by this central conviction that the condition of the human will is such that only the grace of God can suffice to enable one to realize the Christian ideal of life.[3] And Hindu philosophy is pervaded by the conviction that one can never develop proper detachment and attachment in the life

---

[3] See the excellent and extended treatment of the relation of philosophical and Christian ethics in George Thomas, *Christian Ethics and Moral Philosophy* (New York: Charles Scribner's Sons, 1955), and Paul Ramsey, *Basic Christian Ethics* (New York: Charles Scribner's Sons, 1950).

of desire unless he becomes aware of, or realizes, his inner unity and identity with the One, Brahman. On the other hand, much in Buddha's thought, as well as in that of his followers, recoils from appeal to a transcendent power and emphasizes what man himself can do to be free from self-absorption or enslavment to self-indulgent desires.

One might also urge that all psychotherapy is, in the last analysis, concerned with this problem of helping persons to be free from the weaknesses that keep them from being what they can be. And different schools of psychological thought, as we have seen, will give different answers. Many naturalistically minded psychotherapists act on some form of the belief that once unconscious emotional blocks have been removed the person can act rationally; but they would make no reference to "willing." They simply seem to assume that if we know enough about ourselves, if we have some positive aim in life, we can control ourselves and overcome temptation.

Plato's solution, while bearing some resemblance to that of both the naturalists and supernaturalists, moves, as we have seen, on a different plane of theorizing about man. He would reject the Pauline thesis that sin has so weakened man that he cannot lift himself up by his own bootstraps.[4] The spirited element, Plato holds, is on the side of reason to begin with. The human problem is to resist the temptation to side with inclination and passion, so that the reason can go on knowing and appreciating the values that will enrich human existence. Yet this does not mean that, for Plato, "will" simply lifted one by his own bootstraps. Why? Because the person does not live in a world cut off from value or "the Good." Every person is "akin" to the Good and the Beautiful, which can so nourish his life that he can resist the deceptive lure of unstructured inclinations.

Reason for Plato, in other words, is not "merely" human; it is capable of a deeper insight into (because it has kinship with) the nature of "the Good." Thus man is not estranged from the ultimate Good for Plato; he may become seduced if the spirited element and reason do not cooperate in guiding the individual. For St. Paul, Augustine, and most Christian thinkers, on the other hand, Plato's view is much too unrealistic in view of man's constant surrender of

---

[4] See the stimulating discussion of the Platonic perspective in Robert E. Cushman, *Therapeia: Plato's Conception of Philosophy* (Chapel Hill: University of North Carolina Press, 1958).

his ideals. The will is in a state of estrangement from the rational good and God, and there is no hope of creative fulfillment by man's will unaided by grace.[5]

We shall not try to arbitrate this issue here, but the reader should realize that in making honesty and courage, or reason and will, the source of growth in character, we are on the side of Plato, and not on the side of the naturalistic psychotherapist or the psychotherapy of the supernaturalist, *as that side is usually stated.* Although much needs to be said in favor of removing emotional blocks or of salvation from sin through the grace of God, and although other sources of nourishment besides "willing and reason" are important to the total life of a person, our argument thus far commits us to the thesis that the development of character (not of the total personality!) is focused on the moral imperative to will the best I know.

Obligation to the best I know is a factor in human experience along with reason, will, and desire. This view of obligation has not been recognized by naturalistic therapy, and supernaturalistic therapy has neglected it. The problem of "strengthening" the will still exists for us. But its solution will take a different form. Here we are making honesty and courage twin dynamos in the life of character. Character, the crucible of moral creativity, has aims of its own; so do the aesthetic, the scientific, the social, the religious have their own aims, even as each affects and is affected by the other constituents of life. Whatever else we say about a person's character, this is one area that is ultimately his alone to form, although, as we have insisted, it is not separated from the total personality and all that nourishes its growth. This must suffice on this particular point here.[6]

But still another comment must re-enforce our contention that the life of character is an intrinsic value, an independent or autonomous source of value, though affected by the rest of personality and vice versa. The autonomy of the virtues is illustrated by the fact that even when we do not admire or approve the values to which a person may direct his virtues, we do admire and approve his virtues. We admire and approve Brutus' and Marc Antony's honesty and

---

[5] The student is urged to read the writings of Reinhold Niebuhr, Dietrich Bonhoeffer, Paul Tillich, Sören Kierkegaard, and Jean-Paul Sartre, as well as Martin Buber, for provocative treatments of this whole problem. It is interesting to note Gandhi's conviction at this point: "To see the universal and all-prevailing Spirit of Truth face to face one must be able to love the meanest of creation as oneself. . . . God can never be realized by one who is not pure of heart" (*op. cit.*, p. 504).

[6] See Chapter 30 below and also Peter A. Bertocci, *Free Will, Responsibility, and Grace* (New York: Abingdon Press, 1957).

courage even if we do not agree with their objectives. In general, the courage of the enemy is admired and approved, though most of his objectives are disapproved and blamed. Again, we may feel hostile to an offender but admire him when he is honest. On the other hand, if a person is courageous and honest in his pursuit of values that we do critically approve, we rejoice with him all the more wholeheartedly. And what is here said about our first two virtues can be said about all the rest. We think of each as a source of some excellence in life, even if we cannot always approve of the ends that they service.

Finally, if we look for support to our basic contention with regard to the centrality of virtues of honesty and courage, we can find it in as distinguished an ethicist as Nicolai Hartmann. "Wisdom," he writes, "is a value which spurs man on to the choice of ends: bravery to the execution of them." [7] Courage and honesty are the core of this system of virtues because wisdom protects our needs for understanding our values and their relationship to all being, while courage keeps a person in constant encounter with the risks that are forever present in life. That both honesty and courage are involved in every other value venture in life will be further evident as we attempt to define other virtues.

C. *Gratitude*

The third moral virtue-trait is *gratitude*. Gratitude arises as the honest way of dealing with a specific human situation, namely, the fact that we enjoy values that we ourselves did little, if anything, to merit. Nothing a person can do merits the loyalty and love of parents and friends, the harmonies and delights of sense, feeling, and thought, the many goods made available to him when no one knew whether he would use them responsibly or not. In such situations the trait to be willed is gratitude.

When the word "gratitude" is used, we immediately associate it with a "glad" feeling or an emotional state that wells up within us when some wanted value becomes ours as the result of no special effort of our own, or beyond what our effort deserves.[8] But although our feeling of gratitude may grow out of voluntary actions in the

---

[7] Nicolai Hartmann, *Ethics*, trans. Stanton Coit, Intro. by J. Muirhead (New York: Macmillan Co., 1932), II, 246.

[8] See Mandelbaum, *op. cit.*, p. 143, for a contrasting view.

past, we can hardly call any present emotional state a virtue. This is not to say that the feeling of gratefulness is not a value. It is to say that a feeling of gratefulness is not a virtue. It is to say that this feeling, or any other, does not as such have *moral* value. For a person may or may not feel grateful dependent upon his present psychological orientation and mood, and he can hardly be held responsible for the earlier conditions leading to this emotional reaction. Yet, clearly, if he stops to think about the situation in which he does not feel gratitude, he may realize that *he ought to be grateful,* whether he now feels that emotion or not.

Accordingly, we define the virtue of *gratitude* as the *willingness to recognize the unearned increments of value in one's experience, whether the emotional response of gratitude is present or not, by thought and action suitable to the value received.* Thus, school children may not *feel* grateful at a given moment to their teachers, but we urge them to acknowledge at least with a "Thank you!" services rendered them. We thus distinguish between the spontaneous flow of emotional gratitude and the purposeful acknowledgment in thought and action of undeserved or not necessarily deserved goods. Although no doubt we enjoy a richer experience if we feel grateful when we acknowledge unearned increments, the moral value that we would stress is the willingness properly to acknowledge good beyond desert. Not to acknowledge an unearned good because one does not feel grateful is a *moral* weakness, whatever one's emotional response. Dante placed the ungrateful in the frozen ice of heartlessness in his deepest hell.

Moral gratitude, clearly, involves an extension of the virtue of honesty. For it involves clearly recognizing the sources of goodness, and taking courageously the proper moral stance toward the source of goodness. There is no one action that is "proper," but the grateful person tries in varying situations to discover what it is that may express his sense of appreciation or indebtedness. It is for this reason, largely, that the person whose trait of gratitude allows him to become aware of the constant flow of unmerited good in life is better prepared to become temperate and meek.

D. *Temperance*

The fourth personal virtue is *temperance.* The English word "self-control" is too broad for the specific trait of character envisioned here. After all, each of the virtues involves self-control. A more definite kind of control is necessary if a human being is to deal honestly with the sheer conflict, which he will often find in his life, between feelings, wants, and abilities. The conflict, as such, can keep the person from appreciating the possible good in the opposing elements. *Temperance is the willingness to deal with actual and possible conflict within a given life by seeking to harmonize the different elements in accordance with their own potential and the good of the personality as a whole.* Lest we think of each virtue as a separate part of personality, let us remember that temperance is the person trying to bring each phase of his life to function in accordance with the utmost harmony and growth of the whole. It may help to think of "tempered" steel, that is, steel treated to perform a function completely.

There are several tempting ways of dealing with conflict. It is tempting, for example, to bring an end to a conflict by allowing one of the conflicting elements to win the battle. If one can become ascetic and just put something out of his life so that he will never be bothered by it again, he may have "peace of mind." Yet this had better not be done without extreme caution. One does not need to be a Freudian to warn about the danger of repression. The person who tries to avoid conflict by rejecting unwanted tendencies before they can become forceful factors in conscious experience will never gain the experience of knowing what it is that is objectionable about them and of dealing with them openly. Debilitating anxiety may result from trying to avoid a battle. Who knows whether he may not have to meet the same enemy under less favorable circumstances?

Yet it will not do simply to allow conflict to "take care of itself" by allowing the strongest forces to win the day. As we have had occasion to repeat, although human powers do not lead necessarily to goodness or to evil, they need to be assessed in relation to each other. The aim of being temperate is to bring this inner coordination, or proper subordination, out of varied components of life. There is an assumption made by the man temperate in this sense: nothing in life is to receive an automatic veto, and yet no phase of life can be allowed to set its own terms.

Indeed, as we emphasized in discussing the Aristotlelian doctrine of the mean, the concern of the temperate man is essentially positive. Grateful for the actual and potential goods in his complex and changing nature, he seeks to avoid needless and unfruitful conflict.

This is not to smother the emotions of life, ranging from fear to joy, under a constant wet blanket. Without emotions life loses its savor. The temperate man seeks to protect the savor of things from the discomforts of indigestion. This means firm direction in the light of what we know about each element in experience and its connections.

The temperate man, accordingly, is trying to "temper" every aspect of his life, not refusing to allow any one to be out-shouted by the strident demands of any other. To say "everything in proportion" results *not* in a dull average and a convenient mediocrity, but in a strong total person who knows how to woo the promise of all parts into the common venture of mutual support. The temperate man is not one who cannot take strong stands; he is a man who takes a strong stand for inner teamwork! Surely without such temperance it would be impossible to achieve the kind of self-actualization demanded by Maslow, the responsible self-regulating freedom urged by Fromm, and the maturity of personality favored by Allport. We might say that the temperate man, in his skill in subordinating part to whole for the sake of maximum value of effect, is the moral man as artist.

E. *Humility*

Courage, we have said, is needed for situations involving sincerity and sacrifice, gratitude for situations in which there is an unlearned increment of good, temperance whenever there is need for inner harmony and positive order—and each of these is impossible without honest self-analysis. Yet insight into one's own nature brings us face to face with a persistent situation that calls for *humility.*

Humility is the willingness to recognize one's shortcomings and one's assets, without minimizing the one or maximizing the other, in the realization of the responsibility that both involve. The price of making too much of one's assets is a false sense of one's relation to the world in which he lives and of what he can achieve in it. To allow a misconception of oneself to grow is to encourage oneself to play the wrong role. Most of the evil in both a superiority complex and an inferiority complex stems, in the last analysis, from an unwillingness to accept the role one *can* play as opposed to the role one would like to play despite abilities and opportunities. To be sure, a human being never knows exactly what he can do. All the greater is the need for humility, the willingness to live with the assessment of one's powers as his experience brings them to light.

When Plato says that it is each man's duty to find out what he can do best and then govern his private and social life by whatever that may be, he is asking for what we are here calling humility. It is Plato's conviction that one's deeper satisfaction would spring from actually doing what his abilities allow him to do, even though he might like to do (or attach greater social prestige to) something else. For example, the rulers (or philosopher-kings, as Plato called them) are to be selected not because they like to rule or enjoy political power, but because a life-long process of educational training and screening indicates that they have the ability to rule. Underlying Plato's whole thought is the conviction that rulers and everyone else in the state will find a unique kind of lasting fulfillment open to them if they guide themselves by tried abilities rather than by desire as such. The life of desire, unguided by honest assessment of ability and by acceptance of that station in life which ability and opportunities make possible, is a parasitic life dependent on the vagaries of happenstance.

This brief description of humility may serve to strengthen our contention that the virtues cannot be cut away from each other with even the sharpest scalpel. Each, as we have urged, *is the person as a whole trying to solve an inescapable problem, which itself is one phase of the many-sided problem of finding oneself and one's relationship to the world.* A moment's reflection reveals that humility will open the way for gratitude. For the humble person is spared the uncertainty of pretending; he gains the quiet confidence that his goods are rooted in sober capacity. On the other hand, the positive heightening of one's sense of life that gratitude brings will help one to recognize shortcomings in the proper spirit.

Nevertheless, even a balanced self-concept as a basis for everyday living will fail to cover all situations. A special problem comes up when one confronts undeserved evil. Another personal moral value is now needed.

F. Meekness

Too often meekness is linked with humility, and both are associated with a kind of inability to call one's soul his own. Yet, as we have just seen, humility is not self-negation. Nor is meekness self-degradation. *Meekness is the willingness to accept the undeserved evil in life without exaggerating that evil or the degree of one's competence to deal with it.*

As here envisaged, this virtue is concerned with the same problem "solved" by the Epicureans and the Stoics (as well as the Buddhists) in different ways. These schools of philosophy realized that there is much evil in life that was not within one's control. The Epicurean developed the state of mind called *ataraxia* (self-composure). He urged: "Live in the realization that most of your worries are rooted in false or exaggerated fears and in your effort to extend yourself in accepting responsibilities for others that are really none of your business. Concern for others will bring you uncertainty and grief, because you cannot control what others do sufficiently to guarantee your own peace of mind. Therefore, analyze the sources of your pleasures and pains accurately, and then so order your life that you will cut away the pleasures that lead to pain and accept pains that lead to greater pleasure. Accordingly, so far as possible, retire to your garden with a few kindred spirits for whom you take no responsibility, and there sip the cup of life in drafts that will keep the balance as far as possible on the side of pleasantness."

In contrast, the Stoics encouraged the state of mind called *apathia,* to whose meaning our word "apathy" is a poor guide. Perhaps their underlying belief about man and his relation to the universe was responsible for their different attitude toward undeserved suffering. The Epicurean believed that man was adrift in a universe that had no inner ultimate rationale or purpose; one could trust the universe no more than one could trust other pleasure-loving men! The Stoics, however, believed that the universe was a dependable rational structure in which man could feel at home insofar as he was true to the reason within him. Accordingly, for the Stoic, as for the follower of Buddha, one's worst mistake consists in thinking of himself as an isolated unit whose job it is to fit the world and others into his own pleasure pattern. Man's worst sin is to try to draw away from cosmic or social responsibility into the Epicurean's secluded garden.

Thus, when the Stoic finds himself confronted with much evil not in his power, what attitude does he take toward it? He does not go about wailing and bemoaning the fact—or asking: "Why did it have to happen to me?" For, if anything, this attitude simply depletes his emotional energy. On the other hand, it does no good to attack all evils in Don Quixote fashion when one simply cannot do anything about them. There is only one rational answer. "Decide what evils you can do something about, and what evils you cannot do anything about. Refuse to worry about the latter and concentrate on doing the good within your power."

If one does this, he prevents the evil confronting him from entering into his own private fortress. To maintain *apathia* is not to be apathetic or indifferent to evil. It is to keep a resolute control of one's own will, so that one does not capitulate to self-pity and thus open himself to the infection of moral disease. The least one can do is to quarantine evil and keep it from spreading both in his own life and that of others. In the last analysis, one's own character is vulnerable only if he lets down the drawbridge to the inner fortress. (The reader will note that much of what we said earlier concerning the relation of character to happiness reflects Stoic teaching.)

Yet is the Stoic attitude toward evil one consistent with the phrase "accepts the undeserved evil" in our definition of meekness? Not quite. From our perspective both the Epicurean and the Stoic attitudes reveal, despite their seeming differences, the same inner flaw. (We may be slightly unfair to the Stoic virtue.) Both attitudes, in different degrees, seem basically intent on keeping evil from hurting the person, me. The Epicurean flees to his neatly planned garden, and the Stoic retreats to a strongly built fortress within that will resist the attacks of evil. But is prudent fear of evil or proud contempt of it the best way to deal with undeserved evil? Both of these ways invite rigidity and both discourage resiliency in living.

We may suggest the higher virtue that we have in mind by saying: See an evil situation for what it is—quite often a mixture of evil and good. In this situation, rather than abhorring evil so much that you allow it to frighten you away even from the possible good, be willing to "live with" an evil situation, constructively encouraging the good in it. In this way the evil-making factors may indeed be quarantined without quarantining the good also. One can be too "skittish" about evil. If one is intent only on keeping his fortress intact, he may become blind to the good that can come by conquering evil.

Once more, it may be that the Stoic view could embrace this positive concern expressed in Jesus' injunction to "overcome evil with good." Surely it is good to quarantine evil by refusing to yield to it in self-pity. Inescapable and undeserved evil must not be allowed to produce more evil by killing the spirit of the person affected. But a person can become so concerned about his "unconquerable soul," he can so prize his own "indomitable will" that he works overtime keeping himself in antiseptic condition. Thus, even though he does not escape to an Epicurean garden, he may well succumb to the temptation to isolate himself from the evil round about him. He thereby allows evil to take deeper root than it would if he left his fortress to meet evil where it is.

Perhaps the real weakness in the Stoic attitude lies in the misconception that the evil can be neatly severed from the good and dealt with separately. Consequently, it is easy for Stoic *apathia* itself to become a source of evil, for it tends to oversimplify the way in which evil can hurt a person. On the other hand, meekness, as we see it, is the willingness to endure evil along with good in such a way that evil may be quarantined and the good sustained in every situation. The meek person is fighting the "extremes" of self-pity and a Pollyanna naïveté.

After this discussion of the virtue of meekness, we are ready to move beyond the personal virtues to the social virtues: kindness, forbearance, forgiveness, and sense of humor. But first we must justify the distinction we are drawing between the social and personal virtues.

The distinction must not be taken to mean that the personal virtues do not have social consequences. Indeed, the social virtues stem from the personal virtues. What is emphasized by the distinction is a fact easily overlooked, especially by those who think of personality and goodness in strictly social terms. What is this fact? It is that every individual, even if he were the only one on a desert island, would have to solve the kind of problem resolved by the personal virtues. Honesty, courage, gratitude, temperance, humility, and meekness are needed by any person who would improve the quality of his life. No one of them depends upon the existence of other persons. To be sure, success or failure in developing personal virtues are all the more important because they involve other people. But the situations that the personal virtues confront arise from the very fact that a person is a human being with an assortment of different needs and abilities that must interact with each other and with the nonhuman environment.

II. *THE SOCIAL VIRTUES*

In the first place, the social virtues further illustrate our theme that every virtue ultimately involves the willingness to seek and live in the light of truth (honesty). But the social virtues rest also on the psychological fact that, in Donne's famous words, "no man is an island." Far-reaching consequences stem from the fact that human beings are born, helpless, into some sort of family, some sort of society, and some sort of political order. The most self-reliant individual still needs others not only to survive but to realize some of the highest qualities that justify survival. The social moral values (social virtues) protect values, and presuppose personal virtue, but they also add quality to the life of the individual. They arise as a person honestly confronts what is involved in his interaction with other persons as he tries to fulfill the imperative "I ought to do the best I know."

A. *Justice*

The moment a person begins to reflect about the relation of other people to himself and to ask "How should I treat them?" a number of alternatives suggest themselves: (a) I can use them to get what I want, (b) I can make sure that they do not hurt me, (c) I will not hurt them, unless I have to, in order to get what I want, (d) I will not have any fixed policy but will not try particularly to help or to hurt, and see how things go. These four are by no means the only alternatives, and they are suggested here simply to bring us to the crucial question. On what grounds can one reasonably justify the use of any person by another person *only* as a means to an end? To personalize the question: Why should anyone assume that I can be used as if my purpose in life is simply to serve him (and vice versa)? That persons do treat other persons very much as they treat things, that they accept no responsibility for others and use them simply as convenient means to their own ends—this is not what is being contested. But an honest person must justify the theoretical assumptions on which he acts.

We would stress that the argument here is not: "Well, I would not want anyone to treat me as if I were a thing, or as a means only."

Perhaps the so-called "Golden Rule," "Do unto others as you would like to have them do to you," can be taken this way. But sooner or later one would have to indicate why he would be justified in not wanting to be treated as if he were a mere means to another's end. If the Golden Rule is to be justified at all, it must make explicit the assumption that persons have the same basic abilities and wants. A proponent of the Golden Rule could then argue: "If A is good for me, unless I can show that A is bad for another person like me, then I have to assume that, *other things being equal,* my desire for A is justified. But no one has reason, where there is a conflict of interests, to give priority either to himself or to another without justification." At the heart of this reasoning, we must note, is the thesis that if and to the extent that persons are the same, they merit equal treatment.

Because persons are capable of reason, they can reflect upon their experience and they can be consulted about value preference. When we deal with subhuman living beings we cannot reason with them and are thus forced to treat them in the light of whatever we can infer about their wants and abilities. Animals (and plants) cannot become ends-to-themselves because they do not have the reflective self-consciousness that would enable them to become so. We cannot expect them ever to organize their living purposefully from within, although the learning process does result in "selectivity," which is hardly reflective even in the highest animals. However it may be with animals, the fact that human beings can be reflective opens the way to cooperative criticism and evaluation of alternative paths of value, with a view to apportioning good and evil. This, we believe, is the underlying justification for one of the Kantian versions of the Categorical Imperative: "So act as to treat humanity whether in thine own person or in that of any other, in every case as an end withal, never as means only." [9] For when another being can become an end to himself, on what grounds can he be treated as if he were a being who could not possibly suffer and enjoy as we do, make this fact evident to us, and participate in the variety of values open to him as a human being? Whatever else the definition of altruism may involve, it takes root in this fundamental capacity of human beings to be ends to themselves.

In the light of these considerations, we may define the virtue of justice: *Justice is the willingness to make no exception of oneself in*

[9] Immanuel Kant, *Critique of Practical Reason and Other Works,* trans. Thomas E. Abbott (London: Longmans, Green & Co. 1873, 1909), p. 47.

the distribution of either goods or evils, unless one can show good reason for doing so. The "good reason" would be defined in terms of the value system espoused and would consist in showing that when preference is given to some person or persons it will in fact preserve the optimum value of the majority, at least, of the persons concerned.

The individual who develops the trait of justice is the person who is constantly looking for ways in which the various individuals and groups can share values and disvalues so that no one will profit unnecessarily at the expense of others. The wisdom of Solomon is needed to work out the details. Further understanding of altruism and justice as a *principle* will have to await discussion in Chapter 27. But we shall, as we consider other social virtues, realize that the minimal demands of justice, as stated above, cannot be overlooked, even though justice is not the last word in concern for others.

B. *Repentance*

The inclusion of repentance as a social moral value may seem doubtful because of the religious connotations the term evokes. The virtues here depicted do not presuppose either the existence or the nonexistence of God. If a person believes, as Christians of all types do, that he and God stand in a special relationship of trust, then there is, indeed, need for repentance when man is disloyal to God. But whether God exists or not, the discussion at this point assumes only that the individual acknowledges his own responsibility for justice among men. Even so, what one repents having done depends on the ideal of the good life to which he feels obligated.

Repentance is the willingness to make explicit one's realization of evil consciously perpetrated, to ask the person or persons wronged for forgiveness, and to make amends as far as possible for the evil done. Just as gratitude may be attended by "feeling grateful," so repentance may be attended by "feeling sorry." But repentance, we wish to urge, should not be dependent upon an emotional state any more than gratitude should depend on feeling. Furthermore, one may feel sorry for all evils, whereas repentance, we suggest, is related only to evil for which the individual holds himself responsible.

Once more, in discussing any virtue, our concern is not with the total feeling-emotional state, important as that is. In this instance, whatever one's emotional state may be, he ought to *will* to make the evil he has done explicit, to right the wrong he has done as far as possible, and thus seek to re-establish the proper relationship (as envisioned in the ideal of life) with the person or persons wronged. I may admire and praise a repentant person (just as I do a brave act), even though I cannot approve of that for which he is repentant. The obligation to repent grows from an honest facing of the responsibility a person has to others (for justice at least).

We continue to lay our stress on the fact that human relations cannot be left at the mercy of emotional responses. Nevertheless, this is not to condemn emotions but simply to recognize that our emotional attachments often spring from nonrational conditioning and associations and themselves call for evaluation. We often say: "I know I should be sorry, but I am not." Yet we expect others to repent even if they are not sorry. We approve of them if they are "sorry" also, but we do not expect them to act on the basis of their emotional state alone.

Once more we have struck the very difficult problem, psychologically and ethically, of the relation of virtues to emotions, and we are not entirely satisfied with our present solution. We must leave this whole matter to a better moral psychology. We may further observe, however, that the trait of being willing to recognize and make amends for one's moral faults is a power-releasing disposition within the repenting personality. Although it may not be possible to will a given emotional state into being at a given time, being willing to repent may well set the stage for emotional responses and may heal a wounded human relationship.

C. *Kindness*

An inescapable fact in the human situation is the inequality among persons caused by differences in ability, financial background, and sheer luck and all the other accidents of circumstances. There is no denying the burden imposed on those who, through no fault of their own, find themselves unable to achieve ends that would be good for them if only timely help were forthcoming. There come to mind, of course, the infirm, the poor, the jobless, the lonely, the misunderstood —but who of us does not have limitations and infirmities that he cannot escape unaided. Kindness has specifically to do with deficits and burdens insofar as they are caused, largely at least, by no purposeful actions on the part of the individual.

We may, accordingly, define the virtues of kindness as *the willing-*

ness to help others who are needy (owing to nonmoral deficits in their lives) *in such a way that they may still experience values of which they are capable.* Once more, to be kind is not to act from some favorable emotional predisposition, for example, sympathy or tenderness, toward a person, though to feel these emotions *also* may brighten the total experience of both giver and receiver. The kind person heeds not his own emotional state, but the other person's needs.

The reader may, at this point, almost take offense at what may seem the "cold calculation" in "doing" kindness. But far from trying to put a damper on the overflow of generosity on the part of the giver, we mean only to urge the full consideration of the needs of the person to be helped. It is so easy to be "merely sentimental" about giving! How often we give so that we shall not ourselves "feel bad"? And then how often do we think of ourselves as "deserving gratitude" for "giving so much"? Objective and intelligent expression of concern is true kindness, and it requires much more than a susceptibility to emotion. Yet we must not forget that feeling, intelligence, will, and ought fuse in the response and action of a person. In other words, to distinguish the emotive from the volitional roots of a person's response is not to neglect the fact that emotion and will, intelligence and obligation, are phase activities of the unified person.

D. *Forgiveness*

We are now thinking of situations in which persons purposefully inflict harm upon each other. They connive for power over others; they disobey the imperatives of justice, of repentance, and of kindness. They retaliate for injustice done them.

Vindictiveness is the willingness to deal with the evil-doer in a way that will "pay him back" for the evil he has done. Persons often seek to justify such vindictiveness as a kind of justice, because, as they would hold, the evil-doer has been unjust. They plead for "balancing the scales." But does vindictiveness in fact do justice either to the evil-doer or to the victim? Being just is not a matter of mathematical equality. An optician causes a ditchdigger the loss of an eye. But to take the optician's eye in revenge would mean incapacitating him for his work to a greater degree than the ditchdigger. Thus, to follow the maxim "An eye for an eye and a tooth for a tooth" would usually create greater injustice.

Vindictive "justice," obviously, is not fair to the complexity of factors in moral situations. The fundamental obligation is to others who may be hurt, to ourselves, and to the culprit who must be kept from doing further damage. Accordingly, to forgive a person cannot mean to overlook the fact that he may continue to perpetrate the evil in question. The acute problem in dealing with a person who is guilty of a criminal act is: How do we stop the evil without discouraging the good? One thing seems clear: we cannot simply seek a mathematical "equality" in the distribution of good and evil; we must minimize the evil and maximize the good in the situations in which evil has been deliberately done.

With these considerations in mind, we define *forgiveness as the willingness to treat the person by whom one has been purposely wronged with a view to increasing the values in his life and in all our mutual relationships and not simply to punish evil.* To be vindictive and unforgiving is to be willing to arrest evil without regard to the impact of our measures on the culprit's total good. To be vindictive means that one is himself purposely willing to inflict evil that need not occur if he is willing, for example, to take a larger view of the culprit and his own relationship to him and to try to understand the whole situation, good and bad, both in his own life history and in that of the culprit. If recent psychology teaches us anything, it teaches us that to encourage hostility either in ourselves or in others is to set forces at work in personality that can fester and lead to personal and social evil. It was not sentimentality that led Plato to conclude in the *Gorgias:* "It is better to suffer injustice than to do it."

To speak positively, the forgiving person aims at removing the psychological and moral barriers that purposeful evil-doing creates. His concern is to recognize the good in the evil-doer, to release the "good-making" potentialities in his life, and to help in any way he can to keep the evil that has occurred from spreading. If the evil-doer can believe that the harm he has done will not be exaggerated or charged against him in a way that will unnecessarily destroy values in his own life, he will be encouraged to formulate more constructive plans for living.

To forgive successfully calls for more sensitivity and patient intelligence than any other virtue. How easy it is for the "forgiver" to be ungracious, to drive "subtle bargains," and to allow this relation of "forgiving" to keep him from remembering his own sins! On the other hand, he must keep from being sentimental and try to analyze his total relationship to the evil-doer in a way that will encourage moral growth and an increase in value in all the lives concerned. "To err is human; to forgive divine" is true enough. But we might well add "In effect, the purpose of forgiveness will take divine patience, insight, and generosity."

The larger the number of persons involved, the greater are the problems to be faced in the attempt to be forgiving. It is no wonder that the art of compromise and reconciliation so often meets insuperable obstacles when large social units are at odds with each other.

Reverting to person-to-person situations, the question may be raised: Should one forgive when the evil-doer does not repent? It seems clear that without repentance on the part of the evil-doer the aim of forgiveness cannot be *fully* realized. If evil is acknowledged, but there is no disposition on the part of the culprit either to repent or to make restitution (if, and to the extent, that this is possible), the hands of the would-be forgiver are tied. For how can he forgive and forget the evil act if the disposition to repent of it is lacking or if the culprit does not accept any responsibility for the willful harm he has done? Jesus could do more with the repentant thief hanging on the cross beside him than for his unrepentant executioners, who "know not what they do."

Yet, often the very act of forgiving, imaginatively executed, may call forth the perpetrator's desire to change his way of life and the willingness to make whatever restitution is desirable. The "forgiver," nevertheless, is not interested in verbal repentance, but in the change of mind that must be brought about if evil is to be wiped out and goodness encouraged. Clearly there is no simple formula for working out the ideal human relationship sought by means of the dispositions to be just and to be forgiving. The relationship between forgiveness, justice, and repentance will call for risks that must be courageously accepted if all the human beings in a given situation are to accept responsibility for the best possible. (See also Chapter 27.)

III. *SITUATIONAL AND POLITICAL VIRTUES*

We have now sketched out four social virtues and six personal virtues. Because they are responses to pervasive and fairly universal situations that call for moral solutions, we have considered them *cardinal* virtues and would give them centrality in the normative structure of character. Yet anyone enjoying the cardinal virtues will need to develop others as auxiliaries in more specific situations. Surely industriousness, patience, persistence, cheerfulness, aggressiveness, courteousness, optimism, and others are important traits in many personal and social situations. Furthermore, there are even more specific virtues needed for success in specific vocations and pursuits. The doctor, the teacher, the salesman, the merchant, the technician, the manual laborer, the clergyman, the housewife—all need to develop moral traits without which they would be unreliable in their vocation. Some of these *situational* virtue-traits might be largely personal and others largely social, in the sense defined above.

But we must mention in passing at least three more virtue-traits, which we designate *political*. These virtues are developments of personal and social virtue-traits as human beings face problems in their larger communal and societal relationships. These virtues are: *independence,* the willingness to work persistently although in a minority for the values one believes to be the ideal ends for all persons; *tolerance,* the willingness to protect freedom of speech, of worship, and of conscience for all members of the body-politic; and *cooperation,* the willingness to leave no stone unturned to enhance the sharing of all goods and evils that will help members of the community to live in mutual respect. These virtues, developing out of the cardinal personal and social virtues, would, we believe, promote and serve the ideal of the democratic form of political organization. A more adequate discussion of them will ensue in Part IV and in Chapter 28.

IV. *WHY IS LOVE NOT A VIRTUE?*

There is one seeming omission in this list of virtues; for some it will vitiate the whole scheme. Love cannot be found in it. The main reason for this is our conviction that love is not one virtue among others, but the *style of life* that is willed in and through each of the virtues. *Love is the total orientation of a person's thinking, feeling, and willing insofar as his controlling commitment is the ideal growth of personality in himself and in all other persons.*

Our definition assumes a distinction between love as a sentiment and love as an ethical style of life. Love as a sentiment concentrates feeling and emotion on a being or an entity that the person highly prizes. The range of experiences covered by love, in this sense, is simply enormous. Our ordinary English usage moves from such expressions as "I'd love to," "I'd love it," "I just love dancing" (or other activities), to love of self, sweetheart, wife, parents, children, school, state, country, freedom, truth, beauty, and God. We cannot begin here to compare and contrast the different kinds of love—erotic, romantic, ethical, religious, and so on. Still, do they have anything in common?

Our own reflection suggests that wherever there is "love" there is a strongly felt dedication of the person to some supremely valued entity. Speaking psychologically, whatever a person loves constitutes the object of that person's most positive commitment. Love, as a complex psychic state, is the strongest favorable orientation a person can feel toward an object highly valued by him. (Hate is the opposite psychic state.) Because love does involve a fused concentration of one's pro emotions (such as sympathy, tenderness, respect, elation, wonder) on the highly valued object (sweetheart, child, neighbor), the person in love feels in himself a power that gives the object of love right of way when there are conflicts of allegiance.

It will be obvious, however, that while love is concentrated on a highly valued "object" in a given life, that object, critically appraised, may in fact not deserve love. At any one point in a person's life, as we have repeatedly urged, there may be a struggle between what a person critically favors and what he actually finds himself engaged to, between what one does love and what one ought to love. The biblical injunction. "Thou shalt love the Lord thy God with all thy heart and with all thy soul, and with all thy strength, and with all thy mind; and thy neighbor as thyself" expresses the struggle between what ought to engage our love and what actually does.

The ethical problem, in other words, has to do not with the psychological state as such, but with the discovery of the object or objects worthy of emotional dedication. From an ethical point of view we must ask why love as a sentiment ought to be the preferred psychical state under certain conditions. The ethicist cannot assume that any felt state is the object of moral preference until adequate analysis indicates that it is. Therefore, for him both the object pole of the sentiment and the emotional pole must be evaluated in every situation. The girl whom one loves may not be deserving of that love; or the girl whom one does not love may deserve to be loved. Perhaps it is now evident why we cannot consider *sentiment-love* a virtue or a vice without further evaluation of the values involved. And perhaps we can see the point of distinguishing love as a sentiment from love as style of life [10] (the willingness to serve the growth of values in others at one's own expense, if necessary).

But because *ethical love* cannot restrict itself to any one value or virtue at the expense of others, we may wonder how virtues and values are related to it. Our suggestion is that the virtues, as here defined, though not identical with love, are *stages* or *foci* in the life of a person who wills to love. The scheme of virtues is the backbone of the loving character. And the pattern (or symphony) of values, inclusive of character values, is the skeleton of moral personality that activates the loving person.

Thus, in answer to the original question "Why does love not appear in the scheme of virtues"? we reply: Because love *as an ethical norm* is not *one* virtue but a *way of life*, which needs at least the scheme of virtues and values suggested for its fulfillment. Ethical love of others will end in failure to the extent that the virtues are not realized; and there will be no ideal values to guide the character apart from the symphony of values, which, together with the virtues, define the ideal person. The actual development of a loving personality will be the by-product of all the volitional and nonvolitional factors in a personality insofar as the person succeeds in overcoming outer and inner obstacles to the ideal of personality.

Finally, our discussion of values in Chapter 15 showed that values interpenetrate and normatively enter into a system. In this chapter, although we have attempted, in defining virtues, to keep distinctions between the virtues clear, it is apparent that they cannot exist or develop in a vacuum and that they merge into each other and overlap. For they are different ways in which the unified person tries to meet his problems.

Once more, then, analytically we move from part to whole; psychologically and ethically, we are actually defining foci or aspects in the total active response of a person. A personality is always more than the sum of its parts. It should surprise none that love, as a style of life, is the pervasive motive and intention, which at once inspires and is the product of such virtues and values as we have defined.

Much more, in Parts IV and V, will be said about the ideal person, the ideal society, and the nature of the values and virtues that they

[10] For religious persons in the Judeo-Christian tradition at least, and for others, love as a moral style of life is accompanied by and reinforced by love as a sentiment toward God conceived as the loving and forgiving Father of all men. Once more, religious sentiment may initiate and fuse with morally critical action.

express and encourage. It will also become clearer that the emotional and conative facts of human nature are not to be depreciated. Until the whole person can be organized creatively, so that the optimum in value experience (including emotional and feeling states) open to a given person is actualized, the moral will has a task to perform. The main concern in this chapter has been to develop the realization of Aristotle that while virtue may collaborate with emotional or conative disposition, it is to be moved by deliberate principle in the development of new dispositions.[11] Love, as a *moral style of life,* is the whole of which the virtues are expressions; and the virtues are the will to realize the symphonic ideal of personality.

V. *THE MORAL STRUGGLE AND RELIGION*

We bring this chapter to a close by referring to several comments made by Mahatma Gandhi in the final chapter of that autobiography which tells of his "experiments with truth." They not only bring us back to a major point and problem in these chapters on the virtues, but they focus our attention on a consideration that cannot be neglected even in a brief account of the moral struggle. Earlier in his tale Gandhi comments that in all of his experience with many creeds and racial communities "my heart has been incapable of making any such [discriminatory] distinctions." He does not claim the trait of tolerance as a "special virtue, as it is in my very nature, rather than as a result of any effort on my part." On the other hand, when it comes to developing *"ahimsa* [non-violence], *brahmacharya* [celibacy], *aparigraha* [non-possession], and other cardinal virtues, I am fully conscious of a continuous striving for their cultivation." [12]

But Gandhi, like St. Paul, Augustine, and indeed everyone who takes the moral struggle seriously, realizes that his actual achievement falls short of the moral ideal he has set for himself, so he asks the same fundamental question: How can I bring myself, with my entrenched self-love, to become the loving servant of other persons? And Gandhi, like so many other moral prophets the world over, gives a tantalizing answer. It is only a direct experience of that Principle or Power which embraces both him and others that brings him power in his struggle "to love the meanest of creation as oneself." [13] In his

---

[11] Thomson, *op. cit.,* p. 169.
[12] Gandhi, *op. cit.,* p. 276.
[13] *Ibid.,* p. 504.

own words, "little fleeting glimpses . . . of the indescribable lustre of Truth, a million times more intense than that of the sun we daily see with our eyes" have sustained his moral experiments. At the same time, "To see the universal and all-pervading Spirit of Truth face to face one must be able to love the meanest of creation as oneself." [14]

On this view, clearly, there is constant interaction between growth in the realization of the ethical ideal and growth in the realization of God. The moral anguish that a deeply moral person feels in his failure to realize the ideal is bearable because he experiences an abiding kinship with an even greater Source of Value than lies within him and his fellowmen. At the same time, without his own willingness to believe that his own most excruciating and yet most rewarding value experience will be his actual realization of God, God will remain a stranger to him.

We find ourselves at the heart of the problem of the relation between the ethical and the religious life. For many minds any attempt even to define the ethical ideal apart from religious experience cuts the life of morality off from the source of moral power. For such minds this chapter will exhibit a vain attempt to lift oneself by one's own bootstraps. Other minds will interpret any appeal to religion as the tell-tale sign of moral infancy. Obviously the whole question needs to be studied in a larger context. We shall defer further discussion to Chapter 30.

VI. REFLECTIVE SUMMARY

Since virtue-traits are vital components in the growth and preservation of other values, we ask: What are the cardinal virtues? Do they form a system?

We discover a scheme of virtues as we note that personal virtues exhibit a network, which in turn supports, and is enriched by, social and political virtues. Any virtue isolated from the rest becomes a vice.

Without repeating the scheme suggested, we may note the kind of interpenetration that takes place when the virtues are at work in a life. Without the truth-seeking implicit in honesty, all the other virtues and values wither. Yet one cannot accept the insecurities and sacrifice of truth-seeking without courage. Together, honesty and courage, by enabling man to "face reality" in its various forms, en-

[14] *Ibid.*

courage and give vitality to all the other virtues—although each virtue solves a different problem in personal, social, and political life.

Emotional states (such as gratefulness and sympathy) should not be confused with virtue-traits (such as *gratitude* and *forgiveness*), however much they do add to the total quality of personality. This confusion must be avoided especially in relation to love as a sentiment and love as a style of life. For, as the intentional style of life, love is expressed in the scheme of virtues. Such love is the personal commitment to fulfill one's own life in and through objective concern for the criticized values of others. Emotional love, without dedication to the symphony of values and the scheme of virtues as the ideal of personality, can easily become a passionate striving for short-lived and narrow values.

PART IV

Principles of Ethical Choice

18

Are There Principles for
Guiding Moral Choice?

$\sim\sim\sim\sim\sim\sim\sim\sim\sim\sim\sim\sim\sim\sim\sim\sim\sim\sim\sim\sim\sim$

I. *THE MORAL SITUATION*

For man there seems to be no short cut to happiness and the life good to live. Unlike that of the traditional and perhaps much maligned pig, man's happiness is not assured or necessarily even approached in a state of sheer physical satiation or relatively static adjustment to his immediate environment. The person who merely accepts and remains in a state of total dependence on others, emotionally and socially, the person for whom conformity to his group is the major concern is likely to be neither emotionally nor intellectually mature. In most cases, the person who passively adjusts to every demand made upon him, like the person who refuses to adjust or compromise at all, is a person who has stopped growing because he will not or cannot face conflicts and problems as they arise.

Paradoxically, the happy life or the life good to live cannot be equated with a life of unrestricted satisfaction of desires, wants, and valuations. It became evident very quickly in our discussion of values in Chapter 14 that not only preanalytic value claims but criticized values themselves may and often do come into conflict with each other. Like Faust we cannot stand still in present satisfaction. We constantly find ourselves forced to choose among alternatives; if we do not choose, the choice is made for us. One of the first conditions of the possibility of the good or happy life, as we have already discovered, lies in reflective evaluation of our value experiences themselves, in the development of a symphony of values.

Even as the good life cannot be equated with unrestricted satisfaction of desires, so also the good life can hardly be equated with the uncritical obedience to feelings of obligation or of ought. We discovered in Chapter 9 the qualitatively different character that ought adds to experience. The feeling of ought is the *sine qua non* of any experience that is to be fully moral. Only insofar as I choose or do not choose what I feel I ought to do can my action be held to be morally blameworthy or praiseworthy.

But also, in our consideration of the nature and source of obligation, as in the critique of the Freudian superego, we discovered that by the time we approach maturity our feelings of obligation have become attached to a heterogeneous mixture of precepts, actions, and ideas borrowed from or inculcated by parents, such institutions as church and school, playmates, and associates and by our practice in satisfying our own desires. Not surprisingly, our uncritical feelings of obligation are frequently confused and contradictory, as are the guilt feelings that our violations of them engender. Yet, despite the anxiety, frustration, and neurosis to which such unreflective ought and guilt feelings may give rise, our very ability to feel obligation and guilt increases the range of our sensitivity to each other. Moreover, it is the basis for the possibility of responsible interaction and cooperatively enjoyed growth and fulfillment. To do away with the feeling of obligation, if it were possible to do so, would substantially decrease the range and quality of values obtainable, as we saw in our discussion of the symphony of values and the scheme of virtues. The price of increased potentiality for value is indeed increased potentiality for disvalue and suffering; but the price of giving up the potentiality for disvalue would seem to be reduction to the subhuman level. Thus, again, the real problem, upon whose solution depends the possibility of the good and the happy life, lies in critical evaluation of our ought claims themselves. What ought we to do rationally?

What gives their practical meaning to value consideration and feelings of obligation is the fact of choice itself with ensuing action (cf. Chapter 8). We not only do and must choose; it is in our acts of choice that we continue to grow or retrogress. In the act of choice lies our creativity, our moral growing edge; through choice we realize our potentialities or we dissipate them. But unlike most of our animal ancestors, we not only act and select among alternatives, we are able to think, to anticipate actions and alternatives beforehand, and to reconsider them in memory after the act. As a result we can compare actions and choices and evaluate them critically—in the light of our value concepts and feelings of obligation and in the light of many other actions and their consequences. Thus, at least within limits, we can influence our own development.

II. EVALUATION AND MORAL SITUATIONS: PRINCIPLES OR LAWS

In all three aspects of a moral situation—valuing, oughting, and choosing—the fundamental question remains the same. Are there any principles of critical evaluation and action that are adequate guides to the life good to live? But as soon as this question is asked, a series of closely related questions arises: If there are such principles, how can they be characterized? What justification do we have for searching for such principles anyway? What is their source and their status? These much discussed questions actually resolve themselves into the blunt and not always welcome query: Is there such a thing as ethical (or moral) law or principle, and do the terms "law" and "principle" in this sense, that is, the moral sense, have any meaning?

III. POSSIBLE MEANINGS OF "LAW" OR "PRINCIPLE"

No sooner do we ask the question "Are ethical laws or principles possible?" than we seem faced with the age-old controversy that we have already met in connection with values in Chapters 10 to 14, the controversy between ethical relativism and ethical absolutism. What adds to the confusion is the considerable ambiguity in the use of the terms "law" and "principle" themselves. The authors have already discussed what seem to them the major weaknesses that make extreme relativism and social relativism untenable theories of value and of principles of conduct. More to the point of our present concern is the question: Just what do the terms "law" and "principle" mean in an ethical context?

A. *Customs*

At least four different meanings of the term "law" seem, each of them, at one time or another to have been synonymous with moral principle. First, "law" may refer to the customs (mores) of a particular group, society, or culture. Law in this sense has the binding force of the approval or disapproval of the group itself. Its content includes the group's taboo system and its positive and negative injunctions regarding specific actions. Such law varies notoriously from group to group and in the same group from time to time. The change in our conception over the last fifty years of what constitutes decency and proper modesty in women's dress rather nicely illustrates shifting customary morality within the same group. If moral principles be identified with customary law, then the cultural relativist is correct. Unless we are to engage in a vicious ethnocentrism and assert that our present customs ought to be the customs of all people (a position not without its advocates even in such an august body as the United States Senate), we would have to admit that what is customarily right is wholly relative to the group to which the customs belong.

B. *Legal Enactments*

Closely related to customary law is law as legal enactment by a society's governing body. The more important aspects of customary law for the perpetuation of the group and for efficiency of group management are usually enacted into civil law, where they carry not only the sanctions of social approval and disapproval but also definite penalties prescribed by the law itself. But again, as with customary laws, civil laws are relative to the enacting group. To confuse either customary law or civil law with moral principles is by definition to make immoral any opposition to the *status quo* or the governing power. As a result of such an identification Karl Marx, paradoxically, and in the name of what he considered social justice, rejected morality itself as one of "so many bourgeois prejudices, behind which lurk so many bourgeois interests." [1] The history of communism and communist methods in the twentieth century might have been very different had Marx explicitly recognized the difference between moral principles and civil and customary law.

[1] *Manifesto of the Communist Party* (New York: International Publishers, 1932), p. 20.

Further, to confuse customary and civil law with moral principles not only makes the existing customs and laws necessarily right but makes every group equally right no matter how much the laws and customs of different societies may conflict. Because each group is by definition right, the only recourse in intergroup conflict is force. As a result, right itself becomes something very close to the will of the stronger. And yet surely, as intelligent beings capable of criticizing our own value claims and feelings of obligation, we can (meaningfully) insist that some customs and some enacted laws are not what they ought to be either in our own society or in other societies. Insofar as we do so insist, we are in fact (regardless of theory) appealing to moral principles, whose character is different from that of custom and civil law. The very possibility of a critique of customs and civil laws points beyond customs and civil laws to a more objective standard of judgment. Such a critique at the same time indicates a positive relation between the ethical standard and the laws and customs, a relation to which we shall have to return later.

C. *Scientific Law*

A third meaning of the term "law," sometimes confused with moral principle, is scientific law or what is loosely called natural law as discovered in the physical and social sciences. Such laws may be characterized as descriptions of regular sequence among, within, and between things and organisms. They do not prescribe what ought to be. Nor, strictly speaking, do they tell us what must be. Rather they are ideal generalizations about what in fact does take place. Given certain events, all other things being equal, certain other events invariably follow. Because all other things are not always equal (for example, friction modifies the effect of gravitational attraction on a feather falling to earth even though it does not modify the attraction itself), complete invariability has to be assumed rather than proven. Hence these laws have to be called ideal generalizations. "Ideal" in this sense does not mean "ought to be" but "under optimum conditions," and its force is: Under such conditions events, x, y, and z do occur. Thus, such laws as the law of gravity, the laws of motion and of thermodynamics are primarily descriptive statements of uniform sequences of events held to be roughly universal. Insofar as they do hold, we cannot violate them; and the results of trying to violate the law of gravity are predictable to a degree approaching certainty. On the surface, such laws would seem to have very little in common with what might be called moral principles. In terms of their content, they seem to have little or nothing to do with moral decision. The law of gravity will continue to operate whether I want it to, or decide it ought to, or not. Indeed, if I try to break it, I illustrate it!

And yet the relation between scientific natural law and principles of moral action may be closer than it might at first appear. Although worthiness of intent in action and knowledge of the natural order are not equivalent to each other, nor necessarily assurances of each other, the person who attempts to disregard natural scientific law is likely to be, at the least, morally ineffective. The person who has taken lessons in first aid but tries to move a man injured in an accident into his car instead of covering him up warmly and calling for an ambulance may be responding to his feeling of "ought to help that man," but he is certainly running counter to the laws of physiology that he presumably studied in his course on first aid.

D. *Principles of Scientific Investigation*

Another positive relation between natural scientific law and moral principles calls for special note and offers an important clue to the possible character of moral principles themselves. The very possibility of the discovery of scientific natural law and the extension of scientific knowledge depends upon recognition by the scientist or investigator of certain more or less invariable norms or ideals or principles as obligating him as scientist. These principles are the very conditions of the possibility of scientific investigation itself. For example, if he is to be a scientist, the investigator must be willing to approach his subject matter, whether it be in physics or psychology, with an open mind, that is without a fixed or unyielding prejudgment as to what his results will be. He must be willing to follow his investigation through to its logical conclusion in light of the evidence, regardless of whether or not the conclusion conflicts with his cherished beliefs and prejudices. He must be willing to follow the principles of logic and scientific method. He must, in other words, impose upon himself the conditions of rational investigation.

Now these conditions or principles of scientific investigation are not themselves scientific laws, that is, descriptive generalizations discovered by scientists *in* events. The norms of scientific method are not, like the law of gravitation, found or observed in events that occur whether we like it or not. Neither are they, nor can they be, simply laws that we legislate for ourselves. In fact, one of the surest means of stifling scientific investigation has been the attempt to legislate or legally decree how scientists shall proceed and the conclusions they shall draw. The heresy trial of Galileo and the more recent purge of geneticists in Russia are striking cases in point.

Nor are the principles of scientific investigation simply the customs of a particular group, society, or culture. In one sense, one might say that they are the customs of scientists as scientists. But, if so, the term "custom" has taken on a most unorthodox meaning, for the impera- tive character of such principles of investigation does not depend on the fact that they are practiced by scientists, nor does their force derive primarily from the approval or disapproval of other scientists. Rather their validity and force stems from the fact that without them we would have no scientific investigation and advance. They are guiding lines that scientists propose to follow even before they know that they will lead to the discovery of truth in any particular scientific investigation. The experience of previous scientists or investigators has suggested these lines of procedure to scientists who were anxious to improve their procedures, but they were not (a) forced on them as "gravitation" is, nor (b) were they simply arbitrary inventions. Whether a scientist is a Hottentot, a Bostonian, or a Muscovite is irrelevant. In this sense the principles of scientific investigation are universal, not as divorced from all scientists, but as the condition of being a scientist anywhere or any time.

Not only are the conditions of the possibility of scientific investiga- tion universal; in the nature of the case they have to be self-imposed if they are imposed at all. In this sense they constitute specific "oughts" and not "musts." Although it is true that if one is to be a scientist he "must" abide by them, there is no necessity involved for any particular person. No one "has" to be a scientist (as he has to be a male or female); and, significantly, no one can make some one else into a scientist unless that person voluntarily accepts as binding upon himself the principles that are the conditions of scientific in- vestigation. But by the same token a man may have a list of degrees a column long, have the term "scientist" painted on his door, and yet, if he has not imposed upon himself the conditions of scientific investigation, that is, the morality of the scientist in relation to his science, he is simply not a scientist.

The ancient Stoics saw a further relation between scientific law, or what they called the "law of nature," and moral law. In harmony with Socrates, Plato, and Aristotle, the Stoics recognized that the factor in man that enables him to bring order and meaningfulness into his own life is his reason. Through his ability to see connections, to deliberate, to reason, man can gain control over his impulses and appetites; he can, as a matter of fact, discover what is and what is not within his power. It is this capacity which most clearly draws the line between man and the rest of the animal kingdom. In harmony with the scientists whom we have been considering, the Stoics pointed out that the discovery of what is actually under our control, the discovery of the limiting effects of Nature on action, is a function of reason. Reason, then, not only consists of the principles that guide our investigation of Nature but it imposes upon the reasoner his own discovered limitations. The Stoics drew a most interesting additional conclusion from this acknowledgment. Because for the Stoics, our own nature is a part of Nature, to use reason to investigate Nature is itself a fulfillment of a law of Nature in us. The result of investigation is the discovery of the laws of Nature or its ordering principles—what the Stoics called the "reason" of Nature, including man. Thus, for the Stoics, scientific law, the conditions for discovering scientific law, and moral law are ultimately one and the same in kind—laws of reason and Nature, human and otherwise.

The Stoic conclusion would seem too hasty. Our discussion has indicated a real difference in kind between the laws of natural events and the principles or conditions of scientific investigation. The former are not self-imposed or under our control; the latter, while not arbitrary, are self-imposed and their application is under our control. The former are primarily descriptive and predictive; the latter are primarily normative or prescriptive. But one aspect of the Stoic insight, the aspect borrowed from the Socratic tradition and in harmony with recognition of the conditions of scientific investigation, is extremely noteworthy. It points not only to a fifth type of law—law in the sense of universal principles for guiding moral choice —but to the character and justification of such law or principles as well.

E. *Principles of Rational Action*

Almost a hundred years before the founding of the Stoa, Socrates, while on trial for his life, had insisted that the unexamined life is not worth living. What Socrates saw far more clearly than any of his predecessors and many of his successors was that the life that is not subject to the self-discipline of rational control is a life of internal contradictions, frustration, chaos, and meaninglessness. Perhaps the major contribution to western ethical thought of the major Greek thinkers —Socrates, Plato, Aristotle, and the Stoics—was this conviction that man is a rational animal and that his very fulfillment and growth depend upon the exercise of his reason in control of life. What they were saying was not, as is sometimes claimed, that man is always rational, nor that he is necessarily rational, nor that he is only rational, nor that the good life is solely the life of intellectual contemplation. Men quite obviously are not always or necessarily rational. We all too easily can act and think irrationally. Although we may be potentially rational animals, we are also creatures of impulse, feeling, want, and desire. It is true that for Aristotle and for Plato, the highest values tended to be the contemplative values, but they did not hold that the good life as a whole is synonymous with the contemplative life. What the Greek thinkers were insisting upon is that the basic condition of order, of meaningfulness, of the happy and good life is intelligent or rational control of impulse and action. The fundamental prerequisite of responsible action is at least some order by which we guide our choices.

IV. *THE MEANING OF "MORAL LAWS OR PRINCIPLES"*

The relation between meaningfulness in life, responsibility, the good life, and reasonableness has become evident as we considered the need for criticizing value claims and ought imperatives and for resolving conflict on the psychological and social levels. The quest for moral principles, or principles for guiding moral choice, cannot end in the pressures of custom or in civic or scientific law. The quest is for principles of rational action. We have noted that the principles of scientific investigation hold regardless of, and as the conditions of, whatever particular discoveries scientists make. What we need are similar principles to guide our choices, principles that are applicable to all areas of our lives including the area of scientific investigation. Such principles of reasonable action, like the principles of scientific investigation, have to be self-imposed. But they would be universal oughts, and they would be both the human conditions of scientific investigation and the conditions of orderly, intelligent, and meaning-ful choice. Thus, if there are such things as moral principles or moral laws, they *would be universal principles in accordance with which a potentially rational person ought to make his choices.* Only by follow-ing these moral laws as well as he can could such a person be consid-ered reasonable in choosing. Furthermore, his choice could be intel-ligible to himself and others only on the basis of some such moral law.

Once one sees what the conception of moral law involves, both the importance and the justification of the search for such principles, on the one hand, and their imperative character, on the other hand, is not at all hard to grasp. The basic postulate on which moral princi-ples rest is that the good, the happy, the ethical life is at least the reasonable life. And the reasonable life is the life that involves both coherent criticism of value claims and of conflicting oughts, that is, reasonable decision, and consequent action enlightened by critical awareness of the circumstances in which the action takes place.

A. *Justification of the Search for Moral Principles*

Indeed, the justification of the search for moral principles is exactly the same and exactly as valid (and no more so) as the justification for the search for intelligibility and knowledge in any other area of experience. Every approximately normal human being is faced with a basic alternative, whether he has ever formulated it as such or not. He can recognize that it is better (in any sense) to be reasonable and to act coherently, or he can decide that it is better to be unreasonable and to act incoherently. If one takes the first alternative, he thereby obligates himself to search for and act in accordance with the most adequate principles of coherent action he possibly can find. On the other hand, if he decides it is better to be incoherent, he cannot justify any search for moral principles. If he really chooses incoher-ence, he is not even required to give himself a coherent account of his choice of incoherence. Such an individual shuts himself off from any intelligible discourse or rational persuasion. On the other hand, if one does take the first alternative and yet does not search for the conditions of coherent action or, having found such principles, does not act in accordance with them, he is in effect accepting incoherence and irrationality as much as if he had chosen them as principles.

B. *Reasonableness and Coherent Action*

But what does it mean to be reasonable or to act coherently? An adequate answer to this question would depend upon the discovery and elaboration of moral principles themselves, if, as we have suggested, moral principles are themselves the conditions of coherent action. But there is a prior problem of developing some idea of what "coherence" itself means.

"Reasonable" or "coherent" is not something we always are, either in thought or action. In fact, one of the major contributions of Freud and his successors has been to indicate how frequently, even when we believe we are being rational, our motivation springs from unrecognized, uncriticized, and irrational motivational sources. Quite apart from unrecognized, irrational motivations, the Socratic conception that knowledge is virtue, that to know what is right and reasonable itself assures right and reasonable action, is not borne out in experience. The hoary conversation piece to the effect that more ethics books are stolen than any other class of books in the library is not without its element of truth. The power of irrationality in human action is at least one of the factors that traditional Christianity has attempted to account for in the doctrine of original sin. In the light of such behavior, there are those who would insist that rationality and coherence have very little, if anything, to do with morality.

And yet, reasonableness and morality, we suggest, are inextricably bound up together. In fact, in the broadest sense the first would seem to be the condition of the possibility of the second. We have noted that, in practice, regardless of theory, psychoanalytic therapy rests upon the assumption that the only effective correction for irrational, chaotic, and debilitating motivational conflict lies in bringing the chaotic motivational sources to the surface, understanding them, and thereby disarming them. The psychotic or neurotic personality is, to the extent that it is psychotic or neurotic, "irrational." It would seem that the very possibility of normal personality and personality growth (for theories that range from Freud to Allport) lies in rational control or ordering of the nonrational motivational bases of action. "Where the id is," we repeat with Freud, "there shall the ego be!"

But one question persists: What constitutes rationality or reasonableness in this sense? It will be noted that we have used the terms "coherent" and "reasonable" as more or less synonymous. This usage is quite intentional, for the term "reason" has sometimes been taken in a far too restricted sense. Reasonableness or rationality applies most clearly to thought—to investigation, problem solving, and the attempt to understand. But, insofar as choice and action involve or follow from deliberation and awareness, reason applies to choice and action as well.

Now reasoning, first of all, involves logical consistency. In fact, "reason," used in the restricted sense, usually means "logic," that is, logical consistency alone and the deductive processes that the principles of logical consistency warrant. To think consistently involves keeping the meanings of one's terms constant, avoiding contradiction, and recognizing or working out the necessary relations or implications of the meanings of the terms employed. Thus if I say "Jean does better work than Joe," and "Joe does better work than Bill," it necessarily follows that Jean does better work than Bill. If, however, I mean something quite different by "better work" in the second sentence than in the first, or if I assert, "But Bill actually does better work than Jean," I have been inconsistent, and my assertions lose validity—I do not "make sense." Further, if I act on the basis of contradictory or inconsistent assertions, my actions will be as inconsistent as the assertions themselves.

"Reason," in the sense of formal consistency, is the prerequisite of intelligibility. Whenever we detect inconsistency in ourselves or others we can be sure that something is wrong. But it can be pointed out immediately that this is not all that we mean by "reason." In fact, if "reason" is taken in such a restricted sense, the claim that morality involves far more than reason is painfully evident.

An argument may be logically correct and yet the conclusion false. The following argument is a case in point: "All swimmers are ducks. All men are swimmers. Therefore all men are ducks." Here the conclusion necessarily ("logically") follows from the premises and yet the premises do not conform to experience. Without consistency, to be sure, no intelligible thought, conversation, or action is possible. But more than consistency is required before thought, conversation, or action can be considered "reasonable." One may well say of a person that he is logical but not reasonable!

What, in addition to formal consistency, does "reason" demand? The clue lies in the difficulty that we noted in the conclusion, "All men are ducks." To be reasonable means that one's beliefs or conclusions also conform to experience—that in arriving at beliefs one has taken into account as many different but relevant aspects of experience as possible and that the belief is consistent with the aspects or facts of experience included. To act reasonably thus also means to act in the light of past, present, and anticipated experience. A person who stores gasoline cans next to a furnace is acting no more reasonably than a European who concludes from a visit to Atlanta that all Americans talk with a Southern accent.

But even noting the facts of experience and proceeding with care to see that one's beliefs and actions are consistent with, that is, are not contradicted by, the facts—even this does not constitute sufficient guarantee of reasonableness. Reason also involves considering whether one's beliefs and actions are relevant to the facts included; whether the beliefs actually relate, or interrelate, the aspects of experience more clearly than any other set of beliefs based upon them; and whether the actions following from beliefs are ordered or structured with the facts clearly in mind. Finally, to be reasonable includes noting the continuing effect and relation of beliefs and action to experience as it proceeds, and being willing to modify and revise action and belief as changing conditions and additional facts make necessary.

It is reason in this sense of involving striving for consistency, inclusiveness, systematic relevance, and fruitfulness that can be considered synonymous with coherence or what might be more easily called "experiental coherence." It is in this sense also that we are concerned with moral principles as the conditions of coherent choice and action.

Just as no one can force anyone else to abide by the conditions of sound scientific investigation, so no one can force anyone else to be coherent in his actions. No legislature or governor can enact or decree that I shall be rational. No social group as such, by all the force of its approval or disapproval, can make a person consider his actions coherently, although a group may encourage or discourage such coherence. Only an individual can consent to try to be reasonable in his actions and thereby impose the conditions of coherent choice and action upon himself. Moral principles in their very nature have to be self-imposed. But by virtue of their self-imposed character, like the conditions of scientific investigation, such principles are universal in the sense that they are proposed as applying to all potentially reasonable persons engaged in the same search.

C. *"Self-imposed" Character of Moral Principles*

An additional word needs to be said about the meaning of "self-imposed." Self-imposed as applied either to the principles of scientific investigation or to moral principles does not mean that the principles in question are arbitrary or matters of whim. In the case of the principles of scientific investigation, the scientist does not know that the scientific method will, in fact, bring success. Yet, trusting in logic and reason as it applies to the solution of scientific problems, he decides on certain principles to guide him. These principles appear to be not the scientist's arbitrary impositions on events, nor the one-way imposition of "natural events" on him; they are principles that he believes that his own interaction with the world is recommending to him as a guide to truth. So also, moral principles are neither arbitrary impositions nor matters of whim. Rather they are what persons who choose come to believe from experience are constitutive conditions that their experiments in living reveal to them (but do not force upon them) if they are to live as fully and meaningfully as possible. We cannot find happiness or truth any old way; its principles are to be discovered in and through life experiences; and we ought to live by them if we are to live as meaningfully or coherently as possible.

D. *"Universal" Character of Moral Principles*

As soon as the term "universal" is applied to moral principles, several objections are likely to arise. First, our old friends the relativists remind us of a very discouraging situation. The actual moral rules of people do vary to such an extent that not only between cultures, but even in a single culture, no one type of action is approved in all circumstances. Probably most individuals have been dismayed to discover for themselves that what is seemingly right at one time and in one place may not be at all right in another place and time. Even such commandments as "Thou shalt not kill" and "Thou shalt not steal" may have their exceptions.

Again, what the relativist points to is an important fact, but he draws from it an unnecessarily defeatist conclusion. The situation to which he surrenders serves in fact only to emphasize the importance of drawing a clear distinction between *rules* regarding specific acts and the *principles* in terms of which specific acts and choices can be considered moral and reasonable. But this distinction between rules and principles is itself a key to the universality of moral principles. The very fact that many of us do recognize circumstances when the right and moral thing to do might very well be to kill indicates that we do both recognize and appeal to certain principles or conditions of coherent action that are far more fundamental than any specific rules of action.

Let us consider only one example of the character and force of such a principle: Regardless of who I am, I can hardly consider my actions either coherent or moral and thus intelligently responsible if I fail to take into account the specific situation in which I find myself. Indeed, because every act does take place in a culture, at a time, and on some occasion, I rationally ought to take into account the specific conditions of action. Interestingly and ironically enough, some of the major defenders of relativism have actually been so concerned that this principle of specification (as one might call it) not be violated that they have forgotten that they are really urging the universality of the principle of specification itself (cf. Chapter 24). We may well admit that whether *particular acts* are right or wrong is relative to the persons, circumstances, and occasions of their performance, but for this very reason we would insist that the principles for determining whether they are right or wrong are universal.

E. *"Formal" Character of Moral Principles*

Another and opposite type of objection is likely to arise once we contend that moral principles are not rules regarding particular types of action. If moral principles do not command particular acts as such, we might be asked, do they not become so general and so formal as to be empty? It is well and good to say "Act reasonably!" but does this help the truck driver when a pedestrian steps out from behind a parked car in a narrow and crowded street? Or does it help the doctor who must decide whether to save the mother or the expected child in an emergency when he knows he cannot save both? Do such moral principles really have any content?

In one respect it must be admitted that moral principles are formal. That is, in themselves they are not lists of specific "Do's" and "Don'ts." Life may never be simple enough to make such absolute rules and listings tenable. But it must also be remembered that moral principles are only moral as applied to actual changing life situations. They are guides, not formulas, which, like rubber stamps, can be pressed onto living. They indicate the conditions of reasonable action but do not sanction actions in the abstract apart from the context of action. The two things fatal to the truck driver and the doctor would be (1) losing their heads and (2) indecision. The content to which moral principles apply is the whole of our experiences as these bear upon choice. Moral principles might well be considered as analogous to the laws of logic and the rules of syntax, whereas specific acts are like the terms used in propositions. If I am to make sense, I must apply the laws of logic and the rules of syntax regardless of the specific subject matter or terms employed in conversation. Moral principles might be said to be the conditions for making sense in our choosing.

Granted that at least some of the acts we perform and the choices we make may be reasonable, then it would follow that there must be conditions of the reasonableness of action in the light of which our choices and actions may be appropriately guided. Our task now becomes that of attempting to discover more specifically what some of the most pertinent of these principles may be.

V. *REFLECTIVE SUMMARY*

In Part IV we are looking at the problem of moral choice with a view to answering the questions of this chapter: Are there principles for guiding moral choice? In the process of developing our answers, we shall have occasion to refer to and use data and ideas already advanced in this book. We hope that, as the Principles are developed, their systematic connection with each other will be clear. Furthermore, we believe that the truth in different ethical perspectives is accommodated in some such suggested system of moral laws, whose ultimate justification is their capacity to clarify and connect the different facets of moral choice. But first we must, in this preliminary chapter, suggest what we mean by holding that there are principles or laws that can guide us as we choose among value experiences and obligation.

If these principles were the pressures of custom or the outright prescription of civil law, they would not be adequate guides. For ethical action is not necessarily action in conformity to social expectancy or even to law. Indeed, the good on such views would reduce to the wish of the majority or of the stronger.

Nor can the principles we seek be scientific laws. For scientific laws describe the regular sequences between events. What we seek are ideals, and "ideal" in the scientific realm means "what may be expected to occur under optimum conditions." Furthermore, uniform natural sequences cannot be "broken" (as can ethical laws), and they operate without dependence on moral decisions. Nevertheless, we learn several illuminating things by analyzing the nature of scientific laws.

Basic is the realization that the sequences in the natural world are discovered by scientists only as they govern themselves by man-made scientific method. This method does not operate itself, but calls for thought and action in accordance with such ideals as objectivity, courage, and honesty (which are not themselves scientific descriptions). In other words, the principles of scientific method, can be broken, because they are human ideals of investigation; but they cannot be persistently disregarded by him who would discover truth about the world. In short, although these principles are man-made, and not "in the events," as persons we legislate them for ourselves, regardless of cultural differences, because we have discovered them to be appropriate to satisfying intellectual and practical needs. Thus, scientific principles of investigation are self-imposed universal conditions for guiding scientific research, anywhere, at any time.

The principles for guiding moral action must also be self-imposed and universal. But unlike scientific laws, they will tell us not what is, has been, and will be, but what ought to be in every area of life. Such principles, like the principles of scientific investigation, cannot be forced on anyone who is not capable of reason and who does not wish to be coherent. But, our contention is this: ethical choice and ethical action are invalid on any other basis and will suffer to the extent that such universal principles are not followed. For these principles, though not forced upon man arbitrarily, are "suggestions" made to him and critically developed by him in the process of his interaction with the world.

Finally, moral principles are universal without being rules of action in specific situations. On the other hand, they are guides for deciding what rules and what specific actions are most reasonable in choice situations.

With this meaning for "moral principle" in mind, we proceed to suggest a series of principles, which, like the symphony of values and the scheme of virtues, are interpenetrating and cannot be used "in part" without serious loss of value.

19

Consistency—A First Condition of Ethical Choice

~~~~~~

I. PRACTICAL INCONSISTENCY

On foreign policy, we Americans like to think of ourselves as acting out of a real and disinterested concern for the well-being of the world as a whole. We have traditions, of independence, a high standard of living, and democracy that we believe other nations and peoples of the world ought to have the opportunity to develop. We feel that we ought to help them to take advantage of this opportunity, whether in fact they do develop them or not. To be sure, we remind ourselves that we should be realistic about this and not flagrantly disregard our own welfare and interests in the process of helping the oppressed, the starving, and those struggling for freedom, but we are willing to make sacrifices when the need is urgent. On the whole, we insist that we have no major axes to grind and thus are in a position to exert moral and humanitarian leadership throughout the world.

But we have in the past offered grain to India in time of famine on the condition that India change its foreign policy to conform more closely to our own. We did support France militarily in the Indo-Chinese War without insisting or even urging very strongly that France grant independence to the Indo-Chinese. We sent economic aid to European nations but in some cases insisted that aid be spent for American products; in the meantime we increased tariffs so that European products could not compete with our own in the American market. We diminished the Point Four program of technical aid to a minimum while increasing our own arms program to the limit. Then we wonder why we were accused of fostering colonialism, of being imperialistically minded. We could not understand why industrial recovery was not more rapid among some of our European allies. We did not see why our motives were looked upon with suspicion, and were often misinterpreted.

In our own country we realize the importance of education. We recognize that there has never been a period in which clear thinking on the part of all citizens is more important than the present, if democracy itself is to survive. We provided for the education of those who served in the armed forces in the Second World War and the Korean conflict. Many parents deprive themselves of other things that they desire in order to send their children to college. Most parents take pride in the academic achievements of their children at every level in the educational process. Most parents and citizens support and believe in the extension and improvement of public education.

And yet at the same time we are suspicious of "brain-trusters." We seriously propose censoring books in university libraries. We criticize a presidential candidate for being an intellectual, an "egghead." Teachers' salaries remain so low that many well-qualified teachers are forced into other lines of work. All too many of us nod in agreement when someone voices the popular legend that those people become teachers who cannot do anything else. "Otherwise," we are apt to add, "why are they not out making money?"

This anti-intellectual bias is not confined to the uneducated and less affluent members of our society. One of the wealthiest men in the country, a Texas oil millionaire in the $200-million to $300-million class, is reputed to have included college professors, eggheads, and longhairs of all types and varieties, along with card-carrying Communists among the termites destroying the American way of life.[1] And then we wonder why our schools are not more effective, why our citizenry is not better informed, why some of the people elected to office get there, and why we do not attract higher caliber teachers.

[1] Cf. *Fortune* (May 1954) for a fascinating discussion of the political views of some of the wealthiest men in the country.

We insist on the right of every individual to make up his mind for himself. We pride ourselves on a history of religious, political, and academic freedom. We believe that an informed citizen is a good citizen and that the best protection for our "way of life" lies in being informed, not only about men of like opinion with us, but also about those who disagree. We believe that the average citizen will make up his mind intelligently if he has access to both sides of every question. Yet a leading Boston newspaper seriously proposed keeping under lock and key all books on Communism and by communistic authors in the Boston Public Library and also specially recording the names of persons requesting any of these books. And then we wonder why the average American knows so little about the Communism he opposes other than the fact that he opposes it.

A great many students begin the college semester with high resolve to get the most they can out of college educationally. They have worked hard during the summer to earn the means for studying. But the early fall weather is felt to be not very conducive to studying. Football games, dances, trips to the country, all worthwhile and important in their place, seem much more urgent than "hitting the books." The night before the first quiz a particularly important fraternity meeting is scheduled, to which, of course, one has to go. Then such a student is likely to wonder why he is on probation rather than the Dean's list. Often he seeks to rise above such a contretemps by references to "boring courses," "ghastly texts," or by such gems of sophomoric wisdom as "after all, education is not restricted to the classroom."

II. ACTION NONSENSE

One need not be an "egghead" to discern a common pattern running through the above examples. Each of them illustrates basic inconsistency in choice itself—inconsistency between goals or ends chosen, or inconsistency between ends chosen and the means chosen to attain them, or both. And the result in each case is the same: failure in regard to basic aim itself leads to irrational and inconsistent action and chaos. Probably every reader could multiply examples of such failure on every level of human behavior. They are marked not primarily by unavoidable failure or misfortune essentially due to conditions beyond the control of the persons concerned. Rather the failure in each case has a peculiarly moral character. It is based on contradictory choices, choices of conflicting value claims at one and the same time, choice of wants in opposition to oughts. The series of actions involved in each example does not make what we might call action sense.

Our task at this stage is not that of deciding which of the alternatives in any case is correct or even objectively right. Our aim is more fundamental: to determine how we can begin to make action sense, or moral sense when choices are possible. If, as we have indicated, moral principles are the conditions of reasonable or coherent action, what we are now asking is not "When is an action fully ethical?" but, "What is the first or minimum condition of action sense or coherent action?"

Both the nature of our question and the examples cited above point rather clearly to such a minimum or first condition of action sense. In order to make sense in communication or in my own thoughts, there must be a consistency of my thoughts or my communicated ideas with each other. Insofar as my thoughts contradict each other, they are nonsense thoughts. Insofar as my statements contradict each other, I do not make sense: I talk nonsense. In the same way, insofar as my intentions, my choices, and my actions contradict each other, I fall into nonsensical action, chaos, and moral failure.

III. *PRINCIPLE OF CONSISTENCY*

There must, then, be a first or minimum condition of effective and meaningful choice, and we can state it in the form of a moral principle as follows: *Each person ought to choose consistently or logically;* in other words, he ought not to choose on the basis of conflicting and contradictory intentions, or choose conflicting and contradictory actions, or choose conflicting and contradictory means and ends.[2]

This Principle of Consistency in choosing is actually so fundamental and at the same time so simple a principle that one may overlook it entirely on the level of popular moral discussion. Often we take it for granted without adequate recognition of its implication, or we acknowledge it only after the failure to remember it has

[2] Cf. E. S. Brightman, *Moral Laws* (New York: The Abingdon Press, 1933), p. 98.

wrought havoc in our lives. And yet it takes no great depth of insight to recognize that on this simple principle rests the very possibility of controlled and effective action. To choose contradictories is equivalent to not choosing at all or, worse, to choosing chaos itself. My intentions may be of the highest order, and yet if I do not implement them by consistent choice, they remain morally worthless and only add to my own sense of frustration and confusion. Insofar as I fail to choose consistently, I find myself a victim of the strongest inclination, desire, or social pressure of the moment. I lose whatever freedom and self-control I might be capable of, and I become the plaything of forces within me or outside me over which I have progressively less control.

A. *Consistency and Psychological Health*

This need for consistency comes about as close as anything could to being a fundamental need of the human mind itself. Consistency of ends and consistency of ends and means, are required not only on the level of moral consideration but for the very maintenance of psychological health. The sick mind would often seem to be the mind that has given in to unnecessary conflict involving logically unresolvable contradictions. Freud rather clearly pointed out that mental illness follows to the degree that a person withdraws into the world of fantasy primarily to avoid the seeming contradictions between the reality around it and its own desire for pleasure.

The failure to choose consistently is, according to H. A. Overstreet, one of the major characteristics and causes of emotional and psychological immaturity. To the extent that an individual is

> unreasonable—a creature of impulse, of prejudice, of rationalizations—he passes judgments and performs actions that do not comport with the realities of his environment. Therefore, in a multitude of ways, he does what he ought not to do and leaves undone what he ought to have done—thereby compounding friction rather than harmony.[3]

Although Overstreet has more in mind in this passage than consistency of choice alone, he does make it quite clear that the root of the difficulty lies in irrationality.[4] Positively, he suggests that the

[3] *The Mature Mind* (New York: W. W. Norton and Company, Inc., 1949), p. 105.
[4] *Ibid.*

ability to see logical implications, to overcome inconsistencies, is a prime condition (though not the only condition) of emotional maturity.

> The human mind has, as one of its most unique potentials, the capacity to see such logical implications. If it develops healthily from infancy through childhood, and on into adulthood, this inborn capacity becomes a more and more adequately developed tool.[5]

Admittedly, the development of the potential for seeing logical implications and recognizing contradictions is not automatic, and it may be, in fact is, frequently checked along the way by what Overstreet calls "emotional road blocks," such as unconscious or unrecognized sources of conflict. And yet, unless the individual does use the ability he does have for grasping logical relations and does choose as consistently as he can, the possibility of self-direction and continued growth toward maturity is lost. Further, once self-direction is seriously weakened, the very possibility [6] of return to health depends to a large extent upon the help the psychoanalyst may give in uncovering the conflicting or contradictory motivational sources and in helping the individual to regain confidence in his own capacity for self-direction. Only the patient who can see the conflicts or contradictions for what they are is likely to overcome them.

B. *Rationalization*

Our human nature's basic demand for consistency is rather nicely illustrated in our very defense mechanisms against our own inconsistencies. Even when we have not chosen consistently, becoming aware of the fact, we seem to be impelled to give our inconsistent choices the appearance of consistency. We set up patterns or sequences of events that our acts presumably followed, or we reinterpret our actions in a favorable order or context, whether or not that order or context existed when we made our choice. This is the all too familiar process of rationalization, a process of pseudo-justification to meet the unsatisfied demand for consistency.

Erich Fromm [7] in particular has stressed the fact that the mind

---

[5] *Ibid.,* pp. 106–7.

[6] See the essay by Carl Rogers. "The Meaning of the Good Life," in Alfred E. Kuenzli (ed.), *Reconstruction in Religion* (Boston: Beacon Press, 1961), pp. 173–89.

[7] *Man for Himself* (New York: Rinehart and Company, Inc., 1947), pp. 39–41, and *Escape from Freedom* (New York: Rinehart and Company, Inc., 1941), pp. 33 ff.

cannot remain passive in the fact of incompatibilities, incongruities, and contradictions of its own making or otherwise. If the individual cannot solve the conflicts or remove the contradictions, he denies that they exist at all. In effect, rationalization is exactly such a denial. The case we have cited of students who claimed that courses were boring and their textbooks impossible and who yet sought comfort in the thought that education is not confined to the classroom beautifully illustrates the attempt to rationalize the inconsistencies of their own choices. Blaming failures of foreign policy on the ungratefulness, jealousy, and stupidity of other nations all too often reflects a similar attempt to deny the contradictions in our own attitudes and actions.

Some contemporary existentialists, for example Simone de Beauvoir, maintain that the development and the wide acceptance of such deterministic and materialistic philosophies as Marxism and so-called scientific determinism are themselves examples of an extreme rationalization to avoid the guilt and insecurity inevitably following from our inconsistency and incoherence in choice and attitude, nationally and internationally, and the enduring chaos of the second quarter of the twentieth century.[8] The easiest way to get rid of responsibility is to deny that it exists! The existentialist dismissal of determinism as wholly a rationalization is probably too facile an answer to a very difficult problem. Yet it must be admitted that, after our contradictory choices have brought frustration, failure, and injury to ourselves or others, we do tend to argue that we could not have chosen otherwise in the circumstances, or that we were compelled to act as we did. This is a temptingly easy way of giving our acts an appearance of consistency.

Our tendency to rationalize has sometimes been cited as itself evidence of the impossibility of our ever choosing consistently. Our actions, it is alleged, can only spring from their roots in irrational drives and impulses; to think about them can only give them the look of respectability. We never know the difference between rational action and rationalized action.

It must be admitted that the danger of rationalization is always present. All of us probably rationalize more than we realize or care to admit. Yet the very fact that we are able to recognize rationalization in ourselves and others at least part of the time refutes the

[8] Simone de Beauvoir, *Ethics of Ambiguity,* trans. B. Frechtman (New York: Philosophical Library, 1948), pp. 34, 109.

claim that all thinking about action is rationalization. If all thinking were rationalization, we could never know that we do sometimes rationalize. The very statement that to think a given thought is rationalizing would then itself be rationalization and could not be known to be true. Quite to the contrary, the fact of rationalization and its prevalence underline the psychological as well as the moral need for rationality and its first condition, consistency. The only possible effective check on rationalization is not giving up the attempt to be rational. It is more rationality—that is, from the standpoint of our present concern, more careful consideration before and during action so that our choices—motives, ends and the means to them—may be as consistent with each other as possible.

C. *The Stoics and Kant*

The recognition of the importance of consistency in choice as a minimum condition of moral action goes back again to the ancient Greek and Roman ethicists. As we have pointed out in Chapter 10, Socrates, Plato, Aristotle, and the Stoics all recognized that the foundation of the ethical life lies in the potentially rational nature of men. Only beings who can reason, who can become aware of the meaningfulness and, as the first condition of meaningfulness, the consistency of their actions, can be concerned with the rightness or wrongness, goodness or badness of their actions. Again, it was the Stoics in particular who insisted that what power men do have lies in their willed control of their choice life. We may not control or have power over accidents of nature or those of fame and fortune. We cannot be blamed, nor can we blame ourselves, for the color of our skins, the place of our birth, the oil under our neighbor's land but not under ours. We can, however, be blamed, and we blame ourselves, for the attitudes that we take and what we do about these things—for the consistency or inconsistency of our wills.[9] In fact, carrying this idea to an extreme, the Stoics insisted that, no matter what men or fortune or the gods do to me, I remain the master of my fate as long as I consistently control my own will. Ironically, it was Epictetus, the Roman slave, who said, "What say you, fellow?

---

[9] The Stoics' doctrine of freedom of will was hardly consistent with their theory of reality. But for the essential conviction that man is responsible for what he does about what happens to him, see C. I. Lewis, *The Ground and Nature of the Right* (New York: Columbia University Press, 1955).

Chain me? My leg you will chain—yes, but my will—no, not even Zeus can conquer that." [10]

Among modern philosophers, perhaps Immanuel Kant has more clearly seen the importance of a consistent will than any other thinker. Kant insisted that, except for consistent willing, man is completely determined by forces over which he has no control. Yet man becomes truly human, man attains his freedom and dignity, only through the impartial, consistent performance of his duty. In fact, Kant contended that I ought so to choose that my actions would be consistent with each other, and in such a way that, if the maxim (or principle or basis) on which I acted were made universal, all men could act in the same way without contradiction or destruction of the meaningfulness of the act itself. I should always ask myself: How would I like to have this action, at this juncture, forced upon me as a law of nature?

Thus, for example, before I tell a lie, Kant would insist that I ought to ask whether or not everyone could consistently and meaningfully lie under the circumstances, or whether the very idea of universal lying would not destroy the meaningfulness of lying itself. The force of a lie depends upon the fact that it is believed to be the truth. If every one lied, no one would believe anyone and the very meaning of lying would be destroyed. Stealing will serve equally well as an example. To steal means to take the property of another. If everyone stole, then no one could claim property as his own, and it would be meaningless to call such appropriation stealing.

The similarity of Kant's principle to the Golden Rule is not hard to see. Essentially Kant is insisting that I should so choose that I would be willing to have everyone else choose the same way and not make myself an exception. While Kant's extension of consistency to cover all cases of particular acts involves difficulties of its own, his recognition, along with the Stoics', that consistent willing is the foundation of order in moral choice is of basic importance.

IV. OBJECTIONS TO CONSISTENCY

A. Rigid Consistency and Emerson

Important as consistent willing or choice seems to be, not only for the possibility of moral action, but also for psychological health and

---

[10] *Discourses*, Book I, Chapter I, trans. P. E. Matheson, in Whitney J. Oates (ed.), *The Stoic and Epicurean Philosophers* (New York: Random House, 1940), p. 225.

emotional maturity, at least two closely related objections are often raised against it. One of these objections was strikingly and extremely phrased by Emerson in his essay "Self Reliance." "A foolish consistency," Emerson insisted, "is the hobgoblin of little minds, adored by little statesmen and philosophers and divines. With consistency a great soul has simply nothing to do." [11] Emerson's statement, on the surface at least, would seem to involve the rejection of consistency altogether as an evil and confusing thing. So interpreted, Emerson would have a good many contemporary followers.

But taken in this extreme form, Emerson's statement would reduce thought and action to chaos. The "great soul" in this sense would be the completely undependable soul. Such a soul might have great flashes of insight, but there would be no assurance either that he would act upon them or that he would not in the next breath deny the insight. It is hard to see how such a soul could ever exercise the requisite self-discipline to approach greatness. At best, such a "great soul" would have to be something like the Delphic oracle, whose babblings had to be interpreted by "lesser" men before they had any practical relevance for action. Although Emerson's phraseology in his second sentence would seem to support such an interpretation, it is highly doubtful, when the statement is taken as a whole and in context, that Emerson meant anything so extreme.

The clue to what Emerson probably meant, and an important warning in regard to consistency, lies in the first part of his statement. Emerson was objecting to a "foolish consistency," the kind of rigidness or pettiness of attitude and action that involves the refusal to learn anything new, the refusal to change one's opinions regardless of the situation, the refusal to benefit from experience and failure. It is quite true that such a rigid adherence to preformed premises regardless of experience can and does become a major block not only to greatness but to the moral life in any of its forms. The person who is a "consistent Republican (or Democrat)," no matter what the issues or who the candidates, hardly has the best interests of community or country in mind. To avoid breaking the pattern of his actions, he may even be brought to vote in conflict with his own interests! Emerson notes that "nature is not slow to equip us in the prison-uniform of the party to which we adhere." [12]

Other examples are furnished by the teacher who refuses to try

[11] Ralph Waldo Emerson, *Essays, First Series* (Boston: Houghton, Mifflin Co., 1865), p. 57.
[12] *Ibid.*, p. 55.

new texts or new methods of instruction, the housewife who refuses to try new labor-saving devices or new recipes, the person who has made up his mind on some particular question and refuses to consider new evidence or alternative positions and answers. Such rigid consistency may paradoxically be an escape mechanism from a truly consistent facing of experience. Because, at an earlier stage of life, we could resolve conflict and contradiction in only one way, we have steadily refused to consider any other solution. Such consistency becomes a special form of rationalization. But the rejection of such "foolish consistency" does not constitute a rejection of the Principle of Consistency in choosing. On the contrary, in a very basic way it tends to illustrate it. Choosing consistently itself involves learning from past experience, discovering means consistent with the ends that I chose and choosing them, and choosing ends that are consistent with what I can accomplish.

B. *Life is Deeper Than Logic*

Emerson may have had something more in mind, something that leads to a second and much more pertinent objection to the Principle of Consistency in choosing. Emerson was very much impressed with the potential richness of human life, with the often untapped resources of emotion, imagination, and insight that transcend the limits of strict logical discourse or action based upon calculating logical discrimination alone. The good life, for Emerson, is the whole life of feeling, willing, wanting, attaining, achieving. With such later thinkers as Borden Parker Bowne, William James, Henri Bergson, Alfred North Whitehead, and the contemporary existentialists, Emerson would want to insist that life is deeper than logic.[13] And there would be few men other than the narrowest and most extreme of rationalists who would disagree with him. Our discussion of the symphony of values and the scheme of virtues and the suggestions we shall later make about the place of religion in the good life place the authors firmly on the side of Emerson and Bowne at this point.

What is the conclusion to be drawn from this recognition of the breadth of life and the importance of nonrational factors in the good life? Does it mean that life should be irrational and inconsistent, as some men have concluded? To answer affirmatively is to re-

[13] See Brand Blanshard's chapter "The Rational Temper," in *Reason and Goodness* (New York: The Macmillan Co., 1961), for a balanced discussion of this polarity between "life and logic."

turn to meaninglessness and chaos; it is to give up altogether the quest for the good life and the possibility of moral action. To recognize that life is more than logic is not at all the same thing as to say that life should be illogical or that we should encourage inconsistency. Rather is it to recognize that when one chooses consistently he does not simply choose some abstract thing called "consistency." He chooses courses of action, ends, values, ideals, things, attitudes, virtues. Consistency is simply one condition and a basic condition of choosing meaningfully among the vast variety of possible contents of life; it is the first condition of bringing order out of chaos.

C. *Consistency Not Enough*

The authors willingly concede that mere consistency of choice, important as it is, is not enough in itself for moral or intelligent or mature living. Indeed consistency may produce fanatics at the same time that it produces martyrs. And yet there can be no *strong character* (not personality) without it! It may produce a Gandhi or a Hitler. It needs further guidance, but we become aimless without it. Consistency of choices, we believe, is the first condition, not the sufficient condition, of the good and moral life.

Within limits a man may be consistent in evil as well as in good. The calculating criminal, for example, is usually highly consistent within the framework of his particular desires. All that the Principle of Consistency by itself says is: "Do not vacillate!" "Do not choose means that contradict or destroy or conflict with the ends you have chosen!" "Do not both choose and not choose the same thing at the same time!" It says nothing in itself about the ends I ought to choose, other than that they ought not to contradict each other. Should we be concerned with helping the world's needy or with enlarging our bank balances? Should we support education or support control of an ignorant population through force? Should we do a good job at work or spend all of our time on the social amenities? The Principle of Consistency in itself does not offer much help in deciding these questions. But it can be a dependable guide through the process of choosing.

D. *Consistency, a Minimum Principle*

On the one hand, then, we have discovered a minimum or first principle of moral action. I ought to choose consistently. If I do not, my actions will nullify each other; I lose whatever control and responsibility are potentially mine. This principle meets the conditions to which, we said in the last chapter, a moral principle, in our meaning for that term, must subscribe. It is both self-imposed and universal. Because I am the only one who can make my choices consistent, the principle has to be self-imposed. The principle is universal not in the sense that all men are consistent or have to be consistent, but in the sense that insofar as a man's actions are to accomplish anything more than momentary ends, whether he be a Trobriand Islander or a Gothamite, he needs to choose consistently. We have discovered this principle by recognizing our nature's possibilities in relation to the natures of other people and the nature of the world in which we live. We did not "make it up"; we found it as a condition of introducing order in our lives and reducing chaos, as a condition of strength rather than weakness, as a condition of integration rather than disintegration.

But, on the other hand, we have also discovered that this principle of consistent choice is a minimum principle; it is not enough in itself. I may be consistent and still be far from fully moral or fully rational behavior. With what, then, aside from each other, ought my choices to be consistent? In relationship to what does my responsibility for consistent choice lie? These questions lead to a fundamental question that we must now consider. In the light of what ideals should I choose and what makes them morally binding?

V. REFLECTIVE SUMMARY

Our first hypothesis for a universal principle for guiding moral choice, a principle to be self-imposed and yet by no means "man-made," is this: All persons ought to will consistently. Why?

No matter how ideal one's intentions, if his choice of means is inconsistent with them, or if other intentions are inconsistent with them, his actions will nullify each other, and the weakness born of confusion and failure will ensue.

The thesis that persons cannot reason but can only rationalize reduces the thesis itself to a rationalization that is not to be trusted. The least we can do, as we plan our choice of values, is to organize our goals, motives, and means so that they are not contradictory with each other or in needless conflict.

The Greeks—the Stoics in particular—realized that although men are not responsible for what is beyond their control, they, as reason-capable beings, can at least be responsible for the attitudes that they take toward whatever happens to them. Kant went a step further and declared that a person is ethical only to the extent that he chooses actions whose maxims he would be willing to have enforced (like physical laws) upon himself and upon all other persons at that choice point. Thus, lying is always unethical; if lying were universalized, it would render lies ineffective, because no one would be deceived.

Yet consistency must not be taken to require adherence to a path of action simply because it has dominated the past. Nor does consistency demand that persons turn their backs on the richness of life. To be inconsistent is to be unwilling to organize the riches of life in such a way that as many riches as possible can be realized.

At the same time, by following consistency alone we can never decide what the stuff of living is to be—in what direction we shall seek our values and virtues or our style of life. Although we can never kick consistency out from under us, as we might a ladder, we need further guidance in selecting what "walls of value" we ought to scale.

20

What Makes Ideals Binding?

~~~~~~

I. *BASIS OF MORAL RESPONSIBILITIES*

When one must decide what vocation he ought to choose, how he ought to vote in the next election, whether or not he ought to lend his automobile to a roommate, it may not help much to urge: Will consistently! A person may indeed recognize that inconsistent or contradictory actions are self-defeating, and he soon realizes that he cannot be consistent in a vacuum. His choices occur within the complex context of every-day living, with its many confusing and conflicting alternatives. The crucial question becomes: With what ought one to be consistent? Our immediate problem is not that of attempting to answer the question in full, but rather that of searching for a first step toward an answer.

The search for this first step might take the form of asking several other questions: What is the source of moral authority for me? What determines my responsibility as I see or experience it? Where does my moral responsibility lie? But even these questions need to be rather carefully considered before their full import becomes evident. We are not concerned at this stage with the specific content of one's responsibility. One may or may not feel responsible for telling the truth or feeding the dog. Our question here is not what a person feels responsible for but *how* he comes to feel responsible—the basis of one's responsibility.

A. *Responsibility and Choice*

At the outset we need to distinguish between two different senses of the term "responsible." In a broad sense, one may say that the storm is responsible for the flood or that deterioration of environmental conditions is responsible for the spread of juvenile delinquency or that the man who has a heart attack while driving his automobile is responsible for the ensuing accident. So used, the term seems to mean any state, condition, or occurrence in its relation of contributing cause to any other state of affairs. But so used, it clearly does not indicate moral responsibility, although under certain conditions moral responsibility may be indirectly involved in the flood, the accident, or more directly in the case of juvenile delinquency.

Our discussion of the nature of moral law and the fundamental role of consistency in choice has already indicated that moral responsibility can only be present when recognized choice is possible and events are to some extent believed to be within our control. The control present may in some cases be no more than a control over one's own attitude toward events. But at best this much control, including a choice in regard to attitudes, would seem to be prerequisite to any legitimate assignment or recognition of responsibility.

Neither in the case of the storm nor in the case of the man with a heart attack, insofar as the attack was not intentionally induced or brought on by negligence, is direct or obvious moral responsibility involved. Neither the storm nor the heart attack is a matter of intention or choice. It is doubtful whether any one or any group chooses or intends that there shall be a single juvenile delinquent, not to mention intending that juvenile delinquency shall spread. However, even in the case of the flood following the storm, the situation may be more complex morally than at first appears. The storm itself cannot be held morally responsible for anything, nor can men be held responsible for the storm. But suppose the flood following the storm occurred in an area that had been denuded of trees. Suppose, further, that the trees had been cut for quick profit by men fully aware of the effects of deforestation. Moral responsibility then enters the picture.

Whether or not moral responsibility is present in the case of the spread of juvenile delinquency depends upon what is meant by environmental deterioration. It may well be the case that those who recognized the deteriorating conditions, the dangers and personality destruction involved, and who could have helped improve conditions in the home and community share morally in responsibility for the situation. But where exactly lies the clue to moral responsibility itself?

B. *Responsibility and Ideals*

Something in addition to the abstract possibility of choice with some measure of control is necessary before responsibility becomes morally significant. On an afternoon stroll, whether I take the right hand or the left hand path more often than not is a matter of little moral importance. But whether I cheat in an examination, or spread tales about the next door neighbor, or fail to pay bills, is not by any means a matter of moral indifference. The additional factor necessary for meaningful moral responsibility is the recognition that something ought to be done or, more specifically, that I ought to do something to better the situation. In order to recognize that a situation is not what it could be, that it could be improved, or that some alternative open to me will result in impoverishment or deterioration of the situation, I must have some conception of what ought to be done, some ideal in terms of which my choice is meaningful. In other words, to choose intelligently I must choose in accordance with an ideal. Insofar as I do choose with an ideal in mind, I am morally responsible for my choice, whether I finally choose in accordance with the ideal or not.

We need, obviously, to be clear about what the term "ideal" embraces. An ideal includes *the conception of experiences that individuals value, or the conception that, if realized or actually experienced, would yield dependable values*. The ideal is not the experience of value, but the conception of what that value would be. A man cannot know the value experience of being a mother, but he can be responsible for an ideal of motherhood. He can will responsibly an ideal of justice not yet completely experienced. Thus, for Hitler one ideal evidently was world domination by the Aryan and, in particular, the Germanic race. For a follower of Islam a major ideal would be universal acceptance of Allah with Mohammed as his highest prophet. For some people the economic ideal is free enterprise with no government interference; for other persons the economic ideal is government control of the major means of production. In any conceivable area of experience, we find ourselves faced with ideal claims and counterclaims.

C. *Conflict of Ideals*

Clearly the range of possible ideals, like the range of possible values, includes a virtual infinity of contradictions and contraries. One could not choose in harmony with all possible ideals even if he wished. For example, to choose in the light of ideals of Aryan dominance, of Chinese dominance, and of the dignity and brotherhood of all men at one and the same time simply cannot be done no matter how agile an intellectual contortionist you may be. Rational moral responsibility, then, can arise only in relation to a certain group or class of ideals, that is, those ideals that are somehow binding for oneself. It is these ideals in accordance with which one's moral responsibility is determined and in accordance with which one ought to choose consistently.

But again the question arises as to what ideals are morally binding on us. Aside from the welter of possible ideals, many of which are so remote that they are not seriously entertained, we find that by the time we begin to think for ourselves and can consider our own actions critically, we are faced with a multitude of actual ideal-demands made from a wide range of sources and authorities. For most of us, our parents constituted the first positive and negative sources of an awareness of ideals. At a relatively early age we became aware of what our parents did and did not expect of us. And it must be admitted, entirely too frequently the positive ideal or basis on which the parental "no" rested was never made clear. When it was not, we never actually understood why we were expected to behave in certain ways rather than others, even though we did act as expected. Later we may have found that vague, negative ideals (accompanied, when violated, by irrational feelings of guilt stemming, in large part, from unexplained parental demands in childhood) blocked the development of positive convictions of what we ought to do. As our social contacts increased from the family circle to playmates, to school teachers, to representatives of church and state, and, most important, to our adolescent contemporaries, the range of demands on us and ideals presented to us, with their corresponding action claims, increased. What our parents demanded and what our contemporaries and other accepted authorities demanded often conflicted.

Yet it is in exactly such cases of conflict that decision becomes most difficult and most important. To choose conflicting or contradictory ideals is to give up the attempt to live intelligently; it is to violate the logical principle and to head for serious psychological disturbance. At the same time, to insist on ideals that are clearly beyond a person's ability to realize is to misconstrue the very meaning of responsibility.

1. *Refusal to Face Conflict*

What, then, should a person do when faced with such a conflict of ideals? He may, in fact, do one of three things. First, he may refuse to face the conflict and do nothing. But to do nothing is to lose any control whatsoever over the situation, to give up, to resign responsible, intelligent decision and action, and thus become the plaything or pawn of the strongest force.

2. *Reliance on Authority*

Second, a person faced with conflicting ideals may, without thinking the issue through, let someone else, some institution, or some tradition make his decisions for him. This alternative differs only in degree but hardly in kind from the first. Like the first, it is an abrogation of responsibility. In this case, responsibility is dodged by shifting it from one's own shoulders to someone else's. At an early age most of our decisions may have had to be made by our parents or others; indeed, what better alternative is there? But to continue throughout life to rely on others for one's decisions is to fail to grow up morally, to remain enclosed in the maternal cloak literally or figuratively, although other objects or persons may later fulfill the maternal function.

In some cases the inability to decide for one's self or the willingness to let others decide for one may be the unfortunate result of overly zealous or strict parents who refused to let their children go through the normal process of decision making and discovery of results by trial and error. Whatever the cause, however, persons who continue throughout life to shift responsibility for their decisions to someone else (without full awareness of the meaning of the shift) never reach responsible moral maturity. Such persons are all too easily carried away by propagandists and dictators, or would-be dictators. Their predilections and their conscience, in Fromm's terms, remain authoritarian. At best they tend to be the will-power-less persons, the passively led, the group that Nietzsche described as the many too many, rather than the cooperative, creative members of a community.

We do not mean to imply, however, that to be morally mature is to reject all authority or that the morally mature person makes his decisions either in defiance of or without the aid of other persons, traditions, and institutions. Authorities may and do fulfill the extremely important functions of guiding us in our insight, of bringing to our attention factors or sides of questions we all too easily forget or overlook. They may help us avoid unnecessary detours and pitfalls. In a period as complicated as our own, when the frontiers of human knowledge are constantly expanding and the possibilities of encyclopedic grasp of all knowledge have disappeared, none of us can very well dispense with the help of authorities either in specialized fields or in interdisciplinary problems.

However, critically intelligent use of authority to guide or to fill in lacking information is one thing; uncritical and unquestioning reliance on an authority to make my decisions for me is quite something else. The latter comes dangerously close to giving up my moral selfhood; I become a moral automaton, surrendering my unique birthright as a person. Strictly speaking, just as no one else can be rational for me or can make me rational, so no one else can be moral for me, can make my decisions. The decisions the other person makes are his decisions, not mine, and any moral accomplishment is his and not mine.

This problem of the source of moral authority is often complicated by a confusion between the content of what one accepts as authoritative and that which makes it morally authoritative for him. Indeed, I may decide that the Ten Commandments, the Gospels, the Koran, or Plato is morally binding upon me; that the principles or even the rules by which I ought to be governed are those which my superior officer, or governor, or society commands. In so doing, I make the governor, the rules, the institution or the book authoritative for me. I may accept obedience to any such authority as a primary ideal. But in such cases it is all too easy to overlook the fact that unless I do in fact approve or commit myself to such an authority and the ideal of obedience to it, the time may come when I am asked or forced to conform to the authority in question and then feel no moral obligation so to do.

To put the matter in another way, it is one thing to accept an authority provisionally as a guide to conduct, reserving the right to judge the adequacy of the authority's prescriptions in light of the circumstances. It is something else to accept an authority unquestioningly. But even in the second case the unquestioned authority does not become authoritative for a person unless he accepts it and unless the act of accepting involves his own judgment, his own reason, and thus his autonomy as a thinking individual. A person thus paradoxically has to use his own deciding ability or autonomy even to give up or delegate his power of decision. And because the authority one decides upon will be one among many possible authorities (gang, party leader, officer, boss, church, Bible, sciences), one's own deciding and approval become the source of one's obligation to the authority. This does not mean that he may not be influenced in his decision. Nor does it mean that such influence is to be rejected or that one can reject influence altogether even if he wants to. It does, however, underline the dilemma facing the person who would evade responsibility by surrendering his moral judgment unqualifiedly to some external authority. He can hardly avoid the responsibility for such surrender.

3. Autonomous Decision

The third alternative when a person is faced with the conflict of ideals making claims on him from various sources is to examine critically the ideals themselves, to acknowledge one of the ideals presented as his own or formulate a new one of his own to cover the situation, and then either to act on the basis of it or at least be willing to judge this possible action in terms of it. As a matter of fact, an ideal only becomes an ideal for me as I acknowledge it, as I accept it as a basis for choice. To be consistent in my actions at all, once I acknowledge an ideal I become obligated to act in accordance with it. I thus become morally responsible in relation to my own acknowledged ideals.

The principle involved has already been illustrated in our discussion of the basis of moral principles themselves. We pointed out that insofar as one recognizes the ideal of intelligibility or of rationality of action (that it is better to be and act intelligently), he imposes on himself the obligation to search for the most adequate principles of rational action he can find. Similarly, insofar as one recognizes, let us say, the ideal of racial tolerance, he obligates himself not to discriminate against other persons because of name or skin color. Or again, insofar as one acknowledges the ideal of scientific investigation, he obligates himself to objective consideration of evidence and the use of scientific method. Or insofar as one acknowledges the desirability of veracity he obligates himself not to deceive others intentionally.

The interesting thing about our ideals is that in general they have to be self-imposed if they are to have an "obligatory" bearing on our actions. If one does not himself recognize the ideal of racial tolerance, he feels no obligation to refrain from discrimination. If one does not himself recognize the ideal of justice, he feels no obligation to treat others fairly. In both cases he still may have to refrain from the action in question because of fear of external sanctions (for example, loss of business, jail, social ostracism). On the other hand, insofar as one does accept these ideals but does not act in accordance with them, he is contradicting his own intentions and acting unintelligently.

II. *THE PRINCIPLE OF AUTONOMY*

If, then, we ask the question with which we began: "With what ought I to be consistent in my choosing?" the minimal answer would seem to be: "I ought to be consistent with my own acknowledged ideals (until I find adequate ground for changing them or modifying them)." Or, phrasing the suggested answer again in terms of responsibility, "I am responsible morally at least for acting or not acting in accordance with ideals that I acknowledge." I am responsible for choosing; I am under obligation to choose in the light of my acknowledged ideals; and if I do not do all I can to realize those ideals, I feel guilt, whether I feel social approval or not. Only then do I approach moral maturity. We can phrase this in terms of a second moral principle or law, what we shall call the Principle of Autonomy: *All persons ought to recognize themselves as obligated to choose in accordance with ideals that they acknowledge.*[1]

The Principle of Autonomy is, as the name indicates, in a quite literal sense the principle of moral self-government. It underlines

[1] Cf. E. S. Brightman, *Moral Laws* (New York: Abingdon Press, 1933), p. 106.

the fact that self-rule is the very foundation of morality. Morality is not something that can be dictated to me or legislated for me. This principle stresses the self-imposed character of my duty, the fact that my duty follows from the ideals that I recognize, not from what someone else decides that I ought to do. I may have every reason in the world for not doing what someone else thinks I ought to do, but I have no rational excuse for not doing what I think I ought to do insofar as it lies within my power.

When I violate or refuse to obey the commands of others, I may well be able to say that I have done so on moral grounds, that what was commanded ought not to be done, that it was not in accordance with what I think ought to be done in the situation. In fact, the possibility of responsible social change, the possibility of the give and take of communal discussion that leads to growing moral insight, and the possibility of sincere revolt and resistance rest to a large extent on just such judgments. I may feel that enacted law ought to be changed, that a government ought to be replaced, that the expectations of a group ought to be improved. In just such circumstances, my resistance, or my demand for change, is the assertion of my moral autonomy or moral selfhood, my acceptance of personal responsibility. In fact, even if I later change my mind and feel that the law or command that I opposed is correct and ought to be followed, it still is the fact that my earlier protest was made in the light of ideals that I then acknowledged and thus was a moral protest!

On the other hand, what excuse is there, on moral grounds or grounds of intelligibility, for violating or refusing to obey what at any time I believe to be the best, or my acknowledged ideal? My acknowledgment of an ideal as ideal itself is the very ground for feeling "I ought." Insofar as I do violate, not externally imposed ideals, but my own recognized ideals, I feel my own guilt and as a moral agent face my own self-condemnation.

A. *Duty and Desire*

The recognition that one's duty can only be defined in terms of self-imposed ideals does not mean that duty becomes a matter of momentary whims. Nor does it mean that what constitutes one's duty necessarily or usually runs contrary to what others expect or advise. The Principle of Autonomy is a principle of sincerity, not arbitrariness of choice. To act or choose on the whim of the moment or on impulse or even on deep-rooted desire is not necessarily to act or choose autonomously or on the basis of self-imposed ideals. Both Immanuel Kant and the Stoics (let alone Plato and Aristotle) insisted that it is when acts are performed through sheer inclination that we most frequently act contrary to our moral insight. Impulses, desires, and inclinations, while activities of a person and relevant to intelligent decision, are not the products in most instances of careful decision or recognition of what seems on reflection best to him. Sometimes they are manifestations of basic desires in a passing situation, and often we cannot know whence they come and whither they go, and we certainly cannot tell at first flush to what extent they are within our control. Once we are aware of them and, as far as possible, what they involve, the important thing about impulse, inclination, and desire is what we do about them in the light of our acknowledged ideals.

To put the matter in a slightly different perspective, while the Principle of Autonomy does involve the recognition that my duty, to be morally meaningful, has to be self-imposed, this does not mean that duty is a matter of doing whatever I want to do—having my own way. The concept of autonomy is in itself neither egoistic nor selfish. If "to do what one wants to" or "to have one's own way" is taken to mean acting on the strongest desire of the moment, then autonomy calls for criticizing one's desires by his ideals, controlling his actions by what he thinks best upon reflection.

Some ethicists have been so impressed with the difference between the "I want to do" and "I ought" or "It is my duty" that they deny that any relation exists between them and insist that duty is wholly unique, not to be defined even in terms of realizing what one considers to be good. H. A. Prichard, for example, insists that obligation almost inevitably is the autonomous and unique demand to do what we do not want to do.[2] Although this may be an overstatement on Prichard's part, it nevertheless is rather clearly the case that in some circumstances, what I want at the moment and what I recognize as my duty may be quite at variance.

Yet it would be easy to overemphasize the distinction between want or desire on the one hand and duty or obligation on the other. It is one thing to recognize that they are not synonymous and that in particular cases they may conflict. It is quite a different thing to insist that they are unrelated or always in conflict, or to say that

[2] "Does Moral Philosophy Rest on a Mistake?" *Mind*, XXI (1912), 21.

no act performed on the basis of desire or inclination is an act done from a sense of duty or obligation. Such a conception leads all too easily to a bleak and forbidding conception of morality as a wholly negative affair. This hardly seems to "conform" to the facts of mature moral life. The fact that I enjoy or want to do social work or provide for my children or take care of my aging parents does not mean that I am acting contrary to my duty or that I am acting selfishly. I may thoroughly enjoy doing my duty. In fact if I consistently do not, if duty and want or desire are constantly in conflict, I may indeed suspect that I need to take another look at the ideals to which I feel obligation.

Again, to bring together earlier discussion, if obligation is the peculiar feeling that arises when I consider what I take to be the best, and if I arrive at my conception of the best by a process of critical comparison of desired experience or value claims, then my duty is clearly to conform not to desire and inclination but to criticized desires, to my acknowledged ideals. This process would often lead to temporary frustration of desire but, in the long run, to more fundamental enjoyment.

We must not minimize the real conflict between uncriticized desire on the one hand and critically approved desires on the other. In any given situation, conflicts often arise between uncriticized "oughts" from the point of view of that situation and criticized feelings of obligation, let alone between uncriticized feelings of obligation and criticized desires. This whole problem of the relation between uncriticized and criticized feelings of obligation is essentially the problem of "conscience."

B. *The Problem of Conscience*

As we have seen in Chapters 9, 10, and 11, the nature and function of conscience has been a persistent problem throughout the history of ethical thought. To review rapidly, some thinkers have maintained that conscience is a peculiar faculty in men, giving them direct and unerring insight into rules of right and wrong. At times conscience has been claimed to be the voice of God. Some have insisted that we have a "moral sense," which enables us to perceive the rightness or wrongness of any particular contemplated act.

On the other hand, in psychological and sociological circles especially, conscience has been described as the introjection of parental or societal demands, part of the inhibiting superego (cf. Chapter 2). It has been explained as the effect of custom and tradition forced upon the individual before he was able to think for himself and, again, as the irrational inhibiting influence of habits, the origin of which is long forgotten. It has sometimes been assumed that the key to personal adjustment and mental health lies in releasing the individual from the bondage of conscience with its accompanying irrational feelings of guilt. Freud, while recognizing the superego as a normal function of the total ego structure, nonetheless insists that it dominates the ego with severity and cruelty.[3]

1. *The Uncritical or Automatic Conscience*

Whatever else "conscience" may or may not refer to, it is at least another name for our more persistent feelings of obligation and the guilt reactions that we experience when we violate these. Yet conscience would seem to include more than the feeling of obligation, namely, the accumulated content from past experience. In this perspective, Freud, for example, would be quite right in his view that much of the content of conscience is formed long before a child reaches a level of rational discrimination. By the time we reach an age when we begin to think our problems through for ourselves, we are already equipped with what might be called an automatic or uncritical or, in Erich Fromm's term, an authoritarian conscience, an accumulation of internalized or "introjected" oughts taken over uncritically from parents, teachers, companions, or what have you, and often mixed with our own disguised and unrecognized wants.

Such a complex fusion of particular oughts and musts would be a far cry from a clear single voice or a direct insight into right and wrong. It might more accurately be described as a more or less unified crowd of varied and indistinguishable voices. Its dictates are likely to be primarily negative and, at the crucial junctures of action, rigid or silent or confused. To rely on such a heterogeneous guide may well be equivalent to relying on no other guide than the feeling of the moment and thus in fact surrendering any rational basis for action.

The Principle of Autonomy, however, calls for moral self-government, for acting in accordance with ideals that one acknowledges.

---

[3] Cf. *The Ego and the Id* (London: The Hogarth Press, 1950), pp. 39–40, and *New Introductory Lectures on Psychoanalysis* (New York: W. W. Norton, 1933), pp. 90, 91, 104 ff.

If one is to act as an autonomous moral agent, it is imperative that he become clearly and critically aware of what ideals he feels obligated to and why, that he act for reasons satisfactory to him, and not on the basis of irrational promptings even when they feel imperative. A person is under obligation to evaluate critically his own specific ought claims, to be as fully aware as possible of the ideals that he acknowledges. But it would be easy to misinterpret what this obligation means in regard to conscience. It might seem that on the basis of the Principle of Autonomy we should clean the Augean stables by rejecting or getting rid of our automatic consciences altogether.

Yet the problem of the automatic or uncritical conscience is not so easily disposed of. In the first place, even if one desired to rid himself of his uncritical conscience, it is highly unlikely that he could do so. Too much of his early training and conditioning have contributed to it. We cannot intentionally forget without suffering the consequences of repression. The dismissed uncritical conscience would and does take its revenge in terms of unreasonable antipathies, seemingly unexplained conflicts and dogmatic counteraffirmations. The "liberated" student who vigorously and emotionally condemns all religious believers as stupid victims of superstition or derides any argument for premarital sexual control as old-fashioned prudery, without discussing the questions involved on the basis of arguments and evidence pro and con, is often suffering under the backlash of a repressed uncritical conscience. Even though the beliefs he now affirms may be intrinsically more reasonable than those he held formerly, he is not holding them rationally. Ironically, he tends to be more violently circumscribed in his sympathies and actions than he was under the influence of his uncritical conscience.

In the second place, even if a person could rid himself of his automatic conscience, it is questionable whether it would be desirable for him to do so. As the deposit of parental, social, and institutional influences, the automatic conscience may and usually does contain much of real value. It may be a source of (though not a warrant for) what on closer consideration will turn out to be valid moral guidance. Figuratively, the automatic conscience might be considered a storehouse or reservoir of the practical or common-sense morality of one's group, a heritage from the past.

Therefore, some thinkers who would reject any prompting of the

automatic conscience as a sure guide for action yet would insist that
it does contain immediate and trustworthy insights that certain kinds
of acts are right or wrong. We discover in conscience, it is argued,
self-evident rules regarding these kinds of acts "which are no sooner
understood than they are believed." [4] Rules regarding killing, stealing, and lying would be cases in point. We do not have to reason
about them, it is urged; we recognize them as valid on the promptings of conscience itself. What the holders of such a position are
underlining is the presence of positive and valid conscience content.
Their position represents a critical improvement over the reliance on
any and all promptings of conscience.

2. Development of a Critical or Autonomous Conscience

The advocates of this self-evident moral insight, or common-sense
conception of conscience, do point to the first step in developing
what might be called a *critical* or *autonomous conscience*. We should,
they point out, not rely on any and every prompting of conscience
but only on those that we can clearly formulate and of which we
can grasp the intrinsic meaning. But can we accept this view even as
a satisfactory half-way house?

It is not at all clear, to begin with, that any such moral insights
or rules are logically self-evident. To be self-evident a statement's
contradictory must be inconceivable. There is nothing inconceivable about the opposite of such a rule as "It is morally wrong to
lie." Probably most of us can conceive of circumstances in which the
wrongness of lying is at least open to question, and even Ross (as we
saw on page 241 f.) grants that *prima facie* special duties often ought
not to be obeyed. Furthermore, such rules are likely to be ambiguous, particularly when applied to borderline cases, in which help is
most urgently needed. The applicability of "Do not commit murder" depends on how you define murder. Not all persons are by any
means agreed that all killing—for example, in self-defense—is wrong.
If one defines murder as wrongful killing, one is still left with the
question: When is killing wrong?

Perhaps the most serious difficulty with the common-sense view is
the fact that such a conscience-derived series of rules, originating indirectly from or influenced by one's particular society, may well be
too static and too rigid to meet new circumstances (such as what to

[4] Thomas Reid, *Essays in the Intellectual Powers of Man* (London: Macmillan, 1941),
Essay VI, Chapter IV.

do when one's own radiation-infected son approaches a nuclear shelter for admittance).

On the positive side of the ledger, the advocates of common-sense morality do well to remind us that if we disregard the automatic conscience altogether we may be throwing the kettle away with the soup. The possible insights of the automatic conscience can and should be used as hypotheses for further testing. The ideals so grasped should be compared, criticized, revised, supplemented. A careful application of the Principle of Consistency is a second step in developing a critical conscience, that is, a conscience that consists of feelings of obligation toward ideals that one can clearly and reasonably acknowledge and approve as intelligent bases for action. The Principle of Autonomy calls for a continuous experiment in the improvement of one's ideals, not the affirmation of a hard and fast set of do's and don'ts. In this sense, the development of a critical conscience would seem to be a life-long process of growth in and application of insight, one in which we have both the right and the duty to call into question, to criticize, and to revise any or all of the ideals or specific oughts we hold to date.

Such a process of criticism, revision, and growth is not easy. In extreme cases a person's uncritical conscience may have been so rigidly and irrationally formed by circumstances and persons over which he had no control and before he reached a stage when he began to think for himself that he cannot undertake the task of developing a critical conscience alone. He may need the professional help of the psychiatrist to uncover hidden sources of irrational feelings of ought, guilt, and anguish.

Most persons almost inevitably begin the process of conscience revision by the time they reached adolescence. But there are constant dangers along the way. We may stop the process of revision too soon. We may think that we can do it all at once. There is always the danger of rationalizing uncriticized wants into acknowledged ideals. We can forget the actual social context in which we live and the interplay of ideals in community relations. And yet on this continued development of a critical conscience depend both the attainment of moral and emotional maturity and the possibility of individual and communal psychic health. One of the major stumbling blocks to the life good to live is a confused, contradictory, or static conscience.

This discussion of the fuller development of a critical conscience points beyond the Principles of Consistency and Autonomy to considerations of the limits and consequences of action, to the relation of values to each other, in fact to any other conditions of moral action we may discover. Yet without the sincerity and conscious awareness of ideals called for by the Principle of Autonomy and without the consistency called for by the Logical Principle, it is difficult to see how even a start towards the development of a critical conscience should be made.

C. Democratic Process and the Principle of Autonomy

The Principle of Autonomy has important implications on the level of social or group action as well as on the level of individual moral action. Recognition of and faith in the Principle of Autonomy, it can be urged, is in a very fundamental way a key moral presupposition underlying the possibility of democratic process itself. A democratic society is based on the assumption that the members of the society can and will act as autonomous agents capable of making up their own minds, of noting and acting in accordance with their own acknowledged ideals. Apart from individual responsibility, the concept of group responsibility becomes a contradiction in terms. We assume that, given the issues and the evidence at hand, the majority of individuals in a democratic society can and will critically evaluate the ends and the means involved in any line of social action and then assume the obligation to act in accordance with their ideals so formulated and so acknowledged. Once faith is lost in this ability (not only the ability of the superior citizen but of the average also), the reason and ground for democracy is gone. The far more direct and efficient control of society by tyrannical or totalitarian means justifiably takes its place. To turn the matter around, insofar as there is a moral objection to dictatorship, it lies not in what a dictator or head of a totalitarian state may or may not accomplish but in the fact that dictatorship violates the fundamental capacity and obligation of men to become morally autonomous, to formulate plans, and to act in accordance with ideals they acknowledge.

The implicit recognition of the fundamental nature of the Principle of Autonomy is nowhere better illustrated than in the lip service given to such terms as "freedom" and "democracy" and to the striking attempts to define these terms in totalitarian language by such men as Hitler, Mussolini, and both Stalin and Lenin. Mussolini, for example, informed us that fascism "is the purest form of democracy if the nation be considered—as it should be . . . as the conscience and will of the few, if not indeed of the one, and tending to express itself in the conscience and will of the mass, the whole group ethnically molded by racial and historical conditions into a nation." [5] Hitler argued that "the intimate coupling of nationalism, and feeling of social justice must be planted in the young heart. Then there will someday arise a people of State citizens, bound to one another and forged together by a common love and a common pride, unshakably invincible for all times." [6] And Lenin insisted that "the dictatorship of the proletariat . . . will, for the first time, produce democracy for the people, for the majority, side by side with the necessary suppression of the minority—the exploiters." [7]

Yet the contradiction involved in such statements is not difficult to discover. An individual is not free to make up his mind, to discover and decide intelligently what ideals he does acknowledge (1) if he is not free to criticize at any time he feels like it the ideals, individual and social, he is asked to accept or (2) if the sources of information including knowledge of alternative ideals open to him are arbitrarily restricted. One of the important corollaries of the Principle of Autonomy is not only freedom of thought and decision but also freedom of speech. It is not difficult to see why this is the case.

1. *Freedom of Speech as a Corollary of the Principle of Autonomy*

The Principle of Autonomy underlines the duty and thus the right of each person to criticize and judge for himself the potential value of the individual and social ideals that he feels he ought to realize. Intelligent and adequate decision depends upon free access to relevant sources of information. Such access is only possible in practice if we can hear and assess arguments on all sides of questions, if we can criticize and question and be criticized and questioned. To deny freedom of speech, particularly if we are the ones doing the denying, is tantamount to denying ourselves potential sources of information.

My own right to criticize my own ideals and those of others involves the right of others to do the same. In fact, respect of the mu-

---

[5] *Doctrine of Fascism* (Firenze: Vallecchi, 1935), p. 16.
[6] *Mein Kampf* (New York: Reynal & Hitchcock, 1939), p. 636.
[7] *The State and Revolution* (New York: International Publishers), p. 75.

tual right to speak and criticize is important not only from the informational standpoint but also as a check on overly hasty and dogmatic decision on my part. Although strictly speaking, no one else can determine my moral duty for me, others, if they have the opportunity, may help me to formulate my duty and work out the implications of it once I recognize what my duty is. The denial of the right to others to criticize my position in the hope of persuading me to change my mind removes this safeguard. In addition, if I deny this right of self-decision to others I can hardly expect them to respect it in me.

The problem of conscience and of choice is complicated by the fact that we never determine the ideals we acknowledge in a social vacuum. The ideals I affirm and my actions in light of them affect others and vice versa. Living in community, we need (and must have if the community is to function effectively) common ideals, yet ideals that we all affirm. Without free exchange of information, questioning and counterquestioning, we cannot hope to find common ideals toward which to work and which will serve as the acknowledged bonds of our cooperative coexistence. The danger to discovery of common ends does not lie in difference of opinion or even outright disagreement. The real danger lies in refusal to talk about them.

As long as we can continue talking freely and responsibly, there is a possibility of the meeting of minds, of mutual persuasion, of clarification, and, in the best sense, of compromise. Once discussion ceases, the only way of settling or meeting disagreement is by resort to force. But the resort to force is itself a confession of failure. I may then, if I happen to be in power, terrorize you into silence, lock you up, or have you done away with; but in so doing I have admitted the weakness or inadequacy of my own position. The mere fact that I have got rid of you does not make my position right or the arguments on which it rests true.

Most of us are quite ready to admit the self-defeating character of denying the right to speak and of resorting to force in regard to certain areas of experience. We realize that we cannot apply such tactics to settling questions in the realm of scientific investigation without disastrous results. Stalin's silencing of the opponents of Lysenko did not make Lysenko's views on the transmission of acquired characteristics correct. The refusal in some areas of this country during the first part of this century to allow discussion of the Darwinian evolutionary hypothesis did not prove this thesis false. Most scientists would go further and insist that even the restriction of free exchange of scientific information, for whatever reason, makes more difficult the process of discovering new information. If carried to an extreme, such restriction makes fruitful investigation impossible.

A point that is often overlooked is that denial of the right to speak and the resort to force are equally self-defeating in every field including politics, ethics, and religion. The thing that keeps a moral, a political, or a religious system alive and able to meet changing conditions, a real option, is new and developing insight. Hegel, Bergson, Toynbee and, interestingly enough, Marx, among others, have all pointed to the fact that when insight is dead, when a society is unable to meet the challenge of new conditions, it is headed for extinction. Although other factors may contribute, perhaps the surest way to block insight is to block free discussion, to resort to force rather than to free discussion in order to iron out internal and, in the long run, external difficulties.

Insofar as we recognize the Principle of Autonomy as underlying democratic process, the right to free discussion cannot be limited to the majority (Lenin to the contrary notwithstanding). Insights that later become the majority views start as minority opinion. Minorities constitute both the growing experimental edges of a democratic society and many of the critics who keep the society alive to its own conditions. This is strikingly illustrated by comparing the socialist party platform of the first part of the century in this country with the major party platforms of today. Social security, unemployment insurance, federal power projects, all of which have been enacted into law, were then considered dangerously radical. This is not to say that all minority positions have found their way to majority acceptance. Nor, quite obviously, is it to say that all such opinions should be accepted. But we cannot afford the luxury of refusing to give even the most extreme views a hearing.

2. Free Speech and Tolerance

If free speech is to be effective, in fact if it is to be, along with it must go its correlate, tolerance. Tolerance simply means the disposition to be impartial and fair toward those whose opinions differ from one's own. It is the virtue-trait of a person who persistently applies the Principle of Autonomy to other persons, who respects their right to make up their minds for themselves and their responsibility to the ideals that they acknowledge, even though they happen to disagree with him.

As we suggested in Chapter 17, tolerance interpenetrates with the personal virtue-traits, like honesty, courage, and gratitude; and it grows out of social virtue-traits like justice, forgiveness, and kindness, thus constituting a basic political trait. We must be clear about what it does and does not involve.

Tolerance does not mean, as is sometimes assumed, that the tolerant person must agree with, or approve of, the different positions others hold. Nor does it mean that he holds no position of his own or that he thinks the positions others hold are as valid or as good as his own. A person is not tolerant of the opinions and ideals of someone he agrees with. He simply agrees. Nor is one tolerant if he has no ideals or holds no position relevant to the point in question. He is simply indifferent. To be tolerant he must have convictions of his own and yet respect honest disagreement and the right (both his own and the other person's) to try to change opinions by rational persuasion. Anyone who uses tolerance as a rationalization for refusing to make up his own mind or as an excuse for refusing to meet issues squarely simply shows that he does not know what tolerance involves.

Ironically, one danger involved in tolerance is that of becoming intolerant in the name of tolerance itself. Tolerance can be elevated into a kind of a dogma that involves the condemnation of anyone who believes that his own convictions are valid and ought to prevail. The point was strikingly illustrated by one religiously oriented journal of the 1920's and 1930's that engaged in a crusade against religious intolerance. This particular journal entered into bitter polemic against other types of religious positions that it considered intolerant, and instead of increasing religious tolerance, it gained the reputation of being basically biased and intolerant itself.

The final test of tolerance may well be the ability to be tolerant even of intolerance. Again, this does not mean approving of intolerance but respecting the right of those who are not tolerant to try to persuade me that I am wrong, and reciprocally, my right to try to persuade them that they are wrong. Admittedly, this is not an easy position to hold. It is even conceivable that under such a program intolerance will prevail. But unless we can hold such a position intolerance has in fact already won the day.

Recognition of the importance of free speech and of tolerance, particularly the need for tolerance even of intolerance, leads us directly to the center of one of the most perplexing yet critical problems of our own day. If we believe in free speech, do we have the right to deny it to those who frankly admit that they would not allow such freedom if they were in power? The quick answer would seem to be, yes. Freedom of speech, it is sometimes agreed, is so important that it must be safe-guarded at any cost. Anyone who would destroy it has by this desire already given up his right to it. The body politic has a right to protect itself against its own subversion. The stakes for social well-being are high and drastic measures may be necessary. Further, groups who would deny freedom, insofar as they use persuasion to try to gain power, are usually too clever to argue against free speech directly. Rather, they usually wrap up the denial of free speech with an appeal to the underprivileged, economically, religiously, and socially. In this way, the opponents of freedom persuade the less acute and inexperienced members of society who do not or are not capable of realizing the cost. Appeal to security for the stomach or the soul is likely to seem more immediate and concrete than appeal to freedom and to the longer road of evolutionary social growth. Accordingly, to preserve freedom, it is contended, we must protect the weaker members of society against becoming dupes of such propaganda by silencing its sources.

Although such an argument is tempting, it involves serious difficulties. It is difficult to see how such a procedure differs essentially from what it is aimed against. The argument of those who would deny freedom insofar as the issue is directly joined usually takes much the same form. Such groups usually grant the right to be right (as they see right) but not the right to be wrong. They would also grant that the issues involved are too important to be left to the vagaries of popular decision and that those who do not see the correct view must be protected against error, false propaganda, and their own weakness. Thus, for example, the Soviet Constitution of 1936, in the famous Article 125, grants freedom of speech and of the press, but this was interpreted by Commissar for Justice Krylenko as follows: "We do not wish to be hypocrites. No worker, collective farmer or any other working person will object to the fact that any persons who might wish to bring back the capitalist system are not given either free speech or free press by our constitution." [8]

[8] Anna Louise Strong, *The New Soviet Constitution* (New York: Henry Holt and Company, 1937), p. 111.

To deny freedom of speech to those who would deny it if they were in power is equivalent to denying freedom of speech in the name of not denying it. One has in fact already denied it. The more considered answer to the question: "Do we have a right to deny freedom of speech to such persons or groups?" would seem to be, no.

But the question still remains: "What can and should we do about such groups?" Recognition that denying freedom to such groups destroys the very position that we are defending does not mean that one necessarily allows them to speak and let it go at that—any more than tolerance means that one agrees with or approves of the views he tolerates. One tactical error, to which we Americans seem peculiarly prone at times, is that of thinking that, once we have enacted something into law, things will automatically take care of themselves. Unfortunately this is a rather costly form of wishful thinking.

If we really believe in the importance of freedom of speech, we assume the obligation to keep the issue alive, to educate, and to persuade for freedom. The assumption that, given the facts and arguments, the majority in a democracy can decide intelligently carries with it the obligation to present the facts and arguments, to meet the opposition continually on the level of persuasion. We cannot stand back with Pippa and assume "all's right with the world." It seldom is. If we lose the battle for freedom, it is more likely to be by default than by open defeat.

In a democracy, however, once a group that would deny freedom if it were in power leaves the realm of persuasion and attempts by collusion and force to gain control (that is, when the issue leaves the realm of public debate and becomes a matter of conspiracy, sabotage, or overt attack), then the problem is no longer a matter of freedom of speech. Once the matter becomes one of conspiracy or the illegal use of force, it may have to be met in another and more drastic fashion.

3. Responsible Speech and Limitations on Freedom of Speech

Freedom of speech under the Principle of Autonomy carries with it one other important correlate. The right to speak and criticize fully does not give one the right to speak irresponsibly. In fact, strictly speaking there is no right to free speech as such, for the right involves the proper use of freedom. As an autonomous agent I have the right to formulate critically my own ideals and to try to persuade others to them as long as I am sincere about my acknowledged ideals.

I may be mistaken in my judgment; my information may be incomplete. I may not be to blame for being in error in some circumstances. But error is something quite different from intentional misrepresentation or distortion on the one hand and loose, unconsidered statement on the other. Free speech does not give me the right to libelous speech, nor does it give me the right to voice the whim of the moment regardless of my acknowledged ideals and the circumstances. I have no right to yell "Fire!" in a crowded theater. Nor does a United States Senator visiting abroad have a right to insult his hosts. Regardless of what kind of legal immunity a man may have, he is morally responsible for unsubstantiated attacks on the character of another. In this respect the back fence and a Senate investigating chamber are peculiarly alike. This recognition of responsibility for what one says underlines one further aspect of the freedom of speech problem.

Unlike the Principle of Autonomy, freedom of speech is not what might be called a first-level moral principle. Rather it might be called a second-level application that, on the whole or usually, follows from the Principle of Autonomy. As a potentially intelligent moral individual, I ought always to act in accordance with ideals that I acknowledge; but I cannot so readily say that I ought always to speak freely or condone others for so speaking. We have already noted two cases in which morally the right to speak freely would be highly questionable, in which in fact one ought not or has no right to speak freely. These alone would be sufficient to indicate that free speech lacks the universality of a moral principle.

But there are other instances when free speech would be equally questionable. Arguing about principles is one thing; passing on specific kinds of information to persons incapable of using it wisely, or to groups or persons who threaten the welfare of society, is something quite different. A captured intelligence agent, having assumed the obligations of his job, would have very little right indeed to speak freely to the enemy. The same applies to any person who has taken on the obligation involved in accepting confidences. Other things being equal, he is bound morally not to speak freely regarding them.

Freedom of speech, the authors believe, is indeed a precious value, an ideal, and a right derived, in most circumstances, from the Principle of Autonomy. It carries with it heavy responsibilities, and it is something that has to be exercised judiciously. Both in the individ-

ual and in society its exercise must be in harmony with its parent
principle, the range of values chosen, the circumstances, and its consequences for all affected. Thus in some circumstances one may
morally be obligated to be silent and even to deny others the right
to speak. However, it must not be forgotten that anyone who does
deny free speech to another takes upon himself the full and serious
responsibility for so doing.

In becoming aware of the bearing of the range of values chosen,
of the circumstances and the consequences of choice on the exercise
of free speech we have been in fact referring to factors in guiding
choice not implied by the Principles of Autonomy and Consistency
themselves. Clearly, important as they are, they are not by themselves sufficient guides in moral action. Our next principle will take
us further.

III. *REFLECTIVE SUMMARY*

On the view we have taken, a person is morally responsible only to
the extent that he is free to choose among alternatives conceived to
be within his power. Yet, if this person does not choose ends consistent with each other or means and ends consistent with each other,
his freedom can become vicious and lead to chaos. Yet consistency
can also lead to fanaticism and serious loss of value. Clearly, if freedom and consistency are not to lead us astray, we need to be guided
by ideals, by some conceptions of what values ought to be realized in
our lives. Yet conflict rages among ideals too, and we seem to be at
an impasse.

Can we find a way out by passing the responsibility of choice
among ideals to someone else or to some institution? No, for we
must choose the institution in accordance with some ideal, and the
decision to accept and follow the dictates of that person or institution is still ours.

Insofar as we are free, we choose ideals of some sort, and we feel
morally obligated to execute those ideals which we thus impose
upon ourselves, regardless of what their ultimate origin may be.
Others may even force us to action against our wills, but only we
can acknowledge imposed ideals as ours and thus "impose" them on
ourselves. Accordingly, there is no escaping the responsibility, the
moral obligation, to choose the best (ideals) we know.

The particular ideal that we choose (for example, to follow a certain leader) might well restrict our autonomy, but in choosing him we have been obeying the Law of Autonomy—which obligates us to choose in accordance with whatever we acknowledge to be the best. What makes ideals binding is not that they are objectively "the last word" about the best, but the fact that, confronted by choice, we find ourselves obligated to the ideals that we acknowledge.

Thus, whatever the final ideal may be, whatever the final resolution of conflict among ideals may be, the best we can do is to will as consistently as possible the ideal that seems best. This may not seem to take us far, but it lies at the heart of our experience as moral agents, and it forces upon our attention certain other facts involved in choice.

First, although we are never bound to do what is beyond our power, the line of duty follows neither the shifting of desire nor the pressure of social disapproval nor the nod of social approval. We ought to act in accordance with the best we know, be it liked or disliked, socially disapproved or approved. This does not mean that to be autonomous is to be necessarily self-centered or selfish, for we cannot tell at first flush whether the best involves selfishness or altruism.

Second, it is important to realize that we usually come to choice situations with automatic feelings of ought that are uncritical from the point of view of that situation and are no sure guide to what we ought to do. This automatic "conscience" probably represents an accumulation and fusion of past oughts and musts that might well involve us, if obeyed without further criticism, in unreasonable action.

The Principle of Autonomy, therefore, demands that we become as aware as possible of the conflict between the automatic conscience and the critical conscience in order to free ourselves from what might well be whims and strong but uncriticized desires of the moment. Nevertheless, instead of either dismissing or slavishly following the automatic conscience, we do well to heed its deliverances until examination reveals that they are not the best.

Finally, the Principle of Autonomy has important consequences for the democratic way of life. For the cause of democracy is lost unless persons feel individual responsibility to act consistently with their criticized ideals and accordingly respect the freedom of speech and conscience of others. Without freedom of thought, of speech, and of access to different sides of an issue, and without respect for the freedom of conscience of all, there can be no true democracy. We need to be on our guard against those in our midst and elsewhere who use words like "freedom" and "democracy" only in the sense that persons, as cogs in the larger social order or state, are to live in terms of a pre-established goal that itself is beyond criticism.

The believer in freedom of speech and conscience cannot consistently deny freedom to those who in conscience would argue against it as a basis of government. Difficult and risky as it may be, he must be tolerant of those who do not in principle believe in freedom of speech, and he must confine himself to vigorous criticism and persuasion—as long as disbelievers in freedom of speech do not resort to conspiracy, sabotage, and violent overthrow of the government. But it is clear, as we discuss these questions, that the moral agent must move beyond consistency and conscientiousness as he makes specific choices.

21

Beyond Consistency and Sincerity

~~~~~~

I. *CONSISTENCY AND SINCERITY AS BASIC*

Without sincerity and conscientiousness and at least a minimal ability to choose consistently in the light of our ideals, the way to moral and emotional maturity would seem closed. An inconsistent person nullifies the effectiveness and meaningfulness of his choices. Not only is a person who chooses insincerely choosing inconsistently, but he is also violating his own insight into what he considers best. A person incapable of recognizing or discovering his own ideals, a person who depends or is forced to depend upon the dictates of others is a person incapable of responsibility. The capacity to formulate and act in accordance with ideals that one acknowledges may actually be lacking in some individuals. It is rather clearly lacking in younger children, in the mentally retarded, and to a greater or lesser extent in the mentally ill.

On the positive side, insofar as an individual does choose consistently in the light of what he considers best, regardless of how mistaken we may think his judgment of what is best may be, we admire him for his conscientiousness, his moral stamina. To be sure, our admiration for him on these grounds may at times be clouded. However, such clouded admiration may be due to lack of objectivity on our part, as is notoriously the case in time of war when we refuse to give the best among the enemy their due. At other times, we may be so intent on the fulfillment of immediate desires or "in getting our own way" that we will brook no opposition. Yet, on cooler reflection, we are usually ready to admit that it is just such qualities of sincerity and consistency that distinguish those men to whom we attribute heroic character regardless of the object of their heroism.

II. *IMMANUEL KANT AND THE GOOD WILL*

It is this ability, actual or potential, to act consistently and conscientiously that, Immanuel Kant insisted, makes men worthy of respect. "Autonomy," he maintained, "is thus the basis of the dignity of both human nature and every rational nature." [1] According to Kant, the one thing ultimately worth striving for, the defining character of man at his best, of man as moral, is a good will.

> Nothing in the world—indeed nothing even beyond the world —can possibly be conceived which could be called good without qualification except a good will. Intelligence, wit, judgment, and the other talents of the mind, however they may be named, or courage, resoluteness, and perseverance as qualities of temperament are doubtless in many respects good and desirable. But they can become extremely bad and harmful if the will, which is to make use of these gifts of nature and which in its special constitution is called character, is not good. It is the same with the gifts of fortune. Power, riches, honor, even health, general well-being, and the contentment with one's condition which is called happiness make for pride and even arrogance if there is not a good will to correct their influence on the mind and on its principles of action, so as to make it universally conformable to its end. It need hardly be mentioned that the sight of a being adorned with no feature of a pure and good will yet enjoying uninterrupted prosperity can never give pleasure to a rational impartial observer. Thus the good will seems to constitute the indispensable condition even of worthiness to be happy.[2]

By the good will it is apparent that Kant meant essentially a sincere and consistent will.

[1] *Critique of Practical Reason and Other Writings in Moral Philosophy*, trans. L. W. Beck (Chicago: University of Chicago Press, 1949), p. 93.

[2] *Ibid.*, p. 55.

If one were to ask Kant the question, "Are consistency and sincerity enough for moral living?" he would probably come as close as any other major thinker in the history of ethics to answering, yes. But, he would add, only if one clearly understands what these mean, both in themselves and as applied to action. To see more clearly the basis for Kant's answer and its pertinence for our investigation, it may be helpful to look briefly at Kant's argument.

Other things, Kant points out, besides a good will may be good instrumentally (that is, as means to an end). And some things when linked with a good will may become good intrinsically (that is, good in themselves). But all other things besides a good will can become evil and harmful if the good will is lacking. Power, riches, honor, or health without a good will may produce pride and arrogance. Even intelligence, wit, and self-control when they characterize a villain make him more villainous.

But the pertinent question becomes, what constitutes a good will? Kant's answer is that a good will is one which acts in a uniquely human way. Insofar as a man acts on the basis of inclination, desire, or impulse, his act is not particularly human, for such action characterizes all sentient beings. Nor does an action done for the sake of some specific object meet the conditions of a good will, for selection of objects may rest on desire or selfish inclination. Usefulness will not do, for usefulness is a form of expediency or a habitual means of attaining a specific end. Calculation of consequences is not the key to the good will for such calculation simply extends considerations of usefulness.

The key or "the first proposition of morality," as Kant puts it, "is that to have moral worth an action must be done from duty." [3] The worth of an act done from duty does not lie in the purpose that is to be achieved by means of or through the act. Rather the worth of the act lies in the principle of volition itself, that is, the principle or the maxim by which duty is determined. And the key to the maxim determining duty lies in man's reason, that is, for Kant, in his ability to think consistently and to formulate principles applicable to all similar instances. Men, potentially at least, are rational beings capable of determining their actions by the law or principle of reason itself. Thus the good will, the will that is good in itself, is the rational will. Furthermore, a rational will, unlike a will dominated by inclination and desire or ruled by impulse, is a self-legislative or autonomous will.

[3] *Ibid.,* p. 61.

A. *The Categorical Imperative*

But granted that the good will is a rational will, it might be argued that this still does not furnish us with any guide to action, with any way of determining specifically what constitutes a duty. Granted that we ought to be rational, what in detail does this mean? How am I to be rational in any particular situation?

Kant's answer to these questions would be that we have stopped the analysis too soon. We can find the principle that determines duty in the very conception of a rational will itself. A rational will is one which acts out of respect for law or principle itself; not any law, to be sure, but the self-imposed law of rationality, the principle of rational law itself. Now what makes a law rational in principle, Kant insists, is its universality and consistency—that is, in no way does it contradict itself, and in no way does it fail to apply to all cases in point. Accordingly, to discover whether any particular act is rational, I must test it by this principle: If I formulated the maxim or rule guiding this act, could it consistently apply to all rational beings? Kant himself phrases the principle as follows: "Act only according to that maxim by which you can at the same time will that it should become a universal law." [4]

One's duty as a rational person, Kant argues, is always to act out of respect for and in conformity to this principle. As such the principle of rational duty is an imperative—an ought or command—but a peculiar kind of imperative. Most imperatives are hypothetical, that is, they are what might be called "if" commands or "if" oughts. For example: "If I desire to become a concert pianist, I ought to practice. If I desire an education, I ought to study." In contrast to such hypothetical imperatives, Kant calls the principle of duty a categorical imperative. It contains no ifs, ands, or buts; that is, it commands duty, as duty. More specifically, it does not depend on the ands, ifs, and buts of our desires and inclination at any moment. It is the unconditional command of the rational will itself: A rational will ought to act according to that maxim by which it can at the same time will that it become a universal law.[5] This is the first and basic form of the Categorical Imperative.

How does the Categorical Imperative work out in practice? Does

---

[4] *Ibid.,* p. 80.
[5] Cf. *ibid.,* p. 80.

it really furnish a guide to action? Suppose, to use one of Kant's examples, I am in need of money and the handiest means of attaining it is to borrow it, although I know beforehand that I cannot pay it back. Yet I accept the money, with a promise to repay it, realizing that unless I so promise I would not get it. I want to know whether or not such action is opposed to duty. To test it, I ask myself whether or not the maxim of my act (that is, when I need money I shall borrow and promise to repay although I know I shall never do so) could be made universal law. The answer is clear: "It could never hold as a universal law of nature and be consistent with itself, rather it must necessarily contradict itself." [6] In other words, if everyone did the same thing, no one would believe such promises to repay (they would lose their meaningfulness), and lending itself would become meaningless. If honesty is a duty, then, it is so not if I like it or fear it; it is so whether I happen to like it or not.

The same reasoning could be equally applied to lying in general, to stealing, to murder, and, Kant insists, even to laziness and refusal to help others. Murder universalized would rather nicely do away with the possibility of committing murder because it would leave no one to commit murder or to be murdered. The possibility of stealing depends upon the recognition of restricted or private property. If everyone stole, everyone would help himself to whatever he wanted, with the result that no property would be private. Thus, stealing would become meaningless. To be sure, universalizing laziness does not involve self-contradiction as in the case of stealing and murder, but if it were made into a universal law it would contradict a rational being's will to develop his capacities to the fullest.

Again, in the case of refusal to help others, I must answer the question: "Am I willing to ask no one for help at any time?" Although there is nothing self-contradictory in the idea of no one's helping anyone else, such a refusal to help becomes contradictory when it is universalized from any particular person who realizes that situations may arise in which he himself may need and desire the help and sympathy of others.

The Categorical Imperative thus calls for extending the principle of consistency rigorously to consideration of every particular act in the light of the universal principle involved in it. It would be possible in any particular choice situation to apply the Categorical Imperative and then discover one's duty. While the Imperative may

[6] *Ibid.,* p. 81.

appear rigorous as it stands, Kant goes on to draw further implications from it by reformulating it in a way that underlines its uniquely humane features.

B. *Second Form of the Categorical Imperative*

We have already pointed out that for Kant the ground of all instrumental value, and the only thing unconditionally and intrinsically good in itself, is a good will. This good will is (a) a conscientious will: doing everything in one's power to fulfill one's duty. But (b) doing everything in one's power also means: Be as consistent, reasonable, and universalizing as it is in your power to be. Accordingly, *a good will is a rational will* and the rational will is the will that acts in conformity with the Categorical Imperative.

We are now ready for a new formulation of the Imperative. All potentially rational human beings are potentially good wills. Good wills as intrinsically good are ends, not means, and as ends in themselves they are to be treated with respect and dignity. Now, in Kant's words: "Rational beings are designated 'persons' . . . rather than things . . . because their nature indicates that they are ends in themselves, i.e., things which may not be used merely as means." [7] Clearly, I as a rational being ought to respect my own rational nature as an end and not merely a means, and as the source of my dignity and humanity. If this is so, then, by the first form of the Categorical Imperative, I so ought to respect all other potentially rational human beings or persons. Thus Kant derives from the first form a second form of the Categorical Imperative: "Act so that you treat humanity, whether in your own person or in that of another, always as an end and never as a means *only*." [8]

Kant does not mean that we are not or should never be means to each other's ends. If this were the case, all mutual service and differentiation of labor would cease. The "only" in "never as a means only" is a basic qualifier. What Kant does mean is that we should never consider others merely as means to the ends of our own satisfactions (merely as if persons existed, like so many things, for our own convenience). This would rule out the use of the body or the ability of another simply as a means without regard for the dignity—

[7] *Ibid.*, pp. 86–87.

[8] *Ibid.*, p. 87. Probably the best extended treatment of Kant's ethics is to be found in Herbert J. Paton, *The Categorical Imperative* (New York: Hutchinson's University Library, 1947).

potential or actual—of other persons as rational agents. For what Kant is underlining is that apart from persons capable of exercising rational self-determination, there is neither dignity nor intrinsic value. The concept of person in this sense is not necessarily confined only to human beings but, whenever or however it may elsewhere apply, Kant insists, it at least applies to all fully human beings.

It is not difficult to see how and why the Kantian ethics became and remains a rallying point for those who, on the basis of the worth and dignity of human personality, have fought slavery, economic exploitation, political suppression, and indifference to human suffering and poverty. Nor is it difficult to see how Kant's argument for respect of men as ends in themselves, interpreted, as Kant himself interprets it, in terms of the goal of men joined in a *self-legislative kingdom of ends,* became and remains a basic moral argument for democracy, for peace, and for world federation.[9]

III. *LIMITATIONS OF ETHICAL FORMALISM*

Kant's position represents what has been called Ethical Formalism at its best—that is, an ethics that depends primarily upon the motivation or intention of the actor. Kant is willing to say that, insofar as a person chooses autonomously and applies the test of consistency to the maxim of the act considered objectively, he is choosing from a sense of duty and is right. Insofar as he does not, he is immoral. If he could not possibly have done so, he is amoral. Kant is thus the outstanding modern champion of the supremacy of what we have called the principles of consistency and autonomy. Indeed, as earlier chapters have shown, in our discussion of the nature of obligation, will, and the laws of consistency and autonomy, we have learned much from Kant.

But as clear and important as Kant's position is, we are still left with one question: Are consistency and autonomy enough? In some respects even Kant recognizes that consistency and autonomy must be supplemented by other considerations to discover what they actually involve in any particular case of choice. For example, Kant rejects a sole appeal to usefulness or consequences for the individual alone, yet the actual application of the Categorical Imperative in-

---

[9] See in particular Kant's essay, *Eternal Peace* (Boston: World Peace Foundation, 1914).

volves considering what the consequences would be if the maxim of an act were to be made universal. Killing is wrong because *if* all men killed, there would be no one left to kill.

One might well argue, however, that Kant's appeal to consequences in this sense, in one way, goes too far and, in another way, does not go quite far enough. It would seem to go too far in that the consistency of consequences that would follow if an act were universalized is not the only thing that needs to be taken into account on Kant's own grounds. The second form of the Categorical Imperative calls for respect of persons as ends in themselves. Such respect may rather strikingly come into conflict with the abstract consistency of the consequences of an act universalized without regard for the particular context of both circumstances and persons in which the act occurs. Suppose we take lying as a case in point. Kant argues that lying is always wrong, for if everyone lied no one would believe anyone and lying itself would be meaningless. Suppose, however, that not to tell a lie resulted in the needless destruction of another person? What, then, ought I to do?

Kant, interestingly enough, supplies the answer in reply to a French writer, Benjamin Constant, who had insisted, "This philosopher goes so far as to assert that it would be a crime to lie to a murderer who asked whether our friend who is pursued by him had taken refuge in our house." [10] Kant's answer was that Constant was quite right. Even though it meant the death of the friend the truth must be told. "To be truthful [honest] in all declarations is a sacred and absolutely commanding decree of reason, limited by no expediency." [11] It would seem here at least that persons cease to be ends and become means to the fulfillment of an abstract, and, Kant to the contrary notwithstanding, a not very reasonable duty. One might even say that here the first and second forms of the Categorical Imperative conflict with each other.

This example equally illustrates the way in which it might be charged that Kant's appeal to consequences does not go far enough. Choices and actions do have contexts. The consequences of acts are always what might be called context consequences. If I am to act wisely, the consequences that might follow if the maxim of the act were universalized are at best only a part of the probable conse-

[10] Kant, *Critique of Practical Reason and Other Writings in Moral Philosophy*, p. 346.
   [11] *Ibid.*, p. 348.

quences (and often not very likely ones) that need to be considered. Far more important are the consequences of this act in this particular situation. What can I reasonably foresee will happen if I tell the murderer about my friend? Am I not morally responsible for what I could foresee would be the results?

The real difficulty in the Kantian system at this point goes deeper than the question of consequences. It would seem to touch the level at which Kant applies the Principle of Consistency. In our attempt to formulate the Principle of Consistency, we pointed out that a person ought to choose consistently, that is, his choices ought not to contradict or undermine each other. We had to admit that this principle was only a beginning, but an important beginning, in the attempt to live intelligently. In our discussion of the Principle of Autonomy, it became evident that we ought to be consistent at least with the ideals that we acknowledge. Kant, instead of emphasizing a person's consistency in choosing, locates the consistency in the maxim of the act in abstraction from the chooser as a *whole person* related in many ways to other whole persons. As a result, the first form of the Categorical Imperative sets up abstract consistency as the ideal rather than consistency in relation to one's ideals.

It is thus not surprising that the rigor of the first form of the Categorical Imperative creates a real tension, if not contradiction, in relation to the second form. But a further difficulty arises when one attempts to harmonize duties justified by the Categorical Imperative with each other. In the example of the murderer and our friend, "Do not lie!" and "Respect persons as ends, not means only!" seem to be in conflict. One might say that "Do not commit murder!" is also in conflict here with "Do not lie!" for directing the murderer to our friend's room is tantamount at least to aiding and abetting murder. In other words, on the basis of the Categorical Imperative in such situations, whatever one does is contrary to duty. There must be some mistake in a conception of duty that leads one to this impasse in choice.

Suppose, however, we do not accept the Kantian formulation as it stands. Can we return to the simpler conception of the Principles of Consistency and Autonomy? Can we say that our duty consists in choosing consistently and sincerely in accordance with the ideals we acknowledge? Even such a position would be far from removing all difficulties. It would mean, for example, that anyone who acts with real sincerity and consistency in accordance with whatever ideals he affirms is to that extent doing his duty and is morally praiseworthy. This, on the surface at least, seems to lead to moral chaos. People differ notoriously in regard to the ideals that they acknowledge and correspondingly about what they consider to be their duty. Bertrand Russell points out that "the Quaker and the head-hunter each do [*sic*] right in following his own conscience, the Quaker in not killing when the Government says he should, and the head-hunter in killing when the Government says he should not." [12]

To complicate matters, probably every fanatic in the history of the world has been deadly sincere and consistent. From some of the general Inquisitors to the sincere members of The John Birch Society, the Communist Party, and the American Bund such individuals have, out of a sense of duty, inflicted an incalculable amount of anguish and suffering on their fellow men. Yet, on the Principles of Consistency and Autonomy alone, each could claim he was doing his moral duty, was acting rightly and as he ought to act. We would seem to be back in the impossible impasse of relativism.

IV. *FORMAL VERSUS CRITICAL RIGHTNESS*

Yet the situation is not quite so hopeless as it seems. For we need to distinguish between merely formal rightness on the one hand and what might be called enlightened or critical rightness on the other. The difference is much the same as that between the uncritical and the critical consciences, which we have already discussed in Chapter 20. Technically, a person who does choose consistently in the light of the ideals that he acknowledges is to that extent praiseworthy and doing his duty. Insofar as the Borneo head-hunter or the Eskimo shaman is doing the best that he knows, however we may deplore his lack of knowledge, we must admire his moral fortitude. We can hardly hold either responsible for information not available to him. A judgment in regard to ignorance is not a moral judgment, unless the information lacking is normally available to the ignorant person and he is capable of digesting it but has simply refused to make the effort. Indeed, the head-hunter or shaman may be both critically and formally right. For critical rightness depends upon whether the shaman has carefully thought through what he does in the light of

[12] *Human Society in Ethics and Politics* (London: George Allen & Unwin, Ltd., 1954), pp. 74–75.

the information available to him, not on whether what he does is the theoretically best thing to do apart from the context of his life and his knowledge.

Again, the person who is formally but not critically right may be one of two kinds. First, he may be one who intentionally affirms his ideals and oughts without submitting them to the test of rational consideration and self-criticism. Or, second, he may be a person who has become so absorbed by a particular end or good that he loses perspective in regard to all other ends and the effect of his exclusive emphasis. Most fanatics are examples in point. The end that the fanatic chooses may be a highly desirable one, but by exclusive emphasis on this one end, he sacrifices all other values to it, sometimes with disastrous results for that desired end itself. The person who is so intent upon completing his education that he refuses to eat, sleep, or exercise properly may find that he has destroyed his health and thus undermined the possibility of enjoying the education he attains. The person so consumed with bringing about racial integration or slum clearance, crucially important as these are, that he loses sight of other issues is likely to find himself the dupe of an unscrupulous or opportunistic politician or party using such an issue simply as a springboard to power. Such persons are being unintelligent both in pursuit of their ends and in considering the relationship of their multiple ends to each other.

An additional distinction is often drawn between what is "subjectively right" and what is "objectively right." On this basis, a person who acts from a sense of duty, in light of the ideals that he acknowledges, is subjectively right, although what he does may be objectively wrong—that is, may bring about more harm than good. Although this is undoubtedly a valid distinction, it is questionable whether it is as helpful a distinction as is sometimes thought. Our knowledge of what is objectively right, like our knowledge of anything else, is an evolving affair. After an act is completed, we may discover that it did not have the results we had hoped for. We accordingly decide that it was not so good an act as we had thought. In all such situations, we must remember that, at the time of choice, we have to act on the basis of what we think best. To draw a distinction between subjective and objective right helps us then not at all in deciding what to do, because insofar as I act as I think best, I am acting on the basis of what I believe is objectively right at the time.

V. *AXIOLOGICAL CONSIDERATIONS*

In our discussions of conscience, freedom of speech, Kant's Categorical Imperative, and the conception of formal rightness, it has become progressively evident that if I am intelligently to acknowledge ideals toward which I feel obligated, if I am to develop a critical conscience, if I am to avoid an abstract formulation of duty and the narrow unreasonableness of fanaticism, I must consider not only the intention but the results of my action. Changing our perspective from the ideals that we acknowledge to the values for which they stand, we can see that any choice we make is a choice within a field of values, which may be harmonious or conflicting. Every choice has consequences that may enhance or defeat the end desired and for which, in part at least, we are responsible. Every choice takes place in a concrete context with a limited number of possible alternatives open. To overlook the field of choice, the context of choice, or the consequences of choice is to neglect the conditions of intelligent action. The question now becomes, can we formulate any principles in regard to these factors? Let us be sure we know where we are in the development of our reasoning.

The Principles of Consistency and Autonomy, dealing as they do with consistency and sincerity in choice and thus primarily with intention, are often called Formal Principles. They concern the formal or intentional aspects of choice. Ethical systems like those of Kant and the Stoics are often called Formal ethical systems because they stress the formal principles as the more important, if not the only important, conditions of moral choice. Although we have discovered that they do seem to be the necessary preconditions of morality and intelligent action, it has also become evident that they in themselves are not the sufficient conditions and that we need to consider the field, values, and ends of action. We need, in other words, to see whether or not there are any goods or ends or value principles—what we may call Axiological Principles, or conditions of moral and intelligent action, in contrast to the Formal Principles.

At least one principle regarding ends and values chosen tends to suggest itself immediately—what we might call the principle of value system. The fanatic, as indicated, is consistent and sincere. He gets into difficulty, however, because of his tendency toward an unrealistic and often irrational exclusiveness in choice of values. Clearly, one cannot develop a critical conscience without comparing, contrasting, criticizing, and harmonizing with each other the ideals that he acknowledges. But this involves equally the values for which the ideals stand. Accordingly, just as consistency of choice is the first of the formal principles, so a principle not just of consistent values but of coherent and harmonious values would seem to be the first of the principles applying to the values, ends, and anticipated results of choice. More formally the Axiological Principle could be stated as follows: *All persons ought to choose values that are consistent with each other, harmonious, and coherent, not values that are conflicting, contradictory, or incoherent.*[13]

The Axiological Principle rests upon the nature of value experience and the search for dependable values as discussed in Chapter 14. As we saw, the range of experiences we like, enjoy, desire, or approve is tremendously wide and includes nonharmonious and conflicting experiences as well as experiences that do coalesce or fit together into intelligible and mutually supporting patterns. Such experiences, which stand the test of critical comparision, we called dependable or "true" values in contrast to value claims or preanalytic value experience. The Axiological Principle, therefore, first of all involves recognizing the necessity of winnowing out from the plethora of apparent "values" those that do stand up under the process of criticism and accordingly enter into coherent and mutually sustaining relationships.

What we choose are value experiences—sometimes directly, but more often by way of plans of action or ideals that lead to experiences of value. If the value experiences we choose are conflicting, our choices will be conflicting or inconsistent with resulting loss of effectiveness and failure to attain our ends (as we noted under the Principle of Consistency). Further, if the values we choose are conflicting, then it will follow that there will also be conflict either between the ideals that we acknowledge or between the values that we choose and our ideals. The result in either case is confusion. This occurs, for example, when we say that we want high grades and then actually take on more outside activities than are consistent with our goal. The Principle of Autonomy is also violated, because we are not

[13] See E. S. Brightman, *Moral Laws* (New York: Abingdon Press, 1933), p. 125. The word "axiological" etymologically combines the Greek words for "value" and for "order," hence the use of the word "axiological" for the principle of systematic order among values.

then acting in accordance with an acknowledged ideal. In more than a superficial sense, therefore, the Axiological Principle might be considered an extension of the Principles of Consistency and Autonomy. It would perhaps be more accurate, however, to say that intelligent fulfillment of the Principles of Consistency and Autonomy carries one inevitably beyond the problem of moral motivation into a consideration of the field of choice, the values chosen, and their relation to each other.

The Axiological Principle does add at least two most important correctives to exclusive emphasis on the formal principles. First, it calls for object-oriented consideration. Exclusive concern with one's motives, with analysis of one's ought, guilt, and anxieties can be very dangerous and unrewarding. It all too easily leads to a morbid conscientiousness, to the development of what might almost be called an "introspective jag," along with a somewhat subtle form of masochism. Probably all except the most extroverted of individuals are at least occasionally pulled in this direction.

Particularly in periods when our experiences are expanding emotionally and intellectually we are quite likely to react with a kind of excessive and destructive self-analysis. We begin to realize our inadequacies, to recognize that we have not yet conquered and may never conquer the world. We suddenly become aware of our negative as well as positive influence on others. Our feelings of guilt and failure are magnified. Nobody has suffered quite the way we have. Nobody recognizes how sensitive we actually are. Nobody really understands or appreciates us or knows how empty, how desperate, how tragic life is, suspended as it is over the abyss of nothingness. How beautifully we have failed! We turn the screw a little tighter and revel in the additional twinge of pain.

Where such a progression may end is not difficult to foresee. Like so many progressions this is likely to feed on itself until it leads to a paralysis of action. In more extreme instances, radical methods and professional help may be necessary to break the progression. In others, escape from the progression is found in surrender to authority that will provide us with certainties. The Axiological Principle calls for a constant corrective or counterbalance by shifting concern from past failures and present feelings of inadequacy to the range of values to be realized. It invites us to apply intelligence to developing a reasoned plan of mutually sustaining and realizable values. It makes for the balance of conscientiousness by objectivity and a sense of humor. We fully realize our potentialities only when we move beyond growing self-concern to objective accomplishment. But such accomplishment is feasible only if the values chosen are feasible in relation to each other.

Second, the Axiological Principle demands as a corrective for indecision the development of a positive basis for specific value decision through awareness of the kinds of relations values may have to each other and the construction of one's own symphony or table of values to guide choice. Even among the values that we recognize as "dependable" values, the possible range of selection is likely to be wider than any one person can realize, as a result of limits of time, ability, necessary background, or other factors. I might dream of being an ideal jack-of-all-trades, a chemist, an actor, a concert pianist, a statistician, an historian, all of which are admirable and significant occupations. But the probability that I could be all of them at once is so low as to be negligible. If I cannot make up my mind I shall probably be caught like the donkey between the haystacks. He starved to death because he didn't know which way to turn. Frequently, some values have to be subordinated to others. Most students would like to be educationally, economically, and socially successful—all at the same time. Each of these types of success may well be desirable, but for many persons they are not all possible at once. The attempt to pursue each equally can lead to failure in all three.

Quite often decision cannot be put off. One's choice is seldom between good and bad but among various goods and degrees of good. If I do not decide, circumstances will decide for me, and they may do so in the least desirable way. The Axiological Principle does not call for detailed decision beforehand. Rather it calls for the development of a harmonious value system from among the general types of value—such as our "symphony of values"—a system adapted to the abilities and rationally criticized desires of each individual himself. With such a value system I have a guide for the selection of values and for their subordination to one another in the light of those patterns of value most important to me. Without such a system I merely flounder in a sea of unrealized and (if I continue to flounder) unrealizable value possibilities.

The system of values one develops may be relatively rigid or relatively flexible, relatively rich or relatively simple. The type of integration or style of life that a person achieves will be determined by his system of values. But, we would reemphasize, each person's system of values needs to be tailor-made to fit his potentialities and interests. Among the factors that should enter into construction of one's system of values, the factor that we urge here is intelligent choice in the pursuit of values, the specific realization that one is choosing more than the particular values he is aiming at. Consequences are so important that they require special attention in ethical theory and call for a distinct principle, as we shall see in the next chapter.

VI. REFLECTIVE SUMMARY

The Principle of Consistency and the Principle of Autonomy, as we have stated them, find staunch support, up to a point, in Kant's argument for the Categorical Imperative. We have urged that in themselves autonomy and consistency cannot throw light on specific duties without appeal to some set of values and ideals. To universalize the maxim of an act, without reference to the person, circumstances, and consequences involved, is to make consistency of action an end in itself.

But Kant himself moves from his first formulation of the Categorical Imperative to the second by pointing out that persons capable of consistency and autonomy can never be treated as means to an end. In other words, we need to realize that we are never legislating for acts apart from persons, or for acts apart from consequences for persons in given and emerging contexts of action and choice.

Consideration of consequences by themselves is also inadequate to guide choice, but actions without consequences are unintelligible, and actions outside of particular contexts are meaningless. In a word, if we try to be consistent about the maxim of actions without taking into account the complex agent and the complex persons who will be affected by the actions, we shall fail to treat persons as ends in themselves and never as means only.

What becomes increasingly clear, then, is that in moral choice we must move beyond consistency, as such, to the observation of the concrete value experiences in their relation to each other in the lives of persons and finally to the systematization of values into some pattern of values. This pattern of values—such as our symphony of values—will operate as a general scheme and must not be superimposed like a stencil upon all persons at any stage of growth and in different circumstances.

But without such a pattern of values to guide choice, the individual may become fanatic in thought and action, or morbidly conscientious, or morally paralyzed. The Axiological Principle is the principle of objective balance and perspective both on one's own search for values and on that of others. What remains to be seen more clearly is the part that consideration of consequences plays in achieving balance and perspective without loss of consistency or sincerity.

22

How Important Are Consequences?

~~~~~~

I. *INEVITABILITY OF CONSEQUENCES*

Regardless of how much a person may or may not desire it, every act he performs has consequences that extend indefinitely into the future. A man stops to scratch a mosquito bite while working in the garden. The bite becomes infected. He neglects the infection. Finally the doctor has to be called in. The man is sent to the hospital and misses a week at the office. During that week an important business matter comes up regarding the relocation of a textile factory. Because he was not available to present his case, the factory is moved from New England to another section of the country. This move affects the lives of hundreds of people. Quite obviously, not every instance of scratching a mosquito bite has such striking consequences, but it is essentially of such chains of events that history is made. Each act is like throwing a stone into a pool. The disturbance causes waves going out indefinitely in all directions. If the wind is blowing and the pool is rough, the waves may be slight and even go unnoticed, but the pool is nonetheless permanently different if only by the addition of the stone.

One's actions may, in fact usually do, have wholly unforeseen effects or consequences. From the standpoint of other persons, however, it is the consequences, far more than the intention or the attitude of the person who acts, that are important. And it is most frequently in terms of the consequences of our acts rather than of our original intention that we are actually judged by others. If you throw a stone through my window, it is the broken window that I confront and must do something about, not your intention, even though without your intention to scare away the crow the effect would not have occurred. Furthermore, the consequences that occurred can no more be undone than the act itself. If I run over a child, whether I intended it or not, the child is hurt or dead, and all the regret in the world will not change the fact.

The inevitableness of consequences plus the fact that the good or evil done to others is none other than the consequences of actions force us to conclude that a person who fails to take into account whatever consequences he can is either insensitive or foolish. Many ethicists are so impressed with the importance of consequences as to maintain that right and duty are wholly determined by the consequences that follow from an act.

Ethical positions formulated by such thinkers have been generally classified as teleological ethics (from the Greek term *telos,* meaning "end"), or goods ethics, or utilitarian ethics (stressing the usefulness of acts in producing consequences, in particular pleasure-pain). Such positions, in contrast to *formal* ethics as exemplified by Kant and the Stoics, stress that the value of a virtue or an attitude is to be determined not by anything in the virtue or attitude itself but solely by the consequences, that is, the intrinsic values or disvalues that each produces. Even Kant, as we pointed out, was interested in a particular kind of consequences (those that would follow from universalizing an act).

II. *TELEOLOGICAL ETHICS*

Consequences are more or less public and definite. If we define rightness and duty in terms of consequences as do the teleological ethicists, we avoid the relativistic aspects of depending on intentions or on ideals that we acknowledge. Lucius Garvin offers a typical teleological definition of right and wrong: *"An act is wrong if its total consequences are intrinsically less good than those of some other act that might have been chosen. An act is right if it is not wrong."* [1] This would seem to offer a direct and easily applied principle.

[1] *A Modern Introduction to Ethics* (Boston: Houghton Mifflin Company, 1953), pp. 205–6.

Whether one is considering enthusiasm, lying, giving to a charitable organization, or taking out an insurance policy, one asks whether or not this particular act, taking into account its total consequences, produces more intrinsic value than any alternative act possible in this situation. If it does, the act is right; if it does not, it is wrong.

A. *Ends-Means Relations*

Such a view has much to recommend it, particularly if it is carefully defined. For one thing, it calls for a clear conception of means-ends relationships. The holders of teleological views do subscribe to the formula: the end justifies the means. But they would be the first to insist that this does not commit them to a Machiavellian indifference to means, an indifference to any consideration except that they bring about the desired end. The popular usage of "The end justifies the means" must be clearly distinguished from its ethical usage. Popularly, the phrase is taken to mean that any act is all right so long as it leads to a particular desired end. Thus, in the popular view, oppression, torture, treachery, and even genocide might be condoned if they lead to a strong and powerful state. The defenders of teleological ethics would insist that their position warrants no such conclusion. The Machiavellian position overlooks the fact that all the consequences of an act must be taken into account, not just the one end aimed at, and that these consequences must be weighed in terms of their total intrinsic value against the total intrinsic value of the consequences of the other possible alternatives.

Whether or not to go to war in order to get additional sources of oil, for example, is not a decision that can be made with only the specific end of securing the oil sources in mind. The teleologist would raise a whole series of questions: Can the same end be achieved by negotiation? Even if negotiation takes longer and involves concession and sacrifice, will the expense not be less, in terms of money and the dislocation and suffering caused by fighting? What about the effect of such an action on the confidence of other countries in us? Will fighting not jeopardize the possibility of future negotiations with other nations? If we win, shall we not be in constant danger of sabotage and revolt? What about retaliation from other powers also desirous of oil? If negotiations are impossible, are there no other sources of oil that might be obtained by negotiation? What will the effect of war be on our own internal economy, on

morale, on the possibility of additional and larger wars? In the background looms the shadow of unprecedented mutual atomic or nuclear destruction. All these factors, the teleologist would insist, must
be taken into account before right action can be determined. Furthermore, ends must be considered in relation to each other, too!
We never live for *one* end alone; and what might obtain one end
for us might destroy another.

To be sure, the teleologist would insist in his own special way that
the end does justify the means. In fact, nothing else could possibly
justify a means except the ends it produces, for a means is only a
means in relation to an end. But one must not forget that the means
are also ends and the ends are in turn means to additional ends;
any reckoning must take *all* these ends into account. To take a sample case: suppose I am tempted to cheat on an examination. The
examination is not well proctored. My devices are practically foolproof, and the chances of being caught are very low. The course was
required and never interested me, yet I cannot merely pass it for I
need a good grade to maintain my average. So, I cheat, and I receive
a good grade. I am happy; so is the poor deluded instructor who mis-
takenly thinks I have mastered the material! The end has justified
the means.

But this is not the whole story, the teleological ethicist would insist. You have much more calculating to do if you are to take into
account all the consequences. You must add on the possible consequences in your own life, as well as the external consequences, the
long range results as well as the immediate consequences, for these
also are ends that you must enter in the balance sheet. In the first
place, you were not sure you would not be caught until the examination was returned. Your worry on this score must be put into the
negative column. The fact that you got by with it this time has
lowered to just this extent your resistance to cheating. You are likely
to be more careless next time. You may be caught, and the people
who know about it will lose confidence in you. You will be surprised
how such things get around! The next time you may forfeit both a
grade and the opportunity to continue in the college of your choice.

Furthermore, even if you are not caught now or later, the grade
that you received does not represent your mastery of the subject. It
is a falsified record, a lie, that goes with you permanently. Have you
subtly undermined your own confidence in yourself and your ability
to do honestly what is required of you? Have you started a pattern

easily extended to important matters in your vocational preparation? Will you later find that you do not have the information or skill that you are supposed to have at the crucial points in life when you cannot cheat and others are dependent on you? A doctor performing an operation or an aerial navigator over the Pacific has no one's shoulder to look over.

Still further, can we afford to forget the effect on the other students in the class? The students who did study lose confidence in you, whether they congratulate you or not. They may resent your unfair competition. Some may be tempted to follow your example. Like the effect of the bad apple in the bushel, this progression can increase until no one trusts anyone else and the few honest students are penalized for their honesty. At this point the educational process becomes a farce. Neither you nor fellow students are getting what you are paying and working for, and the value of the degree from your college sinks low in the community. (A number of schools in the country have actually had to abandon the honors system of examinations for this very reason.) You have not justified the means by the ends unless you have taken all these various and sundry factors into account. When you do so, the balance would in most cases raise very serious questions as to either the utility or the rightness of cheating. You probably would find a loss where you assumed a profit.

B. *Jeremy Bentham and the Hedonistic Calculus*

The concept of balancing the desirable against the undesirable consequences of acts in determining their rightness or wrongness has encouraged the hope of some teleological ethicists that ethics might be reduced to an exact science of calculating rightness and wrongness by mathematical means. The classic attempt in this direction was made by the English thinker Jeremy Bentham, who was particularly interested in the use of ethics to institute legislative reform. Bentham, with other teleological ethicists, insisted that "the ends of morality will be on all occasions best served by the habit of comparing the consequences of action." [2] Furthermore, according to Bentham, that action is right, which produces the greatest happiness for the greatest number of people. For Bentham, intrinsic value or happiness is to be equated with pleasure and disvalue with pain. He felt that the

[2] *Deontology* (2 vols.; London: Longmans, Green, 1834) II, 77.

amount of value or pleasure in any particular case could be exactly calculated, and he suggested a series of seven dimensions or elements of value that need to be taken into account in such reckoning: (1) its intensity, (2) its duration, (3) its certainty or uncertainty—likelihood of its occurrence, (4) its propinquity or remoteness, (5) its fecundity, or the chances that a pleasure has of being followed by further pleasure or pain by further pain, (6) its purity, or the chances a pleasure has of not being followed by its opposite, and (7) its extent, the number of persons in society who are affected by it.[3]

With the exception of intensity all of Bentham's dimensions do apply to consequences. We rather obviously can apply them in trying to decide on a vocation. I may well ask: Is this the kind of work I enjoy and shall continue to enjoy (duration)? What chances of success in this line do I have (certainty)? Will it make contacts possible and open up at least some room for related avocations that I shall enjoy (fecundity)? How much chance is there that I shall get bogged down in details and drudgery as opposed to enjoying the positive accomplishments of the work (purity)? Is the work important, that is, does it make a real contribution to society or is it the kind of work that is easily dispensed with in times of social crises (extent)? In fact, unless I have asked such questions about vocations and find that the vocation in question scores highest, then I am choosing blindly.

C. *Actual versus Probable Consequences*

There are, however, a number of general problems regarding this matter of considering consequences that our discussion has not thus far taken into account. In the first place, on a teleological view, is it the actual consequences or the probable consequences that determine the rightness or wrongness of an act? An example may help to make the question clear. Suppose, while driving my car into town, I stop to pick up a neighbor who is waiting for a bus. On the way another car runs through a stop light and crashes into us. The neighbor is killed. Here the actual consequences and the probable consequences of picking up the neighbor are quite different things. The probable consequences were that the neighbor would get into town far more quickly and comfortably by riding with me than by waiting

[3] *An Introduction to the Principles of Morals and Legislation* (Oxford: Clarendon Press, 1879), pp. 29–30. See, for an excellent exposition of Bentham and of hedonism, David Baumgardt, *Bentham and the Ethics of Today* (Princeton: Princeton University Press, 1952).

for a public conveyance. The actual consequences were disastrous. Was the act of picking up the neighbor right or wrong?

Those who insist that only actual consequences determine rightness would have to say that the act of picking up my neighbor was wrong although the consequences were wholly unforeseen and unforeseeable. They might add that although the act was wrong it was morally good, because it was done in the belief that it was right. But this would not make it right, for the total consequences were actually less good than those of some other act that might have been chosen, for example, letting the neighbor take the bus.[4]

Such an analysis brings us back to the difference between subjective right and objective right, discussed in the last chapter. One may define "right" in terms of actual consequences if he wishes. But such a definition would do violence to common usage. In effect, it removes "right" from specifically moral consideration, because intention is no longer relevant to choice. To make the rightness of my act depend upon the intervention of factors among the consequences that I could not have foreseen is to place rightness beyond either my control or responsibility.

Further, if rightness so defined were to be used as a basis of judgment of the act and of the actor, if blame or praise were to rest on such a conception, teleological ethics would, it might be argued, assume a harshness and a rigor exceeding that of the most extreme formalism. Take as an example the parents who have children not by accident but for the best of reasons, who do everything they can to provide adequate and responsible home, community, and school background, and yet whose children, through circumstances beyond control of the parents, turn out as threats to parents and society. Were the parents morally wrong in having children? If actual consequences determine the rightness of acts, one would have so to conclude.

Recognition of the difference between moral goodness and right defined in terms of actual consequences modifies the teleological position in a most interesting way. For surely, my duty is to do what is morally right. But I can hardly have a duty to do any supposed "right" that is beyond my power or of which I cannot know. Whether an act is morally good, and thus morally right, seems to depend upon my intention to bring about the best consequences after considering the probable effects of my act. If this is the case, then in considering the rightness and reasonableness of an act I can no more overlook the

[4] See Garvin, op. cit., p. 238.

formal factors (sincerity and consistency) of intention in considering consequences than the formalist can afford to overlook probable consequences of action in considering intention.

We are, after all, primarily concerned with the conditions and limits of reasonable moral maturity, not with what might be the case if we were omniscient in regard to the future consequences of action —not a usual condition among mortals. A person is far from being either morally or ethically good if he does not take into account the probable value or the probable consequences of his actions. If he does so to the best of his knowledge and ability and as a result decides that the consequences of the act in question, as far as he can critically foresee them, yield more intrinsic value or less disvalue than any other recognizable alternative in the situation, then at least his act is to that extent morally right. That, after all, is our concern as moral beings.

If we make the actual consequences the criterion of both goodness and rightness, we would be in the paradoxical position of having to wait until all the consequences are in before we can decide that any act is right or wrong. Because we could never know that any act is right or wrong at the time of action, moral decision and determination of duty would be impossible. If before a mother could decide that it was right to give her hungry baby a bottle, she had to know whether the baby would grow up to be a gangster or a saint, she probably would feed the baby on impulse or instinct and leave such nonsense as theory of morals to people who did not have hungry babies to feed.

D. *Total versus Foreseeable Consequences*

Even to qualify "right" defined in terms of consequences by talking about the probable value of probable consequences does not remove all of the difficulties. G. E. Moore, a contemporary English ethicist, insists that if consequences (even probable ones) determine duty we should never have any reason to suppose that any action is our duty. Note that in the teleological definition of "right," as quoted earlier, the stipulation is that an act is right if its total consequences are better than those of some other act that might have been chosen. The rub, Moore points out, comes in the "total." It would be utterly impossible to consider the probable total consequences of any act, let alone all the alternative acts that might be performed in the situation, assuming that no accidents intervened! The consequences of every act continue indefinitely. Because Moore himself defines duty in terms of total consequences, he concludes quite logically: "No sufficient reason has ever yet been found for considering one action more right or wrong than another." [5] What rule, then, shall guide our action? His only suggestion is that we follow whatever rules are generally practiced. Unfortunately, as we have already discovered, this gives us no help at all.

To give up the attempt to foresee what consequences I can because I cannot foresee all the consequences of action is equivalent to giving up the search for knowledge altogether because I cannot know everything. Not only would such a procedure be a retreat to relativism and glorification of the *status quo,* but it comes dangerously close to abrogating the demand to be as intelligent as we can. I can assess some of the probable consequences of my actions, and with increased knowledge, my range of correct assessment in turn increases. If this assumption is true, to recognize that probable consequences of one of the alternatives open to me are not desirable and do not conform to what I think best, and yet to choose that alternative over another in which the probable consequences do conform to what I think best is (a) to choose incoherent values, (b) to choose contrary to my own ideals, and (c) to choose inconsistently.

During a recent flood, a private car with a family that included a baby six months old was stranded for about three days on a section of highway between two swollen rivers. Stranded in the same section of road was a food truck containing dairy products and meat. The driver of the truck could rather clearly anticipate the ill effects of lack of food, particularly to the baby, but also to the others including himself. The food did not belong to the driver. Suppose he refused to act in accordance with foreseeable consequences because he could not know the total consequences of his act and instead followed the conventional rule regarding taking and giving away another person's property without that person's consent? The driver's moral intelligence could have been seriously questioned.

We are still left with the question "Can we formulate any reasonable principle regarding consequences?" That consequences need to be considered if one is to act intelligently has been amply illustrated. But we have discovered limitations as to the consequences that can be considered. By the nature of our human situation we cannot consider the total consequences of any particular act, let alone all its

[5] *Principia Ethica* (Cambridge: University Press, 1903), p. 152.

alternatives. And if consideration of consequences is to be at all relevant to choice, we have to work with the probable foreseeable consequences rather than the actual consequences, for the actual consequences cannot be known with certainty until long after any particular act has been executed, if even then.

E. *Choice among Available Alternatives*

One additional factor calls for a further qualification in considering consequences. My duty is to choose values harmonious with the ideals I acknowledge, to choose that act the consequences of which I approve—consequences—that include more intrinsic value or less intrinsic disvalue than any other alternative open at the time. But this can hardly mean that I must unqualifiedly approve of all the probable consequences as I see them. To have to approve of all the foreseeable consequences of acts in most situations would as effectively block decision as the demand that I consider all the consequences or the actual consequences. Situations in which all the foreseeable consequences of any given alternative can be approved wholeheartedly or without qualification are rare indeed. A person must choose in context. Not every element involved in the best available context may be ideal, but choose he must. What he can do as an intelligent and responsible person, and all he is expected to do, is to choose that total context whose consequences, as he can foresee them, he *on the whole* approves, in contrast to the other alternatives open.

III. *THE PRINCIPLE OF CONSEQUENCES*

With the qualifications that we have discovered as integral to it, a Principle of Consequences fundamental to morally responsible and intelligent action does take shape. We might formulate it as follows: *Each person ought to consider and on the whole approve of the foreseeable consequences of his actions.*[6]

A. *"Foreseeable"*

Like the Principle of Autonomy, the Principle of Consequences is particularly rich and immediately practical in its range of implica-

[6] Cf. E. S. Brightman, *Moral Laws* (New York: Abingdon Press, 1933), p. 142.

tions. Suppose we look more closely, to begin with, at the import of the term "foreseeable" as integral to the principle. "Foreseeable" has both positive and negative implications. On the positive side, I am duty-bound to take into account the consequences of my choices insofar as I can reasonably be expected to foresee them in the circumstances of my choice. On the negative side, my moral liability is limited to such foreseeable circumstances. I cannot reasonably be held responsible for what I could not have been expected to foresee.

Failure to recognize this negative limit to responsibility for consequences can frequently lead to an unrealistic, heartless, and, we would like to suggest, immoral condemnation both of oneself and of others. For example, suppose a member of my family is suddenly taken seriously ill. I call the doctor and meanwhile do the very best that I can to make the person comfortable in the light of the experience and information that I have. But the person dies before or shortly after the doctor arrives. Then I begin to berate myself. If only I had recognized the symptoms earlier—if only I had called the doctor five minutes sooner—if only I had had the proper medicine at hand—the person might not have died! Or suppose instead of a sudden illness, it has been a longer affair, but still with disastrous results. Once more I might feel that if only we had gone to a different doctor or a different hospital, or if I had insisted that other doctors be consulted, this consequence might not have happened. All too easily I overlook the fact that I did what I could, that the other "ifs" were not real alternatives at the time. By holding myself responsible, I build up unreasonable feelings of guilt for what I could not help. Consequently, my work, others who may be dependent upon me, even friends who have to put up with me are made to suffer for something neither I nor they could help. Carried to the extreme, such self-condemnation can lead to a permanent scarring of my personality and serious anxieties. And all because I am being neither reasonable nor, in a very real sense, ethical.

To hold others morally responsible for misfortunes occurring in similar circumstances without our having a rather clear knowledge of what was foreseeable under the conditions and for the person involved may be equally unjust and irrational. At a Boston-area hospital, a student nurse started to give a prescribed tranquilizer to a group of patients headed for X-ray. She gave it to the first two patients. They had come to the hospital for diagnostic X-ray only, without being seriously ill. She was about to administer the same dosage to the rest of the patients when the first two became violently ill and died almost immediately. She rechecked the bottles. The drug had been taken from the correctly labeled bottle. It was the right color and seemed to be the right consistency. Yet chemical analysis showed the contents of the bottle to be a deadly compound used for sterilizing instruments. Someone, perhaps out of negligence, had made a most serious mistake. Yet what of the student nurse who had given the lethal dose? Her action had been the cause of the deaths. Testimony indicated that a nurse long experienced in the use of the drug might have noticed a slight difference in the size of the crystals and been suspicious. Was the student nurse to blame for not having had such experience? To have held her negligent and responsible for the unforeseeable consequences of her act would have ruined not only her career in nursing, but probably her life as well.

It would be easy, however, to interpret the term "foreseeable" in too restricted a way. The term "foreseeable" does not offer either a rationalization or an easy excuse for negligence or for not taking into account the consequences that normally, in the circumstances, could have been foreseen. Suppose, in the case of the hospital deaths, one of the pharmacists in the hospital drug room, knowing full well the dangers involved in mixing drugs, had nevertheless grown careless. Instead of labeling the bottles and then pouring the contents in immediately, he poured the contents in the two bottles, one the sterilizer and the other the tranquilizer, but then was interrupted by a phone call. During his absence orders had piled up. He knew he should test, but he seemed to remember which bottle was which. To save time he labeled the bottles as he remembered. The deaths resulted. Could he rightfully plead ignorance? Obviously, there is a difference between such ignorance and the ignorance necessarily due to the inexperience of a student nurse. The druggist did not intentionally mix the labels, but he knew that a mistake could be fatal. Nevertheless, he neglected to make a check. It would be difficult to absolve him morally from the consequences of his act. He did not take the precautions he knew he should.

The range of what is normally foreseeable will obviously differ for different persons and for the same persons in different areas of his experience, and responsibility for consequences will vary accordingly. Some consequences any normal person can be expected to foresee. One does not have to be advanced in years or wisdom to realize the probable consequences of building a fire under a wooden stairway.

The traffic policeman is not likely to be too sympathetic to the local resident who pleads ignorance of traffic regulations, although he may excuse an out-of-state visitor who violates the regulation in question.

In contrast to such generally expected knowledge of consequences, a professional guide on a big-game hunt can be expected to foresee the dangers of firing too soon and inaccurately at a charging bull-elephant whereas the amateur on his first safari may not. A trained chemist can be expected to foresee the results of pouring certain liquids together when the housewife may not. A trained logician and propaganda analyst can be expected to foresee the dangers involved in hasty generalization, or in accusation with inadequate evidence, whereas the man on the street may not. What will be foreseeable consequences in any particular case will depend to a high degree upon past experience and education.

B. *Ethical Importance of Education*

The ethical importance of education as it relates to the Principle of Consequences cannot, therefore, be lightly passed over. Education might be defined as a process of increasing the range of human experience, directly or indirectly, in order to widen our understanding and appreciation of experience and to discover the methods and tools for controlling and making it more worthwhile. As such, education can increase our mastery of our world by increasing our ability to anticipate accurately. But at the same time, education increases our responsibility. The desirability of both understanding and responsibility is not hard to see. Probably more human suffering and anguish have been caused by just plain ignorance and by blundering than by any other single factor. Honest belief in the necessity of burning witches or the need for human sacrifice to ward off the evil spirits that spread diseases or cause drought is only a minor case in point. More serious, morally, than "honest ignorance" is the action of those people who should and could know better, but do not bother to find out. Couples who marry and expect to have children, but never bother to seek information about a child's development illustrate the point. So also do people who pray for peace or social justice but refuse to give much thought to ways and means for bringing about peace and social justice, or to the sacrifices of individuals and groups that such an ideal will require.

It is perhaps the recognition of just such a relation between ignorant good intentions and human suffering (plus the difficulty of knowing intentions) that has tempted some ethicists to define duty and right in terms of actual consequences and to refuse to consider intended probable consequences.[7] We have already indicated the practical inapplicability of such a definition. For similar reasons, we cannot make any particular amount or kind of knowledge or education a precondition of morality. We would then find ourselves in the peculiarly intolerable position of saying, for example, that before men discovered the causal relation between lack of sanitation and certain diseases, there was no basis for their being, or being judged, moral. Persons can only be judged in the light of what they know and, presumably, can know. To say otherwise is to bring into serious question the morality of Socrates, Plato, Jesus, and St. Francis, in many ways. Or, more devastating because the frontiers of knowledge are constantly expanding, if we insisted upon a certain amount or kind of knowledge or education, we should have the uncomfortable suspicion that we had not reached as yet either the requisite amount or kind of knowledge for morality ourselves.

Nonetheless, the striking connection between ignorance and human suffering, disvalue, and personality disintegration is a continual, primary matter of moral concern. While the Principle of Consequences could not include the demand that every person must have a certain specified kind or amount of knowledge or education, yet among its implications would rather clearly seem to be the following: First, on the individual level one is obligated to increase his own knowledge and the areas of his knowledge as much as possible, commensurate with his abilities and tasks. This includes the willingness to continue to search and to learn, with full recognition that such searching and learning is by no means confined to formal education. The failure to do so not only cuts down on "foreseeability" in a foreseeable and morally culpable way, but it also reduces one's competency and effectiveness in attaining his ends or ideals. A physician who knew "all he needed to know" ten years ago when he finished his internship, and who has not kept up with advances in the field of medicine since, is not the man to call when the children are sick. Nor is the physician who knows only about children or about anatomy necessarily the best to call in all cases of sickness.

Second, on the communal level, the Principle of Consequences stresses our obligation to make as much education as possible avail-

[7] See John Stuart Mill's *Utilitarianism* (New York: Liberal Arts Press).

able at as many levels and in as many varieties, as are necessary, and to as many people as can profit from it. This in effect means making available to all persons the kinds of educational experience that are most in line with their capabilities and interests. Not everyone, quite obviously, could profit equally from an education in liberal arts or in business or in engineering or for that matter from a college education of any kind. But any person with anything approaching normal intelligence and above can profit from some type of education, some increase in his insight and effectiveness.

Occasionally one still hears the contention that education is a dangerous thing, and if what is meant is that a little knowledge assumed to be certain or assumed to be all knowledge is dangerous, the argument is undoubtedly correct. But such assumptions mark the end of educability, rather than education. In the light of the complexity and smallness of the modern world, it is far more dangerous for our mutual welfare to have blocks of people anywhere uneducated or poorly educated. We can no longer afford the luxury of lack of concern over illiteracy anywhere.

Third, along with extension of education, the Principle of Consequences calls for improvement in quality of education. We cannot afford second-class education, whatever the area or type, any more than we can afford lack of education. Again, this does not mean that everyone should or could be expected to reach the same but constantly higher level of achievement within any particular educational field. However, if there is a danger in asking for various levels of education available to an ever-growing number of persons, it would seem to lie in a lowering of educational standards, in accepting as the aim of education conformity to the average rather than making the aim maximum achievement of insight for each grade of ability. Without an insistence upon the highest quality of education for each level of ability and interest, there can be very little extension of the frontiers of knowledge and the overcoming of ignorance called for by the Principle of Consequences. This is perhaps the least appropriate time in the world's history to castigate the "eggheads," or for that matter, the technicians. What we need is to encourage the highest quality possible in every area.

Thus, fourth, the Principle of Consequences calls for wholehearted communal and individual encouragement and support of research, scientific and general, as the front line in the fight against ignorance. John Dewey and his followers, among others, have been particularly outspoken in their insistence upon our moral obligation to extend scientific investigation as far as possible. In fact, Dewey insists, the assumption that the natural sciences and moral inquiry are separate and unrelated has undermined moral accomplishment and demoralized the sciences.

> Physics, chemistry, history, statistics, engineering science, are a part of disciplined moral knowledge so far as they enable us to understand the conditions and agencies through which man lives, and on account of which he forms and executes his plans. Moral science is not something with a separate province. It is physical, biological and historic knowledge placed in a human context where it will illuminate and guide the activities of men.[8]

The duty to support research is not, however, limited to research in applied science alone. Effective applied science rests upon advances in pure or theoretical science—scientific inquiry—not devising better washing machines or bombs but satisfying curiosity about how things work. It is such curiosity that is important and not the immediate applicability of the knowledge to which curiosity leads. Without the research activities of the "pure" scientist, the "applied" scientist would soon have nothing to apply.

At the present time, the major funds for research come from industry and government. Although such support is important and valuable, it tends to place a premium on practical results of particular types. The industrialist must satisfy his stockholders over not too long a period of time that the research contributes to profits, and the government official must satisfy the taxpayers and electorate that tax funds are wisely spent in terms of their practical results. In such circumstances, the "pure" scientist is likely to find himself neglected and without adequate funds to follow his research where it leads if it does not seem to contribute to the desired commercial end.

A further danger in the financing of research by private industry or by government lurks in the tendency to restrict the knowledge of the results of research to the supporting concern or agency for either monetary or security reasons. Scientific advance depends on past accomplishment. Withholding of information leads not only to needless duplication but also to a breakdown in the kind of interchange of scientific information that suggests new areas of investiga-

[8] John Dewey, *Human Nature and Conduct* (New York: Henry Holt, 1922), p. 296. Reprinted by permission of Holt, Rinehart and Winston, Inc.

tion. If the urgent battle against ignorance is to continue in full force, both the tendency to emphasize applied science alone and to restrict dissemination of the results of scientific inquiry need to be counteracted.

C. *"On the Whole Approve"*

In explaining the Principle of Consequences we have laid considerable emphasis on the "foreseeable." But there is a second important qualifier: "on the whole approve." As we have already suggested, seldom are all the consequences of any alternative open to me those I would approve wholeheartedly, other things being equal. I can only choose among the real alternatives present. Usually I can imagine an ideal alternative better than any now available. Such an imagined ideal may help me discriminate, but because the imagined ideal is not open, I can have no obligation to choose it.

In fact, the imagined ideal may actually pose a danger to present fulfillment of duty. Insofar as I spend my time imagining an unreal alternative, fulfilling it imaginatively, and regretting the fact that it is not real, my effectiveness in assessing the real alternative is reduced. When the term "idealist" is used in a derogatory sense, it usually applies to persons ineffective and inefficient in exactly this way—the "if only we could" people who never quite come down to earth. Whatever else morality involves, its foundation is practical intelligence, and not an "if only things were different" pseudo-idealism. Such idealism is indeed a false rather than an actual idealism since, more often than not, it is a disguised form either of daydreaming or of rationalization. An actual idealist attempts to discover among the open alternatives the one most in conformity with his ideals, a process requiring practical acumen of a high order, as well as courage to test the ideal by which he is guiding action. Such ability is the mark of the art of living as contrasted with mere living.

In many instances, a person may not approve of any of the alternatives open. And yet he either must choose or have the choice (and consequences of it) made for him. In such circumstances the Principle of Consequences indicates that one still is obligated to choose the least of the evils. Insofar as one has done so, he has done all that he could do and is fulfilling his duty. At the time of the Communist march into South Korea, none of the alternatives open to the President of the United States was particularly desirable. He could have done nothing; but this would have meant letting not only South Korea fall under the yoke of the communists but very possibly all of Asia also. He could have delayed action, at the risk of allowing the Communist forces to grow stronger and the native hope of resistance in other Asiatic countries to be further undermined. A third alternative was to meet the aggression alone. Yet this would involve the United States not only in war but in what would appear to others a strictly American and a possibly colonial war. A fourth alternative was to engage the whole Communist world in a major "preventive war" (a contradiction in terms!). Such a war would not only have meant worldwide suffering and destruction but, very possibly, because of the use of nuclear weapons, the eclipse of civilization. The fifth alternative was to meet the aggression with force in Korea while calling on the other members of the United Nations for a common effort. The result would be a long, costly, frustrating local engagement in which no decisive victory could be won, yet in which it would become clear that we would not sit by while the Asian nations were destroyed and absorbed into the Communist empire by force. Again, none of the alternatives or their consequences was desirable, but the duty of the President was to anticipate the consequences and to act in the situation that appeared to involve the least evil.

A voter may be faced with the same choice between evils. Of two candidates running for office he may approve of neither. Candidate A has a voting record and holds a position of which he does not approve. Candidate B is an opportunist who seems willing to use any means to his particular ends. The voter has a third alternative, not voting at all. What ought he to do? If he fails to vote, he will not prevent the election of one of the candidates, but he may also aid the supporters of the least desirable candidate. The decision again becomes a matter of detecting the lesser of the two evils.

D. *Inaction and Consequences*

Unfortunately one cannot avoid consequences by refusing to act. The failure to act is as much an action from the standpoint of consequences as overt action itself and carries with it the same responsibility for foreseeable consequences. Suppose you accidentally overheard a conversation at the next table in a restaurant in which damaging misinformation regarding a friend of yours is passed on. You fail to do anything about it. In a very real way, you become a party to the continued spread of the misinformation and whatever damage it causes your friend. Quite obviously, to decide what to do in such a case would not be easy. Intelligent action is seldom easy. Other factors need to be taken into account. It will make a difference whether or not you know the people doing the talking; much depends on the character of the misinformation. Probably, the least you could do in most circumstances is warn your friend of what is happening.

What is important is the recognition that inaction as well as action has consequences. We are responsible for the foreseeable consequences of our inaction, and this responsibility must also be taken into account in considering which set of consequences we on the whole approve. Whether we like it or not, we are, from the standpoint of consequences, not only our brothers' keepers but also the makers of the situations among which our brothers must choose. The consequences of my action or inaction may drastically limit or expand the alternatives open to you; what you do helps to determine what I can do.

E. *Consequences and Expediency*

Some more formalistic thinkers have objected to the Principle of Consequences on the grounds that it reduces morality to expediency. It makes morality a matter of a balance sheet. One bets only on what appears to be a sure thing. The moral heroes of the race, objectors would point out, have been men who have acted even though the odds in regard to favorable consequences were against them—men who have been willing to sacrifice everything for the sake of an ideal regardless of consequences. Socrates drank the hemlock; Giordano Bruno died at the stake; Jesus was nailed to the cross.

It must be admitted that concern with consequences taken alone without the sincerity in commitment to ideals demanded by the Principle of Autonomy and the scaling and harmonizing of values of the Axiological Principle, could easily become a calculation to escape difficulty and to work out compromises in order to avoid pain. But, as integrally related to the other principles, the Principle of Consequences has quite a different force. Both Socrates and Jesus were very much aware of consequences, including the consequences of sacrificing their ideals for continued physical comfort or even life itself. As reported in the *Crito,* Socrates refused to escape (1) because of the effect his escape would have on respect for law and (2) because a life in which he could no longer go about trying to awaken critical self-examination on the part of others would not be worth living.

The Principle of Consequences dictates not loss of nerve but awareness of obstacles. (It respects sacrifice sufficiently to insist on maximum value for sacrifice.) Some ideals may be so important in their consequences if attained that they are worth pursuing even though the odds against their attainment are high and pursuit of them involves a certain recklessness. Some ideals may only be attained through self-sacrifice, but unless one is aware of the obstacles, considers the probable consequences (both if the ideal is reached and if it is not), his action rather than being noble and moral is likely to be dangerously foolish and wasteful. In the language of the poker player, to draw to an inside straight when the baby's milk is at stake is neither brave nor moral but a selfish and stupid disregard of consequences.

The Principle of Consequences demands that within the range of my ability I shall recognize and accept the responsibility for the foreseeable consequences of my actions in the light of the real alternatives open to me. It requires dedication to a harmony of the best, critical thought, based upon the fullest possible information, with action motivated by a zeal for the highest value that can be created in and through a given concrete situation.

IV. *REFLECTIVE SUMMARY*

The obligations to be consistent and to will self-imposed ideals may well issue in a rigid, blind, and humorless self-righteousness if they are not linked with the pursuit of range and harmony among value experiences. The Principles of Consistency and of Autonomy, without the Axiological Principle, are empty; but the latter without the other two is blind.

In these three principles, the underlying form and content, motivation and goal of the moral life is spread before us. The remaining principles will help us to guide decision and action in the search for comprehensive harmony in value-experience.

The Principle of Consequences helps us to become aware of the obstacles and the ambiguities that choice must face without allowing us to escape concrete responsibility. Five considerations seem unavoidable.

1. When we discuss the question: "Do ends justify means?" ends

and means must be seen actually as a large network of ends and means and not simply as some one end justifying means to its realization.

2. We cannot be held responsible for consequences that we did not intend or could not foresee.

3. Although we seldom can approve all the foreseeable consequences of a choice, we ought to choose those consequences that we can approve of on the whole.

4. The implementation of the Principle of Consequences puts a premium on the highest quality of varied education for all persons, in accordance with individual differences in ability, need, and interest.

5. One cannot make ethical progress without being willing to adopt courses of action that, although inadequate, may in fact lead to the expected balance of value over disvalue. In the human situation, in which we never know all there is to know and can never control all the consequences, the choice the moral agent often faces is not "Shall I suffer?" but, "For what shall I suffer?"

23

Are There Limits to Duty?

~~~~~~

I. *DUTY AND ABILITY*

We discovered in the last chapter that we should not be held responsible for consequences that we cannot foresee. To foresee as best we can—that is our responsibility. We cannot choose or be held responsible for alternatives that are not open in the particular choice situation, but we are responsible for choosing the best alternative available after realistic assessment of the situation. We may not be responsible for what others think we ought to do; we are responsible for acting in the light of the ideals that we acknowledge. In other words, it has become progressively evident that duty and responsibility are correlated with ability. I cannot reasonably feel obligated to do what I cannot do—to accomplish what lies beyond my power or ability to accomplish. A blind man cannot be held accountable for failing to see a "No Trespassing" sign; a crippled person has no obligation to chase a thief; a nonswimmer has no obligation to jump into water over his head to rescue a drowning person.

This correlation of duty and ability is a truism. But like many truisms, it is easily forgotten and often its implications are not fully grasped. We met the pseudo-idealist—the Walter Mitty type—in the last chapter. He dreams of consequences of alternatives not open to him because of his circumstances or his lack of ability or both.

We may smile at instances where ability does not match "idealism." What shall we say of instances where abilities are not correlated with the duty to make use of them? In contrast with the pseudo-idealist are the "practical" men and women who practice a strange brand of unrealism in the name of realism itself. These are the followers of the so-called "tried and true way" who fail to realize the potential values in a situation because they have allowed themselves to be victimized by ingrained habit patterns and restricted vision. "This is the way we have always done it. Perhaps it is not the best way, but it seems to work, and we are familiar with it. Why change?" The subject under discussion may be study habits, teaching methods, curriculum revision, penal reform, economic investment, foreign policy, racial desegregation, or the electoral system. The actual subject does not make too much difference. Most groups contain at least one such person. "To be sure," he will usually grant, "things are not ideal. I would like to see things improved as much as you. But let's be realistic about it! Just what can we do?" And too frequently this in effect means; "Let's not do anything. Let's coast. Please do not disturb." Lack of energy and imagination passes for "realism."

Close relatives both of the pseudo-idealists and of the pseudo-realists are the "back at Old Si-wash" individuals. "Old Si-wash" may be Cranberry High School, or North College, or East Church, or Heaven Sales, or Contaki Neighborhood Club—for the nostalgic soul, Old Si-wash is anywhere and anytime but the present. Do anything or propose anything new, and you hear the old refrain: That's not the way we would have done it at Old Si-wash. "People are not so friendly. Opportunities are not so great. The regulations and procedures do not make as much sense. If only you had been at Old Si-wash, you would know how things really should be done." And usually the implication is: "That's where the real good fellows were, and I was an important one of them." Meantime, "Old Si-wash" refuses to recognize possible values here and now and stands in the way of others.

Still another group of persons, the "you-can-do-it-too" people, know fairly well what they themselves can do and what possible weaknesses are open to them, but they go romantic when it comes to other people. To believe some fond but otherwise realistic parents, any baby born to them is exceptional. He will at least be the world's outstanding physician if not the President of the United States. Johnny's father was a doctor. Accordingly, his mother looks at her child and decides that Johnny will be a doctor. He may not seem cut out for a doctor, he may not want to be a doctor, but "Johnny, you can do it."

And Johnny, who would have been better fitted to do what an excellent mechanic or bricklayer or artist or mathematician does, is started on a line of preparation in which he either cannot succeed or cannot feel inner contentment in his "successes." Every one involved with him is miserable, and reassessment, if it comes, comes too late for John to realize his best possible values.

II. *PRINCIPLE OF THE BEST POSSIBLE*

In none of the above instances are the fullest potentialities for value realization actualized. Indeed, our fifth principle grows out of the first four. The Principle of Consistency, with its emphasis upon so choosing that we do not annul our values; the Principle of Autonomy with its emphasis upon acknowledged ideals; the Axiological Principle, with its emphasis upon structured, harmonious values; the Principle of Consequences, with its clarification of "foreseeable" and "on the whole" approved values—all need the emphasis on quality in value realization now to be brought into focus. This fifth principle, which deals with realizing the fullest value potential of persons and places, can be presented explicitly as the Principle of the Best Possible: *Each person ought to choose the best possible values in every situation and, hence, if possible, improve every situation.*[1]

This Principle of the Best Possible cuts in two directions. First, it demands of everyone the best possible. Duty, while not obligating more ability than a person has, is commensurate with all his ability. "Old Si-wash" and the so-called "practical man" are not measuring up to the present situation in terms of what they can do. One has not met the moral imperative of the Principle of Consequences unless he has foreseen the consequences to the best of his ability. One has not met the moral imperative of the Axiological Principle unless he has developed as harmonious and integrated a system of values as possible to regulate his choice. Thus the Principle of the Best Possible strengthens all the other principles. But second, at the same time that this principle calls for the best possible, it calls only for the best possible not for some impossible or for a purely theoretical best. This second aspect of the Principle of the Best Possible is hospitable to tolerance and understanding. Let us look more fully at each focus of the principle.

[1] Cf. E. S. Brightman, *Moral Laws* (New York: Abingdon Press, 1933), p. 156.

A. *Failure of the Less than Best Possible*

The moral demand for the best possible includes a warning against being content with half-way and substitute measures. One has not done his best possible when he has only made a gesture in that direction. For example: In earlier days before the development of miners' unions, the average coal miner was almost completely dependent upon the mining company not only for his livelihood but for his housing and provisions. The company owned the mine and paid the miners' wages; it also owned his house (company houses) and controlled his buying (the company store). The miner was laid off when the demand for coal was low. In some cases he was prevented by an intercompany system of blacklisting from finding work at mines with more favorable working conditions, if his services were needed at his home mine. When the miners gained enough strength to protest effectively, some companies did raise wages, improve the company houses, and increase the range of goods carried in the company store. But the miners refused to be satisfied, much to the operators' indignation. At best, the miners argued, these improvements were palliatives and did not correct the root difficulty, namely, the company's paternalistic control over the miners' life. The miners, for example, wanted noncompany competitive stores; for without such competition, once the protest died down, the company store could reduce the items carried and raise the price, thus effectively canceling any raise in pay. Without the "best possible" concession—that of competing stores—the miners felt that they remained in company serfdom.

With increased costs of living, persons on fixed salaries, like college professors, tend to feel economic pressures most strongly. Instead of meeting the real issue through salary increase to the best of the school's ability, some college administrations have introduced in such periods a series of what are called "fringe benefits"—reduced prices for concert series, common purchasing plans with discounts, and increased medical-insurance coverage. Although most such fringe benefits are worthwhile and should be introduced in any circumstances, they are not adequate substitutes for the underlying need, namely, increases in salary.

Some Southerners opposed to desegregation insist, and correctly, that great strides have taken place in the Southern states to equalize Negro education. They point with justifiable pride to the fact that some colored school buildings are superior to adjacent white schools. Yet it still remains the case that certain occupations tend to be closed to colored people as long as they remain in the South. And very often the people who are proud of improvement of colored schools nevertheless object to the activities of organizations that have sought to give legal, financial, and moral aid to Negroes who seemed to be unjustly treated as they pressed for recognition of their constitutional rights. However injudicious such organizations have sometimes been, there is no denying that without their so-called "interference" the significant advances in desegregation or in the general welfare of colored people would have been slower than necessary or desirable. For, as many Americans all over the United States are realizing, less than the "best possible" has been done to give first-class citizenship to the colored American population. Without minimizing the serious obstacles that some sections of the country face in achieving gradual progress, the underlying problem is still an ethical one, for both colored and noncolored citizens have been only too willing to do less than the best possible.

To take another instance of moral leniency, probably every community has well-meaning people who make a special effort at Thanksgiving and Christmas time to prepare baskets for the indigent. Such activity is highly commendable, but far from the best possible. Some of these people not only do nothing to try to correct the causes of poverty but, at times when major relief agencies are collecting funds for continued and organized help, insist that they have done their duty by direct contribution. In this connection one is reminded of Elton Trueblood's remark that the church needs fewer supporters and more active members.

Unfortunately, half-way measures that fall recognizably below the best possible all too frequently create a worse situation than no action at all. Half-way measures leave a guilty conscience in some of the performers, a smug sense of satisfaction in others. Those affected by the action resent it as bad faith. In turn they may make demands that cannot be fulfilled or can be fulfilled only at the cost of bitterness and suffering. The French discovered this on a national level in Indo-China and Africa. We seem to have discovered the same thing in the matter of land adjustment for military bases in Okinawa.

B. *Individual Differences and the Best Possible*

On a more personal level, what constitutes the best possible rather clearly differs from individual to individual and for the same individual in differing circumstances. What may be the best possible for you may not be at all the best possible for me. We must avoid a superficial interpretation of the fact that the best possible for any individual (or group) is "relative" to him—to his abilities, his needs, his circumstances, and (to the extent that his desires conform to his abilities, needs, and circumstances) to his desires. The Principle of the Best Possible is not relativ*istic,* for it emphasizes the universal obligation of every individual (or group) to realize his best possible. What it does not call for is my judging you morally in terms of my own best possible. The mother who judged Johnny in terms of his father's best possible illustrates the point. Nevertheless, the Principle of the Best Possible carries implications that extend far beyond Johnny's case.

Plato long ago recognized the fundamental importance of the psychological principle of individual differences and applied it to equitable distribution of function in the healthy state. A man, argued Plato, in the *Republic* especially, cannot realize his potential unless he is performing the functions for which he is best fitted. For Plato, one determines what these functions are, not primarily by consulting one's likes, but by discovering one's capacities. This can be done by noting what one person can do and comparing it with what others can do. The happy man is not he who simply does what he desires but he who learns to desire what he can best do. On the recognition of this insight depend both the private welfare and the continued development, wealth, and solidarity of the complex social whole.

In recent years psychologists have rediscovered the importance of Plato's insight into individual differences. Evidence piles up showing significant individual differences from birth on, and presumably even in the period of gestation. Hence, to try to fit individuals to the same mold, to expect them all to reach the same external standards of achievement, is to defy the very structure of growth in personality.

Whatever our final views about the universality of basic desires, needs, and tendencies or the need for coherent ordering of life, our thinking about persons must always take into account their distinctive and individual needs and abilities. The Law of the Best Possible demands the best of each of us and this cannot exclude our individual differences.

C. *Stereotyping and Prejudice*

Indeed, whenever we begin to think and talk in terms of groups of people as if they were all alike, we not only overlook the fact of individual differences, but we are on our way to breaking the Principle of the Best Possible. For we tend to form stereotypes of men and lose sight of persons as concrete individuals with their desires, longings, abilities, and expectations. It becomes easier to treat men as abstractions—as lawyers, industrialists, farmers, Protestants, Catholics, Jews, the Swiss, the French, the Russians, Negroes, Orientals, and Caucasians—as though the members of each group were simple carbon copies of each other. Such stereotypes are not the sole cause of prejudice, but they contribute to prejudice and become its vehicle.

To be sure, not all stereotypes are prejudices if we define prejudice with G. W. Allport [2] as a prejudgment that resists change in spite of new knowledge. A stereotype may originate in incomplete knowledge or hasty generalization. It becomes a prejudice when it serves as a vehicle or an outlet for personal aggression and insecurity. Thus most, if not all, prejudice against individuals or groups is focused in stereotypes.

But even when stereotypes are not prejudices, they are damaging, for they become sources of prejudices, misunderstanding, exaggeration, friction, and ill-feeling. Whether we pick out the worst or the best characteristics of some members of a group, we apply these characteristics to every member of the group indiscriminately, and, as we do so, we import into them emotional and valuational overtones. More often than not, we are finding the wrong outlet for our own feelings of insecurity, hostility, and aggression.

To be sure, as some would point out, stereotyping is related to the important and economical process of classification. Only by classifying can we generalize and know what to expect. We cannot afford to forget that legitimate classification rests on careful enumerative analyses in which generalizations are recognized as tentative. Our stereotypes of human beings, however, may rest on little or no evidence. They may grow out of conditioned responses, a single shocking expe-

---

[2] See *The Nature of Prejudice* (Cambridge, Mass.: Addison-Wesley, 1954) for an unusually systematic account of the phenomenon of prejudice and acute insight into its dynamics.

rience, or even parental attitudes. Once such stereotypes are formed —and parents pass their own stereotypes on to their children at a surprisingly early age—they tend to be reinforced by unrecognized or only partly conscious or unconscious motives, for example, distrust of strangers, economic rivalry, and the need for a scapegoat to avoid facing our own shortcomings. Furthermore, having found a convenient stereotype, we unwittingly look through it at others selectively, noticing and remembering only what seems to conform to it. Should we see what does not conform, we conveniently write down these instances as unusual exceptions to the rule! And now our mistaken stereotypes readily become full-fledged prejudices. Our anxieties and fears have created their own image in some offending group or type of people. The vicious circle of prejudice seems so hard to break that one prominent social psychologist insists: "Little can be done about prejudices against minority groups until we die and a new generation comes along." [3]

To admit, however, that stereotyped ways of thinking of others are difficult to overcome does not absolve us from our best effort. Failure to make a real effort means that we hand down our prejudices, unmitigated, to the next generation. In our own lives it marks a defeat in realizing either our own or others' "best possible." We lose the positive values, that each of us has to contribute to our common well-being. No one knows how many Marion Andersons, Ralph Bunches, and George Washington Carvers have been lost to us as a result of stereotyping Negroes, for example. Nor can we calculate the untold frustration and bitterness that has unnecessarily accumulated in the lives of both the prejudiced and the victims of prejudice. This emotional and intellectual cancer at the root of so much neglect of the best possible needs more psychological analysis than is possible here, but several other comments must be made.

We cannot overcome stereotyping unless we put aside once and for all the naive and false belief that people can be fitted into the neat pigeonholes of simple and distinct types. To assume that all people with dark skin are alike in anything except having dark skin is about as reasonable as to assume that all people who have yellow tooth brushes are cowards or that all men over six feet tall are bullies. To be sure, all of us have some similar personality traits, but if we observe carefully, we discover that similar traits in different individ-

[3] Stewart Henderson Britt, *Social Psychology of Modern Life* (New York: Rinehart, Inc., 1941), p. 439.

uals do not lead to identical actions. There seems to be no justification at all for prejudging particular individuals in a group apart from specific acquaintance, except for the one and often arbitrary factor which constitutes them a group, such as their living in Indiana, belonging to the Methodist Church, or being dark skinned.

Even if people could be classified into simple types, could it be assumed that the "type" for any particular person remains constant? We are continually changing, and our modes of behavior may vary strikingly from situation to situation.[4] Our behavior at the beach, in an art gallery, at a football game, and in the classroom usually is decidedly different. We modify with changing experience even more or less permanent personality traits; and, in any case, as we have already said, specific actions cannot be predicted. Few if any individuals in any groups are always sullen or always happy-go-lucky, always serious or always irresponsible, always acquisitively minded or always studiously intent or always "rah-rah" boys. To base personal or public relations on the assumption of constancy of type is to miscalculate the motives for people's behavior because we underestimate the variety and richness of personality.

In sum, the so-called typical American college student or Negro or Jew or college professor or plumber is at best a statistical fiction if he is not an outright fiction. Even such a statistically average man, as we have pointed out, would very soon shift from his status. The Principle of the Best Possible demands for every individual the right to be considered and treated as unique—as a complex changing personality with his own peculiar capabilities, purposes, and habit patterns, with his own background and expectations, his ways of looking at the world and reacting to it, and his own changing best possible as conditioned by all of these. What his personality traits and his best possible will be cannot be determined before the fact by reference to a group stereotype or any convenient rule of thumb.[5]

D. *Substitute and Artificial Standards for Achievement*

Another unfortunate result of failing to recognize individual differences both in area and in level of achievement lies in the tendency of many people to set up unrealistic and artificial, even substitute,

[4] See Britt, *op. cit.*, p. 194, and Chapter 7.
[5] See G. W. Allport, *Pattern and Growth in Personality* (New York: Holt, Rinehart and Winston, 1961), Chapter 15.

standards of achievement for themselves and others. This is perhaps nowhere better illustrated than in the rather widespread emphasis on grades as such, both by many students and by their parents. An academic grading system, it can be argued, has its place and function. If it functions properly, the grade should indicate to the student his comparative level of accomplishment and competency in a particular subject matter. It may in some instances quite legitimately serve as a reminder that he might know some things better if he had not put too many extraneous activities in their place. It may further serve as a key to where the best possible for any particular person lies. A student who consistently received C's and D's in chemistry or chemical engineering would be ill-advised to try to make research chemistry or chemical engineering his career. Any one looking for a research chemist is warned to look elsewhere. At best, then, a grade should be a fairly reliable index of accomplishment and competence in any particular subject matter relative to achievement of one's peers, as judged by the teacher on the basis of his experience of the subject matter and students at a given stage of development. A grade by itself, uninterpreted, tells us little and certainly cannot be an end in itself.

Unfortunately, however, the grade itself rather than an index of the accomplishment frequently becomes the end. No one asks how one gets the grade or in what subject. The grade is the thing! If one happens to learn something about the subject matter, well and good, but it is at best a kind of extra dividend. Last-minute cramming, selecting snap courses or instructors, trying to impress the instructor with a hard-luck story, even cheating—what does it matter whether one has done the work if one has the grade! And if the grade is low when one has "done the work," or at least put in the time, what a weeping, wailing, and gnashing of teeth! The school is no good. The instructor in unfair. Or even more serious, the student considers himself an unqualified failure.

Such an attitude seldom, like Athena, springs full grown from the head of Zeus. In some cases, it may result from a long school experience in which the emphasis has been placed upon the competitive aspects of grades rather than individual accomplishment. In highly competitive school situations, students develop habits of working chiefly with the grade in view, to be obtained at any cost. Excessive grade-consciousness may, as the Adlerian psychologist would remind us, come from basic feelings of insecurity, whatever their sources, and the desire to overcome them by the external signs of success. It may result from exaggerating the importance of grades in determining eligibility for professional or graduate schools. Sometimes its earlier cause is a highly unrealistic attitude on the part of parents toward the abilities and accomplishments of their children.

We indicated earlier how hard it is for some parents to recognize that their offspring are capable human beings and not geniuses. Even the more sensible are tempted to believe, without adequate evidence, that Billy is at least as good, if not better, than Paul next door in everything that Paul undertakes. And unless he beats Paul at everything, Billy is not given credit at home for what he really can do. If Paul brings home a better report card in reading than Billy, the family pride is at stake. Billy has let the family down, his folks feel. Billy thus finds himself from the very outset in a vicious competition not only with Paul but with all the other children of his own age in the neighborhood. No wonder that he substitutes the symbol for the accomplishment, the grade for the growth in intellectual power that it should represent. Such a substitute can be disastrous. A person who presents credentials for accomplishments that he does not have is a living contradiction. Often he cannot hide the fact from himself, and his feeling of insecurity widens and deepens. He cannot continue to live a lie without serious psychological and moral repercussions in his own life and without decreased effectiveness in his relations to others. Thus the grades that were meant to be credentials of achievement become roots of self-distrust and maladjustment.

The Principle of the Best Possible, moreover, has implications for the person charged with grading as well as for those being graded. If the student has done the best he possibly can, obviously he should not be held morally responsible for not having done better. But to have done the best possible does not, in turn, justify a good grade that is supposed to measure superior achievement. The old system of using corporal punishment in the elementary grades as a spur to academic attainment has rightly been discarded as morally and psychologically vicious. But if grades are to perform their legitimate functions as comparative indicators of competence and ability in particular areas, if they are to help students determine the best possible for themselves, then it is equally vicious not to grade *as objectively as possible*. When the teacher allows his grading to be influenced by sympathy for the student having a hard time, or by preference for particular pupils, or by desire to keep his classes full, or by desire to show the overly assertive student that he is not as smart as he thinks he is, he prostitutes the grading system to the injury not only of other students but eventually of the very student who for the moment benefits. In every community there are persons who presumably have "good jobs," but who are in fact overburdened by their own anxieties about their being square pegs trying to fit round holes.

E. *Determining the Best Possible*

We are still left with the general question of how one determines the best possible. Trial and error would seem to be a simple answer, broadly correct but requiring qualification. Forming a conception of the best possible for another person demands all our understanding and a patient tentativeness. We have already discussed some of the unfortunate results of hasty generalizations, stereotypes, and rules of thumb in judging the best possible for others. The alternative is to estimate carefully on the basis of what knowledge we have, keeping the estimate open to revision as we come to know the other person better and, indeed, as our own understanding of abilities and their interrelations increases.

Accuracy in our judgment of others depends on our growth in moral experience and psychological understanding. Examples of the difficulties of a fair estimate are to be found in our frequent failures where our friends are concerned. Seldom, if ever, do we know all the circumstances of choice even of those close to us, including their actual abilities at a given time and the force and quality of the pressures upon them. Although the term "misunderstanding" has popularly become an expression for any discouragement, marriage counselors have discovered that it is quite literally applicable to most cases of marital difficulties, minor as well as major. Yet surely, if common experience is the foundation of understanding, married couples should have the broadest basis for such understanding.

Our tendency to err in estimating others calls not only for tentativeness and tolerance in judgment but also for caution in giving advice. The amateur counselor or parlor psychoanalyst, like the "guard-house lawyer" or the home-remedy physician, can do irreparable damage. This does not mean that no one except the trained counselor or psychoanalyst should give advice when asked, for there are obviously different kinds and levels of advice. Most of us are at least partially competent in some areas of the business of living, but we always need to recognize our own limitations in giving advice and be ready to admit ignorance and suggest more competent resources than ourselves. This is particularly important when choice of a career, mental health, or prolonged and deep-seated marital friction is involved. Certainly a college freshman trying to make a difficult adjustment from a particular home community to the demands of a new environment made up of his or her peers should beware of the upper-class amateur analysts with their not yet digested courses in psychology.

The trial and error answer, then, would seem far more applicable to determining one's own best possible than to trying to determine the best possible for others. Here, too, morality begins at home, and I must busy myself with my own affairs: the best possible for me. This is no simple truth. For I am faced with a double danger. I may set my best possible too low, no higher than the range of what I am sure I can do now because I have done it before. I then run no risk. This is a particularly appealing position at the end of a difficult day. Unfortunately, the assumption that I can stay where I am has little ground in fact. I would not have achieved my present level of accomplishment, whatever that may be, if I had always done only that which I was sure from past experience I could do. The would-be pianist who never tries a more difficult number soon finds he has trouble playing the number he was sure he could play. Not to move on is to slip back and possibly have another cause for frustration. To know my best is to know my past and present achievement, but I am a changing—and perhaps growing—person.

Yet the opposite danger is also a very real one. Suppose, as Emerson suggests, that we try to hitch our wagon to a star, but, in spite of our best efforts, do not go very far in space travel. Should we feel like total failures? Or should we say that the journey, as far as we went, was worth it? It opened perspectives on ourselves and the universe. We grew as we journeyed, and that was the important thing. On our way to the "star" out there, we made valuable discoveries within ourselves and about our relation to the world of possibilities.

We may, of course, get wholly unrealistic ideals for ourselves. Some people grow dizzy at certain heights and will not admit it. We may have a gross misconception of what is possible for us. Our failures should teach us our limits. Yet we should not permit them to sink us in the slough of despondent and discouraged frustration. To have given it "a real try" is always a positive achievement.

As a matter of fact, recognizing one's own limitations is not easy. What is reprehensible is to shift the responsibility or blame to someone or something else, to rationalize the failure without recognizing the limitations, temporary or permanent, in one's own abilities—to do anything rather than face the situation candidly. One's parents were at fault for not having provided adequate training. The group was at fault for not giving adequate support. A friend let us down. Something or somebody was working against us. A statement sometimes heard from Ph.D. candidates who never quite manage to complete their doctoral dissertations is: "After all, I am a perfectionist and I won't turn anything in unless it really represents what I can do." Too frequently these statements literally mean: I have tried and failed; therefore I will not do anything. The other danger, that of setting one's ideals too low, is often a frightened reaction to an original failure due to setting one's ideals too high.

A realistic and intelligent approach to what constitutes one's best possible involves a number of factors. Of first importance is the development of one of the most difficult and yet essential of the virtues, candor in self-assessment. Candor, as Philip Wheelwright suggests, is "simply the frank and fully reflective awareness of oneself; and as reflective self-awareness is what constitutes the very being of a self as distinguished from material objects." [6] It might be objected that this is not so simple, and indeed it is not. We only attain to various degrees of candor. Few of us, as Robert Burns pointed out, have the gift to see ourselves as others see us.

And yet the start towards a candid self-knowledge is the simple reflective self-awareness that all of us experience at times. Such self-awareness begins to develop into self-insight when we practice considering ourselves as objects, that is, with a detachment from our immediate wants and desires. Allport describes the state as a "sense of humor"—"that peculiar detachment of the mature person when he surveys his own pretensions in relation to his abilities, . . . his own equipment in comparison with the equipment of others, and his opinion of himself in relation to the opinions others hold of him." [7] We then begin to develop something of the self-objectivity

[6] *A Critical Introduction to Ethics* (rev. ed.; New York: The Odyssey Press, 1949), p. 231.

[7] Gordon W. Allport, *Personality: A Psychological Interpretation* (New York: Henry Holt and Co., 1937), p. 213.

that makes for reasonable assessment of our best possibles. A person who never experiences at least limited moments of such candor is either already living in a world of fantasy or is headed for a break from the moorings in the real world around him.

Candor concerning oneself might also be described as stopping to take stock or to get one's bearings. One does one's best to be honest with himself. What have I attempted? What have I accomplished? What are my responsibilities? Where do I go from here? We pointed out earlier that the real danger lies not in setting one's ideal too high but in what one does about it when he seriously tries to attain the ideal and fails. Here candor makes the difference between a positive, if partial, success and total failure. When I have done the best I can and yet have not succeeded, candor calls for realistic re-evaluation of the goal, my abilities, and my means or strategy. Instead of beating my head against the low ceiling and blaming the world for the obstruction, I recognize that for me some other perhaps more limited end and a set of means in greater harmony with my critically structured values are the best possible in the situation. To be able to do so is the mark of moral and emotional maturity. We only fail completely when we refuse to profit from our mistakes. But to keep on making the same mistakes out of a lack of candor with ourselves is to turn all potential value into disvalue.

A second factor in an intelligent approach to discovery of my own best possible is the use of all available outside helps to self-appraisal. Here the advice of friends (or even of those who are not so friendly) may be helpful as long as I do not rely on it uncritically but weigh it in the balance with my own self-assessment. Others may recognize aspects of my actions or capabilities and facets of my personality to which I am blind because of my own biases. One should also familiarize himself with the kinds of professional help that are available to aid in discovering abilities and limitations. Testing services and vocational-guidance counselors are present at most colleges and universities. Guidance offices usually have trained counselors to help with personal problems. Not only in most colleges but in most communities competent marriage counselors are available. Many married couples of all ages who are not realizing the best possible in their lives together could be helped if they would only seek the aid of such counselors. In more extreme cases of difficulty in self-assessment, competent psychiatric aid either through college facilities or in the community at large is usually available. There are still too many persons who think nothing of visiting a doctor for aid but who let a misplaced pride keep them from getting the psychological aid now available to them.

A third and equally important factor in realistic assessment of one's own best possible is the recognition of some of the characteristics of the best possible that have emerged in our discussion. For one thing, the best possible constantly changes. One needs to realize and accept the fact that in the flowing stream of life there is and will be change, that even if he could know exactly the amount of ability he has and the kinds of needs that are his, the relation between them will change, especially as environmental demands change. There is no escaping the fact that to be alive is to be insecure. If our whole study points to any truth, it is that to flee from insecurity in search of security is to seek a will-o'-the-wisp. Insecurity can never be wholly eliminated, but it can be made creative as one seeks to discover what he can do and ought to do. The best possible might be called an ever-growing ideal.

As one approaches his best possible, the best possible opens out a farther view and at the same time provides power toward the new perspective. For example, as one increases his knowledge, the scope of what he can know and the capacity to know it are proportionately increased. The mastery of the calculus opens up the hitherto seemingly unapproachable areas of advanced mathematics. Even in such matters as strength and physical coordination, although there are definite limits to the theoretically possible, most of us have untapped resources, which will open to us if we venture in discovery of our best possible.

We are frequently too easily discouraged in our overtures toward friendship, cooperation, and understanding because we do not recognize cause-and-effect relations and "dream" rather than plan. For example, it is usually necessary to be a friend in order to deserve a friend. One should not expect to be "appreciated" immediately! In these areas, as in others, what is possible depends to a large extent on what has been achieved. We desire to jump immediately to the theoretical best instead of climbing the rungs of the ladder.

Indeed, the theoretical best is frequently the enemy of the best possible. For example, we may try to introduce major reform procedures all at once into a fraternal society, an industry, a church, a college, or a country with a traditional or habitual but inefficient mode of operation. The reaction is negative or violent. Instead of doing what we can, of actualizing the best possible now and building toward a new best possible approaching the theoretical ideal, we are likely to give up in discouragement or so alienate those we desire to help that the ideal is moved indefinitely beyond reach.

III. *IS MORALITY COMMON SENSE BECOME SELF-CRITICAL?*

We have sought to describe the intelligent self-assessment and the insight and patience towards other called for by the Principle of the Best Possible. We have dealt with the qualifications of the "foreseeable" and "on the whole approved." The Principle of Consequences keeps morality from becoming a matter of Utopian dreaming on the one hand or an inhuman rigorism on the other. Morality becomes rather the structure of fruitful and intelligent, that is, meaningful, living. Some may find such a morality insufficiently dramatic. But it is certainly keyed to effective and continual action. Such living is not easy, neither is it simple.

There seems to be no rule of thumb or simple formula for intelligent and fruitful living. Life itself is far too complicated and rich in potentialities for disvalue as well as value to be amenable to hasty either-ors, to the melodramatic contrasts of black and white. The conditioning principles of intelligent structuring of life must take into account both the complexity and the limitations of actual practical living. It is exactly these realities of every-day experience that give rise to the Principle of Consequences and the Principle of the Best Possible. Thus one's duty always lies within the range of *the* possible, not just *any* possible. To seek to achieve the best within the range of the possible will be found to give ample scope to heights of aspiration and intensities of inspiration and the real heroism needed to get worthwhile things done. This is not Utopianism but common sense become self-critical. But when we explore through criticism the depths of common sense, we touch upon what a poet has called "reason in its most exalted mood."

IV. *REFLECTIVE SUMMARY*

When we set about to execute the obligations to be consistent, to will the best we know, to will self-imposed ideals, and to be responsible for foreseeable consequences, we confront one fact. At every step in our moral development, we invite needless moral conflict and lose value experience open to us unless we commit our abilities to their utmost. The sincere moral agent can never take the attitude "leave well enough alone" if he is not doing his best. For the ethical life is not a matter of half-hearted affirmations or prohibitions; it is a creative life that transforms for good what *can* be transformed. "Doing my best" means doing my criticized and venturesome best.

It is extremely difficult to practice the art of the best possible. In this chapter, we may have seemed to stress the possible—as opposed to the quixotic "ideal"—so much that the reader may well think we have fallen short of the heroism of Browning's "Ah, but our reach must exceed our grasp, or what's a Heaven for." It is so easy for the "best possible" to become a dull ring and not a clarion call. The possible could be what I consider possible in my unimaginative moments or when I am "running scared" and letting the immediate untoward consequences blind me to the more remote goods.

But the possible to which we are obligated is the best—possible! To adapt one of G. W. Allport's expressions, what we are urging in this chapter is that each person program his own ethical identity. Not only are a person's ideals to be self-imposed, but they are to have the authenticity that stems from a critical estimate of his own abilities and needs in the total situation in which he and others live. The Principle of the Best Possible is in service to the ideal of personality as schematized in the symphony of values and in the scheme of virtues—and to the personal, social, political, and cosmic-religious ideals that issue from taking this principle seriously. When the insecurity of personal development and social change are taken seriously, along with the imaginative, yet realistic and good-humored assessment of abilities and achievement, there will emerge in the individualized moral struggle the kind of heroism that characterizes the human venture at its best.

The "good enough" can be the worst enemy of the best; the "best," uncritically conceived, can be the worst enemy of the good. In the midst of this perpetual struggle in personal and social life, the creative moral agent puts aside both self-pity and delusions of grandeur—and goes to work. And we always go to work in the present.

24

Our Obligations to the Present

~~~~~~

I. *THE CHANGING PRESENT*

One of the most striking and unalterable characteristics of our experience is its changing and passing nature. Every action we perform, every thought we think, every choice we make occur in some present moment or span of attention and are gone. All the feeling, hoping, longing, desiring we do are and then are not. We may continue to hope, to think, to desire, to choose, but our present hoping, thinking, desiring, and choosing, even though it may be about the same objects or conditions, is not the same experience that it was ten years ago, ten minutes ago, or even ten seconds ago. Both the experience and its context have changed, and although the past experience has its effect on the present, the past is over and gone and can never be exactly recaptured or re-experienced as it originally was. Although present experience may be similar to past experience, even if all the other factors in present experience were the same (a highly improbable situation for they now have at least a longer history), the present experience would differ from the past experience by the very fact of its recognized similarity, something that was not true of the past experience itself.

A. *The Unrecoverable Past*

No matter how much I may want to do so, I cannot literally relive or re-experience the past. I can remember within limits, but remembering is a different present act, referring to the past, and not the literal reconstruction of the past.

The ancient Greek philosopher, Heraclitus (circa 505 B.C.), underlined this transient, novel, and unrepeatable character of present experience by pointing out that you cannot step into the same river twice "for other and yet other waters are flowing on." [1] Much more recently the American writer, Thomas Wolfe called the last of his four novels *You Can't Go Home Again*. This was the story of a successful writer who tried to go back to his home town and his old friends, but he found that neither the town nor the friends were as they once were and, most important, neither was he. His friends and the townspeople had not taken kindly to his characterizations of them in his earlier novels. He himself was searching for something that was no more, that could not be recaptured; and the attempt to recapture it left him alone and empty.

All the effort in the world will not enable us to hold onto, to bring back, or to change the past. The attempt to relive the past or to live only in or for the values of the past seems doomed to failure by the very passing character of experience itself. This is one of the recalcitrant, brute, and uncontrollable aspects of our experience. Its tragic dimensions are sometimes illustrated in reunion with an old friend after a long separation. You and the friend are overjoyed to see each other. Recalling together old times and former experiences in common is most pleasant. You "catch up" on what each other has been doing since you last saw each other. But then comes an awkward silence; something seems to be missing. You have both changed. You have different interests and areas of activity. Each has his own life, his own problems, his own hopes. The bonds that held you together no longer exist. You can go on recalling past events and old acquaintances, but after the third chorus of "Old Lang Syne" it becomes an effort. Unless you find a bond in new or continued common interests, as happy as you were to see Joe, as glad as you are to have known Joe, you are not unrelieved to see him leave on the 8:10 for New York.

A person who dwells constantly on the past, as older people frequently do, gradually loses contact with the present and the potentialities for value realization that the present alone can offer. Like

---

[1] Fragments 41–42. See John Burnet, *Early Greek Philosophy* (New York: Meridian, 1957), p. 136.

the "Old Si-wash" we met in the last chapter, the present in which such a person does live and alone can live, is embittered by the shadow of a no longer available past.

B. *The "Not Yet" Future*

To a certain extent the same kind of frustration, even bitterness and disillusionment, is likely to characterize the person who dwells primarily on the future. To be sure, there is a difference and a very important one. The past is determinate; it cannot be changed in any circumstances—although I can change my present and future attitudes toward the past. The future, in contrast, is not yet. From the perspective of the present it is at least to some degree indeterminate. What I do now makes a difference in what the future will be when it becomes present. But I can no more act in the future now than I can now act in the past. And if my dwelling on the future, my expectations, and any hopes that I may have become so absorbing, in contrast with what may seem to be the meager possibilities of the present, that I do nothing about them now, there is little probability that the future I desire will ever be realized. But what has all this talk about the changing present, unchanging past, and indeterminate future got to do with ethics?

C. *The Crucible of Value, the Present*

One can only act or realize values as such in the present. The memory of yesterday and the anticipation of tomorrow, it is true, are integral to my present state of happiness or unhappiness, value or disvalue. But it is memory and anticipation that are present, not yesterday and tomorrow in a literal sense.

1. *Psychological versus Ethical Hedonism*

Probably the hedonists in the history of ethics have recognized the importance of present realization of value as clearly as anyone. Basically, hedonism is the position that equates good with pleasure. In considering the Principle of Consequences, we discussed the hedonistic calculus, or the calculus of pleasure, as proposed by one of the outstanding nineteenth-century hedonists, Jeremy Bentham. Centuries before Bentham, a student of Socrates from the city of

Cyrene, Aristippus (circa 435–356 B.C.) maintained that ultimately the only end or goal (and thus the only underlying motivation for human action) is the attainment of pleasure and the avoidance of pain. In this respect, his position can be described as psychological hedonism—that is, it is a psychological theory of the nature of human motivation and not an ethical theory. A psychological hedonist asserts that men necessarily seek pleasure and avoid pain. Aristippus, however, was also an ethical hedonist. Because the good is pleasure (hedonism), not only do men seek pleasure (psychological hedonism), but it is right that they do. In other words, men ought to seek pleasure (ethical hedonism).

Now it is not too difficult to see that ethical hedonism (men ought to seek pleasure) and psychological hedonism (men can seek only pleasure) are hardly compatible, for if men can seek only pleasure then all men do necessarily what they ought to do. To say men ought to do what they cannot help but do is hardly meaningful. Ought and must become one and the same.

However, even Aristippus, in spite of his psychological hedonism, was not willing to admit that all men do what they ought to do. In this inconsistency he was nevertheless in harmony with our direct experience and with contemporary psychological analyses of motivation. Among psychologists Freud tends toward psychological hedonism in his discussion of the conflict between the reality principle and the pleasure principle; yet careful inspection of his varied writings reveals that he does recognize other factors in motivation. Other factors—lure of superiority, creativity, need for love, self-actualization, and other needs—tend to become dominant in the theories of motivation of other psychologists we have considered. We seem to seek a great many other things besides pleasure, although pleasure may often accompany the attainment of these other ends. Psychological hedonism appears to be a tremendous oversimplification. Even such basic human actions as eating and sleeping can hardly be said to be pursued solely for the sake of pleasure. I eat because I am hungry or want to discover what this particular food tastes like, not just or primarily to please myself. This is not to say that eating is not also usually pleasant, but insofar as there is any case in which I eat for any other reason than pleasure, psychological hedonism is mistaken. For such reasons, G. W. Allport concludes: "In sum, we cannot build a theory of motivation on hedonism, because it is a vague principle, insufficiently supported by evidence or by our own introspection, and because the paralleling of pleasure and goal attainment is not close." [2]

2. Egoistic Hedonism

Aristippus is important for our discussion, however, not for his psychological hedonism but for the reasons he gives in support of the kind of ethical hedonism he upholds. In contrast to Jeremy Bentham's utilitarian or universalistic hedonism (the good equals the greatest pleasure of the greatest number), Aristippus urged an egoistic hedonism of the present moment. Pleasure cannot be experienced in the past or in the future, but only in the present. The one thing, he insisted, that ethics or the art of life can teach us is to enjoy the present, for only the present is ours. And because for Aristippus, pleasures differ only in amount, I should seek the greatest pleasure possible in the present. The one thing that kept Aristippus' view from becoming an unrelieved sensualism was his further recognition that even the pleasures of gratifying appetites are only pleasure so long as it is I, and not my appetites, who am in control. The moment my appetites control me, rather than I them, I become a slave and the pleasure fades.

Aristippus' position has its difficulties. First, too exclusive an emphasis on the pleasure of the moment, particularly if one is unmindful of the kind of pleasure and its consequences, is itself likely to block the possibility of pleasures in future present moments. Second, pleasure by itself is an abstraction. We cannot be pleased in general, nor do we feel "pleasure" in general; rather we enjoy beefsteak, friendship, knowledge, and the sunset. Even if one grants that pleasure is always an ingredient in intrinsic value experience, the value is the experience of the sunset or of friendship, with its positive hedonic tone, and not any pleasure by itself. Third, because friendship and beefsteak are not the same kind of thing, it is a serious misreading of experience to say that values differ only in quantity.

Clearly, and in sum, it is easier to talk about "living for pleasure" than to do so, strictly speaking. If I start out exclusively to find pleasure, I fail (hedonistic paradox). I can, however, seek friends, watch the sunset, or increase my knowledge, and these I find enjoyable.

[2] *Pattern and Growth in Personality* (New York: Holt, Rinehart and Winston, 1961), p. 201.

3. *The Present Tense of Value Experience—The Existential Situation*

As one-sided as his formulation was, Aristippus did nevertheless clearly recognize that values (if one substitutes the more concrete term "value" for "pleasure") not realized in someone's present experience are not values at all. Although his egoistic claim that good is my present value alone overlooks the fact that most values, including the bodily values, are usually increased through sharing, what he seems to be driving at has, as a point of emphasis, an element of truth in it. Granted that many individuals may realize values in communal relation, unless some individuals in the community realize these intrinsic communal values in their own present experiences, there would be no warrant for calling them values. Individuals may be "nothing" apart from society, but society is truly nothing apart from its constituent individuals and their realization of values in specific situations.

Such contemporary existentialist writers as Jean-Paul Sartre, Simone de Beauvoir, Karl Jaspers, who in most respects are at opposite poles from a hedonist like Aristippus, give equal emphasis to the crucial character of the present moment as the center of meaning and whatever fulfillment and achievement are possible in life. As Sartre, for example, insists, the meaning of life does not lie in anguished worrying about and reconstruction of the past. There one only finds himself more and more deeply enmeshed in a web of anxiety and frustration. Nor is the meaning of life to be captured in elaborate and unrealistic hopes and plans for the future. All such hopes and plans are doomed to at least partial failure, again with ensuing frustration and guilt consciousness. Unreasonable hopes only increase the anguish of the present for they engender constant worry and fear that they will not be realized.

Instead, what meaning there is in life, Sartre contends, is to be found in present encounter, in involvement now in what he calls the existential situation (present experience) beyond or without either groundless hope or regret.[3] Although Sartre may fail to pay sufficient attention to the framework of memory and anticipation as a condition

---

[3] See the novel *The Troubled Sleep* (New York: Knopf, 1951) for an extreme development of this thesis and *Existentialism* (New York: Philosophical Library, 1947) for a short philosophic exposition.

of meaningful, present involvement, he and other existentialists, along with the hedonists, help to refocus attention on the present as the birthplace of values.

Neither hedonists nor existentialists would have much sympathy with the college student who thinks of his time in college solely as a period of preparation. What he is studying and doing now (he feels) has little or no relevance to living now. He is preparing to live—and here "to live" can usually be translated more accurately "to make a living." While not very happy about it, such a student is usually willing to put up with "this theoretical stuff" in his major field, for he rather half-heartedly believes that at least some of it may have a bearing on his vocation once he begins to live. As for the general requirements for graduation other than those in his major, these seem to be sheer nonsense, annoying hurdles, which no one in his right mind would take were they not necessary to the acquisition of the degree, the magic passport to "real" living.

A variation of the same theme takes place even among some students who recognize the desirability of overcoming racial and economic prejudices, of advocating extension of civil rights, of increasing intergroup understanding, of budgeting time, or of appreciating and supporting the arts. Indeed, it almost seems sometimes that the vehemence of their talk is in compensating proportion to the anticipatory resignation. "Some day when we actually begin to live, things will be different. Then we will be able to change things!" Meanwhile these students fail to invite students from foreign countries or students without automobiles to house parties. Inviting them might be awkward. Or they feel much too busy to attend the Arts Festival. They "love the masses" and are discourteous and mean to the manual workers in the college and dormitories. They find so many unexpected demands on their time that budgeting it seems hardly practical. They console themselves in the thought that, once they graduate, all this will change!

Unfortunately, matters seldom work out in any such fashion. "Life" seldom begins suddenly on some later day or upon receipt of some particular degree. If one does not at least partially grasp the relevance of what he is doing now, in the present situation, the probability that insight will suddenly come later is low indeed. Those who expect to be transformed, to be quite different persons with wholly different habit patterns upon receipt of a diploma are in for not a little disappointment. But the most tragic waste lies not so much in the future disappointment as in the continuing failure of such persons to realize the values and opportunities present situations afford.

Such attitudes are obviously not confined to college students. Some persons persist in work they do not particularly like, devote all their energies and time to it, expecting that, once they have amassed sufficient wealth, they can retire and begin to enjoy life. Many such individuals, unfortunately, can never bring themselves to feel that they have amassed money enough. And if they do finally stop or are forced to stop by retirement requirements, too many of them find that the interests and talents they have dreamed of fulfilling have atrophied beyond revival. While waiting to "live," they have become working machines. Once the work stops the machine rusts and goes to pieces. With progressive increase in life span, with shorter working hours and mandatory retirement at age sixty-five already in effect, with the probability of increased leisure time in the future, we can even less afford to put off "living now." We must learn to live in the multivalued present situation if we want to remain alive enough to be capable of really living in the future.

II. *THE PRINCIPLE OF SPECIFICATION*

The Principle of the Best Possible called for realizing the best possible values in every situation; the actual process of achieving such values in view of the changing and present character of our experience involves an additional principle, which we shall make explicit. This additional principle calls not just for the best possible in any situation but for the best possible relevant to each specific situation and its potentialities, taking into account the uniqueness of every present experience as a locus of choice and action. We might call this principle the Principle of Specification or the Principle of Situational Uniqueness. It can be formulated as follows: *Each person, in any given situation, ought to develop the value or values specifically relevant to that situation.*[4]

A. *Relevance of "Right" to Specific Conditions*

The Principle of Specification in particular warns us against setting up and holding to rigid rules of action or rules legislating once and for all the rightness or wrongness of specific acts. In the light of

[4] Cf. E. S. Brightman, *Moral Laws* (New York: Abingdon Press, 1933), p. 171.

the changing character of circumstances and the uniqueness of each situation, an action that may be right and rational at one place and at one time may not be appropriate at all in a different set of circumstances. Each situation has its own potential values and disvalues, and one can rule arbitrarily beforehand only about the rightness and wrongness of a particular act at the expense of intelligent assessment of the situation itself.

In some circumstances, to give money to the beggar who asks for it may be both generous and noble. In other circumstances, when, for example, the person who asks is in his needy condition because of an overwhelming appetite for liquor and drugs, to give him money only re-enforces the cause of his need and may be the worst thing one can do. Again, in most circumstances, to kill another person violates all the principles that we have considered thus far and is clearly wrong. But there may be exceptional circumstances in which killing may actually become a moral duty. The few rather striking cases in point are those of service men returned from the Second World War and the Korean campaign who went berserk and fired at random into crowds of people. If the only way to stop such senseless, indiscriminate slaughter were to kill the unfortunate man, one's duty would be unpleasant but fairly obvious. To be sure, killing such a person would not be the abstractly ideal solution. He is sick, not wicked. If he could be disarmed and treated as a sick person, this would be the ideal alternative. But while one waits for the opportunity to disarm him, he goes on killing people. To some extent, one becomes an accomplice in their deaths.

It might be argued that such cases as the alcoholic beggar and the berserk killer are exceptions, which are themselves covered by rules. In a sense this may be true. But, the point of the Principle of Specification is that no act can be judged in the abstract apart from its here and now circumstances or context, that rules regarding particular acts are at best guides to be considered, not prescriptions to be taken absolutely. For example, that one has a right to kill in self-defense is sometimes taken as a rule of exception to the commandment: Do not kill. Yet the exception rule itself may have exceptions, depending on the circumstances. It is one thing to kill when no alternative other than killing is open in staving off a mad man; it is quite a different thing for the cornered thief to kill rather than give himself up to the surrounding police. Yet if the thief killed, he could well argue that he was killing in self-defense.

B. *Empirical Relevance of Moral Judgments*

The one very important insight urged by ethical relativists that those who react against relativism have sometimes tended to overlook or undervalue is exactly this recognition of the relativity of the rightness of specific acts to their circumstances. Relativists may (and, we have tried to show, do) draw an illegitimate conclusion from this fact. It does not follow that there are no principles for determining what is right. Even the relativist implicitly recognizes the universality of the obligation to take the specific situation into account, but the relativist tends to urge this to the exclusion of any other principles. His contention, however, that an act may be right or valuable in one set of circumstances, including place, time, and social group, but may be wrong or of disvalue in another place, time, and social group seems to be quite literally the case.

The Principle of Specification thus acts as a modifier of what might be called conventional or "rule-of-acts" morality. Although it does not involve irrational rejection of conventional rules simply because they are conventional, it does call for replacing conventional and habitual response by insight and intelligent assessment of situations as they arise. It calls for an evolving development of moral insight rather than a strictly formalistic and absolutistic attitude to actions.

To put the matter in still another framework: according to this principle, moral judgment, in order to be enlightened, must be experiential, that is, it must take into account experience and the specific situation that calls for action. In turn, any judgment resting on an experiential analysis is open to revision and must be guided by further experience. To rule beforehand that any particular act will always and categorically be right or wrong is dangerously dogmatic. It can be as destructive of critical behavior and sensitive human relations as categorical answers to physical problems are likely to be destructive of scientific research.

C. *Civil Law and the Principle of Specification*

In the light of its ameliorating influence on rules regarding action, the Principle of Specification has interesting implications for attitudes toward civil laws as well as so-called social codes. It does not undermine the principle of civil law itself. Dependable social functioning and civil justice, including the freedom from arbitrary interference in the lives of individuals and groups, is based upon the continuity, impartiality, and objectivity of civil law and its administration. But the Principle of Specification does involve the realization that there may be circumstances in which I may be morally obligated to violate civil law. A minor example would be the obligation to get a badly injured person to the hospital as quickly as possible regardless of traffic regulations, yet without unnecessarily risking the lives of others.

1. Equity

The principle of exception in the light of circumstances, and more particularly the recognition that no codified set of laws can cover all situations, is incorporated in our legal structure itself under the concept of equity—part of our heritage from English common law. Actually the concept of equity goes back from English law at least to Aristotle, who pointed out that there are cases in which justice according to law may work injustice to particular individuals in given circumstances. The error in such cases is not "in the law nor in the legislator but in the nature of things." [5] The reason for this, Aristotle argued, lies in the character of enacted law, the fact that law has to be stated to cover most cases and thus has the force of universality. "All law is universal but about some things it is not possible to make a universal statement which shall be correct." [6] In such situations, a person has a right to have his case heard on its own merits in the light of the circumstances—a right to equitable rather than legal justice. "And this is the nature of the equitable, a correction of law where it is defective owing to its immobility." [7] Accordingly, for Aristotle, "one who is no stickler for his rights in a bad sense but tends to take less than his share though he has the law on his side, is equitable, and this state of character is equity, which is a sort of justice and not a different state of character." [8]

The development of equity as a specific part of English law came during the fourteenth century with codification of common law and against the growing practice in the courts of interpreting the law absolutely, regardless of changing circumstances. Yet within the Eng-

[5] *Nicomachean Ethics,* 1137b.
[6] *Ibid.*
[7] *Ibid.*
[8] *Ibid.,* 1138a.

lish legal system, it was always recognized that, when undue hardship arose under the law, justice ought to be done and the responsibility for seeing that it was done rested with the king as father of the country. The king in turn delegated this responsibility to his chancellor who became keeper of the king's conscience. The chancellor's court, the court of chancery, became a court of conscience to which any citizen might appeal. The function of the court of chancery in equity decisions was not to replace or correct the law but to deal with inequities under the law. At first, the chancellor, acting under an ideal of justice, rendered decisions in equity independent of precedent and enactment. Gradually, however, decisions in equity themselves developed into a body of codified principles, based on previous decisions. In the last century and particularly since the Judicature Acts of 1873-75, the exercise of equity has been returned to the courts with the recognition that the court may, at its discretion, apply the principles of equity when circumstances or changing conditions make the regular application of law work injustice. In America the courts in many states have, from the beginning, been charged with the administration both of law and of equity.

2. Evolution of Law

Beyond the inclusion in our legal system of the recognition of the Principle of Specification in the concept of equity, the Principle of Specification itself seems to be the moral ground both for continuing review, revision, and amendment of law and, in extreme cases, for revolution. Although special social and political circumstances and conditions may not change with quite the rapidity that individual circumstances and conditions do, yet, in the long run, You Can't Go Home Again applies as much to a society or a nation as to an individual.

The conditions that give rise to legislative enactments change, and the laws need to be changed to meet these changing conditions. Technological advances, shrinking distances, increased knowledge in the social sciences, growth of public awareness on social issues, exhaustion of resources—any of these or many other factors may call for changing the legal structure. The shrinking of distances through increased speed of transportation not only has outmoded traffic laws in some communities, but has made the tremendous diversity of such laws in different states and communities both an inconvenience and a hazard to life and property. Increased knowledge of the nature of the mentally ill, of juvenile delinquents and criminals, for example, have made revision of the laws pertaining to the treatment of these persons mandatory in many states. Increased recognition of common and government responsibility toward the aged, the ill-housed, the unemployed, and the chronically ill has called for legal implementation on local and national levels. Other striking evidence of the degree to which change in social structure and law has occurred is provided by the fact that most of the issues championed by the Socialist Party in the first two decades of this century and at the time considered dangerously radical—social security, emergency price controls, federal housing, regulation of securities and exchanges, federal arbitration in labor-management disputes—have now been accepted as national responsibilities and enacted into law.

Fortunately, the democratic form of government makes possible continuous review and evolution of law through legislative action. This principle extends to the basic framework of American law, the Constitution itself, through the procedure of amendment. One cannot assume, however, that such revision and evolution will take place automatically. There are far too many examples of serious lag between changed conditions and unchanged laws. Far too frequently groups with vested interests in the *status quo,* regardless of the needs of the community, hinder or divert continuing review and revision. The Principle of Specification underlines our moral obligation not simply to demand review and revision in the abstract, but to keep informed of changing conditions, to insist upon public access to relevant sources of information, and to require of legislators a public accounting of both legislative actions and failures to act. We have, in this sense, a moral and political duty not merely to vote but to make our considered opinions felt through whatever channels are legally available. The only guarantee of responsible government in the light of changing conditions lies in an alert and responsive citizenry.

3. *The Right to Revolution*

Suppose, however, that government becomes nonresponsive, that the right to review and revise disappears, that through dominance of special interests the existing structure with its inequities is ossified and made more rigid as a result of suspicious fear of change or even extralegal means. Or suppose that the law is drastically modified by a special-interest group, allegedly "for our own protection," that civil liberties and the franchise are curtailed, that the right to public discussion is denied, and that government is carried on by decree rather than legislative enactment. Suppose further that the prospects of changing the situation by normal means appear exceedingly dim. That such "supposing" may conform to fact has been evidenced not only in Italy, Germany, and Spain prior to World War II, but more recently and far closer to home in Argentina under Peron, Venezuela under Juarez, the Dominican Republic under Trujillo, and Cuba under Batista and Castro. When such conditions obtain, the Principle of Specification underlines the moral right to revolution.

Admittedly revolution is a last resort, and the right to revolution not only should not be taken lightly but does not exist until every normal channel for bringing about evolutionary change has been exhausted. But with normal channels exhausted, revolution may be a moral duty as well as a political right. Those legislators and private citizens in this country who, between 1940 (the passage of the Smith Act) and 1957 (the decision of the Supreme Court overturning the conviction of the West Coast communist leaders), attempted to deny the right to advocate revolution under any conditions—those legislators were in fact rejecting the very principle on which our country itself was founded. The Supreme Court decision of 1957 "reestablished the traditional democratic (and American) concept under which all doctrines, including revolutionary ones, may be lawfully advocated and propagated. In other words, the validity of democracy is no longer a taboo issue that must not be challenged." [9]

The Supreme Court decision of 1957 and, indeed, the American Revolution find theoretical support in John Locke's contention that government rests upon the consent of the governed, that when government creates or perpetrates conditions inimical to the governed, the latter have the right to dissolve the government and constitute a new government to their satisfaction. In his *Essay Concerning the True Original Extent and End of Civil Government,* Locke attempted to spell out what the conditions justifying such dissolution of government would be:

> Whenever the legislators endeavour to take away and destroy the property of the people, or to reduce them to slavery under arbitrary power, they put themselves into a state of war with the people, who are thereupon absolved from any further obedience,

---

[9] William Ebenstein, *Today's Isms* (2nd ed.; New York: Prentice-Hall, 1958), p. 150.

and are left to the common refuge which God hath provided for all men against force and violence. Whensoever, therefore, the legislative shall transgress the fundamental rule of society, and either by ambition, fear, folly, or corruption, endeavour to grasp themselves, or put into the hands of any other, an absolute power over the lives, liberties, and estates of the people, by this breach of trust they forfeit the power the people had put into their hands, for quite contrary ends, and it devolves to the people who have a right to resume their original liberty, and by the establishment of a new legislative (such as they should think fit) provide for their own safety and security, which is the end for which they are in society.[10]

The American Declaration of Independence, in language closely paralleling John Locke, develops the same principle of exception to existing government under extreme conditions:

Prudence, indeed, will dictate that Governments long established should not be changed for light or transient causes; and accordingly all experience hath shown, that mankind are more disposed to suffer, while evils are sufferable, than to right themselves by abolishing the forces to which they are accustomed. But when a long train of abuses and usurpations, pursuing invariably the same Object evinces a design to reduce them under absolute Despotism, it is their right, it is their duty, to throw off such Government, and to provide new Guards for their future security.

And the rest of the Declaration of Independence consists of a bill of particulars to show that such extreme conditions had been reached in the colonies.

Among American statesmen, the one perhaps most concerned with the relevance of changing conditions to change in form of government and in law was one of the authors of the Declaration of Independence, Thomas Jefferson. To ensure that governments conform to changing circumstances Jefferson suggested that occasional rebellion is necessary for the health of a government. In a letter to Madison,[11] Jefferson argued:

[10] Chapter XIV, sec. 222.
[11] January 30, 1787, in S. K. Padover, *The Complete Jefferson* (New York: Tudor Publishing Company, 1943), p. 270.

I hold it, that a little rebellion, now and then, is a good thing, and as necessary in the political world as stones in the physical. Unsuccessful rebellions, indeed, generally establish the encroachments on the rights of the people, which have produced them. An observation of this truth should render honest republican governors so mild in their punishment of rebellions, as not to discourage them too much. It is a medicine necessary to the sound health of the government.

That this statement taken literally is too extreme and might well lead to a paralyzing public unrest and insecurity could hardly be denied. Jefferson may well have had his tongue in cheek as he made it. But that he was quite serious about providing in the basic law of the land for radical revision of government and law to meet changing conditions is indicated by his proposal in a letter to Samuel Kercheval, written after Jefferson had served as President and the country had had twenty-seven years' experience under the Constitution.

Jefferson's proposal in effect was that the Constitution should be amended to provide for a new constitutional convention every nineteen or twenty years. "Laws and institutions," he points out, "must go hand in hand with the progress of the human mind. As that becomes more developed, more enlightened, as new decisions are made, new truths disclosed, and manners and opinions change with the change of circumstances, institutions must advance also, and keep pace with the times." [12] Accordingly, he suggests:

> Each generation . . . has then . . . a right to choose for itself the form of government it believes most promotive of its own happiness; consequently, to accommodate to the circumstances in which it finds itself, that secured from its predecessors; and it is for the peace and good of mankind, that a solemn opportunity of doing this every nineteen or twenty years, should be provided by the constitution; so that it may be handed on, with periodical repairs, from generation to generation, to the end of time, if anything human can so endure.[13]

Only thus, Jefferson argues, can the cycle of oppression, rebellion, and reformation, endlessly repeated, as witnessed in Europe from the period of our revolution to 1816, be avoided.

[12] July 12, 1816, in *ibid.,* p. 291.
[13] *Ibid.,* p. 292.

4. Re-enforcement of Tradition, Code, and Law

In the light of the foregoing, it would be easy to conclude that the Principle of Specification is always the principle of exception, that it can be used as moral excuse for disobeying legal enactment or social code whenever it is more convenient to do so or at least whenever the immediate values to be gained seem high on the scale of priority. Yet so to assume would be to jump to a hasty and unwarranted conclusion. The Principle of Specification, like the Principle of the Best Possible, is a double-edged principle.

While the Principle of Specification does, we have suggested, warn against unrestricted application of social codes and legal enactments regardless of circumstances and thus does underline the possibility of exceptions, on moral grounds, to following such codes and enactments, it does not serve as a basis for violating social code or legal enactment whenever convenient. It does not do so for one very important reason: The principle calls for developing the value or values specifically relevant to that situation, *and* that situation always includes the social codes and civil laws actually in operation. For this reason the Principle of Specification is thus actually and equally a principle of re-enforcement of legal and social structure in most circumstances. The legal and social structures cannot be violated with impunity. They form an integral part of the situation itself and, other things being equal, are part of the conditions of effective action. What does this mean, more concretely?

a. Functions of Tradition and Custom

In discussing conscience (Chapter 20), we had to point out that the uncritical conscience, reflecting, among other things, tradition and custom as it does, could not be taken as a sure guide to right action. At the same time we were forced to recognize that in developing a critical conscience, the uncritical conscience has to serve as our point of departure. Because of mere force of habit in the uncritical conscience and, more important, because custom and tradition do tend to embody the moral insights of our heritage, we cannot summarily dismiss either.

Custom and tradition hold together, to a large extent, the living framework of communal action from the smaller community of the family to the larger community of the nation. Any serious weakening of its traditions and customs leads to social disorganization and chaos, and the eventual loss of the community identity, its "image" of itself. Witness the destructive and debilitating effect both on individuals and communities of the loss of cultural identity among the American Indians, African tribesmen, and even our own Appalachian Mountain population, whose local customs and traditions have been too rapidly and too largely displaced by impinging outside cultures. The customs and traditions tend to embody the more stable values, hopes, and ideals of the group in question. Edmund Burke may have been wrong in his contention that tradition has a binding priority over the present, but he was not far from the truth in his insistence that a present without tradition loses its meaning and perspective.

b. *Traditions as Ingredient in Present Situations*

It follows that, to understand or to act effectively or to realize the values relevant to the present situation, we must take account of the customs, traditions, and legal enactments of the locality and the social group. Examples of the unfortunate results of violation of this aspect of Principle of Specification are legion. We can cite only a few striking, yet typical, cases.

During the latter part of the nineteenth century and the first quarter of the twentieth, Protestant missionary activities originating in this country underwent a rapid period of expansion. Much of the missionary work was well planned and gave due regard to the people and place to which the missionaries were sent. In some instances, however, missionaries with the strongest motivation or "calling" failed to take into account that they were going forth to groups with histories, traditions, beliefs, and religious convictions of their own. In some cases the groups were hostile not only to other religions but to strangers in general. Such missionaries could only be ineffective, and indeed they created far more ill-will than understanding or conversion. More effective were those missionaries who tried to understand the local situation with which they dealt, including the language, laws, and customs of the people, and then worked through the existing structure to try to serve the real needs of the place and time.

The same kind of attitude that characterized the less effective of the missionaries has sometimes also marked American foreign policy as it has related to the spread of democracy. After both the first and second World Wars we attempted to establish democratic forms of government patterned on our own model, almost without regard to local conditions. We tended to forget that effective democratic government is not something that can be expected to work in a vacuum. Democracy requires its own traditions and a certain kind of political sophistication. Where no such traditions exist and where political sophistication either does not exist on a broad enough base or takes a different form, to insist that democratic procedures be followed is to invite chaos, splinter parties, dominance of special-interest groups, reaction, and the breakdown of parliamentary government altogether. The history of the Balkan States and of Germany between the two World Wars and the rise of South American dictatorships are cases in point.

In still another area, American reputation and good will have frequently been seriously damaged by the actions of the "ugly Americans" and some less than tactful American tourists. The Millers of Morning-glory, Massachusetts, are convinced that civilization has reached its peak in the Good Fellows Club of Morning-glory. To bestow the benefits of such civilization upon the Old World they travel abroad. How mighty lucky are all these Frenchmen to have the Millers in their midst! Quaint, these Parisians, but what outdated plumbing! A stubborn "frog," the concierge—but give him another dollar, Joe! All these foreigners have their price—and don't worry about not being able to understand his language! A few encounters with the Millers and their counterparts and "Yankee, go home!" is a rather mild reaction, not fomented by Communist sympathizers. Of course, the reverse takes place when Americans treat their foreign guests in college and university and elsewhere only on the basis of "how lucky you are to be here!"

c. *The Moral-Holiday Phenomenon*

One does not have to go abroad to meet real innocents like the Millers. Such people seem to think that whenever they leave the community in which they are known, some or all restrictions on responsible behavior are removed. One might almost describe this as the moral-holiday phenomenon. A business trip, a convention of the Mystic Knights of the Sea, even a vacation trip, is an occasion for disregard not only of one's own usual modes of behavior but of the customs, the feelings, and even the persons of the area to which one goes. Anonymity removes responsibilty, and one can do exactly as he pleases without worrying about the consequences. Plato in the *Republic* (Book II) tells of Gyges, who found a magic ring by which he could make himself invisible at will. When invisible, Gyges could perform any act he wished without fear of apprehension. Gyges' modern counterpart on a moral holiday may not have the advantage of invisibility, but his mode of reasoning and acting is essentially the same: Injustice if undetected is quite all right. Just do not get caught!

The Principle of Specification radically underlines the fact that there are no moral holidays—that morality does not consist in a set of ready rules to be applied in public, where one is known, or on specific days of the week, but rather in continuing intelligent decision, in the light of the circumstances, which translates one's table or symphony of values into actual accomplishment in the light of situations as they occur. Values that are conflicting without anonymity are equally conflicting with anonymity. Whether one does as the Romans do or not, it is nevertheless the fact that unless one at least understands what the Romans are up to, many of the values of a trip to Rome are lost. And if disregard of the Romans is carried sufficiently far, any possibility for value realization in Rome disappears.

d. *Relation between Theory and Practice*

The relation of Romans to the Principle of Specification brings to the fore still another important aspect of the principle. While the principle calls for action in the light of each unique situation, it also calls for the realization of values in that situation. In this respect, the Principle of Specification is an important warning against a certain type of Utopian thinking—a type closely related to the Walter Mitty variety of thinking mentioned earlier. The danger involved is one that sometimes tends to be fostered by an interest in ethics itself. One may become so fascinated with the theoretical aspects of a study that one overlooks its relevance in fact to action now. There may be a great deal of intellectual and aesthetic enjoyment in working out the abstract relation of value types to each other or in planning the components of "the good society" or in contemplating one's ideals. Any and all are legitimate and important studies. But the Principle of Specification points out that values that are not realized in some actual situation are not in fact values and will not be realized.

In his Theses on Feuerbach [14] Karl Marx with characteristic exag-

[14] Thesis XI. See Karl Marx and Friedrich Engels, *Basic Writings on Politics and Philosophy* (Garden City, New York: Doubleday, 1959), p. 245.

geration commented that philosophers heretofore have only talked about the world, whereas the important thing to do is to change it. What he was driving at is very much to the point in relation to ethical theory. An ethics that has no relevance to action now is at best static and at worst no ethics. Planning for the future may be integral to ethical thinking, but unless such planning can be translated into present oughts and present value realizations, such planning may actually block effective action. The budding actor who refuses to take lesser parts in order to save himself for his major role will, in all likelihood, remain an undeveloped bud. The person out of work who refuses to take minor jobs available because they are not commensurate with his social station is likely to remain out of work. The old saying about opportunity only knocking once may have an element of truth in it, and one at least needs to keep the knocker in working order.

(1) *Practical Ethics*

The Principle of Specification, along with the Principles of the Best Possible and Consequences, removes any excuse for thinking of ethics as impractical or unrelated to the changing circumstances of every day life. In addition these principles remove any justification for an impracticable or unrealistic ethics in which "unrealistic" is taken to mean not applicable under ordinary circumstances. This is not to say that the Formal Principles lose their relevance, for they remain the fundamental conditions of responsible action, but it is to say that unless they can be translated into action, with due regard for consequences and real potentialities and in the light of changing circumstances, they remain purely formal without concrete content.

(2) *Independence of Externals*

It might be argued, in the opposite direction, that the Principles of Specification, Best Possible, and Consequences tend to reduce morality to expediency. In particular it may be argued that morality demands that we rise above circumstances at least to the extent of being able and willing to hold onto our ideals regardless of situations and results.

Here the ideal of the Stoic wise man, who remains independent of externals, might be cited for support. Epictetus, for example, insisted that the good and happy man is not the man who has or desires physical strength, prosperity, property, reputation, or public

offices. On the contrary, the good man remains indifferent to all of
these. He is not perturbed by changing fortune or circumstances.
He does not become involved in the troubles of others, nor does
he reflect upon or worry about what others would consider his own
troubles. To become the slave of changing fortune and circumstances is to lose both one's equanimity and one's reason.[15] Does such
an attitude directly contrast with the concern for realizing present
values, as required by the Principle of Specification? Does it make
of morality something more ennobling by reducing concern for
circumstances to ignoble opportunism?

At first glance this might seem to be so. Yet a closer look both
at the principles under consideration and at Epictetus will change
the picture. To be sure, the Principles of Specification, the Best
Possible, and Consequences do call for concern with the present,
its acts, and their consequences. It must not be forgotten, however,
that they do so in the light of one's self-imposed ideals and in accordance with a concern for the harmonious interrelation of values
chosen. What the principles do make clear is that intelligent or
effective action in the light of such affirmed ideals cannot occur in
the abstract. To be effective, ideals must be realized in specific contexts, including adequate, impartial assessment of consequences, potentialities, and the present situation. If this be expediency, then
it is our contention that there can be no effective morality without
expediency.

To return to Epictetus, does Epictetus really disagree? Admittedly,
the ideals Epictetus affirms are essentially those of an ethical formalist—self-control and steadfastness of will. And yet Epictetus is not
unmindful of circumstances. In fact, the doctrine of the independence of externals calls for careful discrimination in terms both
of consequences and of circumstances. Epictetus was particularly
concerned that we distinguish those things that lie within the exercise of our power from those things that do not. "In our power are
opinion, movement towards a thing, desire, aversion (turning from
a thing); and, in a word, whatever are our own acts: not in our
power are the body, property, reputation, offices (magisterial power),
and in a word, whatever are not our own acts." [16] Epictetus' distinction may be drawn too sharply, but the reason for drawing the dis-

---

[15] Cf. *Discourses of Epictetus with the Encheiridion and Fragmenis,* trans. George
Long (London: George Bell and Sons, 1890).
[16] *Encheiridion* I, in *ibid.,* p. 379.

tinction was his recognition of the importance of exercising the power that is ours wisely in the light of the circumstances (including consequences) in which we find ourselves. This calls for the closest scrutiny of things, occasions, and events in order that the values subject to one's power may be realized. Thus Epictetus admonishes:

> In everything which pleases the soul, or supplies a want, or is loved, remember to add this to the (description, notion); what is the nature of each thing, beginning with the smallest? If you love an earthen vessel, say it is an earthen vessel which you love; for when it is broken you will not be disturbed.[17]

> When you are going to take in hand any act, remind yourself what kind of act it is.[18]

> On the occasion of every accident (event) that befals [sic] you, remember to turn to yourself and inquire what power you have for turning it to use.[19]

It would be hard to find closer parallels to the principles that we have been considering.

e. Of Trees and the Forest

There is, however, a danger in the Principle of Specification—if one were to take it as the sole principle apart from the other principles already considered, or even if one were to take it as the final principle, which included the other principles considered up to this point. The danger lies in becoming so concerned with the present that one loses perspective and direction. One would miss the forest, as the old story goes, because of the trees. To a certain extent this danger is offset by the Principle of Consequences and the Axiological Principle, the latter calling for choice among values that are harmonious. And yet, these in themselves are not quite enough. It might well be possible in a series of specific situations to choose nonconflicting values with an eye to the probable best consequences and yet achieve over-all results that are negligible because they fit no comprehensible, cumulative pattern or direction. Intelligent and effective realization even of the values in the present frequently depends not merely or primarily on the present alternative but upon one's long-

---

[17] *Encheiridion* III, in *ibid.,* p. 381.
[18] *Encheiridion* IV, in *ibid.,* p. 381.
[19] *Encheiridion* X, in *ibid.,* p. 383.

run aims. Accordingly, the Principle of Specification needs to be complemented by what may be described as "the longer view" or a principle of directional concern. It is to the problem of the longer view that we now must turn.

III. *REFLECTIVE SUMMARY*

There are no values without persons, we have argued. We now add that values arise in the crucible of each person's present, a present that is constantly emerging from the past and giving birth to a future-present. Whatever defects hedonism and existentialism may have as final philosophies, they bring us back to this realization that to "live for the future" can be done only in the present. The truth in "Gather ye rosebuds while ye may" must be given its due. Consider foreseeable consequences, yes, but see them as involved in the value experience uniquely available in the present situation. We cannot, in short, live every moment as if it were the last minute; but neither can we live "dead to the present," as if this present with its value possibilities had never existed.

To emphasize that developing persons in successively different situations will have value possibilities *related to* those situations is not to fall into *relativism*. It is to grant the element of truth in the contention that there are differences in the presents of persons that must not be disregarded. Any universal ideal, any best possible, arises in the present experience of unique persons.

Accordingly, to take an act that brings value in certain situations and hastily universalize that specific act for other persons and situations is to break the Principle of Specification. Again, this does not mean that there are no guiding principles of action, but it does mean that there are no specific acts that can be said to be always right (or wrong) in any present without reference to that person's present and the value goals in mind. The development of the concept of legal equity, for example, is the application of the Principle of Specification to the administration of the universal principle of justice. The Principle of Specification, moreover, calls for constant vigilance lest the customary and the habitual lead to neglect of the new needs of the present both in individual and in social life.

This principle has relevance for political democracy, which also illustrates it. One of the advantages of a democratic way of life is that many different people in different situations can feel free to express their respective convictions when they believe that new occasions call for new duties. The Principle of Specification supports the "right" to revolution when a governmental situation exists that is no longer sensitive to and expressive of their wishes and in fact oppresses the people who instituted it in order to protect and increase their values.

However, lest the Principle of Specificity be interpreted to mean that any "change in value" is an end in itself, we need to emphasize that it is the value relevant to the present situation that is to be realized and not necessarily the novelty. The past in the present, or the present as heightening the past, may well be the spice in the life of value.

Once more, then, we note the importance of being aware of and balancing the different facets of the moral venture. There are no "moral holidays," according to the Principle of Specification. Yet every moral situation can bring recreation in value. Growing coherence among values is our criterion, but the coherence will not be growing if the moral agent is insensitive to every present as he alternates between thinking and acting.

25

*The Most Inclusive End
and Self-Realization*

〰〰〰〰〰〰〰〰〰〰〰〰〰〰〰〰〰〰〰〰

I. *TOWARD A TIGHTER UNITY*

Is there any principle in terms of which we can bring together emphasis upon (1) the present of the Principle of Specification, (2) the various individual abilities of the Principle of the Best Possible, (3) the foreseeable results of the Principle of Consequences, and (4) the growth in harmony among values of the Axiological Principle? At first glance the Principle of Specification and the Principle of Consequences do not rest easily together; nor does the Axiological Principle with its emphasis upon most inclusive organization of values easily fit in with the particularity of individual abilities under the Principle of the Best Possible.

Can we show any closer interrelation of these principles than is to be found in them merely as conditions of reasonable moral action? For overemphasis on any one of them alone, as on the Formal Principles alone, may result in serious tension with respect to the others. Furthermore, the symphony of values and the system of virtues, developed in Chapters 15 and 17, while giving substance to our discussion of the Principles of Axiology and Autonomy, need to be more positively related to the specific situation, consequences, and the best possible.

II. *THE PRINCIPLE OF THE MOST INCLUSIVE END*

What seems to be called for is a structural, or balancing, or integrating principle, one in terms of which the various conditions of meaningful action and moral life discussed thus far can be brought into focus in relation to each other and given some further direction. To put the matter succinctly, we might ask: To what purpose do we act conscientiously and consistently and, with the field of values in view, take full cognizance of consequences, our best abilities, and the chances of improving every present situation? We might answer: The purpose is to live reasonably, intelligently, coherently. And yet at this advanced stage in our discussion, to do so is not enough, for we need now to specify more concretely, if we can, what living reasonably entails.

Actually the grounds for such an additional defining principle have already emerged. The Axiological Principle stressed the duty to choose harmonious or coherent values. Under the Principle of the Best Possible we recognize that what constitutes the best possible for any particular person is an ever retreating ideal—one that keeps him functioning creatively. In the earlier discussion of the symphony of values, it became evident that the life best to live at any stage of a person's experience, is the life that keeps a creative and mutually sustaining balance between the largest range of values open to it. The "happy" life is an incorporating growth. Finally, the need for direction has been particularly evident in the discussion of our obligations to the present.

The key to growing harmony among values and the corrective to our own concern with the present lie in the direction afforded by an inclusive life plan.

We suggest, then, the Principle of the Most Inclusive End and would state it as follows: *Each person ought to choose a coherent life in which the widest possible range of values is realized in accordance with a life plan.*[1]

One might object that the Principle of the Most Inclusive End adds nothing new, in that its components have been anticipated in earlier discussions. But this is to overlook both its synthesizing func-

[1] Cf. Brightman, *Moral Laws* (New York: Abingdon Press, 1933), p. 183.

tion and the particularly important addition that takes us beyond consideration of consequences to the duty of actively planning and shaping the future (within the limits of the possible, of course). This is the principle that has been foundational to those ethical systems, from Plato to the present, that have urged self-realization as the highest good. So considered, it is the teleological principle *par excellence*.

A. *The Far View*

Among the most important implications of the Principle of the Most Inclusive End is its emphasis upon the long-range view as a corrective to any excessive concern with the present that might arise from the Principle of Specification. The long range is more than just a concern with consequences. It involves an active concern for and creative shaping of the future. Although we stressed the fact (in the last chapter) that all action takes place in the present, yet to this must be added "with an eye to the future also." The present, while not wholly beyond our control, as is the past, is still largely determined. Present action in its very completion is sealed into the unchangeable past. Yet the present is no less important because the future also is in mind. It is in the creative effects upon future presents that present acts gain a larger part of their significance. As a matter of fact, the major tension in present interests is not usually between the present and the future but between the near future and the more distant future.

1. *Carl G. Jung*

The psychological need for the long-range or far view is strikingly developed in Jung's discussion of prospective aim.[2] Jung contends that the various unconscious forces that form the dynamic motivational base of conscious life—for example, Freudian sexuality and Adlerian will-to-power—can only be healthily sublimated and coordinated into effective channels by what he calls "prospective aim." Prospective aim is the desire for a whole personality or for self-realization, "the bringing into reality of the whole human being—that is, individuation."[3]

---

[2] See Chapter 3. Freud also suggests the importance of an ego-ideal, not synonymous with the superego, as a condition of mature development of a creative life pattern.

[3] Carl G. Jung, *Modern Man in Search of a Soul*, trans. W. Dell and C. Boynes (New York: Harcourt, Brace and Co., 1933), p. 31.

Such prospective aim is the root condition of meaningful life—*in fact the essential development of the healthy personality itself.* Although the need for prospective aim grows out of the dynamics of unconscious motivation, the development of prospective aim itself is a matter of moral decision—of choosing a way, of moral consistency, of perseverance and hope, of the long range view. Jung maintains: "Personality can never develop itself unless the individual chooses his own way consciously and with conscious moral decision. Not only the causal motive, the need, but a conscious, moral decision must lend its strength to the process of the development of personality." [4]

2. Gordon W. Allport

In line with Freud and Jung and with psychologists who show a similar future-oriented concern for self-fulfillment (for example, Adler, Fromm, Maslow, and Rogers), G. W. Allport insists that "intelligent and perspicuous *planning* for the future is always a significant feature of any mature life." [5] Without projective, imaginative goals of some sort, a life remains immature, childish. "Every mature personality may be said to travel toward a port of destination, selected in advance, or to several related ports in succession, the Ego-Ideal always serving to hold the course in view." [6] The directions chosen may vary—relatively definite or relatively indefinite, relatively rich in opportunities for achievement or relatively poor. They may involve attempting to change the world or simply procuring "a comfortable home, a routine vocation." [7] But without direction, life not only remains childish; it lacks significance of any sort for the person in question.

3. Friedrich W. Nietzsche

Among ethicists, no one has more dramatically urged the moral importance of the far view (*Fernstenliebe*) than Friedrich Nietzsche, one of the most fascinating and controversial figures in the history of ethics. He is frequently interpreted as being a thorough ethical iconoclast and an advocate of the most extreme form of ethical rela-

---

[4] *The Integration of Personality,* trans. Stanley Dell (New York: Farrar and Rinehart, 1939), p. 289.

[5] *Personality: A Psychological Interpretation* (New York: Henry Holt and Co., 1937), p. 218. See also Chapter 6 above, Section I, A.

[6] *Ibid.,* p. 219.

[7] *Ibid.,* p. 220.

tivism. Castell, for example, treats Nietzsche under the heading "Alternatives to Ethical Theory" [8] and characterizes him as insisting "that custom guarantees morality, that the laws make anything right." [9]

If one is talking about code-morality or customary morality, Castell's interpretation is correct. Nietzsche had no sympathy with any attempt to make any particular code-morality universal, for code-moralities are to Nietzsche moralities without reflection or passion —are attempts on the part of the weaker members of the group to hold the line against individual initiative and social change. It was in contrast to code-moralism that Nietzsche described himself as an "immoralist." [10] But whether such a negative view of morality is fundamental to Nietzsche is doubtful.

The problem of interpreting Nietzsche is particularly difficult in the light of two characteristics of his writing and thought. First, Nietzsche was stylistically more poet than philosopher. His favorite mode of writing was aphoristic and paradoxical. He constantly tends to extremes of statement and is all too easily quoted out of context to mean something quite different from what he intended. This is tragically illustrated in the Nazis' use of Nietzsche to support militarism, German supermanism, and the totalitarian nationalistic state. Nietzsche did declare war on ignorance, complacency, and weakness: "and if you cannot be saints of knowledge, at least be its warriors. They are the companions and forerunners of such sainthood. I see many soldiers: would that I saw many warriors!" [11] But Nietzsche was an ardent foe of militarism. No more scathing denunciation of the totalitarian nationalistic state could be found than Nietzsche's chapter entitled "The New Idol," in *Thus Spake Zarathustra*.[12] "State is the name of the coldest of all cold monsters. Coldly it tells lies too; and this lie crawls out of its mouth: 'I, the State, am the people.' That is a lie!" [13]

The second difficulty in interpretation arises from the fact that Nietzsche is not alway scrupulously consistent. Part of the reason for

[8] Alburey Castell, *An Elementary Ethics* (New York: Prentice-Hall Inc., 1954), p. 83 ff.

[9] *Ibid.*, p. 89.

[10] Cf. *Beyond Good and Evil*, trans. Helen Zimmern (Edinburgh: T. N. Foulis), Sec. 226 ff.

[11] *Thus Spake Zarathustra*, from *The Portable Nietzsche* edited by Walter Kaufman. Copyright 1954 by The Viking Press, Inc., and reprinted by their permission. P. 159.

[12] *Ibid.*, pp. 160–63.

[13] *Ibid.*, p. 160.

this lack of consistency lies in his lack of faith in what he considered to be the pretensions of an analytic or classifying reason to obtain complete objectivity and to arrive at neat and indubitable descriptions of reality. Nietzsche was not a system-builder, but he was a thinker with brilliant, pregnant flashes of insight. Nor was he as wholly anti-intellectualistic and opposed to reason as he is sometimes made out to be. He says, for example, "The only happiness lies in reason; all the rest of this world is dismal. The brightest reason, however, I see in the work of the artist." [14]

As indicated above, Nietzsche does strikingly underline the relativity of code-moralities. And code-moralities according to Nietzsche are, by the unthinking, identified with morality. Morality so conceived is slavishness to tradition and authority. It is an expression of the herd instinct and fosters commonness, weakness, self-satisfaction, laziness, satisfaction with things as they are, resentment, adaptation, conformity, and negation. Such, Nietzsche insists, is the morality of slaves, not rulers.[15]

But Nietzsche's recognition of the relativism of slave moralities does not mean that he is a relativist in relation to what he thinks man can and ought to be. To Slave-morality, Nietzsche contrasts what he calls Aristocratic-morality, the morality of masters, or the morality of freemen. Men do not have to be cowering members of the herd. Man's enemy is inherent weakness and self-pity. Man's challenge is maturity and affirmation. The only peace that is worth having is that which is obtained through "the expression of maturity and mastery in the midst of doing, creating, working and willing." [16]

To obtain such peace, men as they are with their weaknesses must be transformed. Men as they are tend to be partial men and satisfied with their incompleteness. Love of the present, including love of one's neighbor as he is, is an attempt to escape from responsibility or, in terms used later by Erich Fromm, an attempt to "escape from freedom." In *The Twilight of the Idols*, Nietzsche asks, "For what is freedom?" and answers that "one has the will to accept responsibility as oneself." [17] Accordingly, Nietzsche urges that the minimum condition of true freedom, of responsibility, of becoming whole, of moving

---

[14] *Notes* (1875), in Kaufman, *op. cit.*, p. 50.
[15] See particularly, *The Genealogy of Morals*, trans. H. B. Samuels, in *The Philosophy of Nietzsche* (New York: Modern Library, n.d.), pp. 617–807, and *Twilight of the Idols*, in Kaufman, *op. cit.*, pp. 486–92.
[16] Cf. Kaufman, *op. cit.*, p. 489.
[17] *Ibid.*, p. 542.

beyond man as he is, to the overman, is "love of the furthest." In *Zarathustra*, Nietzsche says, "Sooner I should even recommend flight from neighbor and love of the furthest." [18]

With the long-range view, life takes on direction and meaning: "Your love of life shall be love of your highest hope: and your highest hope shall be the highest thought of life." [19] Without the long-range view, men remain incomplete and uncreative.

> Verily, my friends, I walk among men as among the fragments and limbs of men. This is what is terrible for my eyes, that I find men in ruins and scattered as over a battlefield or a butcher-field. And when my eyes flee from the now to the past, they always find the same: fragments and limbs and dreadful accidents—but no human beings.[20]

It would be difficult to find a more penetrating description of persons without direction or hope, reacting only to present experiences. The description also applies all too aptly to the kind of fragmentation that frequently occurs when a person becomes so bound up with an immediate job or problem or task that he can no longer see how what he is doing is part of a larger whole or is contributing to a continuing process. Its applicability to the individual who is unable to or refuses to relate his business, social, religious, and recreational activities to each other is obvious.

The overcoming of such fragmentation lies, for Nietzsche, in continued growth and creativity disciplined by the long-range view.

> I walk among men as fragments of the future—the future which I envisage. And this is all my creating and striving, that I create and carry together into the One what is fragment and riddle and dreadful accident. And how could I bear to be a man if man were not also a creator and guesser of riddles and a redeemer of accidents? [21]

Again, in counteracting overemphasis on fragmentary, immediate interests, Nietzsche's insistence upon the importance and unifying effect of this long-range view, upon responsible, future-oriented, self-creative activity, is crucial and basic to the Most Inclusive End. In most of us, our wants and desires exceed our abilities. Even amidst

[18] *Ibid.*, p. 173.
[19] *Ibid.*, p. 160.
[20] *Ibid.*, p. 250.
[21] *Ibid.*, p. 251.

value claims that, if realized, would be true values (other things being equal), we are frequently embarrassed by our abundance rather than by scarcity. One might like to be a concert pianist, a chemist, an expert in Slavic literature, an anthropologist, a painter, and an aeronautical engineer, all at once. One's abilities might conceivably allow him to be any one of the above or a combination of some of them. But, except for the extraordinarily gifted, there would be neither the ability nor the time for them all.

It is just at this point that the far view becomes essential as a basis for selection and organization—one might even say, as a principle of economy of choice. Without some long-range plan, the temptation is to choose in the light of whatever happens to be the dominant urge of the moment, to dissipate one's abilities without real creativity or solid accomplishment in any particular area. The result too often is frustration and subjection or slavery to the changing demands of the moment rather than mastery either of oneself or the moment in cumulative directional growth.

Nevertheless, Nietzsche's statement of the acceptance of the far view, as quoted, remains incomplete. With typical Nietzschean one-sidedness, it does not pay enough attention to the Principle of Specification. He is perhaps overly pessimistic about the small number of persons capable of the far view. His conception of adequate content for the far view is too restricted, thus overlooking the "most inclusive" aspect of the principle we are considering. Nicolai Hartmann, commenting on Nietzsche, points out:

> The ideals which we are considering are human ideals. But they are by no means merely ethical. They embrace all sides of humanity. Nietzsche regarded their content as consisting predominantly of vitalistic and aesthetic qualities: strength, fulness of life, beauty and whatever is related to these. These qualities are profoundly important and must not be omitted: but they are one-sided and, on that account, when projected into the Idea, are mis-leading. The Idea of man requires the rounding out of his whole nature, physical as well as spiritual, of capacities and all the splendid possessions which are within his power.[22]

Thus to Nietzsche's insistence upon the far view must be added inclusiveness, so that it becomes the inclusive far view or the most inclusive end.

[22] *Ethics*, trans. Stanton Coit (London: George Allen and Unwin, 1932), II, 325–26. By permission of The Macmillan Co.

B. *Self-Realization*

As we mentioned earlier, the thinkers who have been most cognizant of the Principle of the Most Inclusive End are those who have
insisted that the goal of moral effort is self-realization (ethical per-
fectionism). For the self-realizationist, the Kantian dictum to act in
accordance with duty, the hedonistic demand that we seek pleasure,
the utilitarian concern with consequences and the greatest good of
the greatest number, and even the Nietzschean demand for the far
view—all still remain abstract. These views need to be correlated and
made concrete in terms of a life plan, a style of life, or concept of the
kind of a person I ought to become—my potential fuller self. We shall
return to further implications of the tenets of self-realization in
Chapter 26. At present our concern is with its central contention
that the richest and most inclusive life of which I am capable is one
in accordance with a plan for life realistically developed—in the light
of every bit of information that I can marshall about my own potentialities and capabilities.

In our discussion of the virtues in Chapter 16, we noted the insistence of both Plato and Aristotle that virtues do not hang in mid-
air, that they are not abstract formulations that can be applied without regard to concrete situations confronted by particular persons
with their unique capacities and weaknesses. Rather what makes virtues of courage, temperance, and justice is that they, in the last analysis, are also dispositions conducive to excellence or perfection of
function in the individual with his potentialities. Through the virtues, the widest range of capacities is most completely realized. But
the prerequisite to virtue, excellence, and self-realization is also the
constant probing to discover all of a person's potentialities as a life
plan emerges from and further develops the activities that are virtuous.

1. *Plato*

If anything, Plato dwelt upon the importance of emergent life
plans more fully than did his successor Aristotle. Describing justice
in the *Republic* Plato says:

> Our principle that the born shoemaker or carpenter had better
> stick to his trade turns out to have been an adumbration of jus-
> tice. . . . But in reality justice is not a matter of external be-

havior, but of the inward self and of attending to all that is, in the fullest sense, a man's proper concern. The just man does not allow the several elements in his soul to usurp one another's functions; he is indeed one who sets his house in order, by self-mastery and discipline coming to be at peace with himself. . . . Only when he has . . . made himself one man instead of many, will he be ready to do whatever he may have to do.[23]

For Plato, not only is the just man the man who controls his various capacities in terms of their mutual contribution to the fullest life possible, but the just society is that society which respects individual differences and makes possible the mutual complementation of life plans—both for the enrichment of each citizen and of society as a whole. Plato saw that an adequately formed life plan is not possible apart from social orientation on the one hand and the objective assessment of individual capacities as available to individuals and society on the other. There are questionable authoritarian elements in Plato's total scheme, but in emphasizing harmony within oneself as involving basic social orientation without indifference to individual life plans, Plato has few modern superiors.

The importance of realistic self-assessment was touched upon under our discussion of the Principle of the Best Possible (Chapter 23). Plato would agree that the proper assessment of individual differences needs external aids and checks. For the sake of the person and his happiness, as well as the community and common welfare, one cannot leave the matter wholly to what may be wishful thinking or rationalization. Even the most critical of us is likely to be less than candid when his own interests are involved. We earlier suggested the importance of vocational testing as a helpful factor in formulating one's own best possible. Plato's answer was more complete—testing yes, but as integral to educational differentiation. Starting with common primary education, the process of discovering where abilities lie was to be closely integrated with educational accomplishment. Specialized education would be introduced at whatever level of educational proficiency any individual was able to benefit from it. In this way, coordination of life plan with abilities could be assured. The famous myth of the metals,[24] far from requiring a rigid caste

[23] Plato, *Republic,* IV, 443, trans. F. M. Cornford (London: Oxford University Press, 1945), pp. 141–42. For Plato's underlying theory of value, see Chapter 10 above.
[24] *Republic,* III, in *ibid.,* p. 415.

system, aimed specifically at such differentiation in the light of abilities.

Plato, in other words, was insisting that it is only when one's life is unified—"one man instead of many"—in terms of a life plan realistically arrived at, in the light of actual potentialities or capabilities and with an eye to the complementation of diverse life plans in community, that justice or happiness can be attained. He would add that what is true for individuals applies to the community as well.

Plato has sometimes been criticized on the grounds that his conception of a life plan coordinated with abilities is too rigid. He would seem to want to force persons into life plans according to ability, regardless of their desire, and he does not allow switching from one life plan to another once abilities have been determined. "The born shoemaker or carpenter had better stick to his trade." [25] There is little question but that Plato does not emphasize the Principle of Autonomy as much as might be desirable, that is, the importance of helping the carpenter or shoemaker willingly to accept carpentry or shoemaking as a life plan. Yet the alternative also raises a serious problem. Is it better for a person's own satisfaction in the long run, not to mention his self-realization and his contributions to the community, to embark upon the kind of work in which he can reasonably expect to excel? Or is it better for him to try to do whatever he wants at the outset even at the cost of failure to himself or to society? Are wrong choices of vocation easily remedied?

Plato's answer is at least definite. Only the first alternative is morally right, socially just. Plato was not unaware of the importance of moral autonomy; he recognized that we frequently do not know our own best interests. He was convinced that once we do know, not only do we recognize that we ought to fulfill them, we do in fact act in accordance with them. Hence Plato's insistence upon the importance of education is also an insistence upon developing some adequate self-imposed ideals and some realistic life plans.

Plato was too much a realist to leave to impulse anything so basic as a life plan. It must be formulated reasonably, and distribution of such plans must be under rational control. The danger in Plato's view does not lie in his recognition that a person may have to be educated to understand wherein his potential excellence lies and must then be encouraged to control his impulses and passions in

[25] *Republic*, IV, in *ibid.*, p. 442.

accordance with his insight. At this point, Adler, Jung, Fromm, Maslow, and Allport would be in basic agreement. Rather does the danger lie in vesting too much responsibility for reasonably structuring society in the rulers. Plato, of all men, knew how rare men of the stature and wisdom of philosopher-kings would be; even so, he did not build into his *Republic* enough checks against tyranny. But this danger in no way detracts from his insight relevant to individuals seeking the most inclusive end.

It might be objected that Plato's analysis places too much emphasis upon rank or vocation. After all, the most inclusive end, or a life plan, should include all aspects of life and not be limited to vocation. Yet Plato is fully aware that man is more than a worker. The primary education that all citizens shall have includes poetry, dance, music, physical education, and other activities. Plato, however, is far too realistic not to recognize that vocation occupies the major portion of man's waking life. Unless vocation constitutes the focal point of a life plan in the light of which complementary values are chosen, a person is likely to find himself peculiarly impoverished and frustrated. Examples of such frustration are not hard to find.

The first example is that of a person forced by circumstances (whether of his own making or not) into a vocation not commensurate with his abilities and for which he can engender no enthusiasm. John got married before he had finished his education. Neither he nor his parents had enough funds to enable him to continue his education and support a family. He and his wife had hopes that she would be able to work, and that her income, plus whatever he could earn on a part-time basis, would make it possible for him to continue his education. But his wife became pregnant sooner than they had planned. To complicate matters his father had a stroke and financial help was needed for hospital expenses and his mother's support. The part-time salesman's work that he had taken became full-time. From that point on, every time it appeared that John might be able to return to his studies, new crises arose, responsibilities increased, and the hope of further education grew dimmer. Finally it faded completely.

John found himself "stuck" in a job that he did not enjoy. Even though the job did not tax his abilities, his very lack of interest cut down his efficiency and precluded advancement. At best, the job was a necessary evil to be endured. He began to live only after the day's work. Worse still, John's bitterness toward his job gradually extended to his family, his parents, the community, and life in general.

Consider a second example of the person who never stays with anything long enough to master it. Eddie was a person with varied talents and enthusiasms. In high school he did well in the subjects he liked; the others he let slide. He loved cars and took a part-time job as a mechanic. This he enjoyed until he found he was doing the same kinds of repairs over and over again. He hated routine, so he quit. Eddie seemed to have a natural bent for manipulating electrical equipment. He put together high-fidelity sets, built ham radio stations, and modified television sets. So he began working in a radio shop and then in an electronics concern. But again the work soon became routine, so he quit.

Eddie thought he would try college and was admitted. He loved history but hated the required assignments in mathematics and languages. He neglected completely the subjects that made no strong appeal; consequently he was dropped from college at the end of his freshman year. He repeated the same pattern in commercial art school, in insurance selling, in landscape gardening. A number of people of less native ability than he finished college and became productive and respected members of the community. In no field was Eddie ever able to get past the stage of initial enthusiasm into the stage of steady discipline necessary for accomplishment. Eddie is now convinced that he "never got any breaks." This world, he complains, is filled with fools who refuse to give "a man with ideas" an opportunity.

Plato would point out that in each of these two cases failure spread from vocation to other areas of life and was due to the inability to coordinate abilities in terms of a realistic purpose or life plan. The failure in vocation became failure in self-realization.

2. *Aristotle*

With Plato's analysis Aristotle would heartily agree. In fact, Aristotle defines happiness and goodness in terms of proper functioning:

> And if we declare that the function of man is a certain form of life, and define that form of life as the exercise of the soul's faculties and activities in association with rational principle, and say that the function of a good man is to perform these activities well and rightly, and if a function is well performed when it is

performed in accordance with its own proper excellence—from these it follows that the good for man is the active exercise of his soul's faculties in conformity with excellence or virtue.[26]

Although Aristotle does not stress the role of specific vocation in community as strongly as Plato, he does emphasize the importance of community for self-realization. He points out: "Now a solitary man has a hard life, for it is not easy to keep up continuous activity by oneself; it is easier to do so with the aid of, and in relation to, other people."[27]

3. F. H. Bradley

Among recent philosophers who have urged the acceptance of self-realization in accordance with a life plan as the central ethical norm, two thinkers call for brief but special note: the Englishman, Francis Herbert Bradley (1846–1924), and the American, Josiah Royce (1855–1916).

For Bradley, the most general, in fact the only adequate, conception of an end worth striving for in its own right, is self-realization. "All we can realize is (accident apart) our ends, or the objects we desire; and . . . all we can desire is, in a word self."[28] With Plato and Nietzsche, Bradley insists that the self we strive for is not a collection of parts but a unity, what Bradley calls a "whole self." Such a self, as Bradley conceives it, is not just my present experiences. My whole self includes my past and my future as I attempt to relate these meaningfully to each other and to the present. But Bradley goes on to insist that even these are not enough, for my self-awareness arises in a social situation. Any merely private self is still only a fragment. Going beyond Aristotle, Bradley would insist that a solitary life not only is hard but strictly speaking is impossible. I find my true self only in the larger setting of community. Bradley carries this idea to the extent of saying: "In morality the existence of my mere private self, as such, is something which ought not to be, and which, so far as I am moral, has already ceased."[29]

The implications for Bradley are clear. With his German predecessor Hegel, Bradley insists that I find my true self only in the larger

---

[26] *Nicomachean Ethics*, 1098a. See Chapter 16 above.

[27] *Nicomachean Ethics*, 1170a.

[28] From F. H. Bradley, *Ethical Studies*, copyright © 1951 by The Liberal Arts Press, Inc., reprinted by permission of The Liberal Arts Press Division of The Bobbs-Merrill Company, Inc. P. 11.

[29] *Ibid.*, p. 24.

moral organism, that is, the community or society. My society becomes normative for my selfhood, my self-realization, and my life plan. It is only in the context of what Bradley calls "my station and my duties" that my fullest ethical individuality is attained.

In the realized idea which, superior to me, and yet here and now in and by me, affirms itself in a continuous process, we have found the end, we have found self-realization, duty, and happiness in one; yes, we have found ourselves, when we found our station and its duties, our function as an organ in the social organism.[30]

On the surface, Bradley's position sounds very much like Plato's. We find our fulfillment and happiness through fulfillment of our function in society. These functions (or this function) constitute our life work; unless we discover what our proper stations are, our lives lose meaning, become petty, and atrophy.

Yet, when one looks more closely, Bradley is saying something quite different from Plato—something far more questionable. Granted that the members of society are interdependent and that any complex society involves specialization and differentiation of function, it does not necessarily follow that society is a superorganism or a self more real than the complex of selves who make it up. To say of the state as Bradley does that I am but "a pulsebeat in the whole system" [31] or that this state is "the objective mind which is subjective and conscious in its citizens. . . . It speaks the word of command and gives the field of accomplishment, and in the activity of obedience it has and bestows individual life and satisfaction and happiness" [32]—this is to verge dangerously on fascism. Compare the following from Mussolini:

Fascism conceives of the State as an absolute, in comparison with which all individuals or groups are relative, only to be conceived of in their relation to the State. . . . The Fascist State is itself conscious, and has itself a will and a personality—Thus it may be called the "ethical" State.[33]

To assume that either Bradley, or many others who hold to a Theory

[30] *Ibid.*, p. 101.
[31] *Ibid.*, p. 109.
[32] *Ibid.*, p. 120.
[33] Quoted in Albert R. Chandler, *The Clash of Political Ideals*, (3rd ed.; New York: Appleton-Century-Crofts, 1957), p. 175, from Enciclopedia Italiana, trans. Jane Seames in *Day to Day Pamphlets*, No. 18 (London: Hogarth Press, 1933).

of the Social Self,[34] are fascists in a political sense is, of course, not correct. However, the concept of the organic state as a social self does at least open the way to the kind of totalitarian concepts that would seriously undermine the Principle of Autonomy (see Chapter 20).

The Life Plan and Most Inclusive End under discussion here imply no such organism. The Principle of the Most Inclusive End does not call for a life plan chosen for the individual by the state or even by Plato's philosopher-king. Rather, it demands that each person ought to choose a coherent life in which the widest possible range of value is realized in accordance with a life-plan. It quite obviously does not exclude aid in selection by the state, philosopher-kings, psychoanalysts, psychologists, clergymen, or ethicists, when such aid may be helpful. But it does involve the recognition that no moral responsibility for vocation or individual life plan is present unless the actual decision is made by the person in question.

4. *Josiah Royce*

Although in general Josiah Royce holds to a position not unlike that of Bradley, one aspect of his position serves as an important corrective to Bradley. One might accept it as relevant to the Principle of the Most Inclusive End, even while rejecting Royce's final conclusion that we are all parts of one inclusive self on the same grounds adduced for Bradley's case.[35] Royce insists that a life plan or purpose, though inadequate in any particular case, is fundamental to the very meaning, being, and creativity of any self. Furthermore, Royce maintains that each life plan is unique. Without a unique life plan I never truly become a self. With somewhat romantic overstatement Royce maintains:

> In the manifold lives that the world in its unity embodies, there is one, and only one, whose task is here hinted to me as my task,

[34] Cf. for example, Charles H. Patterson, *Moral Standards* (New York: Ronald Press, 1949), p. 221 ff.

[35] There are obviously other grounds than the ethical Principle of Autonomy for questioning the Absolute Idealism of Bradley and Royce as a metaphysical position. Because our concern here is primarily ethical theory rather than metaphysics or epistemology, we are confining our criticism to the main ethical objection. Insofar as Absolute Idealism does raise serious questions about the moral autonomy of individuals, it is our contention that it also raises serious questions about the possibility of any ethics except the ethics of the Absolute. Because for Bradley the Absolute is impersonal, the ethics of the Absolute would seem to be equally questionable. See E. S. Brightman, *Person and Reality* (New York: Ronald Press, 1958) for a statement of the metaphysical groundwork for the Principle of Autonomy, and Personalistic Idealism.

my life plan,—an ideal whose expression needs indeed the cooperation of countless other Selves, of a social order, or Nature,
and of the whole universe, but whose individual significance remains contrasted with all other individual significance. . . . By
this meaning of my life-plan, by this possession of an ideal, by
this intent always to remain another than my fellows despite my
divinely planned unity with them—by this . . . I am defined
and created a Self.[36]

In the above passage, Royce underlines a very important insight:
What creative capacity I have is to be identified especially in self-
formation in accordance with a life plan. When direction disappears,
the self disintegrates.

C. *The Need for a Flexible Life Plan*

From our discussion of Plato, Aristotle, Bradley, and Royce it
might too easily be assumed that a life plan is a rigid sort of thing—
a once-and-for-all strait jacket decided upon either with or without
help, usually in late adolescence, from which one varies at one's peril
and in terms of which failure or success is wholly to be measured.
Such is far from the case. In fact, such a description might sound like
a limit set to a life plan by a neurotic compulsion. The emphasis
upon the far view and the changing best possible needs to be pointed
up in our picture.

The important factor is not a rigid plan but direction—direction,
however, subject to revision or even outright change in the light of
varying circumstances and newly discovered potentialities. To be
sure, at any stage along the line, one's life plan should be as critically
and carefully developed as possible. Without purpose or direction,
as Plato, Aristotle, Royce, Bradley, Jung, James, Allport, and others
properly insist, life tends to lose meaning and orientation. But with
too rigid a purpose, the danger of too exclusive a formalism and
fanaticism, with attendant susceptibility to failure and frustration,
are introduced.

To put the matter in another way, to go somewhere one needs to
have some idea as to where he is going. The nature of the goal helps
determine the means of getting there. But to hold rigidly to the
means is not to allow for the inevitable detours. We want a latitude

[36] *The World and the Individual* (New York: The Macmillan Company, 1901), II,
276.

permitting the trip to be enriched by side excursions to points of interest along the way. Even the goal needs to be flexible, for we may actually go farther, or not so far, as we planned. In fact, alternate goals may emerge as one proceeds, goals that do not involve backtracking and may be more rewarding than the initial goal. To rule out any of these possibilities would be to pour life into a concrete strait jacket! But it still remains the case that unless one has some direction he will never get started.

The person who at any point can plan out the whole of his subsequent life and is then able to do exactly what he has planned is indeed rare. It is highly questionable whether he is to be envied. Such a life would involve a minimum of surprise, even if the goal itself were adventure. One of us has written about "creative insecurity." [37] Such creative insecurity would indeed be at a minimum in a life so planned. But the corrective for the danger of having things go too well is not to be without plan. Quite the contrary. Without a flexible plan, there is insecurity without creativity; surprises stultify action instead of serving as challenges to continued growth.

Suppose we look at a not too improbable flexible plan: Stephen at two may want to be a fireman, at eleven a salesman like his father, at twelve a doctor, at fourteen a biologist. At seventeen or eighteen, when he is ready for college, he is less certain, but despite a new interest in dramatics, he has a fairly definite idea that he wants to work in the natural sciences. He decides to major in chemistry, in a program developed in such a way that he can either continue with chemistry, or go into medical school, or do graduate work in biology. Here a flexible life plan begins to take shape. His plan is modified as he finds that his abilities and interests are in the direction of biology. On the graduate level new alterations within the more restricted field of biology become desirable; again directional decision must be made. Stephen decides he would like to specialize in cytology and become a teacher rather than limit himself to commercial histological research.

Every major directional or life-plan decision that Stephen makes serves as a basis for coordinating other value decisions. Thus, in view of his varying major interests, Stephen may find it necessary to curtail his participation in plays. More time is required for memorizing roles and for rehearsals than his new interests now allow. Yet his

[37] Cf. Peter A. Bertocci, *Religion as Creative Insecurity* (New York: Association Press, 1958).

previous plan had contributed a lasting enjoyment of the theater. It had increased his knowledge of poetry within the limits of the time and energy available. The values he has to de-emphasize as his life plan changes are not necessarily lost but play a different part in a new whole.

As Stephen completes his graduate work and begins his teaching career, he finds that he is an effective member of a series of integrated communities with diverse functions which he is able to make complementary in his own life in the light of his double life plan. He is a contributing member of the group of scholars working in cytology throughout the world. This group is a smaller group within the larger group of biologists. He is a member of a department of biology within a college faculty. As a biologist he is distinguished by a special interest in the theater and in poetry. The variations can be almost endless, but they remain coordinated and controllable in terms of his developing life plan.

It requires no great acquaintance with the careers of people to see that Stephen's development is not atypical. A meaningful plan itself grows out of experience, is modified in the light of continuing experience, but constantly serves as a principle of economy, control, and structuring within experience. One might now say that the Principle of the Most Inclusive End is in fact the Principle of the Best Possible and Specification applied to each person's life as a whole.

III. *A NEW TENSION*

With a developing life plan, based at every point upon an individual's potentialities as a focal ideal in terms of which the other principles that we have considered can be coordinated, it might seem that we had reached our goal in the study of ethics. The aim of intelligent action is the fullest realization of our potentialities in a coordinated life—a life in which the values have been harmonized and the virtues developed in accordance with a dominant theme or life plan. Such a life would have the fullest possible intrinsic values; it would be, as Bradley insists, the end in itself.

And yet a keen critic could point out almost immediately that we have been skirting and not seriously meeting one very important problem, a problem without an answer to which "self-realization" as a goal must remain abstract and one-sided. This is the problem of the tension between individualism and altruism. It is the problem of the concrete individual in community, of duties to one's self as contrasted with duties to others. Self-realization, as we have discussed it, might be charged with being too egoistic. To be sure, Bradley was quite aware of the seeming tension. But in his radical solution he tended to lose the individual in a personified community. And, ironically, his critics might insist that the motive for realizing the larger self still was "self"-realization and thus selfish.

To avoid what seems to such critics to be the egoistic implications of self-realization, some have insisted that morality is always and only other-regarding, that the only duty one has to himself is to be fully mindful of his duties to others. But this would seem to overlook altogether what we have seen to be the moral importance of autonomy and of the most inclusive life plan.

The need for further consideration of the concrete individual in community does in fact grow out of the cumulative effect of the various principles discussed up to this point. The first two principles, which we called Formal Principles (Consistency and Autonomy), applied primarily to individual intention. The next five—what we have designated Axiological Principles (Axiological, Consequences, Best Possible, Specification, and Most Inclusive End)—have brought the physical and communal environment into the picture by stressing concern with the field and results of action. We have attempted to indicate that the need for the Axiological Principles grows out of awareness of the Formal Principles themselves. But we need now to relate the Formal and Axiological Principles to each other far more specifically in terms of the concrete individual in society. Thus it is to what we might call the Principles of Synthesis or the concrete obligations of persons to themselves and each other (Personalistic Principles) that we now must turn.

IV. *REFLECTIVE SUMMARY*

The distinctive contribution of the Principle of the Most Inclusive End is that it focuses attention on the kind of choice, in executing moral principles, that encourages a life-plan. As Nietzsche said, "He who has a *why* to live can bear almost any *how.*"

But the "why" will never be adequate, given human nature, unless it is the most inclusive end of which the given human being is capable. Plato has taught us that this inclusive end cannot be reached unless individual life plans, worked out primarily in terms of careful assessment of abilities, are also coordinated with the capacities and needs of a society. Neither the individual nor society can afford to be self-indulgent by acting according to "what I like when I like it."

We grant that a most inclusive life plan will necessarily take into account the individual person's relation to the state and the society in which he lives. But it does not follow that the individual is only a "pulse-beat in the whole system," as Bradley and other Hegelians urge. Self-realization, as discussed in this chapter and this book, does not presuppose an encapsulated self, capable of full development of its potential without the aid and challenge of other persons; but neither does it forget that responsible growth is ultimately in the individual who develops his life *in* social and civic enterprises. The State walks on the legs of individual persons who grow as they carry responsibility for the social enterprise into their life plans.

The final problem, as we have seen over and over again, is for the individual to keep *rigor mortis* from settling into a life plan, to keep tensive harmony between flexibility and insightful direction.

26

Duties to One's Self: Individuality

~~~~~~

I. *THE MORAL UNIT*

Strictly speaking, America, Russia, the Ku Klux Klan, the Ladies'
Sodality, Oberlin College, or the First Baptist Church has never done
anything, has felt no obligation, has realized no values. At first, such a
statement sounds clearly contrary to the facts. Has not America recently and uneasily concluded a treaty with Japan? Is not Russia now
dominating half the world? Has not the Ku Klux Klan been a
national disgrace for its enemies and the "best white hope" for its
friends? The answer to these questions is obviously yes, until one
stops to consider.

Take the first question as a case in point. Suppose I say, "America
has recently concluded a treaty with Japan by which it was agreed
that America would come to the aid of Japan if she were attacked
and vice versa." If by this I mean that some being, America, sat down
with some other being, Japan, and concluded a treaty that both beings
then signed, agreeing to come to each other's aid, my statement makes
as much sense as if I were to assert that the unicorn and the centaurs
are playing in the lower part of the garden. What I mean by the
statement about America and Japan is that the President of the
United States and the Prime Minister of Japan, with the aid and
advice of their Secretaries of State and Foreign Ministers respectively,
drew up and signed a treaty that in turn was ratified by the members
of the Japanese Diet and the United States Senate. This treaty sets
forth certain contractual obligations binding directly upon officials

and upon leaders of the armed forces of both countries and indirectly upon the rest of us because of the actions of our authorized representatives.

In other words, the President can act, a legislator can act, you and I can act, and any or all of us can feel individual and collective obligations. Our actions may be in accord with our felt obligations or not. But nowhere are there any obligations or actions that are not felt or carried out by some individuals, no matter how complicated contractual and other relations among individuals may become.

The same considerations apply equally to values and disvalues, benefits and injuries. If, as we have urged, values are the actual experiences of satisfying desires and wants, of liking, enjoying, and preferring objects, states, conditions, then (although dependable values are criticized joint products of individuals and environments) there can be no values apart from individuals.

This is not to say that individuals are absolute atoms independent of "society," or that "society" is an arbitrary term for collections of individuals who happen to be spatially and temporarily juxtaposed. Quite the contrary; individuals in complete isolation from other persons are as inconceivable as society apart from constituent individuals. Our very physical being is the result of a social act. Hegel, Bradley, and others are undoubtedly correct in pointing out that our recognition of ourselves as individuals occurs in social contexts, in the distinctions between mine and thine. Recognized individuality is a function of social interaction. Although potential intelligence, for example, may be present in the new-born infant, its development and content depend upon social interchange. As we have noted, Plato and Aristotle insisted, as do contemporary sociologists and psychologists, that we are fundamentally social beings. Even the "antisocial" individual is so only in relation to society.

In further recognition of the fundamental character of the social context, we will admit (1) that most if not all values occur in social context, that is, are social or affiliative achievements; (2) that most if not all feelings of obligation have social reference either directly or indirectly; and (3) that most if not all actions not only occur in social contexts but are frequently specifically designed to modify the social contexts in question. We feel obligations to ourselves and others, and our felt obligations to others are to others both individually and collectively or in groups bound together by common needs, purposes, and values. I may feel obligations and loyalty to the university, the fraternity, the local community, the state, or the United Nations.

But to recognize all this does not change the fact that it is you, or I, or we who feel such obligations and loyalties, who act and who value. It is not the university, the fraternity, the state, or the United Nations in the abstract who do or feel any of these things. In other words, not societies but individuals in social relations constitute the units of morality.

Now if this is the case, if individuals choose, act, feel obligation and realize values, it follows that the values realized and the obligations accepted by a group or society are those which the individual members of that group or society accept. If values are not realized, if obligations are not accepted, by the individual members of the group, then the group has no values and no obligations. Furthermore, the potential values of the group or society will be directly related to the values of the members or to the values that the members are able to contribute.

It is at this very point, however, that we must not commit the "fallacy of composition." For the values of the group additively do not equal the values of the members of the group taken singly. Such a conclusion does not follow for two reasons: First, conflicting values of different members in the group may negate each other in group effectiveness. Second, and more important, because an effective group is formed for some specific purpose, not all the values of any member of the group are likely to be identifiable with any particular group purpose. For example, my activities and contributions in the Garden Club are not usually to be measured by my activities and contributions to the Air Force Reserve or the American Philosophical Association. This is not to say that for me these are irrelevant to each other. My interests in the various groups may complement each other or, by their conflict, show that I entertain values I cannot reconcile. One interest may in some circumstances enhance the other: thus I may be able to contribute more to the Garden Club because of membership in the Air Force Reserve or the American Philosophical Association, and vice versa. However, no simple one-to-one relationship can be taken for granted.

II. *THE PRINCIPLE OF INDIVIDUALITY*

If values cannot be realized in the abstract, if obligations can be felt only by individuals, if the worth of a group is proportionate to the contributions of the members, if, in other words, the moral unit is the individual, then each individual does have a prime obligation to himself. This obligation is to become in fact a concrete moral unit in society—to underwrite the responsibilities and obligations of the formal and axiological principles by becoming, to the limit of his capacities, a complete and responsible person. We can call this the Principle of Individuality and state it as follows: *Each person ought to realize in his own experience the maximum values of which he is capable in harmony with all other moral principles.*[1]

III. *INDIVIDUALS AND SOCIETY*

Quite clearly the Principle of Individuality raises a series of age-old controversies in ethical theory: egoism versus altruism, self-regarding versus other-regarding obligations, social atomism and nominalism versus social organicism, rugged individualism versus social welfare and socialism.

Each of these controversies reflects the same basic problem stated on different levels and in different perspectives. In the next chapter, we shall consider altruism and the problem of duty to others. In Chapter 28 we shall examine the implications of moral principles for social theory. Here we are concerned with the problem of duties owed to oneself as the moral unit—that is, as the developing individual in society—already foreshadowed in our discussion of the Principle of the Most Inclusive End.

Some moral theorists would go so far as to insist that there are no duties to others, only duties to oneself. Aristippus the Cyrenaic (see Chapter 24 above), for example, would argue that my only duty is to find the greatest pleasure for me at the moment. Others would contend that whatever duties I have to others are derived from duties to myself. Nietzsche, in his reaction against "sentimental" love of neighbor, comes close to this alternative. Others would argue that my duties to myself are derived from my duties to others. And still others would come close to insisting that all self-regard is selfish —that I have no duties to myself, only duties to others.

Our discussions of the Axiological Principles would clearly rule out any strictly egoistic or individualistic conclusion—that is, any conclusion that our duties are only to ourselves. And yet the element of truth that egoism has urged is not to be denied. There can be no

[1] Cf. E. S. Brightman, *Moral Laws* (New York: Abingdon Press, 1933), p. 204.

"good life" that is not somebody's life. Such a life, it has become progressively evident, is not something left to chance; nor is it something that appears automatically without self-direction and control. It is a product of reflective choosing, of developing the character traits known as the virtues, of realizing an appropriate symphony of values. As such the good life is at best the self-conscious realization of value in one's own life; nevertheless, one's own life is a life in community and includes the essential affiliative values. Concern for others may be far more than self-interest, but to be "concern" it must at least be the interest of a self that has reached a level of individuality capable of recognizing the uniqueness and value potential of other individuals. Mere gregariousness and sentiment do not necessarily involve concern.

G. W. Allport has perhaps not overstated the case in saying that "egoism is the incontrovertible philosophy of early childhood," but he adds "in the process of growth and extension of interests, newly adopted codes and manners represent genuine, not superficial, alterations in personality." [2] It is here that Allport's concept of functional autonomy plays a central role (see Chapter 6 above). Selfishness is transformed with the development of mature individuality. But with the alterations in motives necessary for maturity, the very key to understanding lies in individuality and its striving for personal integrity. Man, Allport insists,

> is more than a bundle of habits; more than a nexus of abstract dimensions; more too than a representative of his species. He is more than a citizen of the state, and more than a mere incident in the gigantic movements of mankind. He transcends them all. The individual, striving for his integrity, has existed under many forms of social life. . . . He struggles on even under oppression, always hoping and planning for a more perfect democracy where the dignity and growth of each personality will be prized above all else. [3]

Even though some adherents of self-realization, as we saw in the last chapter, tend to dissolve the particular individual in an all-inclusive Self, the central insight of self-realizationist ethical positions is embodied in the principle of individuality—the realization

[2] G. W. Allport, *Personality: A Psychological Interpretation* (New York: Henry Holt, 1937), p. 169.
[3] *Ibid.*, p. 556. Reprinted by permission of Holt, Rinehart and Winston, Inc.

of the maximum value of which one is capable in one's own life. This is strikingly underlined by a contemporary self-realizationist, Charles H. Patterson, as follows:

> The promotion of one's highest interest as an individual through the proper organization of the impulses, desires, capacities, and other elements of his nature is what is meant by realization of the individual self. It is not an easy goal to achieve, for it aims at the harmonious development of all the elements included in one's personality. It calls for the type of organization which makes it possible for the total meaning of life to be expressed in each of its parts. This involves something more than giving immediate satisfaction to each desire as it appears in consciousness. It means that each desire must be evaluated in terms of what it may contribute toward the development of one's entire personality.[4]

For Patterson, as for Allport, any effective community depends upon effective individuals. To put the matter succinctly: any effective sharing depends upon having something to share. Mere association quickly becomes a disvalue when the persons associating have no inner resources of realized value of their own to bring into association. The affiliative values are among the strongest and at the same time the most fragile of values for this very reason.

Anyone who has ever served on a committee will recognize that unless the purpose of the committee is well defined and the members are either appointed or elected in the light of some coordination of their own interests with the committee purpose, the meetings of the committee become a waste of time and a source of mutual irritation. But regardless of the difficulty of problems, work on the committee can be challenging and the association with the other members highly enjoyable (if not always smooth) insofar as each member can identify himself with the committee's purpose. In fact one might even say that a committee in which such complementation of interests is wholly lacking is no committee.

On a more profound and sustained level the same thing can be said of marriage. Too many Americans have been deluded by the lived-happily-ever-after myth. According to this myth, marriage is that idyllic state growing out of moonlight, rose petals, body chem-

---

[4] Charles H. Patterson, *Moral Standards, an Introduction to Ethics*, second edition. Copyright 1957, The Ronald Press Company, pp. 262-63.

istry, and senior proms, reaching its high point shortly after the strains of *Lohengrin* have faded away. From that point on, marriage is supposed to require no effort. The background music continues. Alas, how dreams can be shattered by pin curls, hair nets, and burned toast!

Marriage can be one of the most continually rewarding of human experiences or one of the most destructive in its effect on the lives and values of the persons involved. To be rewarding marriage depends first of all perhaps on a continued growth in common interest, in common values, in the complementary interplay of the enriched individuality of each person. Otherwise continual association not only diminishes intrinsic values but may develop into positive disvalue.

We have already noted the fallacy in personifying society or the group apart from or in contrast to the individual. One unfortunate result of such personification of the group is the tendency either to divorce one's own interest from that of the group or to consider the group interest as the inevitable antagonist of individual interest. In either case, both the group and the individual tend to be losers. One of the first results of such divorce of interests is frequently the refusal to accept responsibility within the group. This is rather strikingly illustrated in the chaos of French politics both prior to and after the De Gaulle reforms. Even though the French government was duly elected, few Frenchmen seemed to feel any responsibility either for or to the government as elected. This lack made the task of governing France incalculably more difficult than it needed to be.

Another and perhaps more deleterious result for the individual is the ease with which he can use the personified group to rationalize and excuse his failure to realize the maximum values of which he is capable. He can at the same time also dodge responsibility and obligation. Personifying society is a particularly inviting mode of expressing frustration and escape from responsibility in a period as nationally and internationally confused as the present. After all, says the student, we have come into a world we did not make and "it's a mess." The forces unleashed by "Science" have been used by "Society" to drive the world to the brink of destruction. It is not my fault. In fact, what can I do? Nothing. Therefore, why try? How can I even study? And why should I?

Such rationalization is convenient because it can be applied at any level as an excuse for doing or not doing almost anything. During the Hitler regime in Germany, a rather large number of sensitive and capable Germans who were not happy with the turn of events used a variant of the same argument to justify acquiescence.[5] Milton Mayer gives a striking account of how ten ordinary Germans attempted to justify their lack of action in the Hitler period: "We did not bring Hitler to power, world conditions did. Society was at fault, not we. What could one individual do?"

Granted that individuals in given groups react differently or play roles different from those they play separately or within other groups, persons who rationalize by reifying or setting the group up as an entity in its own right overlook two facts: (1) a change in the attitudes or roles played by the members of the group changes the group, and (2) within the limits set by his personality, a person is responsible for the role he has accepted in the group.

IV. *SELF-ACTS AND SELFISH ACTS*

A common and major objection to the Principle of Individuality is that it is essentially a selfish principle—egoistic in impact. Morality, such objectors frequently argue, is the opposite of selfishness—it is other-regarding action. Thus to take into account the more extreme type of objection, the Principle of Individuality, it is sometimes claimed, is no moral principle at all but a statement of immorality. Paul Ramsey, for example, insists that Christian ethics is concerned with "purging away vulturous self-interest." [6] True morality, rooted in Christian love, "comes into existence only by a 'leap' which carries a man beyond enlightened self-interest, beyond all intentional concern for self-realization, beyond the mixture of motives in pursuit of some common good; a leap which breaks entirely the circle of self." [7]

This severe indictment of self-realization in general and the Principle of Individuality in particular is counterbalanced by the insistence of the psychological egoistic hedonists (see Chapter 24) that because man can seek only his own pleasure, all human acts are necessarily selfish. In either case the problem is essentially the same—that is, What constitutes an act selfish?

[5] Milton S. Mayer, *They Thought They Were Free* (Chicago: University of Chicago Press, 1955).

[6] *Basic Christian Ethics* (New York: Charles Scribner's Sons, 1950), p. 111. This book and George F. Thomas's *Christian Ethics and Moral Philosophy* (New York: Charles Scribner's Sons, 1955) should be consulted for insight into the Christian perspectives on selfishness-altruism.

[7] *Ibid.,* pp. 101–2.

It might be suggested that objections to the Principle of Individuality on the grounds that it is selfish are based either on a confusion or on a misleading semantic stress. If by "selfish" is meant an act of a self or even an act that is motivated by the interest of a self, then all noncompulsory acts are selfish. "Selfishness" so defined would be a nonexclusive term and would carry no negative or positive moral connotation. "Selfish" would be a descriptive term designating an interested act of a self. But surely this is not what the term usually means. In fact, it rather clearly is not what Ramsey or the psychological hedonists or La Rochefoucauld, the seventeenth-century arch-misanthrope, mean or meant. So defined, generosity, altruism, self-sacrifice, all would be selfish—that is, they would be interested acts of some self. But this is to say no more than that they are acts.

What La Rochefoucauld meant when he insisted that "our virtues are for the most part only our vices disguised" [8] and that underneath external pretense is the unlovely reality of cunning selfishness was that each act had as its motive not only interest, even self-interest, but exclusive self-aggrandizement—that is, aggrandizement at the expense of others if need be (and as would usually be the case). The claim that all acts are performed exclusively for self-aggrandizement at the expense of others is quite different from the claim that all acts are interested acts of some self. The arguments and evidence against psychological hedonism (Chapter 24) would equally disprove La Rochefoucauld's claim. He seems to be guilty of tremendous psychological oversimplification. But whether all men are selfish in this sense or not, La Rochefoucauld is surely correct in his conception of what constitutes selfishness.

Selfishness, defined in terms of actions performed exclusively for self-aggrandizement at the expense of others, does have strong negative moral impact. In this context we can ask once more: Is self-interest vulturous? Are self-interested acts selfish acts? Are acts that help to realize the potentiality of a self selfish? The answer would rather clearly seem to be no. We must not confuse selfishness, an act of the self committed at the expense of others, with the "selfishness," improperly so-called, that is no more than an act of the self inevitably asserting itself in every action.

With John Dewey we can point out that even acts aimed specifically at one's own future well-being may be far from selfish.

---

[8] Translated from *Les Maximes*. *Les Maximes* is the *epigraph* of the section called *Réflections Morales* (Paris: Hachette, 1883), I, 31.

No one would say that deliberate care for one's own health, efficiency, progress in learning is bad just because it is one's own. It is moral duty upon occasion to look out for oneself in these respects. Such acts acquire the quality of moral selfishness only when they are indulged in so as to manifest obtuseness to the claims of others. An act is not wrong because it advances the well being of the self, but because it is unfair, inconsiderate, in respect to the rights, just claims, of others.[9]

Dewey goes on to insist that self-regarding acts make possible other-regarding acts. "Self-sustaining and self-protective acts are, moreover, conditions of all acts which are of service to others." [10]

Illustrations of Dewey's points are not hard to find: A father who so completely devotes himself to his work for the sake of raising his family in the most comfortable of surroundings that he destroys his own health is not necessarily being fully ethical. Again, because being raised in such comfort is not necessarily best for his children's development, the morality of his actions becomes even more questionable.

A person with the best of intentions jumps into the water to save someone in trouble when he himself cannot swim. He not only may lose his own life but hamper rescue of the one he started out to save.

To take a more complex example: Suppose that the situation in your family were such that only you or your brother were able to continue with advanced education. One of you would have to stay home to take care of the family business and look after a sick parent. It is clear in the light of academic accomplishment to date that you have greater academic potentialities than your brother. The probability that you would become a successful lawyer is greater than that he would become a successful dentist. Although your brother is not enthusiastic about the family business, he has rather a knack for it, even though, other things being equal, he would prefer attempting to become a dentist. Whatever is done, the person who stays at home will have to make some sacrifice of his hopes and plans. What should you do? Would the best thing for you or for the family as a whole be for you to say to your brother: You go ahead, I'll stay home?

[9] John Dewey, *Theory of the Moral Life,* ed. Arnold Isenburg (New York: Holt, Rinehart and Winston, Inc., 1960), p. 158. Reprinted by permission.
[10] *Ibid,*

We shall return to the problem of the grounds for altruism shortly, but even now we do well to remember that "leaping to" one's neighbor's side is not always altruism.

We have recognized so far that effective help to others frequently depends upon intelligent self-interest in realizing one's own potentialities and that such interest cannot be considered selfish in any pejorative sense. We can carry Dewey's point one step further. Acts aimed at my future well-being aside, are those acts necessarily selfish from which I now gain pleasure or which are instrinsically valuable to me now and in which I knowingly indulge at the time I perform them? Again the answer would have to be no. It has sometimes been claimed that the reason for my petting my little black dog is wholly selfish—I enjoy seeing him wag his tail and look at me trustfully with his sad cocker eyes. There is no question but that I do enjoy his responsiveness, and it might be granted (although even this may be questionable) that a child first responds to his dog for limited hedonic reasons. Yet to say that the adult act of petting the dog is selfish or purely self-centered is to oversimplify to the point of falsity. Whatever the *basis* of my first favorable response to dogs may have been, I am now genuinely fond of him and pet him to please him, not just myself.

Here again Allport's concept of functional autonomy is particularly to the point. "Motives being always contemporary should be studied in their present structure," [11] and my present motive is neither selfish nor self-centered even though I continue to enjoy what I am doing. Allport adds:

> Starting life as a completely selfish being, the child would indeed remain entirely wolfish and piggish throughout his days unless genuine transformation of motives took place. Motives being completely alterable, the dogma of Egoism turns out to be a callow and superficial philosophy of behavior, or else a useless redundancy.[12]

In view of our definition of selfish acts as those performed exclusively for self-aggrandizement at the expense of others, then even acts from which I benefit at the time of performing them are not selfish unless by performing them I intentionally impoverish others. Listening to music, relaxing in the sun, eating a hearty meal, paint-

---

[11] Allport, *op. cit.*, p. 206.
[12] *Ibid*. Reprinted by permission of Holt, Rinehart and Winston, Inc.

ing a picture, going for a swim, or reading a novel are not selfish acts so long as doing them is not specifically at the expense of others. There are always individuals or causes in the community or in "darkest Africa" to which I could give every minute I spend listening to music. But my present enjoyment is not intended to hurt them, granted that it will not, immediately at least, help them or anyone else. In fact, at the risk of being misunderstood, we can now turn the situation around and point out that insofar as these or other acts from which I benefit are not specifically and foreseeably harmful to others and yet are commensurate with my life plan and do fit into my symphony of values, I have a moral right and even the moral duty to perform them.

There is perhaps one strongly anti-Kantian qualification that should be added. Granted that I have the right and duty to realize intrinsic values and the maximum values of which I am capable in my own life, nevertheless, when I find myself straining to realize such intrinsic values not because they are intrinsic but because it is my "duty" so to do, something has gone wrong. I am likely to reduce or destroy the intrinsic character of the values themselves when I have to force myself continually to achieve them. How pitiful the person who climbs the ramp of the Guggenheim Museum or listens studiously to Bartok or manfully struggles through a plate of escargots, not because he is curious, or enjoys modern painting, modern music, or French food but because he feels he has a duty to do so as part of his self-realization! This is, as Dewey suggests, to separate artificially the self and the ends pursued.[13] Maximum values in one's own life are obtained not through disinterested pursuit of an abstract self-fulfillment in accordance with an abstract sense of duty, but through the concrete pursuit of ends in which one is genuinely interested for their own sakes as ingredients in the rich and varied experiences of one's symphony of values.

V. INDIVIDUALITY AND SUICIDE

On the surface, there would seem to be two kinds of acts that are either in violent opposition to the Principle of Individuality or definitively out of harmony with it. One of these is the act of taking one's own life, and the other is that of giving one's own life in complete

[13] See op. cit., p. 160.

self-sacrifice. In considering the first, one is faced immediately with a semantic peculiarity. Taking one's own life is usually designated by the term "suicide." If one asks whether suicide is morally wrong, the answer, reinforced by most Western religious traditions, is usually an unqualified yes. But if one inquires further just what such suicide, so unqualifiedly condemned, means, the answer is not so clear.

Etymologically, "suicide" simply means to kill oneself. Now it might be possible to argue that killing oneself under any circumstances is morally wrong. At least it is never morally right. Suicide, it is frequently claimed, is always the act of a sick person who as sick (abnormal) is no longer morally responsible.

But now we begin to run into trouble. Most of those who object to "suicide" on moral grounds also recognize that in some circumstances, killing one's self shows a high sense of moral commitment, is in fact worthy of praise. Without being, in such cases, too severe toward the person who does not take his own life, we look upon the person who does as a hero. The obvious example is the intelligence agent on whom the welfare of a great many others may depend. He has been caught and is faced with torture or other procedures designed to force information out of him. He is quite certain that he will not be able to withstand the torture. To avoid divulging the crucial information, he takes his own life. Such a person is neither considered insane nor immoral.

Let us consider a slightly different case in which taking one's own life might be morally praiseworthy: A statesman in a small country is captured by what appears to the outside world to be a revolution from within dedicated to equality and freedom. The statesman is well known as a man of high integrity and dedicated to these same ends. In fact, however, the so called revolution is a "power grab" by a dictatorial group with no intention of promoting either freedom or equality. The captured statesman is closely guarded and used as a showpiece to convince the outside world that the "revolution" is authentic. The only way the statesman can let the world know the real state of affairs, since escape is cut off, is to take his own life.

Now if it be granted that either or both of these examples are cases in which taking one's own life was justifiable and perhaps morally laudatory, then either suicide is not always wrong or not all taking of one's own life is suicide. Obviously, if one defines suicide as self-murder (as Webster does) and "murder" is defined as wrongfully taking life, then suicide is always wrong by definition. But then also one would have to add, taking one's own life is not always suicide. And the crucial question becomes: When is taking one's life suicide and when is it not, and what is the relation of taking one's own life to the Principle of Individuality?

In the first place, we would have to grant that frequently suicide is the act of a mentally ill person. Insofar as this is so, and the person really is *psychotic,* he is no longer responsible and the act is thus neither moral nor immoral but nonmoral (amoral). It is to help such persons that such organizations as "Rescue" in Boston and elsewhere have been set up. But here again we need to be cautious. The fact that some and possibly the majority of cases of suicide involve abnormality does not support the popular myth that all instances do. Of course, if one defines the normal as the average, then anyone who does anything out of the average is abnormal. But this is semantic legerdemain.

There is ample evidence that taking one's own life can be a deliberate choice in the light of consideration of alternatives. The statesman and the intelligence agent are specific cases in point. The ancient Stoics (as we saw in Chapter 19) developed the doctrine of the Open Door. One learns to know the things that he can control and the things over which he does not have control. If external things—pain, persecution, dishonor—become unbearable, or if one has lived a full life and is ready to retire, the door is always open. This at least, the Stoics insisted, is in one's own power. It is with any and all instances of deliberately taking one's own life that we are concerned.

From the standpoint of the Principle of Individuality, with its insistence upon the duty of realizing maximum values in one's own life, we would have to say that, in most circumstances, to take one's own life is the denial of the principle—suicide in the pejorative sense and morally wrong. The Stoic Open Door is too easily an abdication of responsibility. It becomes the final dogmatism of the person who insists that he knows what in most circumstances he cannot possibly know, that is, that no more positive values can be realized in his own life if he continues to live.

Under such conditions suicide becomes what it is popularly considered to be, the way of the coward. A person who takes his own life to avoid excessive debts, for example, leaves not only the debts but the social (and personal) onus of his act for those to bear who have been dependent upon him. The person who commits suicide rather than face public disgrace, prison, or some other serious end is rejecting the possibility of salvaging some values and creating new ones. Even the person on whom no one is dependent or who has no social obligations (if this is possible) overlooks the positive character of morality and the continuing duty to try to mold and create circumstances rather than become their victim. For these as well as for specifically religious reasons (including the religious claim of the God-given privilege of life) the Judeo-Christian injunctions against suicide as morally and religiously wrong are, as general statements, well in accord with the Principle of Individuality.

However, we are still faced with the cases of the statesman and the intelligence agent and similar situations wherein the lines cannot be sharply drawn. If we grant that there may be circumstances in which it may be morally right to take the life of another (cf. Principle of Consequence and Principle of Specification), we can hardly insist beforehand that there will be no circumstances in which it would be morally right or a moral duty to take one's own life. Here the problem of self-sacrifice and the problem of suicide become virtually bound up together.

Take, for instance, a person afflicted with an incurable disease in which the prognosis is a long, costly, painful, incapacitating terminal illness. He cannot reasonably depend on the discovery of a "wonder drug" or a saving surgical method. He is a member of a family of moderate means, and he is fairly certain that the protracted illness with costs of hospitalization, drugs, operations and transfusions will plunge the family deeply into debt. The debt will jeopardize education for the children in the family. In the meantime, all the members of the family will be subjected to an extended period of suffering as he suffers. Therefore, before his illness reaches the bedridden stage, he decides to take his own life. Clearly, he should not be advised to take his own life. Nor could he in any sense be "blamed" if he did not do so. The question is, is he morally wrong if he does so? Or is he showing moral courage and realizing for himself and those close to him the maximum values possible in the situation? We would at least find it extremely difficult to condemn him.

VI. *INDIVIDUALITY AND SELF-SACRIFICE*

However we may judge the last example, the illustrations of the agent and statesman are rather clearly cases of self-sacrifice. Some cases of suicide, then, would fall into the larger class where we place persons who have knowingly given up their lives for the sake of others. In this much larger group the great majority is made up of individuals who have placed their lives in jeopardy for something they considered more important than their own continued existences. From Socrates and Jesus, through the various kinds of martyrs of different historical ages, to the Japanese Kamikazi pilots and the volunteers among conscientious objectors, as well as the individuals who have offered to be medical guinea pigs for the sake of the health of others, one could marshal an impressive list of human beings who seemingly have found something more important than the continued realization of values in their own lives.

Have such persons, frequently the heroes of the human race, denied or violated the Principle of Individuality? A critic might well assert that the Principle of Individuality is for lesser men not capable of supreme sacrifice. We would have to admit, at least, that an ethical system that could not provide for self-sacrifice is a truncated ethical system at best. But we will go farther. Unless an ethical system is able to show that in some circumstances self-sacrifice is the highest form of fulfillment of moral duty, that system is inadequate to the facts of the moral history of the race.

How shall we, then, relate self-sacrifice to the Principle of Individuality? Let us beware of easy solutions. Shall we dodge this whole question by pointing out that the Principle of Individuality is only one principle that holds in general but has to give way to other principles in exceptional instances? This will not do. If there are real exceptions to the Principle of Individuality, then, in the light of our discussion of the nature of moral principle, it is no principle.

Other positions, like that of an ethical formalist like Kant or that of ethical realists like W. D. Ross or E. Vivas, would seem to offer the clearest grounds for self-sacrifice. Some ethical realists would simply assert that, apart from anything else, there is a *prima facie* duty to sacrifice oneself for the good of others. Kant would insist that insofar as one has a choice between acting in accordance with a universalized maxim that involves self-sacrifice and acting from inclination toward self-preservation, duty always lies with the first alternative. For example, if my choice is between keeping a promise to protect bank funds and giving them to the thief who threatens to shoot me if I do not, then clearly my duty is not to turn over the funds regardless of the results.

But the realist-formalist answer is too pat. We have seen that *prima facie* duties conflict and may not always be reasonable (cf. Chapters 13 and 21). The Kantian solution tends not to take into account the total context of action. In the example cited, the possibility of apprehending the thief may be decreased by my disappearance as a witness. Other people may be so dependent upon me that to allow the thief to kill me sacrifices with me their welfare as well.

At the opposite extreme, one might claim, with some hedonists, that the person who sacrifices himself does so because of the pleasure to be derived from anticipating the results of his act, on the one hand, or the desire to avoid more prolonged pain, on the other. Thus, the martyr anticipates not only the joys of heaven but the future recognition of the importance of his act by his fellow men. Although there may be an element of truth in the hedonist's claim, it would again seem to be a tremendous oversimplification. Not all persons who have sacrificed themselves can be shown to have looked forward to afterlife. Among those who have believed in an afterlife, some at least have shared the suspicion of Thomas à Becket in T. S. Eliot's *Murder in the Cathedral:* this is the greatest temptation—to do the right thing for the wrong reason.

We return, then, to the Law of Individuality itself: Each person ought to realize in his own life the maximum values of which he is capable in harmony with all other moral principles. Does the maximum value of which a person is capable in his own life ever involve giving up his life or dying for others? Here a number of lines of our inquiry converge. The Principles of Consequences, of the Best Possible, and of Specification become particularly relevant to the various aspects of the Principle of Individuality as it relates to this problem of self-sacrifice.

First let us remind ourselves that taking one's own life or giving up one's own life, except in extreme situations, is not necessarily the best and the reasonable alternative and may in fact violate the Principle of Individuality. It is possible for self-sacrifice, as well as suicide, to be pathological. There is an old adage to the effect that where there is life there is hope. It points to the belief that normally the Principles of the Best Possible and of Individuality can be expected to guide to the best values that can be actualized in a given situation and in any future that is related to that situation. Death is a drastic alternative: extreme self-sacrifice, as well as suicide, destroys an individual's further potential for value realization at least in this life.

Nevertheless, granted that self-sacrifice is not always what it seems and is not itself necessarily virtuous, there would seem to be at least two kinds of value situations in which self-sacrifice might well be called for by the Principle of Individuality itself. The first of these we shall call self-sacrifice for preservation of minimal conditions of value, and the second, self-sacrifice for creation of optimal conditions of value.

Self-sacrifice for preservation of minimal conditions of value might be illustrated by Socrates' drinking the hemlock. If the general accuracy of Plato's account in *The Crito* and *The Phaedo* is assumed, Socrates could have escaped. Crito urged Socrates to escape for what seemed a number of good reasons: If Socrates remained in prison to die, he would be deserting his friends who would be accused of cowardice in not helping him, his children whom he would be leaving fatherless, and even his love of virtue, for he would no longer be able to teach and practice.[14]

Socrates' answer is clear and to the point. To escape is to violate the principle of civil law itself. Law is to the state what reason is to man. A society without laws is no society, but chaos; and chaos is not productive of reasonable men. Even bad laws are better than no laws, for they can be modified and they do open up paths in what otherwise would be pure jungle. A life apart from law would be no life worth living. The very values that escape presumably makes possible for the fugitive would be cheapened for him and others, or they would disappear entirely, if the objective societal structure in which they had meaning were to be weakened or destroyed. Socrates throughout his career had upheld the value, the right, and the duty of reasonable and responsible criticism of individuals and society. But such criticism would be neither reasonable nor responsible, in fact would lose its relevance if the rational basis of social interaction were undermined. Accordingly, Socrates insisted that the maximum value of which he was capable in his own life—given the place, the time, the issues, and possibilities—was to die. Thus he preserved the minimal conditions of the meaningfulness of the life that he had led up to that point, and, in the process, he preserved for others the minimal conditions as he saw them of continued effective value realization.

[14] See *Crito*, 45.

The choices of many religious martyrs, although the specific values involved may have been quite different, have not been too unlike that of Socrates. Such persons were willing to die rather than recant, in order to preserve what to them were the minimal conditions of effective value, hoping that through their deaths others would realize the preciousness of the values for which they died. Thus, given the conditions, the time, the place, and the issues, their sacrifices actually were for them means of realizing the maximum values of which they were capable. To such instances one would also have to add the other cases of the intelligence agent and the statesman.

In this group we would also have to include a large number of persons who sacrifice their own lives for other specific individuals. The soldier who throws himself on a hand grenade to save the lives of his companions or a Sydney Carton who substitutes himself for a St. Evrémonde on the trip to the guillotine come to mind. In each instance, the specific act of self-sacrifice has its social reference. It is the preservation of the minimal conditions of value realization for others. At the same time, given the circumstances and conditions, it is a realization of the maximum value of which that person is capable. But we must insist that, given other conditions, the act of self-sacrifice would not necessarily have been the maximum value of which the person in question was capable. Self-sacrifice that makes an unqualified appeal to many people's feelings must also be assessed, like other acts, for its true value.

Instances of supreme self-sacrifice for creation of optimal conditions of value are somewhat rarer than self-sacrifice to preserve minimal conditions of value. They do not for this reason represent a "higher type" of self-sacrifice. The extreme conditions calling for supreme self-sacrifice tend to arise more frequently when values are threatened than in the context of increase of value potential. And yet examples of self-sacrifice for creation of optimal value conditions are not too difficult to find. A Walter Reed experimenting on himself in order to prove that yellow fever is carried by a certain kind of mosquito is a case in point. If he succeeded in his proof, it almost certainly meant his death, for no cure for the disease was known. Yet through Reed's discovery of the carrying agent, control of the disease became possible and countless people were able to live fuller lives, freed from the fear of contacting yellow fever. Reed was not forced into such an action by extremity of circumstances or the need to preserve minimum value conditions. His action was not in the normal line of duty; yet for a man whose value proprium was a certain value for himself and his profession, his action did actualize, we may assume, the maximum ideal of his profession and his own career—an ideal of service for the betterment of human health and welfare. In this sense, his act was in full accord with what he believed to be the essence of his pursuit of value, and thus it illustrated the Principle of Individuality.

We have been primarily concerned with the question of whether supreme self-sacrifice is in accord with the Principle of Individuality. We have thereby put the principle itself to a severe test. Close scrutiny has indicated that, rather than being an exception, such self-sacrifice (when it is not irrational or pathological) not only is in harmony with, but may be commanded by, the Principle of Individuality. Such acts are interested, even passionately interested, acts of selves for maximum meaningfulness of value in their own lives and in the lives of others. But the attempt to understand the nature of true self-sacrifice and its accord with the Principle of Individuality leads us again to underline the relation of the Principle of Individuality to the communal context. Thus the Principle of Altruism appears as necessary for the completion of the Principle of Individuality itself.

VII. *INDIVIDUALITY AND SELF-RESPECT*

The full impact of the Principle of Individuality might be summed up in the term "self-respect." We have pointed out the fact that the principle rests upon the recognition of individual persons as moral units—the loci of values, actions, obligations, and ideals. Self-respect as we define it is not a form of what the French call *amour-propre*. It is not to be confused with self-pride or self-assertiveness or with undue concern for the conventional forms of respect from others. Rather, the essence of self-respect is clear recognition of one's self as the moral unit—as, indeed, a creator of values, a responsible actor, obligated to self-imposed ideals.

It now becomes clear that we had begun to note the importance of such self-respect in the Principle of Autonomy, with its recognition of the crucial character of self-imposed ideals. It appeared also in the

Principle of the Best Possible, in the recognition that candor is a precondition of realistic assessment of what constitutes the best possible for any individual. It was found to be central to effective, directional self-realization as called for under the Principle of the Most Inclusive End. Here it becomes explicit and concrete as the ground of personal dignity and worth. I respect myself as a moral unit, as having value potential, as an actualizer of values, and I recognize that apart from me and others like me in our mutual realizations of value, certain values in particular will not be realized. It is this respect for persons as creative moral units that makes the Principle of Altruism, as we shall soon see, the necessary complement to the Principle of Individuality.

The self-respect called for by the Principle of Individuality is not innate and to be found in all persons. It is a goal to be achieved and, as achieved, is the high mark of the mature individual. Although self-respect does involve self-interest, it is to be rather sharply distinguished—as already noted—from selfishness, self-assertiveness, or self-pride. It would not be too far amiss to suggest that for psychologists like Allport, Maslow, Fromm, and Rank, the key to the concept of the psychically healthy person is not adjustment, important as that is, but self-respect.

Otto Rank, for example, describes three stages in the development of individuality to the fullest realization of its potentialities. The first stage corresponds to action in accordance with the Principle of Autonomy, that is, the individual now wills for himself what earlier he was compelled to choose. The second stage is a level of conflict of ideals in which the developing individual begins to formulate new ideals of his own. We are reminded of Maslow's self-actualizing person when Rank describes the third and mature stage as follows:

> In a word, with this type, from all the accepted, the obligatory, from all the wished for, and the willed, from all the aspirations and the commandments, is formed neither a compromise, nor merely a summation but a newly created whole, the strong personality with its autonomous will, which represent the highest creation of the integration of will and spirit.[15]

The characteristic mark of such a mature individual is that he accepts

[15] Otto Rank, *Will Therapy and Truth and Reality,* trans. Jessie Taft (New York: Alfred A. Knopf, 1945), p. 265.

himself for what he actually is. In contrast to the healthy individual, "the neurotic, no matter whether productive or obstructed, suffers fundamentally from the fact that he cannot or will not accept himself, his own individuality, his own personality." [16]

Erich Fromm, agreeing with Rank on this need for self-respect, underlines the fact that the root of selfishness and self-assertiveness lies not in healthy concern for one's own values but in self-hatred. It is the empty and frustrated person, the person who does not respect or trust himself, who is usually contemptuous of himself and aggressively demands the external forms of respect from others. The unique source of aggressiveness, selfishness, and confusion in the modern world, Fromm contends,

> lies not in its principle of individualism, not in the idea that moral virtue is the same as the pursuit of self interest . . . not in the fact that people are too much concerned with their self-interest, but that they are not concerned enough with the interest of their real self, not in the fact that they are too selfish, but that they do not love themselves.[17]

Immanuel Kant, it will be remembered (see Chapter 21), insisted that men do have dignity and are worthy of respect as potentially rational wills, that is, as capable of acting out of a sense of duty in accordance with the moral law within rather than being impelled by inclination alone. As crucial as it is, Kant's insight, we pointed out earlier, remains abstract until seen in the context of the relation of values to each other and to the value potential of human beings in society. Such self-realizationists as Plato, Bradley, and Royce fully recognized the value potential of human beings in society and the fact that such potential is actualized only through self-realization. But, particularly in the case of Bradley and to a lesser degree in Royce, the self-realizationists ironically tended to lose the self-realizing individual in the self-realizing social whole. The Law of Individuality re-emphasizes Kant's belief in the uniqueness of the individual as the moral unit. It puts new stress on the individual's potential as a realizer of values, as urged by the self-realizationists. But it makes these concrete in terms of the self-respecting person

---

[16] Otto Rank, *Art and Artist,* trans. Charles Francis Atkinson (New York: Alfred A. Knopf, Inc., 1932), p. 27.

[17] Erich Fromm, *Man for Himself* (New York: Rinehart & Company, 1947), p. 139. Reprinted by permission of Holt, Rinehart and Winston, Inc.

fully cognizant of his duty to realize the maximum values of which he is capable, given himself and his social context. To such a person's relation to other persons as moral units and realizers of value, that is, to his value-relations-in-community, we now may turn, for we have already recognized the inconceivability of individuals apart from society.

VIII. *REFLECTIVE SUMMARY*

The unit of morality is not the group but the individual person. Persons are persons in social relations, but it is as persons that they experience, criticize, and enact values. The obligation of each person to realize in his own experience the maximum of values possible cannot be taken lightly, because each person is the growing point of value in any social situation. Indeed, the individual cannot share with others values that he does not have or for which he is not striving. The group, "Society," the "State," the "Church," "Science," cannot be saddled with the responsibility for a person's own growth in value.

Selfish actions are self-acts performed consciously to improve one's own values at the expense of other persons. Actions aimed at developing oneself and at self-enjoyment are not selfish if they are not intended to hurt others, provided that they concretely enrich and enhance one's scheme of life. Personal values involve the values of others sooner or later, to be sure, but to brand an act "selfish," be it self-enjoyment or suicide, is to be arbitrary unless one understands motive and consequence and remembers that in the present lives of persons, and only there, are values born and nourished.

The supreme sacrifice of one's own life is the command of the Principle of Individuality in circumstances where sacrifice of self is the condition of a certain minimal quality of value in one's life. "Martyrdom" may not always be the correct choice. But each individual must decide at what point it would be better for him to die than to live without a certain modicum of value—for himself and others. For many men the supreme self-sacrifice can be "their finest hour," the act that symbolizes the very meaning of their own lives.

In the last analysis each man is to decide for what his life stands, and for him to lose that sense of his own place in the struggle for values is for him to lose self-respect and reduce his life to animal existence. What we need to stress, perhaps, when we "choose ourselves" is that we justly do so when our concern is for ourselves as creators of value, and not as exempt from any responsibility that we have as persons in a given situation.

27

Duties to Others: Altruism

~~~~~~

I. COMMUNITY AND INDIVIDUALITY

In the previous chapter we were primarily concerned with the individual person as the moral unit. Unless individuals realize values, feel obligations, and act, no values will be realized, no obligations recognized, and no actions taken. Thus, the Principle of Individuality stressed the obligation of a person to respect his own potentialities as a moral agent and actualizer of values. But it became evident immediately that while we could not conceive of society apart from individuals, neither could we conceive of significant individuality apart from society. While we can think of persons who have withdrawn from society for varying lengths of time, sometimes for the express purpose of asserting their individuality in revolt against society, the very individuality that they assert and the grounds of their rebelliousness are products of social interaction.

Accordingly, the individuality and self-respect demanded by the Principle of Individuality are a product of personal development and socialization, on the one hand, and social evolution, on the other. We hardly needed the depth psychologists to tell us that many human beings neither recognize nor respect their own individuality; but if there were any doubt on that score the literature of psychotherapy has dispelled it. Still, not all societies have recognized the importance, the effectiveness, or even the existence of individuals as moral units. The concept of the significance of the individual has emerged only

595

through a long, slow, generally difficult, and sometimes bloody evolutionary process. There have been and still are major setbacks in
the process, as evidenced by such events as the practice of genocide,
Apartheid in South Africa, resistance to integration in the United
States, liquidation of the Kulaks in Russia and the landowning class
in China.

Individuality itself is clearly an achievement within community;
but effective *moral* individuality involves and depends upon a revised
and developing sense of community and communal obligation. We
have already (Chapter 25) recognized with Plato and Aristotle that
we are essentially social beings, that most if not all values occur in
social context—as social or affiliative achievements—that most if not
all obligations have social reference directly or indirectly, and that
most if not all actions both occur in social contexts and are often
specifically designed to modify those social contexts. The crucial
questions at this point become: How are we, as self-respecting individuals, to think of community? What are our communal obligations,
and on what do they rest?

To begin with, we merely delude ourselves and furnish ourselves
an easy mode of rationalization if we conceive of community as some
sort of being in the abstract, which acts and has obligations apart
from the individuals who make it up. At the same time, neither can
we think of community as did some of the nineteenth-century liberals
and utilitarians, in a merely additive sense, that is, as the sum of
individuals or as a collection of wholly independent individuals. Still,
the key to a mature and morally effective conception of community
does seem to lie in the effective cooperation, mutual interdependence,
and development of common or at least complementary aims of self-
respecting and mutually respectful individuals. If this is so, then
individuals are neither independent social atoms nor pulse beats in
a larger and somehow "more real" social whole. They are interdependent, mutually involved, mutually responsible actualizers of
value or disvalue, whose very power to realize values functions only
when their relations with other human beings are of a certain quality.
From this standpoint, community and individuality are correlative
terms. We shall look more closely at the implications of this for types
of social and political organizations in Chapter 28. Here we are primarily concerned with the relations of individuals-in-community as
these characterize or include their obligations to each other—with the
problem of altruism.

II. *THE PRINCIPLE OF ALTRUISM*

With Immanuel Kant we have urged that persons as moral units and realizers of value, whether actually or potentially realizing the values of which they are capable, are worthy of respect. We have stressed the importance of self-respect as both the product and condition of significant individuality. The same respect that I ought to develop for myself extends to other selves. For other selves, like me, can value and achieve individuality. Although value is of, or for, individuals, it is generally produced through relations in a social group; while the locus of value is individual, the context is communal. Dependable values especially are joint products of the individual and his environment; the most important part of the environment is other people; and affiliative values, we have seen, are crucial to the enhancement of most other values. Without shared values, the ideals that any individual can realize would be drastically reduced; they might even disappear altogether. Even the antisocial individual who values only power or position or wealth can do so only in a society of men to be ruled or to be impressed.

Accordingly, if the Principle of Individuality is accepted, consistency demands that it be applied to all potential individuals. This is *the rational ground for altruism.* Borrowing from, but adding to, the Kantian formulation, we can state the Principle of Altruism thus: *Each person ought to respect all other persons as ends in themselves and, as far as possible, cooperate with others in the production and enjoyment of shared values.*[1]

III. *PERVASIVENESS OF THE PRINCIPLE OF ALTRUISM*

The Principle of Altruism in one form or another is and has been one of the ethical principles most widely recognized by thinkers of different times and places. This is not to say that it has been universally accepted or that its scope of application has not been drastically limited in many cases. If one turns to attempts to justify it, one finds that such attempts range from divine fiat to sentiment. But

[1] Cf. E. S. Brightman, *Moral Laws* (New York: Abingdon Press, 1933), p. 223.

regardless of how well it has or has not been justified, if one takes regard for others as the central concept in altruism, then the degree of unanimity among divergent ethical systems as to the importance of altruism is most striking.

Perhaps the most familiar and widely quoted formulation of an injunction to altruism in the West is the so-called "Golden Rule." "Therefore, all things whatsoever ye would that men should do to you, do ye even so to them!" [2] The Golden Rule has frequently been taken as the archetype for a Principle of Altruism—so much so that a rather wide range of Western thinkers with highly divergent points of view have tried to show that their own formulations of altruism are essentially restatements of the Golden Rule. Two examples will serve to illustrate this tendency: Kant, the Formalist, clearly thought that his Categorical Imperative (see Chapter 21 above) was such a restatement. But so also did John Stuart Mill, the nineteenth-century British Utilitarian. Mill argued that the principle of utility, the greatest good of the greatest number, is a restatement of the Golden Rule. " 'To do as one would be done by,' and 'to love one's neighbor as oneself,' constitutes the ideal perfection of utilitarian morality." [3]

Quite apart from the Judeo-Christian formulation, in fact five-hundred years before the beginning of the Christian era, Confucius had developed what might be called the negative formulation of the Golden Rule: "What you do not wish others should do unto you, do not do to them." [4] The principle in one form or another has turned up in most of the major world religions. In Hinduism it appears in the *Mahabharata* (13:115:21–22) as "This is the high religion which wise men esteem: the life-giving breaths of other creatures are as dear to them as the breaths of one's own self. Men gifted with intelligence and purified souls should always treat others as they themselves wish to be treated." [5] In Taoism it appears as "Regard your neighbor's gain as your own gain, and regard your neighbor's loss as your own loss." [6] Although no such principle appears in the Koran itself, the

---

[2] Matt. 7:12; cf. also Luke 6:31.

[3] *Utilitarianism*, in A. D. Melden, *Ethical Theories, A Book of Readings* (2nd ed.; Englewood, N. J.: Prentice-Hall, 1955), p. 376.

[4] In Lin Yutang, *The Wisdom of China and India* (New York: Random House, 1942), p. 848.

[5] Trans. by M. N. Dutt (Calcutta: Elysium Press, 1895), quoted in Ross Earle Hoople, Raymond F. Piper, and William P. Tolley, *Preface to Philosophy: A Book of Readings* (New York: The Macmillan Co., 1947), p. 309.

[6] Tai-Shang Kan-Ying Pien, *Treatise on Response and Retribution*, trans. T. Suzuki and Paul Carus (Chicago: Open Court Publishing Co., 1906), p. 53.

following does appear in "The Forty-two Traditions of An-Nawawi": "No one of you is a believer until he loves for his brother what he loves for himself." [7]

To return to the West and England for three further examples of a tendency to identify divergent ethics with the Golden Rule: Appealing to what he considered the clear reasonableness and naturalness of fair play, Richard Cumberland (1631–1718), in the seventeenth century, considered altruism a law of nature.

> Whatever assistance any man rightly and truly believes he may or ought to demand according to right reason, it is equitable and consequently a dictate of right reason that he should think that any other in like circumstances justly may or ought to demand the like things from him.[8]

Bishop Butler, in the eighteenth century, charged that man as social is naturally benevolent: "First, there is a natural principle of *benevolence* in man; which is in the same degree to *society*, what *self-love* is to the individual." [9] To argue as Thomas Hobbes had done that man is only selfish is to fail to read the facts of human nature correctly. Butler continues: "It is as manifest, that *we were made for society, and to promote the happiness of it, as that we were intended to take care of our own life, and health, and private good.*" [10]

For Charles Darwin, in the nineteenth century, morality is a product of evolution as much as is man himself. The fact that man has what Darwin called "a moral sense" [11] is the most striking difference between men and the lower animals from which they are descended. This is not to say that rudimentary moral instincts are not present in lower animals, but in men they are more complex. Man's moral sense has developed particularly out of the "ever-present nature of the social instincts" [12] including love and the distinct emotion of sympathy." [13] These have been strengthened by "the approbation and disapprobation of his fellows" and "the high activity of his mental faculties." [14] The result is that "man is impelled by the same general

[7] *The Moslem World*, April 1939, p. 139. (See Hoople, Piper, and Tolley, *op. cit.*, pp. 309–10, for a comparison of "Golden Rule" statements in twelve religions.

[8] *A Treatise on the Laws of Nature*, trans. John Maxwell (1672), p. 23.

[9] *The Whole Works of Joseph Butler* (London: William Tegg, n.d.) Sermon I, pp. 3–4.

[10] *Ibid.*, p. 10.

[11] *The Descent of Man* (New York: The Modern Library, n.d.), p. 912.

[12] *Ibid.*

[13] *Ibid.*

[14] *Ibid.*, pp. 912–13.

wish to aid his fellows" as the lower animals, but modified by foresight and reason into concern for the happiness of all as "an essential
part of the general good." [15] Furthermore, such reasonable altruistic
concern, itself a product of natural selection, is essential to the preservation and further development of the human race.

Thus, Cumberland, arguing from divine law and inherent reasonableness, Butler, from a fixed nature of man, and Darwin, from evolutionary development and natural selection, all agree on the crucial
importance of altruism. All three also agree, though for quite different reasons, that altruism is natural to man. This striking convergence
of diverse ethical positions with different religious positions in support of altruism is not accidental. For no matter what its rationale,
every ethical or ethico-religious position must deal with the reciprocity of obligation in social context. Even defenders of those positions
usually listed as anti-altruistic have to make some concessions to regard for others, if for no other reason than to insure, at least, some
affiliative values. Epicurus includes friendship among the lasting
pleasures. Thomas Hobbes, while insisting that all men are egocentric, realized that without the minimum conditions of mutual
protection offered by civil law, selfishness is self-destroying. Nietzsche,
who had no use for the kind of love of neighbor that blinds both the
neighbor and the lover to their mutual weaknesses, constantly urged
love of men for what they could be.

In the light of our samples, it becomes obvious that the basic
problem is not acceptance of altruism as somehow ethically crucial,
but rather that of giving altruism more careful definition and concrete content. If we can show what the content of altruism is, we can
thereby justify altruism within an ethical system. To pinpoint the
issue, let us revive a question that has appeared in each of the last
two chapters: Is all other-regarding activity necessarily moral simply
because it is other-regarding? If the answer to this question is negative, then the crucial question becomes: What kind of other-regarding
is morally obligatory?

IV. ALTRUISM AND INDIVIDUALITY

While Kant feels that the second form of the Categorical Imperative—
"Act so that you treat humanity, whether in thine own person or that

[15] *Ibid.*, p. 913.

of another, always as an end and never as a means only" [16]—carries the spirit of the biblical imperative to altruism, it is significant that he does not refer to the more familiar form of the Golden Rule cited above. Rather he talks about love of neighbor [17] and love of "neighbor as thyself." [18] The statement in Matthew 7:12—"Therefore all things whatsoever ye would that men should do to you, do ye even unto them"—is in one basic respect strikingly different from Kant and also from our statement of the Principle of Altruism above: Each person ought to respect all other persons as ends in themselves and, as far as possible, to cooperate in the production and enjoyment of shared values. The difficulty in the Golden Rule is its lack of any clear specification of what I ought to want men to do to me or how I ought to consider myself. Without such specification, a serious question might be raised as to whether the Golden Rule taken in isolation is an ethical rule at all. All the rule enjoins is that I do for others what I would like to have them do for me. Suppose I am a dope addict? Or a masochist? Or, as is more likely the case, I really do not like myself very well? The results of applying the rule thus interpreted might be disastrous for all concerned. In such cases, the Confucian negative formulation would be less dangerous.

Thus, the Golden Rule, if it is to be a clear and workable formulation of the Principle of Altruism, must presuppose another and more frequently repeated biblical statement, one to which Kant, in fact, refers. It occurs first in the Torah (Lev. 19:18): "Thou shalt love thy neighbor as thyself." The same statement appears six times in the New Testament (Matt. 19:19, Matt. 22:39, Luke 10:27, Mark 12:31, Romans 13:9, Galatians 5:14). When this statement is taken literally and as the context of the one in Matthew, the so-called Golden Rule becomes less ambiguous and more concrete.

What is most striking about the Torah formulation, which is repeated in the New Testament, is its clear recognition that neighbor-love must rest on love of self. The kind of self-love or of neighbor-love called for is not to be confused with eroticism or sentimentality. It is something much closer to the willed love as a style of life that we suggested in Chapter 17 and to the critical respect for self as a potential realizer of value called for by the Principle of Individuality. It is on such reflective respect that cooperative communal action, as

---

[16] *Critique of Practical Reason and Other Writings in Moral Philosophy*, trans. L. W. Beck (Chicago: University of Chicago Press, 1949), p. 87.

[17] *Ibid.*, p. 60.

[18] *Ibid.*, p. 190.

opposed to emotional gregariousness, rests. It is in terms of such respect that my concern for others is really a concern for their welfare and not merely an attempt to escape from my own loneliness. It is through such mutual respect that we work together for our common growth, development, and good rather than our mutual destruction through individual self-aggrandizement.

In Chapter 26 we pointed to Erich Fromm's insistence that the lack of productive self-love or self-respect is one of the major roots of confusion and frustration in contemporary Western culture. Fromm also insists not only that there is no real conflict between self-love and love of others but that each is impossible without the other.

> Love of others and love of ourselves are not alternatives. On the contrary, an attitude of love toward themselves will be found in all those who are capable of loving others. Love, in principle, *is indivisible as far as the connection between "objects" and one's own self is concerned.* Genuine love is an expression of productiveness and implies care, respect, responsibility, and knowledge.[19]

In contrast to some Christian ethicists on the one hand and Hobbes on the other, we are suggesting with Fromm that although indiscriminate other-regarding and selfishness *are* incompatible, effective individualism and altruism require each other.

We can restate this mutuality in terms of the Principles of Individualism and Altruism themselves. The ground of altruism lies in ethical individuality, but effective individuality cannot be attained apart from altruism. Basically the force of the Principle of Altruism rests upon one's realization of the universality of the Principle of Individuality. As a moral unit, a realizer of values or disvalues, I must recognize others as the bearers of a similar capacity for valuing and must attribute to them my own need of self-respect. This extension to others of what I know in myself is supported when I discover that I am unable to realize the values of which I am capable apart from the respect of others and their cooperation in the production and employment of shared values. Conversely, unless I do genuinely respect others and do cooperate with them in attaining affiliative values, I progressively decrease both my own and others' potential for value attainment.

---

[19] *Man for Himself* (New York: Rinehart & Company, Inc., 1947), p. 129. Reprinted by permission of Holt, Rinehart and Winston, Inc.

The necessity for mutuality in protecting the value potentials of persons is fundamental to the argument for altruism. We see the loss of mutual value graphically illustrated in the unfortunate effect of neighborhood feuds on all parties to the feud or, by extension, in the devastating effect of warfare in the modern world where both victor and vanquished lose. An example of the first may also serve as an analogy of the second.

Down the street from one of the authors live two neighbors with abutting back yards. Both are on the whole pleasant and capable people. Both have beautiful yards. One neighbor, a lawyer, decided to put in a rail and post fence to fit the landscape scheme of his yard. The fence would have enhanced the other neighbor's yard also, because the type of landscape in the two yards was quite different and the fence would have made a clean line of demarcation. A fence, however, has a way of making property lines appear precise. The lawyer hired a surveyor and when the surveyor completed his work, this neighbor proceeded to start his fence. The second neighbor nevertheless decided that the line was not where the fence was being built. He proceeded to call in the town fence-viewer (a peculiarly New England town official appointed by the aldermen to settle minor boundary disputes). The fence-viewer agreed with the second neighbor and claimed that the surveyor had not taken into account a two foot strip of land that the town had taken for a street widening in front of the lawyer's house. The surveyor had therefore set the line two feet beyond the point where it was supposed to be and thus on the second neighbor's property.

Instead of attempting to resolve the issue either by talking it over as intelligent human beings or by getting the fence-viewer and the surveyor together to settle the matter, each neighbor accused the other of bad faith, stealing, and other assorted vices. The second neighbor threatened to bring suit unless the fence building was halted immediately. It was. The fence has remained unfinished for eight years. The neighbors refuse to speak. Each has an eyesore to look at. The second neighbor refuses to use the back part of his own yard and chases the lawyer's children away if they so much as set foot on the land. He will not even return balls that stray over the line. The children reciprocate by making things as unpleasant as possible for the second neighbor—particularly at Halloween.

The whole neighborhood has become infected by the feud. It is almost impossible to remain friends with both neighbors, for a visit to or with one engenders a decidedly frigid response from the other. To a surprising extent other people in the neighborhood are divided into factions siding with one or the other of the two principals. Everyone involved has lost, and no end is in sight until one of the abutting neighbors moves or dies.

Such cases of mutual loss on a much larger scale can be illustrated repeatedly in Western history. The France of the *ancien régime* never quite recovered from the revocation of the Edict of Nantes by Louis XIV in 1685. This deprived the French Huguenots of their right to worship and educate their children in non-Catholic schools. The result was a wholesale emigration of artisans, men of letters, and even some military leaders to Holland, England, and America. Germany during the nineteenth century lost a great many able people to other parts of the world through political oppression. The most striking recent example was the loss to Germany and the world of Jewish scientists, artists, scholars, business men, and other capable human beings. The 1961–62 Berlin-wall incident at least in part was a desperate effort by East Germany to hold on to technicians, scholars, and others who, by fleeing from political oppression, were weakening the viability of the East German state.

All these examples—and many others one might use—simply illustrate and stress individual and societal loss that inevitably occurs whenever people lose mutual respect and refuse to cooperate in the production or enjoyment of shareable values. But at this point we need to be particularly careful that our ground or basis for altruism is kept clear. We have argued that without the sharing of values in accordance with the Principle of Altruism, one cannot realize the maximum values of which one is capable, as called for by the Principle of Individuality. This dependence of maximum values for the individual on shared values clearly is the case. But our examples of mutual sharing must not tempt us to conclude that the ground for altruism is only enlightened self-interest, for this conclusion results only from serious oversimplification.

To be sure, enlightened self-interest is never possible without the shared values. But self-interest alone might very well disregard the Kantian injunction in the Principle of Altruism to regard other persons as ends in themselves and never as means only. Again, we must emphasize that while enlightened self-interest does lead to recognition of oneself as a moral unit worthy of respect, it is this respect for moral units individually and in community that is the ground for altruism and not the self-interest alone. Altruism involves interest and is reinforced by interest, and interest is the interest of a self; but the interests of a self far exceed mere interest in oneself. The interests of a self are by no means all interests in oneself but include genuine interest in other selves and their values.

A second confusion about the ground or basis of altruism at this point might arise out of our earlier statement that altruism rests upon consistent application of the Principle of Individuality to all persons, or upon a generalization of that principle to cover all individuals. It might on the surface seem that we were doing much the same kind of thing that John Stuart Mill did in attempting to ground the prinple of utility (the good equals the greatest happiness of the greatest number) in individual desire for happiness.

We have already called attention to the fact that Mill thought that the principle of utility was a restatement of the Golden Rule. In justification, Mill had insisted that

> the happiness which forms the utilitarian standard of what is right in conduct is not the agent's own happiness but that of all concerned. As between his own happiness and that of others, utilitarianism requires him to be as strictly impartial as a disinterested and benevolent spectator.[20]

The question here is not whether happiness is an adequate definition of value.

The question at this point concerns Mill's basis for arguing that the happiness of all concerned or what he also calls the "general happiness" is or ought to be sought over my individual happiness. Here Mill's argument takes a most interesting turn. He says:

> No reason can be given why the general happiness is desirable, except that each person, so far as he believes it to be attainable, desires his own happiness. This, however, being a fact, we have not only all the proof the case admits of, but all which it is possible to acquire, that happiness is a good; that each person's happiness is good to that person, and the general happiness, therefore, a good to the aggregate of all persons.[21]

Mill's argument contains two rather startling weaknesses. The first lies in his assumption that the desired and the desirable can be

[20] *Utilitarianism,* in Melden, *op. cit.,* p. 376.
[21] *Ibid.,* p. 388.

equated. That such an equation cannot be effected without remainder has already become evident in our discussion of the difference between value claim and tested values (Chapter 14).

The second difficulty is the one that particularly concerns us here. Mill seems to have committed the logical fallacy of composition, for he argues illicitly from a characteristic of a part to a characteristic of a whole. It does not follow that because each man desires his own happiness, men desire the happiness of all. Succinctly: general desire for happiness does not imply desire for general happiness. It is quite possible for the happiness of different persons to be mutually exclusive (as when you and I both want to be president of the company) or for individual happiness and general happiness to be mutually exclusive (if I want to control the country through dictatorial power).

The generalization of the Principle of Individuality in the Principle of Altruism is a very different kind of generalization from Mill's generalization of individual happiness to general happiness. The respect and cooperation encouraged by the Principle of Altruism is based on the self-respect called for in the Principle of Individuality. But that respect, once more, is respect for myself as a person and a possible creator of values and not "for me just because I'm me," as it were. The fact that this kind of respect is extended in turn to all individuals in community in the light of their potential individualities keeps the extension from being an illicit jump from a characteristic of a part to a characteristic of a whole. The Principle of Altruism is based on a recognition of a common characteristic of all the parts and makes emphatic that insofar as persons are similar, respect cannot be arbitrarily confined to the values of one person at the expense of another.

V. *ALTRUISM AND ITS COUNTERFEITS*

If we confine the term "altruism" to the kind of respect for others and cooperation with them in production of shared values, then we need to point out more explicitly that a number of types of other-regarding activities that seem "altruistic" superficially may in fact be destructive of genuine altruism. These types of pseudo-altruism run the gamut from relatively harmless sentimentality to exceedingly dangerous possessiveness.

Suppose we take, as a starting point, the seemingly simple act of giving money to a beggar whom we encounter on the street. Such an act may be genuinely altruistic, but the chances of its being so are rather slim. In the first place, there is no way of knowing the actual situation of the beggar. He could be a man in real need, but if his need is genuine there are various social agencies to which he could go for help. Such agencies are usually able to give him not only emergency aid at the time but long range help and rehabilitation. The passer-by in giving him money does not help overcome the real difficulties. He may in fact aggravate them by delaying the time when the beggar will be compelled to seek the aid he really needs. All too frequently what the giver is doing is helping the alcoholic to obtain more alcohol or the drug addict to obtain more drugs. In addition, the record includes many persons who have made of begging a highly profitable profession.

Most persons who give money to beggars are fully aware of all this or would be if they gave the matter serious thought. The act of giving under such conditions is hardly an act of respect for the beggar or for society; it may result not only in superficial treatment of the need but in shallowness of emotional response.

Such confusion of uncritical sentiment and altruism can go much further than giving to beggars. Perhaps it reaches its most extreme form in the objections raised in principle to the use of animals in medical research for the purpose of alleviating human suffering, on the grounds that the poor animals have no way of protecting themselves.

Furthermore, the impulsive sentiment that bestows a gift upon some needy person who crosses my path may not, in fact, be quite so innocent as it seems. Its purpose may be to salve my own conscience —my guilt feelings. "I just did not quite get around to sending in my check to the community fund this year. I will make up for it by distributing some charity on my own. Besides, in this way I am sure the money gets directly to the needy person. If I had given money to the community fund, or the Red Cross, or some other organization, a lot of it would have gone into overhead, or to pay high salaries of directors or who knows what other fripperies. These charitable organizations need to be investigated and cleaned up." So the rationalization continues.

This matter of performing seemingly altruistic acts for conscience-salving reasons can reach major proportions in some philanthropists who give major gifts or establish charitable foundations with money obtained through rentals of slum property or by crushing competitors by any means available, whether just within the law or just beyond it. The use of such funds may well make major contributions to society or segments of it, but this does not change the fact that the gift had far other than altruistic motives behind it. This is not to suggest that all philanthropy is conscience-salving, but it is to suggest that conscience-salving philanthropy, based on an uncritical conscience and designed mainly to give oneself relief, is not to be confused with altruism.

But we can use "alms-giving" as an example of another manifestation of pseudo-altruism. My gift to the beggar may be neither a burst of sentiment, nor a matter of salving my own conscience, but a matter of "public relations." The real aim is to convince not the beggar but others how really generous I actually am. Public relations have their place, and there is no inherent reason why public relations cannot be altruistic; but altruism and public relations as "public relations" are clearly not the same thing.

Indeed "public relations," like "giving of alms," can be a gross violation of the Principle of Altruism. The public and the beggar can be used essentially as a means for impressing others. The larger the public or the more important the individual we seek to impress, the more the beggar is likely to receive. The people who behave in this way are usually those who are quite willing to take the credit if somebody else will do the work. They are quite willing to lead the alumni association or the community-fund drive if it will help their law or insurance business, their sales, or their political ambitions. They are excellent friends as long as the friends are the "right" people and there is promise of personal advantage.

Closely related to the giver for the sake of public relations is the person who gives to the underprivileged to cultivate his own sense of superiority to them. This is the psychologically sick giver who seeks by his gift to force respect from others in order to make up for lack of respect for himself. Perhaps it is the suspicion that such motivation may be the basis of the gift that frequently leads the recipient of charity to anything but gratitude toward the giver.

With typical overstatement Nietszche suggested that pity is one of the most dangerous of human emotions,[22] for it leads not to an attempt to change things but to an insidious satisfaction with things as they are. The person who pities too readily looks down on the

[22] See particularly *The Antichrist, First Book* (secs. 2 ff).

person pitied. "There but for the grace of God go I" may mean something far different from humility in the face of circumstances. Few people in trouble want either pity or charity. What they want and what altruism would dictate are understanding and help—given out of respect and not from the desire to be held superior.

Finally, and still further away from genuine altruism, is the kind of other-regarding activity designed either consciously or unconsciously to force the dependence of the person or persons cared for upon oneself. It is as though, in one way or another, we were beggaring others in order to play the controlling role among dependents. Overly possessive parents may persuade themselves that they are attempting to make certain that Johnny does not have to face the hardships they did; in fact, this feeling may be a subterfuge for attempting to hold on to Johnny by delaying or even destroying his ability to establish his own independence. It is not accidental that the business practice of more than meeting workers' demands as long as they do not organize into a union or protest general company policy has been called paternalism. It is not surprising that such paternalism is strongly resented, for its aim is not usually establishing mutual concern and regard for employees as human beings, but insuring dependence of the employees upon the company.

In the United States, we tend to be shocked and resentful when some of the "underdeveloped" nations of the world, particularly our Latin American neighbors, seem to be less than grateful for our offers of aid, military and financial. But it is not too difficult to see why our motives are questioned; this aid has so frequently been offered, not in response to specific needs in the countries in question, but rather in response to a threat to markets or sources of supply. This is not to suggest that aid has been offered only in such circumstances or that offering aid in such circumstances is always or necessarily wrong. It does mean that we should not pass off self-interest for altruism and that we should ask ourselves whether sometimes the real motive of what we like to call altruism is not to keep the recipient dependent upon us. One thing is certain: namely, we shall not receive or merit their respect until we convince them that we care for their development as such.

In the previous chapter we pointed out that Nietzsche had little use for certain kinds of love of neighbor. The examples we have considered make it not at all difficult to see why. Such types of concern for others are a credit neither to the loving person nor to his neigh-

bors. Essentially, Nietzsche felt, these are ways of escape, self-delu-
sions, or, if they are reciprocated, ways of mutual indulgence and
stagnation. In Neitzsche's words:

> You cannot endure yourselves and do not love yourselves
> enough: now you want to seduce your neighbor to love, and then
> gild yourselves with his error. One man goes to his neighbor
> because he seeks himself; another because he would lose him-
> self. Your bad love of yourselves turns your solitude into a
> prison.[23]

Nietzsche had no objection to the love of neighbor for what he might
become. The kind of love of neighbor based on the right kind of
love of self—the love of self rooted in self-respect—results not just in
pity alone, nor in charity alone, nor in indulgence, but in understanding and intelligent help. Anything else is a counterfeit of altruism.

In this section, we have suggested further justification for distinguishing, as we did in our treatment of the virtues in Chapter 17,
between action done from emotion or sentiment, and action in accordance with virtue, or willed action. It may be well to repeat, in
this context, that we are not urging that all emotional action is fitful
or that emotional responses consistent with virtuous action do not
make the person and the act more valuable. We are emphasizing
rather that actions proceeding from emotion alone, with no guidance
from a reflective ideal of personality for oneself and others, can
create more problems than they solve.

The discussion in this chapter purposely does not presuppose the
particular symphony of values and scheme of virtues suggested earlier,
for we are here interested in Principles and the rational justification
for the Principle of Altruism in particular. But it should be clear that
the particular actions that one will take in self-respect and in respect
of others will depend on the ideal of personality or the good one believes to be obligatory. In a word, there is no point to saying that I
love my neighbor if I do not know what in him (or in myself) I love.
Nor, as we shall see further, can we know what being just to our
neighbor means concretely without the aid of some pattern of values
and virtues. The community created by the Principle of Altruism, as

---

[23] *Thus Spake Zarathustra*, from *The Portable Nietzsche*, edited by Walter Kaufman. Copyright 1954 by The Viking Press, Inc., and reprinted by their permission.
P. 173.

we see it, is one in which moral agents become co-creators in values they each can reach, given their capacity for realizing and contributing to the "commonwealth" of values.

VI. *ALTRUISM AND JUSTICE*

An understanding and intelligent helpfulness is central to any adequate conception of justice when justice is seen within the context of the Principle of Altruism. We first introduced justice in our discussion of historical views of the virtues in Chapter 16. In Chapter 17 justice was recognized as essential to any adequate scheme of virtues and as the basic virtue among the social virtues. We then defined justice as "the willingness to make no exception of oneself in the distribution of either goods or evils, unless one can show good reason for doing so" (pp. 397–98). It was fairly evident then and should be clearly evident now that unless it fosters and supports mutual respect and strives to develop the shared values of the Principle of Altruism, justice remains an empty formula.

Any society is made up of many persons in complex interrelation, interdependence, and mutual involvement. What any one person does affects to a greater or less degree all other persons in his society. Conversely, what any one person can do or become depends to a very high degree on what others do, how they act, what they expect. This basic fact has been illustrated repeatedly in our discussion to this point. From birth to death, and regardless of how diverse the roles any of us find ourselves filling, we are embedded in a social milieu in which the values any one of us can realize are circumscribed and conditioned or opened up by what we do intentionally or unintentionally to each other. Whether we like it or not, the welfare of each cannot be divorced from the welfare of all. To be sure, given a large enough social framework, subsocieties within the social whole can continue to exist for some time in spite of mutual deprivation, conflict, and parasitism. But to the extent that such exploitations of the whole by the part occur, the society as a whole and each member in it are impoverished proportionately in relation to the values that might have been realized. The element of truth in Hobbes's position was his clear recognition that any society in which concern for others is basically lacking is no society; it is a jungle in which no one can achieve more than momentary satisfaction. In this sense at least, a communal altruism is not just an ideal, but a necessary condition of individual and communal survival and development. Justice is both the individual and institutional recognition of this fact.

Justice, like altruism itself, rests upon mutual respect. The conception of justice in a society tends to develop with increasing communal awareness on the one hand and increasing recognition of the potentialities of individuals in community on the other. Melvin Rader has insisted "that justice and self-realization are more or less interdependent, that they reciprocally determine and enhance one another.[24] To the extent that this is the case, one should be able to distinguish different levels or kinds of justice.

Minimal justice is what might be described as *corrective* or *retributive justice*. Such justice calls for impartiality in arbitration of disputes—an impartiality that involves considering the disputants not as friends, enemies, or relatives, but as responsible human beings with due claims to be adjudicated on the basis of the evidence. Even the old eye for an eye and tooth for a tooth formula, as inadequate as it is, rested upon the assumption that each individual had as an individual a right to equality of treatment—whether positive or negative. Insofar as one of the parties to the dispute may be the group itself, the principle of corrective justice involves the right of every individual, as over against the group, to be considered in his own right and awarded, condemned, or exonerated on the basis of rules of evidence that are relevant to his own situation. As applied to every person, such justice becomes embodied in the legal system of a society. In addition, as a matter of individual practice and expectation in regard to others, it illustrates and defines the minimal virtue of justice.

Closely allied to corrective and retributive justice, but involving more than redress and correction, is *distributive justice*. Distributive justice is much more difficult to deal with, for it involves impartiality in the distribution of goods and services. Just what such impartiality is, or what its basis is, is not always clear. If distributive justice entailed equal sharing of goods and services to every person, not only would it be impracticable, but, more seriously, it would fail to take into account differences in needs, abilities, foresight, motivation, and responsibility. Clearly we are not all alike or equal in natural endowments or in what we do with these. To fail to recognize such differences is not to treat them with the requisite respect. To be sure, the

[24] M. Rader, *Ethics and Society* (New York: Henry Holt & Company, 1950), p. 200.

opposite extreme, in which some persons secure most of the goods and other symbols of success (such as money) while other persons gain almost none, also violates regard for individuals. Indeed the capabilities both of the "have nots" and the "haves" may be so reduced that the society and its members become incapable of further striving and development. The net result is progressive approximation to social suicide.

If, therefore, distributive justice can mean neither equal distribution nor allowing one group to amass all the real wealth, what does it mean? On what kind of impartiality does it rest? At least one suggested answer would seem to lie in the very recognition of individual differences themselves. There probably is a minimal amount of goods and services without which a person is able neither to retain his self respect nor to develop the capabilities that he has. But beyond this minimal amount, distributive justice does call for impartial consideration of needs, abilities, foresight, motivation, contribution, responsibility and related factors. It is this problem of distributing rewards (and punishment) with full awareness of complex and variable facts that confronts college officials awarding scholarships or a committee, departmental chairman, or dean considering faculty raises and promotions, or a business executive in personnel development, or a governmental executive making out a pay scale for his area. Justice in this sense calls for the utmost impartiality possible in assessment of individuals in the light of their capabilities, rather than reliance on personal predilection and hunches.

Distributive justice within any particular society or group may well have to be redefined in such a way as to be relevant to that group, its potentialities, and its problems. It is far too easy to devise a general formula as to what would constitute economic justice in abstraction from actual conditions. It may in fact be the case that any group or society only approximates more or less closely what would constitute distributive economic justice for that group or society. One can, however, point out a number of relevant factors that need to be taken into account in developing a more adequate specific conception of economic distributive justice.

First, it is quite clear that distributive justice cannot be thought of in local terms only. The world has shrunk to the point that no society is completely isolated from any other society, and distributive justice must take into account the relation of societies to each other. We can no longer be smug in our own affluence while Indians or

Chinese die from hunger or Peruvian peasant children are unable to learn in school because of malnutrition while their landlords are enjoying the cafés of Paris.

Second, the assumption that business is business, that "economic man" can be divorced from moral man is sheer mythology. Man in business is just as much a moral agent and as subject to the Principles of Consequences, Specification, Individuality, and Altruism as man engaged in any other kind of activity.

Third, because the possibility of enlightened community and in-dividual self-development depend upon mutual respect and coopera-tion under the Principle of Altruism, any economic system based on the assumption that men are only consumers or units on the labor market, to be used as means for accumulation of profit or power, is not only immoral but over a period of time even self-destructive. This is not to say that men are not also means to a great variety of ends, including profits, and legitimately so. But it is to emphasize the fact that at the point at which men become *only* means to ends, they are being exploited as persons, and everyone is impoverished, in-cluding the exploiter. This statement applies not merely to economic exploitation but to every type of human exploitation as well.

The types of justice that we have been considering so far—correc-tive and distributive—are in a sense minimal conditions presented by the Principle of Altruism. But the Principle of Altruism clearly goes further than they do. It is a principle of cooperation, of mutual respect and enhancement. It calls for a conception of justice that is more than a negative or "no exception" virtue, and in social practice it involves more than the judicial impartiality of the courts. What is called for is a positive conception of justice as the responsible con-cern of cooperating, mutually respecting individuals with the welfare of the inclusive community. Such a conception of justice is not far from what Plato had in mind in his insistence that the just state is one in which every part functions adequately in contributing to the welfare of the whole.[25]

Justice, so conceived, involves the recognition of our common or mutual responsibility for overcoming the conditions that give rise to juvenile delinquency, providing for improvement of education in some less affluent areas of the community, making it possible for able students to receive higher education, providing medical aid to the aged and the indigent, slum clearance, and reducing poverty wherever

[25] Cf. *Republic*, IV, 432–34, 444.

it occurs. These are only some examples of positive justice—a justice whose full implications we have only come to recognize in the United States in the last forty years. Such justice cannot be restricted to the small community or the family or even the nation, for it involves taking seriously the injunction to treat persons as ends in themselves and to cooperate with them in the production and enjoyment of shared values wherever such persons may be. It is not based upon a desire to interfere with others' affairs or upon a desire for paternalistic control, but upon mutual respect and cooperation. Although we shall return to further discussion of the implications of positive justice in the next chapter, it is of basic importance to recognize at this time its foundation in the Principle of Altruism. Furthermore, such altruism, unless it translates itself into a reasoned conception of improved society and into action in accordance with such a conception, is not in fact altruism but a return to sentimentality.

In discussing the virtues, we discussed briefly the nature of forgiveness and its relation to repentance. We would refer the reader back to that discussion (pp. 398–400) now, for in forgiveness we are concerned with the problem of "loving" and of doing justice, in the light of the ideal of personality and community, to persons who have knowingly hurt other persons.

The kind of justice that is involved in forgiveness brings to the fore what must be seen as the core of every altruistic act in which, in the attempt to realize a greater good for the agents involved, there is danger of losing good already in hand. In every altruistic act in which the objective is the creation of a new community of value at the risk of losing well-earned gains, there is a venture, an act of reasonable faith, if you will, that is consonant with the obligation to the best we know. The willingness to sacrifice new values in order that new heights may be scaled is not outside altruism but is its "fine excess" to use Keats's phrase. The human obligation to increase values is literally impossible in the imperfect human world without the common creative ventures of persons striving together for the more than ordinary.

VII. *IDEAL OF PERSONALITY*

With the Principle of Altruism we have completed our discussion of some of the principles guiding moral choice. These are principles

of intelligibility or coherence in action, guides to effective and coherent living, to the fullest development of value and meaning in
life, individually and communally. The principles themselves are obviously not original with us but have emerged out of the continuing
quest for ethical insight by philosophic investigators at least from
Socrates and Plato to the present. We have suggested that these principles also have a peculiar relevance to the development of recent
psychology of personality and the search for emotional, mental, and
social health and maturity. We hold no brief for the particular formulation of these principles given here, nor would we claim that our
list is necessarily exhaustive. We have insisted that moral principles
are not casuistic rules of thumb; they are statements of some of the
universal conditions relevant to effective decision-making for the
fulfillment of human potentialities.

It has become clear in our discussion that morality is not an easy
thing; there is no quick formula to the good life. To make lists of
particular actions supposed to be always good or bad is an extremely
dangerous oversimplification. On the contrary, if we have discovered
anything, it is that the sphere of morality is the business of every-day
living and involvement, of frustration and success, of achievement
and failure, of growth and regression. The moral quest is not a matter
of following the will-o'-the-wisp of Truth, Beauty, and Goodness in
the abstract or as Platonic Ideas divorced from the mire and turmoil
of every-day life. It is the application of enlightened, mutual, common
concern and intelligence in continuing decision-making. This does
require consistency, acceptance of responsibility, seeing values in
relation, taking into account consequences, accepting the challenge
and the limits of the possible, keeping in view the specific situation
and its relevance, and also having some long-range direction in terms
of which to judge. Finally, it involves developing a healthy respect
for oneself as a realizer of values and extending this respect to others
in the cooperative development of shared values.

We have stated these conditions as principles, and we have discovered that as principles for guiding choice, they do form a system in
the sense that each has bearing on the others and no one of them
alone assures moral accomplishment. Each requires the others. Together they do add up to what might be described as a concrete ideal
of personal and communal action. E. S. Brightman felt that this ideal
should itself be stated as an additional principle. We would prefer
to call it a summary statement stressing the fact that its content is

the whole system of principles developed to date. So considered, it is not a formula, nor is it an additional law, but an injunction to the fullest self-realization of personality in community: *Each person ought to judge and guide all his acts by his ideal conception of what his whole personality ought to become both individually and socially.*[26]

The task remaining to us in the closing chapters is to indicate the relevance of the ideal of personality and the system of moral principles to selected areas of personal and social development.

VIII. *REFLECTIVE SUMMARY*

At this stage in our deliberations, we hardly need to remind ourselves that the individual personality is a by-product of social interaction and that the person as the moral unit realizes most of his values in community. But apart from the fact that many values actually depend on mutual cooperation between persons, the rational ground for respecting all other persons as ends in themselves (and, as far as possible, for cooperating with them in the creation and enjoyment of shared values) is the Principle of Consistency. In my search for the best I know, I cannot with reason favor myself, as a bearer of value, without respecting other bearers of value.

The more specific problem arises in deciding what it means concretely to respect another person or "to love my neighbor as myself." Much sentimentality is avoided if we realize that in "loving," the moral agent is to be guided by the same ideal of personality in dealing with himself and with others. I may help another person because I like him, but if I am to help him, I must be guided by a critically approved pattern of values that I believe all persons, including him and me, can and ought to realize as far as possible.

It may seem, on the surface, that altruism is in the last analysis enlightened self-interest, that helping another is only another way of helping myself. But we are not seduced by the ambiguity of "self-interest" if we realize (a) that on the view of human nature presupposed here one cannot be interested in self without interest in others, and (b) that the rational basis for interest in others is not the mere fact that we need each other in many ways but that other persons merit my respect as ends in themselves. Again, just as the Principle

[26] Cf. E. S. Brightman, *Moral Laws* (New York: Abingdon Press, 1933), p. 242.

of Individuality holds me to realizing the best that *I* as a bearer of value can realize, not what I "please" when I "please" it, so the Principle of Altruism holds all bearers of value in a network of respect for that criticized pattern of values that they can create with and for each other. Indeed, without this constant emphasis on the careful and cooperative analysis of persons and values in the light of a coherent pattern of values, it is easy for "altruism" to be in fact seductive and hypocritical selfishness.

Genuine justice, in the last analysis, is guided by the concern that persons share the values of life in such a way that no person is unnecessarily deprived of what he can realize as a member of a community of mutual concern. No two persons are equal in the mathematical sense, so every attempt must be made to help each person to contribute all he can to the growth of value in community. Only then can each person realize the optimum of value in his own life and suffer as little as possible from the evils that come either through accident or through moral imperfection and failure. Justice, in a word, is the best way of being merciful—if one is guided by the ideal of persons in a community of concern and not by "formula." Justice is not a way of taking risk or sacrifice from the moral venture; it is a way of sharing risk and sacrifice as constructively as possible.

PART V

The Good in Social and Religious Perspective

28

The Responsible Society in Ethical Perspective

~~~~~~

I. *ETHICS AND SOCIAL PHILOSOPHY*

To ask where ethics stops and social philosophy begins comes close to asking a question that is unanswerable in principle. Why? Insofar as ethics is concerned with human conduct, it is concerned with human beings interacting in social contexts and thus with social structures, means, and ends. Insofar as social philosophy is concerned with the rationale of social structures, including social and political means and ends, it is concerned with human beings acting in the light of their ideals, individual and social. Inevitably one's social philosophy is an extension of one's ethics and one's ethics is a specification of one's social philosophy. It is no accident that the *Republic* brings together in one work Plato's ethics, social philosophy, and theory of reality (metaphysics). For Aristotle the *Nicomachean Ethics* is Part I of a total work of which Part II is *Politics*. Although ethics and social philosophy are distinguishable in terms of emphasis, they are not separable in subject.

This recognition of the mutual involvement of ethics and social philosophy should not, however, be taken to mean that persons may not hold conflicting individual and societal goals. Indeed, some deny the relevance of morality to politics, or vice versa. Morris Ginsburg in discussing "The Moral Basis of Political Conflicts" points out:

In approaching this question we have at the outset to face the view that moral differences, if they exist, are really irrelevant to the situation today. The forces engaged in the struggle for mastery are, it will be said, strictly amoral. No doubt both sides talk in moral terms and claim to be acting in defence of their rights. But this moral appeal is only made, so it is suggested, because it is psychologically useful. . . . The moral appeal is thus used as a ruse for the multitude to hide the naked search for power.[1]

Plato's Thrasymachus and Callicles had argued in similar fashion and, in denying the relevance of morals to social philosophy, had become characters in masterpieces that involved both!

II. *SOCIAL ISSUES AND MORAL PRINCIPLES*

From the outset of our discussion of the possibility of moral principles through our treatment of the Principle of Altruism, we have witnessed the inevitable interrelation of ethical, political, and social issues. It may be well, before we consider the norms for a responsible society, to bring together in this section different suggestions that have come out of our analysis of the moral principles advanced in Part IV.

A. *Moral Principles and Civil Law*

In Chapter 18 we distinguished customs and legal enactments from moral principles. Without this distinction, a meaningful critique of enacted law (with an eye to its improvement) is hardly possible. If enacted law is identified with moral principle, then enacted law defines the morally right, and it is meaningless to say that the laws ought to be improved. But to recognize the difference is also to underscore the positive relation between the two.

Although some laws may be specifically unjust in the legislators' intent—that is, enacted for restrictive, repressive, or selfish ends— the ethical critique of law rests on the assumption that law is devised to promote the welfare of persons in society. Effective enactment depends upon and is conducive to a clear ideal of what a given group

[1] Reprinted from *Scrutiny*, Vol. XVI, No. 1. (March 1949), in Milton K. Munitz, *A Modern Introduction to Ethics* (Glencoe, Illinois: The Free Press, 1958), p. 508.

ought to be socially and politically. However, what social ideals should be and how to apply them are as subject to review and criticism in the light of moral principles as is any individual ideal. Societal ideals require all the more careful consideration in the light of moral principles than do personal ideals because the ideals operative in a society drastically affect the ideals of all the individuals within the society.

B. *Autonomy and Social Responsibility*

In Chapter 20 we discovered that the Principle of Autonomy is the key ethical presupposition underlying the possibility of democratic process itself. If individuals are not capable of making up their minds for themselves, of acknowledging ideals and judging their own acts in the light of their acknowledged ideals, then there can be no such thing as a self-determining community, and democracy loses all excuse for being. It follows that unless individuals are free to exchange, criticize, and reformulate ideas and ideals, that is, unless they are free to think and speak responsibly, effective autonomy and democracy are curtailed.

Clearly, emotional, moral, and political maturity and sophistication go hand in hand. Therefore in discussing the Principle of Autonomy and, later, the Principle of Specification, we did not suggest that all groups and societies are at a stage appropriate to political democracy. We do not do so now. Nor would we hold that there is a single correct form of democratic organization for those groups and societies in which democracy is appropriate.

We did, however, urge that it should be the aim of both the individual and the community to achieve the kind of moral and political maturity that makes democracy possible. Moral maturity and political maturity are not only in accord with the Principle of Autonomy, but they are also the preconditions of that mature sense of social responsibility which gives rise to a responsible society itself. The only effective way of developing such maturity, we pointed out, is through practice—that is, through actual participation in individual and communal decision-making.

Attainment of autonomous maturity takes time. It does not occur by command. Rather does it involve learning to associate consequences with decision through increasing self-involvement, through discovering the importance of tolerance, compromise, rational persuasion, and mutual accommodation. Under emergency conditions, even in a developed society, public discussion and participation may have to be curtailed in favor of rapid decisions by duly constituted leaders. Nevertheless, the health and continuing maturity of the body politic depends upon adequate constitutional safeguards against usurpation of power after the emergency has passed. The power of exercising autonomous judgment, if not used by the electorate, tends to atrophy. The danger in having Platonic philosopher-kings, military juntas, or interim dictators lies not so much in their intentions as in the ease with which such rulers, for the sake of efficiency in the service of the "common good," either fail to educate their followers in political responsibility or fail to return power to a presumably immature electorate.

We do not hold, then, that morality ceases when political democracy is curtailed or that morality does not exist where political democracy has not been developed. But we recognize that moral autonomy does have political implications and that some forms of political organization are more, and some less, conducive to the attainment of emotional, moral, and political maturity by their constituent members. Here again Hegel and Bradley would seem to be quite right in their insistence that personal morality and sociopolitical context are inseparable.

C. *Action in Context*

In Chapter 21 we followed Kant's argument for human dignity, based upon the recognition of man's potential moral autonomy. Men as ends in themselves are worthy of respect; ideally they should be united in a society in which they are never treated as means only. But we also saw the danger, political as well as personal, of exclusive emphasis upon any one goal or even any set of goals, because all goals need to be considered in the context of other possible value realization. That a sincere but misguided fanatic can produce havoc in his own life, in the life of others, or in a whole society, history makes abundantly clear.

Therefore, in Chapter 22 we turned to the field of action and its results—the evaluation of consequences. Here we were faced immediately with the old problem of how ends and means affect both sociopolitical contexts and individual desires. We noted that only an end justifies a means, of course. But what the Machiavellian and the fanatic overlook is that all means are also ends (have intrinsic value or disvalue in themselves) and all ends are also means (have further desirable or undesirable consequences). Thus, in order to be politically realistic, let alone ethical, the total value system has to be taken into account. Otherwise the means to the desired end and the consequences of that end destroy whatever value the end taken by itself might have. For example, to try to preserve freedom of speech by denying it to those who disagree with you as to what freedom of speech means is to endanger what you set out to preserve. Or to overcome private exploitation of agricultural workers by state exploitation still leaves agricultural workers exploited.

D. *Education*

The average citizen as well as the political leaders must have the necessary information, and they must be able to assess facts as a basis for intelligent action. Clearly, the moral imperative to increase both education and research is both individual and sociopolitical.

Sheer ignorance and not inherent malevolence is all too frequently at the base of some of the most inhuman actions—witch burning, voodoo, arbitrary segregation, persecution of minorities. Accordingly, in Chapter 23 we stressed the tragic results of wedding such ignorance with frustration, envy, anxiety, and fear, thus turning stereotypes into strong prejudices. We noted the waste of human potential and the increase in human suffering caused by the failure to take individual differences adequately into account. Here Plato's recognition that a just society, whatever else it may be, is at least a society in which each individual has the opportunity to do the kind of work he is best fitted to do took on new relevance.

E. *Societal Uniqueness*

In Chapter 24 we urged the uniqueness of every historical situation. The fact of individual difference must be kept in mind as we consider the good of societies in their historical, economic, political, and geographical characteristics. One cannot decide on the best political organization of a society without considering the peculiar characteristics and problems of that society's context and stage of historical and educational development. A feudal society cannot be changed into a democracy by decree.

Furthermore, within every society, the Principle of Specification, while realizing the essential character of legal continuity, stresses nevertheless the importance of flexibility, provision for evolution, and change of law to suit changing circumstances. Custom and tradition are essential if a society is to continue; but these traditions must be living, changing, and relevant to new developments. Otherwise *rigor mortis* sets in, and the society inhibits rather than enhances the mature potential of its members. In more extreme cases of repression, the repressed have a moral right to revolution.

F. *Planning*

In Chapter 25 we enlarged on the importance of social as well as individual planning, for the latter is literally impossible apart from the former. One's vocation, for example, is both a mode of social accommodation and a means of contributing to one's society. Indeed, no self can be realized if even conceived, in isolation from society. We did resist the tendency of some self-realizationists so to emphasize the social dimensions of the self as to lose track of the individual in the social whole. Yet there is no denying that vocation is a meaningless concept apart from social structure and that an adequate social structure is impossible without the mutual complementation of vocations.

G. *Individuals in Community*

Our discussion of Individuality and Altruism, in Chapters 26 and 27, never lost sight of the interdependence of individuals in society. The individual, to be sure, is the moral unit, the realizer of values, the one who feels obligation and responds in action. But once more, he is all of these only in community.

Actually we must keep in mind always that any individual is a member of a number of communities or societies or groups, some voluntary and some not. Some of these communities are what they are because people live in the same locations, others because people have common needs; frequently, and in the most closely knit communities, they have common goals. There may be combinations of all three factors or of any two. But regardless of the base of the community or the degree of unity in the community, the value of any member to the community is directly related to what he contributes to that communal base through the values he realizes, or can realize, in his own life. Thus the imperative holds for each individual: realize the maximum values of which one is capable.

At the same time, the maximum values of which any individual is capable depend upon community—on the realization of shared values. Thus the imperative holds: treat others as moral units and cooperate with them in the production and enjoyment of values. To this extent —and the extent approaches all-inclusiveness—"individual" and "community" are reciprocal terms.

The Principle of Individuality articulated the crucial importance of self-respect. And the kind of self-respect engendered in the Principle of Individuality re-enforces and, in fact, is an extension of the acceptance of responsibility demanded by the Principle of Autonomy. It is the Principle of Altruism, however, that brings us to the realization that neither self-respect nor responsibility is significant apart from community. Can we really conceive of self-respect or responsibility (except in most unsual and temporary circumstances) as significant apart from communal respect and responsibility? However, because society in the abstract realizes no values and feels no obligation, it follows that a society, be it as small as a family or as large as a nation, is only as responsible as its constituent members are and can only recognize communal obligation to the extent that its constituent members do.

We are aware that in particular societies those who recognize group responsibility or communal obligation may be limited to a very few. In some cases a group may be forced together by external constraints. Or it may be controlled by socially irresponsible individuals interested only in self-aggrandizement. It is even possible for groups to form irresponsibly, or for irresponsible ends, as is exemplified by a lynching mob or a street gang. Not only for the members of such groups but for the larger societies in which they appear, the immediate results are disaster or at least serious curtailment of value.

Groups or societies in which only a limited number of persons recognize group responsibility and communal obligations are more frequent and more complex. Undoubtedly, in most groups or societies the degree of recognition of responsibility will range from the disaffected and the neutral to the highly dedicated. In some instances, one highly dedicated person (regardless of the reason for his dedication) may keep an otherwise moribund group from dying. But when such groups lose the dedicated person they either dissolve or become prey to other groups.

Again, other things being equal, the effectiveness and the sense of responsibility of a group does seem to be proportional to the acceptance of responsibility and communal obligation by the constituent members. It is not accidental that, when voter apathy is high, political corruption tends to flourish. Both the apathetic voters and the community as a whole lose. The sad fact is that the apathetic citizen too easily becomes the prey to an unscrupulous leader who perverts the society for his own ends and involves the apathetic citizen too deeply for withdrawal. Those who tolerated Hitler or Mussolini out of apathy, or in protest against apathy, found themselves enmeshed in fascism.

H. *Groups in Communities*

All of us are involved in many groups and in societies within a society, and this multiplicity complicates social interaction and responsibility. Within the various groups to which we belong, we are asked to fill various roles that we frequently have difficulty harmonizing. We do not, and perhaps should not, feel equal responsibility in all roles and to each group. Almost every mail brings invitations to join or support additional groups. The calls made upon us, and often the groups to which we belong, have partially or, in some instances, largely conflicting goals. The company one works for, the school he attends, his neighborhood group, his church, his political party, his country club, the Friends of the Library, his fraternity, his professional society, the alumni organization, his family, his country, and an indefinite number of other groups have goals that are not always mutually supporting.

Nevertheless, unless he is what might be described as a pathological joiner, one feels at least some obligation or responsibility to each of the groups to which he belongs. There is clearly a point beyond which joining itself is irresponsible, that is, when it is no longer possible to participate responsibly in given groups or societies. Up to that point, the problem of complementary responsibilities for any individual needs to be solved in the light of the Principle of the Most Inclusive End and of a life plan that keeps affiliative values central.

III. *THE RESPONSIBLE SOCIETY*

By different paths, then, we are brought to the concept of a responsible society in the larger sense that includes smaller groups, the society frequently referred to as the body politic. The cumulative effect of the moral principles, coming to a focus in the Principles of Individuality and Altruism, calls for a general conception of the responsible society considered as a goal or norm. In minimal terms, such a society is described by the conception of positive justice developed in the last chapter, that is, a society characterized by the responsible concern on the part of cooperating, mutually respecting, autonomous individuals for the welfare of the inclusive community.

At this point we could readily agree with the definition of a responsible society developed by the World Council of Churches in its Amsterdam Assembly of 1948 (if slightly modified to delete its theological implications).

> A responsible society is one where freedom is the freedom of men who acknowledge responsibility to justice and public order, and where those who hold political authority or economic power are responsible for its exercise to . . . the people whose welfare is affected by it.[2]

The responsible society so conceived is a structure approaching the Kantian self-legislative kingdom of ends. *First,* it encourages the respect of persons for each other as ends in themselves—the mutual respect of cooperating and competing persons. *Second,* it includes the freedom of morally autonomous individuals to make up their minds for themselves within the framework of social responsibility. Such freedom allows the right to disagree, to criticize, and to work toward change in society and government and toward adequate protection of these rights. *Third,* it includes faith and reliance upon rational persuasion, as opposed to brute force in influencing social and political change, both internally within a society and externally between societies. *Fourth,* it embraces the recognition of the importance not

[2] From the Amsterdam Assembly, *The Church and the Disorder of Society* (1948), p. 192, as quoted in Walter G. Muelder, *Foundations of the Responsible Society* (New York: Abingdon Press, 1959), p. 19. See Muelder's book itself for an excellent discussion of various aspects and implications of the concept of the responsible society in its religious, theological, and ethical context.

only of corrective and distributive justice but also of positive justice in economic and political terms—a justice based upon a developing conception of human welfare and of the right of every human being to the conditions commensurate with minimal security and self-respect. *Fifth,* in the light of individual differences in abilities, needs and interests, and the diversity of such legitimate and structurable interests, it is an open, pluralistic society that encourages diversification of voluntary groups and subsocieties. From the continuous interplay of such groups healthy criticism, change, and development can emerge. *Sixth* it is committed to government by law—law subject to revision and amendment, but law rather than whim, caprice, favoritism, force or fad—law impartially administered and representatively developed. *Seventh,* and finally, a responsible society is one in which the importance of education and its diversification, again in the light of individual differences, is fully recognized and made available to all its citizens.

IV. *EVOLUTION OF ALTERNATE CONCEPTIONS OF SOCIETY*

In Chapter 27 we suggested that the concept of the significance of the individual has emerged only after a long and difficult social evolution. Individuality has not always been a high intrinsic value and the key to effective morality, nor is it always recognized as such even today. People must be educated to the idea of a responsible society as a kingdom of ends—a society characterized by the responsible concern for the welfare of the inclusive community by cooperating, mutually respecting, free individuals. Such social education is all the more imperative because the alternate historical conceptions of society remain still very much alive today and offer a serious challenge.

A. *Social Organicisms*

Perhaps the oldest functioning conception of both the structure and the goal of society might be described as the organic conception. Society is likened to a biological organism in which individuals might be compared to cells in the total organism. Cells have no separate existence; their function is to contribute to the health of the organism as a whole. Although there can be no organism without cells, yet the characteristics of the cells are determined by the structure of the organism. The organism is always more than the sum of its cells and any particular cell or group of cells is expendable. It is the survival of the organism and the attainment of its potentialities that are important, and the cells are incidental to this total organic function. Any cell or group of cells that does not conform to the structure of the organism must be cut off for the sake of the health of the whole.

1. *Primitive Organicisms*

While the analogy between society and a biological organism is complex and modern, the practice of social organicism is as ancient as men. To a very large extent, marginal and so-called primitive societies are and have been highly organic in character and for a very basic, though unformulated reason, namely, survival. The conception of the noble, independent, presocietal savage so popular in the eighteenth century comes quite close to being sheer mythology. Primitive societies tended to require an almost absolute allegiance to the group, for only the group was able to cope with a threatening environment. Food, shelter, protection against the elements, natural enemies, supernatural enemies, and all forms of danger caused the highest priority to be given to group security. The rebel could not be tolerated. Membership in the group was not to be taken lightly and most social practices and beliefs were modes of re-enforcing group identification.

In totemic tribal societies, for example, the totem, usually an animal or plant, sometimes was little more than a name linkage to identify members of a particular group. But far more frequently, the totem meant a great deal more—it was that to which the tribe traced its ancestry, the continuing source of the tribe's existence, the symbol or embodiment of its unity and organization, its strength and vitality, and its link to a continuing place in nature. A threat to the totem was a threat to the tribe itself. In service of the totemic conception elaborate rites and rules frequently developed—initiations, taboos, ceremonial cleansings, totemic meals, strict control of marriage groups.[3]

[3] See Robert H. Lowie, *An Introduction to Cultural Anthropology*, rev. ed. (New York: Farrar and Rinehart, Inc. 1934, 1940), p. 257 f. copyright 1934 by Robert H. Lowie, copyright 1962 by Luella Cole Lowie; and Melville J. Herskovits, *Cultural Anthropology* (New York: Alfred A. Knopf, 1955), p. 175 f.

The carry-over of some of these totemic rites in modern society is testimony to their effectiveness as means of reenforcing group cohesion.

2. Modern Organicisms—Totalitarianism

We have already encountered one form of modern organicism in Bradley's conception of a man's station and its duties. In its more aggressive manifestations on the political level, modern organicism has culminated in the conception of the totalitarian state. The more extreme defenders of the totalitarian state assert that the state has complete control over all aspects of the lives of its subjects: economic, moral, cultural, religious, and even marital. The state has a being and personality of its own; its subjects have their existence only in and through the state. Koya Nakamura, writing a history of Japan in 1939, describes the pre-World War II Japanese nation as follows:

> The relation between the Imperial House and the people today may therefore be likened to those between the trunk and the branches of a gigantic tree, for if we were to trace the genealogy of each Japanese subject, we would find that he belongs to a family which centuries ago was either a direct or indirect off-shoot of the Imperial Family. . . . In other words, the Imperial Family and the people having a common ancestor in Amaterasu Omikami, our sovereign and his subjects are completely united like one man to form the Japanese nation and state.[4]

The state and the state alone is the final moral arbiter—the source of morality, but itself above any moral commitment or demand. Alfredo Rocco, writing in support of Italian Fascism says:

> For Fascism, *society is the end, the individuals are the means, and its whole life consists in using individuals for its social ends.* Individual rights are recognized only in so far as they are implied in the rights of the State. In this preeminence of duty we find the highest ethical value of Fascism. Individuals come into being, grow, and die, followed by others unceasingly; social unity remains always identical to itself.[5]

[4] Quoted in Robert O. Ballou, *Shinto, The Unconquered Enemy* (New York: The Viking Press, 1945), pp. 188–89. Reprinted by permission.

[5] Quoted in Joseph A. Leighton, *Social Philosophies in Conflict* (New York: D Appleton-Century Company, 1937), p. 15, from Alfredo Rocco, *The Political Doctrine of Fascism*, International Conciliation Pamphlets, No. 223.

Mussolini in *The Doctrine of Fascism* described the fascist organic state in the following way:

> The State, as conceived and realized by Fascism, is a spiritual and ethical entity for securing the political, juridical, and economic organisation of the nation, an organisation which in its origin and growth is a manifestation of the spirit. . . . Transcending the individual's brief spell of life, the State stands for the immanent conscience of the nation. . . . The Fascist State, as a higher and more powerful expression of personality, is a force, but a spiritual one. It sums up all the manifestations of the moral life of man. . . . The Fascist conception of the State is all-embracing; outside of it no human or spiritual values can exist, much less have value. Thus understood, Fascism is totalitarian, and the Fascist state—a synthesis and unit of all values—interprets, develops, and potentiates the whole life of a people.[6]

While Hitler was nowhere near as able a theoretician as his Italian counterpart and constantly tended to confuse his anti-Semitism with his organicism, he too was a thoroughgoing organicist.

> The intimate coupling of nationalism and feeling of social justice must be planted in the young heart. Then there will some day arise a people of State citizens, bound to one another and forged together by a common love and a common pride, unshakeable and invincible for all times.[7]

Leighton very nicely summarizes the general organic mystique of the Nazi apologists as follows:

> The Nazi apologists stress the Germanic Nature or Essence (*Deutsche Wesen*), Germanness (*Deutschheit*), the unity of Germanic souls (*Einheit deutscher Seelen*), the German people—totality of the German people (*deutsche Volkstum*). . . . Soul of the Race (*Rassenseele*). Folkness (*Volkheit*)—is defined as the unity of the comradeship of the people in a spiritual Reality.[8]

Lest one be tempted to think that such extreme organicism and its advocates died with World War II, the following statement circulated in 1962 in a throw-away leaflet of the American Nazi Party

[6] In Leighton, *op. cit.*, pp. 16–18.
[7] *Mein Kampf* (New York: Reynal & Hitchcock, 1940), p. 636.
[8] *Op. cit.* p. 37.

under the signature of Lincoln Rockwell, Commander, World Union of Free Enterprise National Socialists, Arlington, Virginia:

> *WE BELIEVE that society can function successfully and there-fore happily, only as an ORGANISM:* That all parts benefit when each part performs that function for which it is best suited to produce a unified, a single-purposed WHOLE, which is then capable of out-performing any single part, the whole thus vastly increasing the powers of all cooperating parts, and the parts, therefore subordinating a part of their freedom to the whole; that the whole perishes and all parts therefore suffer whenever one part fails to perform its own function, usurps the function or interferes with the function of another part, or like a cancer, devours all the nourishment and grows wildly and selfishly out of proportion to its task—which latter is exactly the effect on society of the parasitic Jews and their Marxism.

It should be pointed out that modern organicism may not in its inception take on strictly nationalistic lines. It may be race organi-cism—the Aryans—or class organicism—the Proletariat in the interim phase. However, whether it begins as nationalistic or not, the organic group becomes what might be characterized as a nation or state sur-rogate and, in its ascendency, assumes the role of total society includ-ing State functions.

3. *Critique of Organicisms*

If one looks at organicism historically, the reasons for its persist-ence, and its persuasiveness, at least in its less extreme forms, are not hard to see. Organicism does clearly recognize the embeddedness of every individual in society. It does underline the strength possible through social unity. It fully recognizes (in fact, it plays upon) the human need for belonging, for identification with the group, and upon the sense of security (whether security in fact is present or not) that such identification may bring. Just as primitive organicisms were modes of protection against a hostile environment, so modern or-ganicisms tend to flourish in periods of unrest, threat (real or imag-ined) from without, paralysis of political commitment and action within a society, or breakdown of individual and social morale. Organicism is usually advocated as a radical solution to radical ills.

The question remains whether modern organicism as a solution to social ills does not in fact destroy the patient. Our whole discussion of moral principles thus far would seem to refute the organic conception. For the autonomous individual is swallowed up in the social whole. He becomes an automaton, a means rather than an end in himself—a means to the deification of an abstraction. Far too frequently the individual, instead of being integrated into society, feeling that he belongs, and gaining security and strength in the whole, is in fact relieved of his responsibility, terrorized, crushed, and left far more insecure than he was before. Instead of responsible individuals in a responsible society, organicism results from and then encourages individual and national loss of responsibility.

B. *Social Atomism*

The opposite extreme of organicism and, to a certain extent, a reaction against it, as history shows, is what might be called the atomic conception of society or *social atomism*. The social atomist stresses the revolt of the individual against the group. He thinks of society not as a biological organism but as a name for the collection of individuals.

The model for social atomism is suggested by the hard, independent atoms of classical physics. Society is no more than the particular arrangement of atoms in relation to each other at any particular time. While such atomism, in its more extreme forms, is not as pressing an alternative today as the various forms of organicism, it is the conception of society that underlay the classical liberalism of Bentham, the classical capitalism of Adam Smith and the Manchester school, and the anarchism of Godwin, Proudhon, and Bakunin. In a rather fascinating way, what was the liberalism of the nineteenth century has tended to become the conservatism of today, so that the present advocates of a moderate social atomism tend to be those who object in principle to the further extension of the federal government in matters of education, welfare, and economic control.

1. *Emergence of Individualism*

The development of social atomism depended upon the emergence of the individual out of the social whole. It is not correct to say that there was no recognition of individuality in primitive societies or in more recent organic societies. But it would not be too far amiss to suggest that the folk heroes, legendary figures, and even historical persons who stood out as individuals did so primarily as symbols of the group and its virtues. Abraham, Samson, Hercules, Ulysses, Jason are significant instances. However, the very process of hero formation also helped to focus attention on the individual and his function in relation to the group. When the hero revolted against the group—as Prometheus did against the gods—significant individuality was born.

As the ancient world became more sophisticated philosophically and religiously, the individual as a self-conscious moral unit stood out in ever bolder relief. The revolt of the Old Testament prophets against the institutionalism of the priests was an important step. In Greece the sophist movement, having begun with an attack on the possibility of universal truth, ended with man taking his own measure with his devaluated reason. Protagoras, the sophistic relativist, stated: "Man is the measure." Relativism, interestingly enough, contributed to man-centeredness. The Socratic insistence on self-knowledge as the precondition of all knowledge carried the argument beyond relativism. Both the New Testament and the Stoic insistence on the brotherhood of man and the fatherhood of God further highlighted the importance of the individual. Democritus, meanwhile, had developed the concept of physical atomism. The Stoics, insofar as they emphasized the capacity of man within his inner fortress of the self to remain unaffected by what happened outside the self, came close to developing moral atomism.

The factors giving rise to the rebirth and development of individualism in the modern world are far too many to enumerate here. Only a few major ones can be mentioned. The Renaissance humanists in rediscovering antiquity rediscovered the individual man. The Reformation emphasized the individual's direct relation to God. The breakdown of feudalism, the industrial revolution, the emergence of scientific inquiry, the rise of a middle class, the rise of laissez-faire capitalism, all contributed to individualism. By the time of the American Revolution, "natural and inalienable rights" were considered by the founding fathers to characterize each individual as an individual and to set the limits beyond which government could not rightfully go.

It became clear in our discussion of the relation between the responsible society and the Principles of Individuality and Altruism that individualism does not necessarily imply social atomism. Nevertheless, from the recognition of the importance of the individual it is not far to the conclusion—albeit hasty—that individuals alone exist, that society is but a name for the sum of individuals at any particular time and place. And it must be admitted that, apart from a developed conception of individuals, social atomism would not be conceivable. But as we might expect, about as many different forms of social atomism have developed as there are conceptions of the nature of the social atoms. These various forms might lead to radically different conclusions. A few examples will serve as illustration.

2. *Thomas Hobbes—Egoistic Atomism*

For Thomas Hobbes the human atoms are exactly analogous to classical physical atoms, that is, they are independent bodies in constant motion in space. In the "state of nature," such human atoms are amoral, insatiably self-assertive, but not invulnerable to the attack of other men. Because each man wants all he can get, all men are natural enemies to each other, are in a constant state of warfare: "Such a warre," Hobbes says, "as is of every man, against every man." [9] Man is thus without security, in constant danger of attack, incapable of preserving his gains: "And the life of man, solitary, poore, nasty, brutish, and short." [10] The only solution, according to Hobbes, is formation of an all but irrevocable social contract setting up an absolute sovereign to force men into society and protect them against each other. In a most fascinating way and starting from assumptions diametrically opposite those of the organicists, Hobbes concludes with a totalitarian state as monolithic as that of the most extreme organicists. Hobbes considered such a move the only means of holding the warring atoms together. The warring atoms can be held together by a force men consent to apply from outside.

3. *William Godwin—Ethical Anarchism*

Within atomism, the opposite extreme in conception of the nature of men as social atoms is represented by the ethical anarchists. William Godwin, writing at the end of the eighteenth century, serves as an example.[11] Men are basically good and are capable of indefinite improvement. Godwin believed that men are corrupted by social institutions. Any form of compulsion interferes with man's goodness and growth and results, not in improvement, but in slavery and misery. However, if left alone, if freed from institutional controls,

---

[9] *Leviathan* (Everyman's Library; London: J. M. Dent & Sons, Ltd., 1914), p. 64.
[10] *Ibid.*, p. 65.
[11] *Enquiry Concerning Political Justice and Its Influence on General Virtue and Happiness* (New York: Alfred A. Knopf, 1926), written in 1793.

legal or customary, human goodness would reassert itself and all men, rid of inhibitions, could live together enjoying the common welfare. Thus, to reform men, we must do away with government, taxation, penal systems, marriage, and organized religion.

4. Bentham—Hedonic Atomism

Most atomists have fallen somewhere between Hobbes and Godwin in their conception of men and prescription for social welfare. Jeremy Bentham, for example, considered men "under the governance of two sovereign masters, *pain* and *pleasure*." [12] Further, as we have already pointed out (Chapter 22), for Bentham pleasure is to be measured quantitatively and the good determined by addition. As pleasures are additive, so are the people who experience pleasure. Thus, society is additive in character. "The community is a fictitious *body,* composed of the individual persons who are considered as constituting as it were its *members.* The interest of the community then, is what?—the sum of the interests of the several members who compose it." [13] Thus the good, legislative advantage, economic advantage, public policy, all are to be determined by counting each person as one and balancing the sum of pleasure and the sum of pain. Social control is reinforced by pleasure-pain sanctions. Bentham thus argues:

> A measure of government (which is but a particular kind of action, performed by a particular person or persons) may be said to be conformable to or dictated by the principle of utility, when in like manner the tendency which it has to augment the happiness of the community is greater than any which it has to diminish it.[14]

5. Adam Smith—Classical Capitalism

When translated into economic terms, atomistic liberalism has had perhaps its most profound and continuing effect upon all of us. Adam Smith, falling historically between Hobbes and Bentham, argued that the economic welfare of a country depends upon the competitive self-interest of its citizens.

[12] *An Introduction to the Principles of Morals and Legislation* (new ed.; Oxford, 1823), in Oliver A. Johnson, *Ethics: A Source Book* (New York: The Dryden Press, 1958), p. 202.
[13] *Ibid.,* p. 204.
[14] *Ibid.*

It is not from benevolence of the butcher, the brewer, or the baker that we expect our dinner, but from their regard of their own interest. We address ourselves not to their humanity, but to their self-love, and never to talk to them of our own necessities, but of their advantage.[15]

It is our competitive self-interest, translated in terms of utility in the satisfaction of our wants, that is the root of economic process and progress. With his French predecessors, Smith agreed, furthermore, that, given the division of labor and the market mechanism, the key to national as well as individual wealth was what he described as natural liberty or noninterference with the competitive interaction of economic atoms.

All systems, either of preference or restraint, therefore, being thus completely taken away, the obvious and simple system of natural liberty establishes itself of its own accord. Every man, as soon as he does not violate the law of justice, is left perfectly free to pursue his own interests in his own way, and to bring both his industry and his capital into competition with those of any other man or order of men.[16]

Through such individual competition and search for private advantage, society as a whole benefits.

Every individual is continually exerting himself to find out the most advantageous employment for whatever capital he can command. It is his own advantage, indeed, and not that of society, which he has in view. But the study of his own advantage naturally, or rather, necessarily, leads him to prefer that employment which is most advantageous to the society.[17]

Adam Smith represents what might be described as the classical capitalistic position both in Europe and America. Such a position rather nicely coalesces with a position of states rights, local autonomy, and nongovernmental interference in general.

Basically, on such a view, government has three functions. First, government is a policing agency designed to protect life and property individually in times of peace and collectively in times of war. Sec-

---

[15] *The Wealth of Nations*, Intro. by E. R. A. Selzer (Everyman's Library; London: J. M. Dent & Sons, Ltd., 1947), I, ix, written in 1776.
[16] *Ibid.*, I, XI, ii.
[17] *Ibid.*, V, p. 398.

ond, government serves as an arbitrator, a supposedly impartial referee in disputes between individuals and corporations. According to Herbert Hoover, this is *the* important function of government:

> Looked at as the umpire in our social system, our Government has maintained an equality before the law and a development of legal justice and an authority in restraint of evil instincts that support this social system and its ideals so far as the imperfections of developing human institutions permit.[18]

Third, government operates or manages certain services considered in the public domain, including post office, highways, public health, and public schools. It must be pointed out, however, that each of these services has been admitted as part of the public domain only over serious opposition from those who accused the government of encroaching on private affairs. Other things being equal, the defenders of the classical capitalist view argue: that government is best which governs least.

It must be admitted that an unrestricted capitalism or economic atomism of the Smith variety has never been fully in operation. What we call capitalism today in this country is very much modified. Our concern at this point is not with a critique of capitalism as an economic system but with atomism as a conception of society. However, at least a word or two needs to be said about the relation of classical capitalistic theory to practice in the light of its atomistic assumptions. First, the Smith position seems far too optimistic about the coincidence of private and public advantages. There seems to be no necessary coincidence between short-term private advantage and long-term public advantages. The history of abuse of natural resources in this country prior to governmental control all too sadly illustrates the point. Even Hoover recognizes the importance of "an authority in restraint of evil instinct that support[s] this social system."

Second, and following from the first, the one thing that Smith overlooks—perhaps most strikingly—is the tendency of unlimited and uncontrolled competition to destroy itself. Because money makes money, those who have money are always at a comparative advantage, and without internal checks the system leads inevitably to concentration of wealth in a progressively more restricted group of individuals.

---

[18] *American Individualism* (New York: Doubleday, Doran & Co., Inc., 1922), pp. 50–51.

The final success for any competitor is elimination of competition or achievement of monopoly. To work at all, the system has to be modified to keep that competition alive by inheritance taxes, antitrust laws, and similar devices.

Third, because humanitarian concerns are no part of the system as such, the system itself tends to encourage persons to treat other persons as means to profit, not as ends, and thus also tends to the sacrifice of all other freedoms for the sake of economic freedom for a very few.

6. Critique of Atomism

To return to social atomism in general, as a reaction against organicism it has performed some extremely important functions. First, from the seventeenth century on, it has served as a protest and a focus of revolt against tyranny and authoritarianism. The convergence of political, economic, and scientific atomism (which are somewhat uneasy bedfellows) has given to the various social atomisms sufficient dimensions to attack organicism on every level. Second, the development of social atomism, in spite of its more egoistic and deterministic forms, has in fact tended to put a premium upon individuality and personality and has thus raised individuality to a sociopolitical category. The various atomisms have put forward individuals as the units of society and thus have been effective counteragents against the social, class, or group-mind myths. Third, by freeing individuals from absorption into the social whole, the various atomisms have tended to encourage uniqueness, initiative, a sense of individual importance and, Hobbes and Smith to the contrary, a sense of individual responsibility for social conditions. Fourth, perhaps one of the most important contributions of atomism has been to develop freedom into something far more than a psychological and ethical question, that is, into an accepted social, economic, and political goal.

Social atomism, however, seems to be as much an exaggeration of the human situation as we found organicism to be. First, whereas organicism tended to dissolve or lose sight of the parts in the social whole, atomism tends to overlook the fact that wholes do have characteristics that the parts separately do not have. It is one thing to say that society is a meaningless abstraction apart from the individuals who make it up. It is a very different thing to say that society is simply a term for the individuals additively.

We have had to recognize again and again that the individual in isolation from his social context is as much an abstraction as society would be apart from individuals. While the individual is the moral and social unit, his characteristics as an individual are derived to a very large extent from the groups out of which he emerges—his family, his peer groups, his vocational group, his national and cultural groups.

Furthermore, there can be little question that these groups, while made up of individuals, do as groups have characteristics that the individuals taken separately do not have—the productive capacity of a factory, the harmonic blending of an orchestra, the thoroughness of a research team. This does not mean that the groups become extra-personal entities, but it does mean that the relation of persons in groups is *more than* additive.

Second, because he fails to recognize the unique characteristics of groups, the atomist also seriously underestimates the dependence of individuals on the group. Frequently, we are not aware of the degree to which we depend upon societal relations until these are challenged or disrupted. Quite apart from the societal basis of life and language, complex societal diversification has so increased dependence of individuals on societies as to make the average city dweller rather helpless if any part of the vast supporting systems in the modern city breaks down—transportation, water, electricity, food, clothing, shelter, credit, and education. Quite literally, a rugged individualist and a self-made man are contradictions in terms.

Third, social atomism does tend to encourage social irresponsibility by its very failure to recognize complex interdependence. Today the continuing appeal of atomism tends to be unrealistic nostalgia or blind reaction to frustration. We cannot go back with Thoreau to Walden Pond or proceed with Godwin to a governmentless paradise. To assume we can do either is to deceive ourselves. We cannot retreat into isolation for our country or for our hemisphere. Our protective walls as individuals, communities, or countries no longer exist. We are part of a world community so close that any one of us can talk to a man in Australia or Moscow as though he were sitting in a chair nearby. Armageddon is as close as a flock of geese passing in front of a radar screen in Labrador or the overly itchy finger of a minor official in a control center in Washington or Moscow. What happens in Brazzaville tonight may tomorrow change all our plans about what we will be doing next summer. Although we may still be strangers, none of us can ever be alone.

C. *Organic Pluralism*

Fortunately there is a middle ground between atomism and organicism. We earlier suggested the outlines of the third alternative in developing the conception of a responsible society. In contrast to organicism and atomism we might describe the third alternative as organic pluralism. Organic pluralism attempts to go beyond organicism on the one hand and beyond atomism on the other without denying the important emphases in each.

Thus, basically, it embodies a principle of cooperation, in contrast to the compulsion of organicism and the competition of atomism. It presupposes both voluntary and involuntary cooperation of individuals with each other, which is implicit in atomism, and voluntary and involuntary cooperation of groups with each other and individuals, which is implicit in organicism. With organicism, it recognizes the overwhelming social interdependence of individuals in the contemporary world that makes social egoism and rugged individualism anachronisms. At the same time, with atomism, it recognizes that the goal of social process is the realization of the potentialities of autonomous individuals in social interaction.

With these facts in mind, we can define *organic pluralism as that conception of society and social process directed toward the organization of society with optimum freedom for individuals in their relation to each other and with such unity as is required by group existence and by social intelligence in choosing means toward social ends.* The organic pluralist would not hold with the organicist that the state is the all-inclusive group, nor would he agree with the atomist that the state is only a name for the larger additive social units. Rather, the organic pluralist recognizes that the state is perhaps the most important and, at present, most inclusive form of social organization; yet the state is still one among many forms of social organization with obligations through its members to other and reciprocating groups. Within this concept of mixed voluntary and involuntary group cooperation and competition, there is room for a wide variety of differences of opinion regarding both means and ends; there is also a fundamental agreement, as opposed both to totalitarianism and atomism, about the value of a wide variety of cooperating and competing groups, each one contributing to the wide variety of human values and accomplishments.

In a significant way, the federal system in the United States represents an experiment exemplifying organic pluralism. The central federal government is concerned, on the one hand, with the common welfare of all states and localities in the country, including their common external relations to other countries; it is concerned, on the other hand, with the internal welfare of the states and communities in relation to each other. The federal government has specific obligations to the states and the states to the federal government. But each state in turn has its primary area of internal responsibility; each contributes, through the effective development of its own welfare, to the national welfare. The particular form of political organization within the separate states is determined (within limits) by the particular states. While such self-determination does lead to some conflict, confusion, and even to some inequalities in comparable regulations in different states, it also helps to preserve the uniqueness of character and contribution of each state in the national picture.

When to this complexity of governmental units is added the vast variety of other kinds of groups that cut across governmental divisions —religious groups, political parties, educational groups, industrial and business complexes, professional organizations, all with some degree of autonomy, the spectrum seems chaotic. Yet the very variety opens up the opportunity for development of the complex interests and values of human beings in society itself. The one norm that the organic pluralist would urge is that each group in the complex of societies making up society accept the challenge of becoming a dependable society, first, in relation to its own goals and the means of attaining them and, second, in its interaction with all other groups and societies.

We might also suggest that the organic pluralistic conception underlies the possibility of an effective United Nations or family of nations. A strong United Nations does not necessarily involve the loss of the individual function and character of its constituent nations. It would do so only if its basic conception were organic and its goal a totalitarian state of all mankind. To date, however, as a result of the weakness of the coordinating society itself, the United Nations has, if anything, tended too much in the direction of atomism —the juxtaposition of completely independent national units. In conception, the United Nations involves the complementation and cooperation of states in promoting human welfare. There is nothing contradictory in the idea of a responsible society of nations—each with its own internal political and cultural forms, according to the unique situation of that nation, its stage of development, historical background, and cultural goals—united for the purpose of promoting common welfare, peace, cooperation, and the very uniqueness of each of its constituent members. In fact, at this stage in world development, apart from such a responsible organic pluralism, we all stand in constant jeopardy of mutual destruction. Such an effective United Nations is no longer an idealistic dream but a hard necessity and an essential norm if we are to survive.

V. DEMOCRACY

We are left with the question of the relation of the responsible society and organic pluralism to democracy. Is democracy itself a distinct sociopolitical norm along with the responsible society and organic pluralism? Is democracy the organic pluralistic responsible society in action? Or is it not a norm at all but only a euphemistic, emotionally charged term without content? Or only a term denoting a somewhat rare historical political form?

The answer to these questions depends upon how one defines democracy. We have already had occasion to point out that the term "democracy" has been claimed as applying to his own system by everyone from Mussolini to Stalin (Chapter 20, Sec. C). Surely the "democracy" of Mussolini, Stalin, Jefferson, Eisenhower, and Kennedy can hardly be identical, and one is almost left with the suspicion that the term has become merely honorific. Yet the question remains, why should the term have such emotional appeal?

If we think of "democracy" primarily as a term denoting a form of political organization and then insist that only what might be called a "pure" democracy is in fact a democracy, we would have to define democracy as James Madison does in *The Federalist* (No. X): "a society consisting of a small number of citizens, who assemble and administer the government in person." [19] We would then also need to point out that such governments have not been numerous and that what we have in the United States is not democracy but republicanism. From Plato through Madison, "pure democracy" has been criticized as being unduly subject to demagoguery, factionalism, and

---

[19] Albert R. Chandler, *Clash of Political Ideals* (3rd ed.; New York: Appleton-Century-Crofts, Inc. 1957), p. 68.

arbitrary disregard of the rights of minorities. Plato, of course, presented the trial of Socrates as a vivid case in point.

Such a restrictive definition of democracy even as a political form seems, however, to be highly arbitrary. If we broaden the definition to the generic type of which "pure" democracy would be one species, then many of the objections lose their power. We can then use James Bryce's recent but classic definition and say that a democracy "is that form of government in which the ruling power of the state is legally vested not in any particular class or classes, but in the members of the community as a whole." [20] Aristotle called such a government a constitutional polity and described it as follows: "But when the citizens at large administer the state for the common interest, the government is called by the generic term—constitution." [21] Democracy in this sense would include Madison's republic—"the delegation of government . . . to a small number of citizens elected by the rest." [22] Regardless of the species, probably Lincoln's description in the Gettysburg Address of a government "of the people, for the people, and by the people" comes as close to defining the essential tenets of political democracy as it is possible to come.

Considered only as a political form, democracy no doubt has its serious dangers. It can in fact become the mobocracy that Plato hated. There is danger of the tyranny of the majority over the minority that Rousseau among others feared. There is the danger of reducing everyone to the lowest common denominator, particularly if democracy is too closely linked with social atomism.

But even on a political level democracy has shown itself able to develop correctives for its weaknesses and excesses. Effective democracy as a political form does require, among other things, recognition of the supremacy of law for the very protection of the political form itself. Aristotle, in harmony with the Socrates of the *Crito*, insists that a constitutional polity requires that law be supreme, and this is the safeguard against mobocracy or democracy in Plato's sense:

> He who bids the law rule, may be deemed to bid God and Reason alone rule, but he who bids man rule adds an element of the beast; for desire is a wild beast, and passion perverts the minds of rulers, even when they are the best of man. The law is reason unaffected by desire.[23]

[20] *Modern Democracy* (New York: The Macmillan Co., 1921), I, 20.
[21] *Politics*, 1279 a 39.
[22] In Chandler, *op. cit.*, p. 69.
[23] *Politics*, 1287a 34.

Somewhat ironically, the very effectiveness of the law as a protector of individuals and their rights within a democracy lies in formulating the law in as impersonal and thus impartial a manner as possible.

Democracy, however, would seem to be more than just a political form. Indeed, its effectiveness as a political form rests upon more than purely political bases. What these are we have already discussed. First, the citizens must be capable of judgment and acceptance of responsibility; that is, they must have moral autonomy. Second, they must be capable of some degree of objectivity—subject to rational persuasion in the light of evidence. Third, they must have a sufficient degree of maturity not to rush to arms over any disagreement—to respect each other enough to reach reasonable compromises. Fourth, they must have enough faith in each other to delegate responsibility to their elected officials. Thus it becomes evident that in describing democracy we are talking, in fact, about the responsible society and organic pluralism in action—as applied to the body politic as a whole.

Accordingly, democracy in the fullest sense is not only a political form, but also an ethical and social ideal. And its effectiveness as a political form is directly proportional to the degree to which the ethical and social ideal is approximated. Democracy cannot be fully actualized where there are second-class citizens, or where respect of the individuals, for themselves and for each other as individuals and members of diverse cooperating and competing groups, does not exist. Nor can democracy be actualized where any considerable body of citizens refuses to accept responsibility and concern for the common welfare.

VI. *THE ARISTOCRATIC IDEAL*

Two major types of criticism of democracy call for special note. One of these is the aristocratic criticism, and the other is the Communist or Marxist criticism. The aristocratic ideal, shared by thinkers as different as Plato, Nietzsche, and Santayana, involves the rejection of what might be described as the tyranny of mediocrity. The aristocratic ideal is excellence. Excellence in government cannot be encouraged by reducing everyone to a common level. The aristocrat contends that society should be so organized as to develop superior individuals, who are, as Plato insists, by nature the fewest. According to Melvin Rader, the aristocrat "contends that democracy involves sharing without excellence. Its effect, he declares, is to popularize and thus vulgarize. In its lust for equality, it levels all distinctions and exults in the average." [24]

The aristocrat would have little use for "the watering down" of culture through mass media, for choosing political candidates on the basis of their popular appeal, or for giving equal weight at the ballot box to the town illiterates and the college professors. George Santayana has stated strikingly the seeming impossibility of joining democracy and excellence together as follows:

> Culture is on the horns of this dilemma: if profound and noble it must remain rare, if common it must become mean. These alternatives can never be eluded until some purified and high-bred race succeeds the promiscuous bipeds that now blacken the planet.[25]

It would be folly to deny the relevance of excellence as a social ideal, just as it would be folly to deny individual differences. We have already pointed out that equality under justice and equality as a democratic ideal can hardly mean literally equal distribution of goods and services any more than it can mean equality of ability. Democratic equality, then, cannot mean what simply is not true: that everyone is equal in every respect. Nor does it mean reduction of everyone and everything to the lowest common denominator. Rather it does mean impartiality before the law. Democracy as the ideal of a responsible society means equal opportunity for every grade of ability to express and realize itself. A conception of equality that acknowledges the right of every man to an adequate opportunity to actualize his potential is not in conflict with the ideal of excellence. Indeed, it encourages every man to achieve and to take satisfaction in his form of excellence. In a word, excellence, if defined as efficiency only, is hardly excellence!

The democratic ideal thus challenges each person and group to attain its full and proper excellence. Excellence itself, to be meaningful, must be defined in terms of the Principle of the Best Possible. So conceived, excellence can both be approximated and shared. What is more, in accordance with the nature of affiliative values, to attain to the democratic ideal is to have shared in process the benefits of one's success. As Rader puts it: "Democracy, as a way of life, is the

---

[24] *Ethics and Society* (New York: Henry Holt & Company, 1950), p. 245.
[25] *The Life of Reason* (New York: Charles Scribner's Sons, 1905), II, 111.

self-realization of cooperative human beings—the interpenetrations of excellence and sharing." [26]

VII. *THE COMMUNIST CHALLENGE*

The Communist or Marxist critique of democracy raises a different set of problems. It must be remembered that contemporary communists call their societies "peoples' democracies." Stalin, in defending the Soviet Constitution before the Eighth Congress of Soviets in 1936 argued:

> In the U.S.S.R. there are only two classes, workers and peasants, whose interests not only are not antagonistic but, on the contrary, amicable. Consequently there are no grounds for the existence of several parties, and therefore for the existence of freedom of such parties in the U.S.S.R. There are grounds for only one party, the Communist Party, in the U.S.S.R. Only one party can exist. . . . They [Western democracies] talk about democracy. But what is democracy? Democracy in capitalist countries where there are antagonistic classes is in the last analysis the democracy for the strong, democracy for the propertied minority. Democracy in the U.S.S.R., on the contrary, is democracy for all.[27]

The most obvious comment on Stalin's statement is that the conception of democracy he is offering involves a monolithic party-class, organic in character and totalitarian in range of control. As such, it violates both the norm of a responsible society and the norm of organic pluralism; it becomes in principle the tyranny of the majority, if one assumes that the party does in fact have majority support. The very conception of man on which it is based tends to exclude the possibility of a meaningful democracy. This rather strange inversion of terms has its origin in Karl Marx himself.

In the *Communist Manifesto,* Marx begins in what appears to be a thoroughly Kantian fashion. He presents a scathing bill of particulars against the laissez-faire bourgeois society of his time. Many of the items Marx raised are very much to the point and have in fact helped lead to some of the modifications of the classical capitalism we noted earlier. The heart of Marx's critique is contained in the following:

[26] Rader, *op. cit.,* p. 263.
[27] *Stalin on the Soviet Constitution* (New York: International Publishers, 1936), pp. 22–23, quoted in Chandler, *op. cit.,* p. 217.

The bourgeoisie . . . has resolved personal worth into exchange value, and in place of the numberless indefeasible chartered freedoms, has set up that single, unconscionable freedom—Free Trade. In one word, for exploitation, veiled by religious and political illusions, it has substituted naked, shameless, direct, brutal exploitation.[28]

Marx's critique, then, was sensitive to the treatment of man as means only by early nineteenth-century capitalism, as "an appendage of the machine," and not as an end in himself.[29] Marx was carried away by the force of indignation in his own critique. The bourgeoisie has, according to Marx, betrayed man's aspirations, conscience, and reason. As a result "law, morality, religion, are to him [the proletarian] so many bourgeois prejudices, behind which lurk in ambush just as many bourgeois interests." [30] Refusing to be deceived by such moral disguises, the proletarian must take power into his own hands, and force will probably be necessary. The goal to be attained after the class struggle is resolved is what Marx calls the Realm of Freedom, but about this realm, Marx says surprisingly little. "In place of the old bourgeois society with its classes and class antagonism we shall have an association in which the free development of each is the condition for the free development of all." [31]

Of the method by which this goal is to be reached Marx has a great deal to say. It will be attained through the immutable and determined historical process of class conflict—the dialectic, a conflict in nature and in the material process of production. Because the process is inevitable, what men think and do will be determined by the process, dialectical materialism, and not vice versa. The very tone of Marx's later questions in *The Manifesto* takes for granted the absolute dependence of what man thinks on his mode of production and his social class.

Does it require deep intuition to comprehend that man's ideas, views, and conceptions, in one word, man's consciousness changes with every change in the conditions of his material existence, in his social relations and in his social life?

[28] Karl Marx and Frederick Engels, *The Communist Manifesto*, in Chandler, *The Clash of Political Ideals* (3rd ed.; New York: Appleton-Century-Crofts, Inc., 1957), p. 92.
[29] *Ibid.*, p. 95.
[30] *Ibid.*, p. 99.
[31] *Ibid.*, p. 109.

What else does the history of ideas prove, than that intellectual production changes its character in proportion as material production is changed? [32]

In *Capital* Marx adds: "My dialectic is not only different from the Hegelian, but its direct opposite . . . with me . . . the ideal is nothing else than the material world reflected in the human mind, and translated into forms of thought." [33]

Finally, in *The Critique of Political Economy*, Marx argues:

The mode of production in material life determines the general character of the social, political, and spiritual process of life. It is not the consciousness of men that determines their existence, but, on the contrary, their social existence determines their consciousness.[34]

Let us dwell for a moment on such a radical perspective. Men have no moral or intellectual autonomy. Human consciousness is an after-effect of materio-economic process; it does not initiate and therefore cannot be responsible. Ideas themselves are effects, not causes. While the final stage of the dialectic will be called The Realm of Freedom, it is a bit difficult to discover what this could possibly mean, for men, if Marx is correct, are incapable of freedom. At any rate, before such a realm is reached, there must be class conflict and the proletariat must assume a dictatorship in the period of revolution and consolidation. Marx, beginning with an indignant protest against an old system that had failed to treat men as ends themselves, rescues them only to install them in a brave new world where they can no more than before attain to the dignity of ends. Even in the world after revolution men are only integers in a process and not responsive agents. "Democracy" in this context could only be a self-contradictory term.

VIII. *COALESCENCE OF SOCIAL IDEALS*

From our investigations in this chapter three basic social ideals have emerged, which were really implicit in our previous principles themselves. They are (1) the ideal of a responsible society, (2) the

[32] *Ibid.*, pp. 106–7.
[33] *Capital* (rev. ed.; New York: The Modern Library [1906]), p. 25.
[34] *A Contribution to the Critique of Political Economy* (Chicago: Charles H. Ken & Co., 1904), p. 12.

ideal of organic pluralism as its mode of organization, and (3) democracy as its way of political life. Only in the coalescence of the three,
we think, can society approach a realization of maximum potentiality in community.

IX. *REFLECTIVE SUMMARY*

The responsible society—we have been paving the way to an adequate
definition of it from the first page of this book. For we have been
aware that no person is an island. Yet to consider him no more than
a part of any mainland is to threaten the uniqueness of his personality, the autonomy of his responsibility, and the creative contribution
he can and ought to make, freely, to the whole.

It is our thesis that the person lives and thrives in community, not
in organicistic unity or atomistic pluralism. Organic pluralism as a
social philosophy seeks to realize the kinds of dependence—biological,
psychological, social, and political—that do exist among persons
(individually and in organized groups), and the moral imperatives of
the ideal of personality.

We realize, concretely, that the unique organization of values
and virtues that gives content to the ideal of personality is not possible if persons confine themselves to cooperating with other persons
on more or less intimate and temporary terms. Without the under-
girding structures—customs, institutions, and laws—of a state and
society that sustain and encourage the realization of values that he
holds supreme, the individual moral agent will remain impoverished,
for all his valiant efforts. He needs other persons and social institutions in which to develop and to challenge his potential. Yet without
the individual's imaginative and creative loyalty, social institutions
lose their dynamic for value production; they become oppressive—
if they do not die.

Therefore, in a society that is an organic pluralism the essential
unity must be one of cooperative purposes dedicated to the common
purpose of creating and recreating personalities—always as ends in
themselves and never as means only. In a society that is an organic
pluralism, persons accept responsibility for their freedom—in the promotion of a democratic commonwealth of responsive-responsible
freedom.

29

Sex, Love, and Marriage in Psychological and Ethical Perspective

~~~~~~

No ethical insight into sex, love, or marriage is possible unless we see each in relation to the other and to the realization of the symphony of values. This is our hypothesis, and we hope to confirm it by the basic facts, or what we believe to be basic facts, about sex, love, and marriage. For we are now in an area where so-called factual studies are riddled with valuations, and valuations are often based on "facts" that turn out to be fictions. Nevertheless, we shall do the best we can in one chapter to articulate what we hold to be the facts and values upon which our hypothesis rests. We begin with an interpretation of sex.

I. *SEX IN PSYCHOLOGICAL PERSPECTIVE*

Psychologists do not speak with one mind about the dynamics of sexual life. They do agree that sex (however differently they define it) is an unlearned drive, need, or motive. In minimal terms, we may say that every "normal" person experiences inner stirrings that render him especially sensitive to certain stimuli, usually provided by the opposite sex. Even such a minimum is open to question, and we must be satisfied to submit what we believe is defensible.

Sex is not, as Freud would have it, so generic an urge that every other motive and action stems directly or indirectly from it. We need not deny that infants gain pleasure through stimulation of the erogenous zones of the body, but we question the wisdom of considering these pleasures sexual. At the same time, we suspect that there is enough evidence to support Freud in the contention that the sex impulse is not focused once and for all on members of the opposite sex only. Initial psychophysiological deficiency may be the cause of some homosexuality. There is little doubt, however, that homosexuality is also a learned mode of response. It seems better to say that, while the sexual urge is usually directed toward members of the opposite sex, there is no fixed predisposition against homosexuality.[1]

Sex, we therefore suggest, is an unlearned psychophysiological urge that motivates the individual usually to approach members of the opposite sex with a view to releasing the inner tension felt. This inner tension is felt (beginning at puberty when sexual organic functions have matured) as an affective-emotional state of lust (not love), and it predisposes the individual to sexual activity. Sex-lust *as felt* is not geared to the preserving of the species.

We have made a number of seemingly simple assertions that we need to clarify. First, this definition of sex attempts to describe the sexual impulse as experienced at the human level. As in defining other innate motives (Chapter 7), so in defining the sex-lust urge we inspect what is felt consciously by the person internally. We do not assume that human tendencies are only extensions or complications of animal instincts. If we are correct, not before puberty does the individual experience the distinctive emotion of lust, which involves psychophysiological preparation for sexual activity.

Some will object to the use of the word "lust" for this inner stirred-up state, because the word carries negative moralistic associations for them. But we know no better word to indicate this powerful, unlearned, irreducible emotion that generates so much imaginative and overt activity for good and evil in human experience. Furthermore, if we use a specific word for the uniquely sexual emotion, we shall

---

[1] It is the conviction of the authors that the present treatment of the homosexual, legally and socially, should be subjected to the most careful ethical scrutiny. Treating a person who may have a congenital deficiency as if he were a criminal is like blaming a blind person for not seeing. Homosexuals should not be thrown into one category and treated as moral perverts when they may be physiological and psychological deviates. At the same time, even when his deficiency is congenital, it does not follow that the homosexual must give vent to his homosexuality.

be able to avoid the use of the word "love" for the experience and expression of sexual emotion. The fact is that persons may be in lust with each other without being in love with each other.

Second, we also wish to avoid the assumption that, because sexual activity results in progeny, this is the "natural" or only "proper" aim of sex in human experience. The release of sex-lust in itself, whatever the specific means of release, brings pleasure—whether or not the objective is the production of children. The means of gratification, the quality of sex-lust pleasure, will usually vary with the degree of release and the circumstances surrounding release. What we wish to stress here is that, whatever other factors enter into the final evaluation of sexual release, it is important to remember that sexual release is a value experience initially. There is nothing about sex-lust as such that is bad.

In other words, sex-lust pleasure is not a by-product of any other function, for example, the production of children. This does not mean, of course, that its value may not be increased or decreased by other considerations. But we do not adequately cope with the dynamics of sex if we minimize its power as a felt need or tension in its own right. We cannot but be grateful to Freud and psychoanalysis for opening our eyes to the complicated dynamics of sexual activity and to the consequences that occur when we unintelligently neglect the demands that it makes on the human being.

Third, we must not overlook the plasticity or flexibility of the sexual urge in human experience. Although fertilization of the ovum presupposes sexual intercourse (barring artificial insemination), the gratification of sex-lust can take an indefinite number of forms and need not be geared to reproduction. What requires special note at the human level is that there is room for much experimentation and learning and therefore for much artistry in the expression of the sexual urge. Because sex-lust is loosely geared to any specific mode of insuring reproduction, the individual as he grows can develop psychological habits that will facilitate or impede not only the eventual success of sexual intercourse as a reproductive act, but also the enjoyment of sexual expression. At the human level, we cannot assume that the individual will enter marriage and, by built-in, automatic activities, proceed either to adequate sexual enjoyment for himself or for his partner.

It is unfortunate, therefore, to suppose that children have been provided with proper sex education when all they know is how babies

are born. Sexual information falls far short of sexual education unless the growing child and adolescent are taught what physiological,
emotional, and ethical dispositions are likely to prepare him best for
the fulfillment of sex in his life in relation to the other values he
espouses.

It is, accordingly, a deceptive understatement that conceives of
sexual experience as rooted solely in rhythmic physiological predispositions that set up a peculiar hunger which must be served in some
way or other. To repeat, the strength and importance of the psychophysiological demands must not be minimized. To seek to spiritual-
ize sex without taking adequate account of almost sheerly physiological
sexual hunger can produce needless bodily and mental harm. Yet
much harm has been done by thinking of human sexual passion on
the model of animal sexual activity, without making proper allowance
for human sensitivity and flexibility.

It is no exaggeration to say that the harm is parallel to what would
result if the gratification of animal hunger were made the model for
the gratification of human hunger. Human beings eat to gratify
hunger, but, except in extremes, they are equally concerned about
the manner in which they eat, what they eat, with whom they eat.
For them eating readily comes to serve social, aesthetic, and religious
purposes. Indeed, all that distinguishes persons from animals—in the
way of perception, imagination, intelligence, and in the capacity for
art, sociality, and religious activity—makes it impossible for them to
treat the sexual urge either as a restricted biological demand for
reproduction or as an animal chain of reflexes. No human being
experiences his sexual impulses without infusing them with meanings
and values that arise from the relationships he finds to exist between
his sexual urge, his other propensities, and the values placed upon
them in his home and social environment.

Thus, even apart from any criticism of the adequacy of the statistical procedures, the underlying fallacy that subtly ruins the courageous
ınd important work in the Kinsey reports [2] is Kinsey's root-conception
of sex as an almost completely biological demand, without adequate
attention to the fusions that play such an important part in human
expression. The number or quantity of "sexual outlets," to use his
give-away term, is hardly as important as the quality of sexual experi-

[2] Alfred Charles Kinsey, *Sexual Behavior in the Human Female* (Philadelphia:
Saunders, 1953), and *Sexual Behavior in the Human Male* (Philadelphia: Saunders,
1948).

ence. For example, a kiss may be a sexual outlet, but when in a particular person's life it comes to mean an easy way out of a social conflict, its impact is much greater than that of a biological outlet alone. In human experience generally, every manifestation (or lack of manifestation) of the sexual impulse may have meanings and values that outrun its biological roots and transform its impact in a given life.

Finally, the sexual urge has purposely been defined without specifying any generic difference between male and female. Obviously, the parts played in the reproductive process by male and female are different, and there will be differences in the pattern of sexual excitement and response. But we have deliberately avoided even suggesting any generic differences in the strength of the sexual urge and of the pattern of arousal and stimulation.

For, in the light of the data at hand, it seems better to lay the emphasis on individual differences rather than on supposedly generic differences between men and women. A particular female may be much more responsive sexually or more sensitive to sexual stimulation than a particular male. Learning, involving one's individual response to the role that may be expected of male or female in a given society, counts for so much in human experience as to warn against a stereotype of what is to be expected from a member of the opposite sex. Preconceived ideas about what another can or should enjoy in and through sexual behavior have kept men and women, even in marriage, from the fullest enjoyment of the sexual act. The person who can learn to control his own responses in a way that will help him to be an active, cooperative partner will have gone far toward removing some of the obstacles to harmonious and rewarding sexual responsiveness.

It will be obvious that what we believe to be the facts about sex will play an important part in the decisions a person makes about the kind of control he should exercise in dealing with his own sexual tensions. We are now ready for the question: On the basis of the description suggested, toward what goal may one aim in sexual training?

A final answer to this question is impossible without taking other needs and values into account, but, isolating the nature of the sexual experience as far as possible, we now propose a specific value judgment by which sexual training may be guided. It is this: The quality of enjoyment in sexual responses is increased to the extent that one's action is acceptable to and reciprocated by the partner so as to achieve mutual harmony in sexual responsiveness. There are various ways of simply relieving sexual tension; through nocturnal emission, through masturbation, through petting, through mere sexual intercourse. But human experience indicates that the fullest enjoyment of sexual activity, even as purely sexual activity, comes when two persons can so cooperate in their individual responsiveness that the climax each enjoys in orgasm can be simultaneous. We judge such unison of response highly valuable.

From this qualitative point of view, much sexual experience, in and out of marriage, probably falls far short of the goal. The sad fact is not that human beings have had illicit sexual experience, but that, licit or illicit, they have not known sexual quality. Why? Because they have not been able to meet the psychophysiological conditions (if we remain at this level) needed for a harmonious experience. Much more is involved than can be spelled out in one chapter, but, we repeat, rigid stereotypes about sex, and conditioning of sexual responses through petting and premarital sexual intercourse may well be impediments, at the "purely sexual" level, to the responsiveness that two persons need to enjoy in marriage.

Again, too often the negative feelings that individuals have toward sex result from earlier disappointment with relatively tawdry sexual experience (from petting to sexual intercourse). What is too easily minimized is the fact that one's future sexual responses are affected by the mental, physical, and emotional habits and "set" produced by his past experience with sex. For example, the quality of sexual experience that newly-weds have, regardless of how well suited they are in other ways, will depend on what psychophysiological habits they bring to sexual intercourse. To suppose that cause and effect do not operate here and that "love conquers all" is to be naively sentimental.

To put our point positively, the ideal preparation for harmonious sexual intercourse in marriage—still staying at the level of physiological response—is a set of psychophysiological predispositions sufficiently free and flexible to enable the partners to accommodate themselves to each other as they learn to meet each other's sexual requirements. There will probably always be some hurdles to overcome because of the inevitable individual differences, but basic self-confidence in one's capacity to control one's self, emotional freedom sexually, and mutual tolerance will reduce these obstacles—especially when the sexual act itself is a symbol of a couple's unity in other respects. Qualitative harmony in sexual experience is not a goal easily achieved; yet, as a high point in the partners' value experience, it is also a source of confidence in their other relationships.

It follows, then, that the argument for or against premarital sexual experimentation and intercourse must be related at least to the quality or value that can come into life through harmonious sexual intercourse. We cannot know to what extent sex is to be controlled or what "control" means unless we are clear about what is involved in productive sexual fulfillment itself and how it is related to other values. It is to this larger question that we must now turn our attention.

II. *SEX AND LOVE*

We have been treating sex-lust as an irreducible urge that makes its own distinctive demand on—and can make a distinctive contribution to—human experience. Without forgetting this fact, we must now consider essential factors that (a) decrease its value and (b) increase its value.

We shall preface our discussion by dealing with the suggestion in some quarters that the person who does not gratify his sexual urge may become mentally ill. Now, there is no denying that the sexual urge is very strong, that its control to the point of inhibition is very difficult. This fact encourages the "fiction" that gratification of the urge is needed for mental health. We use the word "fiction" purposely, because this conclusion is not, to begin with, consistent even with evidence we have daily before our eyes. After all, we all know many human beings who have knowingly denied themselves sexual experience, not because they had no desire, but because it could not be fitted into the total pattern of preferred values in their lives. Such persons are no less "healthy" personalities than others, and frequently they are more healthy than many who have had "illicit" sexual experience.

The problem, in fact is not one of either expression or inhibition.[3] Persons who inhibit sexual response for the wrong reasons may in-

[3] There is probably no fuzzier psychological notion than that of sublimation. We confess that the only sense we can make of it is that the emotional and mental energy that a person has not used for a given purpose is available for other purposes. But to suppose that an urge like sex can be gratified by being directed toward some other object involves "mechanical" assumptions that are difficult to conceive and nowhere, to our knowledge, adequately justified. For this reason we make no use of this mechanism.

deed face serious personality problems. But so do those who express their sexual urge for the wrong reason. We must grant, for example, that the person who without understanding the nature of the sexual urge, puts it away from him in horror as something nasty, may find that such drastic treatment of sex (*repression*) will lead to unsuspected trouble. For, having dealt with a very strong need violently and uncritically, "once and for all," he never comes to any knowledge of ways in which it can be adequately controlled. Because such a strong desire cannot simply be put away and forgotten, he may well live in constant anxiety lest this "black demon" be unleashed. Such repression can cause anxiety of one sort; but irresponsible expression can set up anxieties too and result in personality problems which bar fulfillment of both sexual and other needs.

The choice, in other words, is not between "expression or inhibition," because both can lead to more problems than they solve. Another alternative is open; control, the conscious inhibition of sex-lust—with a full realization of possible values lost, but with a willingness to forego some value for the sake of others.

To generalize, there is no truth in the statement often heard that there are dire consequences if one leads a life "without sex," for the consequences of either inhibition or repression will depend upon the other values, or the constellation of need gratification, in a particular person. Again, it is not a question in the last analysis—within or outside marriage—of "sex or no sex" but of the quality of sex in terms of the total life pattern.

All the more, then, we must ask the questions: What is likely to decrease the value of sex? What is likely to increase it? We are now definitely passing from psychophysiological fact to evaluation, and the best we can do is to keep the relation of valuation to facts clear.

A. *Factors Causing Diminishing Satisfaction*

At any point in the continuum from petting to sexual intercourse, there is pleasure in the release of tension—other things being equal. But the individual is likely to find that, especially if sexual expression is made an end in itself, the release-pleasure experienced at any one point will be more difficult to achieve by remaining at that point. To be specific, is it not true that the kissing that may yield gratifying expression for a while will not continue to be an adequate means of relief? Will the individual not find himself needing to caress the body or to extend the area of petting, in order to achieve about the same degree of release earlier achieved through kissing? Elsewhere [4] this psychological sequence has been called *the sexual progression.*

The sexual progression pinpoints a fact that cannot be overlooked if we are to understand the reason for persons frequently finding themselves controlled by sex rather than controlling sex. Too often, for example, the adolescent thinks that his problem will be solved if he can find release from his sexual tension at a given point. Much to his surprise he finds that he has been pouring oil on the fire he had hoped to extinguish. Again, many young people, seduced by the sexual progression, have found that while "petting" to a certain point released tension, it was only for a while.

Kinsey reports [5] that many college young people deal with their sexual tensions not by intercourse but by petting to a climax or orgasm. It is safe to generalize that orgasm becomes more difficult to achieve (and this applies to masturbation as well). The result is that persons who pet to a point short of sexual intercourse, especially when release of sexual tension is conceived of as an end in itself, find themselves confronted all over again with the need to shift to a new point of gratification in order to achieve sexual pleasure. Thus, sex gratification by itself may well have created a problem greater than the problem that it solved.

Obviously, from the fact of the sexual progression itself, we do not have a tidy answer in black-and-white to the question: "To pet or not to pet?" Each person must answer that question within the larger context of value. But any valuation needs to take into account this fact of diminishing returns and progression of release-point and the probable intensification of the problem of control.

Another question readily comes to mind now. Does the sexual progression apply to sexual intercourse itself, within or outside marriage? One hesitates to make sweeping generalizations on matters on which there is little trustworthy data. But on what psychological grounds would we assume otherwise? Until we have reliable data to the contrary, the inference may be drawn from what we see generally taking place in human experience that sexual intercourse, if sought solely or mainly as a source of sexual release and exploitation, will bring diminishing returns. To be explicit, we suggest that persons

[4] Cf. Peter A. Bertocci, *The Human Venture in Sex, Love, and Marriage* (New York: Association Press, 1949), Chapter 1.

[5] See Kinsey, *Sexual Behavior in the Human Male.*

who use sexual intercourse purely or largely for sexual release and exploitation find themselves seeking new forms of titillation, new persons who will bring release; they find themselves not freer from sexual tensions, but chained to the need for variety in the source of sexual stimulation and release. The sexual progression, left to itself, might well lead to sexual perversion.

In any case, as long as one's orientation toward sexual experience (be it within or outside marriage) is the self-centered gratification of the desire for its own sake, there is negligible, if any, improvement in the quality of the experience. Indeed, the individual may lose correspondingly in self-confidence with regard to his capacity to control his sexual demands. Furthermore, persons who marry in the hope of relief from sexual tension may well discover that such relief is only temporary. They soon find themselves caught again in the progression—even if their habits of self-centered sex gratification should still allow them to meet the demands of the partner. It is no exaggeration to say that marriage, far from solving the problem of sexual control, may well increase it.

To summarize: sheer quantity of sexual experience does not give to the individual the freedom from tension that he hopes for, and it certainly does not improve the quality of sexual relief. What does?

B. *Factors Causing Increasing Satisfaction*

Before answering this question, let us first warn against misunderstanding. We are not about to suggest an escape from the progression of sex. As we see it, the progression describes the evolution of a psychic response pattern, which, confronting the individual at every phase of his sexual life, is by no means a necessary evil. The sexual progression can indeed serve to enrich the total sexual experience of compatible partners and, in cooperation with other factors to be mentioned, can be controlled in accordance with the values both partners prefer.

Second, approaching the answer to our question: Under what conditions is there increase of sexual pleasure and quality? We must note that often the gratification of any urge is all the more satisfactory if it can become the occasion for gratifying other significant interests of the person. For example, while fish tastes "good" to the hungry man, it tastes "better" if he has caught the fish himself. It tastes "best" if he can prepare it with a friend in appropriate surroundings and flavor it with good conversation and companionship. When a family meets together around a table on such memorial days as Thanksgiving, the eating of food becomes the occasion for gratifying a whole complex of needs and interests. Turkey is never so good as at Thanksgiving because we eat with a special spirit. The gratification of hunger thus takes on a much larger meaning than appeasing physical hunger or appetite.

We can now suggest the answer to our question, for an analogous enlargement takes place with regard to sex-lust. The meaning and value of sex in a person's life enlarges in accordance with its capacity to be a focus of or means of expression for other values. If anything is noteworthy about the history of sex, it is the way sex has served as a medium for and a companion to the expression of other interests, such as art and religion.[6] That this should be so is not surprising if we remember that sex-lust is in fact one focus in the complex need-life of a person and that it necessarily exists in—and cannot be ripped out of—the matrix of other conative tendencies in a life. Need we point out that curiosity, mastery, succor, tenderness, respect, and creativity are singly or conjointly involved whenever sexual expression of any sort takes place? Sex-lust lives as a phase in the total conative life of a person, and its meaning in his life will depend on whether it is a threat to or a partner of the gratification of other interests. To take one notable instance, the way in which sex-experience is connected with the desire for children will greatly affect the meaning it will have for partners.

Indeed, although we shall not discuss the matter here, the whole discussion of the desirability of the use of birth-control methods needs to be infused with concern for the quality in sexual experience and the effect of use or nonuse of the particular contraceptive methods on the individual concerned. Fear lest conception take place, or

---

[6] "The intimate association between man and woman is religious meditation, the recognition of sex, not as an evil to flee from but as an uplifting force to be utilized in a partnership of the spirit, raises sex adjustment from an instinctive level, and marriage from a mere physiological contrivance. It fixes the greatest and the best thing in man, namely, love, upon the supreme object, namely God. Man cannot achieve perfection if he leaves love out of account or distributes his life in segregated compartments of earthly affection and spirituality. Sex thus has to be evaluated in terms of religious experience. Therefore, man will pray to be delivered not from sex, but its temptations; he will import into normal sexual life a religious partnership so that moments of the greatest intimacy will cease to be exciting, and a serene tranquility and full vitality will be associated together without detriment to either" (Radhakamal Mukerjee, *The Theory of Art and Mysticism* [Bombay: Asia Publishing House, 1960], p. 259).

anxiety that one is breaking norms that one respects by using contraceptives, may destroy possibilities of value in the sex experience.
On the other hand, two persons who enter upon intercourse in the
hope of becoming parents to a child they both desire can enjoy an
experience of union that goes far beyond, and yet is heightened by,
the harmony of their mutual responses.

Other considerations, as we shall see, support our main theme, that
the positive value of sex-lust and its expression will depend upon the
capacity to be harmonious with, or become a means of expression for,
the other values in a person's life. In a word, one never gets out of
sex more than he brings to it. When sex is a means of expressing
mutual love, its total meaning is enhanced, for the sexual act now
becomes a means of unifying symbolically two persons who feel unified in their value structures. The gratifying of sex-lust, far from being a narcissistic form of self-indulgence, far from using another
person as a means to one's own gratification, now becomes a way of
celebrating all that love and life mean to the participating persons.
It is time, clearly, that we developed the meaning of love in this
connection.

III. SEX, SENTIMENTAL LOVE, AND
ETHICAL LOVE

In a larger ethical context, we have suggested that love is not to be
conceived of essentially as a particular emotional state or sentiment
but as an ethical style of life, which ought to pervade all the trait-
values (see Chapter 17). At the same time we pointed out that while
the virtues themselves are to be conceived of as chosen volitional dispositions, the truly fortunate individual is the one who can depend
on emotional support for the volitional intent. Happy is the man
who finds his emotions strongly on the side of his duty. Of course,
there is no separating of volitional from emotional states in the
matrix of personality, but we all know the inner situation expressed
in this sentence: "I love him, but because he is not the type of person
I ought to marry, in fairness to both of us I will not marry him." In
other words, a person can feel a sentiment of love that may, or may
not, conflict with the larger value system. It is important for us to
underscore this fact, even if we have no clear psychological insight
into the relation of sentimental love to ethical love.

Still, is it not fair to say that when we feel sentimental (romantic) love for a person, we are so strongly predisposed emotionally in favor of that person that we "can't do enough for him"? Whatever the differences between ethical and sentimental love, in both the person finds satisfaction in acting in a way that will bring greater unity between himself and the loved person. Yet we want to admit that it is the rare person who finds that his sentimental love conforms at every stage to the full demands of volitional-ethical love.

Very difficult moral choices present themselves when a person feels the conflict between emotional loyalty toward those he loves and the requirements of a loving style of life. For a loving style of life may well demand that he treat generously those for whom he feels no sentimental attraction. Sometimes the very fact that we especially enjoy "doing things" for some people may lead us to a certain neglect of them in order that we may concentrate our energies in the service of those to whom we owe a duty in spite of the lack of an immediate sentimental bond. Again, in the case of sentimental love, we must guard against pleasing ourselves or the other in such a way as to spoil him for his best growth.

We have said enough to account for some of the major conflicts between sex-lust, love, and marriage. Yet here we would stress the positive and creative contribution that is made when sex-lust and sentimental love can be means of expressing, celebrating, and deepening ethical love. For, when the motive of sex-lust is in harmony with other emotions fused in the sentiment of love, and when the sentiment of love is in harmony with the dominant ethical involvement of the persons concerned, the lovers may look forward to a peak experience that symbolizes, celebrates, cements, and deepens the unity thus far forged in their lives. Let us put all this more concretely.

John and Mary, seventeen years old, meet and "fall in love" with each other. They enjoy being with each other, exchanging ideas and appreciations, and doing things together. They soon need to decide to what extent their sexual attraction and mutual affection for each other is to be physically expressed. Let us assume that they pet, that as time passes they approach the point of sexual intercourse, and that they decide against it, despite difficulties in self-control. As the days go on, they find themselves increasingly indifferent or even hostile to each other's ideas. Even their activities tend to become an escape from the realization that they have little more to say to each other.

They have in fact begun to sense a rift in their deeper interests and values. They feel miserable about it and yet cannot seem to give each other up. For their "going together" still serves to solve other problems, and the mutual enjoyment of such sexuality as they experience, along with what common interests they do have, keeps them together. In other words, their sentimental love keeps them together and in hope of closing the gap they feel between their longer-range interests.

Nevertheless, even though John protests his love for her, Mary finds that in important ways earlier not obvious to her, he is self-centered in his relation to his parents and his peers. He has become quite possessive about her. His work at school is needlessly a barely passing grade, and it betrays his lack of long-range ambition. Still, he dances well, is physically attractive, has social *savoir faire,* and keeps conversation going, as long as topics are not explored very far. Accordingly, she keeps up her relationship with him even though she may say to herself, "When I really think about him, I cannot respect him." And the fact is borne in upon her that while their mutual endearments are pleasant, there is more sexual demand in both of them than she can reasonably approve. Let us assume that she comes to the point at which she realizes that, difficult as it may be to break up this "compatible" social arrangement, it would be better for them both to discontinue seeing each other.

Now, on our thesis, to the extent that their basic interests and values do not harmonize, there is a threat to the quality of enjoyment that John and Mary get from petting. This cannot be a symbol of their togetherness. Yet, insofar as their sexual affection is pleasant for its own sake, they have greater difficulty in checking the sexual progression. Indeed, they are tempted to accelerate the sexual progression in order to fight that something which has come between them. Let us assume that they decide to have sexual intercourse and that it is relatively harmonious. How long will it continue as an experience that can celebrate any larger unity? And if the sexual experience is, to begin with, so gratifying to both that it seems to be the main point at which they "speak" to each other, how long will they be likely to feel exalted in their experience? If we are correct, the quality of their experience will diminish, but the strength of sexual desire will not decrease. They will find it difficult to return to petting and achieve adequate release without sexual intercourse.

In short, persons who seek to hold each other through sexual gratification seem bound to be disappointed. For even apart from worry lest conception occur, they are running against something about sex experience that is just as much fact as any biological fact. Namely, sex experience, to escape diminishing returns, must become the symbolic expression of the other values in the lives of the persons involved. Sentimental love, inclusive of sex, may be an encouragement to volitional love, but it grows in stability and depth only as it expresses effectively the search for greater harmony activating the two lovers.

IV. *IS PREMARITAL INTERCOURSE ETHICAL?*

It is with these considerations and with the argument of this chapter in mind that we now face a question as serious as the poignant situation that it often expresses in the lives of many lovers.

Let us assume that John and Mary, in their late teens or early twenties, are in love and feel basic harmony among their values. "Why," they ask, "should we wait until we get married to engage in sexual intercourse? We are beyond the point where sex is exploitation or personal aggrandizement. Yet we cannot afford to be married. Why wait?"

Any full consideration of this question cannot overlook the fact that at the time of writing there is no contraceptive method that is one-hundred per cent successful other than a physiological operation, although there is a strong scholarly support for a class of drugs that approach one-hundred per cent for persons who are able to understand the conditions of use. In order to strengthen John's and Mary's case, we shall assume that there are foolproof contraceptives and also that they need not be bothered by all the serious problems that would face them if pregnancy occurred. Our argument against premarital sexual intercourse even between engaged couples is to be built around the concern to protect the quality of sexual experience and love now and in the foreseeable future.

First, it is important for John and Mary to realize fully what their demand for even "safe" sexual intercourse apart from marriage actually means. It means that they are expecting to express their love for each other sexually without binding their lives to each other socially, economically, or legally. If married, they would accept responsibility for each other in the eyes of their fellow men and of the

state at least. Furthermore, as they shared the same living quarters
and worked out the daily problems that any two persons have to face
as they settle into the tasks of housekeeping and making their way in
the community, their love would be put to work.

Marriage leaves few areas of the personality untouched, and the
constant sharing of satisfactions and disappointments involves and
challenges value schemes in ways impossible for John and Mary as
unmarried persons. Love in marriage is forced to develop new roots,
which take firm grip on the value soil that nourishes the lovers. Indeed their love will not survive without growing and embracing
more of their lives as persons. Nothing can bring out what the quality of love is better than marriage. Marriage can break love faster
than anything else. But it can also feed its growth. If John and
Mary fail in marriage, they can feel that they have at least tried to
live with mutual responsibility in every area of their lives.

These considerations, lightly sketched over what is really an extremely complex background, underlie our belief that premarital
intercourse, even between lovers, invites sexual disappointment.
Such action isolates sexual experience from the total pattern of their
values. When sex is an experience that two people can have in the
midst of their other joys and sorrows, it contributes to the ongoing
interlocking of both lives and develops a quality it cannot otherwise
have. For now it both encourages and symbolically expresses the
growth in unity that John and Mary experience in every area of
their lives. Sexual intercourse before marriage is no preparation for
marriage; it really "tests" very little, for it is a so-called "marital"
intercourse out of the real context of marriage.

We are not suggesting that John and Mary, having been in love
for a number of months, let us say, cannot possibly find in their first
premarital experiences of sexual intercourse a new point of unity
for that particular stage in their relationship. This will depend upon
their past sexual conditioning, on their capacity to quiet (for good or
ill) the scruples that may well beset them in the light of their moral
training and sense of social responsibility—in brief, on the content
of their consciences at that time. But John will do well to bear in
mind that, if he does love Mary and wants to help nourish her self-
respect and confidence in her capacity for being a good partner,
there is danger, as well as a lack of generosity, in the demand for
premarital sexual intercourse. For he may be exacting more from
her than she can psychologically afford to give, however willing she

is to give of herself in the name of love. And the same applies to Mary in her relation to John.

Furthermore, John and Mary, on having sexual intercourse, may not enjoy unity of mutual response, either owing to interfering moral scruples or to the difference in responsiveness. Generalizations are dangerous, but is it psychologically far-fetched to urge that a young couple will need even in marriage to take some pains in working out their responses to each other? If John and Mary are married and encounter difficulties in sexual adjustment, the total conditions under which they live will provide both incentive and opportunity to improve their relationship. In addition, marriage provides many ways in which any temporary deficit in sexual mutuality may be made up to each other. If, on the other hand, John and Mary are unmarried and find their experience less than satisfactory, they are likely to consider it more of a problem than it would actually be in better circumstances, and they may falsely conclude that they are not suited to each other. Thus the experience that was to unify them further actually creates problems and may lead to separation.

In sum, the sexual experience deserves every emotional and circumstantial encouragement it can get if it is to be a growing experience of enrichment. The tragedy of so much premarital sexual experience is not that it is premarital, but that it is shockingly disappointing and destructive of confidence. John and Mary want to be one; often, without realizing it, they both actually want a quality of joy that sexual release itself cannot give; and when they do not find it, they can be more deeply disappointed than they are readily willing to admit. What they are likely to neglect is the all-important fact that, if sexual experience is to be an increasing source of unity, a bearer of joy and creativity, the lovers must bring to it the imagination and the discipline that any art demands.

No art is developed without thought, patience, and self-forgetfulness. Many young people have in principle decided against premarital sexual intercourse and, frankly facing the difficulty of self-control, have learned to help each other meet the problem as their courtship developed. Such young people have not felt that they loved each other less, and indeed they have come to understand better the springs of their love for each other. Early in their love lives, they have learned to forego immediate self-gratification in the interest of other values. Such knowledge can be a source of confidence; it can discourage suspicion and jealousy during stretches of married life when absence or illness make sexual intercourse impossible.

In order to consider another possibility, however, let us go so far as to assume that sexual conditioning (or what we might call the content of sexual conscience at the time) is such that John and Mary can enjoy a high quality of mutuality even in their early sexual experience. The question we would now ask is: How long will John and Mary continue to keep the experience high in quality, growing in quality, a binding force between them, if, unmarried, they are not sharing the other investments in their lives?

We need not urge again that the sexual experience needs encouraging conditions if mutuality is to be encouraged. Once the early bloom of a new experience wears off, John and Mary may well find it more difficult to maintain the earlier "mood" and zest, with the result that qualitative decrease sets in. Married persons testify to the fact that it is not a simple matter to be emotionally and otherwise prepared for the kind of fulfilling sexual experience that is more than sexual release. But what will John and Mary experience when, unmarried, they cannot possibly have the other sources of mutuality, strength, and growth that will, on the one hand, compensate for less fulfilling sexual experience and, on the other hand, provide sources for richer experience?

In short, why should John and Mary expect that the rules for sexual success should not be the same as for other desires? Quality of gratification is lost where larger meaning cannot be expressed. Sex needs marriage, both sex and love need marriage, just as art needs fundamental formal restrictions if the product is to have the much desired values of enduring growth in power and meaning.

Before passing on, let us draw a conclusion from our analysis that applies to a question asked by many worried people: What will happen to chastity once contraceptives have removed the fear of pregnancy with its economic and social consequences?

Psychological and moral chastity is not sensitively defined, in the last analysis, in terms of whether a person has or has not had sexual intercourse. Chastity basically consists in the motivation and practice that keeps sex from being self-centered and self-indulgent and that constantly dedicates it to the growth of value. Chastity, if it is worth protecting, must be protected within the marriage bond as well as outside it. That is, neither the husband nor the wife is chaste as long as one uses the other simply or largely as a means of sexual gratification. Sex in itself is prostituted when it becomes a source of self-enslavement and not a growing phase in the total development of mutual concern between two people. As long as chastity stems from fear of progeny and social disgrace alone, the emphasis will tend to be placed on whether sexual intercourse is licit or not, rather than on the conditions that make for quality in and through sexual experience. Thus persons will continue to lose a creative source of goodness in their lives.[7]

V. SEX, LOVE, AND MONOGAMY

A. The Progression of Love

The sexual progression highlights the fact that human experience, made an end in itself, not only brings diminishing returns, but also becomes the source of more psychic tensions than it resolves. What we might now call the progression of love occurs when sex becomes a way not only of saying "I love you!" but also of symbolizing common loyalty to a larger scheme of values. When John and Mary can respect each other as persons, when their patterns of value are basically congruent [8] with each other and expressive of a loving style of life, the sexual experience finds support in the total impetus of both personalities, and at the same time it celebrates the communion that John and Mary have already achieved. Yet even love of this quality, an integral part of ethical love, cannot stand still. John and Mary cannot remain "lovers"; marriage and home are needed to keep their love new and fresh as other values enter the compass of their lives.

What is emerging here is a conception of marriage not mainly as a way of assuring posterity, economic security, or even social stability, but as the best way of challenging and encouraging the full growth of persons. In marriage John and Mary put their love to work in the common pursuit of mutual growth through the whole

[7] The literature that deals with sex and love in a critical psycho-ethical manner, without presupposing theological norms, is difficult to come by. In significant similarity and contrast with what is suggested in this chapter is William Graham Cole's *Sex in Christianity and Psychoanalysis* (New York: Oxford University Press, 1955). The following works are also helpful in this context: Sylvanus M. Duvall, *Men, Women, and Morals* (New York: Association Press, 1952), Clarence Leuba, *Ethics in Sex Conduct* (New York: Association Press, 1948), and Alexander Magoun, *Love and Marriage* (New York: Harper and Brothers, 1948).

[8] See Peter A. Bertocci, *op. cit.*, Chapter 4.

range of values possible in their new world. It is this theme that now needs further development.

B. *Monogamy, the Matrix of Growth in Personality*

The thesis that we would expound briefly in this last section is that monogamy best serves the needs of personality growth once a society has been able to solve the economic and biological problems that protect survival. There are, of course, economic, psychological, social, and other grounds for monogamy. Mukerjee puts it well when he says:

> It is a monogamy of a lasting kind, buttressed by art, religion, social etiquette and manners, that throws open the highest opportunities of personality development of normal man and woman, who all the time can fuse their sex urges with relatively unlimited interests and values in life.[9]

We shall restrict ourselves here to a line of argument consistent with the dominant theme of this chapter.

We turn at once to the difference between an ethical home, nourishing its family with an ever richer psychological knowledge, and the house that shelters the biological animal. It is all too easy to suppose that a well-built, spacious, nicely appointed house in a hygienic community is an adequate foundation of a home. For a human child, however, a home is not simply a place in which he can be safe from harm and disease, important as this is. A home is an atmosphere permeated by understanding concern and intelligent love for him as a person with his own needs and abilities. If we have learned anything from our psychological studies, it is that the child needs to be loved for himself, that he is not to be treated simply as a possible source of economic and social security for the family and larger social group. In the midst of his discouragements as he faces his growth problems, the child needs the encouragements that understanding kindness and forgiveness bring. But above all the child needs to be guided in his ventures in living, in relating himself, his needs, and his abilities to the support and growth of others, both in his own family and beyond.

Obviously, this kind of moral education requires more than a

[9] Radhakamal Mukerjee, *The Horizon of Marriage* (Bombay: Asia Publishing House, 1957), p. 12.

good house and parents who are "in love" with each other. It calls for lovers whose own ventures in life include the having and the nurturing of children as persons. For such parents children are not the "by-products" of sexual experience, but integral to their very conception of what makes for high achievement. Such parents are aware that nothing will more readily bring out the strength and weakness in their own schemes of values than their attempt to rear children. Fewer experiences can bring them more insecurity along the whole length of their lives; at the same time fewer experiences can yield more joy and creativity. The love they had for each other up to the time children were born will be challenged to its very roots as they find themselves needing imagination, self-control, and goodwill (indeed, what virtue does not stand them in good stead?), such as few other ventures in living demand.

The family in the last analysis is the crucible into which parents and children pour their assets and liabilities. The personalities that result will depend first upon the capacity of parents to modify and develop habits, attitudes, sentiments, traits, values, and styles of life in such a way as to take adequate account of the needs and abilities of their children, and in the growing child's world as well as their own. The fundamental argument in favor of family planning stems from the psycho-ethical conditions required for the nourishment and growth of personality, both in parents and in children.

With these requirements in mind for the growth of love, for a home in which each person can feel a participant member, does it take much argument to show why monogamous marriage is better than any other form? For a monogamous union affords two persons the opportunity they need to concentrate their energies on developing a quality of home life dedicated to the growth of persons. It is no mean task to be a resourceful, sensitive, and loving partner of one man or woman. The commitment "for better or worse till death us do part" is not a commitment needed for economic or social safety, but a commitment required if two persons are to grow together and develop as they face their problems as human beings and as parents.

Furthermore, as we have seen, only two persons whose styles of life are suffused by fundamentally congruent values can provide a psycho-ethical environment or a home in which each is encouraged to make commitments consistent with his abilities and the needs of others. No doubt, there are societies in which the struggle for survival must take place at such a marginal economic level that non-monogamous forms of marriage seem required. But whatever advantages such schemes have, they invariably involve regrettable sacrifice and suffocation of human interests and abilities. They demand subordination of some members of the family to others in rigid ways that cannot be sanctioned the moment that it is not absolutely necessary for survival. What justifies the ethical ideal of monogamy is the fact, we suggest, that everything considered, it affords the best opportunities for parents to nourish, respect, and love each other as persons and for them to share the responsibility and satisfactions for nourishing, respecting, and loving their children as persons.

Perhaps we can now all the more readily see, to hark back to the place of sex in life, why Mukerjee says:

> In monogamy sex, indeed, recedes from the centre of human relationships and penetrates into the ever-widening fields of unifying satisfaction based on the original and normal ground of honour, self-control, and fidelity. Such are the opportunities that monogamy offers for sexual behaviour to get as close to the ideal of integrating the personalities of the partners and promoting tenderness, charity and altruistic relationship in society.[10]

VI. *UNFINISHED QUESTIONS*

To bring a chapter like this to a close is to realize how much more needs to be said to assure adequate balance in perspective. Yet even in a more extended treatment we would wish to plead that sex, love, marriage, and the home must be seen in interrelation. We have hardly touched upon the relation of the family to the social order, which at once nourishes, challenges, and threatens it. We should want to argue that the attempt to isolate the home—even if it were possible—will lead to stagnation of its members. But we would add immediately that no society will be stronger than the homes in which persons can be nurtured as nowhere else.

Also, we have not paid adequate attention to the part religion can play in challenging the narrowness of loyalties that can develop in one's home, state, and society. We cannot forget, however, that for many persons mutual loyalty to each other in marriage, and love of

[10] *Ibid.*, p. 16.

family becomes a unifying force and a substitute for religion and God. Whether this ought to be so will depend on the truth or falsity of religion and on the religious beliefs that two lovers bring into marriage and their home. What is certain is that their experiences in sex, love, marriage, and the home will not only lead them to "ultimate questions" but also challenge their beliefs about God and the destiny of human values in the universe.[11]

But this much can also be said at this point, briefly. In and through sex, love, marriage, and the home, we suggest, two persons are constantly sinking new shafts into the subsoils of value possibility in their own personalities, and they do so consciously or unconsciously within the framework of their ultimate faith in the sources of creativity. No person coming into intimate interaction with a loved one, with the birth, growth, hopes, disappointments, dreams, and accomplishments of children, can escape a haunting sense of the unfathomed possibilities for good and evil in the world. The nature of the religious commitment that two persons bring to each other and to their home will infiltrate the whole texture of their love for each other, their children, and their neighbors. If parents indeed are often forced to "play God" to their children, the kind of God that their actions suggest will depend on the kind of God that unites them in worship. Obviously, there is no limit to the kinds of ventures in value that love in marriage at once stimulates and celebrates.

VII. *REFLECTIVE SUMMARY*

We cannot think clearly about sex, love, and marriage without understanding the relation of each to the other. The fundamental thesis here is that while sex-lust is not intrinsically bad, its value in the life of a person will be enhanced by its capacity to symbolize and express a wider range of values in the lives of the persons involved.

The fundamental problem is not "sex or no sex" but quality of sex. Inhibition or expression of sex for the wrong reason can keep sex from being the creative source of value that it can be in personality. The expression of sex simply to release actual tension involves one in a sexual progression in which the release point be-

[11] See *Sex and Religion Today,* ed. Simon Doniger (New York: Association Press, 1953).

comes more difficult to achieve. Thus, the sexual progression may lead one from pillar to post seeking a sexual release that in fact brings less satisfaction.

Furthermore, sexual expression for self-gratification can lead to habits and emotional sets that may interfere with the achievement of unison in sexual response in marriage. Indeed, the person who has made sex a matter of self-indulgence or of mastery over another will not find it easy, to say the least, to shift to the other-regarding modes of response demanded if marital sexual experience is to be mutually satisfactory.

It is important for persons to enter marriage, if possible, in control of their sexual responses, without blocks caused by relatively rigid habits of emotional and physical response. They can thus more readily achieve harmony in sexual response and experience a mutuality that beautifully symbolizes their spiritual unity. The crucial fact seems to be that when sexual experience can be mutual and become a symbol of other shared values in the lives of married people, it takes on a high value that it cannot by itself yield.

Premarital sexual intercourse between persons sincerely in love can create more problems than it solves. It is certainly no realistic preparation for marriage, for without the support of the other values that marriage brings, sexual intercourse can easily degenerate into an experience that has little sensitive and creative value for the participants. Broadly speaking, the transition from "I am in lust with you" to "I love you" is a transition that can be measured only in terms of the value schemes to which two persons are dedicated. Insofar as lovers are concerned to share other values responsibly with each other, to that extent will they be willing so to control their sexual expression, before marriage and in marriage, that they make sexual intercourse a fitting way of expressing and symbolizing their need for each other in their total venture in value realization.

Marriage, on this view, is the putting of mutual love to work in the growth of value, both in and beyond family relationships. Monogamous marriage provides the best environment for growth in personality both for husband and wife and for children. Thus, sex and love, invested in monogamous marriage, grow in quality and value; they inspire and are inspired by the creative process of making a home in which persons can trust each other—as ends and never as means only.

30

Religious Experience and the Life Good to Live

〜〜〜〜〜〜〜〜〜〜〜〜〜〜〜〜〜〜〜〜〜〜〜〜

At this stage in our inquiry we can confirm Charles Stevenson's assertion that "potentially *any* belief has a bearing in ethics." [1] No set of beliefs has been more influential and controversial than those about the relation of religion to the good life. For, as Royce says: "A man who propounds a religious system must have a moral code, an emotional life, and some theory of things to offer us. . . . He need not, indeed, know or pretend to know very much about our wonderful world, but he must know something, and that something must be of definite value." [2]

Because we are confined to one chapter, it seems best to limit the scope of our discussion and move from a descriptive account of religious experience to the problem of its proper place in the good life. We begin, then, not with the analysis of some system of religious beliefs, but with *beliefs about what happens in religious experience.* We shall not differentiate here between religious experience and mysticism, for mysticism may be considered a "peak moment" of religious experience.

---

[1] Charles L. Stevenson, *Ethics and Language* (New Haven: Yale University Press, 1944), p. 12.

[2] Josiah Royce, as quoted in Maurice Mandelbaum *et al., Philosophical Problems* (New York: Macmillan, 1957), p. 519.

I. *PEAK MOMENTS OF RELIGIOUS EXPERIENCE*

Many readers will already be familiar with Wordsworth's lines from "Tintern Abbey":

> . . . and I have felt
> A presence that disturbs me with the joy
> Of elevated thoughts; a sense sublime
> Of something far more deeply interfused,
> Whose dwelling is the light of setting suns,
> And the round ocean and the living air,
> And the blue sky, and in the mind of man . . .[3]

It is this same Wordsworth who said:

> The religious man values what he sees chiefly as an imperfect shadowing forth of what he is incapable of seeing. The concerns of religion refer to indefinite objects, and are too weighty for the mind to support them without resting a great part of the burden on words and symbols, by a process whereby much is represented in little, and the infinite Being accommodates Himself to a finite capacity.[4]

Another "presence" is identified by St. Teresa of Avila (1515–82) as that of Christ himself.

> For if I say that I see Him neither with the eyes of the body nor those of the soul—because it was not an imaginary vision—how is it that I can understand and maintain that He stands beside me, and be *more certain of it than if I saw Him.* . . . He renders himself present to the soul by a certain knowledge of Himself which is more clear than the sun.[5]

But Plotinus (circa A.D. 205–70) will not speak of the One he experiences as a person:

[3] Quoted in Walter Houston Clark, *Psychology of Religion* (New York: Macmillan, 1958), pp. 264–65.

[4] Quoted in W. R. Inge, *Mysticism in Religion* (Chicago: University of Chicago Press, 1948), p. 70.

[5] As quoted in Evelyn Underhill, *Mysticism: A Study in the Nature and Development of Man's Spiritual Consciousness* (New York: E. P. Dutton, Paperback Series, n. d.), pp. 341–42.

The soul must remove from itself good and evil and everything else, that it may receive the One alone, as the One is alone. When the soul is so blessed, and is come to it, or rather when it manifests its presence, when the soul turns away from visible things and makes itself as beautiful as possible and becomes like the One (the manner of preparation and adornment is known to those who practice it); and seeing the One suddenly appearing in itself, for there is nothing between, nor are there any longer two but one, for you cannot distinguish between them while the vision lasts: it is that union of which the union of earthly lovers, who blend their being with each other, is a copy. The soul is no longer conscious of the body, and cannot tell whether it is a man or a living being or anything real at all. . . . When in this state the soul would exchange its present condition for nothing, no, not for the very heaven of heavens, for there is nothing better, nothing more blessed than this. . . . All the things that once pleased it, power, wealth, beauty, science, it declares that it despises; it fears no evil, while it is with the One. . . .[6]

Aurobindo, an Indian mystic, emphasizes the paradoxical basis of individuality and self-confidence involved in religious experience when he says: "But the true essence of sacrifice is not self-immolation, it is self-giving; its object not self-effacement, but self-fulfillment. . . . Our sacrifice is not a giving without any return or any fruitful acceptance from the other side." [7]

And, Tagore, the Indian poet, reiterates: "Joy! Joy! I triumph! Now no more I know Myself as a simple me. I burn with Love. The Center is within me, and its wonder Lies as a circle everywhere about me." [8]

Alfred North Whitehead, whose view of God would differ in important respects from that of any of the other persons quoted in this chapter, defines the nature and significance of religious worship, when, in a famous passage, he defines religion as:

[6] As quoted in W. R. Inge, *op. cit.*, p. 119.

[7] Sri Aurobindo, *The Synthesis of Yoga* (Madras, 1948), p. 71, as quoted in *Mysticism and the Modern Mind* edited by Alfred P. Stiernotte, copyright © 1959 by The Liberal Arts Press, Inc., and reprinted by permission of The Liberal Arts Press Division of The Bobbs-Merrill Company, Inc.

[8] Stiernotte, *op. cit.*, p. 123, quoting from Curdial Malik, *Divine Dwellers in the Desert* (Bombay, 1949), p. 11.

the vision of something which stands beyond, behind, and within
the passing flux of immediate things; something which is real,
and yet waiting to be realized; something which is a remote
possibility, and yet the greatest of present facts; something that
gives meaning to all that passes, and yet eludes apprehension;
something whose possession is the final good, and yet is beyond
all reach; something which is the ultimate ideal, and the hopeless quest. . . .

The immediate reaction of human nature to the religious
vision is worship. . . . The fact of the religious vision, and its
history of persistent expansion, is our one ground for optimism.
Apart from it, human life is a flash of occasional enjoyments
lighting up a mass of pain and misery, a bagatelle of transient
experience.

The vision claims nothing but worship; and worship is a surrender to the claim for assimilation, urged with the motive force
of mutual love.[9]

Henry Nelson Wieman, a contemporary American philosopher of
religion, for whom the Divine is the creative process in the world,
describes a religious experience he had during postgraduate college
days when he seemed overcome by a feeling of failure, worthlessness,
and futility.

Gradually there emerged within me a spreading sense of peace
and rest. . . . Then I found myself . . . almost laughing and
crying with joy. Joy about what? I could not tell. I only knew
my pain was gone, and I was full of great gladness, courage and
peace. . . . I simply knew that I was glad, and ready and fit to
go ahead and do whatever I might find to do and take the consequences whatever they might be. . . . The strong emotion of
gladness gradually passed away in the course of days, but the
courage, peace, readiness to meet any fortune with equanimity,
and joy in living did not go away. The old anguish did not return.[10]

Suzuki, the Zen Buddhist, is accordingly quoted favorably by Wieman:

[9] Stiernotte, *op. cit.*, p. 60, quoting Whitehead's *Science and the Modern World*
(New York: The Macmillan Co., 1948), p. 275; and p. 65, quoting *ibid.*, p. 275.

[10] Stiernotte, *op. cit.*, p. 24, quoting from Henry Nelson Wieman, *Religious Experience and Scientific Method* (New York: The Macmillan Co., 1926), pp. 225–28.

The individual shell in which my personality is so solidly en-
cased explodes at the moment of sartori. Not, necessarily, that I
get unified with a being greater than myself or absorbed in it,
but that my individuality, which I found rigidly held together
and definitely kept separate from other individual existences,
becomes loosened somehow from its tightening grip and melts
away into something indescribable, something which is of quite
a different order from what I am accustomed to. The feeling that
follows is that of a complete release or a complete rest—the feeling that one has arrived finally at the destination.[11]

Turning now to a more naturalistic analysis of religious experience, we observe in two examples how a "Naturalistic" Humanist
would describe the experience:

There are moments when the sheerest and simplest sensual
experience wears a golden significance. Suddenly, as the atmosphere is crystal clear after a rain, objects take on a naked, trans-
parent meaning. . . . We are stabbed by the isness, the thatness
of things, and there comes a fresh and splendid sense of existence.
These experiences differ from those in which we become absorbed, in that they shock us into self-awareness, as we are sharply
moved to acknowledge the individuality, the shattering presence
of something outside ourselves. . . .

There comes a time when we are so used by other men, so
privy to their sorrows and satisfactions in our years of companionship, that we know within us the meaning of the mass
and misery of the whole race. This is mysticism, a mysticism of
man in nature.

It comes from the rest of nature around us, converging and
coalescing within that whirlpool of nature which is a human
body and person. The universe gathers within a man, speaks
and wonders and ponders within him, and then declares to itself the revelation of its own being.[12]

These samples of religious peak experiences suggest the reason for
the claim that without evaluating such high moments, no justice can
be done to the question: What is the life good to live? It is clear that

[11] Stiernotte, *op. cit.*, p. 26, quoting from D. T. Suzuki, *Essays in Zen Buddhism*
(2nd Series; London: 1950), pp. 31–32.
[12] Kenneth L. Patton, "Mysticism and Naturalistic Humanism," quoted in Stiernotte,
op. cit., pp. 78, 80–81.

such experiences make a "shattering" difference to the persons who have them.

But the same would have to be said for what, with William James, we might call the other "half of mysticism," namely, "a sort of religious mysticism turned upside down." Here, as in psychological delusional states like paranoia, "ineffable importance" is attached to "the smallest events, the same texts . . . the same voices . . . the same controlling by extraneous powers." In this "half of mysticism," however, "the emotion is pessimistic" for instead of consolations we have desolations, and "the powers are enemies to life." [13]

Indeed, even from our few samples, we can see why James concluded that mystical experience itself could not be used as the last word for any particular view of the universe. To quote what to us is a crucial passage:

> The fact is that the mystical feeling of enlargement, union, and emancipation has *no specific intellectual content whatever of its own*. It is capable of forming matrimonial alliances with material furnished by the most diverse philosophies and theologies, provided only they can find a place in their framework for its peculiar emotional mood. We have no right, therefore, to invoke its prestige as *distinctively in favor of any special belief*. . . .[14]

Considering the possible nature of the psychological dynamics involved, James comments that "the classic mysticism and these lower mysticisms spring from the same mental level, from that great subliminal or transmarginal region" or unconscious that can house every kind of "agency." And James concludes, "to come from thence is no infallible credential." [15]

All the more, then, as James says, must we sift and test religious experiences, demanding that they "run the gauntlet of confrontation with the total context of experience, just like what comes from the outer world of sense." [16]

More particularly, we must be careful not to identify prematurely the *psychological power* that religious experiences characteristically release or the *psychological authority* they carry with them in the lives of the experients, and their value in the good life. There is no

[13] William James, *Varieties of Religious Experience* (New York: Longmans, Green & Co., 1902), p. 426.
[14] *Ibid.*, pp. 425–26 (italics added).
[15] *Ibid.*, p. 426.
[16] *Ibid.*, pp. 426–27.

doubt, on the whole, of the new power and zest that religious experiences bring into the lives of those who have them. But if we face all the facts squarely, we must realize that in the name of such intimate experiences, in the name of the Power believed to be present in such experiences, great good and great evil have been committed. The ethicist cannot take these religious value claims at face value; nor can he neglect an experience that can be so life-transforming. Therefore, we pause to suggest minimal considerations we must keep in mind as a basis for judging the truth of these claims.[17]

II. *VALUES OF RELIGIOUS EXPERIENCE*

It is clear from our samples that although the religious experience yields knowledge, in some degree, to the person having it, the event itself always outruns any verbal description and expression; it is ineffable. The experience at its height does not last long, "half an hour, or at most an hour or two," as James says. But what characterizes different descriptions of the experience? The individual feels peculiarly gripped by a power not himself. However we finally come to interpret it, the person is convinced that he could not have produced the transformation that he feels taking place within him by himself, as he normally conceives himself and his nature.

Accordingly, the religious experience, in startling fashion in deeper ecstatic moments, and in a less stirring way in most experiences of meditation and prayer, stands as a challenge to the view of either man or the world as "natural," in a one-dimensional sense, or in the sense in which the physical, biological, and social sciences usually use the word "natural." The religious experience, in James' words, "absolutely overthrows the pretension of non-mystical states to be the sole and ultimate dictators of what we may believe." [18] Stating the matter positively, Rufus Jones, another student of mysticism, says: "a person feels an overmastering conviction that actual contact is attained with a divine, life-giving, joy-bringing Presence." [19]

[17] Rudolph Otto, *Mysticism East and West* (New York: Meridian Books, 1957). D. T. Suzuki, *Mysticism: Christian and Buddhist* (New York: Harper & Brothers, 1957). David Baumgardt, *Great Western Mystics* (New York: Columbia University Press, 1961). Paul Tillich, *Dynamics of Faith* (New York: Harper & Brothers, 1957). H. D. Lewis, *Our Experience of God* (New York: The Macmillan Co., 1960). See also W. T. Stace, *Mysticism and Philosophy* (Philadelphia: J. B. Lippincott, Co., 1960).

[18] James, *op. cit.*, p. 427.

[19] Quoted in Mandelbaum, *op. cit.*, p. 578.

But apart from the immediate, "enjoyed" quality of the religious experience, apart from the cognitive assurance felt by the experient, apart from the feeling of being gripped and transformed, one effect is central, and no one who is fair to the facts can deny it. Religious experience brings, in Rufus Jones's terms, "a vastly increased stock of energy to live by." There results "an enrichment of the individual mind, an increase of its range and depth, an enlarged outlook on life, an intensification of insight, a heightening of personality." [20] " 'Interior plenitude' is on the whole a greater gain than is the bare accumulation of information" or "ready-made communications." [21] Perhaps we can now express, in our own way, what seems to us to be a core of truth that, whatever else may be claimed, cannot be ignored by a person interested in the development of the good life.

The religious life, when religion is an "acute fever," is one in which the person is committed to what he believes is a Source of the highest, if not of every, value worth having. It matters little at the moment whether we speak of religious experience in terms of union, or "creature feeling," [22] or of objective Presence. There is no denying a peak commitment in which the person feels that the best in his life is at stake, is heightened, or is confirmed. What is characteristic of all religious people—including even those who believe in God not as an independent Power in the universe making for righteousness, but as a dedication to the good of man in the realm of Nature—is a feeling of unity-within-an-all-pervading-Source of goodness. They may not express it this way, but in and through this belief they find strength and power to bear what they feel they could not have borne otherwise; and on the positive side, they prize a kind of partnership or sense of union, which brings out the best in them, as they see it, and enhances all the other values in their lives, which now assume a "proper place" in their striving for power and for goodness.

On our view, then, the most pervasive characteristic of religious persons, underlying even radical differences in beliefs about values and God, is their unifying sense of purpose, their sense of involvement in a larger, somehow controlling scheme of things. And if power, unity, and integration were in themselves the highest values, we could find no better source of them than religious belief.

We have been saying that the religious experience is a source of

20 *Ibid.*, p. 580.
21 *Ibid.*, p. 582.
22 See Rudolph Otto, *The Idea of the Holy* (London: Oxford University Press, 1926).

power in life. But we would not leave the impression that it is therefore only instrumental to other values, to be reduced to or replaced by them. The religious experience is neither a kind of moral experience nor a kind of aesthetic experience; it brings its own unique quality into the life of a person, just as do moral obligation and aesthetic response. We shall therefore designate this kind of experience "the holy," remembering that it will, as part of the total response of a person, have an effect upon and be affected by the other dimensions of his life.[23]

Our purpose here keeps us from entering the debate as to whether a universal, qualitative datum can be ascribed to this experience. Surely the words used to describe the holy invariably reflect the experient's own beliefs about the nature of the Source of the experience. A Christian finds "Christ" present in the experience, whereas a Hindu does not. Thus we cannot assume that *the belief* resulting from the experience does not in good part at least have its source in the experient's earlier beliefs. Let it suffice for our purpose here to stress a minimum: the empowering effect of the experience, its unique qualitative nature as felt by the experient, and its capacity of creating and strengthening the individual's conviction that he is in intimate relation to the Source of good in his life.

Indeed, the holy can so grip a person that, for its sake, he may neglect other areas of value. Thus he may "deny the world" for the sake of his "flight from the alone to the Alone," or he may affirm both the flight and the return to the world. There is no telling exactly what the effect upon the life of the individual will be; we have seen that Freud thinks that religion represents immaturity in the life of a person, whereas G. W. Allport differentiates mature from immature religion and stresses the enriching and unifying effect of a mature religious sentiment.

We come back once more to the realization that "religion" or "religious experience" is a factor in the good life that can have momentous effects both for good and for evil, depending upon the standard of values by which one is judging the personality involved in religious experience. And this takes us to the next question we must consider. For assuming that the religious experience can make an important difference to the content and development of personality, the all-important question becomes: How shall we know

[23] See Peter A. Bertocci, *Religion as Creative Insecurity* (New York: Association Press, 1958), Chapter I.

whether the Source felt to be present in the experience of the holy does in fact exist, and what it is in its own nature? In what follows, we can outline only one approach to the answer to this question, but one which fills out, perhaps, the conception of value as developed in this book.[24]

III. *ARE VALUES A CLUE TO THE STRUCTURE OF THINGS?*

We begin our argument with a review of our earlier analysis of value experience. Dependable values, we found, are the joint products of persons in their interaction with the value possibilities in the world beyond themselves. The fundamental fact upon which we base our argument is that we human beings do not ultimately create ourselves. Yet we, and not animals, not atoms, not cabbages, are able to think about, to will, to enjoy the satisfaction of our varied needs. This ability is also a fact that we must not underrate. There may be many other kinds of beings in other realms spatial or celestial; yet it is the human person alone who, as far as we know, can guide himself by moral principles and be creative in the ways we have designated in the symphony of values and scheme of virtues. It is persons, with their activities and potential, their actual value experiences and their reaching for more creative developments, who are sustained by the world in which they live and with which they interact.

That persons, capable of this kind of value experience and potential, should have *arrived* in the evolutionary process *and survived* is, we hold, as much a fact about the world as that eclipses occur. How, then, may we, taking the whole range of human experience into account, reasonably conceive of the probable structure of this world?

There are two important theoretical objections that must be met before we can proceed to answer this question. A keen critic will ask: Because the only evidence we have is the one run of events that constitutes the one realm of Nature and the kind of persons we know, have you any theoretical right to judge "probabilities"? Generally we infer that an event will probably occur if we have seen it, or another event like it, happen under given conditions. Must you not

[24] For a more complete presentation of the argument for God suggested here, see Peter A. Bertocci, *Introduction to Philosophy of Religion* (New York: Prentice Hall, 1950), especially Chapters 1–4 and 11–20.

judge "the probable" only after you have witnessed a whole series of runs?

We realize that we are not, as it were, cosmic observers, who watch a cosmic Creator "positing" or creating a sufficient series of universes to enable us to calculate the *statistical* probability of what the next creation would be. If it is statistical probability we are after, it is obvious that we can never ask any questions, like ours, about the universe as a whole. For, of course, all we do know is this one run of events we call our world.

But in the first part of this chapter we have seen that it is important for us to know, as far as possible, whether there is any truth in religious experience and the various affirmations proceeding from it. Our answer, therefore, to this first objection is to admit that our conclusion will not meet the demands of statistical probability. Our next task is to make clearer what is involved in the question we are asking.

Our question takes the form: Is this universe in which we live one whose structure is such that it supports the best that we find in human experience? Or is it such that human values have no grounding apart from their presence in human nature? The "probable" answer we are seeking is not a statistical probability but, to use Butler's phrase, the "probability which is the guide of life." That is, we live here, in the midst of this order of things, and we inescapably venture in value creation, choosing some values and not others, developing certain convictions in the course of our thought, feeling, and action. Are any of these convictions or hypotheses more indicative of the structure of the world as we know it than others?

Our reply raises the second objection. Because, in order to survive, man had to adjust to this order, why of course it had to support him. Those beings it did not support are dead!

This objection builds on the idea that only the fit survive, but it too misses the target. For what puzzles us is not man's survival but his arrival. In a world that presumably was mindless and careless of value experience, the arrival of a creature like man is anomalous, to say the least. What the objector must make credible is not simply that man should survive but that man who is supposed to have arrived purposelessly should then *survive with value quality only upon condition that he does certain things and avoids others.*

The objector expects us to believe in the happy conjunction of two accidents, the first that man should arrive without purpose, the second that having arrived without purpose man should have it in him to adjust to an accidental set of conditions that nevertheless determine whether he should survive and achieve value. It is the objector who strains probability.

Man did not have to arrive, and he certainly did not have to survive as he has. Indeed, history shows in general—what individual experience shows in particular—that some kinds of choices lead not only to extinction but to a quality of existence that makes survival "nasty, brutish and short." The person, a unity of ventures in thinking, feeling, willing, oughting, and aesthetic and religious responses was born in a world in which the orders of physical and biological nature, taken by themselves, gave no hint of the creature he is. For he can guide himself by laws of logic and of evidence, and he can choose value experiences open to his nature, in accordance with or in defiance of his felt obligation to do the best. All that is involved in the life good to live, as we have seen it, has no facsimile in the lower orders of life. And although man does not have to choose such a life, although he often chooses under the most difficult conditions, the fact still remains that unless his choice is along these lines, he endangers the goods that he already has and that he thinks he can afford.

And now we can take another main step in our argument. From what we do know we can infer that, if man was to survive at all as a reasoning being, he had to have an environment that encouraged and supported his ventures in reasoning. In a word, he needed a realm of Nature that would not defy but challenge the logical and mathematical demands he made upon it, and he needed a realm of Nature within which he could dependably predict the future in the light of the past. Even to make possible his sheer physiological existence as a complicated animal, the sequences in his own nature and in the world needed to be orderly enough and coordinated enough for him to expect them, predict them, and to some extent control them in accordance with the range of his needs and abilities.

On the other hand, had the order of Nature and his own humanity been so fixed that every event was unalterably fixed in a network of being, without either flexibility or plasticity, there would be no possibility of freely directed growth. Actually, free will-agency leads to sheer chaos unless it takes place within a larger structure of order not inconsistent with growth. For if man was to choose as a moral creature, he needed the cognitive capacity to observe, remember, organize, predict—and in a stable, sequential order of Nature that allowed for alternatives and yet was geared to his own needs and capacities.

But man's moral problem begins essentially at this point. The world stage is set for the human ethical venture the moment there is will-agency and plasticity within order. Conative selectivity and willed choice are possible only as man can come to know and to control within limits what will happen to him and his fellow men in this kind of world. He cannot guide his ethical ventures if the values he experiences are not themselves grounded in the more or less stable rhythm of events in his own psychophysiological being and in the world. Only thus can he come to understand that certain value choices seem to be favored by the nature of things and produce goodness of life, whereas other choices are discouraged, ultimately under pain of death.

To summarize: If man had arrived in a world without regularities and possibilities of change; if he had arrived without certain needs and abilities which could be altered within limits to avoid destructive clashes with other animals, men, and the forces of nature; and if he had not been able to choose within limits, without being a complete victim of his past habits or present environment, there would have been no human culture in any of its forms. As things stand, man did arrive with his abilities and needs in a world that made a variety of modes of survival possible. The important thing is that more than one pattern of values has always been open to him. His problem has been to discover that pattern of values and virtues, that style of life, which decreased chaos and fostered increasingly the dependable values in his life.

In our earlier discussion, what have we discovered about the search for values? First, that dependable values exist neither independent of the desires and needs of human beings nor dependent solely on human whim, desire, need, or emotion. Second, that the value experiences that can reasonably be approved in the symphony of values dependably enhance the potential of the person in his relation to other persons and the world.

The underlying reason for preferring one pattern of value experiences to another is that in addition to evoking the person's intrinsic enjoyment, that pattern, better than any other, proves to be rooted in and conserves and develops the more enduring potential of the individual's needs and abilities as he interacts with others and the world. In the last analysis, our guide in selecting the pattern of moral and nonmoral values in the symphony of values and in the process of orchestrating our value choices is our conception of what our natures allow in relation to the nurturant and challenging environment. This means, if we interpret our data right, that our highest values are statements not simply about what we are, but statements about what we, given our natures, can become in this kind of world. Our ideal values, then, are the products of our native potentialities interacting with the world's possibilities.

At the risk of needless repetition, let us illustrate. What do we mean when we say that an apple has health-value? We mean that, basically, the biological structure of the apple is such that it can sustain and preserve our physiological nature. If our bodies were not the kind of bodies they are, if the apple had a different biological nature, the value we call "health-value of an apple" could not exist. And the health-value of apple-eating is greater than the value, say, of apple-blossom-eating, because the apple and not the blossom will better nourish such bodies as ours.

Again, let us assume that we prize love (both loving and being loved) above riches. This means that although a large quantity of money can make available food and a vast range of physiological and mental values (from housing to travel and schooling), there are some values that money cannot buy and without which even the values that money can buy become dangerous. By tracing the psychological causes and effects in personality, we know that the person who is loved and loves can enjoy and sustain experiences more important to creative social harmony than he could if he had wealth but was neither loved nor loving. We need not try to justify this particular conclusion here (we have treated love as a style of life especially in Chapters 17 and 29). But the kind of argument it illustrates is crucial. The basis for treating one value as more valuable than another is neither a whim of men nor an accident of Nature, but the dependable relationship we have discovered between human beings and the kind of environment in which they are fostered.

If our reasoning is correct, we can now generalize. We conclude that a certain pattern of human values gives the clue to what "the structure of things" favors. Have we not discovered that without the search for knowledge (cognitive values), for beauty (aesthetic values), for character (moral values), for mutually cooperative and creative concern between persons (social or affiliative values), none of the other values (for example, the economic and health values) is possible in this kind of world? Can we not reasonably (if not demonstrably) infer that, as far as the evidence permits, it is more probable that the universe supports and sustains these values than any other?

Our thesis is, in essence, that if human beings, given their needs and abilities, given will-agency and a sense of moral obligation, can make the most of themselves and of the lawful structure of the natural world only if they choose love and not sheer power, truth and not error, aesthetic and not unaesthetic experience, mental and physiological balance rather than anarchy, then we have the right to believe that the universe is not indifferent to these values. For only insofar as human beings move from relative chaos toward harmony of interests, from relatively uncritical conviction to reasonably justified conclusions, from relatively self-absorbed and selfish interests to a broader insight into self and to unselfish concern, from relatively irresponsible, whimsical choice to creative self-discipline in the light of the best that they know, only thus can they find or realize *in this kind of world* the best their natures allow.

True, in this human-natural world, there are configurations of selfish power, hate, and ignorance, which, armed with economic and military power, flourish for a while and seem to survive through a force of inertia. But those who know love, knowledge, and beauty would rather suffer physical deprivation and other disadvantages than sacrifice them to such "power values." It is, we repeat, from this kind of experience and from such empirically observed concatenations between values that we move to the belief that our highest values are embedded in a cosmic norm.

The issue reduces itself concretely to one question. The world in which we live is one that, whatever else has happened in history, has produced (to limit ourselves to the Western Graeco-Roman-Christian world) Homer, Socrates, Plato, Aristotle, Moses, Hosea, Spinoza, Kant, Jesus, Paul, Augustine, Dante, Da Vinci, Michelangelo, Bach, Beethoven, Galileo, Copernicus, Newton, Einstein, Lincoln, Schweitzer, Shakespeare. Now for the question. Have such lives, and a host of others in every part of the world, no real evidence to offer of what can be done in this kind of world? Does their experience make no valid report upon any central tendency of the world experienced? Do they not take the measure of the universe as well as of man?

Without such men and the intimations of what life is and can be to which their experience points, we would have had to agree that life is "nasty, brutish, and short." If we deny the findings of these, our explorers into the high possibilities of an overarching world to whose laws man is adapted morally, or if we fail to respond sufficiently by espousing harmoniously the basic values that their lives confirmed, then we shall indeed find ourselves peering out of prison cells with narrow openings upon the universe. Endanger the values that such men have identified and sooner or later you endanger everything that man can hold dear in this kind of world—including his very existence, as the twentieth century knows.

Such is our conviction; but let us review the evidence for it. We have given a certain weight to religious experience, though we have found it inconclusive of itself. We have sought the grounds on which we could consider the universe itself involved in the support of the values to which man, if we are correct, ought to be loyal as he chooses among the alternatives open to him. And we have urged that only insofar as men devote themselves to and join with one another in a search for a harmonious pattern of values can they at once realize, preserve, and increase the range of value experiences open to them in this kind of world. Man, we saw, was not merely a creature wandering about in a world that made everything possible. There was a geography and a map implicit where everything seemed uncharted. There was a "lay of the land," and the rivers flowed down to the sea. We gradually realized that, given man's potentialities, he would be challenged to protect and develop a sense of obligation to the values that he could thrive upon in community. Other patterns offered themselves—there were many alluring paths as he went his way. Yet to follow these patterns was to feel "estranged" and "alienated" because they did not lead to the highest that his given nature and the given universe made possible.

For the world seems to exhibit norms, or broad guidelines by which man must direct his life if he is to be creative in his search for values. He is free within limits to choose; but the outcomes, the results, the kind of growth and decay do not depend upon him but upon the patterns that the universe allows. Man is free to hate and to remain in relative ignorance; but if he does, he cannot avoid certain effects and results of his choice. The psychological and physical "laws" of Nature are not such that man has no choice; but if man is to realize the best they make possible, he must take advantage of certain possibilities and avoid others. For example, he must avoid hate and ignorance for their own sakes and pursue love and knowledge for their own sakes if he is to protect value-realizing in himself in relation to Nature.

His moral values and moral laws, in a word, must be consistent with what we may now call the *norms for value realization,* which do not depend upon him for their existence.

This means not that love and knowing, as human beings experience them, exist independently of man, but that the universe may be said to have *norms for value,* to which the value experiences of knowing and loving are geared—nay, without which knowing and loving would not be possible as value experiences for man.

To this conclusion, we can add a consequence. These *norms for value experience* may be conceived as the purposes that are intrinsic to the nature of a cosmic Mind or Person, who creates and sustains the universe. In other words, our line of argument, we believe, is most consistent with philosophical theism. According to this view, God, in accordance with the norms of reason and love, created the orderly world and free persons. He sustains both with the ultimate purpose that men should develop their own characters creatively as they learn to know and love and appreciate each other and God in God's world.

This is not the place to develop this hypothesis in rounded fashion, for other philosophical considerations should be adduced to support the view that God is a Person and a Creator. But some such argument as we have developed in this chapter would, we believe, be needed to substantiate the claim that a Creator-Person is good. In fact, to say that the cosmic Creator is good is to say that (in a properly defined sense of the terms) He *knows* eternally the norms of truth, goodness, beauty, and fruitful creativity and that He *wills* to create Nature and free persons in such a way that they may enter into creative fellowship with each other and with Him.[25]

Pantheism would be denied on this view because it dissolves human individuality and freedom into a cosmic One, however creative the One might be. But we must be satisfied here only to suggest our final metaphysical view of God and his relation to the world and man and

[25] Obviously the problem of evil needs to be faced before the goodness of God can be adequately substantiated. But this much can be said here. We cannot know what we mean by evil without some norm and standard of goodness. And it seems to us that, while the facts of evil do call for modification of the traditional theistic view of God, the case for the goodness of God stands on the fundamental fact-value that this is the kind of universe in which persons have and can develop the kinds and patterns of value which have been discussed in this book. See E. S. Brightman, *A Philosophy of Religion* (New York: Prentice-Hall, 1940); Peter A. Bertocci, *Religion as Creative Insecurity* and *Introduction to the Philosophy of Religion;* and W. P. Montague, *Belief Unbound* (New Haven: Yale University Press, 1930).

to argue this view from only minimal considerations. Yet, because we believe that the independent evidence supports a theistic rather than a pantheistic view of God, we would not favor the pantheistic interpretation of religious experience. The "union with God" so often felt in religious experience we would interpret not as absorption of individuality in the One Absolute but as the feeling of harmony between the purpose of the finite person and the cosmic Person.

IV. *RELIGION AS CREATIVE FELLOWSHIP*

We are now ready to reconsider briefly, and again only in bare essentials, the nature of the relation between the good life and religion.

In the last section we were searching first for some independent evidence, not arising from the experience of the holy itself, for taking the essential import of the religious experience seriously. Assuming that the highest human (nonreligious) values do establish a reasonable base for *belief* in a theistic God, we can now say that the conviction born of religious experience is sustained: man is in the presence of, and gripped by, a Being who is the Source of those values. *What we can know by our reason thus directs, not our intuitions, but our interpretation of them.*

By this route, also, we may assert that the criteria of ethical values, although directing and guiding our interpretation of religious "mandates," are, on this view, not allowed to determine without further exploration what the religious reaches of man's experience are and what man's proper relation to God and his purposes may be. There is simply too much transforming power generated by religious experience for the ethicist, at this point, to consider the experience of the holy an addendum to the good life that may be left simply to the taste of the individual. Thus the conclusion suggested is that the complete meaning of the good life itself in all of its ramifications, both for the individual and for society, cannot be discovered without dedication to the religious quest.

For, as we have seen in Sections I and II of this chapter, the experience of the holy is both an intrinsically worthwhile experience and a generative source of zest, inspiration, growth of purpose, and vision. Those who have experience of the holy feel that something is happening to them that they cannot and should not be required to do without. In the most general terms, they also feel that they are in a responsible relation to their Source of Values, a relationship that they should cherish for its own sake and to which they should be loyal in thought, feeling, and action. The particular way in which they conceive their relation to this Source is reflected in the way in which they express their loyalty. But for them the religious experience is *confirmatory,* even when it is not itself alone creative of their faith in a cosmic Ground. For them it is a challenge to further growth, and vital to their larger venture in goodness.

Not out of vanity or for the sake of security do such religious persons gratefully dedicate their lives and all that is theirs to God. It is not simply "aesthetic fun" for them to build their houses of worship and their cathedrals. And it is not simply "so that we may encourage goodness in society" that they develop their programs of religious education and responsibility. Whether they retire to their closets to pray or join in communal fellowship with other seekers after God, they feel a new unity, at once sobering and creative, with the sustaining Purpose pervading their lives and the realm of Nature.

In a final summary, how may the ethicist ultimately relate the good life to the religious quest? Our present answer in this book is that the search for the nonreligious values in life does not depend *for its validity* upon belief in God. Unlike Ivan in Dostoevsky's *Brothers Karamazov,* we do not hold that without belief in God "everything is permitted." The moral quest and the assertion of what is good and evil do not logically depend upon belief in God. But religious experience and the values that center in and proceed from it are so crucial to the growth of values and personality and to the inner victory over evil that the sensitive moral agent cannot set the religious quest aside, once and for all, as meaningless.

There is simply no gainsaying the power generated by the conviction that in the struggle for personal and social fulfillment one is realizing his inner kinship with the divine Will. Indeed, as we have said, this very fact makes religious conviction fanatic and evil when it is uncritical. Let one believe, as the religious person in some way or other believes, that in the best he knows and in the highest he experiences, he is sharing God's creativity, and there are released in him energies not known by those to whom the religious venture is closed.

There is no demonstrable proof that God is responsible for this change. But may it not be that such transformation and power depend in the last analysis on the act of faith itself? It may well be that religious assurance and truth is not given once and for all, that it is never given in such a way that the responsibility for discovery does not lie in the willingness of the moral agent to commit himself to the God his total experience indicates.

In the realization and development of truth, of character, of aesthetic value, and of love, only the venturesome and creative souls reach the peak experiences. Why should it be otherwise in religion? Religious faith, when it is mature and correlated with other value ventures, may well be the peak experience in creativity. For now the person humbly and gratefully determines that his life and his values shall always be seen and enjoyed under commitment to the ultimate Creativity that is God.

V. *REFLECTIVE SUMMARY*

The Reflective Summaries in this book were written with an eye to providing a review of the ground we have covered. If they are now reread, it will be seen that at no point have we justified or grounded any ethical conclusion on belief in God. Yet there are those who argue that there is no ultimate theoretical justification and no adequate psychological motivation for the good life apart from belief in God. And there are those who claim that religious belief is no more than a psychological crutch for immature or crippled persons only. There are also those who differentiate between immature and mature religious belief and who hold that the mature religious sentiment can be both the cause and the crown of the healthy, creative personality.

The contention in this book is that while ethical life (in its non-religious values) does not logically depend for its validity on belief in God, a definition of the ethical life remains incomplete until one assesses the place of the holy in the symphony of values. Our own conclusion, reasoned in skeletal form here, is that the religious experience, while it is a transforming source of power, cannot by itself bear the burden of belief in God or any specific view of God. However, supported and guided by evidence from the total human search for values, the religious experience and belief in God can bring the believer to the highest levels of value realization.

Basic to the argument of this chapter are two general conclusions. First, the religious experience, despite variety in its quality and disagreement about its interpretation, is a source of power in the life of the experient. Second, the moral agent, in his realization of dependable values, is a fact about the universe that cannot be overlooked in any reasonable account of its structure.

If man, given the kind of nature he has, finds that he lives in a universe that supports certain ventures in value and not others, he may reasonably conclude that his life and values are not accidents of a "step-motherly Nature," but rather are themselves indications of what this universe can become *in him*. The highest human values, accordingly, are statements about man and the universe. Indeed, the scope of man's values and his moral principles may be reasonably taken as evidence for cosmic norms for value realization. Viewed theistically, these norms may be reasonably interpreted as purposes of God for man, purposes that involve man's free cooperation in fulfillment of them.

In this perspective, religious experience and theistic belief may be seen as themselves creative acts that in fact unleash powers in personality not otherwise available. The *religious* man is the good man, willing to explore and commit himself to the conviction that this world is itself grounded in the creation of the most inclusive values. And the *good* man is the religious man, seeking to discover the fullest meaning of God in the creative realization and sharing of his value experience.

Index of Names

~~~~~~~~~~~~~~~~~~~~~~~~~~~~~~~

698

Index of Subjects

~~~~~~~~~~~~~~~~~~~~~~~~~~~~~~~~~~~~~~